See How They Grow

Infants & Toddlers

Sue Martin

Centennial College

THOMSON
—◆—
NELSON

Australia   Canada   Mexico   Singapore   Spain   United Kingdom   United States

THOMSON

★

NELSON

See How They Grow: Infants and Toddlers
Sue Martin

Editorial Director and Publisher: Evelyn Veitch	**Production Editor:** Tammy Scherer	**Creative Director:** Angela Cluer
Executive Acquisitions Editor: Joanna Cotton	**Production Coordinator:** Hedy Sellers	**Interior Design Modifications:** Peggy Rhodes
Senior Marketing Manager: Chantal Lanning	**Copy Editor:** Susan James	**Cover Design:** Peggy Rhodes
Developmental Editor: Alwynn Pinard	**Proofreaders:** Susan James and Bob Kohlmeier	**Cover Image:** Andrea Nord
Permissions Coordinator: Alwynn Pinard	**Indexer:** Maura Brown	**Compositor:** Carol Magee
		Printer: Phoenix Color

National Library of Canada Cataloguing in Publication

Martin, Sue
    See how they grow : infants and toddlers / Sue Martin

Includes bibliographical references and index.
ISBN 0-7747-3587-2

1. Infant psychology.   2. Infants—Development.   3. Toddlers.
I. Title.

BF719.M37 2003   155.42'2
C2003-901489-4

Dedication

To my mother, Audrey Finnie née Stott (1923–2000), who taught me to be a mother through her example and knew intuitively about unconditional love.

The ultimate lesson we all have to learn is unconditional love.
—Elisabeth Kübler-Ross

Contents

Preface

See How They Grow takes a new approach to looking at babies and very young children—a perspective that leads to a more human and responsive understanding of each child.

Readers of this book may already have an appreciation of the stages of infant and toddler development from either theoretical learning or practical experience. This text offers an overview of that development, presented in a holistic and sympathetic way. It is also likely that readers will have taken time to look at babies and toddlers because they enjoy seeing the baby's emerging personality and are intrigued by the amazing complexities of this small person's behaviour. *See How They Grow* is designed to help the reader sharpen these observation skills; it offers a variety of strategies for recording and analyzing pertinent information.

Understanding why infants and toddlers behave the way they do is a continuing source of fascination for all those immersed in the experience of early childhood. The book provides a variety of interpretations for such behaviour. Theories and principles of development that have demonstrated lasting value are presented alongside newer explanations. In particular, though recent brain research contributes to ways of explaining behaviour, it is not left to stand alone but is presented along with a novel form of phenomenology that enables the adult to enter the life-world of the very young child.

The philosophy of *See How They Grow* borrows from both older and newer perspectives of childhood, taking the best from several world views. The analogy of the garden and gardener is used to explain the role of the adult and of the child. Froebel's *Kindergarten* offers a useful image of the growing and unfolding of the child, with nurturance and tender loving support emanating from the adult. Here the infant and toddler's garden supports the emergence of the seedling in a way that helps it become its own unique self, and the gardener takes special care to see to its changing needs, and so spends time to understand the seedling.

As a reader, you might have gained experience and skills in working and being with infants, toddlers, and 2-year-olds as a parent, volunteer, student, or professional. Whatever your background, so long as you want to explore the experience of very early childhood, this book should offer you new perspectives as well as knowledge.

Typically, this text will be useful for:

- student early childhood educators
- practising early childhood educators
- family child-care providers
- home visitors
- pre-service infant and toddler specialists
- parents
- parent educators
- resource teachers working with infants, toddlers, or 2-year-olds
- early interventionists working with very young children and their families

It may also be of interest to individuals studying educational psychology, parenting skills, philosophy of care and education, child development, or other related areas of human studies.

Learning Outcomes are listed at the beginning of each chapter so that the reader can see clearly what will be achieved. These outcomes may be matched with course or program learning outcomes, competencies or standards, in accordance with the educational practice of an institution.

Reader are drawn into each chapter by a scene that offers some discussion that is likely to bring their existing understanding into sharper focus. From this point, new ideas are offered and explained in relation to understanding the pertinent issues of the chapter. A similar format is used for each chapter, to enable the reader to navigate the material more easily.

Research into what constitutes quality care is presented with special emphasis on how to recognize and respond to individual, familial, and cultural differences, as well as the necessity for respecting all babies, toddlers, families, and caregivers. The term "caregiver" is never used as a label for the doer of only practical, routine work. The terms caregiver, educator, nurturer, teacher, educarer, or other names for the adult role are used interchangeably without indicating that any part of the role is more important than another. Caring, educating, nurturing, and being with very young children are all of equal merit and importance.

Adult–child relationships comprise many roles: the parent role, of course, as well as home child-care provider, early childhood educator, nursery assistant, teacher, therapist, nurse, nursery nurse, or other professional with direct responsibility for one or more infants, toddlers, or 2-year-olds. Again, each person is equally important in the life of the child, except for the parent, who is always considered the most important figure.

Chapters 1 to 3 offer the background needed to fully appreciate the remaining chapters. Starting with an overview of the philosophy of care and education as it relates to babies and toddlers, Chapter 1 challenges readers to examine their own values and approach to their work and to determine the underlying philosophy of different programs. Chapter 2 opens with an explanation of why observation must be at the core of good practice. The skills and methods of recording are described and discussed; the reader will find clear principles here that require attention. The concept that there are many ways of seeing children is also introduced: the scientific method is one approach; phenomenology provides another. Chapter 3 gives an overview of the schools of developmental theory; the key argument is that there are many ways to interpret behaviour!

Phenomenology may be a new philosophy to some readers, or one not previously applied to early childhood. Phenomenology is a way of understanding the phenomenon of very early childhood. Instead of studying childhood only from the outside (by applying theories to the child), we also try to understand what it is like to *be* a baby or toddler! Getting into the conscious world of the very young child is not easy, but we start by identifying their levels of alertness and use this understanding to try to enter their world. The work of the phenomenologist has to be undertaken by the adult involved. It goes beyond academic study—the work involves being an observer and learning to *be with* the child (rather than to *do to* the child). Because a set theory doesn't apply across the experience of different individuals, this can be challenging. It is fruitful, however. It is not suggested that the educator as phenomenologist should take over from the adult as scientist, psychologist, or theorist; but working together they can offer the child the best possible experience.

The text takes special care to avoid reinforcing the notion that there is a rigid timetable or schedule for development, and makes it clear that children should not be measured against norms in a manner that finds any child intrinsically deficient or advanced.

Chapters 4 to 12 offer outlines of the growth and behavioural changes that are likely to be observable through each of the stages of development. These are not profiles of what *should* occur but rather a guide to what might be observed. The emphasis is on considering young children competent! Developmental perspectives are offered in each of these chapters in such a way as to lead the reader to become more responsive to each individual young child. Rather than offer separate information on developmental stages, infant and toddler curriculum, and guidance strategies, the text merges these concepts in such a way that adults learn to tune in to children and enter their life-world. The curriculum of the child is seen as everything that the child experiences. Guidance includes every aspect of the adult's involvement in the child's world. Clearly the adult has responsibility for both curriculum and guidance; the reader is shown how to carry out this important combined responsibility.

The innovative way of presenting the material mirrors the phenomenological philosophy within which each chapter is situated. Leading from the observable characteristics of human development, the reader learns to identify these features of development within each individual child and to get in tune with them. Responses to the child originate from the adult's interpretation of the child's developmental stage, style, cues, and awareness. Curriculum originates with the child rather than the adult.

The adult is not passive in this process. As each chapter unfolds, the reader learns to become actively engaged with the young child in a way that assists her to participate within her own environment. Interpreting the infant's or toddler's cues is central to each chapter from Chapter 4 to Chap-ter 12. How the adult meets the child *where she is* is explained sensitively. Knowing how to help her elaborate her perceptions of the world follows naturally. The text explains how the adult takes steps to act within the child's world and to introduce new experiences. Depending on the child's responses and state of awareness, the adult is shown how to extend or limit stimulation.

The features of each chapter follow a similar sequence; each is designed to help readers increase their observational skills, apply their developmental understanding, get in tune with very young children, meet the children's individual needs, respond sensitively and appropriately, offer children experiences that fit their world, and expand children's skills and knowledge of the world. Each chapter offers practical advice along with ideas for further activities and selecting suitable play materials.

As part of understanding the needs of infants and toddlers within a broader context, other features of the text deal with the broader responsibilities of the adult working with infants and toddlers. One important feature concerns the conditions for health that are framed as indicators for healthy development. Readers are introduced to some of the individual and special needs of infants, toddlers, and 2-year-olds. Various conditions are introduced and explained so that the breadth of developmental variation can be appreciated. An unusual approach is taken to understanding issues of potential neglect and child abuse. Although there are common strands of information about this sensitive and troubling subject, the text shows that manifestations of both abuse and neglect may be connected with the stage of the young child's development. This issue centres on the way that the power dynamic between adult and child can be distorted.

The biggest shift from knowledge to action is made in each chapter in the "Starting Points for Response" and "Getting in Tune" sections. These sections set the stage for responsivity, the core concept of the book, which combines care and education. Examples of the practicalities of responses are made in the "Responding to Changing Needs" section of each chapter. These are followed by further responses that might be made as the appropriate situations arise. These are not recipes for activities, as may be found in other curriculum books. Instead, they provide concrete ideas on how to support and facilitate the child's skills as they emerge. What was traditionally understood as curriculum and guidance is presented in a truly developmental way, so that the adult can enter the child's world and provide meaningful experiences. The material is presented in a way that leads the reader to be able to appreciate how to individualize responsiveness—with understanding of the familial and cultural perspectives that contribute to each child's individuality. The child is not considered an entirely separate entity, but part of a family and a complex social system.

Further features of the text lead readers to think critically about what they have read and how they might apply some of the ideas. Chapter summaries appear near the end of each chapter to help the reader to distill the material. Key terms are identified as they appear, and are defined in the end-of-book glossary. Useful further readings are suggested at the ends of the chapters.

Both learners and instructors will find the material logically sequenced, easy to read, visually appealing, and supported by a wide variety of learning aids. The information it provides will enable both professionals and parents to work more effectively and more empathetically with the babies and young children in their care.

Special Acknowledgements

Cathy Coulthard, a staff educator at the YMCA of Greater Toronto, has contributed significantly to the content and editing of the text and provided timely support when deadlines loomed. She has demonstrated what I write about and has crystallized all the experiences that are included in Chapters 4 to 12. Thank you, Cathy, for your expertise, humour, and encouragement. Dr. Patricia Corson, Professor of Early Childhood Education at Ryerson Polytechnic University, provided me with an enormous amount of personal and professional assistance during the writing of this book. Thanks, Pat! My professional links with the Association for Early Childhood Educators, Ontario (AECEO), have sustained my enthusiasm throughout the writing process. I wish to thank my friends in the Association of Childhood Education International (ACEI) and my fellow board members, who have helped me to understand that there are many good ways of nurturing very young children and that anybody who claims to have the perfect recipe for educating or caring for children must be wrong!

Parts of this book were written while I was on secondment to the YMCA of Greater Toronto as Manager of Training and Development for Children's Services. I want to thank my colleagues there for their input and for the opportunity to photograph children in the Family Development Centre. I thank my colleagues at Centennial College for their professionalism and all they have taught me. I would also like to thank the following people, who provided valuable comments and suggestions during the development of this book: Gordon Beckett, Sheridan College; Diane Hamilton, Conestoga College; Laura Oyama, Humber College; Claude Painter, Langara College; Brenda Pollock, Vanier College; Ann Stone, Langara College; Lisa Teskey, Georgian College; Lynn Traynor, Malaspina University College; Marian Warwick, Fanshawe College; and Connie Winder, George Brown College. The people I have worked with at Nelson have been marvellous; I have had a wonderful and encouraging relationship with Joanna Cotton, Executive Editor; and Alwynn Pinard, Developmental Editor, has been diligent and patient. Thanks to a fabulous publishing team.

CHAPTER 1

Caregiving and Educating: Philosophy and Practice

Not all babies receive the loving, nurturing care that they need. This mother and her baby show us the mutual delight of early attachment.

Learning Outcomes

After reading and studying this chapter, you should be able to:

- discuss the core issues that contribute to the development of a philosophy of care and education
- articulate a philosophy of care for infants, toddlers, and 2-year-olds
- determine the characteristics of high-quality programs for infants and toddlers
- identify the principles of effective caregiving, nurturance, guidance, and developmental support for infants, toddlers, and 2-year-olds

Scene: A small group of early childhood education students discuss infant and toddler program philosophies in a seminar class.

"A few months ago I didn't think about philosophy very much—but I am happy to tell you that when a parent asked about the philosophy of the centre where I am doing my placement, I could tell her the important points without even looking at its philosophy statement," said Karima, a second-year early childhood education (ECE) student.

The professor replied, "Well done. Your familiarity with the philosophy of the child-care centre is important for several reasons. It guides you in your work with the children. It enables you to co-ordinate your actions with others in meeting the needs of the children. It also helps you to communicate in a meaningful way with parents concerned about the care their children receive."

Karima responded, "Thanks. I can see how philosophy makes a difference to what I do, but I couldn't write my own philosophy statement."

"You will, in time," the professor assured her. "But you'll keep changing your ideas as time goes by!"

By the time we are on the path to a professional role in working with young children, we have been exposed to a variety of philosophical approaches to care and education, even if we can't label each approach. Our own childhood has provided us with a framework for thinking about the **values** that underpin these approaches: we tend to compare later experiences with those of our own childhood.

If your parents, teachers, and caregivers encouraged you to be independent and discover things for yourself, it is very likely that your experience was "designed" based on values of personal autonomy and self-direction. Not all approaches are as obvious, particularly if the experience was inconsistent. Moreover, not all child-rearing or education approaches are well thought out. Sometimes traditional patterns of interactions are repeated without conscious reference to a philosophical approach. Yet that, in itself, carries an unspoken value.

Added to our experience as children is our adult learning in the values and philosophy of child care and education. Simply observing parents and other adults interacting with children exposes us to a variety of perspectives. Some of these perspectives are labelled—Montessori, Reggio Emilia, Waldorf, cognitive, or self-directed, for example. If they are true to these labels, they will have clearly defined values and principles of practice. Additionally, we may have studied the great philosophers, such as Plato, Rousseau, Kant, or Sartre. Although it's unlikely that any program would claim to be a "Plato Program," familiarity with the insights of these philosophers helps us appreciate the values on which we do base our programs. These might be profound values, such as belief in education as a process of social reform or in childhood as a distinct stage in human development.

No program or family can be value-free. We need to know what the values are, how they translate into practice, and how we might influence the shaping of values. We also need to learn how to determine a philosophical perspective by observing programs.

One principle common to the philosophy of many child-care centres is **child-centredness** (putting the child at the centre of practice). We will be looking closely at the idea of child-centredness, because it reflects current thinking about what very young children really need.

This chapter will provide you with some ideas about developing your own **philosophy** of care and education for infants, toddlers, and 2-year-olds as it outlines the philosophical approach that is threaded through the book. You are encouraged to think critically, examine your own beliefs and values, and keep an open mind about different viewpoints about very young children—this may ultimately mean that you will disagree with the text's perspective! However, the overall approach is one of respecting children and families and understanding what the professional person can contribute to the life of the young child, so it is unlikely that you will disagree with that concept, even if you might show respect differently. In addition, the style of the book is to offer research, theories, ideas, and experiences to help you develop your role as one offering responsive caregiving.

It is generally assumed that observing infants and toddlers, engaging in experiences with them, extending your knowledge base, and interpreting what you observe and experience will all contribute to developing your own philosophy. You cannot expect to have a clearly defined "carved in stone" philosophy at the end of this chapter, but you will be several steps closer to clarifying your own stance. In time, you may want to revisit some of the ideas found here to challenge and refresh your personal philosophy.

▶ Translating Values into Practice

As early childhood educators, it is important for us to be aware of our beliefs and values about children, families, and child care. Box 1.1 lists the kinds of things we need to think about in order to determine our values in the key areas of parents and families, societal expectations, personal knowledge/beliefs, and the caregiver role.

However, if we want our actions to be consistent with our values, we must do more than just be aware of our values. We need to work out what they mean in practice. If, for example, you value the right of parents to make choices about their child, then you will have to find ways to support those choices. You might, for example, follow the parents' instructions about the foods their child is to be fed or enable the child to sleep because she was awake late at night. Some things you can do easily; others are more difficult. You might find that one parent's choice has an impact on the choice of another parent. In such cases, you would have to decide whether to compromise or try to meet everyone's conflicting needs.

▶ Beyond Instinct

Some people who do not work with young children wonder why it is necessary to study for a job that they think relies on common sense and instinct. Many parents, they argue, have no education in parenting and yet bring up children adequately; some home child-care providers may have only a little training and

---

BOX 1.1

EXAMINING YOUR BELIEFS AND VALUES

Listed below are items you should consider when examining your views about parents and families, social expectations, your personal knowledge and beliefs, and the practitioner's role.

Parents and Families
- how you perceive the parental role and parental choices
- the respect you have for young children and their families
- how you perceive the adult's role in parenting, caregiving, and educating infants and toddlers

Societal Expectations
- what society wants for its children
- how society values life and the rights of the child
- how society accommodates the diverse abilities of children
- what environments society considers appropriate for young children

Personal Knowledge/Beliefs
- what you believe about the child as a separate person (or part of a larger unit, such as a family or a society)
- how you view power and control or empowerment and freedom
- how you perceive the future
- how you understand the process of change through life
- what you believe about why children exist and the purpose of life
- how you understand the notion of personal reality and the nature of experience
- what you believe about equality and hierarchy
- what you understand about human biology, psychology, and other scientific or theoretical explanations of childhood
- what you understand about how children learn
- how you perceive success
- what you believe about human potential and how it can be achieved

Caregiver Role
- how you consider your own needs and goals as a professional
- how you enter into the life experience of the infant and toddler
- what you understand about the relationships between educators and families and how they can support very young children

seem to do well enough with the children in their care. Why, then, is a philosophy of caregiving and a knowledge of child development necessary?

Instinctive behaviour can be useful, but it won't help in all situations. For example, our instincts might lead us to protect young children, but they won't help us to understand the safety issues related to modern transportation and the need for child restraints in cars. Our instincts might also assist us in helping a child learn a new skill, but knowledge of the child's thinking patterns might help us do a better job. On the other hand, sometimes our instincts can help us out of difficult situations. For example, when a child is in distress, an adult might instinctively make the comforting sounds and movements that no textbook could teach.

Instinctive behaviour on the part of the adult is a primitive mechanism for survival. But as educators we have much higher goals than survival. We need to articulate what we really want for children, and be clear about how we will attempt to achieve it. This is accomplished through a philosophy of practice that takes into account the needs of young children at each stage of development.

▶ Challenging Assumptions and Familiar Perceptions about Infants and Toddlers

In this short section we take a few minutes to think about some of the ideas that we might already have about infants and toddlers. Here we are not trying to define a philosophy, just to challenge some of the assumptions that might lead us in the wrong direction. Critical thinking helps refine our philosophy and makes sure that we are reasonably free from automatically accepting familiar perceptions as correct. They may have merit, but we need to critique some of our views; then if we hold on to them it is intentional.

• The way I was brought up—what was wrong with that?

We usually accept the way we were brought up by our own families as normal. We also tend to internalize the values associated with the practices of nurturing that we experienced. Childhood experience can lead to passive acceptance of a certain philosophical approach. The challenge for us as professionals is to question our assumptions and to become aware of and review everything that we do. With reflection and a thoughtful philosophical approach, our practice can improve significantly.

• I was trained for the job—isn't that good enough?

Our values relating to child care are influenced by more than our own experiences: professional training also contributes to a standardized view of what practice should be. All training and education reflects the values of the time and place in which it occurs. The early childhood educators who studied in the 1950s will have a different mindset from those who studied in the 1980s or 1990s, or those who are studying now. Programs preparing adults to work with infants and toddlers reflect not only the current knowledge and research about children but also differing values and societal influences.

Knowledge is increasing at a fast pace: it's difficult to keep up with current research or even to know what to believe. Although educators can help facilitate your learning, you will need to be open to new ideas, think critically, make up your own mind, and be prepared to challenge your own values. There is more than a single right way to approach most things; the care and education of infants is no exception. An unfamiliar child-rearing practice may have some merit, and something to teach us, although we shouldn't imitate it without reflection and examination of its applicability.

Current trends in infant and toddler care and education lead us to value relationships between adults and children, but researchers have not spent much time looking at child-to-child interactions. Similarly, emphasis on toddler independence has made us look toward supporting autonomy rather than interdependence.

• Isn't "child-centred" good?

Many of us have experienced child-centred programs where children are encouraged to be self-directed.

But there are great differences among programs that claim to be child-centred. For some, child-centred means taking a "hands-off" approach, where the young children play independently; self-direction may be expected, but in these programs the adults are less involved with the children's activity. In other programs self-direction—on the part of the young child—allows the adult to follow the child's lead; here the adult is likely to be much more involved in the child's play. How the term "child-centred" is interpreted makes a significant difference—if you use the term, be sure you define exactly what you mean by it. In general, however, you will need to think about the idea of self-direction as a part of child-centredness.

Some researchers now wonder if this neglects the ability of children to learn in other ways, and to accept greater adult direction. This is a significant issue and we will return to it.

• More toys must make for a better program—mustn't they?

Of course, a focus on the child is essential!

Providing infants and toddlers with toys and play material so that their learning potential can be realized has been the goal of many teachers who appreciate the fact that stimulation improves cognitive functioning. But some teachers and parents now question an approach to stimulation that involves purchasing large numbers of toys, perhaps encouraging children to become mere consumers.

• Don't young children need sensory play—food is safe, isn't it?

Some people criticize the use of food as play material when many of the world's children are starving. How will you respond when presented with these controversies?

• Development is divided into domains—has that changed?

Recently educators, researchers, and philosophers have been challenging some long-held beliefs about children's growth development and how the way we study these subjects shapes our thinking (Penn, 1999; Kilbride, 1997). For example, the concept of **developmental domains**, readily accepted by many, is really an artificial notion created as a way to provide more detailed information about particular aspects of development. Although domains of development are usually reviewed as parts of the whole, the concept of the whole is, in fact, rarely represented. Clearly, **holistic development** focuses on "who the child is" rather than what the child can do in each developmental area. What is the solution? An acceptable approach might be to combine the holistic view with the concept of domains, presenting the child as a whole person, but one who can be viewed from many angles.

• How can developmentally appropriate practice be out of fashion?

Designing and delivering programs that are appropriate for the developmental level of the child seems like a logical way of programming. Bredekamp's research and creation of what does, and does not, constitute **developmentally appropriate practice (DAP)** was influential in shaping how programs should be individually child-centred and suitable for the child's stage of development—the concept is easy to understand and offered guidelines for implementation that were followed in recent years. However, the

publication of the first DAP document by the National Association for the Education of Young Children (NAEYC) was critiqued in such a way that it was found to be insufficiently inclusive from a cultural perspective—what was thought to developmentally appropriate was actually limited to a monocultural point of view. Some practitioners thought that the DAP document provided a benchmark for ages and stages of development and used it to assess the development of children; this was not its purpose.

The concept, which posits that education be guided largely by age-related characteristics, is criticized by many because of its apparent limitations. Some people think it excludes the necessity for more individualized practice; others think it is insufficiently sensitive to cultural or familial differences. Still other critics focus on DAP's values, and argue that, as a North American creation, it is not applicable in other contexts. Yet even when we progress beyond such approaches, we must recognize that these frameworks for thinking form a significant part of our professional heritage and may us help along the road to new understandings.

• Is direct instruction wrong?

Developmentally appropriate practice is based on the idea of underpinning emerging skills by providing suitable experiences that support development. Children have always played, given the opportunity and materials; they don't usually need to be taught to play. Interestingly, adults have always tried to teach even young children by offering clear emphasis on new words or providing a strategy to help solve a problem; they were not wrong to do this. Parents and other adults have met with some success in instructing children. Research supports this; children do learn in structured environments. This might appear to contradict DAP, but it does not. Appropriate learning experiences can be mediated by adults, and they are most successful if the intervention is supplied at the right time developmentally and in a way that is mindful of the learning that has already occurred. Our philosophy doesn't have to be at either end of the structured-versus-unstructured continuum if we are well informed. DAP and **direct instruction** can be combined if we think this meets children's needs.

After thinking about these issues you might have shifted in your position—or you might hold on to what you thought at the beginning. What you might realize is that you'll need to become better informed before you can define your own philosophy. The remaining chapters of this book should assist you, but remember that *See How They Grow* has its own stated philosophy, outlined below. It is quite acceptable to disagree with the conclusions that are made here—but make sure that you have thought through your ideas and are basing them on sound research.

▶ Why Do We Need a Philosophy of Practice?

It is necessary to have a philosophy of care for infants and toddlers because we need a sense of direction and purpose in this work. Philosophy serves as a guide to practice. The philosophy should be based on the educated views and beliefs of all the people involved in the care of the children. Where people are meeting the needs of children by working as a team, there must be a shared commitment to the children and a common set of beliefs about how that commitment will be honoured. Creating a well-thought-out and clearly written **philosophy statement** helps people to develop common understandings and to work together successfully. Most importantly, a philosophy statement can help educators consistently meet the needs of the children. If we can decide on a philosophy, then we can shape everything we do to the principles it contains.

Some of the concepts mentioned in this outline might be new to you. As each chapter of See How They

Grow unfolds, you will find each concept discussed as it relates to child development, observation skills, and responses to infants, toddlers, and 2-year-olds.

PHILOSOPHICAL ROOTS

The Garden Analogy

The very young child is like a seed that is just beginning to sprout. Adults have the responsibility to protect this young life and nurture its growth, just as a gardener would tend a plant. The environment in which the young life grows is the garden, over which the adult has stewardship. The style of garden management may vary, as do the young plants themselves, but each plant develops according to an inner direction that is shaped by encounters in the garden. Each adapts to the changing seasons as it gains knowledge and skills for life. As it develops, the plant changes, sometimes with rapid strides, but at other times in slower incremental stages, moving through to the next step in the cycle of life. Some days the plant will need greater support and will flourish if it receives it. Because each young plant may have different needs and patterns of behaviour, the gardener should read each plant's cues and deliver the individual care required.

The garden analogy is rooted largely in the Froebelian principles of the Kindergarten (*Kinder*

BOX 1.2

WAYS TO SHOW RESPECT FOR INFANTS AND TODDLERS

- Tell the baby what you are about to do before you pick her up.
- Accommodate differing schedules for sleeping and feeding.
- Take time to tune in to the child's activity before you interrupt her with your ideas.
- Use developmentally appropriate guidance (e.g., do not ask a toddler to "use his words" when he has little language).
- Enable a child to have a meal alone with the caregiver if he eats better that way.
- Accept that crying tells you something and see that persistent crying is a repeated request, not a deliberate annoyance.
- When faced with a frustrated toddler, acknowledge his feelings before you try to distract him away from the frustration.
- Acknowledge that some children take longer than others to get used to new people and surroundings and be prepared to spend the extra time nurturing a child who needs it.
- Have pictures and books that look like people from each child's culture.
- Remain calm and make time immediately with the toddler who always comes late and doesn't settle easily.
- Show empathy for the child who is hurt, even if he seems to cry longer than you think the hurt warranted.
- Work more diligently with the child who arrives unwashed and dishevelled and who sits by herself without seeking attention.

means children in German and *garten* means garden). Friedrich Froebel saw the child as developing in stages in the garden of life, and the adult as bearing responsibility for how that happened. This philosophy has been extended to embrace the need for individual nurturing; the garden image endures, providing us with a "back to nature" appreciation of the child as having special qualities in mind, spirit, and body. Ultimately the garden is only a part of the child's world, but it represents the part over which adults have responsibility and a small degree of control, if only to create the positive backdrop against which the child can thrive. From Froebel to new research in neuroscience, the garden analogy needs no reshaping: it fits 21st-century cutting-edge science as well as it fit 20th-century developmental theory and 19th-century idealism.

Respect for Very Young Children

At the root of the philosophy of *See How They Grow* is a deep respect for each child. Magda Gerber did not invent respect for infants and toddlers, but she showed us *how* to respect them. With her sensitive approach of viewing experiences from the perspective of the baby, Gerber's attitude toward infants was refreshingly different. Avoiding sentimentality or the race to acquire skills early, Gerber respected the individual style and rhythm of each child. She mirrored

the baby's pace and responded to its cues, in an effort to maximize communication and meet the needs of the baby. Drawing on Gerber, Box 1.2 outlines some of the ways adults can show respect for young children. Gerber is a significant contributor to our understanding of early childhood, and her principles are reflected in this book.

Respect is an attitude as well as a set of behaviours. Very young children know without being told whether they are accepted and loved. Our every action speaks loudly to children about how we value them and how we value the task of caring. In turn, this contributes to children's sense of self-worth and shapes their perspective on the world.

Respect for Families

As adults who care for and educate very young children, we often say we have respect for families. But that is easier to state in theory than to demonstrate in practice, especially when the parents' views conflict with our own. Kilbride (1997) states that "families are our partners in the great enterprise of teaching and caring for children" (p. 21). Partnership requires a relationship of give-and-take.

Respect for families shows in most of the things that we do professionally, not only the things that parents see us do (see Box 1.3 for ways to show respect for families). Sometimes our attitude of respect may be

---

BOX 1.3

WAYS TO SHOW RESPECT FOR FAMILIES

- Greet family members in their own language.
- Celebrate their joys with families and commiserate with them in times of sadness.
- Welcome parents and siblings into the centre.
- Ask the parent about her or his day.
- Accept without question that, after a day at work, a parent wants to do the grocery shopping without the child.
- Ensure that family members are included in the program wherever practicable.
- Represent all types of diversity in the environment, particularly the ethnic mix of the children.
- Accept lifestyles that differ from your own.
- Support families that are undergoing stress, such as separation, culture shock, moving home, or caring for elderly relatives.
- Provide resources such as names and phone numbers for families in need of social services, religious supports, or referrals for assessments.
- Explain why you have a "no nuts" policy; the parent may not know about extreme allergies.
- Ask parents/families for their expertise.
- Keep parents up to date.
- Tell parents the truth when they ask how their child is doing.
- Stop gossip in its tracks when you hear anyone talking behind a parent's back.

challenged by parental views that are contrary to our own personal value system. Yet under no circumstances can our behaviour indicate bias, favouritism, or personal preferences, nor can we shun those with whom we disagree. Even subtle behaviours can belie the respect that we must try to show. The professional role requires deep sensitivity, based on knowledge and a readiness to admit our mistakes.

Safety

Safety is the most essential part of the adult's responsibility to the very young child. It requires an unceasing observation of the child and the child's environment. Because all elements of safety change according to the mobility, needs, and abilities of the child, the adult needs to understand child development principles in order to ensure physical and emotional security.

Safety is as much an attitude as a list of things to remember. Safe practice requires that the caregiver make wise choices about all items in the environment, observe continuously, intervene when necessary, be aware of developmental stages and appropriateness of activities, and avoid potential problems. A list of things to watch for can help safe practice, but vigilance in every part of every activity is the only way to avoid incidents. Each chapter of *See How They Grow* that deals with an age/stage of development indicates some potential hazards and how they can be addressed.

▶ Determining the Philosophy of a Centre

The process of creating a philosophy of practice requires that the writers identify their values and beliefs and articulate how they will be demonstrated. As a result of a reflective process, the philosophy statement acts as a reference point for all aspects of working with young children. In other business environments, the equivalent would be a company's mission, vision, and values statements. In the child-care environment, the philosophy statement precipitates the formation of a plan of action, policies, and indicators of **best practices** (characteristics of successful programs). As such, the philosophy statement provides the backdrop for the business of child care.

PERSONAL AND CENTRE-BASED PHILOSOPHIES

Personal philosophies of infant and toddler caregiving and education are formed as you learn about, and work in, various child-care settings. These experiences influence how you perceive your role and the ways in which children's needs can be met. You may encounter a child-care centre that demonstrates values you do not share and practices that you do not feel comfortable with. Part of your ongoing learning is to observe carefully and to ask questions about what you see and why certain practices are followed. Although staff members should be open to such questions, you will need to ask them appropriately and at the right time. These communications might help you come to appreciate a different way of looking at things. Explanations may lead you to change your mind or become clearer about your own values and beliefs concerning practice. It is important to be respectful of the experience of centre staff, whether or not you share their perspectives. Just as there are different ways of doing things "right" as a parent, there are different approaches to caregiving that might also be appropriate. When seeking a job, it is desirable to match the potential employer's philosophy with your own, so that you will find the centre a comfortable place to work in.

Only if there is an abuse of power, an experience of neglect, or the employment of a practice that harms the child should a philosophy be considered wrong. Even then, the practice might be wrong while there is some merit to the philosophy. Read the comments about potential abuse later in the text before taking any action; it is not for you to judge—only to pass on your observations to the appropriate authorities for their action.

TERMS USED IN PHILOSOPHY STATEMENTS

Many child-care centres and programs for very young children claim to have an eclectic philosophy and practice—that is, one drawing from many different philosophical and theoretical approaches. Typically you may encounter the following terms used to describe a philosophy: "developmentally appropriate," "sensory," "play-based," "developmental," "discovery," "child-directed," "nurturing," "primary-caregiver," or "social curriculum." In practice, most of these hint at a more responsive caregiving model than "enriched," "rigorous," "structured," or "educational" models. Other terminology might alert you to the values of the program. Centres that speak of "guidance" rather than "discipline" will usually be more developmentally appropriate and nurturing. "Discipline" has connotations of greater teacher direction and attempts to control children's behaviour. Centres that mention "moral learning" might emphasize particular religious beliefs, but they may also have a heightened awareness of social responsibility. "Pro-social skills" can be construed in various ways in practice: the term might mean an emphasis on positive role-modelling or an insistence that toddlers "share" things. Recently there have been aspirations to an "anti-violent" approach. This does not mean that any other approach is pro-violence, but that children are encouraged to use nonviolent approaches to problem-solving. Many child-care centres take a positive approach to peacemaking. The intent is to arm children with strategies for solving conflicts. With the advent of new policies in schools of zero tolerance toward violence, there is an added incentive to help children learn to use positive actions and words. This can be role-modelled and reinforced with young infants and toddlers.

Emphasis on one domain of development or another seems common in philosophy statements. You might see the terms "cognitively focused curriculum" or a "social-emotional focus" in their literature. Some programs promise an ideal that is unattainable or use rhetoric and fancy brochures designed to impress parents.

Terms such as "inclusion," "diversity," and "nature" may be used in a variety of ways in philosophy statements. Some programs that claim to be "inclusive" fail to live up to the term in any way other than including all children in activities. The goal may not be to include all children regardless of background, social class, ethnicity, or ability. Programs claiming "diversity" might include children with special needs. Specialist staff may be available for developmental support or intervention. Alternatively, the term might be used to indicate an anti-bias perspective in the curriculum. The word "nature" or "natural" might indicate a setting with aesthetically pleasing use of light, wood, colours, fresh air, and textures or a

"scientific discovery" program. It might mean that only natural, not plastic, materials are used.

A centre's reputation may be a guide, but to determine the philosophy of a centre for infants and toddlers, you need to consider the elements outlined in Activity 1.1. This section raises some of the major issues that you should consider in evaluating a centre.

Avoid judging what you see until you are sure you have all the information. There may be reasons why a child is handled a certain way or why the routine has been disrupted. Asking open questions may be helpful, but the centre staff may be concentrating on meeting the children's needs, not yours. A centre offering good quality care, whatever its philosophy, will find time for answering questions from students or parents, but that time may be after the program has finished for the day. Ask to read any information that the centre has prepared about its own programs. This might include the centre's policies, history, and its relationship with its community. Some centres will have newsletters. Although public libraries might have general information about centres, you will need to visit the centres themselves to understand just what they offer and what values they hold.

Many child-care centres or private home child-care settings are run by large companies, agents, or other associations. These may share a philosophy as well as administration. In these settings it is important to examine the central philosophy as well as the local or site-based philosophy and practice. Large organizations can find it difficult to ensure consistency of philosophy because so many individuals with differing views are working for the same employer. Activity 1.1 provides a checklist for helping you figure out the philosophy of a centre by observing its practices.

Activity 1.1

Philosophy in Practice

A. Visit an infant and toddler child-care centre and determine its philosophy by observing elements of its practice. Using the chart below, enter the words or phrases that characterize each program area listed on the left.

Program Area	Characteristics (use words or phrases)
1. Relationships with children	
2. Relationships with parents	
3. Communication style with parents	
4. Use of colour and light in design	
5. Use of physical space	

6.   Furniture type and/or style
7.   Qualifications of staff
8.   Professional development provisions for staff
9.   Range or type of play materials available
10. Flexibility or rigidity of routine
11. Approach to child independence
12. Demonstration of values
13. Emphasis on cooperation
14. Accommodation of children with special needs
15. Quality of welcome and/or inclusion
16. Parental involvement and/or partnership
17. Teacher involvement with individuals
18. Teacher involvement with groups
19. Program evaluation
20. Affiliations with organizations
21. Affiliations with businesses, associations
22. Accommodation of children from diverse backgrounds
23. Discipline and/or guidance strategies
24. Freedom of movement and/or direction

B. Select the six words or phrases that best characterize the centre, placing the top item in the middle.

Philosophy Web

C. Write your own philosophy of care and education. You can begin by thinking about the following questions:
1.   What is the purpose of infant and toddler care and education?
2.   What is the role of a non-parental adult in the life of an infant or toddler?
3.   What do you think is the key to a positive relationship with parents?
4.   How do young children learn?
5.   How do children become competent adults, and what constitutes a competent adult?

Then repeat the exercises in Part A and B, providing responses that reflect your own philosophy of care. The philosophy web you create in Part B will form the backbone of your philosophy statement. Flesh it out with the responses to the other questions that you consider most relevant.

Guidelines:
1.   Review the philosophy statements of various centres—but do not copy them (see sample).
2.   Review the elements in Box 1.4 (page 13) and try to picture what your ideal program would look like.
3.   Analyze this vision to determine what your core beliefs and values are.
4.   Decide on a structure for your statement. Use headings and then fill in the sections with descriptions.
5.   You might want to choose a quotation that sums up or captures the essence of your philosophy.
6.   Use clear language, and whenever you use an educator's term include a translation into everyday language.
7.   Offer the broad outline, not the specific details, of implementation.
8.   Edit your work; it should get to the point rather than meander through pages of flowery description.

D. Share and discuss your philosophy statement with other class members or edit and refine it on your own.

E. Identify the similarities and differences between your own philosophy and that of the centre you visited. Discuss with your class how you could work in the centre, whether or not your own philosophy and that of the centre are similar.

Sample Philosophy: Cradle-Care Centre

Process for Developing Our Philosophy Statement

In keeping with our philosophy, we have undertaken a detailed process to determine our philosophy. This process involved gaining input from parents, board members, and staff through focus groups, general parent meetings, and surveys. We have gathered together a large amount of material that a small ad hoc group has filtered and presented to all stakeholders for their editing. The result is the following statement, which will shape every part of practice in the coming years.

What We Believe about Families

We think that families are the most important part of our children's lives. The wishes of parents should be uppermost when decisions are being made. Whenever possible parental wishes should be met. Communication between parents and staff will be made regularly, initiated by both parties and responded to readily.

The extended family is important in our community and families will work with staff to embrace all generations in the children's program. Parents, grandparents, aunts, uncles, and siblings are welcomed into the centre, but the needs of the infants and toddlers will determine the level of involvement of family members.

Although the centre serves a small rural community without significant cultural diversity, we are open to the values and practices of others if they are consistent with the centre's valuing of family life. Religious teaching is not part of the centre's curriculum, but there will be support of each child's spiritual, physical, and psychological development, based on values of mutual respect and respect for nature. The families in our community share a connection with the land as a source of life and growth, the seasons of life through which all plants, animals, and people develop, and acknowledge the special responsibilities of people as they use the world's resources. These things will be reflected in the centre's program.

What Is Expected of Them

Childhood is a time for families to get to know their children as well as for children to get to know their families. Separating children from families is harmful. Learning needs to take place within our community as in an extended family.

What We Believe about Caregivers and Teachers

The caregivers and teachers of our children are special and have a special role in the development of our children and families. They should be well prepared for their task and have the wisdom of our elders to look after the children. Their job is to work with the families, not only the children.

What We Believe about Children

We believe that our children are our future. They are born into families and need to know where they belong. Self-identity is more important than self-esteem. Achievement is individual, but true self-worth comes from personal achievements, however small.

The period of early childhood is special because it can shape how the older child and adult will develop. The rate of early development is fast and the adult needs to pay close attention to the changing needs of each child. Although individual accomplishment and independence are important, children need to be socialized into appreciating their place in a group. They need to become interdependent to become effective team members and work collaboratively.

Young children need experience with real materials. Their actions are part of their learning and they help to reinforce understanding. Children need to learn to make choices and experience consequences for them.

Stories are part of our children's heritage. The oral traditions of our community are an important link to their past and help children to know who they are.

The caregivers and teachers must respect our ways, demonstrate their commitment to the community, and love our children.

The safety of the very young children always comes first, but the children must be able to take small risks and experience the consequences. The caregiver's guidance must be clear but loving. Punishment is not appropriate for babies and toddlers.

Conclusion

Cradle-Care Centre is an important part of our community and plays a significant role in nurturing our children and preparing them to be part of our unpredictable future.

INDICATORS OF QUALITY CARE AND EDUCATION

Earlier sections of this chapter have suggested some of the components of quality care and education. We need to expand this information by understanding the research that has been done to determine the characteristics of effective programs that deliver high-quality care and education. Research into **quality care indicators** for infants and toddlers highlights the following issues:

- *The ratio of children to adults.* Lower ratios tend to allow for better communication and attention and a better ability to meet children's needs.

Determining the adult's role in caregiving can be one of the indicators of philosophy in practice. Here, the adult helps the infant hold a book and recognize images. With guidance, the child can become increasingly independent.

- *The size of the group of children.* Smaller groups are more likely than larger groups to offer the context for appropriate nurturance and learning.
- *The education of the caregiver or educator.* Higher levels of education are equated with higher-quality care.
- *The amount of attention each child receives from an attentive adult.* The longer the attention, the better the experience for the child.
- *The communication style and methods used by the agency.* Open communication with parents and multiple approaches to giving and receiving information are most effective.
- *Continuity of care.* When very young children consistently have the same caregiver, they are more likely to make and keep secure attachments. Continuity is even more important for young children whose home experience is poor.
- *Parental involvement.* Where parental involvement is high, there is likely to be a better outcome for the young child.
- *Remuneration.* The pay and benefits of the child-care employee have an indirect, but clear, relationship to the overall quality of care that is offered.
- *The environment.* The adequacy of the physical environment and the access to appropriate materials is associated with quality care and education.
- *The climate.* The emotional well-being of staff, children, and parents directly influences the quality of care and nurturance offered.
- *The administration.* Quality child care is financed, organized, and evaluated effectively and efficiently.

If current research makes it relatively easy to answer the question of what constitutes good care, it is more difficult to determine what actually constitutes a good program. The answer to the latter question will depend on what you are seeking and what fits with your beliefs about children's development. Exactly how the care is delivered is secondary to its quality, and programs with different philosophies can deliver equally good care.

OTHER ELEMENTS OF PRACTICE

Developmentally appropriate practice (DAP) has, for some years, been thought to be the essence of good practice—as we mentioned earlier. Even with a broader definition of DAP that includes cultural and contextual perspectives (Bredekamp and Copple, 1997), there is now a veil of doubt surrounding the usefulness of the practice. One professor, Roberts-Fiati (1997), who represents an increasingly common view, is deeply critical of DAP, suggesting that the practice is unhelpful because the context of each child's development differs. She also believes that what is developmentally "appropriate" becomes an expectation of development and therefore the criteria for assessing a child. Here, she may be mixing two ideas: DAP as practice to support development and DAP as a profile of expectations about development. Clearly, children's experience needs to be appropriate for their development, but the notion that particular behaviours are expected at a particular stage is a departure from the intention of DAP as presented by Bredekamp and Copple (1997). For our purposes, DAP for infants and toddlers involves observing the individual development of each child and providing for all the young child's needs, according to that individual's developmental stages, whatever those might be.

We will return to assessment issues in later chapters.

RESPONSIVE CAREGIVING

Responsive caregiving is an approach to meeting the child's needs that is mindful of how young children grow and develop and how the adult can support this process. Responsivity involves respect rather than power, nurturance rather than simply meeting physical needs, and reading the infant's cues rather than providing a set routine of care. Box 1.4 provides some guiding principles for responsive caregiving.

Infants and toddlers do not need the kind of planned curriculum that older children need, and they should not be exposed to a watered-down version of a curriculum designed for more mature children. Adult involvement is, perhaps, more important than any other element of "curriculum." The responsive adult *becomes* the curriculum. Adult observation and assessment should lead to responses that improve the child's experience of life, support the child's emotional well-being, show understanding of the individual child's temperamental style, adjust environments to maximize learning potential, reinforce the child's emotional attachments, provide social experiences that are appropriate and supported, aid in the acquisition of language and communication skills, and ascertain the child's specific and individual needs. Clearly, responsive caregiving requires sensitivity.

In Chapters 4 through 12, you will see how responsive caregiving can be offered in relation to the developing young child. As the child matures, the process remains the same, but the practicalities alter. This is why an understanding of development is as essential as being able to read the child's cues. Although practical responses should be linked to the development of the child, there are general standards for what is and what is not responsive caregiving. Box 1.5 (page 14) lists some behaviours that are not consistent with responsive caregiving.

SOCIAL CONTEXTS OF DEVELOPMENT

The **social context** for every child is unique and changing constantly. Each young child will experience the environment differently and interact with it

---

BOX 1.4

GUIDING PRINCIPLES FOR RESPONSIVE CAREGIVING

The following are guiding principles for "being" and "doing" with infants, toddlers, and families.

1. Behaviour is meaningful.
2. Everyone wants things to be better.
3. You are yourself and your role.
4. Don't just do something—stand there and pay attention.
5. Remember relationships.
6. Do unto others as you would have others do unto others.

Source: J. Pawl and M. St. John (1998), How You are Is as Important as What You Do, in Making a Positive Difference for Infants, Toddlers, and Their Families *(Washington, DC: Zero to Three), p. 7.*

BOX 1.5

BEHAVIOURS INCONSISTENT WITH RESPONSIVE CAREGIVING

While all of the following adult behaviours are inappropriate, some constitute abuse or neglect.

- letting a child cry until she goes to sleep
- forcing a child to eat
- handling a child roughly
- requiring prolonged attention to an activity
- punishing a child (emotionally or physically)
- failing to explain to a child what you are about to do
- interpreting a child's activity rudely
- keeping a child awake (so he'll sleep later)
- looking down on the child (rather than being on her level)
- neglecting to change a child when he is wet or soiled
- providing inadequate (insufficient or inappropriate) stimulation
- denying a child's basic needs
- failing to provide physical contact, eye contact, and cuddling
- not talking to a child
- failing to provide proper supervision
- ignoring a child's cues
- jeopardizing a child's physical or emotional safety
- handing a child to an impaired parent or guardian
- ignoring signs of neglect or abuse
- failing to seek professional assistance
- giving parents wrong or incomplete information
- reprimanding a child for behaviour related to skills not yet acquired
- imposing adult ideas rather than picking up on the child's interests
- providing watered-down preschool curriculum
- laughing at a child
- choosing children on the basis of gender or ethnicity
- having favourites
- sharing materials unfairly
- enclosing a child in a small space
- leaving a child unattended
- exposing a child to chemicals and harmful substances
- using undue physical force
- failing to make accommodations for children with individual or special needs
- imposing rigid routines

---

individually. Every element of a child's environment influences that individual's development. Indeed, as Urie Bronfenbrenner (1979) says, human development happens as "a result of a person's exposure to and interaction with the environment" (p. 9).

As we will see in Chapter 3, Bronfenbrenner designed a model to illustrate the systems of the environment that are influential. These systems include the people, institutions, and values that the child comes in contact with. As caregivers, we are responsible for some parts of that social environment. Given its significant influence on the child, we must ensure

that this environment is as positive as possible. To accomplish this, we must be able to appreciate how the child perceives the environment and adapts to it.

CULTURAL EXPERIENCE AND DEVELOPMENT

The cultural style of caregiving influences the child's perception of the world, and this seems entirely desirable. The range of human experiences is part of what makes us different. As we will discuss at several points in the book, **phenomenology** is a

Ecological System

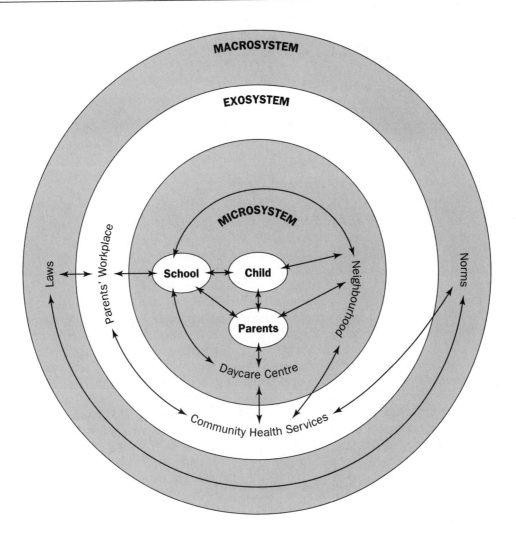

Ecological Theory: **Nested Environments**

Ecological theory is best known for its diagram of nested environments—the micro, the meso, the exo, and the macro.

Micro = individual or family environment
Meso = interactions of micro environments
Exo = an outer level that operates indirectly on the micro environment
Macro = outermost level, such as national society

The ecological model looks for interaction and interdependence among the environmental levels.

Source: N. Hale.

school of thought in which people value the essence of the individual's human experience; they remind us that, although experience is essentially individual, the creation of the experience is shaped by the values and attitudes that surround the developing child.

Whether or not we live in a diverse community, we need to have some sensitivity to the wide variety of experiences of very young children. While there is wide cultural variation of experience, convincing evidence exists that almost all infants and toddlers go through the same stages of development in similar sequences.

Children may differ in their patterns of development for both ethno-cultural (ethnic origin and cultural experience) and individual reasons. One must be sensitive to possible cultural variations and not approach the issue with rigid expectations. There are many possible variations. (See Box 1.6.)

Culturally Sensitive Programs

Cultural sensitivity to families and young children can be reflected in an **anti-bias curriculum**, as discussed above. The core of good practice in this area is based on the attitudes and values that are held by all the adults in the child's life and how effectively and consistently these are transmitted in the choices made by the caregivers. When planning any activity or experience, you might want to consider how well it fits the **individual** in a cultural as well as a developmental sense. For example, visual information is significant to infants and toddlers, so images of people should always include ones with an ethnic or cultural similarity to each child.

To ensure that our programs are culturally sensitive, we might wish to incorporate an anti-bias approach to our work. In recent years there have been some excellent resources available to help educators challenge their thinking and practices in relation to understanding and accommodating children, families, and coworkers of **culturally diverse** backgrounds. Nadia Saderman Hall and Valerie Rhomberg (1995) offer a useful model for implementing an anti-bias affective curriculum for young children. As the diagrammatic representation of their approach on the next page shows, a complex set of adult skills is required.

Hall and Rhomberg's sensitivity to both individuals and families is completely consistent with the philosophy of See How They Grow. What might be different between the two philosophies is that Hall and Rhomberg state that they are "taking a stand against unfair treatment associated with one of the areas of diversity where bias may exist" (p. 2); this addresses bias in a head-on manner. In contrast, although See How They Grow might appear idealistic, this book's philosophy assumes that any of these biases are quashed within a respectful, caring, supportive, individually focused, nurturing, accepting environment. There is no hint that anti-bias work is wrong; indeed its success allows us to move forward with a pro-diversity attitude—one that accepts and celebrates the breadth of human culture and experience.

However much we might want a perfect world, we cannot assume that bias has been removed in all aspects of our work. Hall and Rhomberg identify the following aspects of potential bias: ability, age, appearance, belief, class, culture, family composition, gender, race, and sexuality. Each of these must be understood, and addressed, in order that a pro-diversity philosophy is incorporated into every aspect of our practice.

It is assumed that the reader is sympathetic to the idea that adults should be respectful to all people, but how you might express this trait could differ. Think carefully about the stance you take, after examining the underlying beliefs that you hold.

Familiar items that offer comfort and continuity should be part of the child's environment. In time, the child's world can enlarge to allow for discovery of new

---

CULTURAL SHAPING OF DEVELOPMENT

An extended family in Vancouver was characterized by its close-knit functioning, its high expectations for the four children, and the joy that the children gave their parents and grandparents. The grandparents, who were not born in Canada, had brought with them many of the ways of life from the old country. Many of these familiar values and practices were kept alive because the family lived among others of the same culture. Mary, the family's youngest child, was nearly 2 years old. She was dressed carefully and told not to spoil her nice clothes. Playing on her grandmother's knee, she learned songs in a language other than English. Mary learned quickly and pleased her family. She became familiar with the alphabet of the old country and acquired the socially acceptable behaviours of her family's and neighbourhood's culture. She looked to the adults and older children to help her, so she didn't learn to tie her shoes or button her coat. When she started nursery school, Mary had not yet learned to feed herself or mastered any of the self-help skills that many other children had.

At nursery school Mary's development was recognized for what it was—culturally shaped. How could the teachers accommodate her developmental needs?

Affective Skill Building

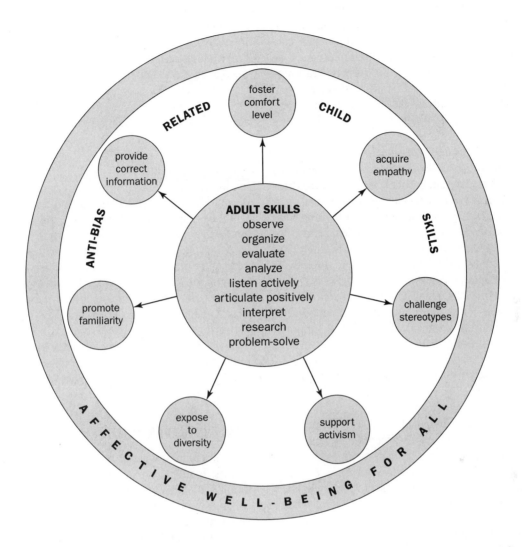

Source: Based on Nadia Saderman Hall and Valerie Rhomberg (1995), *The Affective Curriculum: Teaching the Anti-Bias Approach to Young Children* (Scarborough, ON: Nelson).

materials and different objects. Because the sensory perceptions of very young children are their means of discovering the world, this should be gradual, and should provide items that are without bias and that support cultural values. How this is done might depend on the cultural makeup of the group.

CHILD-CARE SETTINGS

Child care takes place in a variety of settings—in the home environment, with parent, family, or nanny care; in full-day and part-time childcare and drop-in centres; and in private home daycare settings, or any combination of these. It is the quality and continuity of the caregiving experienced by the young child that is important, not where that care occurs. Any of these arrangements can meet the child's needs, depending on the skills of the caregivers involved.

Types of Child-care Services for Infants and Toddlers and Their Families

Most people will probably mention child care as the most obvious service for young children and parents. Within this category, there are private, nonprofit, municipal, workplace, laboratory school, or school-based services. These may have affiliations with churches, synagogues, temples, or other religious organizations. They may also be linked with philanthropic associations and charities. Group child care can take many forms. The programming may be age/stage-linked, multi-age, or intergenerational. Centre care in Canada must be licensed according to provincial or territorial legislation. In 1999, there were nearly 330,000 spaces in regulated child-care centres (both full-time and part-time), and a further 70,000 spaces in regulated family daycare centres. (There were also 155,000 regulated spaces for school-age children.)

In addition to daycare centres, family resource programs might have drop-in facilities, toy libraries, playrooms, resource availability, infant massage workshops, discussion groups, therapies, classes for parents with their young children, and breast-feeding support. Family development centres are a relatively recent concept in the delivery of responsive programming. They may offer a wide variety of support and opportunities for children and families. Mental- and physical-health programs provide medical supports, interventions, and mental-health resources. These can involve "well baby" clinics or be designed to support babies with medical conditions or special needs. Health programs vary considerably across Canada and may include a variety of therapies.

Within the home, the infant or toddler may be cared for by one parent or both, or by a grandparent, qualified nanny, family friend, or baby-sitter. Home child care can also be offered in someone else's home in either a licensed or unlicensed setting by a qualified professional, trained home care provider, or baby-sitter.

Aboriginal Child Care

Another variation in child-care services in Canada stems from the needs of the Aboriginal population. In the 1996 census, there were 71,000 First Nations, 23,000 Métis, and over 6,000 Inuit children under the age of 4. Ensuring that the needs of these children are met has been a struggle: "The maintenance of indigenous culture is a major concern for all aboriginal peoples" (*Child Care in Canada: Provinces and Territories, 1995*, p. 87). Consequently, Aboriginal people wish to control and operate child care and to ensure that their cultural practices are enmeshed in these services. There has been a strong push toward having the Aboriginal communities determine early childhood education services for themselves. Lack of trained staff, poor family structures, and issues concerning the cultural perspectives of the staff and the program and the inflexible standards have all con-

tributed to insufficient and inadequate child-care operations for Aboriginal Canadians.

Two federal initiatives are intended to support Aboriginal child care. Aboriginal Head Start is an early intervention approach supported by Health Canada. The First Nations/Inuit Child Care Initiative is a Human Resources Development Canada program aimed at raising both the quantity and the quality of child care in Aboriginal communities. Organizations of First Nations and Inuit people have taken responsibility for managing and administering the latter initiative.

DEVELOPMENTAL DIVERSITY

As noted earlier, individual variation in development is to be expected and accepted. When we have become familiar with a large number of children, we tend to have some idea of what constitutes typical development. There are some dangers with this, because the sample of children that we have observed may not be appropriate for basing conclusions on what is really the **norm** or what should be cause for concern. Yet if we rely on comparing the child's behaviour to a well-researched norm, this too can be problematic. The norms can give us some reference point, but they are only one piece of the developmental puzzle.

EARLY INTERVENTION

Early intervention programs are those that support infants, toddlers, and their families when they are thought to be at risk. This category might include children in poverty, babies born prematurely, or parents who are drug- or alcohol-dependent or mentally ill. Erickson and Kurz-Riemer (1999) indicate that intervention must be broad-based, driven by family needs, and evaluated regularly.

By addressing family needs and providing the resources that are most likely to lead to positive outcomes for the children, many child-care programs are, in effect, offering **early intervention**. Specific programs build on parental strengths and assist in parental decision-making skills. From the child's perspective, interventions are geared toward providing positive developmental outcomes, supporting emotional well-being, and offering protective mechanisms that address the risk factors. An example of successful early intervention is provided in Box 1.7.

When Tyler was slow to walk, his mother thought it was because he was overweight. All of Tyler's peers could walk, but at 15 months he would sit placidly and make little attempt to crawl, much less walk. The

<hr />

BOX 1.7

EARLY INTERVENTION

Research into the effectiveness of early intervention programs leads us to have the following understandings:

- Most young children who receive early intervention services do make progress. (How much of that progress is actually due to the early intervention services rather than other factors is still open to question.)
- There is more evidence attesting to the effectiveness of intervention with children who are environmentally at risk than those who are biologically at risk.
- Intervention leads to greater progress for children who are higher functioning at the time of entry into the program. And for children with disabilities, the more severe the impairment, the less progress is evident in response to the intervention.
- Intelligence is enhanced in some children.
- The effectiveness of the program depends on the duration of the program and the child's age of entry. The earlier the better; longer interventions appear to be more beneficial.
- More intensive interventions tend to be more effective than less intensive interventions.
- Gains in each developmental domain are evident as a result of very early intervention.
- Dependency and institutionalization are reduced as a result of intervention.
- There is a reduction in the need for special educational services for children when they reach school age.
- Health, social service, and education costs may be reduced when early intervention is successful.

Adapted from: A. Widerstrom, B.A. Mowder, & S.R. Sandall (1997) Infant Development and Risk: An Introduction, *2nd ed. (Baltimore, MD: Brookes); M.F. Erickson & K. Kurz-Riemer (1999),* Infants, Toddlers and Families: A Framework for Support and Intervention *(New York, NY: The Guilford Press).*

educator at Tyler's child-care centre suggested that his mother make an appointment with her pediatrician to have her son examined. The doctor concluded that Tyler did not have a physical problem, but was mildly below average in intellectual functioning. Tyler needed extra cognitive stimulation, a moderately reduced diet, and some specific assistance and encouragement to walk. The educator and Tyler's parents provided all of these on a consistent basis. Without this early intervention, Tyler would not have achieved as much as he did. He was able to stay with his peers in the child-care centre and has sustained his place in the mainstream at elementary school.

Early intervention, as the term implies, focuses on ensuring that the child's issues are considered and accommodated in the first days or months of life. The earlier the intervention, the more likely it is that there will be a positive result. Types of early intervention include supporting attachment behaviours, providing parents with developmental information, assisting parents to be advocates for their child, and offering language supports and play experiences. The interventions might be offered in the child's home, a clinical setting, a parenting centre, or a child-care centre. Play therapists, early childhood educators, occupational therapists, psychologists, social workers, psychiatrists, speech-language pathologists, and pediatricians may work separately or in combination to deliver the intervention.

Basing our philosophy of care and education on sound research is important, especially in the area of meeting the needs of children with diverse developmental needs. If we appreciate the effectiveness of intervention programs, then we will endeavour to work with parents to ensure the best possible outcome for their child. This might mean that an integral part of our program will be careful observation and identification of any concerns. Erickson and Kurtz-Reimer's recommendations for policy and practice are useful when developing a philosophy of practice for children.

1. Intervention programs should be designed within clearly defined conceptual and theoretical frameworks and should be based on the latest knowledge about effective intervention.
2. Interventions should be broad-based, recognizing the multiple contexts in which families and children function, and should avoid working with a child or family in isolation.
3. Interventions should be driven by the family's needs to the greatest extent possible, rather than by pre-planned activities or curricula.
4. Early interventionists must conduct evaluations of their programs.
5. Early intervention programs should consider working collaboratively with other programs to further research.

Educators and caregivers must work closely with parents to ensure that appropriate referrals are made. Cooperating effectively with interventionists and other professionals may lead to increased supports within your program and the opportunity to work with a range of specialists; it may also assist you in developing individualized programming that meets the child's needs. As Erickson and Kurtz-Reimer point out, using prepared curricula is unlikely to meet the needs of the child; you may want to examine your practice in relation to adopting manufactured materials that claim developmental support in favour of creating your own responsive curricula that meet the needs of the individual child and her family. To make sure that the intervention is successful you might also need to be flexible about working within a team, communicating effectively between team members, keeping scrupulous documentation, welcoming others into "your" program and being open about how you deliver the program. Your philosophy of practice needs to extend to this collaboration

This section has addressed some of the issues related to infants' and toddlers' individual needs, and young children who have **special** or **exceptional needs**. We use either of the terms, "special " or "exceptional" needs, to refer to those children whose development is atypical—outside the range of what is typical for the majority of children at their stage. Some children may have diagnosed disabilities—we discuss these throughout the book—but at this point it is more fruitful to think of every young child as having different individual needs. If caregivers and educators are trained well enough, and there are sufficient human and practical supports, most children with special needs can be accommodated within a regular pro-

gram for infants and toddlers. This approach to inclusion is not the philosophy of all programs, although current policy directions tend to force the issue. Caregivers may be concerned that they are not supported well enough to offer an inclusive program. However, the benefits for children and families are enormous. In brief, the benefits of inclusion are:

- emphasis on ability rather than disability
- better integration into society throughout the child's life
- increased family involvement throughout the program
- acceptance of developmental diversity among children, families, and society
- improved support for the holistic development of the child who has a special need
- higher-functioning peers as role models, play partners, and communicators
- emphasis on individual programming for all children within the program
- collaborative program planning with specialist supports

The philosophy you adopt on inclusion will influence many aspects of the rest of your program. We are addressing not only the child who has the special need, but the society we all live in.

▶ The Role of the Adult as Educator and Caregiver

The educator is in a privileged position in taking responsibility for very young children. Unfortunately, many people think that working with young children is merely "baby-sitting" and that caregivers need neither education nor significant skills. The reality is that being an educator requires acquiring and applying knowledge from many areas, including biology, sociology, child development, observation and assessment, psychology, philosophy, curriculum design, health and safety, and responsive caregiving. In addition, the educator must be an excellent communicator, be able to articulate a clear philosophy of education and caregiving, and be able to provide a positive role model. The personal characteristics and attitudes that the educator must demonstrate include caring, responsiveness to needs, the ability to act swiftly to avert dangers, tolerance and understanding for challenging behaviours and situations, sensitivity to children's individual temperaments, respect for all families and children, and acceptance of a variety of different lifestyles and preferences among family members. In addition, educators must remain positive whatever the circumstances, keep information confidential, perform their roles as professionals, accommodate developmental differ-

ences, respond to a variety of social cues, and remain flexible in solving problems.

The table below and on pages 22 and 23 gives an outline of the three main philosophical models.

▶ Adults in the Lives of Infants, Toddlers, and 2-Year-Olds

Responsive Caregiving	The Core of the Adult's Role	Supportive Guidance
The science of meeting the child's needs—a research-based approach	**The core competencies of the adult's role—a practical approach**	**The art of entering the child's world— a phenomenological approach**
• responding to physical and basic needs • viewing the child as somewhat dependent and in need of developmental support	• meeting the child's irreducible needs • viewing the child as part of the future of society • the needs of the group override individual needs	• meeting emotional and psychological needs • viewing the child as a competent human being • the individual's and family's needs are of greatest importance
• reading cues and responding • emphasizing the physical and socio-emotional aspects of development	• sharing experiences • building community • circle time	• observing before moving into the child's space • entering the child's own world
• providing appropriate experiences • designing a curriculum for very young children • sanitizing, sterilizing, and being hygienic	• working with families • supporting / facilitating children's development • observing children individually and collectively and responding accordingly	• supporting human goals • sharing beliefs and values • tuning in and connecting • synchronizing rhythms with the baby • seeing the child's world from her perspective
• assessing development using normative measures • evaluating the environment using valid and reliable tools	• advocating for the rights of children • ensuring practice is ethical • acting as a source and resource for families	• nurturing • being in the dance of communication • being part of the baby's world and giving her personal space
• providing appropriate experiences with the developmentally appropriate model (DAP)	• designing and implementing programs that suit the cultural context of the community	• sharing values and beliefs • accepting the range and diversity of human competence as seen in every child
• following policies, procedures, and protocols	• applying current research to practice • emphasizing professional conduct	• developing a shared vision with families • making meaningful connections with family members
• protecting from harm	• implementing programs for groups and individual children	• respecting differences—valuing diversity • honouring cultural patterns
• changing, diapering, washing, bathing, toileting	• accommodating children with special needs	• responding to each child individually • extending play behaviours
• giving information to parents	• conducting regular program evaluation and planning for improvement	• loving and offering physical contact

ADULTS IN THE LIVES OF INFANTS, TODDLERS, AND 2-YEAR-OLDS (continued)

Responsive Caregiving	The Core of the Adult's Role	Supportive Guidance
The science of meeting the child's needs—a research-based approach	The core competencies of the adult's role—a practical approach	The art of entering the child's world—a phenomenological approach
· planning meetings	· using a variety of communication approaches to reach all parents	· massaging and providing physical comfort
· determining temperament styles, patterns of behaviour, and individual cycles—and planning to accommodate them	· practising universal precautions	· working collaboratively in a team of caregivers to ensure continuity for the child
		· providing a climate of mutual respect that is role-modelled in all adult–child and adult-to-adult interactions
		· collaborating as equals with all staff, professionals, and parents
· documenting progress of the individual and group of children	· demonstrating program accountability	· encouraging curiosity and risk-taking
		· offering genuine choices
		· emphasizing emotional well-being and personal fulfillment
· implementing activities	· supporting the child's development of pro-social skills	· getting messy with the children
· providing leadership to the team	· accessing a range of materials for play and discovery	· having fun within the child's view of the world
· ensuring minimum ratios	· meeting legislative requirements	· empathizing with a child's feelings
		· discouraging competition between children or parents
		· valuing spiritual aspects of human experience
· following individual program plans	· developing a hierarchy of staff with differentiated roles	· linking home and child-care experiences
· collecting, storing, and accessing contextual and health data	· engineering natural and logical consequences for staff, parent, and child's actions	· encouraging sensory experience while engaging with the child to mediate the child's understanding
· displaying the products of the child's work		· using everyday domestic materials, recycling used materials and accessing found materials
· demonstrating professional behaviour	· preparing children for the next step in their development	· feeling for, and with, a child in distress
		· accepting failure as part of learning
· making sure staff get adequate breaks	· reinforcing progress, building on successes	· giving warnings about what is going to happen
· purchasing appropriate materials and organizing and storing materials	· supplying manufactured toys, play materials	· respecting when a child doesn't want something—food, sleep, or activity
· recognizing children's responses to situations	· accepting natural competition	· providing parameters for behaviour
· adapting to differing approaches to learning—as directed by the child		

ADULTS IN THE LIVES OF INFANTS, TODDLERS, AND 2-YEAR-OLDS (continued)

Responsive Caregiving	The Core of the Adult's Role	Supportive Guidance
The science of meeting the child's needs—a research-based approach	The core competencies of the adult's role—a practical approach	The art of entering the child's world—a phenomenological approach
• developing policies and practices for appropriate guidance (discipline)	• predicting the next developmental stage and planning for it	• being flexible about policies when necessary
• evaluating the program's effectiveness • aesthetics are valued • routines are organized to meet the needs of children, parents and the professional team	• emphasizing the physical, cognitive, and socio-emotional aspects of development	• reflecting on interactions with each child • routines are flexible and match the child's own pace • parent–staff meetings are frequent and organized
• providing a positive role model	• using newsletters and bulletin boards to deliver information	• taking time, avoiding a rush
• identifying the child's developmental stage and providing developmentally appropriate toys	• regular parent–staff meetings are scheduled	• emphasizing the process of discovery • valuing spontaneity
• identifying and responding to a child's special needs • providing resources for families as they are needed	• the process and products of learning are valued	• learning more about child development with the aim to be more successful in understanding children and meeting their needs

See How They Grow draws on elements of each of these models. They are not presented as "right" or "wrong" ways of being in the lives of very young children. There are merits to each one, and most programs for children draw on a variety of differing approaches to create what they think is best. Although the scientific approach—often called the "medical model"—has been critiqued as being insufficiently responsive, our modern version of responsive caregiving embraces current research. Thus the scientific approach has developed over the years into something quite different from the medical model of the 1940s to 1970s, where cleanliness was considered the paramount virtue. Current research emphasizes the development of the brain (what could be more scientific?), but the application of the research leads us to acknowledge the role of attachments and relationships. You will notice that each approach's attributes are listed, but they are not comparable as you look from one column to the next—this is deliberate, because they have developed from different worldviews that cannot easily be categorized.

These concepts—the responsive caregiving approach, the practical approach, and the supportive guidance approach—challenge what we believe about the nature of how and what we need to be in the lives of children. This is a philosophical, practical, and scientific issue.

The following list is an example of how the philosophy was developed for one child-care centre.

Key Characteristics

- holistic support of children and families
- a human, research-based practical philosophy
- a balance of individual and collective rights/needs
- spontaneous and planned activities
- an environment that is hygienic and pleasant
- shared values, being flexible when necessary
- clear, simple policies
- cooperative staff group
- culturally and developmentally appropriate
- sympathetic and empathetic to individuals
- accepting and accommodating of diversity
- observation, assessment, and regular program evaluation
- responsive to individual children
- respectful of children and families
- warm and inviting, use of natural materials

The staff, parents, and community representatives came together to develop a common vision for the Rosegarden Infant and Toddler Centre. Using three models—responsive caregiving, the practical approach, and the phenomenological approach—the group discussed the approach they wanted to take. (The characteristics of Rosegarden are shown in the

Adults in the Lives of Infants, Toddlers, and 2-Year-Olds

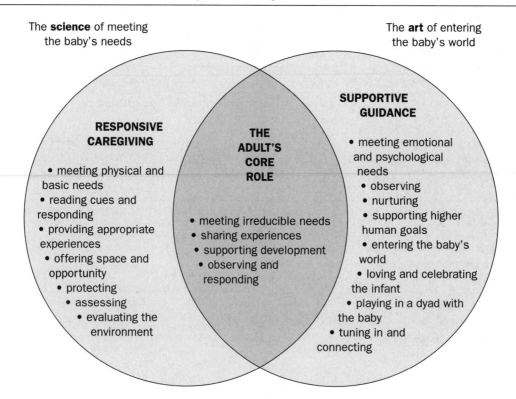

The **science** of meeting the baby's needs

The **art** of entering the baby's world

RESPONSIVE CAREGIVING

- meeting physical and basic needs
- reading cues and responding
- providing appropriate experiences
- offering space and opportunity
- protecting
- assessing
- evaluating the environment

THE ADULT'S CORE ROLE

- meeting irreducible needs
- sharing experiences
- supporting development
- observing and responding

SUPPORTIVE GUIDANCE

- meeting emotional and psychological needs
- observing
- nurturing
- supporting higher human goals
- entering the baby's world
- loving and celebrating the infant
- playing in a dyad with the baby
- tuning in and connecting

At the centre of the adult's role is meeting the child's irreducible needs (see Brazelton & Greenspan, 2000). This includes being aware of and meeting the most basic physical needs and entering into the child's world—combining the art and science of being in the life of the child.

diagrammatic representation of their view, above.) This will help them keep their goals clear as they work with architects, design the children's environments, and plan their program. They have articulated their intentions and now have their own model that will help keep them focused.

The role of the caregiver seems to be much more complex than those in careers outside the human service field. Consequently, early childhood educators need not only a sound preparatory education but also a variety of opportunities for mentored experience in working directly with infants and toddlers. This learning takes time and must be supported by those who have already gained competence.

WORKING WITH VERY YOUNG CHILDREN: WHO IS THE RIGHT PERSON?

It is not enough to say that working with very young children requires patience and a liking for children. These attributes may be essential, but they are only the beginning. Educational institutions and employers use a variety of tools to help them decide who should enter a program or be offered employment. Selection for study at a college or university usually requires the demonstration of academic achievements at previous levels in subjects of study. Where there is "open access," a program may accept candidates on a first-come, first-served basis. The majority of educational institutions require academic credits. Some forward-thinking organizations will enroll students after assessment of their experiential learning—that is, the learning they gained through work or related experience. This is called Prior Learning Assessment and Recognition (PLA or PLAR). This is a useful process because it can enable learners to progress more rapidly and employers to hire staff more readily.

Variations exist across the provinces and territories of Canada in terms of the programs offered, the competencies for entry to practice, and the legislated requirements for employment. Typically there are one- or two-year community college programs that lead to certificates or diplomas in early childhood education as well as university programs leading to bachelor's degrees in ECE, applied arts, child studies, or related fields. These programs often include both academic content and field placements in infant and toddler settings, but this is not always the case. Post-diploma programs are offered by some colleges in infant and toddler studies, or with a focus on young children with special needs. Each province or territory is responsible for its own training and legislation and for the establishment of qualification equivalency for those trained externally.

Across the United States, there are even wider variations in the preparatory programs offered for entry to work with very young children. Legislation varies enormously as to the level of preparation required, and the regulations associated with differing child-care settings. To some extent, the academic and practical preparation required of those who are to work with infants and toddlers indicates the values of that society, as well as what they can afford. Finland and some other European countries that stress parental leave and demand high levels of preparation for care-givers and teachers of young children clearly value the importance of the early years, and are prepared to pay to maintain high standards.

Academic qualifications usually indicate that the holder of the diploma or degree will have certain competencies and will be able to demonstrate the appropriate knowledge, skills, and dispositions for a job in the field. However, academic qualifications alone are rarely reliable predictors of successful practice; additional personal qualities, motivations, and inner directions are also important factors. Working with infants and toddlers is specialized and stressful, and carries a high level of responsibility. Measuring the attributes required for such work is very difficult for employers because they appear to require subjective assessment. With team-based program delivery, the same hiring considerations that apply to early childhood educators also apply to individuals from the fields of nursing, education, medicine, social work, or occupational therapy who work with young children.

Screening processes such as criminal reference checks with the police provide employers with the information necessary to exclude people who have been convicted of criminal offences, particularly those related to children. These are not indicators of competence, only filters to screen out inappropriate people.

College and university programs that articulate their program's learning outcomes offer some indication of the levels of knowledge, skills, and attitudes necessary for working with very young children.

Some of these have been developed carefully, keeping in mind the needs of the community as well as the specific **competencies** required of the early childhood practitioner. They can provide a useful profile for employers who are looking at the competencies required for the job. However, the outcomes are usually stated at a minimum level, rather than the optimal level that an employer might desire.

There are some useful tools being developed by Canadian Child Care Federation (CCCF) and its partners that will help clarify the specifics of the role. The CCCF's **occupational standards** are a written statement of what is required so that a person entering the occupation can do the job in a safe, competent fashion. Occupational standards have three components: (1) description of the core knowledge required, (2) description of the required skills and abilities, and (3) a written code of ethics (CCCF, 2002). While the standards apply to work in any setting other than the home environment, they acknowledge that certain types of settings and ages of children will be associated with additional competencies.

Further competency profiles can be accessed from provincial and territorial professional associations across Canada. In addition, three organizations in the U.S. offer useful documentation: the National Association for Early Childhood Education (NAEYC), the Child Development Associate (CDA) at the Council for Professional Recognition, and Zero to Three. Australia, the United Kingdom, Jamaica, and many other countries have developed their own competency profiles, entry to practice standards, and training standards. Although (and because) they are articulated in different ways, it can be helpful and interesting to review them.

The competencies necessary for working with very young children are not all captured in formal statements, even though each competency document will try to capture the essence of what such work is about. Working with infants, toddlers and 2-year-olds requires a genuine liking for children, not just a sentimental view of their "cuteness." It necessitates addressing your own needs, for the sake of the children, not instead of their needs, because if you are not healthy and balanced you cannot offer them what they need. Caring for and nurturing children requires patience, not merely sitting and waiting for development to occur. Constant observation, knowing what to look for, and what to make of what you see is at the core of the work. It demands a sense of fun and a sense of the ridiculous. Seeing the world at the child's level is another part of the educator's abilities—without being condescending or patronizing. Educating involves anticipating what the children are about to do and then responding when they do the unexpected. Vast knowledge about children's development is necessary and it must be applied very quickly when the occasion arises. Communication and advocacy skills are an asset—applied so as to relate to the real context of children and families. Having respect for all people is vital even when they think differently or hold challenging beliefs. The early childhood practitioner must lead children to independence while sustaining a two-way attachment with them. Above all, practitioners need to honour the opportunity to be involved in the lives of other human beings. They must also "let go" when the time comes and accept that things don't always work out as they had hoped. Can all these things be measured? Not easily!

▶ Practical Experience for the Student Educator

Preparation for working with young children consists of two major elements: academic study and practical experience. After students have studied theory, philosophy, and child development, among other subjects, it is important that they gain experience in the field. Ideally, such experience begins with an opportunity for observation and discussion and progresses to actual participation in the program of a centre. This section reviews some of the important issues that surround student placements, including consideration of the children's needs, the experience that students should gain, and the expectations of the centres involved.

PUTTING THE CHILDREN FIRST

The cardinal rule when working with young children is that the child comes first. Students need to learn by participating in practical situations, but this must never occur at the expense of the children's health or well-being. Learning situations must entail no risk to the children. Meeting the children's needs may mean that the student's needs are put aside for awhile. It is a good idea to chat with the centre's supervisor and the school's supervising faculty to create strategies that support the learning needs of the student educator.

BEING A LEARNER

If there is a practicum manual, placement guide, or other type of field practice document, the student should become familiar with it and make sure that the

college, the centre, and the students share common understandings about expectations. If there is a college field faculty supervisor, this person will take a role in supporting the student's learning. If the supervisor has particular requirements or expectations, these should be clarified.

Ideally, students start the preparation for their study with extended periods of non-participatory observation and with opportunities to discuss their observations with an experienced practitioner. Even prior to this non-participatory phase, however, students should have taken courses in child development, philosophy, and sociology. In-depth study must also occur concurrently with field practice, so that students can make reasonable inferences about the children's needs as they become apparent. Understanding helps to make the student's role clear.

Observation is one of the most important ways of learning about infants and toddlers and about the program that is designed to meet their needs. Students have a responsibility to acquire skills in observing and recording pertinent developmental information. The methods of recording are likely to be learned in the college classroom, but the larger part of the task is accomplished at the centre, learning to look very carefully, to record objectively what is seen, and then to interpret the observations. This process leads to a better understanding of the development of infants and toddlers, increased understanding of their needs, and an expanded repertoire of skills in responsivity. It also improves the student's appreciation of how the children's environment should be constructed. Observation skills are discussed in detail in Chapter 2.

In addition to providing opportunities to observe the children, the centre also provides an opportunity for students to learn from observing professional child-care workers in action. The student educator can learn a great deal from the role models provided by the qualified staff members. Students also have the opportunity to ask appropriate questions about what they see in the centre. Some practices may require explanation or demonstration if the student is to learn them successfully. Students will benefit from an environment that encourages asking questions about any aspect of practice.

Not all staff members will be equally open to answering students' questions or to providing feedback on student performance. Students should be prepared to request feedback if necessary, as this is a very important part of the learning process. In addition, students must be aware of what is going on at the centre and be reflective about their efforts to fit into the program and meet the children's needs. An important prerequisite for fitting in is reading and understanding the agency's philosophy statement and observing and asking questions about how it translates into practice.

WORKING WITH THE AGENCY

Centre supervisors or directors may have particular requirements of students. Students are more likely to be successful if they find out what these requirements are and how they translate into practical procedures. For example, ways in which parents are to be contacted, the style of programming, and the type of record-keeping that students are expected to do may differ from place to place.

The amount of preparation that students will do depends on the stage of their learning, the success of previous plans, and the responsivity of the philosophy of the centres at which they are placed. Students will need to make sure that they understand the extent of their responsibility for the program. Along with this, students must be sure to document their learning in the way required by the agency and the college. Some centres will want all activities planned and evaluated. At others, spontaneous interactions are more important.

Child-care programs may emphasize a particular aspect of curriculum or be more responsive to particular developmental domains. This may influence aspects of the caregiver's role. Some programs focus on intellectual stimulation, while others may highlight emotional attachments or meeting physical needs. Students may find that the program does not fit their personal philosophy. However, a student must be slow to make judgments about the program or about how children are handled; they may not be in possession of key information. For this reason, students should ask questions about what they see. This is a key part of their learning.

Students will sometimes find that they are given practical tasks to do, such as making play materials, changing diapers, cleaning infant chairs, or other such work. These are all part of the learning experience and should not be resisted. However, there can be times when students are asked to focus on practical jobs rather than being with the children. If this becomes excessive, students should talk to their supervisors about their own learning needs. This can be a difficult issue because there may be an expectation that students have to "pay their dues." A balance needs to be negotiated between this expectation and satisfying the students' learning needs.

The student educator has the opportunity to work as a member of a team of educators and other professionals. All members of the team must be able to listen to one another's perspectives and to discuss issues and negotiate appropriately. Although the student's perspective is valid, it is based on less experience. Thus, the student should remember that qualified staff will always be responsible for making decisions. However, depending on the centre, students frequently have input into the process. Despite variations among centres, all student educators will learn how groups function and how they can contribute to the practice within the centre.

Students may also wish to gain experience in evaluating and planning environments for infants and toddlers. However, a student must gain knowledge of research related to indicators of high-quality environments for young children before she can start planning or rearranging the placement environment. The student might want to observe the environment for several reasons, including improving its use, evaluating the room to identify safety concerns, or assessing the success of the setting in stimulating intellectual curiosity. To what extent the student is able to influence elements of the environment is the choice of the agency staff, but this opportunity will help the student to gain skill in this area.

As students' skills are developed, there will probably be greater opportunity to use those skills in an integrated and responsive way. At no time should students be left alone with one or more children. Qualified staff must always be present, even if the students appear to be competent. There are several reasons for this, including insurance requirements, legal liability, parental expectations, and undue risk. Students should not be used as extra staff. Toward the end of the placement it is likely that students will want to take responsibility for the program and see if they can stretch themselves to perform all the competencies of the job. This may be possible, and desirable, as long as qualified staff are readily available to assist and offer the students feedback.

WORKING WITH THE CHILDREN

The most enjoyable part of the student's role is being involved directly with the young children. This role should be enjoyable. Remember that others will pick up on and respond to the student's attitude in working with the children. Although aspects of the work should be fun, students should remember that their first responsibility is to meet the children's needs.

The heart of the role of the students is responding to the developmental needs of the infants and toddlers in their care. To do this well, students will need to apply what they have learned in their academic courses. Understanding what is happening with the children and why they are behaving in particular ways is essential. Students should use the theoretical parts of study to help explain what they observe. Based on this observation and analysis, students need to learn how to fulfill the infants' and toddlers' needs. Chapter 3 details the principles of child development, and subsequent chapters describe the stages of development throughout the early years.

Although infants and toddlers in group care have individual needs, they may not receive constant one-on-one attention. Student educators must learn how to manage the group and facilitate collective needs while making sure individual needs are met. Frequently, student educators will learn to support one child at a time before they have responsibility for a whole group of infants and toddlers.

The emphasis on *individual* care and education for babies and toddlers might lead us to think that only two-way communication can be effective. Undoubtedly, this dyad allows for close attachments and the building of trust, but it should not exclude other relationships. Indeed, in a homecare or child-care setting, people are not paired off to the exclusion of other relationships. The dynamics of groups can allow for communication across pairs and allow for three-way (or more) connections.

The adult can see to the needs of one child while anticipating the needs of a second and reaching out to a third. This takes skill and a clear understanding of the attachment and relationship process, requiring the maintenance of individualized responses. The complexities of attachment behaviours will be discussed in subsequent chapters. Meeting the needs of several young children at once is challenging. It helps to understand the stages of child development, so that you can determine their needs more effectively. An effective adult with a calm disposition will be able to facilitate conversations that embrace a group, scan the environment and activities to see when intervention is necessary, and facilitate playful interactions while doing so.

Student educators will also be expected to take responsibility for their own general health and to contribute to the agency's task of ensuring an optimal environment for the physical and mental health of the young children. Responsibility for personal health requires consideration of immunizations, chest X-rays, screening for health conditions, regular physical examinations, exercise, good nutrition, dental health, general cleanliness, frequent hand-washing, and stress management.

The agency will want to reduce the possibility of spreading infection. Students can help with this if they look after their own health. In addition, they will need to follow required protocols for diapering and the personal hygiene of infants and toddlers. Preparation of formula and other foods, as well as actual feeding, requires scrupulous care. Student educators must follow instructions as well as respond to the needs of the infants and toddlers.

Safety considerations include protection of the infants or toddlers in every way. Students must be aware of general safety issues and make sure they are mindful of particular hazards that are situational or concern a particular child. Health, infection control, and safety are covered in detail in chapters 4 to 12.

WORKING WITH PARENTS

Not all child-care centres are comfortable with letting inexperienced student educators approach parents or answer their questions.

Reasons for this hesitation include fears that students might convey inappropriate or inaccurate information, might not know important pieces of confidential information about the family, could undermine a fragile relationship of trust, might provide an inappropriate role model, or might not convey information to centre staff. In addition, there could be legal, insurance, or ethical implications for direct student–parent contact.

Despite these considerations, it is important for students to learn how to listen to parents and how to respond to parental requests. The best way to acquire a new skill is to see it in action and then to try it out. Student educators need to have exposure to parents in varying situations so that they can become effective communicators.

Students should consider the following strategies:

- Ask the agency for permission to work with one or two selected families.
- Request supervision in all parent interactions.
- Attempt to obtain information about families through indirect contact, such as questionnaires.
- Ask qualified staff to review all communications (i.e., bulletin boards, newsletters, curriculum packages, health information) before the student posts or distributes them.
- Create a developmental portfolio that can be shared with the parent with the help of qualified staff.

- Role-play situations involving interaction with parents.
- View videotapes of "ideal" parent interviews or communications between qualified staff and parents.
- Prepare daily reports that can be presented to parents via qualified staff.
- Ask qualified staff to show parents photographs or videotapes of the student working with their young child.

PROFESSIONAL CONDUCT

Professionalism is expected from student educators. This will include:
- punctuality

- confidentiality

- appropriate clothing, shoes, outdoor protection, hairstyles, nail length, and personal presentation for the type of work (see Box 1.8)
- demonstrated respect for families and young children
- respect shown to staff and fellow students
- high standards of personal hygiene
- appropriate styles of communication
- demonstrated acceptance and inclusion of all young children.

Working with very young children is demanding. It is likely that, while working with children, students will also have to keep up with college assignments and personal commitments. Time management skills are absolutely essential for success. It is helpful to keep an organizer/date book so that commitments can be scheduled.

BOX 1.8

A PRACTICAL YET PROFESSIONAL APPEARANCE

Working with infants and toddlers can be messy. When considering clothing and accessories, student educators have to find a balance between what is practical and what still looks professional. Suggestions include:

- clean, tidy, well-presented, and practical washable clothes
- pants, longer skirts, knee-length shorts, saris, and other ethnic dress
- sweaters, sweatshirts, shirts, blouses, T-shirts
- cotton or poly-cotton fabrics
- flat shoes (separate indoor and outdoor)
- sandals with ankle straps and enclosed toes
- climate-appropriate coats, hats, gloves
- sun hats and sunglasses when necessary
- sunscreen when necessary
- safe name badges
- fanny packs for emergency kits
- aprons for messy tasks
- unbreakable lenses in glasses

In addition, it is important to wash regularly and pay attention to personal grooming. Some centre settings might be uncomfortable with:

- tattoos
- body piercing
- brightly dyed hair
- some messages on T-shirts
- transparent tops
- jeans or other denim items
- track pants and sweatshirts
- leggings
- eccentric clothes

- unwashed/wrinkled items
- biker jackets
- clinging dresses or skirts
- short shorts or short skirts
- uncovered arms
- religious and some other symbols
- bare feet or legs
- nail polish/long nails
- clunky jewellery

Student educators should avoid:

- flowing scarves
- wool/angora items
- tank tops
- advertising on garments
- bare bellies
- formal suits
- constrictive clothing
- uniforms or medical coats
- flip-flops or slippers
- sun exposure
- cold or wind exposure

- high-heeled shoes
- heavy makeup
- long nails
- perfume
- uncovered cuts, sores, warts
- purses
- sharp brooches or pins
- dangling earrings, bracelets, or necklaces
- sharp or heavy rings
- big hairdos or long loose hair

Consider the reasons for avoiding these items. How might they apply to your work setting?

Just balancing day-to-day work demands can be a challenge for the student educator. In addition, the student must be prepared for extraordinary situations. For example, a student might observe a situation that appears to involve either neglect or inappropriate handling of young children. The student must be aware of the agency's policies on these situations. It is not for the student to make judgments, approach parents, or tell tales to staff members or people outside the agency. If there is a possibility of child abuse of any kind, the internal policy of the centre must be adhered to. This is likely to involve contacting the local child protection agency. The student must offer any written documentation or observations (not proof) of a potential concern. The agency will treat the inquiry in confidence and follow up as it sees fit.

It is not only in a child protection situation that students need to maintain confidentiality. In any placement, students will have access to information about infants, toddlers, and their families. When they are working with qualified educators, it might be appropriate to discuss an issue that is related to confidential information. However, this should be done only if it is in the interest of the child, not because the student wants to gossip. The professional behaviour expected of a student includes avoidance of sharing any information outside the agency.

Confidentiality also applies to observations, assignments, learning logs, and any other written or spoken information about the children, staff, and parents at the agency. Sometimes students will need to share information in class about a child or situation or write an assignment related to the agency or children. The best way to deal with this is to use pseudonyms (i.e., change the names of the individuals

involved) and remove some identifying details if necessary.

▶ The Role of the Professional Educator

After successful placement experiences, the student educators will be ready to take on the role of a practising educator by accepting primary responsibility for a group of infants and toddlers. Professional educators have the responsibility to:

- articulate a philosophy of care and education for infants and toddlers and determine the practical demonstration of such a philosophy.
- meet the physical needs of the infants and toddlers in their care.
- communicate effectively with parents and meet their requests.
- observe and record pertinent developmental information and make appropriate assessments about each child's development.
- document and store personal, family, health, and emergency data, as well as demonstrations of developmental change about each child.
- design and implement a program that is developmentally appropriate for each young child.
- provide individually responsive curriculum and guidance.
- support infants' and toddlers' emerging skills.
- organize, manage, and facilitate young children in a small group.
- respond to the individual cues of infants and toddlers.
- stimulate infants and toddlers appropriately using sensory activities and experiences.

- design individual program plans, including activity plans.
- provide continuity of care, nurturance, and support for infants and toddlers.
- work collectively and collaboratively with team members to provide an appropriate program.
- communicate effectively with human service professionals.
- comply with all legislation, regulations, and guidelines pertaining to the profession.
- accommodate children of different abilities, backgrounds, and cultures, and promote an anti-bias environment.
- promote healthy attachments and provide emotional support for each child.
- design a professional development plan and keep a professional portfolio of learning and achievements.
- support the learning of student educators when possible.

- promote professionalism, advocate for the rights of children, and become an active member of a professional body supporting educators.

Before we leave the role of professional educator, let's think about what it is to be part of the lives of young children and their families. Rather than outline what this means to you in the context of your role and responsibilities, read the following selections from a transcription of a videotape. This might help you appreciate what your role is—although the relationship described is one between a well-know infant clinician and a mother, you are likely to glean from it a greater depth of meaning than can be conveyed by merely listing the requirements of your role. After reading the transcript, try to interpret how this approach might affect your own work, where you have different responsibilities but ones with similar importance. You might also identify some elements of the author's work that are not within your role.

A Story That May Influence How You See Your Role

I remember a lot of time when we came here, there was this doll that my daughter loved.

She named her Baby Lyn.

And every time we'd come, that doll was there.

I remember one particular day when we came, the doll wasn't there, and she was so broken-hearted.

And it was like, "Let's find Baby Lyn. We have to find Baby Lyn!"

I was like, "Wow!—You're really going to look for a stupid doll for my daughter to make her feel good?"

I just thought it was really great.

You got into looking for this doll—seriously—asking everybody—"Have they seen this doll?"—everybody.

And you found her.

And I was like wow! All this for a doll?

And you let my daughter bring her home, and that doll was—the centre of her world.

Baby Lyn sat at the table and ate with us.

She was just there, all the time, right up under her arm.

Walking around with her.

She was the show-and-tell doll—every Friday. "This is Baby Lyn."

And when Baby Lyn's face got a little smudge on it, I had to give Baby Lyn a bath.

She was so excited about this doll that it was just like—I guess a part of here came home with us for her—and for me.

I saw a change in my child.

It was something good that came home, that I learned from my daughter and her doll.

Like if she hurt, she pointed to the doll's arm.

(. . . continued)

Or if a tooth was coming in and hurt, Baby Lyn's mouth "hurt right here."

I thought it was so great—I was learning what's hurting on her, from her doll.

You came over and I was really surprised . . .

You came in my neighbourhood.

You weren't afraid.

On a day that I was really, really sick and missed an appointment, you were determined to keep our appointment, no matter what.

And it was—OK—that really felt good that somebody cared enough to come and see us.

Antricia was running up and down the stairs, excited, saying:

"Oh, Jeree's here, Jeree's here. She has a present! She has a present!"

I said, "Calm down, girl!"

I was really surprised and taken aback that, you know, you came to my neighbourhood and to see me.

And the walls started tumbling down, and I could trust a little bit more.

I was surprised at everything that you did.

Because growing up, for me, nobody was ever there, and—as I said before—I never trusted anybody.

Everything was the opposite of what I thought.

Like when you came over in my neighbourhood, it was just—I never thought you would do that.

When you let my daughter have Baby Lyn from the program, I was like, "She would never give this doll away."

And I was like, "Take good care of this doll, you know, we can't get her dirty."

I learned something from my daughter—that it's OK to take what people are giving you, if it is in a good way.

And it's OK if you mess up. It was different . . .

When you stepped in, it was like, OK, this is something that I really did need.

You were just yourself.

You weren't afraid to speak up and let me know that there are things that I shouldn't be doing.

Most people are afraid to let people know those things. You can't be hitting, you can't be doing this.

Right off the bat—you didn't hold back.

So it was really great that you were honest and you were *there*.

You had feelings.

It was like a handshake.

It was a strong handshake.

It was real.

I told you once when I was upset and hit my daughter and you just came right out and said, "We can't have that."

And I thought, "What? Excuse me? This is my child. You can't tell me what to do."

(This is all in my mind—like "No!", you know.)

I was just blown away, it just tickled me.

Wow! She's yelling at me.

(. . . continued)

It was so cute—it really struck me as funny.

Because you didn't hold your tongue.

Most people—I feel that they're afraid of the consequences . . . they'll stop, and then there will be, "Well, I'm just going to have to take your child from you."

That's not the way to go about it.

It's . . . not helpful.

When you said, "You just can't do that, you know, I won't have it," it was like, "OK, wow."

I felt like a three-year-old, but it just felt really good that you weren't afraid to say that to me.

And it was easy to say, "OK, I won't hit her no more."

And I haven't.

Which is good.

Sometimes I really want to just tear her up.

But I've learned—and she's learned—that hitting isn't the way to raise a child.

Now when she's sixteen and wants to do something wrong, I'm going to bring her here and say, "OK, I never hit her. Take care of this situation!"

At first, I couldn't read you.

I couldn't crack you.

No matter what I did, you were there.

You were just hanging on.

And because I didn't trust, I didn't think you liked me.

But once I started to trust in something, it felt comfortable . . .

I did feel that you liked me . . .

It was just me, and the way I was feeling anyway.

It's not what you do, it's how you do it that made a difference.

And I think if you're one of those people that smile in people's faces and then aren't really there for them, no matter how much you smile, you can see under that, no matter how bad you're feeling.

And with you, it wasn't like that.

Everything was real.

I remember one night you took my daughter and me out to dinner, and I was totally blown away.

It was my birthday, too, and I never had a party.

I never celebrated my birthday; it was like just another day.

And here we were going out this night, and it was the day I was born.

It was like a little birthday celebration, and my daughter was there.

She was surprised that a birthday can be so intimate and small.

This birthday made me feel good inside.

I liked it.

That day, you were there after five.

It was like, "Wow, I'm so special!"

It was great . . . it was something I know that you didn't have to do, and I didn't feel that you were making yourself sit here and have dinner, and it just made me feel really special.

Another time I was having a real hard time.

(. . . continued)

You had come over.

I had called you.

You had given me your home phone number.

I was, like, "OK, she gave me her home phone number. I'm going to use it!"

I was feeling really, really down, and I called you and you came over, even though I knew by your voice that you were—you have your own life, and everything, but you came over, and it was like, "Oh, wow, she's here, she's actually here."

I was basically testing the waters.

I needed somebody with me that day.

You were there.

You really didn't have to be, but you were.

I've been through a lot of programs, and ran into a lot of people on the mental health highway, and you run into a lot of people that are just there for the money, if it's money, or whatever it is.

They're not there because they want to be there to help people.

And they're really rude, and nasty.

They don't give a damn about you . . .

They can really build a . . . plexiglass thing between you . . .

It's like . . . they're at this high desk, and you're at this low desk and chair, and they're looking down on you, and they really make you feel bad.

And it's like—yuck. I don't know if I can trust this person with my life, because they're not really there.

Well, actually, I just feel that they should be on the other side of this plexiglass—with me.

You and my other therapist were mother figures for me.

I really didn't know how to raise this little, tiny baby.

I didn't know what to do aside from changing diapers and feeding and burping.

That's not all there's to it.

I didn't know.

With your help . . . for me it felt like having two mother figures help me along with my child.

Not having that from my own family . . .

I feel that if I can raise my child properly, then maybe she'll be a better person to her kid.

It's like breaking the cycle.

I wasn't raised properly, and learning something from you and my therapist helped me to raise my child properly.

Even though I was like 27, 26, hey, I was being raised . . .

You can be raised over, no matter how old you are.

You guys taught me how to love.

You taught me how to speak—speak softly—with a big voice.

You taught me how to care.

And those were things that weren't inside of me.

Excerpt from Jeree H. Pawl (February/March 1995), The Therapeutic Relationship as Human Connectedness: Being Held in Another's Mind, *Zero to Three.*

PROFESSIONAL DEVELOPMENT

Successful early childhood educators are lifelong learners. They continue to learn on the job and by involving themselves in professional development opportunities. As with any kind of learning, self-direction in which each person takes responsibility for her or his own learning and career development leads to a more successful outcome.

It is desirable that employers take a role and support the professional development (PD) of their staff with money and time. The cost will be recovered in terms of staff retention, personal refreshment, lifelong learning, increased quality of service delivery, and improved parental satisfaction.

Large organizations such as the YMCA, YWCA, professional associations, colleges, and universities can offer in-house training, coaching, and professional supports for their staff working in child care. Smaller operators combine their professional development efforts or "buy in" to the resources offered through commercial organizations, professional associations, and large conferences. The Canadian Child Care Federation (CCCF), the Canadian Association for Young Children (CAYC), the National Association for the Education of Young Children (NAEYC), Zero to Three, and the Association for Childhood Education International (ACEI) offer some of the best professional development opportunities through conferences, symposiums, distance learning, and training institutes.

The most accessible learning materials are the books and journals that are available in the education, parenting, and child-care sections of bookstores.

Early childhood research data are available from many Canadian, American, and European sources, including government departments, universities, interest and advocacy groups, and research institutes. Particularly useful are statistical data from Statistics Canada and research information provided by the Childcare Resource and Research Unit at the University of Toronto and by Human Resources Development Canada.

Concept Media, Resources in Education (RIE), and other filmmakers offer video training materials that can be excellent support. With CD-ROM and Internet access, the amount of information available is enormous. Even so, many educators find that interactive learning is more effective. Professional development must be timely, pertinent, reinforced, and applicable, and must have follow-up supports if it is to be really helpful.

The Philosophy of See How They Grow

At the centre of the philosophy of See How They Grow is the valuing of individual infants and toddlers for who they are, what they can do, and for the families they are based in. Each young child is an individual with diverse abilities, interests, and experiences. Children may be parented according to a range of values and beliefs, but each needs to be fully accepted and respected. Specifically, See How They Grow is based on the following beliefs:

- Babies are amazingly complex human beings.
- Babies and toddlers are competent and have incredible potential to make relationships, learn, and adapt.
- Parents are the most important adults in their children's lives.
- Parents are the caregivers' partners in supporting the needs of their young children.
- Respect for young children and their families is at the core of all aspects of practice.
- Safety and protection from harm are the first priorities of caregivers.
- Maintaining the infants' and toddlers' health and well-being is essential to caregiving strategies.
- Infants and toddlers are individuals in terms of their growth, rhythms, patterns of development, temperament styles, and needs.
- The study of infant and toddler development through observation, research, and application of theoretical models is essential for furthering understanding and meeting the needs of young children more effectively.
- The development of infants and toddlers is holistic, even though we may study its domains and issues separately.

- Infants and toddlers have the right to have all their basic physical and psychological needs met.
- Infants are born into cultural and familial contexts, and their development must be viewed within those contexts.
- There are many ways of nurturing children, most of which should be openly accepted.
- Infants and toddlers of varying abilities, of differing appearances, from any culture or ethnic background, from any social or economic class, and from either gender are equally deserving of high-quality care and nurturance, although their needs may differ.
- Infants and toddlers must be in an environment that meets their needs for **attachment** and continuity of care.
- Observational, health, and contextual information should be kept up to date, and recorded and stored in a confidential manner.
- Guidance strategies used with infants and toddlers must support the individual developmental needs of the child.
- Adults act as mediators in many aspects of the young child's learning.
- Including children of all abilities is beneficial to all.
- It can be more important to "be" with children than to "do" with them.
- Abuse of young children stems from inappropriate power dynamics in adult–child relationships; how this abuse is demonstrated frequently relates to the child's developmental stage.
- Preparation for and evaluation of the caregiving role must be thorough and ongoing.
- Caregivers are responsible for their own health and well-being in the performance of their role.
- An infant's and toddler's curriculum involves every aspect of the child's experience, both planned and unplanned.

▶ Summary

A statement of philosophy contains the values and beliefs about children that drive all aspects of practice in a child-care centre. The philosophy must be carefully considered, discussed, and articulated so that it is understandable and becomes a living document that shapes all activity within an agency.

How a centre arrives at the statement that contains its philosophy takes time and effort for both research and reflection. It will involve looking at beliefs about children, best practices, and examining current knowledge of child development, and seeking indicators of high-quality service delivery.

A field placement is an opportunity for students to put their understanding of theory into practice. Learning about the program, fitting into its philosophy, getting along with the staff, and working with the children require observation, communication, and a real effort to be appropriate in behaviour and attitudes.

As students become practising educators, they will continue on their path of lifelong learning. Maturity, experience, and reflective practice combine to allow the educator to be an increasingly responsive person delivering high-quality care and education.

▶ KEY TERMS

anti-bias curriculum
attachment
best practices
child-centredness
competencies
culturally diverse
developmental domains
developmentally appropriate practice (DAP)
direct instruction
early intervention
ecological system
ethics
holistic development
individual
norm
occupational standards
phenomenology
philosophy
philosophy statement
quality care indicators
responsive caregiving
social context
special needs (exceptional needs)
values

▶ DISCUSSION QUESTIONS

1. Where do your own beliefs about young children come from?
2. What would an ideal infant or toddler environment look like?
3. If parents and educators have differing views about children's needs and development, what compromise could be acceptable?
4. Looking at your society in general and the media in particular, what images of childhood are projected?
5. How do your beliefs about young children compare with society's view?

▶ ADDITIONAL RESOURCES

▶ Further Reading

Doherty-Derkowski, G. (1995). *Quality Matters: Excellence in Early Childhood Programs.* Don Mills, ON: Addison-Wesley.

Erickson, M., and K. Kurz-Riemer. (1999). *Infants, Toddlers and Families.* New York, NY: Guilford Press.

Gerber, M. (ed.). (1987). *A Manual for Parents and Professionals.* Los Angeles, CA: Resources for Infant Educators.

Ideas: Emotional Well-Being in Child Care. *Interaction.* Canadian Child Care Federation. George Brown College, Toronto, ON.

Phillips, D.A. (ed.). (1988). *Quality in Child Care: What Does the Research Tell Us?* Washington, DC: National Association for the Education of Young Children.

Chandler, K. (2003). *Administering for Quality: Canadian Early Childhood Development Programs.* Toronto, ON: Prentice Hall.

David, M., & G. Appell. (1973). *LOCZY: An Unusual Approach to Mothering.* (Trans. J.M. Clark, from *Lóczy ou le materage insolite*). Los Angeles, CA: Resources for Infant Educators.

Doherty, G., & M. Friendly. (2002). *Making the Best Use of the You Bet I Care! Data Sets: Final Report on a Research Forum.* Toronto, ON: Childcare Resource & Research Unit.

Feeney, S., & N. Freeman. (1999). *Ethics and the Early Childhood Educator: Using the NAEYC Code.* Washington, DC: NAEYC.

Gerber, M. (1991). *The RIE Manual for Parents and Professionals: A Basic Introduction to RIE.* Los Angeles, CA: Resources for Infant Educators.

Hewes, J. (1995). *Many Ways to Grow: Responding to Cultural Diversity in Early Childhood Settings.* Edmonton, AB: Alberta Association for Young Children.

NICHD Early Child Care Research Network. (2002). Child Care Structure, Process, Outcome: Direct and Indirect Effects of Child Care Quality on Young Children's Development. *Psychological Science 13*(3).

Wardle, F. (2003). *Introduction to Early Childhood Education: A Multi-Dimensional Approach to Child-Centered Care and Learning.* Boston, MA: Allyn & Bacon.

▶ Useful Web sites

Canadian Child Care Federation (CCCF)
www.cfc-ef.ca/cccf

Child Care Resource and Research Unit
www.childcarecanada.org

Zero to Three
www.zerotothree.org

Association for Childhood Education International (ACEI)
www.udel.edu/bateman/acei/

National Association for the Education of Young Children (NAEYC)
www.naeyc.org

Educarers: World of Infants
www.educarer.com/index.htm

CHAPTER 2

Getting in Focus: Observing Infants, Toddlers, and Twos

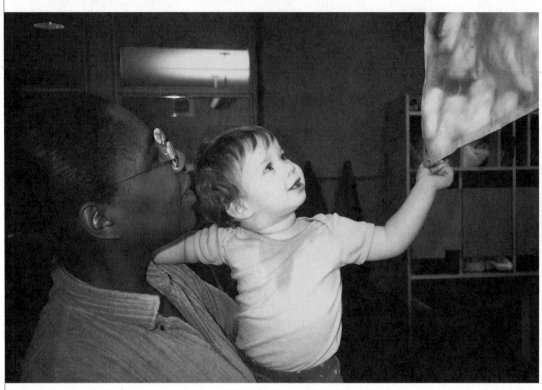

Following the child's lead means that we have to observe his behaviour carefully and respond to *his* time frame, not ours.

Learning Outcomes

After reading and studying this chapter, you should be able to:

- explain why it is important to observe and record pertinent information about the behaviour of infants and toddlers
- identify the characteristics of effective observation strategies for infants and toddlers
- describe the use of developmental portfolios as authentic assessment tools for infants and toddlers
- develop a system for assessing the development of very young children that aligns with your philosophy of care and education

Scene: An art class taken by a variety of learners, including early childhood students—this is an elective course.

"Ways of seeing are not just a matter of using your eyes," explained a university teacher. "It's not what your eyes see, but what your brain processes, and that's an issue related to your previous experience and beliefs." The teacher was addressing perception as it relates to appreciating art, but several listeners who were also early childhood education students felt that the notion applied to observing children, too.

Perception is a subject of interest to artists, philosophers, psychologists, medical professionals, and, of course, educators. The principles in each discipline are equally valid. Artists consider perception from an aesthetic perspective; philosophers approach it as a way of understanding values and beliefs. Psychologists study the role of the brain in perceptual functioning, and medical practitioners report new leaps forward in applications of perception in health care. Finally, educators examine perception and **reflective practice** when teaching methodologies of observation and recording.

A Professional Cycle of Reflective Practice

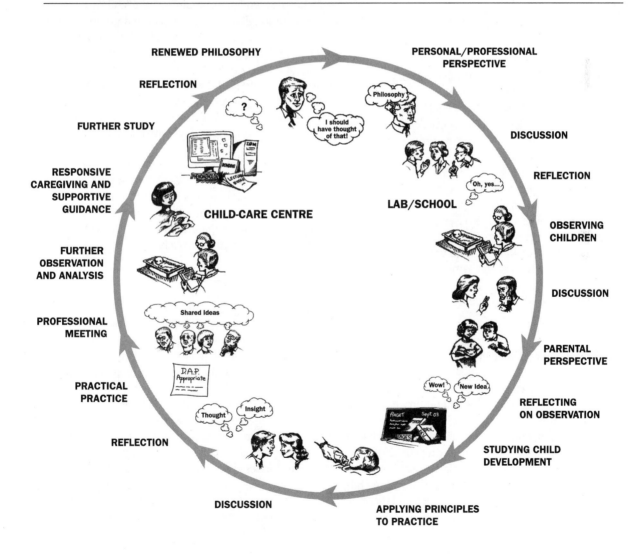

▶ Why Observe?

"What's the point of learning all that stuff about observation methods. I can see, can't I?" asked a student at the start of my observational skills class. My response was "I'll ask *you* the same question at the end of the course." As it turned out, I did ask her the question as she handed in her last observation assignment. She replied, "Well, I didn't know before that the more I look, the more I see . . . and now I've learned something about child development I know what to look for . . . The trouble is, the more I know about children the more I know I need to learn about them . . . and as I observe more, I know I need to do more with the children."

That is the core of our challenge. We need to practise **observation** to learn about children. As we observe and study, we learn more about what to look for. We apply what we know about children and can then find improved ways of supporting them. An ongoing circle of action—that is, observing, interpreting, responding, and continuing to observe—will lead you to be an effective caregiver for infants and toddlers. You will become skilled in observing, increase your knowledge of child development to help you interpret what you see, learn to respond sensitively, learn ways to support and protect, interact positively, and provide experiences for each individual child. In many caregiver preparation programs in colleges and universities, these skills are taught as separate subjects: observation skills, infant and toddler development, curriculum for young children, and guidance. This book illustrates how you can learn the skills and apply them at the same time. This chapter will begin with observation, because it will be the basis of every other part of your work.

▶ What to Observe

The more we observe, the better we respond; the more we know about developmental processes, the better we know what to look for. The essential pathway to knowing what to observe is practising your observation skills and reviewing the effectiveness of the responses that you make, based on what you see. Increasing your experience with young children and studying developmental stages and theories allows you to appreciate the behavioural details that you might otherwise miss.

Focusing your attention, however well intentioned, is inadequate if you know little about what you are looking at. The trained educator becomes increasingly able to pay attention to behaviours that help to explain what is going on for that child.

▶ When to Observe

No time of day is more important than another for observational purposes. Even the sleep times of infants and toddlers can provide you with interesting observations. Feeding, diaper-changing, bathing, and dressing times, as well as transitions and separations from the parents, are as significant as the times when the infant or toddler is playing or interacting with other people. Ensure that you informally observe all aspects of the young child's day. Also plan more organized systems for observation so that you can record sufficient information about all aspects of the child's day and all domains of the child's development. Although developmental domains can help you review all aspects of the child's development, you must remember that you are recording information about a whole human being. All children are deserving of respect, confidentiality, and an appreciation of their wholeness. Detailed information need not be cold and clinical; the purpose is to support the amazing, dynamic, and individual process of human development.

Remember that all the information you collect will need to be reviewed afterward so that you can consider what development is being demonstrated, what the individual needs might be, and how you can respond. Always separate the objectively recorded information from your analysis.

PERMISSION

Educators, caregivers, and students should always seek **permission** from the parents to observe, record information, or make evaluations about any child. Sometimes permission is given as an integral part of enrollment in a child-care centre, but this should always be checked. If the permission is not up to date, it should be requested again. Figure 2.1 shows a sample permission form. Before any observations are recorded, parental permission must be obtained. When parents enroll their children in a centre, the observation and assessment processes should be discussed with them. This usually means that it becomes an accepted part of practice for educators to observe and record information about individual children. Parents need to understand this and become active in participating in the observational protocols. It should be part of the interviewing process for parents to sign a form giving their consent for appropriate observations to be

FIGURE 2.1

Sample Permission Form

Permission Form for Observations and Portfolios
An agreement between students and parents or caregivers and parents.

Parents are asked to give permission to students and teachers to make observations about the children in our centre. This provides the students with an important learning opportunity and assists them with their college courses.

Please complete the lower half of this form, indicating your preferences about documenting your child's developmental progress and allowing access to information about your family.

TO BE COMPLETED BEFORE HANDING TO PARENT

I, _____ (student/teacher name), will not document any information about your child without your signed consent. I will abide by your requirements for storing and accessing this information. Such information will be recorded objectively and sensitively. If you wish to review this documentation at any reasonable time, this will be facilitated.

Signed   Dated

_____   _____

I/we _____ (parent's name(s)), _____ (date),

_____ (phone #), agree to have _____ (child's name)

observed   _____

photographed   _____

audiotaped   _____

videotaped   _____

Please initial the categories above that are acceptable.

In addition, I/we will be comfortable if we are approached to provide any of the following information:

health history   _____

family information _____   Please initial the categories that are acceptable.

I/we agree to the student/teacher collecting any of the following:

artwork samples   _____

handprints   _____

footprints   _____   Please initial the categories that are acceptable.

Please return this form to _____.

THANKS FOR YOUR HELP.

Parent's signature _____

recorded and stored. They should always be given reasonable access to any of this documentation.

Students who are learning about children, and acquiring skills in documentation, will need to seek, and gain, written permission from parents before undertaking their work. Sometimes permission is granted by the parent on the original form on enrollment, but this cannot be assumed. As with any other research, permission should always be requested when it concerns human subjects—including children. Any recordings should be discussed with parents only after the student educator has checked with the supervisor or mentor. Any inferences made must be checked before parents see the material or hear the educator's opinion. This is because, like a doctor's diagnosis, professional opinions must be reliable.

▶ Getting Started

Informal observation should be the starting point for all interactions with young children and should guide all planning and responses. Observing and responding to very young children is an entirely natural activity (see Box 2.1). When a baby goes by, you are likely to turn to look. If the baby is in a stroller, you might pause for a few moments and peer at her while you make odd facial expressions. Given more time, you might talk to the baby in short sentences in a high-pitched voice while you try to maintain eye contact. Given the opportunity, you may reach out to the baby and put your finger in the palm of her small hand or tweak the chubby flesh of her leg.

If the baby starts to get agitated, you may feel glad that you are not alone with her. Her cry may upset you. However, if you are left alone with the crying baby you might pick her up, rock her, or try singing a song, whether or not you have been exposed to many babies. Even people who are not familiar with infants are likely to do similar things. One reason for this is that babies have inborn mechanisms to ensure that their needs are met, and adults have instinctive behaviours relating to caring for the young of the species.

You can observe children while you are involved with their activity and while you are responsible for them. This is called **participant observation**. This can give you a feeling for what is happening, but it is impossible to record what is happening—unless you have a video camera catching your participation and children's behaviour. **Non-participant observation** requires the observer to be free of direct responsibility or involvement with the children. There are advantages to being a non-participant because you can focus all your attention on your observation.

We are attracted to the faces of very young children (Morris, 1995) because they appeal to us, draw us toward them, and cause us to feel that we want to protect them. This may be nature's way of ensuring that they are cared for. When we watch young children, we can see their individual personalities and emerging skills, and then become more responsive to their needs. We respond both emotionally and practically. We provide comfort and reassurance and ensure that no harm comes to the young child. As the processes of the infant's maturation continue, there is an inner drive toward self-help along with adult responses to support independence. We support the unfolding stages of the child's development. Both child and adult grow together: the toddler's mobility and activity get our attention and, protectively, we anticipate the dangers that are not understood by the toddler. From very little information, we understand

---

BOX 2.1

EXAMPLE OF INFORMAL OBSERVATION AND INTUITIVE RESPONSE

Jamie was coming home from college on the bus after several hours in the classroom. He was tired, but noticed that the woman in front of him had a baby on her lap. For a while the baby snuggled into the woman's chest with closed eyes. Gradually the baby became more alert and, holding onto the woman, looked over her shoulder at Jamie. The baby's face had little expression, but Jamie smiled at her. Jamie wondered if he had done the wrong thing, because the baby held onto the woman's shoulder more tightly and cuddled into the woman, hiding her face. Several minutes later the baby looked over the woman's shoulder again and stared at Jamie. This time his smile and was rewarded with a smiling response. She hid from sight several more times and kept coming back for a smile. Soon Jamie was playing peek-a-boo. He got off the bus at the next stop and waved good-bye. The baby held up one hand and wiggled her fingers at Jamie.

that the toddler cannot predict things. Even without study, we have some insight into a toddler's thinking skills; this kind of knowledge replicates some of the wisdom of our ancestors, who were more ready to rely on practical skills, common sense, and instincts than most of us are today.

HAVING A PURPOSE IN OBSERVING

When we observe infants and toddlers, we may have more than one intention. We may be enjoying who we are looking at because we are enchanted by their incredible abilities. Often we are observing because we are responsible for the child's safety; we are ensuring that a child's curiosity does not lead to an accident or that a small baby does not roll off a change table onto the floor.

While we are doing this, we may also notice what interests the child or how his skills have increased. We may be looking for specific developmental information to assure us that everything is progressing well. Possibly we will notice behaviours that indicate something about the child's thinking abilities. Attachments to adults and relationships with other children can be observed; these can inform us about some emotional aspects of development. Listening to the child's early language can tell us about his expressive language skills. Watching responses to language can frequently let us know about the child's receptive language and what he understands.

If we are trying to be in tune with the baby or toddler, then we observe the child to help us pick up his cues. Personality and temperamental styles are also observable and can help us to meet the child's needs for certain kinds of caregiving responses. Another reason for observing may be that there is cause for concern about a child's changing health status. For example, we may notice patterns of behaviour that are different from the ones the child usually exhibits, or perhaps that his appearance has changed.

BUILDING SKILLS

Educators, caregivers, and parents can perform their roles more effectively if they build up their observation skills. They can create their **guidance strategies** and activity plans, enjoy the child's development more richly by entering into the child's world more meaningfully, and become better attuned to the child and thus more able to support her needs. Developing these skills requires a lot of practice, but it is both intriguing and satisfying.

How we see the young child depends on what we are looking for. What we know about developmental sequences, health, personality styles, and so on helps us to observe more usefully. Our perceptions of what we observe are far more significant than the actual visual information that we receive.

We learn about development from observing, and we observe more effectively by understanding the principles and patterns of development. This two-way process continues through our professional lives.

▶ Selecting Observation Methods

The main categories of observational recordings are as follows:

Narratives: any written accounts of behaviour, including:

1. **running records**: long, detailed descriptions of everything a child says or does and the way the child performs actions over a predetermined length of time, recording whatever happens to occur

2. **anecdotal records**: written descriptions of an individual child or children's group activity, selected for recording after the event because the observing adult thinks something significant happened during the activity

3. **diary records**: a series of anecdotal records recorded on a regular basis about one or more children

4. **specimen records**: very detailed descriptions of a child's activity, including all language, behaviour, and expressions (usually created by trained psychologists or specialists)

5. **observation documentation**: written descriptions of a child's or children's activity that include the reflections and considerations of the educator, usually accompanied by photographs

Samplings: focused observations that seek to record events or patterns of behaviour:

1. **time sampling**: recordings made of a child's behaviour at preset time intervals to determine behavioural patterns

2. **event sampling**: recordings of a child's demonstration of a specified behaviour to determine its frequency, duration, and significance

Checklists: any listing of behaviours or attributes used to gauge the demonstration or absence of each item—checklists require interpretation of behaviour to compare it to each item listed.

1. **prepared checklists**: checklists containing items that have been evaluated to be valid and reliable measures of what is being recorded.
2. **homemade checklists**: checklists containing items chosen by the user—usually behaviours or attributes that are considered important.

Rating Scales: listings of attributes or behaviours with a scale attached to measure the *degree* to which the item is demonstrated—their use involves significant interpretation of behaviour.

1. **numerical scale**: a list of items in which numbers indicate the degree of behaviour or attitude demonstrated.
2. **semantic differential scale**: a list of items with a sliding scale of responses, such as "high incidence—average incidence—low incidence."

Chart: any record of observations using prepared columns and categories.

There is a range of standard methods for observing children, and each method has a different use and purpose. Familiarizing yourself with the various methods can make the task of observation more efficient and markedly more effective. Narratives offer the opportunity for detailed "open-ended" recordings; samplings can help us to recognize behaviour patterns; checklists can provide an overview of behavioural progress or evaluation of the environment; and rating scales help us to indicate the level of significance of various behaviours. These methods, and more, are presented in Table 2.1. You should familiarize yourself with these methods, using the information in the table to identify their characteristics, purposes, strengths, and challenges. In addition, you can consult the resources listed at the end of this chapter for more detail on these methods and the kinds of information they can provide.

TABLE 2.1

▶ Observational Recording Methods for Infants and Toddlers

Method	Description	Features
Narratives	Written accounts of behaviour	Naturalistic descriptive recordings
1. Running records	Detailed record of everything the child says/does	Holistic view of development
2. Anecdotal records	Selected recording of behaviours/events that the adult considers pertinent	Efficient way to document pertinent behaviours
3. Diary records	Regular recordings detailing important developmental progressions, regressions, or activities	Identify individualized pattern of development
4. Specimen records	Very detailed, usually coded, account of behaviours	Used by psychologists for close analysis
Samplings	Prepared formats used to determine occurrences of behaviour	Identify behaviour patterns
1. Time samplings	Behaviour is described in a snapshot at predetermined time intervals	Patterns of play, sleep, etc., may be identified
2. Event samplings	A specific behaviour is identified, defined, and charted	The duration, severity, causality, and frequency of the behaviour may become evident
Checklists	Lists of behaviours that are checked off	Offers an overview of development
1. Prepared checklists	Valid and reliable listing of skills/behaviours, usually normative- and/or criterion-referenced	Can identify the child's developmental level and performance in relation to the norm
2. Self-designed checklists	Lists of skills/behaviours considered relevant to the caregiver	May offer indications of progress and overall development

TABLE 2.1 OBSERVATIONAL RECORDING METHODS FOR INFANTS AND TODDLERS (continued)

Method	Description	Features
Rating scales	A way of recording the degree to which a behaviour, trait, or skill is demonstrated	Can offer a profile of individual temperament, skill levels, or development
1. Semantic differentials	Word opposites offer a way of indicating preferences or styles	These may offer a qualitative approach to identifying individual styles
2. Numerical scales	Numbers are used to indicate the degree to which a behaviour is observable or a characteristic is thought applicable	Qualitative information may be helpful in detailing a personal profile
Charts	Pictorial or written data recorded on prepared sheets	Efficient way of recording personal functions and patterns
1. Daily log charts	Prepared chart indicating activity of the day	May provide an overview of the child's day, including feeding, diaper-changing, and play
2. Activity charts	Prepared chart to record interests, activities, play discovery, and learning	Offer an overview of the child's activity
3. Pictorial representations	Pie charts, bar graphs, diagrams, or other visual presentation of information	A way to make large amounts of data manageable and understandable
Media-Assisted	Electronic or technologically aided recording processes	Can provide ways of recording and storing large amounts of information about individual children, group functioning, and the program
1. Video recordings	Video camera is used to record individual skills, play sequences, and group activities	Provide detailed material for later analysis regarding play, communication, and other activities.
2. Audio recordings	Tape recorder is used to record vocalizations, use of language, musical activities, singing, or any other sound	Useful for analysis of language development, rhythm, pitch, etc.
3. Photographs	Photographs are used to capture the changing bodies, size, skills, and the process and products of discovery	Provide visual documentation of development
4. Computer recordings	Used for storing information gleaned from traditional methods or as direct process of documenting information	Provide storage and retrieval of data

RECORDING INFORMATION

Not all observations are recorded. If they were, it would be impossible to do anything other than observe! However, recording observations is a very important part of the educator's role. Because it is a time-consuming task, it must be done as efficiently and effectively as possible so it enhances the child's life. Even if the method used is fairly open-ended, there must be a sense of purpose for the recording. A working knowledge of standard recording methods will allow you to choose the method that best suits your purpose.

Observations should always be recorded as soon as possible after they are made. Some methods require observing and recording simultaneously; this enables the observer to record small details that might otherwise be forgotten. Recording immediately after observation may help promote accuracy while avoiding the distraction of recording during observation. There will always be some small differences between what actually happened and what you recorded. You will not have intended this, but, as we saw above, your perception of the occurrence is a personal one. If some time elapses between the observation and the recording, the likelihood of misrepresentation will be even greater.

Efficiency can be boosted if you use prepared observation sheets. These will help you focus on what you are seeing; they also cut down on writing time and can produce more readable results without the need for rewriting.

Figure 2.2 shows a continuum, with **objectivity** and **subjectivity** at opposite poles. Most perceptions drawn from observational information are neither purely objective nor subjective; they lie on a continuum somewhere between the two. Objectivity in observation is usually considered desirable because it demands the rigour of science and logic. It helps the observer avoid judgments and assumptions. However, under some circumstances, objectivity should be tempered with a degree of subjectivity, to allow for a more empathic and holistic understanding of the child being observed.

DEALING WITH OBSERVER BIAS

If you were to ask two people to observe the same child at the same time using the same method, you would likely end up with two quite different records. This is because all observers have some sort of **bias**. Although you cannot always help your biases or know how they were formed, you must examine your perspective to see if some of your biases need to be reconsidered. When you begin to observe young children, you may find that it is hard to avoid some assumptions and even a few judgments that you didn't mean to make. Reviewing your recordings will help you eliminate comments that stem from such assumptions.

Police officers come across this daily when they review the evidence offered to them by people who appear to be very reliable and objective witnesses. Frequently these people will have made assumptions, as their minds attempt to "fill in the blanks" when they

are unsure of something. They don't realize that their need to make sense of something may cause them to draw an incorrect conclusion. Thus, it is particularly important to recognize the difference between a proven fact and an *interpretation* of the facts.

Observed information is purely visual and auditory data until our brains make some sense of the information. Perception involves the processing of visual and auditory data. Consequently, as noted above, no perception can be completely objective.

▶ Assessment

Most of our thinking necessarily involves making inferences or interpretations—we are all trying to make sense of our world. Observation and **assessment** are two distinct processes that require the separation of seeing and perceiving. The first tries to avoid inferences and focuses on mere facts; the second involves making some sense of the facts, usually by comparing them to a norm, pattern, or theory to explain the observation.

MAKING INFERENCES

Assessments of behaviour should only be made using well-recorded observations; otherwise the result is an assumption, not an assessment. An **inference** is a deduction or explanatory statement. The core of the assessment process is explaining the young child's behaviour by making inferences based on current understandings about child development. An inference might explain behaviour using a theoretical explanation, such as inferring that a child is in the sensory-motor stage. Another way of explaining behaviour is to match it to a normative profile, to see if the behaviour indicates an age-level performance.

FIGURE 2.2

Objectivity–Subjectivity Continuum

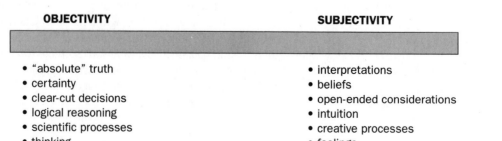

OBJECTIVITY	SUBJECTIVITY
• "absolute" truth	• interpretations
• certainty	• beliefs
• clear-cut decisions	• open-ended considerations
• logical reasoning	• intuition
• scientific processes	• creative processes
• thinking	• feelings

Doing this, we might infer that a particular child is using the two-word phrases typical of an 18-month-old toddler. Other explanations for behaviour might factor in pieces of contextual information. We might infer that an infant's irritability is caused by a low-grade infection or that a toddler is becoming more comfortable with his mother leaving. Box 2.2 illustrates the types of inferences that might be made after observing the behaviour of a toddler.

VALIDATING YOUR INFERENCES

An assessment involves making inferences, but it doesn't stop there. It also requires **validation** of those statements: we need to check to see if our inferences are correct. To be valid, the inferences must include reasons that are carefully considered and are supported in some way. It is best to validate inferences using reliable sources, such as books that offer well-researched information. You might use a normative reference, apply a theory, or use a pattern to validate your inference. Box 2.3 (page 48) illustrates a running record observation that includes both inferences and validations.

Validating inferences involves checking them through to see if they are likely to be correct. If the inferences that you make cannot be supported, they should not be stated—or they should be deleted. To make sure that you are making good inferences:

- check each inference with the perceptions of another professional—does the other person agree with you?

BOX 2.2

EXAMPLE OF OBSERVATION: INTERPRETING WHAT YOU SEE

John, 21 months, was standing by the activity table holding a large football to his chest while other toddlers were finger-painting. With his arms clasped around the ball, he leaned forward, leaning over another child's painting. John dropped the ball. Looking down, he saw it roll across the table, bounce off the table, and roll across the room. John ran around to the other side of the table, but the ball was now out of his sight. He knelt under the table at the far side of the room, then crawled under the table, going out of sight for a moment or two. He came out crawling, while he rolled the ball forward, pushing it with his left hand.

Some possible interpretations of these observations are as follows:

—John has gross motor skills typical of his age: he can stand, run, and crawl.

—His fine motor skills enabled him to pick up the ball, but he carried the ball with outstretched arms rather than using a more refined grasp.

—John did not concern himself with the activity of the other children but stayed focused on the task of looking for the ball until he found it. He is able to hold in mind what he is looking for and has the concept of permanence of the object.

Not all of our inferences will be correct. Some of them might turn out to be incorrect when we try testing them. Inferences that are made for assessment purposes tend to do one of the following things:

- compare the child's current behaviour with her previous behaviour (example of an inference: today she looked for a missing piece of the puzzle, whereas last week she didn't seek the missing item)
- use a theoretical idea to explain a behaviour or set of behaviours (example of an inference: Tanya has become attached to her caregiver, Suzanne)
- compare a child's behaviour with a normative profile (example of an inference: Gordie's ability to balance four blocks on top of each other is beyond the expectations for his age, 9 months)
- determine a child's need (example of an inference: Yasmin's confident walk around the edge of the low fence is an indication that she might soon walk without the wall if she is given encouragement)
- indicate that a new stage is being entered (example of an inference: Damien's frequent temper tantrums show that he is striving to be independent—he is entering the autonomy stage)

- consider how you can support your inference—can you come up with sound reasoning to back your inference?
- think—what research supports your interpretation?
- use valid and reliable measures (such as norms, if you think they are useful) as benchmarks for your inferences about a child's behaviour.

- match the behaviour you have seen, and your inference related to it, with a recognized theory that might explain it.

The more of these processes you follow, the more likely you are to reach a good strong inference—but it remains *your perspective*, not absolute truth!

BOX 2.3

SAMPLE RUNNING RECORD OBSERVATION

The following is a short running record observation of Shaila (7 months) in an infant room in child care shortly before her mother leaves for work.

Running Record:
Shaila lies on the change table pushing downward with both her legs, kicking her mother's abdomen with both legs simultaneously. She does this repeatedly at the same time that both of her arms are swivelling outward with clenched fists. Her face is distorted, her eyes are almost closed and are somewhat watery. With reddened facial skin Shaila cries with a high-pitched sound, pausing only for quick gasps of air. Mom talks quietly as she removes her wet diaper. Gradually her legs cease their kicking and her arms continue to swivel outward, but they do so more slowly. The crying stops for a moment but starts again, this time more softly. Shaila's eyes open and settle on the gaze of her mother. Her colouring changes to a pink tone, although her eyes are still wet. Shaila changes her sound production to a gentle cooing, which is repeated by her mother. Now Shaila smiles weakly. She continues to gaze toward mother, but she sucks on the soother, which mother puts in her mouth.

Inference:
Shaila has an attachment to her mother.

Validation:
Ainsworth's attachment theory. There were indicators of Shaila's attachment to her mother. It was likely that Shaila's cry was an attempt to get attention because she was uncomfortable. There appeared to be some degree of trust that her mother would respond to her. She was able to be calmed by her mother and there was some taking turns in communicating. Shaila returned her mother's gaze and offered her a weak social smile. Ainsworth describes these behaviours as indicators of attachment; she researched the link between babies crying and mother's responses and saw greater attachment when the mother was responsive to the infant.

Inference:
Shaila's emotional development is typical for her age (Allen and Marotz, 1994, p. 57).

Validation:
Greenspan's research into emotional development and Allen and Marotz's developmental profiles. Shaila demonstrated a rhythm of initiating communications and responding that Greenspan describes as "falling in love" and "developing intentional communication." At 7 months Shaila's development, in terms of her age and stage, falls between two stages of Greenspan's milestones. The behaviours that indicate that her emotional development is typical for her age include seeking attention, smiling when she is smiled at, gazing with interest, and seeking comfort. In addition, the Allen and Marotz profile for 4-to-8-month old infants states that typically at this time infants establish a trust relationship if their needs are met consistently.

It is important to realize that *validating your inferences does not mean that they have been proved.* Although supporting an inference does not prove it to be right, it does show that you have applied theory to practice and are, therefore, more likely to be right than if you did not attempt that process. If educators always went through this process and avoided making inferences that they couldn't validate, assessments would be much more reliable.

The inferences in part A of Box 2.4 are quite likely to be correct, but they need support. Support can come from additional observation, asking other edu-cators for their perceptions, applying a theory and seeing whether it fits, or looking up a developmental profile to see if the inference matches items in the profile. Even after you establish such support for an inference, it is still possible that the inference is incorrect. Part B of Box 2.4 shows some common inferences that may be incorrect. However, the risk of making a mistake shouldn't stop us from using crit-ical thinking skills; it means we need to practise to become better at it and to study child development so that we have a broader knowledge base for our decision-making.

BOX 2.4

POSSIBLE CORRECT INFERENCES AND COMMON MISTAKES

A. Inferences That Might Be Correct

Observation	Possibly correct inferences
A newborn baby turns her head when her cheek is stroked.	She is showing a rooting reflex.
A toddler shouts "no!"	The toddler wants autonomy.
An infant cries persistently and draws her legs up and down, extending her legs.	The infant is experiencing colic.
As he lies in his crib, a baby passes items from hand to hand.	He is showing an example of the proximo-distal sequence of skill development, with physical control now extending to his arms and hands.
An infant of 9 months always rolls to the side when put into a sitting position.	The infant appears to have less back control than most infants her age.
A toddler swishes her hands in the bathtub and tries to pick up some bubbles on the surface of the water.	The toddler is in the sensory-motor stage of development.
At 12 months, the infant pulls himself to standing, cruises alongside a large box, and takes three steps toward the caregiver before falling to the floor.	The infant is demonstrating gross motor skills typical for his age.

B. Common Mistakes

Observation	Possibly incorrect inferences
The child is 30 months old.	The child is in the pre-operational stage.
An infant plays in a solitary way.	The infant cannot play with others.
A toddler separates from a parent.	The toddler is securely attached.
A baby refuses his bottle.	The baby is sick.
A baby turns to the mother.	The baby's hearing is good.
The child does not follow simple instructions.	The child doesn't understand the instructions.
An infant responds to black-and-white images.	The infant prefers black-and-white images.
A toddler takes longer than his peers to become "toilet-trained."	The toddler is fixated on the anal stage.

At an early stage of observing and recording information about children's behaviour you will not be able to make sound inferences or validate them. It's important to go through this process so that we don't make assessments before we have sufficient knowledge. This knowledge comes gradually, from experience and study.

▶ Principles of Professional Observation

When we observe infants and toddlers professionally, a number of principles apply. We must conduct ourselves properly so we are not thought to be nosy or busybodies and we must be seen to behave ethically according to our professional commitments.

CONFIDENTIALITY AND PROFESSIONALISM

We will address each component of professionalism, but we will start with a broad statement. The professional observer must have permission to observe and must respect the **confidentiality** of those being observed—making sure information is stored and shared discreetly. In addition, professional observation requires purpose, understanding of the role of the observer, the selection of appropriate observation methods, and an appreciation of recording issues. The observer must approach the task with objectivity and be prepared to address the issue of bias. Skill-building and the ability to classify and interpret data and to initiate responsive planning are indispensable.

▶ Authentic Assessment

Authenticity usually refers to philosophical approaches that include respect for children and an appreciation for assessing them in everyday, naturalistic situations. The term is used by those who have difficulty with a medical approach to testing. They feel that clinical-type assessment has its place for diagnosis when things go wrong, but that ongoing support for development works better using an approach that celebrates the individual nature of development as it gathers essential information. Authenticity demands a "sympathetic understanding of the child" (a phrase used in the title of a book by David Elkind). The assessment must be based on appropriate criteria and must be carried out without bias. The data must be collected in an organized manner using methods that fit the purpose. The assessment should be entirely congruent with other parts of practice, such as curriculum and guidance, and it should involve teamwork, using both critical thinking and reflective feeling. Authentic assessment leads to the identification of the child's needs and connects to how the caregiver can respond to those needs.

The caregiver should view observation as being at the core of all assessment techniques and work toward **authentic assessment** of children—that is, assessment that considers each child in his or her own individual context.

Most educators appear to value objectivity in observing and recording (the belief that there is a truth to what happened and that that truth must be sought). It is a good idea to start observing with the idea of trying to be as factual as possible and recording only what you see. It is impossible to be entirely objective—and it may not be completely desirable. Human beings process information as they absorb it and, at times, subjective perceptions can be meaningful and useful. This does not mean that observers should be sloppy sentimentalists, but they might become increasingly reflective and honour their feeling responses as much as their factual ones. When trying to increase observational and recording skills, the aim of objectivity can serve the observer well, but as observers become more thoughtful and reflective about their recordings, subjective thoughts might provide further insight. As part of an authentic approach to assessment, one that is mindful of the child and how she is being assessed, both objective thought and subjective feeling responses can be valid—but the educator must be able to tell one from the other.

CONFIDENTIALITY

Confidentiality is needed to protect the privacy of children and their families. When you are writing observations, do so in a professional manner that observes confidentiality. Your recordings may assist your planning or some other part of your caregiving and educating. Whatever the reasons for making them, they should be shared with the parents and stored in a secure place.

Teamwork is essential in infant and toddler care. However, the need to communicate information within the team can breach confidentiality. Each member of the team needs to know the essential details of the child's health status, some contextual information about the child's family and background, and information from team members about recent occurrences. Along with the recorded observational information, this represents a lot of personal data.

Parents have differing ideas about what constitutes privacy for their family. Some might not want an observation chart that details their child's bowel movements. For others, this is no problem. The professional caregiver has to find ways to meet the needs of all families for privacy. Information about the child's family, health, and home must not be accessible, in any form, to anyone other than the family concerned and the professionals who are working with them.

Whatever the family's attitudes, it is always essential to protect all family information as confidential. For example, if you receive information about parents separating, this is not to be shared. If you have any observational information, this too must not be shared with anyone, unless permission has been granted.

Students sometimes face particular challenges with confidentiality issues. Sometimes caregivers are rightly reluctant to give students contextual information, even if it would help them to understand the child's behaviour. If a child-care agency is open to student fieldwork, it helps if it has a signed parent-release form that gives permission to students to access the information stored in files. If students are allowed access to this information, then they, too, must keep it absolutely confidential.

▶ Participant and Non-Participant Observation

Observations can be categorized as either participant or non-participant—that is, you are either involved in the situation with the child or you are standing apart observing. Observing while participating is something that you should be doing all the time when working with young children. Non-participant observation leaves you free to see some details of behaviour and interactions with others that you might miss if you were more directly involved. If you need to record information as well as observe, you may need to organize non-participant opportunities. Realistically, most adults working with young children do not get much non-participant time, so they need to establish ways to observe and then record soon after the action.

Most observations that are recorded of very young children are made in **naturalistic settings**—that is, in the child's normal, everyday environment. On occasion, it may be necessary to set up testing-type situations so that you can observe particular skills or behaviours. These situations should be kept to a min-

imum, because they can be stressful for both the young child and the adult. It is more likely that an individual will perform well in situations that are without stress: play behaviours, social interactions, and cognitive skills may appear less well developed in structured scenarios. Do your observing when the child is comfortable and in her usual environment.

▶ Portfolios

A single observation is helpful, but it cannot give a holistic picture of the very young child. Much of who the child is and how she behaves is shaped by her family and the culture in which she is nurtured. It is therefore very helpful to find out whatever you can to put the observations in a context. Parents should be approached with the utmost respect and with the knowledge that they might decline access to the information. Explaining your goals to the parents and building a trusting relationship with them is the key to success.

As illustrated in Figure 2.3 (page 52), a **portfolio** is a collection of observations plus information on health, family background, and other personal matters. When combined, this information allows for the review of the child's development within the context of individual experience. As the child grows, the portfolio will include a variety of items made by the child, along with photographs and other memorabilia that document her life. Interspersed will be regular contributions from all the stakeholders in the child's life, updates, new observations, and ongoing assessments and individual plans.

Blending observation of the individual within the group and interpreting the significance of those observations is a method of documenting development preferred by some professionals. Although open to accusations of subjectivity, and lacking the validation of other methods, it can be useful for experienced professionals who are already skilled at objective recording and **analysis of observation**, as outlined above.

The observational material might be shared with a group of parents and with other professionals, leading these adults to be responsive to the needs of the children as a group. Examples of this approach can be seen in the Reggio Emilia programs for toddlers and older children, in which the educator records what she thinks is important about the children's activities and how they present an opportunity for demonstrating the children's emerging skills.

FIGURE 2.3

Child Portfolio

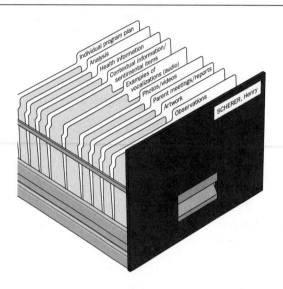

▶ A Phenomenological Approach to the Study of Infants and Toddlers

In most studies of infants and toddlers, the child is a subject to be studied according to scientific methodology. This approach has given us significant knowledge about children and their development. Criticism of the scientific approach centres on its limitations in seeing and responding to the child with respect and humanity.

The **phenomenological approach**, rooted in phenomenological studies undertaken in the 19th century, looks at the child's "experience of being." Phenomenological studies try to get at what it's like to be, think like, and function as the child being studied. Phenomenologists consider the *meaning* of the experience of the child being studied. A phenomenologist considers the child's experience from the child's perspective and contributes an additional construction of meaning as an individual with her own experience meeting the child's experience. The new meaning is a crossover between the phenomenologist's perspective and the child's perspective. Table 2.2 offers a concise comparison between the phenomenological and scientific approaches to the study of infants and toddlers.

When studying young children, the phenomenologist observes, interacts with, and "lives" side-by-side with the child. This might sound subjective when compared with the scientific method described above,

but phenomenologists would argue that subjective feeling and intuitive and interpretive responses are the keys to understanding. To accomplish their goal, phenomenologists must have an entirely nonjudgemental respect for their subject. Because the child's experience is an entirely personal and individual process, the phenomenologist meets this experience through her own eyes rather than through the distancing lenses of the scientist.

Child-care practice that is influenced by phenomenology is respectful, supportive, child-centred, and child-directed, with adults taking a role of observation and careful engagement with each child. You can begin to experience the phenomenological approach to young children by undertaking the last exercise in Activity 2.1 (page 54).

▶ Developmental Screening and Assessment

Caregivers can contribute to the formal assessments carried out by medical staff, health personnel, developmental specialists, and psychologists. The role of the parents and educators is to seek assistance if there are behavioural changes in or developmental concerns about a young child or if other signs or symptoms cause concern. In most situations, parents have the responsibility to approach these professionals, but the caregivers' observations can be very useful. The caregivers might tell the parents that they are con-

TABLE 2.2

▶ A Comparison between Science and Phenomenology

Approach	Science	Phenomenology
Focus	Behaviours	Lived experience
Attempts to explain	Forms, functions, and processes	Living and being
	What and why	How
Methodologies	Experiments/controlled observation	Naturalistic observation
	Analysis	Shared experience
		Reflection
Orientation	Objective	Subjective/intuitive
Values	"Hard" evidence	Holistic understanding
Uses	Contributes to fact-finding	Contributes to human understanding

cerned about the child. To this the parents will, most often, contribute their own perceptions. Alternatively, they might be the first to think there is a need for professional help and relay these thoughts to the caregivers.

Health and developmental screenings identify the need for further investigation. These are usually conducted by the child's pediatrician or other health professional, although developmental assessments are also carried out by professionals with special skills. Screenings may be part of regular checks, or they may be conducted because the educators or caregivers have identified a particular problem. Usually there is an opportunity to offer observations and to answer the questions of the assessor; parents, and caregivers if the parents agree, may attend a meeting for this purpose. The child's needs are more likely to be met by a team that includes parents, caregivers, and the health or developmental professional. Follow-up plans may be developed for the child that can be carried out cooperatively by the parents and caregivers. Some young children may need regular assessments and have curriculum or special devices that are designed to meet their specific needs.

▶ Responding to Assessment Results

There are many different ways of meeting the needs of very young children. The educator's task is to respond to the individual in the most appropriate manner. This section outlines some of the most common compo-

nents of caregivers' responses to assessment, whether based on their own observation or on the work of health and developmental professionals.

COMMUNICATION WITH PARENTS

Throughout the observation and assessment process, and on a daily basis, the educator should share information with parents and listen with sensitivity to parental observations, perceptions, and needs. The educator should work with parents to find ways of helping their child that fit into their lifestyle and family needs.

Educators must treat parents as partners in supporting their children. Although this seems obvious, parents are too frequently considered at the end of the assessment process rather than as an integral part of it. Assessment information should never be presented to parents without ongoing consultation. In contrast to a summative assessment—that is, an assessment at the end of a set period of time—a formative, in-process assessment allows for ongoing communication and for quickly changing issues to receive the response they need.

Assessments may indicate the emergence of skills that can be encouraged or challenges that can be addressed. If parents and educators both agree on the best strategies to support the child's development, then they are more likely to be successful. Consistency between parents and educators has clear advantages for the child.

However, educators may find themselves in a situation where parents are unable to grasp a potential

---

Activity 2.1

Practising Portfolios and Phenomenology

A. Profiling a Young Child

Select a baby or toddler to be the subject of a portfolio profile. After obtaining parental permission, gather a variety of items and observations that capture who the child is. The portfolio can include any of the following:

- photographs of the young child in action
- the child's birth story (from the parent)
- information about the child's health history
- thoughts of the parents, grandparents, and friends about the child's likes and dislikes
- a map of the child's social relationships
- observations of the child (e.g., running records)
- characteristics of the child's temperament and style
- what the parents hope for their child
- checklist of skills
- video of behaviour and/or interactions

B. Celebrating the Young Child

Celebrate the infant or toddler by sharing this information with the child's caregivers and parents.

C. Phenomenology

Return to the child and, with permission, spend a day or more with him or her. After spending this time at the child's level, interacting, playing, and communicating with him or her, record your thoughts and feelings about the experience (an example follows). What meanings can you draw from the experience?

Thoughts/Observations	Feelings/Interpretations	Meanings
Julie pulled herself to standing and peered around her, smiling when she caught the gaze of her caregiver.	Julie is pleased with herself and enjoys the approval of adults. She has a sense of autonomy and is demonstrating a trusting relationship. It was delightful to see her feeling positive above herself.	Julie's physical skills are developing as might be expected. From Julie's perspective, she is seeing the world from an upright position. There seems to be an inner drive in Julie that pushes her to become independent. Fulfillment of this leads her to experience joy.

---

health or developmental concern. The parents may, therefore, not understand the need for extra help for the infant or toddler and may refuse permission for such help. In such cases, the caregiver may find it helpful to talk to the centre supervisor and licensing agency. If you do speak to anyone about the issue, you must treat the matter confidentially and not use the child's or family's name or identifying characteristics.

RESOURCE TEACHERS AND SPECIAL EDUCATORS

In some situations, **resource teachers** with specialized knowledge of children with special needs may assist the child one-on-one within the child-care centre. The special educator might be a regular visitor or an extra member of the caregiving team in the infant or toddler room.

As a team, the caregivers can work together and learn from one another to support the child. Developmental diversity can be accommodated within a child-care centre if the staff are willing and suitably prepared. This may mean that the specialized staff demonstrate particular strategies or techniques to the staff so that they become sufficiently skilled to provide nurturance, health support, and stimulation.

EARLY INTERVENTION PROGRAMS

Parents are likely to be actively involved with an **early intervention** program. It may be directed specifically to such challenges as parent–child relationship difficulties or particular developmental issues. It is likely that such a program will a focus on physical or psychological health and well-being.

Infant intervention programs may assist a young child who has a general developmental delay or a diagnosed special need. Specialists may visit the child on a regular basis, or the child may visit them for extra support. Early intervention is thought to be desirable where early support to address a particular challenge can be offered. In some cases, early intervention programs can assist significantly so that later, more serious, problems are avoided.

CREATING AN INDIVIDUAL PROGRAM PLAN

An **individual program plan (IPP)** can be designed for any child after thorough observation and assessment. In some agencies, IPPs are used only to assist those with special health or developmental needs. The IPP is a natural progression from the assessment, taking the process from what has been inferred to what will be done about it.

Although the IPP may be written in different formats, the intention is always the same. The IPP indicates what development is observed, how it can be supported, and what experiences will be provided to do this. Some IPPs formalize this information with clearly stated goals and objectives, but most take the form of a simple outline of current and emerging skills, a review of what needs to be done, and some ideas on how this will be achieved.

Authentic assessment approaches use IPPs that are updated regularly. It is usually preferable to support the child's emerging skills, rather than focus attention on what is anticipated to be the next stage. Accurate assessment is not dependent on a normative concept. Authentic program plans provide for more open-ended activities so that the child can operate successfully at her own level.

RESPONSIVE CAREGIVING

Infants and toddlers respond well to responsive caregivers who can read their cues and appreciate their stages of development. If educators observe and interpret carefully, they will be able to provide more appropriate responses than if they were to design activities before such individual observation.

If assessment is ongoing, responsiveness can be rapid. Daily observations allow the educator to notice subtle advances and changing needs and then to respond in a way that fits the individual.

Responsiveness is the heart of the educator's role. If the process of becoming more responsive is the intention of the educator, observation skills need to be practised and finely tuned.

Interpreting a child's behaviours is a necessary part of responsive caregiving. Here, a toddler uses a coordinated set of skills to open a shed door.

DESIGNING ACTIVITIES AND EXPERIENCES

The term "design" may make the process of planning activities sound more time-consuming and cumbersome than it really is. Ideally, any design should be based on the individual child's observed needs and interests. Yet, because educators work in a group setting, they must be prepared to offer a wide variety of activities and experiences that are open-ended and generally developmentally appropriate. It is important to note that such considerations are not an excuse for pre-planning themes months in advance. This type of planning is not suitable for infants and toddlers.

Instead, it is essential to prepare sensory activities that can be enjoyed in a variety of ways or to have ready some experiences that can be modified according to particular needs as they arise. Having a "bag of tricks" at your disposal can be useful as a starting point. Then you can observe responses and engineer the experience to fit a child precisely.

As a response to observed behaviour, the educator will need to make some small modifications to the program to fit the children's changing needs. Looking at the infants and toddlers and how they respond to changes is important. Some infants will be happy when stimulated by environmental changes, but other infants prefer consistency and will be confused and unsettled by the changes.

An educator needs to be able to meet the needs of infants and toddlers individually even though they are in a group. This means that the observations educators make should take into account collective as well as individual needs. Moreover, educators must plan for early social interactions, which means observing children in their group context. Planning for the group should strike a balance between recognition of the developmental health of the children in the group and the need to cater to all the children simultaneously.

ACCESSING COMMUNITY RESOURCES

Resources likely exist in the community that can help educators with their task of responding to observed development and assist them in understanding assessments that have been made by a professional team. Organizations that support and advocate for particular disability groups can be of particular help if understanding a diagnosed condition is necessary. Health practitioners, volunteers, information services, and college faculty can also be helpful. For print resources, try the local library, a specialist library, an Internet site, or a community resource centre. Materials can be accessed from toy libraries, resource centres, libraries, special-interest groups, specialist catalogue suppliers, or regular stores.

MAKING REFERRALS TO OTHER PROFESSIONALS

Educators must be competent in their role, and must also know when a situation requires knowledge outside their own skill set. Health care and social work are two of the professions most frequently contacted to assist both parents and educators. Referrals are often facilitated by child-care centre staff, but they must be done with the full involvement and approval of the child's parents.

ACCOMMODATING DIVERSITY

To promote the emergence of a healthy self-concept, educators should ensure that infants and toddlers are in an environment that reflects their own physical appearance and includes culturally familiar objects.

Caregivers should make sure that the centre has a wide range of books, toys, decorations, and foods, so that all children can find things that are familiar and reflect their cultural experience. To provide comfort and familiarity for the child, the educator must be aware of a great many issues pertaining to family lifestyle and cultural background. These are illustrated in Figure 2.4. In addition, Box 2.5 (page 58) lists some considerations that may help caregivers deal with cultural differences among children and their families.

Communicating with parents must be done in a culturally sensitive and inclusive manner. Observations of families and their interactions, as well as of the child, should help educators refine their cultural sensitivity and improve cross-cultural communication.

Box 2.5 lists some examples of situations that call for accommodation. Box 2.6 (page 60) lists some methods of accommodating individual, family, and cultural differences.

GUIDANCE STRATEGIES

One of the most important parts of program planning, resulting from the educator's observations, are the **guidance strategies** that are developed for the young child. These strategies may include identifying boundaries for behaviours, determining the adult's response to the child's patterns of action, planning the consequences of behaviours, and deciding which actions to encourage. Rather than disciplining the child, emphasizing the re-shaping of negative behaviours, positive

FIGURE 2.4

Aspects of a Child's Family and Culture that May Require Sensitive Understanding and Response

Family and Self

physical type
appearance
experience
relationships
temperaments/styles
physical needs
emotions/emotional control
physical contact
self-perceptions
self-actualization
self-definition of culture
personal rhythms
ethnicity
sense of belonging
membership in social groups

Family Living

lifestyle
accommodation
food
clothing
hygiene
employment/standard of living
time management
playing/play material
sleeping
leisure activities
child-care/eldercare arrangements
space
communication styles
behaviour guidance
relationships
exposure to the media
grooming
food/mealtimes

Family Relationships

engagement with child
personal space
roles
power dynamics
family interactions
interactions with staff
nurturing style
support system
time spent together
expressions of love/caring
attachments

Parental Perceptions of Program

welcome
inclusion/invitation to participate
centre's values/philosophy
acceptance/tolerance/being wanted
    and valued
accommodation of needs
pervading culture
accessibility
politics
caring
stimulation/learning/play approaches
physical environment
safety
atmosphere
other children and families
communications

Family Rituals and Practices

symbols
artifacts
holy days
religious practices
celebrations
culturally shaped behaviours
modes of dress
play behaviours
transition behaviours
mealtimes
domestic processes
routines
rites of passage

Values and Beliefs

expectations
views of childhood
what constitutes best practices
type and quality of parental involvement
gender roles and responsibilities
independence/interdependence/depend-
    ence
social responsibility
guidance/discipline
goals for children
social class values
ways of caring
responsibility for children
love and caring
concept of family/extended family
power dynamics/authority
respect/duty
meaningfulness
actualization
priorities

guidance strategies build from what the child does well and what is socially acceptable.

Infants and toddlers respond best if they experience consistent styles of guidance, nurturance, and adult interaction. Guidance strategies can be used to assist children in learning and to support them in their development. Specific strategies are based on the observational information that the educator has gathered. Sometimes educators will try out a way of guiding behaviour and find that it was unsuccessful. Although

EXAMPLES OF SITUATIONS THAT CALL FOR SENSITIVITY AND ACCOMMODATION

Time

Kinga's first reaction to Leena's late arrival every morning was annoyance. She thought that Leena was missing some of the fun that the other toddlers were having. When Leena's mother found out that all the other toddlers came in early, she explained. "I need you to understand," she said, "that I work two shifts and the only time I have to sleep is between 5 A.M. and 9 A.M."

Climate

"Back in my home country," explained a parent, "we didn't take our babies outside if it was cold." "But we wrap them up really well," said the caregiver. "Yes, but what's the need to go out when there's snow on the ground?" replied the parent.

Parent Interviews

Tim was new to the infant room, having recently graduated from a college program. When reviewing his experiences during his first week of work, he told the director, "I just don't understand why Jenna's mom won't look at me when I talk to her. It's like she is ignoring what I say." The director suggested that this might be a sign of respect, not rejection.

Independence

"Don't all children learn to help themselves to do things? They need to learn, and life is much easier when they can dress themselves," said one of the teachers from the toddler room as she talked to parents about the program. "We think that learning to get along with each other is far more important than learning to put a jacket on," replied a parent. "They'll learn to dress themselves as they get older."

Lifestyle

"When I spent time in the centre I noticed that lots of the children's books show parents that are white, with a male daddy and female mommy. My family is not like that. My partner is female and I'm of Afro-Caribbean heritage," explained one of the mothers.

Transitions

"I'm not okay to say a quick good-bye and then leave," said one of the parents. "That's the advice I was given. After Nathan has settled I'm supposed to get up, say goodbye, and leave," he continued. "I think that Nathan enjoys our leaving each other when I make a fuss over him and we have lots of hugs and kisses."

Guidance

"No, I don't believe that smacking toddlers really works; they just cry more," said a dad to a caregiver. "You know, I don't like it when you use that type of discipline. It doesn't do any good." The caregiver thought for a few minutes and outlined the guidance policy that was a required standard of practice.

Mealtimes

"There is too much wasted food," said a parent, confiding in her child's caregiver. She continued, as the caregiver listened, "At 18 months my daughter should be eating up what she's given."

Bedtime

"Grace likes to take her bottle to bed with her. It helps her to get to sleep," explained a mom. "I don't think that will do Grace's teeth any good," replied the student teacher. "She hasn't got any teeth yet," said the mom. "What's your problem?"

Touristic Curriculum

"When I told you we come from Japan I didn't expect you to have a Japan Week," said a critical mom. "You have pictures of kimonos. Do you really think that Midori will recognize these? She's only 26 months old."

Commercialism

"Why do you have Disney cartoons on the walls?" asked a parent as he toured the centre prior to having his child put on a waiting list. "We think that they are friendly—all kids seem to love them," said the centre director lightheartedly. The parent's face became more serious. "Have you thought about the commercialistic and materialistic values behind such images?" he asked.

Language Barriers

Soheila entered the centre. It was her first visit to a North American child-care centre. She brought her 9-year-old son along as her interpreter. When she spoke to him behind her hand, the boy frowned but looked up to the centre director, who was waiting expectantly. "Why do you have a row of toilets without walls or doors?" he said, as he looked down at the floor.

Celebrations

"Can you leave my child out of your birthday celebrations? I don't believe in making a fuss. It encourages behaviours that are not in keeping with what we think. What's more, our religion says that they're not okay," said a mother of a toddler approaching 2 years old.

Values

"When they're grown up, these kids are going to have to fend for themselves. Telling them to 'be gentle' or to 'use your words' (a guidance strategy suitable for pre-school children) doesn't help toddlers get a grip on the real world." This statement came from a mother managing to provide for three children as a single mom.

Special Needs

"Do you really think that you're doing the right thing by having those two special kids here?" asked a mother of a child newly enrolled in a toddler program. "Won't they hold up the others? Anyway, they'll take up so much time that there won't be enough for my child."

Allergens

"We have a 'no perfume' policy in the centre," explained the supervisor of an infant and toddler centre to a mom who wanted to leave her infant with a silky scarf perfumed with the mother's usual scent.

Food

"We don't eat pork," said a mother with dark skin. "Oh, are you Jewish?" asked the caregiver. "No, I'm not. I'm Muslim, if you really want to know," replied the mother.

BOX 2.6

RESPONDING TO INDIVIDUAL, FAMILY, AND CULTURAL DIFFERENCES

- Show respect for all families and children.
- Listen and wait patiently for comments and questions.
- Notice body language, but interpret it cautiously.
- Offer times and places for confidential discussions.
- Avoid confrontations by encouraging open communication.
- Be clear about what is a standard of practice and which program elements can be adjusted.
- Check your personal biases and avoid judgments.
- Use cross-cultural communication skills to assist shared meanings.
- Explain why parts of the program are offered in a particular way.
- Use informal opportunities to enhance parent education.
- Be prepared to learn from parents and children.
- Use questions from parents as a tool to evaluate the program's values and practices.
- Avoid making assumptions about specific cultures or reinforcing stereotypes.
- Acknowledge profound beliefs and do not attempt to change them.
- Use a variety of human and practical resources in support families.
- Be quick to apologize for your mistakes.
- Don't let differences paralyze your actions.
- Consider individual and collective needs and how you will meet them.

---

it does not always result in success, this trial-and-error approach is quite suitable. Although there are some generally accepted guidance policies, individual interactions must be based on the communication and temperament styles of the children involved.

HEALTH CONCERNS

When the educator identifies changes in the infant's or toddler's behaviour or observes signs or symptoms of a health concern, then appropriate action must be taken. With very young infants, response must be particularly rapid because the child is extremely vulnerable. Daily baseline observations will give the educator a frame of reference for later observations. Some conditions require rapid response; others are less pressing. In all cases, parents must be informed of an educator's health concerns. Educators must remember that they cannot diagnose an ailment or provide medical intervention. Parental permission is required for every aspect of health care.

RESPONDING TO POTENTIAL CHILD ABUSE

The primary role of caregivers is to ensure that children are healthy and that their needs are met. Caregivers and teachers have a legal responsibility to contact a child protection agency when they have a reasonable suspicion that a child has been abused. As such, they need to be vigilant about noticing and doc-

umenting signs of abuse. In cases where abuse is suspected, they must follow the protocol of their child-care centre. In addition, they should write down all observations that indicate potential abuse.

It is important to note that caregivers do not conclude on their own that abuse has taken place. They simply report the indicators they have seen to a child protection agency. This can be done anonymously, or the child-care centre and caregiver may directly indicate their cause for concern. Any action is the responsibility of the child protection agency, not the caregiver or the centre.

▶ Summary

Observation is an essential part of the educator's role. It must be done continuously so that the children are always safety nurtured and supported in their development.

Educators need to use formal methods of observing and recording developmental information about infants and toddlers so that they can document important changes and respond to the children appropriately. Infants and toddlers must be observed and assessed in ways that capture their true competence and take into account contextual information.

Making authentic assessments involves observing infants and toddlers in their natural settings and documenting their development over an extended period of time. The most effective way to do this is by creating a portfolio about each child. Parents, who are our partners in providing care and education for each child, need to be involved in all aspects of the child's program, including making contributions to the observation and assessment process.

Naturalistic observation is an integral part of a child-centred philosophy. It can lead us to a better understanding of developmental processes and, most importantly, enable us to provide appropriate experiences and supportive guidance.

▶ KEY TERMS

- analysis of observation
- anecdotal records
- assessment
- authentic assessment
- bias
- charts
- checklists
- confidentiality
- diary records
- early intervention
- event sampling
- guidance strategy
- homemade checklists
- individual program plan (IPP)
- inference
- informal observation
- narratives
- naturalistic setting
- non-participant observation
- numerical scale
- objectivity
- observation
- observation documentation
- participant observation
- permission
- phenomenological approach
- portfolio
- prepared checklists
- rating scales
- reflective practice
- resource teachers
- running records
- samplings
- semantic differential scale
- specimen records
- subjectivity
- time sampling
- validation

▶ DISCUSSION QUESTIONS

1. To what extent can you be unbiased about what you observe?
2. If you were to see an infant you didn't know in a supermarket, what would you look for to tell you what age or stage the baby had reached?
3. If you were to set up a new system for observation and record-keeping in an infant or toddler room, what would it include?
4. How might you encourage parents to share their observations of their child with you?
5. If you had some concerns about a 15-month-old child who was not yet walking or saying any words, what might you do?

▶ ADDITIONAL RESOURCES

▶ Further Reading

Billman, J., & J. Sherman. (2003). *Observation and Participation in Early Childhood Settings: A Practicum Guide.* 2nd ed. Boston, MA: Allyn & Bacon.

Dotsch, J. (1999). *Non-Biased Children's Assessments.* Toronto, ON: Bias-Free Early Childhood Services.

Langford, R. (1999). *Checklist for Quality Inclusive Education: A Self-Assessment Tool and Manual for Early Childhood Settings.* Barrie, ON: Early Childhood Resource Teacher Network of Ontario.

Martin, S. (2003). *Take a Look: Observation and Portfolio Assessment in Early Childhood.* 3rd ed. Don Mills, ON: Addison Wesley Longman.

Morris, D. (1995). *Illustrated Babywatching.* London: Ebury Press.

Wortham, S. (2001). *Assessment in Early Childhood Education.* 3rd ed. Upper Saddle River, NJ: Prentice Hall.

Wylie, S. (1999). *Observing Young Children: A Guide for Early Childhood Educators in Canada.* Toronto: Harcourt Brace.

▶ Useful Web sites

Child and Family Canada DAE-DAP
 Collections.ic.gc.ca/child/docs/00000083.htm
The Consultative Group on Early Childhood Care and Development
 ww.ecdgroup.com/download/cc107bci.pdf
NCREL
 www.ncrel.org/sdrs/areas/issues/students/earlycld/
Head Start
 www.bmcc.edu/Headstart/Trngds/Observation/

CHAPTER 3

Explaining Behaviour: Understanding Growth and Development

The rate of development is so rapid for most young children that the adult has to pay close attention to notice all the emerging skills. Within a few months, this infant has progressed in a wide variety of ways.

Learning Outcomes

After reading and studying this chapter, you should be able to:

- describe the domains of development of infants and toddlers and how they interact in a holistic manner
- compare and contrast a range of schools of thought about infancy and toddlerhood
- apply principles of development to infants and toddlers
- discuss theoretical explanations for observed characteristics of the development of infants and toddlers
- respond to the needs of infants and toddlers

"My mother knows more about babies than anyone," said Kylie's mom. "She had eight of them!" The way we were raised, which likely reflected our mothers' views of what children need at different stages of development, is extremely important to our own understanding about how children develop and the context in which this happens.

In the 1950s, parents and educators were taught that young children should always be cared for in the home by the mother. Our parents and grandparents were likely influenced by this thinking. Twenty years later, "evidence" was produced that group care was an acceptable, indeed desirable, way of nurturing young children. Our own beliefs have been moulded by a combination of our traditions and the way societies shape knowledge.

We know that a mother's firsthand experience, the values and beliefs held by a culture, the dominant scientific view, and a variety of others ways of knowing, all contribute to our collective knowledge base about the development of young children. It is likely that you have heard arguments in favour of each perspective. "Nonprofessionals" sometimes pour scorn on the jargon and "facts" presented by scientists, labelling such views "edu-babble." For their part, professionals sometimes believe that their knowledge is superior and represents a deeper understanding. As well, representatives from different cultures may find that their values clash with what professionals advocate. They may mistrust scientific "interference" in the way they raise their children. Faith in progress often leads people to believe that today's knowledge base must be better and more accurate than yesterday's. As educators, we must guard against all such certainties.

▶ Growth and Development

"She's grown a lot" is a typical comment from an adult who has not seen a young child for even a short period of time. Usually the adult is commenting on how much bigger the child is, but with this growth comes increased capacity to do things.

The term **growth** relates only to the first element, the way the child is getting bigger. Growth means an increase in size, change in bodily proportions, and alteration of internal systems that account for that growth. These alterations include skeletal changes of **ossification** and **calcification** as the bones become stronger and harder. Muscular changes brought about by **myelination** allow for better coordination. Hormonal changes support the increase in size and bodily functioning, and changes in the central nervous system promote chemical and electrical communications within the body. All parts of the body undergo changes associated with growth. Most aspects of growth are measurable: height, weight, and head circumference are the easiest to observe and measure. Figure 3.1 (page 65) illustrates typical growth patterns in North American children.

"He's developing into a fine young man," usually means that the child is growing up. He is not only bigger, but more mature and better able to handle the world. Infant and toddler development, like all aspects of human development, is in a constant state of complex change. **Development** is somewhat dependent upon growth, but the term relates more specifically to the increasing skills of the individual and the processes that enable the individual to adapt to life's experiences.

Development involves changes in complexity of functioning. As infants develop, they increase their range of actions. This involves making connections between the mind and the body. Gradually, random actions become deliberate movements. At first the movements need to be thought about, but later they become more automatic. All development involves action, whether external or internal. Although external action is easier to observe than internal action, they are equally important.

▶ Infant and Toddler Development

THE NEEDS OF INFANTS AND TODDLERS

Certain conditions must exist for an infant or very young child to grow and develop. The most obvious **physical needs** are:

- appropriate nutrition
- clean air
- suitable clothing
- moderate temperature/climate
- protection from harm and disease

Even when these basic needs are supplied, the infant or toddler may not thrive. Young children have **psychological needs** as well. These include:

- physical contact
- consistency of caregivers and enduring relationships

- predictability of environment
- encouragement
- **accommodation** to personal style and temperament type
- respect
- unconditional love
- acceptance of individuality
- appropriate guidance and support
- positive role models
- individual care and attention
- resolution of emotional conflicts
- a sense of belonging to the family and group

To support the infant's and toddler's **cognitive needs**, children also require:

- responses to their behavioural cues
- sensory experiences
- sensitivity to personal learning style
- opportunity to explore, experiment, and pursue curiosity
- adults who support learning
- adults who provide language in a reciprocal relationship
- appropriate toys and playthings
- time, space, and opportunity to play
- contrasts of experience
- challenges that are achievable
- one-on-one attention

In addition, for **optimal development**—the best possible development and the realization of the infant's and toddler's potential—the child needs:

- a positive and stimulating learning environment
- harmonious parent and caregiver involvement
- high but attainable expectations
- individualized and responsive programming
- a stress-controlled environment
- emotional safety
- a primary caregiving model of child care
- experiences that promote creative thought and problem-solving
- clear parameters for behaviour
- the demonstration of clear and consistent values
- careful observation, assessment, and responses
- an aesthetically sensitive environment
- acceptance of personal style

The idea of identifying the needs of individuals is not new, but there have been some recent attempts at refining them. Brazelton and Greenspan (2000) have combined their wisdom, born of experience with many very young children and their families, and developed a short list of what they call **irreducible needs**. These factors do not address the most obvious basic needs, but rather address "the fundamental building blocks for our higher level emotional, social, and intellectual abilities." This is the list of the seven irreducible needs:

1. the need for ongoing nurturing relationships
2. the need for physical protection, safety, and regulation
3. the need for experiences tailored to individual differences
4. the need for developmentally appropriate experiences
5. the need for limit-setting, structure, and expectations
6. the need for stable, supportive communications and cultural continuity
7. the need to protect the future

It is noticeable that the list of needs is holistic in that it addresses each part of the child's development in a combined entity. There is a concept of the child within the context of her community—and it is a cultural context in which the child needs to function. Freedoms and responsibilities are seen as being essential and coexisting—the child needs parameters but also needs to know about functioning within the world. Each of the needs relates to the child's environment, which is dependent upon both positive relationships and appropriate experiences. It is therefore necessary to understand that the adults in the life of the child—primarily parents, but also professionals—are directly responsible for making sure these needs are met. In the "irreducible needs" model, Brazelton and Greenspan take the view that the professional practitioner's responsibilities include a multidisciplinary team of care providers. Ultimately, they see their concepts, including those of the "Touchpoints" framework—"periods during the first three years of life during which children's spurts in development result in pronounced disruption in the family system" (page 184)—as being models that might influence the delivery of services for children and provide a structure for reporting society's success in supporting very young children and their families.

FIGURE 3.1

How to read and interpret growth charts

There is no such thing as a definitive growth chart. Babies are born with different weights, heights, and head circumferences, and they grow at different rates. Nationality, ethnicity, age of the mother, age of the child at birth, standard of living, feeding habits and arrangements, and gender will all influence that growth. Charts will only reflect the data collected at the time they were compiled, and so when and where that is done will affect the results. How the data are plotted on the chart is also relevant. Unless arithmetically averaged, they will probably be presented by percentile. For example, the 10th percentile is the point at which 10 percent are below and 90 percent are above the numbers shown at that point.

The charts on pages 65–66 are compiled from the growth charts of the National Center for Health Statistics (NCHS) in the U.S., using the ranges between the 10th and 90th percentiles for each stage. If you need more specific data, you should consult the NCHS charts, which are available online.

These NCHS charts have very definite limitations that are worth mentioning. For instance, First Nations children (indeed, most children from non-Caucasian families) have growth patterns that differ somewhat from those plotted in these charts. They tend to be heavier at birth, and their weight–height ratio is greater than the 50th percentile for other populations. However, the diversity of First Nations people across Canada is such that the Canadian Paediatric Society believes that no single chart could be produced for them, and that individual growth charts for different tribal or cultural areas would be based on such small numbers as to be unreliable.

BOYS

Age	Weight	Length/Height	Head Circumference
Newborn	2.8 kg – 4.2 kg [6.2 – 9.2 lb]	47 – 53 cm [18 – 21 in.]	33.2 – 38.0 cm [13.1 – 15.0 in.]
6 weeks	4.1 – 5.8 kg [9.0 – 12.7 lb]	53 – 60 cm [21 – 24 in.]	37.2 – 41.2 cm [14.6 – 16.2 in.]
3 months	5.1 – 7.1 kg [11.2 – 15.6 lb]	58 – 64 cm [23 – 25 in.]	9.4 – 43.0 cm [16.0 – 17.5 in.]
6 months	6.8 – 9.2 kg [15.0 – 20.2 lb]	64 – 71 cm [25 – 28 in.]	42.0 – 45.4 cm [16.5 – 17.9 in.]
9 months	8.0 – 10.8 kg [17.6 – 23.7 lb]	68 – 76 cm [27 – 30 in.]	43.6 – 47.0 cm [17.2 – 18.5 in.]
12 months	9.0 – 11.9 kg [19.8 – 26.2 lb]	72 – 79 cm [28 – 31 in.]	44.8 – 48.4cm [17.6 – 19.1 in.]
15 months	9.6 – 12.8 kg [21.1 – 28.2 lb]	75 – 83 cm [30 – 33 in.]	45.6 – 49.0 cm [18.0 – 19.3 in.]
18 months	10.2 – 13.5 kg [22.4 – 29.7 lb]	78 – 86 cm [31 – 34 in.]	46.2 – 49.4 cm [18.2 – 19.4 in.]
24 months	11.2 – 14.6 kg [24.6 – 32.1 lb]	83 – 92 cm [33 – 36 in.]	46.8 – 50.4 cm [18.4 – 19.8 in.]
36 months	12.5 – 16.6 kg [27.5 – 36.5 lb]	91 – 101 cm [36 – 40 in.]	47.5 – 51.6 cm [18.7 – 20.3 in.]

FIGURE 3.1

HOW TO READ AND INTERPRET GROWTH CHARTS (continued)

GIRLS

Age	Weight	Length/Height	Head Circumference
Newborn	2.7 – 4.0 kg *[5.0 – 8.8 lb]*	46 – 53 cm *[18 – 21 in.]*	32.4 – 37.0 cm *[12.8 – 14.6 in.]*
6 weeks	3.8 – 5.4 kg *[8.4 – 11.9 lb]*	52 – 59 cm *[21 – 23 in.]*	36.2 – 40.0 cm *[14.3 – 15.7 in.]*
3 months	4.8 – 6.6 kg *[10.6 – 14.5 lb]*	56 – 62 cm *[22 – 24 in.]*	38.2 – 41.8 cm *[15.0 – 16.5 in.]*
6 months	6.2 – 8.4 kg *[13.6 – 18.5 lb]*	62 – 68 cm *[24 – 27 in.]*	40.8 – 44.2 cm *[16.1 – 17.4 in.]*
9 months	7.2 – 9.8kg *[15.8 – 21.6 lb]*	66 – 73 cm *[26 – 29 in.]*	42.4 – 45.6 cm *[16.7 – 18.0 in.]*
12 months	8.3 – 11.0 kg *[18.3 – 24.2 lb]*	70 – 77 cm *[28 – 30 in.]*	43.4 – 46.8 cm *[17.1 – 18.4 in.]*
15 months	9.0 – 11.8 kg *[19.8 – 26.0 lb]*	73 – 81 cm *[29 – 32 in.]*	44.2 – 47.6 cm *[17.4 – 18.7 in.]*
18 months	9.6 – 12.6 kg *[21.1 – 27.7 lb]*	76 – 84 cm *[30 – 33 in.]*	44.8 – 48.2 cm *[17.6 – 19.0 in.]*
24 months	10.6 – 14.0 kg *[23.3 – 30.8 lb]*	81– 90 cm *[32 – 35 in.]*	45.6 – 49.2 cm *[18.0 – 19.4 in.]*
36 months	12.0 – 16.4 kg *[16.4 – 36.1 lb]*	90 – 100 *[35 – 40 in.]*	46.6 – 50.6 cm *[18.3 – 19.9 in.]*

DEVELOPMENTAL DOMAINS

For purposes of understanding development more thoroughly, we sometimes divide the study into different **developmental domains**, or aspects of development. For example, we might isolate cognitive development or language skills. This is often an effective strategy for research and can lead to useful information, but it can also present us with a problem. After we look at development in segments, we need to put the interacting segments back together so that we can see that we are dealing with a whole human being.

Developmental domains are the categories or aspects of development that, together, make up the whole child. Experts in developmental studies use different categories depending upon their perspectives.

"Physical," "cognitive," "social," "emotional," and "language development" together constitute an example of one set of domains.

Developmental domains can be studied by analyzing observable characteristics and indicators of change in each area. Theories that explain how this development occurs are extremely helpful for the educator. If we understand how a phenomenon occurs, we are more likely to be able to make informed decisions about what our role should be.

Physical Development

Physical development concerns the changes in skill development of the body. It depends on growth, including observable increases in size, proportion, weight, and head circumference. Physical development is driven by physiological changes in the body, particularly in the brain and nervous system. Without adequate nutrition and the satisfaction of all the basic needs, the very young child will not gain mastery of physical skills.

The two strands of physical development relate to increasing refinement of control of the large and small muscles of the body. **Gross motor skills** involve control of the large muscles of the body that allow sitting, crawling, walking, and so on. **Fine motor skills** concern the skill development of the smaller muscles that allow for hand control and coordination of hand and eye.

Perception and Sensory Development

Infants and toddlers learn through physical exploration of their world. They perform actions and take in information through their five senses: sight, hearing, touch, taste, and smell. Sensory information is processed, or perceived, according to what was previously absorbed. Infants have almost completely functioning senses, but lack experience; their processing of sensory information is limited because of their very limited understanding of what they are perceiving.

We can observe the interest infants and toddlers show in the things around them. We can see how items engage their interest, how they respond to a stimulus and then turn away from it when they tire of it. Observing **habituation** (a decline in interest) and **dishabituation** (a renewed level of interest in a stimulus) can be useful for educators trying to support learning by stimulating the senses.

Perception depends on the functioning of the senses and the processing of the information gained by the senses and sent to the brain. The degree to which each of the senses is ready to absorb information, the relative maturity of the nervous system carrying the information, and the readiness of the brain to sort, match, and process that data combine in a way that is extremely complex. Physical development requires increasing refinement of skills aimed at coordinating movement. For this to occur, the muscles must be sufficiently mature to respond to chemical and electrical signals. The drive to become autonomous (independent) leads the baby to make repeated efforts, which result in skill acquisition.

Communication and Language Development

Communication refers to interactions using visual and sound signals, and especially to the acquisition of language—the symbolic system of exchanging thoughts and feelings. **Communication skills** develop from babies' efforts to have their needs met.

The central condition for communication skill development is attachment to the adult.

A wide variety of types of communication can be observed in infants and very young children. They may make sounds, expressions, and gestures. Some of these are deliberate attempts to communicate; others are cues that may be interpreted by an adult, thus beginning the dance of communication. Communication may be initiated by either the adult or the child. To fine-tune the communication process, the child needs to have plenty of opportunity to engage with an adult.

Advocates of **baby signing** believe that early communications enhanced by gesturing will expand the child's understanding by promoting neurological connections, which confers an intellectual advantage. A recent refinement of baby signing, "Sign with Your Baby" (Garcia, 1999), has an extensive vocabulary that appears to be effective. Long-term studies have not yet proven there are any lasting benefits. Communication systems designed to help babies to share meanings before they can speak have recently gained popularity. Although originally created as forms of sign language intended for the deaf or hard-of-hearing child, new methods build on a combination of child-initiated and adult-initiated actions in a way that resembles spoken language.

Language grows by expanding the dance of communication that is already established. **Language acquisition** depends on the child interacting with people and hearing the language. Yet while language acquisition always occurs within a social context, it is believed to be aided by the child's inner ability or **pre-wiring** (Vygotsky, [1934] 1962; Chomsky, 1968).

Considering the complexity of the task, the very young child gains language skills remarkably quickly. As educators, we can facilitate that task if we know something about the process and stages of language acquisition. The adult assists the child to learn language by a scaffolding process (Bruner, 1983) involving sensitive responses to the infant's cues and assistance by providing necessary language structures and vocabulary.

Cognitive Development

Cognitive development concerns how the individual thinks and responds. Cognition depends on sensory input and perceptual processing. The study of this developmental domain centres on how young children come to understand the world they find themselves in, how they adapt to that world, and how they learn to represent it. **Adaptation** is a sophisticated process that requires **assimilation** of new information, accommodation of previously constructed **schemes**, and the urge to balance these responses (equilibrium).

Early cognition occurs in a **sensory-motor** pattern (Piaget, 1952) that is restricted by the child's limited experience, egocentric perspective, memory, and thought capacity. Sensory-motor intelligence involves the young child coordinating physical actions and sensory information. The child creates schemes of understanding that can be considered preliminary concepts. These become increasingly refined with repeated action. During the sensory-motor stage, approximately the first two years of life, young children learn from imitation and hands-on experience. This allows them to perform actions deliberately, understand **object permanence** and some **cause-and-effect** relationships, build some basic concepts, and begin to represent the world symbolically, eventually moving on to **symbolic thought**.

Although cognitive functions are internal, they can be glimpsed through children's behaviour, particularly through the mistakes they make, and, with older toddlers, what they say. Cognitive processes can be challenging to understand because they require detailed observation, an understanding of theoretical explanations, and analysis of an individual child's behaviour. Nonetheless, educators find studying cognitive processes extremely helpful in appreciating how the child sees the world and learns about it. Vygotsky, [1934] 1962) provided a model, called the **zone of proximal development**, that describes the way that the adult can move into the child's learning, identify what requires assistance, and provide supports so that the child can then perform tasks without adult help.

In addition to observing behaviours in ways that lead us to infer what or how the baby is thinking, we now have technologies that allow us to "see" how the brain is functioning from the inside. Brain scans can tell us about cognitive processes and what parts of the brain particular types of thinking occur in.

An extremely useful resource kit is available from the Canadian Child Care Federation: "Nourish, Nurture Neurodevelopment" (Bertrand et al., 2001). It synthesizes the research on brain development and makes it accessible to practitioners such as ourselves. It provides us with a review of recent brain research and offers a clear interpretation of how these groundbreaking studies contribute to our understanding of how young children's brains develop biologically and the environmental conditions that support optimal development. Key findings are that, for a child's brain to grow and flourish, the child needs:

It is easier to observe physical skills than cognitive functioning. Here, the child is trying to bang the drum with alternating hands. The invisible cognitive functioning needed to perform this activity is extremely complex.

- breast milk/breast-feeding: the best food for optimal development
- healthy **attachment**: a strong and nurturing relationship with at least one adult
- responsive care: care that responds to the child's needs and signals
- protection from harm: a childhood as free as possible from negative physical and mental stresses

These four components reinforce what we already appreciate about the psychological or irreducible needs of the child. It is good to know that advances in science underscore the theories that have developed from other branches of child study. What is challenging is that there is little compromise in those four essential conditions for healthy brain development. As parents and professionals working in partnership for very young children, we need to ensure that these needs are met. Providing responsive care requires the caregiver, at the minimum (according to the CCCF meta-study), to:

- watch for the child's own, individual cues and signals and learn to anticipate when it is time for food or for a cuddle, rest, or new activity
- expose the child to new experiences and activities as and when the child is ready
- share the child's activities and follow the child's interests
- watch for moments to extend the child's skills
- express affection and cheer specific accomplishments

The concept of responsive caregiving—which is central to this book—is also the required approach, according to the CCCF. We need to learn to look for these cues more carefully, provide more appropriate experiences, follow the child's lead, and engage with each child in a positive, meaningful way.

Emotional Development

Emotional development concerns children's increasing awareness and control of their feelings. Infants start life with a few basic emotions and develop others as they form social relationships. The most important aspect of infants' emotional development is rooted in the earliest relationships, **attachments** they make with adults (Maccoby, 1980). There are observable stages of attachment (Bowlby, 1965) that are considered dependent upon sustained relationships with only a few adults. The term "bonding" is sometimes used to describe the infant's specific attachment to the mother (Klaus and Kennel, 1982). Attachments will always be challenged by separations from the adult. Very young infants may appear more interested in having their needs met than in who meets them. But older infants and toddlers will be more specifically attached and want particular adults to provide attention. Separation from these key adults can cause **separation anxiety**.

Children face a series of emotional tasks that provide challenges for each stage of development. Early emotional tasks require the individual to gain an identity while developing attachments and, later, striving for independence, or becoming **autonomous**, while needing emotional support (Erikson, 1980). **Self-regulation**, or the ability to calm or otherwise control the self, is another early emotional challenge of infancy (Greenspan and Greenspan, 1985). "Falling in love" is an emotional process that occurs a little later. Developing intentional communication and then developing skills in emotional thinking are later stages of **emotional development**.

Although emotions are inner feelings, they can be interpreted from the very young child's behaviour, particularly from facial expressions, postures, and gestures. Emotional development is very challenging to support because it requires consistency and very sensitive responses to the infant and toddler. Educators need to promote healthy attachments and ease separation difficulties. On a daily basis, they are confronted with emotional challenges. These are better handled when the educator understands their underlying cause. "Caregivers who respond sensitively to the infant's emotional signals help to develop self-regulatory skills," explains Goulet (Spring 2000).

Social Development

Social development concerns the infant's or young child's identity, relationships with others, and understanding of his place within a social environment. Social development is shaped by the very young child's context. Social development starts with the child's understanding that he is a separate human being. The infant develops a concept of self through forming attachments to others. Attachments to adults and the opportunity to form relationships are essential for social development. But the capacity of very young children to relate to others is somewhat limited by their **egocentricity**—that is, their focus on themselves. Gaining skills to operate in social environments is significantly helped if the toddler has positive role models; much of the child's learning will come from observing adults and older children.

The social context of development forms the young child's social reality. The most effective social learning tools for toddlers are imitation and **role-modelling**; for younger babies the social world consists of the adults and children to whom they have some attachment. The adult–child dyad is the centre of the infant's social world; communication within it allows the baby's social skills to flourish.

An infant's social play is largely **solitary play** (Parten, 1932); the infant plays independently, without engaging with others. The egocentricity of young children does not allow them to see the perspectives of others. Gradually, children start to play alongside others in **parallel play**. Some pretend play may be observed in older toddlers, much of it imitating the adults they see.

The educator can help meet the social needs of infants and toddlers by appreciating the need for consistent care, relationship-building, positive role models, and appropriate conditions for social interactions.

Moral Development

Moral development concerns the child's ability to understand right and wrong and to function in a pro-social way—that is, in a manner that is socially positive (Honig, 1983). Moral development depends upon both cognitive and social development because it requires an increasing understanding of people, things, and issues. Sometimes moral development is viewed as a process of social cognition. Although clear evidence of moral development can be seen in the toddler's gradual acquisition of pro-social skills, moral learning starts much earlier. Very young children internalize social views of their world when they observe role models. Because adults encourage some behaviours and discourage others, the very young child learns values and attitudes. What constitutes morality is largely externally driven through social learning, but there appears to be an inner drive that strives for justice, or fairness, in terms that relate to the child's ability to appreciate personal perspectives.

Personality Development

The study of **personality** development considers the temperament types of children and how they remain surprisingly constant through life. **Temperament** is considered the raw material of personality (Berger, 1982). Researchers have isolated nine components of temperament that affect the different styles of response of individuals to the environment (Thomas and Chess, 1977; Campos et al., 1983). The nine categories of components of temperament are:

1. activity level—the degree of energy in movement
2. rhythmicity—the regularity of eating, toileting, and sleeping
3. approach or withdrawal—the ease of approaching situations and people
4. adaptability—the ease of tolerating change in routines
5. threshold of responsiveness—the point at which there is a response
6. intensity of reaction—the degree to which there is a reaction to stimuli
7. quality of mood—the degree of affect (demonstration of emotion)
8. distractability—the ease of being distracted
9. attention span and persistence—the focus of attention or period spent focusing on an activity

In the majority of newborn infants, one of three temperament constellations can be observed. Each constellation is a cluster of several of the nine components. The three temperament constellations are: regular, positive approach responses to new stimuli, high adaptability to change, and mild or moderately intense mood that is preponderantly positive; irregularity in biological function, negative withdrawal responses to new stimuli, non-adaptability to change, and intense mood expressions that are frequently negative; and a combination of negative responses of mild intensity to new stimuli with slow adaptability after repeated contact (Chess and Thomas, 1996). A simplified view of temperament categories places temperament in three rough groups: "the easy child," "the difficult child," and "the slow-to-warm-up child."

Maturity of personality refers to children's ability to recognize their own style and learn to use it to advantage. Many views of personality development emphasize the importance of the child's early years and early experiences (Freud, 1940; Erikson, 1963). **Self-actualization** approaches (Maslow, 1970) focus on the child's growing concept of self and emphasize the child's personal motivation as the tool for personal success. Researchers are beginning to understand the link between physiological makeup and behavioural patterns as well as the ways that young children are shaped by genetic predisposition. It is likely, for example, that hormones influence temperament styles.

Categorizing Information by Domain

Now that you are familiar with the various **developmental domains**, you should proceed to Activity 3.1, which asks you to categorize observed information about these domains.

THE WHOLE CHILD

When we refer to **the whole child**, we are usually inferring that we appreciate that the child is a human being who is an individual and not just a subject who is splintered into developmental domains. Clearly, each domain overlaps and interrelates with the others. Consequently, it is important to study the interactions among all domains. For example, both language acquisition and emotional development have a social context. In addition, all the domains are, in one way or another, influenced by the child's physical status.

THE CONTEXT OF DEVELOPMENT

Contextual factors can shape the process of development. Where the child is born and how the child is nurtured can make an enormous difference to how the child develops. Similarly, the culture in which the child is raised will influence motivation, encouragement, values, and many aspects of learning. Different backgrounds can also play a part in what language or

Activity 3.1

Categorizing Information about Developmental Domains

Categorizing Skills

Review the contents of the profile you created in response to the activity in Chapter 2 and categorize the information according to developmental domains. Using the diagram below, list the observable characteristics or skills under each category.

Development Profile

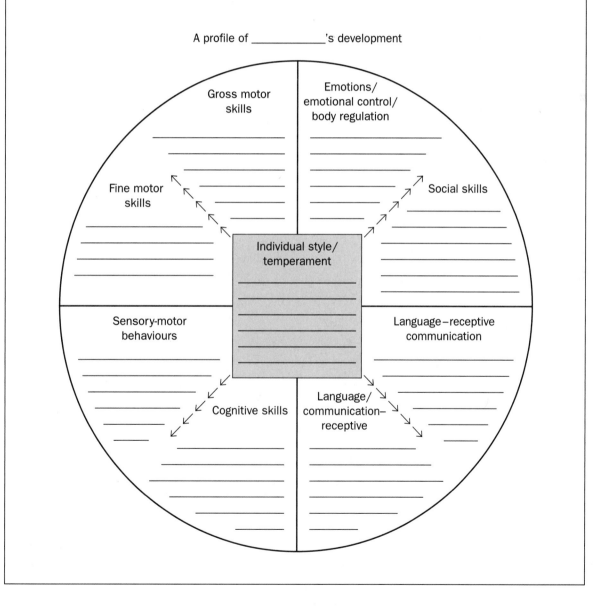

A profile of _____'s development

Gross motor skills

Emotions/ emotional control/ body regulation

Fine motor skills

Social skills

Individual style/ temperament

Sensory-motor behaviours

Language–receptive communication

Cognitive skills

Language/ communication– receptive

languages are acquired; usually there is also an element of cultural learning embedded in learning a language. Poverty or affluence is likely to make a difference to the child's immediate environment, nutrition, and the meeting of needs. The child's family composition, lifestyle, level of education, and housing can also influence the very young child's development. The most important part of the very young child's context is not the quality of the physical environment, although that is a factor, but the quality of adult interaction and consistency of treatment. In a child-care centre, the contextual issue includes the quality of interactions between parents and educators and the consistency of the child's treatment in the agency and the home.

DEVELOPMENT WITHIN AN ECOLOGICAL SYSTEM

Human development occurs within a social system. Infants' and toddlers' development may be driven by biological processes, but the possibility of realizing personal potential lies in the complex social network in which very young children find themselves

We looked at Bronfenbrenner's work in Chapter 1, but we need to see his approach as being theoretical as well as philosophical.

Bronfenbrenner (1979) offers a useful illustration of the interactions among the different aspects of an individual's social system, or what he calls the **bio-ecological system**. As illustrated in Figure 3.2, the **ecological system** consists of three concentric circles, with the child at the centre. Bronfenbrenner labels these circles the microsystem, the exosystem, and the macrosystem. These represent, respectively, the layers of people, institutions, and values with which the individual interacts. Each person's ecological system is different, although there are similarities, particularly between family members. However, even two very young children growing up in the same family experience life from different perspectives.

FIGURE 3.2

The Ecological System

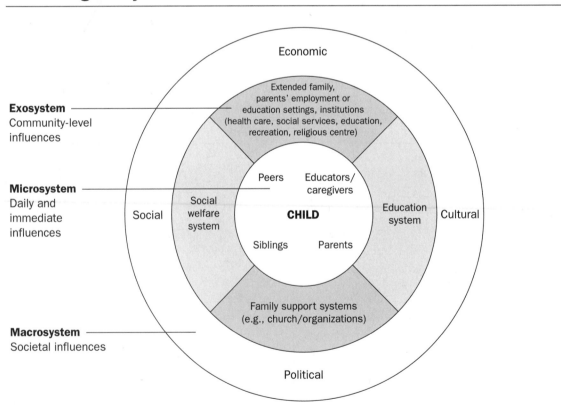

Source: Based on U. Bronfenbrenner (1979), The Ecology of Human Development: Experiments by Nature and Design *(Cambridge, MA: Harvard University Press); and D. Petes and S. Kontos (1987),* Continuity and Discontinuity of Experience in Child Care *(Norwood, NJ: Ablex Publishing).*

Because every child is born into a social structure and is influenced by the various aspects of this structure, understanding the actual *context* of a child's development helps us to appreciate the child's development patterns.

▶ Theories of Development

The term *theory* tends to intimidate people when they start to study development. It need not be so difficult. A theory is just a model that helps us to understand what we observe. For example, we frequently make explanations for why a child is behaving in a particular way. This is a theory, an explanation for a phenomenon. Developmental theories attempt to explain what is occurring for an individual. Studying theories can be a challenge because there are so many of them and they often use complex terms. Ainsworth, Bandura, Bowlby, Bronfenbrenner, Bruner, Chomsky, Erikson, Fantz, Freud, Gardner, Izard, Kagan, Piaget, and Vygotsky are a few of the important theorists who have offered significant models that attempt to explain young children's behaviour.

Theorists arrive at their ideas through various methods of study. Most of the major theorists used approaches involving forms of observation. These included naturalistic observations and contrived observations in formal experiments. From these observations, explanations of development were hypothesized and then tested.

What we understand about children can be shaped by several important theoretical schools of thought about human cognition and behaviour. People who follow different schools will observe an infant or toddler and see the same behaviour but likely interpret it differently. Educators frequently pick and choose aspects from a number of schools rather than identify with one particular approach. They may explain one behaviour with reference to a particular school but find that another behaviour is best explained by a different school. We call this an **eclectic** approach—where we put together aspects of different schools. Most educators use an eclectic way of explaining behaviour.

APPLYING THEORY TO WHAT WE OBSERVE

Some of the theoretical models that are particularly useful to us as early childhood educators involve the development that we see every day. These theories can help us understand observable development. They tell us:

- why very young children repeat actions

- why young children need love as well as physical care
- how new skills are learned
- how infants make connections with an adult
- what enables or drives toddlers to walk
- why newborns have reflexes that disappear
- why babies are interested in looking at visual contrasts
- when infants can understand symbols
- how language is learned
- why very young children have faces that attract attention
- why there can be difficulties in babies separating from adults
- when a toddler might learn to walk
- why toddlers are dependent on adults yet strive for independence
- how infants make sense of objects
- why babies look for lost items
- why toddlers seem self-centred

MAINTAINING A QUESTIONING ATTITUDE ABOUT THEORIES OF DEVELOPMENT

Theories will help you in your job of caring and educating. The results of someone else's detailed observing, recording, and hypothesizing may lead you to an understanding of a behaviour that you might not have been able to think of on your own. Theoretical models are not always correct, though. Moreover, they can be incorrectly applied. Use your common sense when testing the applicability of a theory, but don't dismiss a theory too quickly. Tread carefully through new concepts and test them out in ways that are harmless to the children. A theory may seem far-fetched at the start, but you might eventually find that it explains a behaviour in a meaningful, if not obvious, way.

For example, when Piaget (1952) postulated that infants built internal **mental schemes** of understanding from their actions, people were dubious at first. This new view of infancy didn't fit their understanding. When Bowlby (1965) introduced the concept of bonding, many scorned the theory. People are resistant to changing their ideas. Often, the implications of a new theory mean that parents and caregivers need to modify the way they care for infants.

At the same time that you study child development theories, you should examine norms of behaviour. Both of these areas will make more sense if you apply the knowledge to the infants or toddlers in your care. Theoretical explanations and **normative profiles** can work together to assist our understanding of infants and toddlers.

▶ Principles of Development

The **principles of development** are the pathways or **patterns of development** that have been observed by experts. Although most child development theorists agree that there is merit to each of the principles, each expert is likely to emphasize one principle over another.

MATURATION

Maturation refers to a sequence of biological elements that reflect growth and development. The pattern of growth and sequence of skill acquisition for young children is largely determined before birth. Much of a child's developmental map is created by genetic information from the parents. If a child's parents are both tall, she will likely be tall. If members of her family were relatively late learning to walk, that too may be a familial pattern. Further developmental mapping may be determined by broader evolutionary processes. For example, the reflexes that are typical of a newborn infant appear and then disappear. They do this regardless of the genes from the parents. This is a pattern of development that may reflect the general need to survive, or it is perhaps an adaptation to the environment that was a necessity at an earlier time. Infants tend to follow a similar pattern of development in that they usually acquire skills in the same order. Yet individual schedules mean that children may acquire these skills earlier or later than their peers. For example, babies learn to sit before they learn to walk, but the ages at which they gain the skill of sitting or walking may be different. Some children gain more quickly in some domains and more slowly in others.

The above discussion may make it seem that we can do little about children's developmental achievements. However, the milestones can be achieved only if the child experiences conditions conducive to development. If children have insufficient food or love, they will not reach their potential in growth or any other area of development. So, while caregivers should know typical patterns of development, it is more important to provide the **optimal conditions** for growth and healthy development.

In recent years, some educators have moved away from the use of developmental profiles or schedules, citing reasons such as cultural bias. Although these reasons seem valid, there is a danger in abandoning such profiles. Without them, we would have only limited understanding of developmental sequences and norms. Developmental profiles or schedules enable us to appreciate changes in the developmental process from a theoretical perspective.

The seasons of life are reflected in writings of the main religions and in legends and poetry that are centuries old. The concept of the cycle of life is evident in nature and is an inescapable truth. We are all born, live, and die. How we do that, where we live out that cycle, and our frame of mind about why are highly individual and depend on the interaction among the clocks and among the domains of development. The discovery of the seasons of life requires, perhaps, adult consciousness, but the infant is as much a part of the cycle as the middle-aged or elderly person!

THE HUMAN LIFE CYCLE

Infants and toddlers are at the start of their **life cycle**. Their experiences are likely to shape their later growth and development. Life-cycle theorists suggest that three clocks drive human development: the **social clock**, the **biological clock**, and the **psychological clock**. The social clock reflects the influences of expectation. The biological clock reflects the maturational process that drives developmental change. The psychological clock concerns ability to think according to increasingly complex inner structures. The concept of the three clocks is illustrated in Figure 3.2. Examples of the workings of each clock, and possible conflicts between them, are given in Box 3.1.

AGES AND STAGES

The actual chronological age of a child provides a marker for adult expectations of the child. This is a problem for at least two reasons. First, people who make age-related remarks are often not familiar with "typical" development for that age. Second, age-related comments may label the child. These labels—slow, advanced, smart, and so on—can affect the future expectation that adults have of the child and that the child has of himself.

In contrast to chronological age, a **stage** is usually thought of as a set of behavioural indicators that, together, constitute an identified step in the development process. Stages are even less precise than ages in developmental terms. For example, infancy is considered to be a stage, but it is defined in different ways by different theorists. Despite these differences, stages can give us give an idea about the typical sequence of developmental advances, understand why a child is behaving the way she is, help adults support the child to the next step, or stage, and help educators identify possible developmental difficulties.

FIGURE 3.3

Life-Cycle Clocks

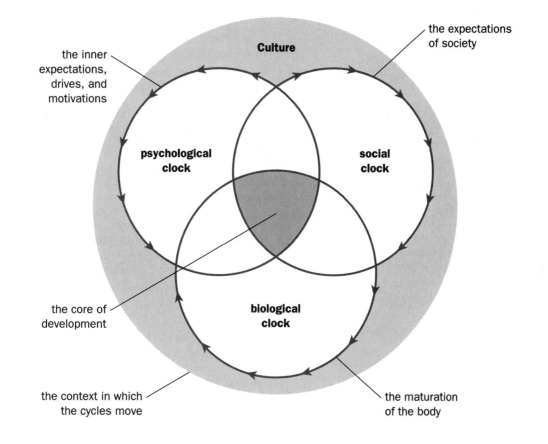

BOX 3.1

CHILD DEVELOPMENT "BY THE CLOCK"

Social Clock

Khalid, 26 months, likes to drink from his bottle rather than from a cup. Although he is able to use the cup quite well, he prefers the bottle. Khalid's parents think it's time to put away the bottle. How could this conflict be resolved? Should Khalid have to use the cup?

Biological Clock

Jon, 9 months, sits on his mother's lap in the waiting room of the doctor's office. His mother is concerned that he does not yet crawl. His older brother could crawl at about 8 months. What might the doctor say about this? Why hasn't Jon started to crawl?

Psychological Clock

Mandy, 20 months, has been copying adult language and behaviours for a long time. This week the caregiver notices Mandy demonstrating a different kind of activity. She is acting out the role of her mother in the dramatic play area. What change has occurred in Mandy's thinking? Why didn't she do this before?

Interaction of the Life-Cycle Clocks

Frequently, development change reflects the interaction of the three different clocks. For example, Dawn, 30 months, has had bowel and bladder control through the whole day for some time. At night she has a diaper, because she has "accidents." Dawn's father thinks it is time for her to be able to get through the night without a diaper. "These diapers cost a lot," he says. "Surely she is big enough now to have grown out of them." Dawn is distressed that she wets herself at night. She hides at bedtime when her father comes up to kiss her goodnight. Dawn has internalized the social expectations of her father and feels grown up enough not to have diapers at night. Yet her biological readiness hasn't kept up.

Can you identify the issues that reflect the social, biological, and psychological clocks? How might the apparent conflict between them be addressed?

HEALTHY DEVELOPMENT

The term **healthy development** is being used more and more often by researchers to emphasize the need for positive development outcomes. Healthy development is not a perfect state, but it indicates that the child's process of development is progressing positively.

Health is a physical, emotional, and psychological process and it requires careful planning and promotion. Pimento and Kernested (2000, p. 7) indicate that, although attention is paid to the health care system, the most significant determinants of health are in fact social and economic. These include "income/social status, healthy child development, freedom from discrimination, and communication and life skills."

INDIVIDUALITY

Each child's experience of family, society, and culture is as individual as a fingerprint or DNA. Even the child's position in the family contributes to her individual context. Although her experience may have many features in common with that of other family members, it is unique. Box 3.2 shows how children raised in the same family have individual contexts for development.

▶ Norms of Development

Earlier we discussed the philosophy of normative assessment; here we will look at where **norms** come from.

The study of development has been heavily dependent upon research that tells us what most children can do at a particular age. Arnold Gesell pioneered work in development by taking a sample of children and determining the average ages at which they demonstrated skills. More recently, researchers have tried to determine norms of development based on much wider samples of children. These profiles, including those by Allen and Marotz (1994), Sheridan (1997) and Illingworth (1992), are used primarily for screening and assessment.

When used as criteria for evaluating a child's developmental progress, developmental norms can offer useful information. For assessment of infants or toddlers, they may provide a developmental profile of a child that leads to specific action or intervention. However, using norms is a limited process that is open to abuse. Critics have strongly condemned the overuse of normative assessments and have questioned their validity and reliability. Some think that norms should not be relied upon for measuring performances of children from different cultures, because their patterns of development may vary or their opportunity to develop skills may be somewhat different. Another complication centres on the sample of children from which the norm is derived. It could be too small or poorly representative of some cultural groups. For these reasons, we need to think seriously about what criteria we use for assessment. Norm referencing should, perhaps, be used only as one part of a much more comprehensive approach to assessment.

Despite these cautions, norms should not be dismissed because of the challenges they present. We need to ensure that the research sample is appropriate in size and representation. We also need to make sure that we use the norms as a yardstick for measurement rather than as an indication of failure. Normative tools can offer means for gathering some quantitative assessment information, data that are presented in numerical or otherwise measurable forms. Quantitative data involve measurable information,

---

BOX 3.2

INDIVIDUAL CONTEXTS FOR DEVELOPMENT

Justin was the first child of Christine and Ralph. He was born in Jamaica, four years before his family moved to Toronto. His younger sister, Kesha, was also born in Jamaica, but only five months before the move. The family now has a new baby, James, who is 7 months old.

Kesha's experience of family life and relationships is totally different from that of her brothers. She is a middle child, with an older and a younger brother. For a time, Kesha was treated as the baby of the family, but the arrival of James changed the family dynamic. As a girl, Kesha is expected to behave differently than her brothers. When she arrived, her parents were a little older, more experienced, and more financially secure than they were when Justin was born. After the move from Jamaica, Kesha lost immediate access to her extended family, who had contributed so much to the care of Justin in his first few years.

The timing of the move from Jamaica had a different impact on Justin and Kesha. Justin remembers his old home and his friends and family there. Although Kesha has heard stories and seen visiting relatives, she does not remember her birthplace. Such experience also contributes to the different contexts of the two children.

---

such as the child's height or how the child is performing at a particular age level. It is important to supplement such data with information specific to the child's context. With access to both normative and contextual information, we will have the most helpful combination.

DEVELOPMENTAL PROFILES

The **developmental profile** is a complex listing of norms across all domains of development in a way that emphasizes the notion of "stage." A stage relates to a set of behaviours rather than single actions; together they indicate a general level of functioning. For example, a norm might indicate that at 6 months of age an infant will hold items to her mouth. The stage approach sees this as just one of many behaviours that indicate that the infant is in the sensory-motor stage. The developmental profile acknowledges that the domains of development interact and that there are deep structures underlying the observable characteristics of behaviour.

The authors of stage profiles often present their structure of stages as progressive steps that may have some approximation to ages, but the focus is the stage rather than the age. Both Erikson and Piaget offer stage models that have significant usefulness to us as educators.

Some of these profiles of development have led people to think that if a child is not demonstrating the supposed "right" level of performance, there is something wrong. This is usually not the case. But the profiles can give us a good idea about what to expect in terms of the sequences and patterns of development for most children. They can assist us in making assessments that involve identification of atypical skill levels. Although these atypical levels should be noted, they do not necessarily mean there is anything troubling. It is always important to bear in mind that children have individual patterns. If you keep observing and responding to "where the child is now," you are likely to find that what you have observed was an individual quirk rather than a problem. If your continued observations suggest that the child's behaviour is not what you might have expected, check your perceptions with normative profiles and with other professionals.

It is entirely possible to use profiles of development without making inappropriate judgments and labelling the child as "behind" or "ahead." A well-researched and culturally inclusive profile can help caregivers and health providers appreciate and document the individual's development in a way that no other tool can.

DEVELOPMENTAL PROGRESSION

Another process that can be used to gauge skill acquisition uses the child's own pattern of change as markers for developmental **progression**. To assess a child's performance, the child's earlier skill performance level would be used as a point of reference for current assessment. Although this exercise is helpful to some extent, it tells us only what gains have been made, not whether the performance level is typical for the child's age. Sometimes **regressions** will also be evident; they are often part of ordinary development.

LIVED EXPERIENCE

Every child's experience is different, even if they are identical twins living in the same family. Ultimately we don't know what other people's experiences or their mental constructions of those experiences are. Instead of studying children on the premise that all behaviour can be interpreted, the phenomenologist (as described in Chapter 2) greets the person of study by immersing herself in the life of the subject. One principle of studying development is to understand that there are many approaches, each of which has strengths and limitations. Counteracting scientific method may be a way of reaching a different level of "knowing" children, neither more nor less important in what it might reveal, or the process by which it was revealed.

NATURE AND NURTURE

Individual patterns of development occur whatever the circumstances of life. Identical twins may have the closest shared reality and a similar schedule for maturation, but even they have differing perspectives as they see each other and the rest of the world. The interaction of **nature and nurture** influences the pattern of each child's development, ensuring that development is truly individual.

Nature determines the individual's genetic map. Children inherit genes from their parents that set out the potential for each domain of development. Whether or not this potential is realized depends on the circumstances of individual life experience—what we call nurture.

Shakila's parents are dark-haired, brown-eyed, relatively short, and not very athletic. Growing up, neither of her parents had had access to plentiful, nutritious food. Her mother is quiet and shy, her father more outgoing. Shakila seems to take after her father in personality. At 18 months, she was below the norm for height but, because of her parent's stature, her pediatrician wasn't concerned. The toddler has a good appetite, and her parents are able to provide her with excellent food, unlike their own experience as children. Shakila takes advantage of the play opportunity at her daycare centre and has become more physically active than was expected by her parents. She has put on weight and has a sturdier build than her parents.

We don't know how Shakila would have developed in different circumstances, but we can see that her development was shaped both by her genes and by the experiences that were open to her.

Whether or not the "nature versus nurture" debate remains pertinent is open. Some modern theorists believe the dual concepts to be redundant. If the truth lies in the combination of the two, the explanation for development is that it is a dynamic interaction between the biological potential of the individual and every aspect of that person's experience. Consideration of both forces appears to remain relevant while we grapple with understanding genetic inheritance and the changeable components of life experience.

Twin Studies

One way of studying whether components of development are determined more by nature or nurture is by comparing identical twins who have grown up separately with those who have been brought up together—twin studies. Of course, identical twins are not often raised separately, and it would be a big ethical problem to split twins for the sake of an experiment. Galton (1875) was the first person to consider using twins to determine the outcome of the nature-versus-nurture debate. Siemens' book *Die Zwillingspathologie* (1924) was the first systematic description of the classical twin study design. Since then, many researchers have used variants of this methodology to see if particular attributes were determined by nature or nurture. When identical twins—that is, those who have the same genetic material—are reared apart, they still display some striking similarities. It has been found that various characteristics as well as diseases are heritable. Physical pattern of growth, personality attributes, and behavioural styles can all be heritable. In one study, male identical twins separated at birth met again in adulthood. They had chosen wives with the same names and similar looks, purchased similar models of car, lived in houses of similar style, and had numerous other similarities, including clothing and their choice of toiletries. Other than their fingerprints, there was little difference between them. Not all twin studies have offered such clear indication that attributes are heritable. There is agreement, though, that some characteristics and potentialities are genetically determined.

CONTINUITY AND DISCONTINUITY

Development continues throughout childhood and beyond, but not always at the same rate. A period of accelerated progression may be followed by a plateau, during which time little change occurs. Educators and parents are likely to notice when a new skill is acquired rapidly, but they may not notice a period of slower development. The toddler who is toilet-trained almost overnight provides a good example of rapid development.

Some domains of development appear to follow a continuous path of skill increase—**continuity**. Others may follow patterns of **discontinuity**. A toddler may swing between periods of intense effort to be independent and a reliance on an adult for some self-help skills, showing us that development may be accompanied by inner conflicts.

DIRECTIONS OF DEVELOPMENT

The sequence of physical skill acquisition is similar in all children. The pattern involves increasing bodily control that starts at the top of the body and progresses downward (**cephalocaudal sequence**) and from the centre of the body outward toward the extremities (**proximodistal sequence**). Thus, infants first learn to hold up their heads, then sit, stand, and walk, and so on.

Children may be ready to perform a skill, but they need time and opportunity to practise the action until mastery is achieved. This process of skill refinement continues for a long time after the core skill is demonstrated and enables the child to perform actions more accurately and purposefully.

CRITICAL PERIODS

Some experiences need to occur naturally, or be provided, for infants and toddlers at the correct time of their development. There are **critical periods** during which infants and toddlers gain particular skills and understanding. Sadly, children who miss having the right kind of learning opportunity at the right time may not manage to acquire some learning even if they have enriched experiences later on.

Research has shown that the brain is particularly receptive at certain times (Shatz and O'Reilly, 1990). One of the most important periods is the first three months of life. The newborn's brain contains the possibility of billions of neurological connections. These connections can happen only if the appropriate stimulation is provided. Without the stimulation, the possibility of the connections is lost.

There are also critical periods for damage. An infant who has very limited exposure to adults, and is therefore unable to make attachments, may have long-term, if not permanent, emotional difficulties. Meeting some basic needs for survival may seem to be enough for a child to develop satisfactorily, but research indicates that very young children need to have physical contact and love in their first months or they may be unable to grow and acquire skills. Spitz (1945) called this a **failure to thrive** and captured harrowing film of infants and toddlers who were

underdeveloped in every domain, despite apparent meeting of basic needs. More recently, follow-up with European and American families who adopted very young children from Romanian orphanages shows that families are contending with severely withdrawn older children. Although these children have been given love and nurturance since they were adopted, institutionalization for the first months of their lives did irreparable damage. Further adoption studies have highlighted difficulties in addressing developmental issues and providing meaningful compensation.

DEVELOPMENTAL "CATCHING UP"

The concept of the critical period can lead people to believe that nothing can be done for children whose development is delayed or for whom early experience was relatively poor. To a limited extent, it is possible to **catch up** in some areas of development. This is noticeable in infants and older children who have been hospitalized or institutionalized for a short period of time. Such children can reach the developmental level of their peers if their experience is not too long or traumatic. This may seem to contradict some of the things described above, but we are talking now about *limited* periods of time spent in poor environments.

It is difficult to predict what amount of damage is done to a child whose learning experience is limited. It appears that temperament, emotional attachments, and compensatory experience may be deciding factors in the child's ultimate development.

READINESS

Educators and parents frequently talk about a young child's readiness. It might be readiness for weaning or for using a toilet. Whatever the skill, the notion of readiness assumes that because a child is competent in one area, he will automatically be "ready" for the next step. It may be a mistake to make this assessment even if you are familiar with the child and with typical stages of development. Usually children will indicate readiness by demonstrating an emerging skill that is related to the one for which they might be ready. For example, if a toddler is ready to use a potty he may indicate this by using appropriate actions and possibly some imitation of another child or adult.

Readiness is a concept used by some educators who believe that they can enhance the child's development by setting goals to achieve the next step. Readiness assessment is carried out in various settings, including child-care centres. The most serious difficulty with readiness assessment is that there are very few ways of predicting the future abilities of children. Current performance is not always an indicator of future potential.

Researchers use the concept of **developmental outcomes** as measurable indicators of what children know and can do. There is a belief that achieving desired outcomes within a time frame or at the end of a period of education and nurturing is a useful predictor, or sign of readiness, for the next stage. This supposes that the developmental steps are achievable progressions and that gaining any one level indicates the potential for achieving the next. This is, to some extent, questionable. Wanting or not wanting to take the next step may be an issue. Also, as is the case with any type of skill acquisition, perhaps the optimal level or the maximum possible for that individual has already been reached!

MOTIVATION

Children's interests shape their learning. If they are **motivated**, their attention span is likely to be longer and they are more likely to attend to details. This principle is more obvious in older than younger children, but it is relevant to infants and toddlers.

Various elements interact in determining what might motivate a very young child. Some biological pre-wiring leads infants and toddlers to be interested in particular things at particular stages. For example, an infant is keenly interested in looking at faces or face-like patterns. Observing visual preferences tells us much about the child's interests. Differences in perceptual and cognitive functioning lead some children to pay more attention to some things than others. Children who have a lower level of cognitive functioning are less likely to be curious and persist at a task.

Success in a particular area tends to be a strong reinforcer. Also, the infant or toddler is likely to want to be involved in an activity where there is some reward. Temperamental differences also play a part in motivating the child. Some toddlers will be more independent than others just because of their personal style. Older infants and toddlers can be motivated by their mothers to do things that they had refused to do alone (Tronick, 1989). This could be because the relationship of trust allows the child to believe that the mother's request is all right. The adult's emotional responses can shape the child's interests. Approval or disapproval expressed on a parent's face may be enough to encourage or halt a child's interests.

Rewards and punishments can act as external motivators. Although less likely to be successful for the right reason, such inducements or negative reinforcers have some effect. Even infants can have their behaviour modified as a result of adult approval or disapproval. For toddlers the need to please can be a strong motivator. But stronger still can be the young child's inner drive for control and **autonomy**. This motivator is difficult to influence, but it is not desirable to try to break the child's will to do something. Adult intervention needs to work *with* the intrinsic motivation, not in opposition to it.

MUTUAL INTERACTIONS

Development occurs in a reciprocal manner—that is, the infant's behaviour influences the adult's as much as the adult's influences the child's. When we observe the interactions between adults and very young children—**mutual interactions**—we can see how much the child's behaviour affects the adult's behaviour and vice versa. This reciprocity allows for mutual attachments, complex relationships, a variety of learning experiences, two-way emotional comfort, and the creation of successful family and social groups.

THE BIOLOGY OF DEVELOPMENT

Early views of the "nature" argument of development tended to focus on the potential that was indicated in an individual's genetic makeup. Recent advances in genetics as well as neurobiology lead us to understand that, rather than being *limited* by our supposed potential, individuals have a much greater potential than they are ever likely to realize. Our biology could let us be smarter than Einstein if we let it. This is not an argument for pushing children to achieve an adult conception of success. Rather, we need to provide the optimal environment and all the appropriate support, love, and guidance to allow children to stretch their own boundaries of success. Instead of adopting a finite view of potential, we should look at infant and toddler development as a flexible process.

We can improve our ability to provide optimal circumstances for development by increasing our knowledge of biology and health issues. Biological processes that drive the way the body receives nutrients, benefits from activity, repairs itself, requires sleep, deals with stress, undergoes aging, and so on, all influence patterns of development.

DEPRIVATION AND RESILIENCE

Deprivation refers to any condition in which the child's needs are not met in a serious or ongoing manner. It is not necessarily equated with poverty, although a family's limited financial resources can affect how well it provides the basic elements of life to children. Deprivation can involve physical, cognitive, or psychological damage, or a combination of these. Consequences of deprivation can be varied and are somewhat unpredictable.

Some children appear to be more **resilient** to deprivations than others, and are less affected for little apparent reason. Steinhauer (1996) suggests that children's resiliency can be enhanced if they have external supports and internal mechanisms that act as protection from negative experiences. Although some personality types are more likely to have increased vulnerability, inner emotional resources are likely to ameliorate the effects of poor circumstances. However resilient the child is, her development is highly to be affected detrimentally if she is deprived of basic needs.

Steinhauer defines resiliency as "unusually good adaptation in the face of severe stress, and/or an ability of the stressed person to rebound to the pre-stress level of adaptation." To enable children to be resilient to whatever life puts in their path is difficult, because it demands that their living conditions and relationships are such that they develop healthily. This is extremely challenging for large numbers of families—perhaps one in four Canadian children lives in poverty. Steinhauer suggested that there are several protective factors that foster resilience:

- personal characteristics, including social competence, problem-solving skills, autonomy, perseverance, and an optimistic outlook
- families that have the strength to cope and endure despite chronic stress and repeated crises
- families and schools that provide care and support, high but achievable expectations, and opportunities for children to participate and contribute
- caring communities and nations that support the family and see children as a shared and precious resource[1]

DEVELOPMENT AND CULTURE

As mentioned above, part of the child's context concerns culture. Culture is not only an environmental factor: it relates to the moral, ethical, and social values that underpin every aspect of the child's experience. Because they shape so many parts of the child's development, cultural contexts of develop-

ment must be appreciated by educators. Without this understanding, it is impossible to interpret the child's behaviour. One of the cultural issues that influences how children develop is their exposure to the expectations of the adults around them. For example, in a culture that values independence, you may observe toddlers gaining self-help skills much earlier than those whose parents feel that toddlers need to be dressed or fed by adults.

You must avoid making judgments about the beliefs of parents. Without respect and consistency of treatment, the very young child will be confused.

TYPICAL AND ATYPICAL DEVELOPMENT

The concepts of **typical** and **atypical development** are contentious because of their judgmental tone. While it is crucial for adults working with very young children to appreciate the details of behaviour of children at different ages and stages, care must be taken when such terms are used. They can lead to labelling and the lowering of expectations of the child about whom the statement is made.

Adults must balance their understanding of what constitutes typical behaviours with their appreciation of the broad range of what is "normal" or individual, as well as the context and culture in which the child lives and the way that might shape key behaviours.

Whether their behaviour is typical or atypical, children need to have appropriate experiences and interactions. When a child's behaviour appears to match that of children of a younger age, you will need to observe and record developmental information very carefully. If, after consulting with the parents, you have a common concern, you may suggest accessing professional help. This may also be advisable if the child is particularly ahead in skill development. Whatever their developmental patterns, children need, and deserve, individualized support.

Children whose behaviour is atypical are likely to have special need of support of their development. Various special needs can be accommodated within a regular child-care setting, but some specialized expertise may be needed to make sure that the children's needs are fully understood and accommodated.

Developmental diversity can include physical, social, and cognitive disabilities and delays as well as special aptitudes, talents, and giftedness. There may be associated health concerns and particular stress on the child's family. A particular condition may not, in and of itself, be the cause of developmental challenges; the condition may create mobility, social, or other difficulties that, in turn, result in an interrelated developmental issue. It should be remembered that

---

1. Source: Sparrow Lake Alliance, "Methods for Developing Resiliency in Children from Disadvantaged Populations," prepared for the National Forum on Health by Paul Steinhauer, March 31, 1996.

there is very wide developmental variation within the population as a whole. The majority of children who are cared for in group settings can, and should, be supported in an inclusive child-care environment and by skilled educators working collaboratively with the children's parents.

▶ Studies and Government Initiatives

Recently in Canada, several new studies and toddler initiatives have targeted the area of childhood development. The National Longitudinal Survey of Children and Youth (NLSCY) is a government-funded study of Canadians from birth to adulthood. The first year of data collection was 1994, from a sample of 22,831 children aged 0 to 11. The survey is designed to provide data about holistic developmental processes and to consider the indicators of both positive and negative outcomes for children. From it, child-related policies will be developed, designed to "help young people follow healthy, active, and rewarding life paths."

Growing Up in Canada is the 1996 report of the NLSCY study; it presents some preliminary analyses of NLSCY data. This Human Resources Development Canada and Statistics Canada report offers a series of important papers that deal with some of the issues affecting Canadian children and their development. The longitudinal survey will continue to provide meaningful data "the analytic potential of which will grow enormously in years to come as further survey cycles are completed" (Cappe and Fellegi, 1996, Prologue/*Growing Up in Canada*).

The National Children's Agenda appears, at face value, to be an initiative that holds the promise of providing the support for Canadian children and families that is essential for their healthy development. The February 2000 budget speech, given by then-Finance Minister Paul Martin, seemed positive. "An important key to our children's success is the strength of the communities in which they live. That is why the federal and provincial governments agreed to develop a National Children's Agenda." However, there is fear the initiative is insufficiently specific. Writing in *The Globe and Mail* on March 4, 2000, Anne McIlroy explained in "The Budget: What about Children?" that it lacked clear strategies and adequate finance; "because it is so vague, the children's agenda currently does not have a lot of support around the cabinet table. Even the most optimistic proponents say they don't expect a large financial investment." While in principle the con-

cept of offering integrated and coordinated services seems ideal, the reality may not, unfortunately, match the initial intention. Child-care advocacy groups have moved quickly to support the National Children's Agenda with the clear message that "Children can't wait" (Child Care Resources Research Unit, April 2000).

"You Bet I Care," funded by the Child Care Visions program of Human Resources Development Canada and sponsored by three Canadian universities, is a series of studies that have followed up "Caring for a Living" (CCCF, 1993) and "Our Child Care Workforce: From Recognition to Remuneration" (Beach et al., 1998), which compiled and synthesized earlier studies. This new series provides original data about the characteristics of child-care centres across Canada and their staffing. From these studies we are already gaining information about the increase in numbers of infants and toddlers in centre-based care, the availability of such care across Canada, and the demographic profile of Canadian child-care centre staff along with their training, workload, and responsibilities.

Some of the "realities" of the "You Bet I Care" study were that:

- Seven out of 10 mothers with children under age 6 are in the paid workforce (*Profiling Canada's Families II*, Vanier Institute of the Family, 2000, p. 86).
- Almost nine out of 10 working women return to work within a year after giving birth (Statistics Canada, *The Daily*, September 1, 1999).
- In 1996, the percentage of husband/wife families who were poor was 10.5 percent; if the wives' earnings were removed, 21.4 percent of husband/wife families would have a family income below the poverty line (Statistics Canada, *Poverty Profile 1996*, National Council on Welfare, 1998, p. 87).

Brain development has been a clear focus for researchers in human development over the last decade. Numerous studies have increased our body of knowledge about how the brain works, how humans think, and what we can do to maximize learning. The majority of these studies point to the significance of the very early years as the critical period for learning. Pinker's work on language uses technologies, including MRI (magnetic resonance imaging), that provide new methods of study as well as new information. The technological approach is not accepted by some of Pinker's critics, but his continuing work certainly contributes to our collective understanding about deduction being the process that distinguishes human language from other forms of communication. This is rooted in the evolution of human beings, he contends, which is more complex than the pre-wiring suggested by Chomsky.

Neuroscience and early child development forms the basis for the final report of McCain and Mustard's "Early Years Study, Reversing the Real Brain Drain" (April 1999). The content and recommendations of the report presented to the Ontario government has brought attention to the need to support healthy development. The co-chairs provided leadership for a collective effort to synthesize current research and argue for an approach to "achieve the goal of improved outcomes for all young children and encourage your government to start the process" (letter to then-Premier Mike Harris on February 16, 1999). By the end of 1999, an Early Years Task Group was formed and had started work to establish or support existing services for children and families. A set of selected exemplary community-based initiatives was chosen to inform the work of the Task Group (Children's Secretariat, Government of Ontario). This appears to be a positive response by the Ontario government, but infant and toddler educators will need to pay attention to the type of services that are supported; these may not be centre-based.

"The most important part of neurological development in the first few years of life is the connecting up of cells to form pathways. Unconnected brain cells have a lot of potential, but are not doing anything," said Steinhauer at a 1998 conference in Alberta, "Linking Research to Practice—A Canadian Forum." After reinforcing the need to understand brain development, attachment research, and readiness to learn, Steinhauer went on to explain the core of his recent research work: what happens when children face poor environments, inadequate attachment figures, and poor learning experiences. His studies have revealed that there are ways of buffering children, or fostering their resilience (Steinhauer, 1996). His definition of disadvantage is not synonymous with economic deprivation, although poverty makes families' distress worse. His recommendations include eliminating child poverty, protecting children and youth through their key stages of development, and focusing community attention on the human and economic costs of failing to protect the development of vulnerable children and families. Steinhauer is insistent that we "make investments in social capital as important as investments in economic capital" (Steinhauer, 1996, Sparrow Lake Alliance Executive Summary).

The Canadian Institute of Child Health (CICH) recently published "Our Promise to Children" (Guy, 1997). This, too, reviews the newest neuro-developmental research and its impact on parents and educators. It clearly indicates four determinants for positive child development, protection, relationships, opportunity and hope, and community. The CICH is a national organization whose mandate is to improve the health of Canadian children and youth. It does this through gathering and disseminating current research in ways that make complex data meaningful.

Here are the three major trends in Canadian child care and early childhood education over the last few years: (1) child care overall is static (at best) or has lost ground and we need a national system of child care; (2) provinces diverged in policy, funding, and services so that inequalities for children and families became more conspicuous; (3) the number of children, especially younger children, is decreasing in most provinces and this offers an opportunity to take action while the child populations are low.

A longitudinal study conducted in the U.S. by the National Institute of Child Health and Human Development has tracked the lives of over 1,300 children through their first seven years of life, starting in 1991. The data have been collected and preliminary findings point to qualitative issues of mother–child (in forming attachments) relationships and correlations between child-care experience and developmental outcomes. Further analysis will provide both qualitative and quantitative information that may assist parents and educators internationally.

"How Should We Care for Babies and Toddlers? An Analysis of Practice Out-of-Home Care for Children under Three" (Penn, 1999) is a significant study of very young children in three different European countries. Rather than focus on measurable developmental outcomes, it sought to reveal the experiences of childhood within the context of family and culture. The study leads the reader to appreciate the values and beliefs underlying the care of babies and toddlers and suggests that there are limitations in using "child development" as the only framework for understanding infancy. As we discussed in Chapter 1, there are many ways of considering childhood, and, in Chapter 2, the experience of being a child is quite different from being an adult observing children. There are also, as Penn argues, many ways of studying infancy and toddlerhood, ways that are shaped by our own values and beliefs. They influence the way we see children and, consequently, the methods we use to study them.

The recent studies add to the body of knowledge that we share about infants, toddlers, and families; in time, even more information will become available.

Activity 3.2

What Would You Like to Learn?

You have now read the first three chapters about philosophical approaches to infant and toddler care and education, observing and recording development, and principles of development. What would you like to learn next? Identify some areas of knowledge that you would like to gain and some skills that you want to acquire. After that, consider strategies that will enable you to gain this knowledge and these skills. What will you do with the learning once you have gained it?

My Learning Plan

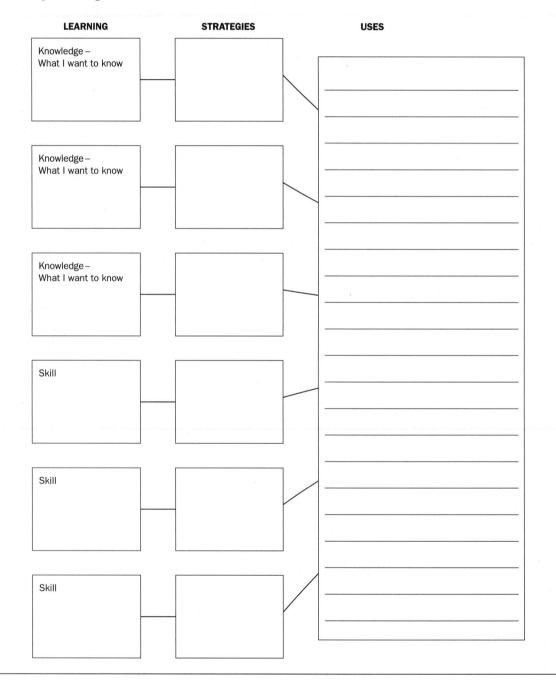

LEARNING   STRATEGIES   USES

Knowledge –
What I want to know

Knowledge –
What I want to know

Knowledge –
What I want to know

Skill

Skill

Skill

As you read and acquire more information, remember that information is not the same as knowledge; you need to make the information your own—construct your own understanding through combining information with experience.

▶ What Comes Next?

Before moving on to the next chapters of the book, which outline specific growth and behavioural changes of infants and young children, pause to think about the material presented in the first three chapters, what you have learned from this material, and what you would like to learn next. Activity 3.2 provides the outline of a learning plan, which you should now take the time to complete.

▶ Summary

We frequently divide aspects of the child's development into domains, to make studying infants and toddlers more manageable. These are artificial constructs, but they enable us to look closely at a child's development. These domains interact dynamically, so that every child progresses in different ways. Without the concept of domains, we may see the child's holistic development more clearly, but we can be overwhelmed by how much is going on simultaneously.

There are some principles that govern how development occurs. Appreciating these is particularly helpful because we can then understand what drives the developmental process. Research into infant and toddler behaviour and biology has provided us with some understanding of how the process of development happens. However, the way that development is explained differs among different schools or traditions of thought. We need to become acquainted with very young children to learn about them, but we also need to apply some of the theories that are considered reliable, so that we can test their applicability. Comparing explanations of development can be confusing, but it assists the educator in understanding the infant's and toddler's needs and how they can be met.

▶ KEY TERMS

accommodation
adaptation
assimilation
attachment
autonomy
baby signing
bioecological system
biological clock
calcification
catch up
cause-and-effect
cephalocaudal/proximodistal sequence
cognitive development
cognitive needs
communication skills
continuity/discontinuity
critical period
deprivation
development
developmental diversity
developmental domains
developmental outcomes
developmental profile
dishabituation
eclectic (approach)
ecological system
egocentricity
emotional development
failure to thrive
fine motor skills
gross motor skills
growth
habituation
healthy development
irreducible needs
language acquisition
life cycle
maturation
mental schemes
moral development
motivation
mutual interactions
myelination
nature/nurture
neuroscience
norms
normative profiles
object permanence
optimal conditions
optimal development
ossification
parallel play
patterns of development
perception
personality
physical development

physical needs
pre-wiring
principles of development
progression
proximodistal sequence
psychological clock
psychological needs
readiness
regression
resilient
role-modelling
schemes
self-actualization
self-regulation
sensory-motor
separation anxiety
social clock
social development
solitary play
stages
symbolic thought
temperament
the whole child
typical development/atypical development
zone of proximal development

▶ DISCUSSION QUESTIONS

1. Consider your own development. If you categorized it according to domains, how much would this help you understand its complexities? Also, how much would it help you to appreciate "who you are"?

2. When you see toddlers playing with new sensory materials, how is their learning occurring?

3. Children's hunger, deprivation, and abandonment are disturbing. How might you predict the future for such children if you knew that, from today, they were going to receive appropriate nutrition, medical treatment, stimulation, and lots of love?

4. Research work leads us to better understanding children's development. What ethical limits should there be on experimentation, observation, and other types of research?

5. What do we need to know about infants and toddlers that research work has not yet been able to provide?

▶ ADDITIONAL RESOURCES

▶ Further Reading

Berk, L. (2002). *Infants and Children: Pre-Natal through Middle Childhood.* Needham Heights, MA: Allyn & Bacon.

Bertrand, J., et al. (2001). *Nourish, Nurture, Neurodevelopment Resource Kit.* Ottawa, ON: Canadian Child Care Federation & Canadian Institute of Child Health.

Brazelton, T., and S. Greenspan. (2000). *The Irreducible Needs of Children: What Every Child Must Have to Grow, Learn, and Flourish.* Cambridge, MA: Perseus Publishing.

Fabes, R., and C. Martin. (2003). *Exploring Child Development.* 2nd ed. Boston, MA: Allyn & Bacon.

Fogel, A. (2001). *Infancy: Infant, Family, and Society.* 4th ed. St. Paul, MN: West.

Ramey, C.T., and S.L. Ramey. (1999). *Right from Birth: Building Your Child's Foundation for Life: Birth to 18 Months.* New York, NY: Goddard Press.

Snow, C.W. (1998). *Infant Development.* 2nd ed. Englewood Cliffs, NJ: Prentice Hall.

▶ Useful Web sites

The Consultative Group on Early Childhood Care and Development
www.ecdgroup.com/aboutus.asp
All you need to know about psychology
psychology.about.com/cs/child/
Amy Glenn's lecture notes for child development
socialscience.tyler.cc.tx.us/agle/partone.htm
ECE Web Guide
www.ecewebguide.com/specific.html
The Human Early Learning Partnership (HELP)
www.earlylearning.ubc.ca/index.html
Canadian Policy Research Network
www.cprn.org
The Early Years Study: Reversing the Real Brain Drain.
www.childcarecanada.org/policy/polstudies/
can/earlyyrs.html
Better Beginnings
www.opc.on.ca/bbbf/
ERIC Clearinghouse on Elementary and Early Childhood Education
ericeece.org

CHAPTER 4

New Beginnings: Newborn Infants

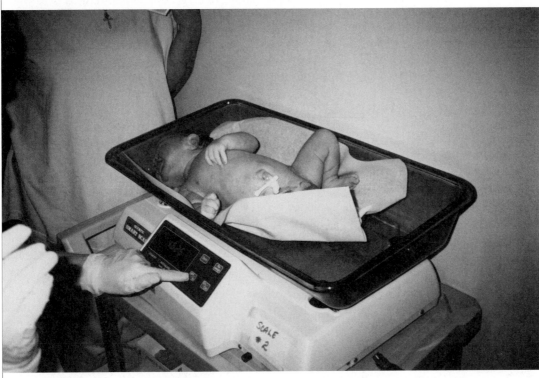

The medical experience of hospitals is many babies' introduction to life. Some people want a gentler and less medicalized birth and neonatal period for their babies.

Learning Outcomes

After reading and studying this chapter, you should be able to:

- identify the observable characteristics of newborn infants
- explain the significance of newborn infant behaviours in a development context
- recognize and respond to the developmental diversity of neonates
- respond to the neonate's health, safety, and development with appropriate protection and caregiving
- discuss the need for research into infant abilities and how that may shape the caregiving strategies of parents and educators
- develop strategies to work with parents as partners in the care and education of their children

Scene: A couple about to become parents discuss their concerns about the coming baby.

Conner explains his nervousness about having their first baby: "I'm the youngest child in my family and I've not really had the opportunity even to hold a baby, never mind look after one 24 hours a day." "That's not my worry," says his partner, Dahlia. "I just want the baby to be all right. I've read all those magazines about all the things that can go wrong. Just last night I saw on the box [television] a program about Siamese twins." Conner tries to reassure her, "The chances of that happening are so small we shouldn't even think about it." Then, "Let's try to think positively," Conner suggests.

Adults tend to have a few common reactions to newborn babies. "I'm afraid I'll drop her" or "He cries all the time" are perhaps the most frequently heard remarks. But how accurate are they? Newborns are, of course, **vulnerable** in a lot of ways, but they are probably more resilient than you might imagine. Think of the tough challenge they have gone through to be born. They can't be all that fragile. And although it may sometimes *seem* that they cry all the time, babies sleep for some of the night and during the day; even when they're awake there are times when they're not crying.

Wet and slippery when born, you might have thought that babies are always washed and dried before being handed to the parents. Not so; the **vernix**, a white waxy stuff covering the baby, may be left to dry and is likely to flake off. The baby may not look quite as you expected!

Many people think that babies can't do very much because they haven't had time to learn. Others know that they can show a wide range of automatic movements, called **reflexes**, including the ability to suck, grasp, and step. The stepping reflex is particularly amazing. Long after babies have lost this instinct, they will have to learn how to walk.

The way the baby looks may cause you to wonder whether the newborn really belongs to the parents.

Babies' skin tone and hair colour may differ at first from those of their parents. Skin may be lighter in colour or different in texture from that of the parents. In time the colouring will alter, and we are more likely to see a family resemblance.

You may notice that the infant's head seems oddly shaped—this is a result of the birth process. Depending upon whether newborns are premature, post-mature, or on time, their appearance is likely to be a little different. Perhaps you have noticed that average-sized babies have some roundness to their bodies because of their stored fat. Premature or low-birth-weight babies may be smaller, and they are also likely to be less filled-out.

▶ What to Look For

You may be wondering why you need to be aware of the development of newborns. Such young babies are rarely seen at child-care centres. Why, then, is this chapter included in this book? Box 4.1 provides some of the answers.

BORN INTO A FAMILY

For most families, welcoming a new baby is a time of great joy and fulfillment. Parents may behave in ways not typical of their usual style. They will spend time with their babies and enjoy a sense of the miraculous when they look at them. However, some parents are be slower than others at falling in love with their babies. Reasons for this may include hormonal changes and trouble adjusting to the enormous impact the new baby is having on their lifestyle. Once they have some time together to get to know each other, almost all babies find a way into the hearts of their mothers and fathers. Belsky and Kelly (1994) identified six abilities of parents that can help make the transition to parenthood a positive one. These include being able to give up individual goals and work as a team, resolve differences about sharing tasks, handle stress successfully, understand that the

---

BOX 4.1

WHY DO WE NEED TO KNOW ABOUT NEWBORNS?

The period from the cutting of the umbilical cord through the first two, four, or even six weeks is the **neonatal** stage, sometimes referred to as the postpartum period. In this chapter we consider the newborn to be a **neonate** for approximately the first six weeks of life. The events of birth and early life experience lead us to have sensitivity for each baby. Understanding neonatal development helps us to set the stage for appreciating later progressions.

good elements of a partnership will relate to different things after the baby, and communicate in ways that nurture their partnership. If parents can be supported to do these things, they are more likely to become effective parents and meet the needs of their infants.

GROWTH AND PHYSICAL CHARACTERISTICS

At birth, infants are examined for an early assessment of their general health. The first assessment is likely to be the **Apgar Scale** (Apgar, 1953), which evaluates heart rate, respiratory effort, reflexes, muscle tone, and colour at one and five minutes after birth. This assessment is done by the attending medical personnel to see if the baby is in good physical condition. Further checks of these functions will continue, but in a less formalized way.

Size

The baby, at birth, is, on average, about 46–53 cm long (18–21 inches) and weighs between 2.8 and 4.2 kg (6.2–9.2 pounds). Boys tend to be little longer and heavier than girls, but the differences are small. Although a little weight is lost in the first few days, this is quickly regained.

The Neonate's Head

At birth, the **neonatal** baby's head is about one-quarter of the length of the body. As the baby develops, the proportion gradually changes: by adulthood the head is only one-eighth to one-tenth of the height of the body.

The large head allows for greater development of the infant's brain than other parts of the body. Because the head was likely to have been squeezed and moulded during birth, it is probably somewhat pointed. Movement of the skull bones allows for a safe birth. Soon after birth, the head gains a more rounded appearance.

On the top of the head, the diamond-shaped anterior and posterior **fontanels**, or soft spots, are visible. There are four more fontanels, but they are harder to locate. While fontanels are less vulnerable than you might imagine, they do indicate parts of the brain that are not covered by the skull bones. These gradually close as the skull hardens.

The hair on the baby's head may be thick, fine, curly, or straight. Many babies are bald at birth, and some lose what hair they do have. Some babies may get a bald patch where they have been resting their heads, but this is not a long-term problem. Sometimes the infant's whole body is covered with soft hair, called **lanugo**. This usually results from a delayed fetal condition and falls out in the first few weeks. It is no cause for concern unless the mother had been taking a steroid-type drug.

Heart and Lungs

The newborn's heart weighs less than an ounce. Despite its small size, it can pump blood at a pulse rate from 140 to 180 beats per minute. Most babies breathe within a few moments of birth. Up to that time, the baby receives oxygen from the mother through the umbilical cord. The first breath is a reflex triggered by cold air. Breathing can be hindered if the lungs contain fluid. Sometimes babies have to have the fluid suctioned off to enable them to breathe easily.

Appeal to Adults

Babies are not always very attractive to anyone but their parents—indeed, some parents might even think that their offspring look a little weird, at first! After the first few days babies put on weight in ways that tend to make them more attractive. Researchers believe that babies have large eyes, rounded cheeks, deep foreheads, and round faces to make them appealing to adults so that we will protect them. Berman (1980) and Morris (1995) have suggested that babies' appearance makes us want to pick them up and pay attention to them. Their appearance is an in-built means of survival.

Responses

The type of delivery may influence the behaviour you can observe in the newborn baby. An uncomplicated home birth may provide a calmer and quieter environment than would be possible in a noisy hospital. If the birth was a positive experience for the mother, the baby may also be more calm. However, it is hard to predict how the mother's labour will progress and exactly how that experience will affect her baby.

Reflexes

Reflexes are the inborn, automatic behaviours that show us that the baby is physically and intellectually healthy and that the nervous system is working well. Some of the reflexes, such as rooting, sucking, and swallowing, are necessary for survival; others serve only to tell us that the infant is healthy.

All reflexes probably had a purpose at some point during human evolution, but the need for some may be less clear today. Without reflexive behaviours, it may be that later physical or cognitive skills would not develop. As deliberate bodily control increases, many of the reflexes disappear. They seem to serve their purpose and then go away.

Senses

At birth, all five senses are in working order. The infant's sense of touch is well developed: they can be seen to respond in different ways according to the way they are touched or to other tactile experiences. Some babies do not like being touched as much as others, so the infant's cues must be heeded. Although **sensory stimulation** is important, the baby can be **overstimulated**. The neonate has sensitivity to pain, but it is thought that this is less in the first couple of days of life than later on. Newborn babies are unable to regulate their own temperature. However, they will respond to temperature changes.

As though programmed to like breast milk, newborns like the sweet taste of lactose in milk. They may also respond differently to salty, bitter, and sour tastes. Like their sense of taste, their sense of smell leads neonates to prefer the odour of a lactating—that is, milk-producing—mother. Newborns may make a face at or turn away from what they perceive as unpleasant smells, and they can sometimes locate the source of an odour.

Hearing is essential for many later skill developments. The newborn can hear a range of sounds and will prefer the sound of the mother to other sounds. Often the neonate responds more positively to complex sounds than to single tones. Babies' hearing ability enables them to hear their own sound production, which will ultimately allow them to learn language.

Vision is less well developed than the other senses in human neonates. They have some ability to see in colour, but this is not yet well refined. Their focusing ability also takes time to develop. Babies try to focus on and scan objects in an effort to see them. Early focusing is possible if the object or person is close. The ideal focusing distance is about the space between an adult and a baby held in the adult's arms. Infants' eye movements are relatively slow and not very specific. Yet it will only take a few weeks for them to be able to see at a greater distance and with better connection between both eyes. Their eyes will stop wandering as much. Significantly, they will be able to see in three dimensions, because of the coordination of the eye muscles for **binocular vision**. With a month, newborns will fixate on an object or face and will scan it with eye movements that allow them to take in visual information.

Perception

There is a difference between taking in information from the senses and perceiving. What the young baby sees may be different from what we see because we process the information differently. Adults have spent years experiencing what things look like, smell like, and so on, and can recognize things and people. Lack of experience means that the baby perceives differently.

For most of the time that babies are awake and alert, more than one of their senses will be stimulated. They will hear while they see, for example, or feel something as they hear it. This kind of sensory information is called **multimodality**, because several senses are stimulated simultaneously. Infants have to learn to sort out all these bits of information in an attempt to understand what is happening. When they become familiar with a particular form of stimulation they may tire of it and look away. This **habituation** is significant: it tells us that an important type of neurological activity is happening.

Newborn Competence

Newborn babies' abilities are amazing. Recent experiments have shown that neonates have the ability to use all their senses and do sophisticated things like imitate a facial expression. For example, a baby can copy someone putting out his tongue by putting out her own. This behaviour is remarkable—it may be reflexive, we don't know. She does not know what she is doing, and the skill may not be very important, but the fact that she can do it shows another type of complex neurological activity that was not previously recognized until recently.

Numerous studies are currently being conducted into various functions of the neonatal brain. Theories about how babies are preprogrammed for various types of learning are likely to offer us some useful explanations for how learning happens. Most important for us as caregivers is to know that observable behaviours indicate significant advancements. These may help us to know what we should provide for babies to support their learning potential.

Yet the field of infant research has its share of disagreements. For example, recent work that looked at the link between physical skills and neurological development has led some people to believe that it is a good idea to help the baby practise reflexive movements. The thinking is that practising stepping would lead to earlier walking. Others think that there is no long-term benefit for the baby. Another research project suggests that if physical skills are encouraged and practised, intellectual powers will be increased as well. The traditional perspective is that physical skills will happen when the child is ready, and that they should be supported at that time, not pushed prematurely. In the case of such disagreements, it may be best to let common sense prevail until we get really clear evidence.

Sleep and Wakefulness

More easily observable than neurological activity are the infant's states of arousal or awareness. Wolff (1966) identified several stages of sleep and wakefulness: regular sleep that is calm and relaxed; irregular sleep that is jerky, with changing facial expressions; periodic sleep that happens between regular and irregular sleep; drowsiness that is seen with an unfocused stare or closed eyes; alert inactivity, where the baby is awake and curious; waking activity, where the baby has bursts of activity; and the state of crying. Other observers describe these states more simply as uptime, downtime, trance, and sleep (Quilliam, 1994). Whichever model we use to help us interpret the infant's states, it is clear that there are many levels of awareness and receptiveness. We need to recognize these if we are to find the right way to respond. Any number of variable conditions can influence the infant's state. Noise, hunger, calming words, a pacifier, being swaddled, or being in a safety carrier in the back seat of the car can all make a difference. Moreover, babies differ in their patterns of wakefulness and sleep. Unhappily for some parents, most newborn babies do not appear to have a predictable pattern. After the parents become used to getting up several times a night, the baby will unexpectedly sleep through to morning; this will have the parents running in to see if everything is all right!

Routines and Patterns

Each family deals with **routine** in different ways. Some parents think that infants should determine their own routines and eat and sleep when they like, but other parents prefer a more organized schedule. The problem is that the baby doesn't listen to the parents' requests for a full night's sleep. Establishing a routine is a gradual process whereby the infant's needs are met while the parents try to manipulate the timing. After about six weeks most families have established a workable pattern, even if they manage it by sharing the care and the interruptions during the night. You might observe parents suffering from a lack of sleep and feeling irritable as a result.

Crying

Crying is one behaviour of infants that is particularly designed to reach the ears of adults. This is their way of communicating, but it might pose a challenge to a tired parent or to any caregiver when it doesn't seem to stop. Types and intensities of crying vary from infant to infant. Mothers may be able to identify their own baby's cries even when other babies are crying. This may be an evolutionary characteristic that supports attachment and survival. The cries are also heard by the adult in different ways, depending on circumstances—for instance, whether they have just fed the baby, or they themselves feel tired. All infants cry; typically, neonates cry for about two hours a day. This doesn't mean anything unusual is happening. At six weeks, crying may increase to about three hours a day (Shelov, 1993).

Parents may think that the cries of their own babies are endless; the emotional tie between parent and child does not make the crying any easier to deal with. Between the second and fourth week, crying may increase because of **colic**, a condition that produces a high-pitched cry. Its real cause is not entirely understood, but it concerns the gastrointestinal tract. Colic may be indicated by clenched fists, extended or drawn-up legs, and extended periods of crying that do not respond to comforting.

Feeding

Newborn infants' feeding patterns will be as varied as their other patterns. Some babies are self-regulated and feed at predictable times. They may also then sleep in patterns more agreeable to the parents. Other babies feed irregularly. In addition to variations in when and how often they feed, babies do not consume the same volume. Some are breast-fed while others are given formula.

There are many advantages to breast-feeding a baby. The infant receives antibodies in the breast milk. It is less expensive, requires no preparation, is at the correct temperature, and presents fewer hygiene problems than formula preparation. Breast milk is "designer" milk made especially to meet the human baby's nutritional needs. Research suggests there is lower incidence of sudden infant death syndrome (SIDS) among breast-fed babies. The hormones produced by breast-feeding help to cement the mother–child attachment. Even a short breast-feeding period is beneficial to the infant. The **colostrum**—that is, the pre-milk fluid—is rich in antibodies and provides essential nutrients.

Another extremely important issue related to breast-feeding is one that has been discovered relative recently; breast milk and breast-feeding are beneficial for brain development (Canadian Child Care Federation 2001). In fact it is one of four major factors in ensuring healthy neurological development.

Although social attitudes about breast-feeding have changed, some people continue to view it in a negative way. They may feel that breast-feeding in public is unacceptable. This may be because in North American culture breasts tend to be perceived in a sexual way.

We may observe mothers establishing close relationships by breast-feeding their babies. Yet a similar quality of attachment can be observed with non-breast-feeding mothers and also between fathers and newborns. Formula-feeding parents who spend time cuddling their babies and tuning into them by watching, listening, and responding to their cues do form strong attachments. Much has been written about the psychological benefits of breast-feeding for the infant, and there is some evidence that indicates that breast-fed babies are better off in later life. However, caregivers need to respect the decision of the mother to breast-feed or formula feed and offer any support they can to aid the mother in her decision.

Bladder and Bowel Function

The neonate is not aware of passing urine. Only in time will the baby realize what causes the warm, wet sensation. Since a baby urinates every couple of hours, a conscientious caregiver might change the baby eight, 10, or 12 times a day. Diapers that take the wetness away from contact with the baby's skin make diaper-changing less urgent, but the commercials describing diapers that "keep baby dry" are not always to be trusted!

One of the first diaper changes may be a surprise, because it will reveal **meconium**, a greenish-black substance that contains mucus, bile, and amniotic fluid. This is usually eliminated within 24 hours of birth. Later stools will be soft, yellowish, and inoffensive, particularly if the baby is breast-fed. Babies vary in their bowel movements. Observing the individual baby's usual pattern is useful; we can then identify any changes to that pattern that could indicate a potential problem.

Newborn babies' skin is sensitive and will usually need some measures to prevent skin rash on the buttocks. Skin ointment should be applied only after the skin is cleaned. Otherwise, bacteria may be trapped underneath it. When adults dispense cream or ointment, they should not scoop it from the jar with their hands, because they could contaminate the contents. Instead, use a fresh spatula to scoop a small amount and apply it carefully.

Cleanliness is essential in all parts of caregiving. Diaper-changing presents the greatest dangers. Thorough and regular hand-washing is absolutely essential and is the most effective way of reducing the spread of infection (Canadian Paediatric Society 1992).

The Newborn's Genitalia

Baby boys will typically have fully descended testicles and their maleness will be obvious with a penis that functions for urination. Their genitals may look rather large and red, but this will correct itself without treatment. Some parents have their boys circumcised for religious or cultural reasons or because they believe it leads to better hygiene. Circumcision is controversial in terms of the pain endured by the baby and the procedure's supposed benefits.

Female babies will usually have pronounced labia, or genital folds, and a clitoris. They may have a white discharge from the vagina; it may even be slightly bloodstained because of hormonal changes. The breasts of newborn boys and girls may be a little fuller than you expected. Again, shifting hormonal levels are the cause, and this will normalize in a few days.

Skin and Temperature Regulation

Because of their sensitivity, newborn babies are susceptible to skin problems. **Milia**, small white spots seen mostly on the nose of the newborn, are blocked sebacious glands and will disappear without treatment. Other rashes, such as heat rash or **urticaria**, are caused by environmental conditions and allergies, so they call for careful observation and a quick response. Scaly patches on parts of the body may indicate dryness that can be dealt with easily, but cradle cap, on the baby's scalp, may need medical attention. Because the baby cannot shiver or sweat, and will not show a drop or significant rise in body temperature, it is necessary to moderate room temperatures carefully and dress the infant appropriately.

The Navel

The stump left on the baby's navel is the end of the umbilical cord, which was clamped and cut soon after birth. The stump needs little attention as long as it is kept clean and dry; it will usually fall away after five to 10 days.

Twins and Multiples

Babies who are born one at a time are called singletons. A small number of babies, about one in 80, are born as twins. There are two types of twins: monozygotic (from a single egg that has split into two), and dizygotic (twins that develop from two separate eggs).

Twins and multiples, although born one after the other, may be very different in their birth weights and developmental needs. Although some parents might like to dress their twins and multiples alike, they soon come to understand that they are raising children with very different temperaments. Their patterns of sleep and wakefulness can vary to such an extent that they are never asleep at the same time.

There are increasing numbers of triplets and multiples being born; this is thought to be because of the increased use of fertility drugs among women experiencing fertility problems. There are several organizations in Canada, Europe, and the U.S. that offer advice, information, emotional support, and practical supports such as exchanges of clothes. It can be very expensive to raise twins and multiples, but the greatest challenge is meeting the needs of each child while remaining healthy and getting sufficient sleep. It is quite possible to breast-feed twins or even triplets, but there are a variety of demands put upon the mother, father, and other caregivers. It becomes essential to focus on the babies and try to ignore less important things such as housework!

Caregivers of multiples in a child-care or home situation must meet the needs of each child and make suitable accommodations to ensure that each baby is supported in every domain of his development. It can be too easy to focus only on the caregiving elements of being with the infants. Take time, just as you would with other babies, to enter their space and appreciate their differing interests and patterns of alertness.

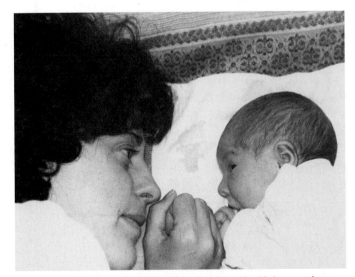

This new mother is getting acquainted with her newborn. She has set the stage for early bonding. This is the time for relationship-building, leading to a secure attachment.

Attachment and Emotional Development

If the cutting of the umbilical cord was the first real separation of the baby and the mother, other aspects of attachment and separation occur in psychological as well as physical ways. Kaplan (1978) suggested that mending the "rupture" between mother and child is the major task of the "mother and newborn couple." Closeness and early **bonding**—making a stable relationship—are thought to have sensitive periods, such as the time immediately after birth. Many studies have shown the long-term advantages of making and sustaining these early relationships. Klaus, Kennell, and Klaus (1995) insist that time needs to be made available for mother and child to connect with each other. It has been shown that mothers who have this time to bond are less likely to experience parenting problems months, and perhaps years, later. Clearly, it is the strength and continuity of this primary relationship that allows the infant to become conscious of being an important and a separate person while enabling the parents to do their job effectively and joyously. This bond is the beginning that allows the infant to reach her or his potential in the years ahead.

▶ Particular Needs

The essential role of the adult in caring for newborn babies is to ensure that all their needs, both practical and emotional, are met. Newborns are not impressed with an expensively decorated room, but they respond well to comfort and feeding.

Basic needs include feeding, changing after urination or a bowel movement, shelter and a comfortable environment that provides protection, scrupulous hygiene, warmth and avoidance of extreme weather, suitable clothing that allows movement and growth, a balance between sensory stimulation and calming surroundings, and some degree of quiet and opportunity for making close relationships. Time and a calm, responsive caregiver are the best insurance that the needs of the newborn baby are being met.

HEALTH ASSESSMENT

Newborns are at a very vulnerable stage of development and have recently undergone one of the most traumatic events of their life, birthing. A variety of bodily functions need to be checked soon after birth and will need to be watched until the baby is obviously stable and settled into a pattern of waking and sleeping, feeding and playing, being active and passive. Close observation is necessary for the first hours and days.

PROTECTION FROM INFECTION

Although many babies are exposed to numerous people without incident, the possibility of exposure to life-threatening infection exists. Some parents are cautious, particularly with premature babies or those who have experienced difficulties, but others may not see the risk to a healthy newborn. The rise of bacteria such as streptococcus that are resistant to some antibiotic treatment presents an increasing risk to the newborn infant. Consequently, we must consider the issue of exposure to infection and appreciate that vulnerable newborns need to be protected. Their immune systems are immature, and they may be unable to fight infections that pose little risk to older children and adults.

HYGIENE AND CLEANLINESS

Hygiene is particularly important at this stage to maintain a high level of cleanliness. A sterile environment is not necessary, but caregivers must be scrupulous about cleanliness. The most significant thing that adults can do is to wash their hands frequently and appropriately (Pimento and Kernested, 2000). Diaper-changing procedures should be carefully considered so that cross-infection is avoided. All baby equipment must be kept clean. Bleach solutions are the most effective sanitizing agents and should be used daily. Items that are in contact with the infant must be washed regularly; hot, soapy water and a rinse is usually all that is required.

Bottles and all feeding equipment are breeding grounds for bacteria. These must be washed, rinsed, and sterilized in accordance with manufacturers' directions and stored where they cannot be contaminated. Because of the growth of microorganisms, used bottles should not be reheated. Microwave ovens should be avoided for warming milk: the milk continues to heat after the power is shut off (Canadian Paediatric Society, 1992), and, microwaves may cause hot spots in the formula or cause steam to collect at the top of the bottle, which might scald the baby. According to some studies, microwaves might also damage the formula's composition. Microwave use may also be associated with careless re-warming of formula, presenting bacterial problems. Newborns must be protected from these hazards.

PHYSICAL PROTECTION

Safety issues are particularly pertinent to the newborn (see "Everyday Safety Issues," on page 100, for details). Because newborns are so small and unable to protect themselves by moving away from dangers, they are vulnerable to situations that would present little risk to older children. Careful observation, supervision, and involvement with the baby are necessary even after all potential dangers are removed.

RESPONSE TO CUES

The mother, father, and other caregivers need to learn the **infant's cues**. Such learning often occurs through trial and error. From time to time, the mother may seem to know intuitively what the baby needs; at other times, it may be difficult to tune in, but persistence is essential. Box 4.2 provides a list of some infant cues.

BOX 4.2

DEFINITION OF INFANT CUES

I. Subtle **engagement** cues
    A. Alerting—Increased muscle tone of face, possibly with flushing to cheeks, eyes usually sparkle
    B. Brow-raising—Elevating of eyebrows and formation of horizontal lines in forehead
    C. Feeding posture—Moderate abduction of the lower arms, forearm flexion, and fisted hands held palm inward
    D. Head-raising—Elevation of head with eyes directed upward toward caregiver

II. Potent engagement cues
    A. Facing gaze—Looking at the parent's face
    B. Mutual gaze—Sustained eye-to-eye contact

III. Subtle **disengagement** cues
   A.   Facial grimace—Combination of a frown, eye-tightening, and upper-lip-raising
   B.   Eyes clenched—Eyes tightly shut
   C.   Gaze aversion—Eyes turned away from caregiver or object
   D.   Diffuse body movements—Motor movement of arms and legs, usually tight or close in toward torso; movements can be jerky and give the impression that the infant is struggling
   E.   Immobility—Can be either positive or disengagement cue; a stilling of movement of arms or legs, as if in anticipation of something to come
   F.   Head lowering—Chin brought in toward chest, eyes usually lowered as well
   G.   Hand to ear, neck, or behind neck

IV. Potent disengagement cues
   A.   Crying (three types)
      1.   Hunger or ordinary cry: somewhat low in volume, of short duration (one–two seconds); rhythmical, with vocalization and one–two-second pause, vocalization and one–two-second pause, and so forth
      2.   Angry cry: a far more forceful version of the hunger or ordinary cry; remains rhythmical
      3.   Pain cry: a vocalization of sudden onset, of long duration (approximately seven seconds); loud, followed by audible expelling of air, gulping in air, repetition of above
   B.   Whining—A prolonged, high-pitched, somewhat nasal sound; not rhythmical, uttered by itself and repeated a few times in succession
   C.   Fussing—Staccato, short, low-pitched vocalizations; not rhythmical
   D.   Spitting—Spitting up small amounts of food, without gagging or forceful projection
   E.   Pulling away—Removing torso and/or head away from caregiver or object; that is, withdrawing and increasing distance from caregiver or object
   F.   Tray pound—Hitting the surface of highchair tray or tabletop with the palm of the hand
   G.   Lateral head shake—Turning head from side to side as if saying no

Adapted from partial list of Sumner and Spietz, in Erickson and Kurz-Reimer. G. Sumner and A. Spietz (1994), NCAST Caregiver/Parent-Child Interaction Feeding Manual *(Seattle: NCAST Publications, University of Washington School of Nursing). For more information, contact NCAST, Box 35790, University of Washington, Seattle, WA, 98195-7920; fax: (206) 685-3285.*

Quick responses to the baby's needs are essential for building relationships of trust. Newborns are not too particular about who meets their needs, as long as they are met. Although they can differentiate between people and prefer those who are familiar, they can be calmed by the relaxed manner of a stranger's care. When infants send out messages to adults, they may persist until we understand them. However, adults cannot rely on the infant's persistence and should always be alert to the cues the infant is giving.

STIMULATION AND RELAXATION

Although sensory stimulation is necessary, it is important to recognize the baby's signs when she is telling you she has had enough. She will attempt to ignore information overload, but she does not have the ability to organize her thoughts or regulate her behaviour. At birth, babies need little more stimulation than would come naturally from everyday interactions and domestic surroundings. Overstimulation does not produce babies who are more intelligent. Rather, overstimulated babies may become irritable and confused.

However, babies can become used to sleeping with a noisy background. A baby who is used to a certain amount of sound may not be able to sleep in quieter places and may need music or white noise.

SUPPORTING THE CAREGIVER

Primary caregivers cannot offer high-quality care to newborns if their own needs are not adequately met. These needs include nutrition, sleep, and exercise, as well as time to do what makes them feel peaceful and whole. All of these contribute to the psychosocial health of the individual (Donatelle and Davis, 1997).

Thus, as the backdrop to providing good care and responsiveness to infants, caregivers need to be proactive in ensuring that their own needs are met.

Mothers may need particular consideration. Their bodies have undergone the changes of pregnancy, labour, and birthing and are experiencing hormonal changes; they are trying to adjust to a new role; and they then have multiple responsibilities during the day. These all have an impact on the way the mother is able to cope and to form attachments. The process is normal, but that does not mean it is easy. The mother may find that she needs practical assistance in domestic matters or a break from caregiving. Such assistance, outlined in Box 4.3, may prevent some difficulties for both mother and baby. It may even protect the infant from the kind of neglect or abuse that can result from the mother's stress.

▶ Developmental Variation

Most babies are born healthy and without significant special needs. But variations in prenatal development mean that some babies face particular challenges. Some of the most significant variations of development happen because of length of gestation and the conditions for prenatal development. Many developmental variations stem from genetic inheritance, family patterns, exposure to teratogens such as chemicals or drugs, availability of prenatal care, the birth experience, or from other reasons we cannot determine.

The educator's task is to provide support to both the infant and the family as the baby is diagnosed and directed to necessary supports. Specifically the educator must:

1. observe and record pertinent behaviour of the infant and be prepared to share that information
2. identify any developmental alerts with the assistance of the family
3. seek resources and direct the family to appropriate professionals (it is not the educator's job to intervene or refer the baby directly)
4. support the family through the processes of medical and other professional diagnoses and interventions
5. read the parent's cues and determine when and how to support the family
6. work collaboratively within the parenting and professional team to ensure that the child's needs are met
7. make appropriate accommodations to the program to meet family needs
8. set clear boundaries about the role, and what assistance is appropriate
9. nurture a close and supportive relationship while showing empathy for the family
10. avoid talking to others about any child or family

PREMATURITY AND LOW BIRTH WEIGHT

Preterm babies and those who have low birth weight present particular challenges. A premature infant is one born before the 38th week of development. However, many preterm babies do not face significant developmental challenges. Low-birth-weight babies may have received insufficient nutrition before birth for a variety of reasons, including **placental insufficiency**. With medical intervention, many very tiny and extremely immature babies do survive. Yet this can present an immediate challenge for medical personnel and a long-term challenge for the parents and

---

BOX 4.3

A USEFUL STRATEGY FOR SHARING CARE: SUPPORTING NEW MOTHERS

New mothers do not automatically fall in love with their babies, although most feel some attachment from the time of their birth. Birthing is tiring, hormones are fluctuating, and the new addition to the family may alter the dynamics of the parental relationships. Enabling the mother to feel competent, reassuring her that it is perfectly normal to have feelings of ambivalence, and providing her with a little time to herself for sleep or a change of scenery can be very helpful. Educators can make comments about the mom's competence as they talk to the new baby: "Wow, how beautiful you are, your mommy did a great job to make such a beautiful baby." Or in adult conversation it might be helpful to sit down for coffee and let the mom talk. Reassurance that other parents feel the same stressors and feel that they too are on an emotional roller coaster is supportive. Perhaps you can offer to extend baby care to enable mom to sleep, shop, or take time for herself.

caregivers who will have responsibility for these children as they grow older. Delayed development may well remain evident when the child is in toddler and preschool child care and when the child goes to school (Deiner, 1997).

Respiration difficulties are the most common concern with small babies. They may also suffer vision problems, circulation difficulties, body-regulation concerns, and feeding and digestive problems. Generally, the smaller the preterm infant, the greater the likelihood of there being more significant problems.

CONGENITAL CONDITIONS

Congenital conditions are those that are present at the time of birth. The term does not distinguish the reasons for the condition. Some conditions—especially the more severe ones—are recognizable at birth. Others will not be identifiable until much later. Generally, the more severe the disability, the earlier it will be detected (Allen et al., 1994).

Chromosomal Disorders

Some congenital conditions stem from **chromosomal disorders**. These genetic abnormalities can usually be identified quite early in the infant's life by a range of observable characteristics, called a syndrome. Two commonly known chromosomal disorders are fragile-X syndrome and Down syndrome.

Metabolic Disorders

Some **metabolic disorders** are also genetically determined. One of these, phenylketonuria (PKU), can be detected by conducting a heel-prick test. Following a positive test, the infant is put on a special diet. This prevents the brain damage that is a consequence of the untreated disorder. Other metabolic disorders can cause a wide variety of symptoms that can influence later development.

A number of other congenital conditions are related not to genetic abnormalities but to teratogens. A **teratogen** can be a drug, other chemical, or virus that causes fetal abnormalities. Exposure to environmental toxins such as PCBs or to prescription, over-the-counter, or illegal drugs taken by the mother can result in malformations of limbs, intellectual impairment, and death. Fetal alcohol syndrome (FAS) results from the mother's consumption of alcohol during pregnancy. Characteristics of FAS may be evident at birth, but some impairments may not show up until later, when the child is experiencing learning problems.

Infants suffering from the effects of the mother's addiction to hard drugs present particular challenges. The immediate difficulty confronting health-care workers is weaning the infant off the addictive substance. The baby is likely to suffer some withdrawal difficulties because of a physical dependence on the substance taken by the mother. Later, the long-term challenges may be even harder for parents and educators to manage. The infant may have poor intellectual functioning that cannot be corrected or other developmental challenges that require significant support.

Environmental pollutants, viruses, bacteria, blood incompatibility, smoking, maternal health status, immunization, and a wide range of other factors influence development in the neonatal period. Frequently, when there is one condition causing concern, others are also present. We do need to remember, though, that in Canada, 71 percent of mothers had problem-free pregnancies in 1994 (Canadian Council on Social Development, 1996) and good infant health is related to the mother's health during pregnancy.

HIV/AIDS

Sadly, we are seeing more babies born with the **human immunodeficiency virus (HIV)**. Women of childbearing years are being infected in increasing numbers in Canada (Canadian Council on Social Development, 1996). The virus can be transmitted to the fetus during pregnancy or delivery or transmitted to the infant via breast milk. It is currently estimated that 15 to 30 percent of HIV-infected mothers pass the virus on to their babies. This infection rate can be reduced using newly developed medications.

Research in the field of HIV and AIDS—acquired immune deficiency syndrome, the end stage of HIV infection, when serious illnesses appear—is expanding rapidly, and caregivers should try to keep up to date with published material on this topic. It is possible that you will become a caregiver to a baby with HIV without knowing about the presence of the virus. The practice of **universal precautions**—that is, assuming that infection is present and therefore always adopting hygiene practices to avoid transmission—will ensure that you protect yourself and other infants.

INJURIES AT BIRTH

A number of different types of injury to the infant, before, during, or after birth (the **perinatal** period) can result in minor or major health and developmental challenges. For example, the cord may wrap around the baby's neck during birth. This can stop the flow of oxygen to the baby and can cause anything from mild intellectual impairment to death.

Atypical Birth Presentations or Difficulties

Atypical birth presentations (unusual ways the baby tries to be born), prolonged labour, or pressure on the baby's head causing cerebral irritation can occur. These can cause long-term developmental challenges that may not be obvious at birth. Careful observation of the infant may produce some useful information about the infant's behaviour that can alert you to the need for further assessment.

Babies Exposed to Cocaine and Other Drugs

It is not only illegal street drugs that can cause later developmental challenges. A fetus exposed to physician-prescribed and over-the-counter medications by the mother's ingestion of such substances can be damaged in some way. Advice from medical practitioners can help mothers weigh the possible benefits of particular medications against potential detrimental effects. Generally it is sensible to avoid any substance that might have an effect on the baby. The placenta acts to filter the blood passed to the unborn child, but it does not keep out all substances that are detrimental.

Exposure to cocaine and other street drugs does have a negative effect on later development, and there can be a difficult withdrawal process for babies who are born addicted to drugs taken by their mother. Some years ago the belief was that a baby born to a crack-cocaine-taking mother would have severe developmental difficulties. We now know through extensive research that there is a variable effect and it is difficult to predict exactly how the baby will be damaged. That said, there are likely to be some cognitive difficulties and a possibility of delayed motor skill development (Chasnoff, 1992). It is suggested by some pediatricians, such as Daniel Nuespiel, addressing the issue in *The New York Times*, that parents and professionals avoid the use of the term "crack babies" because the label can be a self-fulfilling prophecy and because it is only a minority of babies who experience significant developmental difficulties.

It should be noted that babies born to drug-addicted mothers also frequently live in poverty and disadvantaged conditions. These conditions are even more likely to be detrimental to the baby than the drug exposure.

Newborn babies may need special physician-prescribed treatment soon after birth to manage their withdrawal from drug exposure. In the early months of life the baby needs close monitoring. Babies who are born addicted to particular substances may be particularly irritable, physically sensitive, and difficult to pacify.

SOCIOECONOMIC CIRCUMSTANCES

Poverty can cause a multitude of problems for the unborn and newborn infant. Malnutrition of the mother, poor prenatal care, unsanitary living conditions, or exposure to inappropriate environments can all affect the infant. Early maternal support can make the outcome much more positive for both mother and infant.

DEVELOPMENTAL ASSESSMENT

All babies, regardless of their health at birth, need ongoing assessment. Information, observation, and formal screenings and assessments are essential to ensure that the developmental needs of the infant are met (Canadian Paediatric Society, 1992).

Schedules for health and developmental checks vary from province to province. One of the most commonly used neonatal tools is the Neonatal Behavioral Assessment Scale (NBAS) (Brazelton, 1995). It requires a trained examiner and can identify a range of concerns. A related tool, the Assessment of Preterm Infant Behavior (APIB) (Widerstrom, Mowder, and Sandall, 1991) can identify intervention needs.

Many of the most serious disorders are likely to be noticed at birth. More mild, but still very significant, defects may be noticed by the parents and caregivers in the first weeks and months of life. Infants' responses to visual and auditory stimulation may indicate challenges in these areas. If these potential problems are observed in naturalistic, everyday situations, they may need further investigation by professionals.

The responsibility of the caregiver is to ensure that all preventive measures are taken to support the child's health and development. Caregivers should ensure that their knowledge of developmental issues is up to date and that they can share this knowledge with the parents and others supporting the infant. Their responsibility includes observing and recording behavioural information and health signs that can assist them and other professionals to identify concerns and support the infant and family. On a day-to-day basis, caregivers need to offer the nurturance, stimulation, and care that fits the newborn's individual needs.

▶ Developmental Alerts

You will see variations in each newborn. Avoid making assumptions about the causes of developmental variations or differences in appearance, but ensure that you respond to any real developmental or health concerns. Any of the following are potential causes for concern, or **developmental alerts**, in the neonatal period:

- absence of reflexive behaviours such as rooting when the cheek is stroked, sucking for milk, and swallowing
- absence of reflexive startle response where baby throws out arms and legs and opens hands
- absence of grasping a finger or small object
- absence of stepping when held upright with bare feet touching a surface

You also should notice when a baby:

- has an asymmetrical appearance
- has asymmetrical movements
- displays prolonged jerkiness of movements
- has high-pitched crying
- does not cry
- shows no response to stimuli
- displays floppiness of the arms or legs
- has severe responses to foods or other substances
- has bulging or sunken fontanels
- has an enlarged head
- fails to feed
- shows prolonged colic/abdominal distress
- has a lack of eye engagement (after two–three weeks)
- displays prolonged distress and irritability

▶ Health Concerns

Health concerns may overlap with developmental alerts. Any of the following observations should receive medical attention:

- no breathing
- rapid respiration (over 60 breaths per minute)
- diminished breath sounds
- no pulse
- heart-rate change (over 180 or under 100 per minute)
- soreness in the diaper area
- raised or lowered body temperature: normal rectal temperature is 38°C (100°F); normal armpit temperature is 36.1–37°C (97–98°F)

- choking
- skin rashes
- navel "weeping" or bleeding
- feeding difficulties
- excessive spitting up
- dehydration (diminished urination, sunken eyes, less skin firmness, quick weight loss, drowsiness, altered breathing)
- swollen or sunken fontanels
- vomiting
- unusual sleepiness or difficulty in waking
- diarrhea, unusual fecal matter, or blood in the stools
- discharge from the vagina
- swollen genitals that do not correct themselves
- unpredicted blueness around the mouth or any part of the body
- yellowing of the skin or any skin-colour changes
- seizures (convulsions)
- white furry mouth or reddened mouth
- adverse reactions to medications
- allergic responses
- breathing difficulties, congestion, or runny nose
- sticky eyes
- bleeding from any part of the body
- signs of injury, including bruising and other marks
- unusual behaviour

In addition, all accidents must be documented and reported to parents. Any resultant breathing difficulty, significant bleeding, loss of consciousness, choking, convulsion, or other significant symptom should receive an immediate first-aid response and referral to a qualified medical practitioner. Enrollment in a specialized infant first-aid and cardiopulmonary resuscitation (CPR) course, such as those offered by the Red Cross or the St. John Ambulance Brigade, is essential for those working with newborns.

▶ Signs of Potential Neglect or Abuse

Abuse is a difficult word to define. Standards of care vary, and the perception of them is somewhat subjective. What is acceptable practice to one parent or caregiver may be thought of as abuse by another. That said, abuse can be defined as an active, aggressive act that causes physical, sexual, or emotional harm. Some believe that there must be a degree of willfulness on the part of the abuser, but this assumes that abuse can occur only when it is deliberate. In infant caregiving, it is entirely possible to abuse an infant by being careless or rough, or by lacking skill.

Neglect can occur in similar ways, but it involves a passive disregard for meeting the needs of the infant.

It is quite easy to create a profile of personal characteristics that might predispose a parent or caregiver to be abusive or neglectful. The majority of people who fit that profile, however, do not harm their infants and are rightly insulted at the suggestion that they might be abusive. It is also important to remember that abuse or neglect of infants is not limited to a particular social class or economic background.

Certain conditions may make abuse more likely. They include, often in combination, a lack of education and skills to meet the needs of the infant, undue stress in personal or sexual relationships, financial hardship, and social isolation. In addition, abusive adults may have a low tolerance for frustration. They may lack an attachment to the infant, see any demands by the infant as willfully intrusive, have early life experience of being abused themselves, or lack strategies to solve problems.

Parental and caregiver behaviour is likely to point to problems, although it is quite unlikely that an adult will be abusive in front of others. Lack of attachment coupled with some physical sign might indicate a potential difficulty. Sometimes the adult will be overly nice to the baby in front of others. At other times, an adult's disregard for the baby might be a signal that help is needed—the adult may be trying to communicate the problem.

The more common forms of infant abuse include shaking and bruising the infant. This usually occurs as a result of adult frustrations. **Shaken baby syndrome** can lead to significant internal damage to the baby's head; it can result in brain damage and death. Marks on the infant's body can be minimal even when there has been major damage. Behavioural changes in the infant—seizures, prolonged jerkiness, floppiness, or altered awareness—may be indicators of a problem. Bruises are easier to detect; sometimes they may even correspond to the shape of the adult's hand. Abuse of very young infants can be hard to identify unless we observe the infant closely and become familiar with individual patterns. We can then notice small changes in appearance or behaviour that might indicate a potential problem.

Premature babies are particularly vulnerable to abuse. They are three times more likely than full-term babies to be abused during infancy and early childhood (Schmitt and Krugman, 1992).

Neglect can take a variety of forms. Because infants require constant care and attention, it can be a real challenge for any parent or caregiver to meet all the baby's needs. Neglect may involve negligence in providing for the infant's basic needs. This can lead to poor growth, lack of responsivity, dehydration, hypothermia, infection, developmental difficulties, and, in extreme situations, death.

The infant's long-term development is likely to be affected by any kind of abuse or neglect. Physically abused and neglected children have a variety of difficulties, including developmental delay, behavioural problems, and excessive hostility. Even though the infant will not have an autobiographical memory detailing the events of abuse or neglect, any negative pattern of interaction and violent events will influence every aspect of the child's later development.

The caregiver needs to ensure that signs of abuse are documented and offered to the child protection agency for investigation. It is not the task of the caregiver to diagnose abuse or assign blame. It is possible that the same signs and symptoms have an explanation other than neglect or abuse.

▶ Everyday Safety Issues

Protection from all kinds of hazards are essential for any baby in the neonatal stage because they are so small, lacking in physical control, and generally vulnerable. The following are some of the most common and significant items the caregiver should consider:

- protecting newborns from extremes of temperature
- using safety constraints while travelling
- removing hazardous small objects and dangling strings
- paying attention to buttons, sharp objects, and drawstrings on clothing
- checking change-table stability and ensuring that the infant cannot fall off the change table
- protecting newborns from pollutants such as tobacco smoke and household chemicals
- ensuring that the crib mattress fits its base, and that the crib is stable, with a secure latching device and a space between the bars of not more than 5.9 cm (2⅜ inches)
- avoiding dangers while holding the newborn (e.g., scalds from coffee, burns from the stove, tripping while walking, dropping)
- ensuring bathtub safety (avoidance of slipping, lowering body temperature, scalding, and drowning)
- checking infant-seat stability, non-slip base, and safety straps
- checking baby-swing stability and safety straps

- ensuring personal security (e.g., guarding against kidnapping, incompetent baby-sitters, or intense sibling rivalry)
- checking baby-carriage and stroller stability and structure to support and protect the head and back
- removing plastic sheets, coverings, and bags that could cause suffocation
- checking baby slings or back-carrier safety (e.g., security against falling out, chafing legs, or bumping the head)
- using non-breakable rattles and playthings (although they probably won't use them yet)
- using stuffed toys that do not have loose stuffing or small detachable parts
- guarding from cats, dogs, and other animals that may pose dangers such as suffocation, scratching, or biting
- being aware of places of safety in emergency situations
- having emergency plans
- checking fire protection, smoke alarms, and carbon monoxide alarms.

A newborn needs to be supervised at all times. Accidents do not happen to newborn infants; all incidents are preventable. Yet a list of preventive measures is only the start of ensuring the infant is safe. Protection involves a constant evaluation of the environment and an awareness of the child's developmental stage and particular vulnerabilities.

▶ Starting Points for Response

RESPONSIVE CAREGIVING

Newborn babies are dependent upon their caregivers in every way, although they have remarkable potentials. Mother and baby usually have opportunities to get to know each other and form a bond. All caregiving strategies need to address this **bonding** process. The most important part of caregiving is in providing for the physical needs of the child. Parents and other caregivers have to learn the baby's cues. Through feeding, changing, holding, cuddling, dressing, bathing, and talking to the baby, and tuning in to the responses, two-way communication can be established.

Although it may seem that the baby responds to experiences more than initiating them, it can be interesting when we pay close attention to the communications that start from her. Two-way communication is dependent upon our reading the cues—identifying the messages that the baby is deliberately, or by chance, sending to us. When we acknowledge the cue, we are trying to engage with the baby—just as she might be trying to engage with us. **Engagement** is the two-way connection that comes about when baby and adult enter each other's consciousness. There is a special communication that doesn't necessarily require words or sounds, but is likely to rely upon facial expression. Sound production from either the baby or adult may enhance this connection; adults may use some high-pitched words to support the engagement, the baby may make cooing or contented noises. The **neonate** does not yet have a social smile, but she is programmed to seek and stare as methods of early engagement.

After a short while the baby's engagement is likely to fade. After all, her concentration span may not be very long. Adults might be surprised at how long the sequences can last, but eventually the baby will **disengage** by looking away, showing another focus, drooling, or showing behaviours unrelated to the engagement.

Babies separated from their mothers can bond successfully with their caregiver, but such a process must be based on responsive physical contact and meeting needs promptly. Box 4.4 on page 102 provides some suggestions to help you tune in to the newborns, read their cues, and respond in a helpful way.

SUPPORTIVE GUIDANCE

The object of **supportive guidance** is to do far more than just make clear where the boundaries are. The intent is to provide a positive framework within which the baby is comfortable, feels safe, and can take small risks. She needs to learn about people in her immediate world and to learn to function effectively in society. This starts with building relationships.

To discipline a newborn baby is inappropriate, but this is the time to establish positive patterns of interaction. Being responsive to the baby's needs is the first guidance strategy that the adult must offer. Later behaviour is dependent upon the social relationships that the baby makes. Time, opportunity, and shared experiences are reinforcers of behaviour.

It is impossible to spoil babies. No effort to meet their needs can be too much. The reciprocal communications between baby and mother (or other adults) provide the backdrop for establishing trust. It would not be an overestimation to say that this relationship provides for the roots of character development, security, self-knowledge, moral understanding, emotional regulation, physical health, and later development.

BOX 4.4

GETTING IN TUNE WITH THE NEWBORN

Below are some starting points for building your **responsivity** skills with a newborn. Tune in with respect and:

- respond to crying promptly
- identify possible causes of discomfort (diaper change, hunger, gas, need for attention)
- notice the type of cry and what that means for this baby
- respond to the baby's state of awareness (uptime, downtime, trance, sleep)
- check the supply of all basic needs (warmth, protection, hunger, comfort)
- tune in to the individual patterns of reaction
- identify the baby's temperament style and provide appropriate responses
- support attachments by offering responses quickly and tenderly
- take time for eye-gazing
- sing lullabies at sleep time and more boisterous songs during uptime
- allow the baby to grasp your finger, stroke the baby's hands, rub the baby's back
- rock the baby in your arms or over your shoulder, whichever the baby prefers
- provide a warm bath and a short massage (stop if the baby doesn't like it)
- observe reactions to stimuli and respond to the baby's preferences
- provide visual stimuli within the baby's focusing ability
- imitate the baby's own sound production
- repeat words using a higher pitch than normal
- take turns in sending and receiving messages
- smile and make faces, watching the response
- put your tongue out and see if the baby copies you
- read signs of tiredness and boredom and then decrease stimulation
- stimulate all five senses, one or two at a time
- keep scarves or objects smelling of Mom close by
- see if the baby likes to be propped up a little to see everyone
- try carrying the baby in different ways to determine personal preference
- take time for feeding and hold her while you do so
- play games, like follow the rattle, until the baby tires of it or responds to something else
- play classical, jazz, folk, or pop music and see the response
- identify the baby's fears and provide support through an emotional response
- make your routine similar to the one at home
- ensure continuity of caregivers
- protect the baby from any danger
- talk, play games, and have an intimate moment during diaper-changing
- take the baby for a walk
- ensure that the baby is dressed for the weather

FACILITATING DEVELOPMENT

When newborns' emotional and physical needs are met, all domains of development are supported. Early brain development occurs rapidly, and newborns need adequate human stimulation more than toys or fancy rooms. Caregivers need to tune in to babies' responses to stimuli and withdraw when necessary. Constant bombardment is confusing rather than helpful.

Supporting parents in both their confidence and competence can be particularly important at this early time. **Facilitating development** is typically the responsibility of parents, but most parents need practical and emotional support so that the baby–adult relationship can get off to a good start. Early relationships between adults and babies can be challenging when their knowledge of each other is insufficient to identify the baby's rhythms and responses. All relationships take time; any efforts to further the relationship provide the foundations for healthy development.

Babies need opportunities to move and to gain physical control over their bodies. They gain preliminary schemes of understanding from the actions they make. The beginnings of understanding about being a separate person arise from the responses the newborn gets from adults and the way they affect her world.

HOLISTIC RESPONSE

Activities 4.1 and 4.2 encourage a **holistic response** to newborns. Activity 4.1 suggests ways of engaging in newborns' experiences and extending your interactions with them. Activity 4.2 helps you to observe each baby and to develop activities that are targeted to individual interests and skill levels.

In this chapter, and in all of the following ones, you will see similar diagrams indicating a range of potentially useful activities appropriate for the age or stage of the infant, toddler, or 2-year-old. Remember, very young children vary tremendously in their stages of development, styles of interaction, interests, and moods of the moment!

Read the diagram carefully, because it contains various key components:

- the central circle indicates your state of constant observation
- within the large circle you will see a sequence of four sections, indicating:
  - how to engage the infant
  - what the experience is
  - how to enter the moment of the activity
  - how to extend the experience if it is successful

At the centre of the diagram, you can see what skills this activity may address—skills that are usually becoming evident at that age/stage. The four outer circles indicate:

- the developmental domain that is most likely to be supported through the activity
- concepts/schemes that may be addressed through the activity
- the language/communication that might be emerge
- any safety issues that are pertinent to the activity

The concept of *See How They Grow* is to develop relationships and offer experiences that support the very young child's optimal development. The core activities that you will have with a newborn will be entirely spontaneous. Because communication is a two-way process, you'll need to merge receiving and initiating communication. The main point of the activity is engagement. As in all relationships, you need to balance sending and receiving messages. You read her messages and you try to enable her to read yours. It's a give-and-take process and she needs to be as much in charge of it as you are.

The following open-ended experiences are some of the adult offerings that might be appropriate for babies in their first weeks of life. Remember that human relationships are more important than materials, particularly at this very early stage. The experiences are starting points for joyful engagement. If the baby is not responsive to the stimulation or appears interested in something else, follow her lead rather than your own! Observe her actions, try offering the experience in a variety of different ways, check her response. If she is engaged with the experience, or anything that happens as a result of your planning, ensure that you enter the moment with her. If she is enjoying the experience, support it with language and calm encouragement. Whenever the experience is successful, try repeating it—babies

Activity 4.1

Responding to the Changing Needs of Newborn Infants

Your interactions with babies must be responsive to their needs and emerging skills. To assist you in engaging in the baby's experience, the activity on page 104 offers suggestions that may extend your interactions. Careful observation is necessary so that you introduce the idea at the right time and in the appropriate way. Each suggestion includes ways the idea can be extended if the baby is ready. This activity also illustrates the safety, communication, conceptual, and developmental issues that you, as a child-care professional, need to hold in mind as you respond to the baby.

Many other activities are appropriate besides the ones listed below. Your skill in developing them will come as your experience and enjoyment increase.

Activity 4.1

Responding to Changing Needs of Newborn Infants

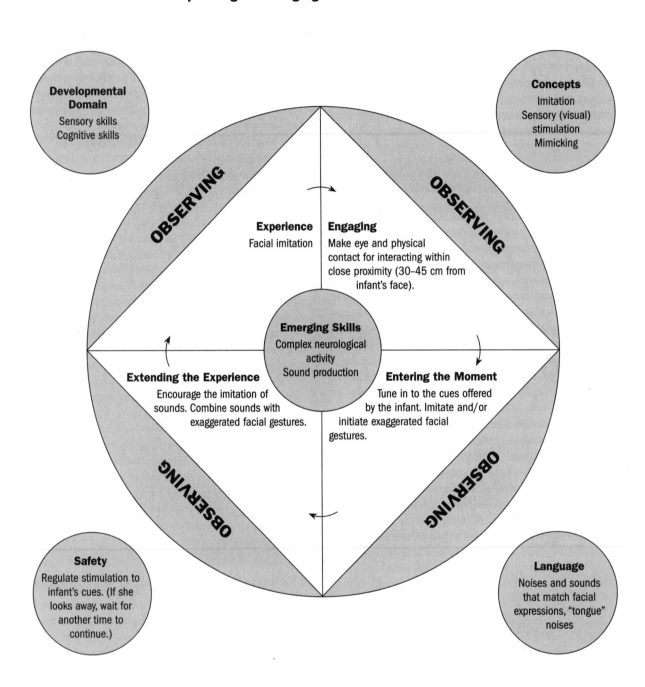

Developmental Domain
Sensory skills
Cognitive skills

Concepts
Imitation
Sensory (visual) stimulation
Mimicking

OBSERVING

OBSERVING

Experience
Facial imitation

Engaging
Make eye and physical contact for interacting within close proximity (30–45 cm from infant's face).

Emerging Skills
Complex neurological activity
Sound production

Extending the Experience
Encourage the imitation of sounds. Combine sounds with exaggerated facial gestures.

Entering the Moment
Tune in to the cues offered by the infant. Imitate and/or initiate exaggerated facial gestures.

OBSERVING

OBSERVING

Safety
Regulate stimulation to infant's cues. (If she looks away, wait for another time to continue.)

Language
Noises and sounds that match facial expressions, "tongue" noises

often respond well to repetition. They learn what to expect, which is gratifying for them. Then, for novelty, try a variation of the activity, with only minor differences. Monitor the response you get from her.

At all times focus on her rather than trying to make your activity successful. Relatively minor activity can prompt positive engagement. Enjoy your interactions!

Activity 4.2

Creating Responsive Curriculum For Newborns

Activities for babies should evolve from their own interests and skill levels. There cannot be a set curriculum. The adult's role is to tune in to the baby's world and create experiences that are mutually enjoyable, that celebrate the baby's current abilities, and that provide opportunity for continued development. The following ideas will help the adult to observe each baby and assist them in providing some meaningful experiences.

With confidence, the adult can extend these ideas yet further.

Developmental Domain	Observation of Emerging Skills (things that you see)	Responsive Experience/Activity
Reflexes	– reflexes gradually disappear (some quickly) as purposeful and deliberate actions become apparent	Carefully try to elicit reflexes from the infant. If you fail to get an expected response, discuss with a physician.
PHYSICAL Gross motor	– holding head up for short periods of time – pulling herself up on her arms for short periods of time while on her stomach	Lay the baby face down on a blanket. Place toys in front of her and talk about the toys. (Be on the floor yourself.)
Fine motor	– swinging arms and hands to the midline while lying on her back – grasping rattles or fingers – looking at her hands and showing some limited voluntary control	Lay the infant on her back and place rattles, mobiles, and toys with different sounds slightly above her shoulder/head. Shake, rattle, and squeeze toys, and encourage the infant to make attempts at swiping for the toys.
COGNITIVE	– integrating the senses (i.e., seeing and hearing, seeing and touching, hearing and touching, etc.) – imitating sounds, facial gestures, etc	Ring bells slightly above and off to the side of the infant, speak to the infant, and watch her scan and locate the source. Allow the infant to grasp the noisemakers.

Developmental Domain	Observation of Emerging Skills (things that you see)	Responsive Experience/Activity
Language	– cooing, making happy sounds, distress sounds	An excellent time for these experiences occurs during diaper-changing, when the infant has the close, undivided attention of the caregiver. Mimic happy and cooing sounds. Respond to distress sounds.
Social/emotional	– forming multiple attachments – self-concept – purposeful responsive smiling	Talk through your actions. Talk with the infant about her body parts (e.g., Where are Riane's toes? Nose?). Sing songs. Dictate your actions as you attend to the infant's needs. Smile while interacting with the infant.

Responding to Changing Needs

Newborn Infants

EXPERIENCE 1

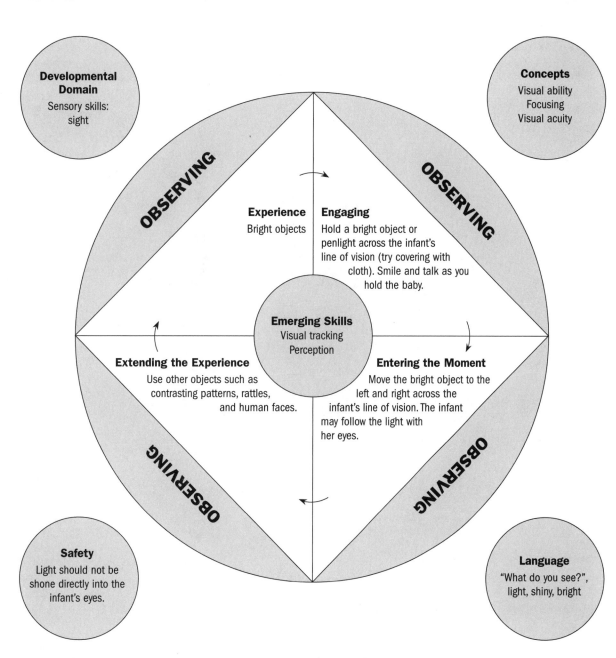

Developmental Domain
Sensory skills: sight

Concepts
Visual ability
Focusing
Visual acuity

OBSERVING

OBSERVING

Experience
Bright objects

Engaging
Hold a bright object or penlight across the infant's line of vision (try covering with cloth). Smile and talk as you hold the baby.

Emerging Skills
Visual tracking
Perception

Extending the Experience
Use other objects such as contrasting patterns, rattles, and human faces.

Entering the Moment
Move the bright object to the left and right across the infant's line of vision. The infant may follow the light with her eyes.

OBSERVING

OBSERVING

Safety
Light should not be shone directly into the infant's eyes.

Language
"What do you see?", light, shiny, bright

Responding to Changing Needs

Newborn Infants

EXPERIENCE 2

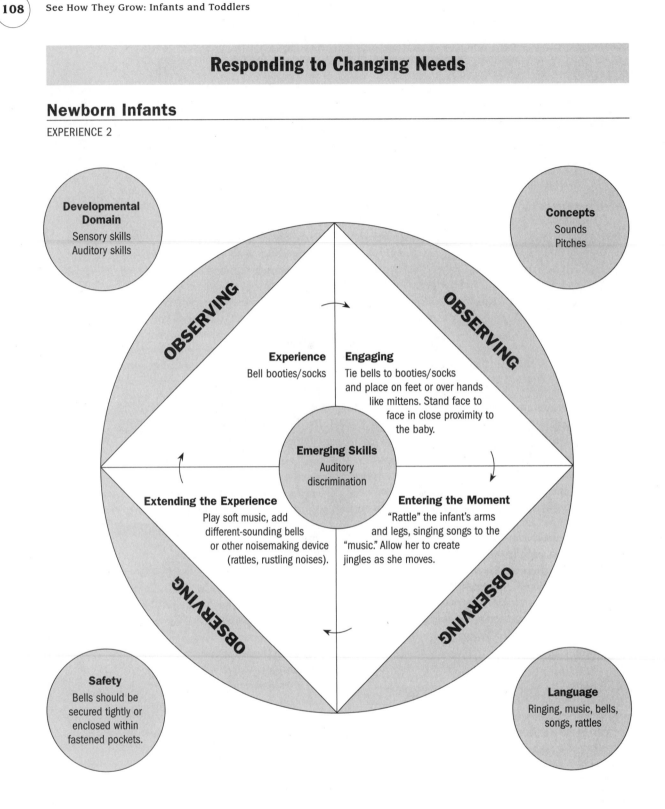

Developmental Domain
Sensory skills
Auditory skills

Concepts
Sounds
Pitches

OBSERVING

OBSERVING

OBSERVING

OBSERVING

Experience
Bell booties/socks

Engaging
Tie bells to booties/socks and place on feet or over hands like mittens. Stand face to face in close proximity to the baby.

Emerging Skills
Auditory discrimination

Extending the Experience
Play soft music, add different-sounding bells or other noisemaking device (rattles, rustling noises).

Entering the Moment
"Rattle" the infant's arms and legs, singing songs to the "music." Allow her to create jingles as she moves.

Safety
Bells should be secured tightly or enclosed within fastened pockets.

Language
Ringing, music, bells, songs, rattles

Responding to Changing Needs

Newborn Infants

EXPERIENCE 3

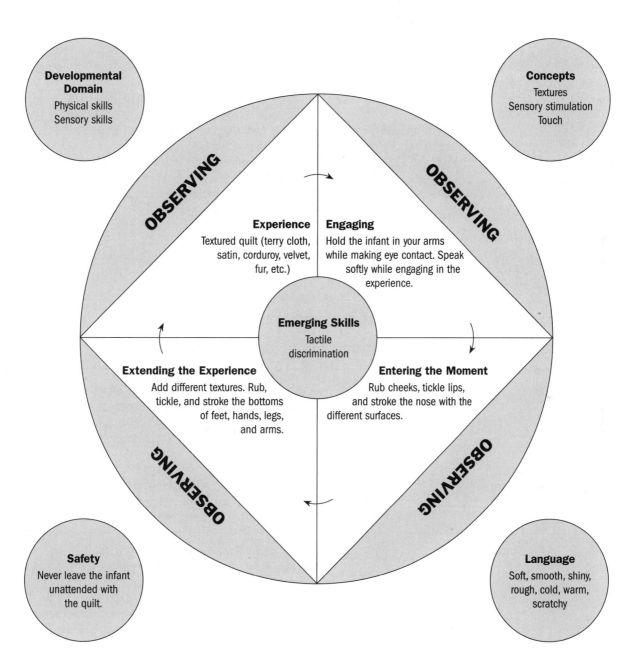

Developmental Domain

Physical skills
Sensory skills

Concepts

Textures
Sensory stimulation
Touch

OBSERVING

OBSERVING

Experience

Textured quilt (terry cloth, satin, corduroy, velvet, fur, etc.)

Engaging

Hold the infant in your arms while making eye contact. Speak softly while engaging in the experience.

Emerging Skills

Tactile discrimination

Extending the Experience

Add different textures. Rub, tickle, and stroke the bottoms of feet, hands, legs, and arms.

Entering the Moment

Rub cheeks, tickle lips, and stroke the nose with the different surfaces.

OBSERVING

OBSERVING

Safety

Never leave the infant unattended with the quilt.

Language

Soft, smooth, shiny, rough, cold, warm, scratchy

Depending upon the responses that you gain from the baby, you might find it helpful to repeat activities 1, 2, or 3, or modify them, adding some of your own ideas. The baby is very focused on her body and physical self—she is gradually gaining control of her body and will, after some time, begin to perform more actions in a deliberate way. To support her physical discovery, which is usually helpful in the early weeks, pay attention to her body. Some babies like that more than others—be guided by her. Arching the back, disengaging, or showing upset tells you she wants something else—or she prefers to engage with you with less physical contact.

Even as a very young infant, the baby needs an adult to support her learning about the human and concrete environment. She is not a passive receiver of information, but an active seeker. She performs actions on her world to help her learn about it and she initiates communications, but she is limited in her mobility and language, even though she has some competence at making attachments. Guiding the baby responsively requires understanding these things and providing a bridge for her between her known world and the world she has yet to learn about.

Although purchasing toys is not an essential part of nurturing babies, many parents and other adults like to buy toys to express their celebration of the child's life. Having a room full of toys is more likely to impress adults than babies, but there are some purchases that are more appropriate than others. Some toys are more suitable for the home environment than for group care, but the expense of some materials can only be justified if the items will have multiple users. The baby stage is so short that some toys are only played with for a very short period in any one child's life. Always check each item for safety and clean it appropriately, especially between its use by one baby and the next.

Further Experiences and Interactions

Further Experiences	Interactions
Baby	Touch, stroke, hold, and rub the baby's arms, legs, feet, toes, hands, fingers, stomach, back, and neck while smiling, talking, and singing to the infant (use lots of powders).
Baby mirrors	Hold a safe, unbreakable mirror 8 to 12 inches from the infant's face. Talk to her about who is in the mirror (facial features).
Grasping fingers	Place and stroke your fingers in the palm of the infant's hands. Her grasping reflex will firmly hold your fingers if you pull up on them.
Textured surfaces	Lay the infant on differently textured surfaces while feeding, playing, resting, and changing her.
Noisemakers (music toys, squeaky toys, etc.)	Slowly move the toys back and forth in front of the baby.

Smile and talk as you hold the baby. Always respond to her signals.

Responsive Guidance for Newborns

Age/Stage: Newborns

Situation	Response
• William cries when adults are making faces at him. • Alexandra doesn't seeem to sustain eye contact with others for long periods of time. • Marilla always falls asleep when visitors come to see her.	**Developmental Issue: Overstimulation** Infants are not capable of physically removing themselves from situations that they are not interested in, not comfortable with, or prefer not to be part of. As signs of overstimulation, infants may cry, tune out, sleep, or withdraw as a way of communicating their displeasure with the situation. Stop the experience until the infant appears to be ready for further stimulation.
• "David is so little. Won't I break him if I'm not careful?" • "Darian is only a couple of weeks old. Can he do anything yet?"	**Developmental Issue: Vulnerability** Newborns are completely dependent upon their caregivers to meet their physical and emotional needs, and though they are vulnerable, they are also very resilient. Normal handling should not harm the infant, provided his head is properly supported. Natural, everyday interactions in a nurturing and safe environment should be sufficient stimulation to inspire their complex genetic potentials. Warm, responsive relationships are important for normal development.

Manufactured Toys and Play Materials for Newborn Infants

Toy/Material	Uses	Group Care	Home
Mobiles	– Place within arm's length (8 to 14 inches) and slightly to the right or left	√	√
Small stuffed animals	– Stroke the baby's arms, legs, and cheeks with the furry material (beware of pop-off eyes, tags, and small pieces on the toy; also, be careful not to leave the infant unattended with the toy) – Squeaks, rattles, or music will entice the infant	√	√

Toy/Material	Uses	Group Care	Home
Tactile easy-to-grab rattles	– Provide multiple grasping areas of different textures that are washable	√	√
Discovery mirrors	– Unbreakable, child-sized and child-shaped mirrors that have soft edges; allow the infant to see herself	√	√
Stroller gyms	– Attach manipulatives (rattles, mirrors, music makers) above the infant's position in the stroller/pram	√	√
Bouncy chairs	– Many come with vibrating motors to simulate car rides, etc., which may soothe the infant	√	√

▶ Summary

Newborns have greater capabilities than we thought even a decade ago. Their sensory activity allows them to take in lots of information from their early experiences of life. Even more significant, infants are born with a wide range of reflexive movements that are innate and somehow allow them to acquire skills later in life. The pre-wiring for learning is present at birth.

Each birthing experience is different. A positive birthing seems to result in fewer emotional difficulties. Early physical contact is essential and helps to cement the bond with the caring adult. The transition to motherhood can present some challenges, and some mothers may need extra support, both physically and psychologically.

The demands of parenting can be considerable. Newborn babies are totally dependent on adults for every aspect of their care. Although newborns may sleep for longer than older babies, they take time to establish a pattern. They thrive on consistent handling and prompt responses to their needs. A feeding routine may not be established for some time.

Infants are unique. They are born into families with differing styles, values, and practices. There are many ways to be an effective parent, and all of them must be respected.

▶ KEY TERMS

abuse
Apgar Scale
atypical birth presentations
binocular vision
bonding
chromosomal disorders
colic
colostrum
congenital conditions
cues
developmental alerts
disengagement
engagement
facilitating development
fontanels
habituation
HIV (human immunodeficiency virus)
holistic response
infant's cues
lanugo
meconium
metabolic disorders
milia

multi-modality (senses)
neglect
neonatal
neonate
overstimulation
perinatal
placental insufficiency
reflexes
responsivity
routine
sensory stimulation
shaken baby syndrome
supportive guidance
teratogen
universal precautions
urticaria
vernix
vulnerability

▶ DISCUSSION QUESTIONS

1. To what extent do you think birthing experiences affect the child's later development?
2. Explain why you think that neonates are competent or incompetent.
3. How urgent is attachment? Do neonates need immediate bonding with an adult?
4. If you were caring for toddlers, what information about their neonatal period might be helpful to your understanding of their development?
5. What difference to the baby is there if the father rather than the mother is the primary caregiver?

▶ ADDITIONAL RESOURCES

▶ Further Reading

Klaus, M.H., and P.H. Klaus. (1999). *Your Amazing Newborn.* Cambridge, MA: Perseus Books.

——. (1994). *The New Baby and Child Care: A Quick Reference Encyclopaedia.* Toronto, ON: Family Communications.

Klaus, M., N. Fox, and M. Keefe. (1998). *Amazing Talents of the Newborn: Emerging Perspectives in Perinatal Care– Reference Guide & Video.* St. Louis, MO: Johnson & Johnson Pediatric Institute.

Henderson, K. (1999). *Newborn.* New York, NY: Dial Books.

Lindsay, J. (2003). *Nurturing Your Newborn: Young Parents' Guide to Baby's First Month.* Buena Park, CA: Morning Glory Press.

Mehren, E. (1998). *Born Too Soon.* New York, NY: Kensington Pub. Corp.

Simkin, P., J. Whalley, and A. Keppler. (2001). *Pregnancy, Childbirth and the Newborn: The Complete Guide.* Deephaven, MN: Meadowbrook/Simon and Schuster.

Zero to Three–Bulletins. National Center for Infants, Toddlers and Families, Washington, DC.

Verny, T.R., and P. Weintraub. (2002). *Tomorrow's Baby: The Art and Science of Parenting from Conception through Infancy.* New York, NY: Simon & Schuster.

WestEd Center for Child and Family Studies. (1998). *Talking Points for Essential Connections.* Sacramento, CA: California Department of Education.

▶ Useful Web sites

Resources for Educarers
www.rie.org/educarer.htm
Neonatology on the Web
www.neonatology.org/classics/default.html
Infant massage
www.cfc-efc.ca/docs/mcca/00000359.htm
Infant massage—Holistic bodyworks
www.holisticbodyworks.com/InfantMassage.htm
Neonatal health screening (BC)
www.healthservices.gov.bc.ca/hlthfile/hfile67.pdf
Congenital conditions
www-hsl.mcmaster.ca/tomflem/birthdefects.html
Example of physical examination (medical)
www.mc.vanderbilt.edu/peds/core/physexam.html
Ask Dr. Sears—Apgar score
askdrsears.com/html/10/T110227.asp
B.C. Reproductive Care Program—Newborn Checklist
www.rcp.gov.bc.ca/Guidelines/Perinatal%20Forms/forms14.pdf
Brazelton's Neonatal Assessment—Outline
www.arts.uwaterloo.ca/~ma3rober/311lecture01_15.pdf
Babycenter—baby and all
www.babycenter.com/newborn
National Network for Childcare—ages/stages
www.nncc.org/Child.Dev/ages.stages.new.one.html
Sure baby information
www.surebaby.com/
Breast-feeding
www.waba.org.br/

CHAPTER 5

Taking Notice: Infants from 6 Weeks to 3 Months

Some babies sleep much more than others. Their personal rhythms can differ, too. Many babies will soon sleep through the night, but for some parents broken nights continue for months or even years.

Learning Outcomes

After reading and studying this chapter, you should be able to:

- identify the observable characteristics of development of infants at the 6-week-to-3-month stage
- explain the significance of behaviours of infants from 6 weeks to 3 months of age in a developmental context
- recognize and respond to the developmental diversity of 6-week-old-to-3-month-old infants
- assess the development of infants in the 6-week-to-3-month stage
- respond to the health, safety, and development of 6-week-old-to-3-month-old infants with appropriate nurturance, activities, protection, and caregiving
- develop strategies to work with parents as partners in the care and education of their young infants

Scene: Early childhood education students are having a break for coffee and are enjoying a chat.

"I thought she would miss her mom," said an early childhood education student, "but my 8-week-old niece was quite happy with me looking after her when my aunt went out shopping." Like this student, you may have noticed that as long as the immediate needs of babies this age are met, they don't seem to mind who is meeting them.

This period, after the sometimes difficult adjustments to a newborn baby, can be rewarding. Said one young mother, "I remember that my son was much more like a real person by the time he was 6 or 7 weeks old. But by then I was feeling a whole lot better after a difficult delivery."

The early days and weeks are a challenging time for many parents and their babies. By about 6 to 8 weeks, there has usually been a settling period, and they may have managed to establish a pattern of sleep, feeding, and activity that suits all family members. "Baby blues," which are sometimes experienced by the mother because of hormonal changes, are likely to have passed, and the physical challenges of birthing are usually behind the mother as well.

You will probably have noticed that babies at this stage have become a little more plumped out, and their head may have a more rounded shape. Their skin will probably be less flaky and will have acclimatized to the new environment.

Protecting very young babies from germs is important, but after a few weeks mothers will typically want to get out and about. Babies will be introduced to friends, extended family, and anyone else who wants to take a look. They generally will respond fairly well to seeing all these new faces, actively scanning their faces. And they don't mind being fed by someone unusual, but they prefer to be comforted by their mother and the people they know best.

▶ What to Look For

"Our youngest babies are about 6 weeks old," explained the centre's supervisor to a new group of students starting their placement in the infant room. "We love it when we have such tiny babies, but it's hard for the moms to leave them." You might be able to imagine what it is like to leave a baby with a caregiver when you are only just getting to know each other. **Separation** is two-sided: the baby separates from the mother, but the mother also has to separate from her baby. While we usually focus on one side of the challenge, we need to remember the reciprocal nature of separation. At this stage, it may be harder for the mother, because infants are more concerned with having their needs met than with who supplies them. The mother's emotional welfare is a significant issue for caregivers, because it directly affects the infant's security and building of trust. If separations are overly emotional, the climate will be tense and difficult for the baby. Watch for the way the separation occurs and try to support both mother and infant.

SOCIAL RELATIONSHIPS

Because infants at this stage are beginning to make associations between things that are pleasurable and the presence of their mother, they are likely to be more comfortable with their mother. Yet this does not mean that they cannot make a transition to multiple caregivers. If the infant's world expands to include other adults, these people must live up to the standard of reliability that exists between mother and baby.

TEMPERAMENT STYLE

Some babies are slow to warm up to new people. You will see that their **temperament** shapes the patterns of interaction they have with adults (Chess and Thomas, 1996). Others are more accepting of changing surroundings and faces; these babies may appear to be easier to care for. The slow-to-warm-up infant may need a slower transition and more comforting. Watch for the kinds of reactions that babies have to new people. Although 6 weeks to 3 months may seem to be a very young age to have a baby cared for by a stranger, some parents report that the change to multiple caregivers is easier at this age than later, when the baby is attached more specifically to one adult.

SELF-REGULATION

At this age, the ability of the baby to control herself in small ways is a major milestone. This process is called **self-regulation** (Greenspan and Greenspan, 1985). During this period, the baby begins to be able to calm herself down, responds to stimuli with recognizable patterns, and tends to feed and sleep with a more discernible cycle. Her interest in the world remains completely **egocentric**—from her own perspective—and she sees everything through her own senses, with only a little knowledge that she is a separate human being, never mind the agent of significant emotional turmoil. So it is important to remember that when a baby appears to be driving an adult to despair, she is not doing it deliberately.

GROWTH PATTERNS

At this stage, infants grow approximately 2.5 cm (1 inch) a month (Allen and Marotz, 2003). The weight gain is more obvious than the relatively small increase in length. Weight will depend upon birth weight, maturity, nurturance, general health, activity level, and nutrition. Most babies will have a more plump appearance than they had in their first weeks. You may see some skin folds on their chubby arms and legs.

Not all babies are like this, though; others will be longer, thinner, and yet perfectly healthy. Steady weight gain and growth are more important than the baby's actual weight.

SLEEP AND WAKEFULNESS

There are many variations in infants' patterns of sleep and wakefulness. Some babies may sleep only four or five hours at a time; others may sleep up to 10 hours. The total amount of sleep per day will vary from infant to infant. Infants may display states of wakefulness that are neither sleep nor alert periods (Quilliam, 1994). They may take many or few naps and be awake for short or prolonged periods.

PHYSICAL DEVELOPMENT

Fine Motor Skills

By about 6 weeks the baby can usually bring her hands to the middle of her body as she lies on her back (Furuno et al., 1993b). She may look at her hands and appear to examine them carefully. She has some limited voluntary control of her hands, which she uses to grasp things, but she cannot deliberately let go. Initially, she is more likely to swipe at an object with her arm. This fine motor skill will not be very precise, but in time and with practice the swinging becomes more controlled.

Gross Motor Skills

When a young infant is placed in a sitting position she may slide down the seat because her back is still rounded. She has not gained the back control necessary for real sitting and will need to be propped up.

She will usually hold her head up without a head lag, but she may not do this for prolonged periods or if she is tired. It takes a lot of physical effort and concentration to achieve the gross and fine motor skills that adults take for granted.

An infant may pull herself up on her arms for short periods if she is lying on her stomach, but she soon collapses and lays her head down again. These little press-ups show the increase in strength in her arms. So far, similar strength and control has not spread to her legs, although she may like to stretch them and kick. A random kick may become more controlled in time. At this stage, the baby may learn to kick her legs and feet deliberately, but this usually comes later.

Babies' physical skills develop gradually, with marked improvement in head control. According to the **cephalocaudal** sequence, physical skills progress from the head downward. Thus, although infants display increasing head control, they do not yet have the ability to sit without support.

As babies gain new bodily control, they will use their skills to discover the world. It is noticeable that children who have a significant cognitive challenge may also have slower than average physical skill acquisition; they will probably have less motivation than other children to make the discoveries about their environments.

Neurologically, physical and cognitive skills are mutually supportive. The brain stem and midbrain, which are called the subcortex, are the most developed parts of the brain of a very young baby. They regulate basic biological functions such as digestion and breathing. The outer layer of the brain, the cortex, allows for many kinds of thinking processes, but it is underdeveloped at birth. In time, the nerve cells that transmit messages from the cerebral cortex become more effective. They need a sheathing of myelin to do this. This process of **myelination** leads to the infant's being able to behave and think.

Reflexes

Reflexes such as stepping, sucking, and the withdrawal from painful stimulus disappear without warning during this stage (Allen and Marotz, 2003). Some of these reflexes, which were present at birth, may have triggered particular skills. For example, babies now do not need to root for food—they know where to find it. Also, their sucking is voluntary rather than reflexive, because they can choose when to suck. Researchers are divided about the purpose of the reflexes, but they are likely the outward sign of neurological pathways in the brain that allow for later developments (Kotulak, 1996).

Some of the baby's actions develop from his reflexes, even when the reflexes have disappeared. Perhaps it is because the neural pathways have been formed that the baby extends reflexive actions from automatic to controlled behaviours. Early deliberate behaviours tend to be repetitive; this too reinforces new neurological connections.

THE SENSES AND PERCEPTION

The sensory information received by the brain needs to be processed. Because this processing takes place internally, it cannot be observed. Nevertheless, we need to understand infants' cognitive processing if we want to be able to interpret subsequent behaviour. Dr. Harry Chugani, a pediatric neurobiologist, has studied this activity by using **positron-emission tomography (PET)**. His exciting discoveries indicate that early experiences, not only pre-wiring, influence how the brain develops. If that is the case, then we have a challenging task to ensure that those experiences are appropriate.

Sight

Visual information can be absorbed only according to the **maturational readiness** of the infant. For example, a baby who cannot yet focus on a mobile will be unable to take in information from it, but the same baby may be able to focus on an adult's face and therefore absorb that information. From the eyes, chemical and electrical messages pass the information to the brain. The process works so fast that the baby can take in many thousands of sensory messages every minute. Visual stimulation can cause different kinds of responses—a reflexive response, such as a blink, driven by the subcortex or a more complicated process of the cortex. This more complicated process may allow the baby to organize information. For example, he might recognize what he sees and compare the visual information with previously understood information. He might even cluster together some thoughts about what he sees; these we call **visual schemes**—early understandings gained through images.

What *we* will see is the infant's fixation on the visual stimulus and his reaction to it. If we become familiar with the baby, we may notice patterns of response and indicators of his familiarity with a particular form of stimulation. We may also notice when the baby looks away from the stimulus, or when he re-engages with it. These may be examples of **habituation**—that is, of the baby's becoming used to a stimulus—and may indicate the need for new stimuli. After lengthy observations of the infant, it will become increasingly clear to us that he is taking in a lot from his environment.

It helps that a baby can use both eyes together to take in visual information. At this age, the eyes will usually be working together, or converging, so that the infant can begin to understand the idea of depth from his **binocular vision**—both eyes working in coordination. The brain has to process the information sent to it. If, at first, the baby has little experience of depth, it is likely that the information is not processed according to that concept. Maturational and experiential influences need to work together; in time, the baby's perception of depth increases. Generally, **visual acuity**—the ability to see—is improving throughout this stage. By about 3 months, the infant will be able to see farther away, perhaps to a mobile hanging from the ceiling or to an adult across the room.

Taste, Smell, and Hearing

The infant is likely to have a preference for sweet tastes, and might refuse water, being more satisfied by breast milk or formula. Not yet ready for solid foods, the baby will probably consume more milk, but at fewer feedings. The infant can discriminate between familiar and unfamiliar smells. New smells are not necessarily disturbing to her, but familiarity tends to be more comforting. During this stage, an infant's hearing will be better than that of a newborn, but not as acute as an adult's. Infants tend to respond to sounds in the higher frequencies.

Touch

As infants mature, they may have increasing sensitivity to touch. Individual responses vary with temperament and sensory sensitivity. You may observe that some infants respond erratically to the same stimulus, others respond in predictable patterns, and still others show little response to their experience of being touched. A baby who is 6 or 8 weeks old may arch his back to show you he dislikes being touched. It may be possible to find ways of communicating and stimulating without emphasis on touch, if that is what is needed.

Some babies are much more cuddly than others. For some mothers, having a baby who does not want

Learning through the senses is the hands-on discovery approach used by all babies and toddlers.

related to their experience. These are the exciting beginnings of learning.

Recent research has offered new understanding about the function of the infant's brain and the child's potential. It is thought that the brain is greedy for information at a very young age, and if optimal conditions are presented to infants, they will achieve much more than if they are understimulated. Some people assume that we should provide intensive experience in subjects of learning for infants during their sensitive periods of neurological activity. David Elkind (2001b) strongly opposes this view, saying it may present a distorted analysis of brain research. He thinks that infants need to be supported in their development and nurtured in accordance with their individual needs rather than being exposed to a subject-based "curriculum." This negativity toward structured curriculum is echoed in Magda Gerber's (1998b) philosophy of responsive caregiving. She argues that infant development is not a race, and that nothing of worth is achieved in the long term if babies are not allowed to be babies.

to be touched or cuddled causes profound disappointment. Adults must observe the baby's responsiveness to each type of stimulation so they can fine-tune their strategies for caregiving. It is important to acknowledge perceived differences in responses and to develop ways of working with all infants rather than ignoring those who have a negative response.

COGNITIVE DEVELOPMENT

When something occurs that the baby likes, such as stroking the texture of her new soft blanket, she repeats the action that caused the sensation. Piaget called this a **primary circular reaction** (Piaget, 1952). To understand this stage in the context of Piaget's series of developmental stages, review the chart on developmental stages found in the Appendix.

Through these repetitive actions, infants build up an inner understanding of their world. They don't have the language to describe it, so they think in terms of physical things. Piaget described this pattern of activity as the second of a series of substages of **sensory-motor development**, the stage of learning through action. Babies at this stage make more use of their senses and are beginning to organize information using the neurological processes available to them. This means that repeated actions are allowing infants to build up **mental schemes**—clusters of ideas—

SELF-CONCEPT

The way a baby perceives and reacts to any situation or person is shaped by her emotional well-being and temperament style. Without adults who are actively engaged with the baby, there will be no opportunity for her to establish a oneness or **separateness** (Kaplan, 1978). In other words, the baby will not develop the notion that she is a separate and complete human being. These ideas are related to the concepts of "self" and "others," and mark the beginning of the emergence of the personhood of the baby.

To know that you are a separate person, you need to be involved in some kind of relationship. Your self-image develops from seeing parts of yourself reflected back in other people. If the reflection of the self is positive, you will conceptualize that part of yourself as positive. This interactive dance allows the baby to shape her world as her world shapes her (Weissbourd and Musick, 1981). It seems a stretch to think of this as a first step of personal empowerment, but that is what it is.

SOCIAL RELATIONSHIPS

Because the baby makes generalized rather than specific attachments at this stage (Ainsworth et al., 1978), caregivers may fail to appreciate the baby's need for predictability and constancy. The baby may appear to be able to deal with changes in caregivers, but that positive response depends on consistency of care, if not of caregiver. This need for predictability probably means that the baby will thrive on the establishment of relationships with a few people he can relate to (Sagi et al., 1994). Some of the implications of this for group child care of young infants are dealt with in Box 5.1.

SIX WEEKS SEEMS YOUNG TO BE IN GROUP CARE: DOES IT DO THE BABY ANY HARM?

A 6-week-old baby does seem young to be in child care. But, realistically, some mothers run out of maternity leave around this time and have to return to work. Also at this stage, the infant is not particularly concerned with who provides his care. High-quality child care can be as good as parental care. For some babies, it may be preferable to being at home. The trouble is, not all infant care is of high quality. Refer to the indicators of high-quality care in Chapter 1 to determine the conditions for acceptable or optimal care.

There is another way of looking at the issue of babies separated from their parents this early. Babies can make **multiple attachments** to the adults in their lives (Bowlby, 1969), and those attachments can be secure (Lamb, Sternberg, and Prodromidis, 1992). As long as the relationships are consistent, it is fine for babies to be cared for by adults other than the parents. Yet a strong caution comes from Burton White, who says that babies will do best when cared for "by someone who is passionately in love with them" (White, 1995, 162). His position against day care for infants and toddlers is rooted in the idea that the young child can make the emotional ties that she needs only in a relationship of "love." White hints that love is found in family connections. Belsky also concluded that "entry into day care in the first year of life is a 'risk factor' for the development of insecure-avoidant attachments in infancy" (Belsky, 1986, 7).

Where do such theories leave us? Clearly, secure multiple attachments *can* be made, but *are* they? There is evidence that the child's emotional needs can be met in high-quality infant and toddler care (Clarke-Stewart, 1989). The crucial issue is that the vulnerabilities of the child at such a young age create responsibilities for educators that they must not neglect. An infant's or toddler's separation from parents must be made in a way that provides security and continuity so that those further attachments can be made.

Educators should not forget the impact of the separation on the parents. It's really hard for parents to leave their babies. When a baby is only 6 weeks old, a caregiver may have greater difficulty dealing with the mother's or father's sense of loss than with the baby's. Parents are likely to need a lot of reassurance that everything is going to be fine.

Regardless of the social or economic reasons for group care of young infants, the caregivers must offer the very best care and education in the most stable way within the most secure and appropriate environment. In addition, they need to share every aspect of it with the infant's parents.

Babies are able to make multiple attachments, but they need the relationships to be emotionally engaging as well as physically responsive. Interestingly, an infant may start to notice other babies at about 2 months of age (Snow, 1989), and may also respond to the social advances of older brothers and sisters at this stage.

When you observe an infant interacting with a variety of caregivers, observe her dance of communication as well as the adults' provision of the baby's basic needs. Look for the transitions from one caregiver to another and how the patterns of communication alter. Although the baby may accept what the various adults offer her, you should be aware of a lack of consistency in the caregivers' responses. In some cases, infants may slow down their social overtures to adults because those adults are unpredictable. You might find that an infant who is apparently adapting well to people and appears to be an easy, undemanding baby, is actually giving up on making relationships.

EMOTIONAL DEVELOPMENT

Emotional damage at a very young age can certainly have lasting effects, even if the infant cannot remember it. Yet not all infants brought up in emotionally deprived circumstances turn out to be emotionally troubled (Werner and Smith, 1992). Nonetheless, a strong correlation exists between the two. However **resilient** some children may seem in the face of emotional deprivation, it remains a serious cause for concern. The deprivation may not be as severe as the "hospitalism" documented by Renee Spitz (1945) or as that seen, more recently, among orphans from countries around the world. But there is significant reason to believe that early emotional deprivation can lead to anything from mildly maladaptive behaviours to extreme violence or even long-term lack of emotional responsiveness.

Happy infants are those who remain active and receptive to people and situations. Although different temperaments lead to a range of responses, babies in trusting relationship with one or more adults are most likely to be secure.

Information about how early experiences can contribute to overall **resilience** is surfacing regularly. Voices for Children (2002) articulates the research in ways that early childhood practitioners can apply. The essence of resilience lies in the solidity and continuity of relationships rather than physical surroundings; but infants do need the healthy environments that are most likely to exist in circumstances where the family lives in relative comfort—certainly without poverty and uncertainty. Emotional development, which shapes emotional well-being for years ahead, is more likely to flourish where there are consistent and strong attachments.

Smiling is a wonderful way for babies to engage adults. First smiles, which occur when a baby is about 6 weeks old, are usually a response to a person—that is, they are connected to a social relationship. Desmond Morris suggests that the very young infant smiles not because she is really happy but because she has learned that smiling gets a positive reaction from adults. Thus, although smiling isn't necessarily a sign of happiness, the social relationship in which it occurs is likely to promote a baby's security, and therefore her happiness.

As the infant grows older, she may initiate a smile as an invitation to the adult to make a social connection, or she may smile to reflect her happiness. This smile may occur without visual stimulation, such as an adult smiling at her. Blind or visually disabled babies smile without having been able to make a visual connection with a person.

The range of emotions that a baby can demonstrate at this stage is not very wide, but he can make his feelings known to the adults around him. Distress, for example, can be seen even in very young babies. Within a few weeks, the range of emotions expands. During this period, babies might show anger and delight. Social situations may cause a baby delight. This is displayed by more than a smile, and often involves whole-body squirming or slight rocking. Anger can be seen when an infant is hungry or uncomfortable, or when his needs are not met immediately. It is quite normal for this emotion to be shown, but adults must respond as quickly as possible. Box 5.2 provides some guidelines for responding to the needs of an infant at this stage.

LANGUAGE AND COMMUNICATION SKILLS

The ability to communicate and use language is pre-wired into the brain, suggested Chomsky (1968). Some recent brain research may have confirmed this, but researchers are divided on the best way to approach the infant's sensitive periods for communication development. All seem to agree, however, that various conditions must be in place before communication skills can develop. Two-way connections are essential. This is the dyad on which all communication is based. The infant needs to be heard and to hear. She also needs to know that she has an effect; for example, her cries must draw an adult response.

In communication, there must be a sender, a receiver, and a message. The baby and the adult can be both sender and receiver. The baby can send the message that he is content, hungry, in need of comfort, and so on. The adult can convey the message that the baby matters and that he is loved and will be responded to.

The infant's attachment to or relationship with one or several adults is essential for the baby to learn to communicate. Communication flourishes in a **reciprocal relationship**. Helping this relationship along is the baby's newfound ability to coo or make happy sounds (Adamson, 1996). The adult enjoys the happy response of the baby, and the flow of communication is enhanced.

There are some other important conditions for communication. The infant must be able to process

BOX 5.2

GETTING IN TUNE WITH INFANTS AT 6 WEEKS TO 3 MONTHS

Below are some starting points for building your responsivity skills with a 6-week-old-to-3-month-old infant. Tune in with respect and:

- ensure that all basic needs are met: diapering, contact, feeding, protection, warmth, etc.
- identify the infant's sensory acuity: visually and through hearing, taste, smell, and responses to touch
- establish the infant's preferences, response patterns, and style, and make all responses in accordance with this style
- observe the infant's patterns of wakefulness and sleep and try to anticipate the need for both quiet and stimulation
- take every opportunity to talk to the baby, and use a high-pitched repetitive way of talking
- sing or talk as you perform many of the domestic tasks in relation to the infant
- respond to gaze and initiate further eye contact
- notice the baby's uptime and provide appropriate stimulation
- observe the baby's trance states and whether they lead to sleep or action
- allow the baby to sleep when she wants to
- feed the baby on demand and as she lies in your arms
- be patient when the baby is slow to feed or has responses that are more irritable than usual
- provide a few visual images for the baby within her field of vision
- if the baby responds positively to being touched, stroke her body
- when the baby has tired of activity, help her refocus her attention
- provide a few objects for handling
- dangle objects that may provide interest for swiping at with her fists
- determine the baby's interest in and response to various smells
- use infant massage techniques in a warm room
- make bath time a warm, pleasant experience with lots of caressing and talking
- dim the lights and notice the responses
- identify different responses to black and white, primary colours, and pastels
- talk through your actions as you change diapers
- play various types of music during the day and determine the responses
- play outside if the weather is favourable, but protect the baby from the cold and the sun
- prop the baby up with cushions or foam wedges to allow her to handle material more easily
- prop the baby up to see adults' domestic activity
- provide the baby with the mother's possessions, which may be comfortingly familiar
- build trust by ensuring continuity of care and attention
- respond to crying promptly and try to read the type of crying
- identify the baby's attempts at seeking someone to communicate with
- notice the baby's body language as cues for your responses
- provide a range of soft, hard, and textured objects for handling
- encourage the baby to look at her own face in a mirror
- ensure that the environment is interesting at the baby's eye level when she is lying down or propped up
- allow for downtime and tuning out from things and people
- protect the infant from any danger and provide a hygienic environment
- place the infant on her back to sleep
- if little you do gets a positive response, seek another adult's support

auditory and visual stimulation to make meaning of it. In addition, he must have the ability to recognize people, to make links between actions and thoughts, and to memorize and recall pieces of information. For language, he must have the capacity to make sounds, imitate vocalizations, and control sound production.

All this may sound rather clinical, but communication is an extremely complicated process involving physical, cognitive, social, and emotional development. Each of these must be synchronized for communication to happen. It is really interesting to appreciate these complexities as you watch the dance of communication between the infant and the adult. Look to see who initiates a communication. Who follows? Does this pattern recur or does the leadership change? Are facial expressions imitated? Are they started by the adult or the infant? How does the adult continue the experience and how does it end? You are observing the essence of the infant's search for meaning.

As you can see highlighted in Box 5.3, communication becomes even more complicated when a second language is involved—a challenge for parents and practitioners, anyway. On the positive side, it may seem surprising that the infant's exposure to more than one language does not lead to complete confusion. The baby is not pre-wired for any particular language and her early communications are not dependent upon spoken language. When she is exposed to a second language there are also distinct intellectual advantages—even if the two (or more) languages get a bit muddled in the short term. At this stage, the baby is still pre-verbal, but being exposed to the sounds of two or more languages may enable her to begin to babble using both sound types—because that's what she hears. Communicating this to parents can be challenging, particularly when their first language is other than English—but it is worthwhile for all parties. Enhanced communication between parents and practitioners, as well as directly with the baby, can make the baby's experience become more meaningful.

▶ Particular Needs

Babies who are 6 weeks to 3 months old must have their needs understood and their cries responded to quickly. The baby is aware of the people around her, is beginning to know that she is a separate person, has some understanding of how to attract adults' attention, is becoming a social person, responds to stimuli, is learning from experience, and has the beginnings of some bodily control that will ultimately lead her to independence. What she needs is to have her stage of development understood as being extremely important, not just a chrysalis stage before the "real" person emerges.

The infant's potential is quite incredible, so the adult must appreciate the infant's ability to take in information and try to make sense of it. Stimulation is important, in ways that the baby can understand. Contrasting stimulation with calm helps the baby to regulate herself. The quality of relationships and their

---

BOX 5.3

BUILDING CROSS-CULTURAL COMMUNICATION SKILLS: ROLE-MODELLING AND DEMONSTRATION

Spoken language can be an enormous barrier if the language spoken in the agency is not understood by the parent. One strategy that can assist communication is practical demonstration and role-modelling. Parents may be familiar with this process for all kinds of learning in a language environment that leaves them feeling left out. Being there can often lead to a good understanding of what happens in the centre. Parents can be given as much opportunity as they wish to observe what happens within the centre, how children are guided, and what activity goes on in the centre. Although the subtleties of conversation would be missing, the tone of voice that is used by the staff, the gentle respect for the young children, and the dynamic learning environment would be demonstrated. If signs are posted in the languages spoken by the parents, these can complement and explain what the parent observes.

consistency are the core requirements for helping her form attachments to adults. Although the baby is more comfortable with familiar adults, her greatest need is for continuity of care and to trust that the available adults will meet her needs.

▶ Developmental Variation

Development may vary according to the infant's gestational age at birth, the birth process, and her health in the neonatal period. Some developmental issues become apparent at 6 weeks, when most infants have established some patterns of sleep, feeding, and activity.

Progression is as important as the **developmental milestones**, which are the significant stages of development. For example, if a baby was floppy in the neonatal period, it is more important that her muscle tone improves than that she acquire particular skills. Infants who are less responsive than average at birth may show development by being more responsive to different kinds of stimulation within a few weeks. A few babies who have experienced particularly difficult births may be more settled now. So the flow of progress must be the focus for the observer of infants at this stage.

You may see some babies who hold up their heads and have more back control than others. These advances do not necessarily indicate a lifelong advantage in gross motor skills. And the baby who begins to swipe at objects and grasp them is no more likely to become a boxer than a baby with later-developing grasping skills!

Caregivers should take notice of individual patterns. These include health indicators and developmental stages. By observing the infant and noticing her particular patterns, the parent and educator can support the infant's needs more effectively and precisely.

▶ Developmental Alerts

PEDIATRIC EXAMINATION

Although **screening** and **assessment** schedules will differ according to the locality, a comprehensive pediatric appraisal of the infant's development usually takes place at about 6 weeks. Pediatricians, particularly those who were involved in the infant's neonatal period or who are informed about significant developmental issues, are able to support parents and infants in a variety of ways. They can provide screenings to exclude the possibility of a variety of health and developmental conditions. They can perform a detailed assessment to establish the child's health status. Other services include providing immunizations, weight checks, and nutrition advice, and assisting the family to meet the needs of the baby.

Most infants show some significant signs or symptoms, or present particular challenges for their parents. The pediatrician can offer advice or refer the parents to other resources. Availability of resources depends on the location. Some parents may be able to access special interventions, nurse practitioners, toy libraries, drop-in centres, child welfare services, parenting classes, and other services that may not exist in some rural, remote, or less advantaged areas. Although all babies with special needs should have access to special services, in reality accessibility varies. Most parents will never require such services, but pediatricians and educators can be successful advocates for those who do.

PARENTAL RESPONSE TO MEDICAL/DEVELOPMENTAL DIAGNOSES

A few infants face special challenges. In such cases, early identification of developmental or health concerns can lead to better understanding, improved caregiving, and, if necessary, an intervention program.

Parents face an enormous hurdle in accepting that their baby is not developing as they had hoped. Frequently parental hopes remain high despite medical opinions that indicate a real or potential developmental challenge for their baby. Parental resistance to such information can be very real and is entirely understandable. Yet most parents want to be as well informed as possible, even if what they hear seems negative. However, a parent who feels stressed, vulnerable, and emotionally tired may have difficulty understanding medical terms and complex discussions about the baby's future. For this reason, parents may want to have someone with them at specialists' appointments.

Coordinating information from several different sources can feel like a full-time job for parents. A little assistance and a team approach can lighten the burden, improve communication, and lead to smoother continuity of care for the child. If the infant is already in a group child-care setting, it is highly desirable that the child's educator be a part of the multidisciplinary team. The educator might have to attend some meetings, offer observational comments, be involved in some problem-solving activities to provide the best care, and facilitate communications with the parents. Parents and educators working together can ensure continuity of care, and each can learn from the other and share their successes.

NEUROLOGICAL PROBLEMS

A difficult birth increases the chance of the infant suffering some degree of neurological damage. Pressure on the head is the obvious cause. After a birthing trauma a doctor may pay particularly close attention to a baby's reactions to stimuli and her general progress. It is not always possible to determine the cause of a brain injury or other neurological problem. Neonates who showed little sign of a problem may demonstrate developmental differences by the time they are 6 weeks old or so.

Typically, brain-injured infants are irritable, hard to settle, and difficult to feed. They may frustrate their caregivers because they don't seem to respond well to the usual calming techniques. Their sleep is fitful and interrupted. These same signs can be seen in babies who are abused, so care should be taken to avoid making any assumptions about why a baby is extremely irritable.

HYDROCEPHALUS AND SPINA BIFIDA

Although these are two separate conditions, they coexist in some children. Hydrocephalus is a condition in which fluid builds up in the brain. This condition may correct itself, but it is more likely to need treatment with a shunt or tube that drains the fluid. This treatment generally prevents cognitive impairments.

Spina bifida varies greatly in severity. It can be anything from a clump of hair covering a cleft at the base of the spine to a condition where part of the spinal cord protrudes from the spine in a sac. Surgery may be essential within a day or two of birth, and in many cases this will prevent later problems. Care of the infant with spina bifida may involve ensuring that the site of the surgery is protected. A few infants with the condition may experience paralysis of the legs. Medical experts can advise parents and educators on how to manage the individual child's specific needs.

▶ Health Concerns

SLEEP AND WAKEFULNESS

Patterns of sleep among infants from 6 weeks to 3 months vary considerably. Some babies at this stage are awake and alert for longer than when they were neonates. Parents may report that their infants are sleeping through the night and have been for some weeks. Other parents who look tired may be dealing with interruptions in their sleep because the baby wakens and wants feeding or other attention.

FEEDING AND WEIGHT GAIN

Similarly, inconsistent feeding habits are common. These may relate to how frequently the baby feeds and how much she eats, which may, in turn, be connected with weight gain. Breast-fed babies may be test-weighed before and after a feeding to determine what they have consumed, but in practice determining the amount of breast milk they have had is difficult. This may be a good thing: it is normal for a baby's appetite to fluctuate and too much attention should not be paid to it. Bottle-fed babies' consumption of formula is easier to monitor, so small and large feedings are easy to detect. More important is the amount of weight the baby is gaining. The typical weight gain is fairly steady, except when she is not feeding well or has an ongoing condition that makes feeding more difficult.

SKIN CARE

By this stage, most of the lumps, bumps, and marks on the newborn's skin have disappeared, and the baby has clear skin. The baby's skin is delicate and needs careful attention, particularly in the diaper area. Adults need to ensure that the baby is not exposed to direct sun; at this stage, the baby is too young to have sunscreens applied. Regardless of their skin tones, babies have skin that easily burns.

BODY TEMPERATURE

Although the baby's ability to regulate his body temperature is improving, he does not have the ability to sweat or to increase his activity to keep warm. Room temperature should be maintained. Checking the baby's hands to see if he is cold is a poor way of assessing temperature. If it is necessary, checking the baby's neck and back would be more accurate. If the baby is low on the ground in a seat or lying on the floor, the surrounding temperature might be lower than you think. Also note that a comfortable room temperature for an active adult might be cooler than what is needed for a young infant. On the other hand, avoid having the room too warm or having too many clothes or blankets on the baby.

EXPOSURE TO PEOPLE

There are differing views about when to introduce the baby to new people. The timing may be dictated by circumstances; if the parent has to return to work, exposure to a much wider range of people happens earlier. Personal preference may also be an issue. Some parents prefer to keep their babies at home for the first few months, while others take their infants to the park, the mall, drop-in centres, parties, and other gatherings. The baby's immunity to the germs of all those people may be sufficient to protect her, but the wider the range of germs, the more likely the baby is to catch something. Yet babies cannot constantly be kept in a germ-free, sterilized environment. Moreover, babies need to have social contact and to make relationships, so exposure to people is essential. Hand-washing, good personal hygiene, and reduced contact with people with colds, flu, and stomach upsets are commonsense precautions.

INFANT SEATS, CAR SEATS, AND STROLLERS

In both home care and group care, caregivers need to be able to move infants from place to place. Sometimes inappropriate equipment, like strollers and inadequate baby seats, are used. At this stage, the infant's back control is likely to be poor. The baby, if put in a seated position, can slump forward with a rounded back, flop sideways, or slide down in an improper seat. The infant needs to have adequate back support and protection. Most babies at this stage need a baby carriage that allows them to lie on their back or be safely propped up. Avoid premature use of strollers that have little support for the back. Similarly, the infant is probably not yet ready for a high or low infant chair unless she is wedged in with foam or pillows. If pillows are used to support a baby in an infant chair, the baby should be closely supervised, as the pillows can present suffocation hazards.

A lie-back baby seat can be a good idea, enabling the baby to have a better look around. But the base of such seats can slide across a surface as the baby's motion causes the seat to move. Thus, babies in lie-back seats should never be left unsupervised, especially if the seat is resting on a table or other piece of furniture.

Extended indoor use of car seats can be inappropriate, even when the baby appears to be comfortable. This is because the baby shouldn't be left in a rounded-back position for unduly long periods. When travelling, the baby must be in a car seat that is approved for his weight and that has been securely anchored in accordance with the manufacturer's instructions.

Car travel puts a baby in danger, and every effort should be made to select, install, and use safety restraints. Take notice of the following considerations when planning to travel with a baby of this age:

- The selection of appropriate restraints should be based on the weight and height of the baby.
- If using secondhand equipment, make sure that it meets current safety standards.
- The back of the car is the safest place for all passengers.
- Although rear-facing car seats are best for younger babies, they should not be placed in front of an air bag on the front seat.
- Follow manufacturers' instructions for fitting baby restraints.
- The baby should not be held in a passenger's arms at any time.
- Straps should be fastened around the baby with room for her movement (put your fingers under the straps to test).
- Blankets (if necessary) should be placed over the baby after securing in the seat—over the straps.
- Accidents are caused by drivers attending to baby's needs while in motion or at stop signs.

SUDDEN INFANT DEATH SYNDROME

Unfortunately, this age range is the peak time for **sudden infant death syndrome (SIDS)**. Caregivers must remember that, although rare, SIDS does happen. In these instances, the parent or caregiver puts the infant down to sleep and returns to find that the baby has stopped breathing. This is a parent's worst nightmare. A thorough investigation of the circumstances must follow, and an autopsy will be performed. If a diagnosis of SIDS is made, it is not a clear explanation for the death. Rather, SIDS remains an unexplained phenomenon. Until researchers provide us with further understanding of SIDS, there is little we can do to guard against it. We do know that breast-fed babies are less likely to die of SIDS. But the best thing a caregiver can do is to lie babies on their backs or sides; these positions are less likely to create conditions in which SIDS occurs.

Alarms that alert adults if the baby's breathing stops can be used, but opinion is divided about their usefulness, their reliability, the frequency of false alarms, and the fact that they cannot prevent the problem. Various causes of SIDS have been theorized, but as yet we have very little indication of the reason why some babies die.

▶ Signs of Potential Neglect or Abuse

SIDS is sometimes mistaken for child abuse. It is very difficult to accept the death of a young infant, and so much harder if the parent is wrongfully accused of abuse. Yet because death does occasionally result from parental abuse or caregiver abuse, we must be vigilant in looking for signs of abuse.

If an educator notices any signs of abuse or neglect, the educator must document any significant behaviours, bodily marks, or other information. Documentation can be used to assist a child protection agency and, in some cases, the police. It is not the role of the educator to "prove" that the indicators point to abuse or neglect.

ADULT FRUSTRATIONS

Here we will consider why babies are sometimes the victims of adult frustrations, rather than look at the baby for signs that frustration has been taken out on her. Some adults manage their emotions better than others—this may be as a result of their own personality, the role models that they have internalized, and the frustrations that they experience. Similar sets of circumstances can lead adults to behave in opposite ways. It is likely that persons' perceptions of their life circumstances are more significant than their actual standard of living, opportunities, and relationships. That said, a person undergoing particularly difficult life transitions, such as divorce, loss of employment, change of location, breakup of relationships, and so

on, is going to experience some significant stressors—how that person might respond cannot be easily predicted. Stressors are prevalent among different socioeconomic groups and responses to those stressors may vary—people from all kinds of backgrounds express their frustrations in inappropriate ways. Lack of control of their behaviour may become an issue and is particularly damaging when directed toward a vulnerable baby.

Frustration can lead to an unhealthy emotional climate in the home—or child-care centre. In both settings, adults can experience frustration. The professional setting may mean that the staff are better prepared, but they too may have challenges in their personal and/or professional lives. Fortunately the group context of child care offers some protection to the children—staff monitor one another's behaviour. But this isn't always a certainty. Staff may try to find excuses for what they see as another staff member's temporary difficulties. Friendships among staff members may also protect the staff member rather than the vulnerable infant.

In both the home and child-care centre—as well as any other situation where the child may be—there is the possibility that an adult may vent his or her anger on the child. Younger babies are particularly at risk from frustrated, uncontrolled adults. Their dependence, demands, and inability to be anything other than a victim, may increase their chance of being targeted. An emotionally charged atmosphere negates the possibility for responsive caregiving—other adults are affected by the climate and this alters their ability to respond effectively to the infants, never mind the creator of the atmosphere. Thus, the environment becomes emotionally polluted. This may cause the baby to cry more, become less easy to settle, and increase the tensions that already exist.

Handling a baby when one is frustrated easily transmits feelings to the baby. Because physical touch is the primary path of communication, the baby may well respond to negativity before the adults even know that is what they are feeling. Frustration may show itself to the baby emotionally, physically, or both ways. Poor handling of the baby, rough management of her needs, or neglect can result from such frustration. Any sign of potential neglect or abuse must be reported to the appropriate authorities without judgment.

Professionals may be able to assist those adults who become frustrated in some way—after all, we all experience those emotions from time to time. Ideally families and professionals can work together to learn to recognize stress buildup and develop strategies for dealing with it in a positive manner, by finding some respite from caregiving and by providing positive role models. All adults need time for themselves, to collect their thoughts and to see to their own needs. Sometimes supplying this time will allow the adult to return to the baby in a more positive frame of mind.

Infant burnout—when adults have given so much of themselves that they need to recharge their own batteries—can happen to both parents and professional practitioners. All of us involved in the lives of very young children need to monitor our own, and each other's, emotional well-being, and support each other in what is very demanding work.

MATERNAL DEPRESSION

A small percentage of mothers, rather more than might be willing to admit it, suffer from postnatal depression. This is a pathological condition that has much greater impact than the **baby blues** experienced by most women two or three days after birth.

Postnatal depression could last for only a few weeks, but it is more likely to last for months and may go on longer than that. The mother is unduly challenged to cope with her baby, other family members, domestic responsibilities, the relationship with her partner, and possibly a work situation. She is overwhelmed by feelings of negativity, poor self-worth, and apathy. She likely has sleep problems and appetite difficulties and is unable to manage daily tasks. At times, she feels low or even suicidal. Isolation, changing family dynamics and altered roles, a diminution in sexual interest, and lack of sleep may increase the depression.

Maternal depression affects the quality and quantity of care the mother is able to offer her infant. She may not realize that her feelings are extreme, and may need supportive adults to help her address the problem and seek help. Support groups, psychotherapy, prescription drug therapy, and a variety of other treatments are available and can be effective, given time. The problem for the infant is that he can't wait. His needs are immediate. He needs to be fed when he is hungry, changed when he is wet, and responded to rapidly and warmly so that he can start building his sense of self and trust in adults. Adults in the mother's life can help the mother–child dyad by removing pressure, by "being there" in a non-judgmental way, providing a positive role model for quality caregiving, praising the mother's efforts at responding to her baby, and ensuring that the child is adequately protected from potential harm.

The long-term effects of maternal depression on infants can be lessened with complementary care from other adults. But the mother's role is so important throughout the child's life that early support is often essential to ensure positive outcomes for the child. Attachments between mother and child may need extra support. This may be expensive and time-consuming, but early intervention may prevent later emotional problems that would require a much larger investment.

Maternal depression does not automatically imply infant abuse. But the depressed mother is at a higher risk of hurting her child because of her frustration and inability to focus away from herself and meet the needs of her child. She is also more likely to neglect her baby. Yet neglect is not an inherent symptom of postnatal depression; it is a potential result of it. Difficulty bonding with the infant and the need for emotional support seem to be parallel issues for the mother suffering from postnatal depression. If support for the mother is offered and accepted, maternal competence is likely to be enhanced, increasing the strength of the mother–infant bond.

Both adult frustration and maternal depression contribute to the profile of the person who commits abusive behaviour or neglects infants and very young children. Although these might seem like clear categories, in practice they are not—because they don't indicate a profile of a likely abuser. This is possibly the most challenging part of the abusive cycle—it can begin any time by almost anyone. While the majority of professionals may wonder how such terrible things occur—and no excuse should be found, only perhaps some reasons as to why it happens—some parents may reflect on their experiences and wonder how they stopped themselves from going over the top. In most of us, fortunately, there is an inner voice that stops us from committing acts that we know are wrong—but it's a voice that is silent at some times for some people.

Frustration and depression are not the only reasons for victimizing infants with abuse or neglect—but they explain many of the circumstances when they might suffer. If we observe either situation, we should see them as prompts for protecting the youngest.

► Everyday Safety Issues

The baby's complete dependence means that adults must ensure that the infant is protected. Parents and educators have to think about the situations and environments that they bring young infants into and make sure that every eventuality is considered. Thinking about the infant's physical environment is the first step.

INFANT EQUIPMENT

Cribs, bassinets, strollers, carriages, baby seats, and car seats (as discussed earlier) must be maintained in safe working order. Although it is a good idea to check the item for a safety tag, visual inspection of the article is always essential. It must not allow the baby's head to become wedged, or toes or fingers to become entrapped. The materials must be non-toxic, smooth, and sturdy. The item should offer firm support with no possibility of suffocating the infant or collapsing. When babies are in their cribs, they may not be supervised every moment of the day and night, so the crib must be entirely reliable.

The appropriateness of the equipment for the infant's size and stage is as important as its condition. What is safe at one stage might present considerable hazards at another. In making this judgment, it is important to remember that babies develop new skills rapidly, and sometimes unexpectedly. In addition, not all babies have the same level of activity. Some particularly boisterous babies might not be safe in seats that others take to well. Individual preferences of the infants might also shape choices: some babies like to be upright; others prefer to lie back. Although these preferences should be a central consideration, safety is of foremost importance. Always be aware of the need to strap infants into their seats and strollers; this is something both parents and educators tend to be lax about.

CHANGE TABLES

Change tables present several potential hazards. As well as the issues of hygiene and cross-infection, there is an additional risk of the baby falling from the table. Adults sometimes assume that because a baby cannot yet sit or crawl, she cannot move enough to fall from a change table. Yet such falls are a real possibility. Diaper-changing procedures need to include a "keep one hand on the baby" rule.

ON-THE-FLOOR PROTECTION

Babies at this stage may be laid on the floor to play or propped up to see what is going on. The floor is a very vulnerable place for the infant. Adults or older children can fall onto the baby, particularly if they are walking around the infant. Avoid stepping over an infant even if there appears to be no obvious danger. Keep equipment away from the infant so nothing can fall on top of her. Make sure that you do not hold objects over the heads of infants on the floor. It is too easy to drop items onto the baby. Rocking chairs are a particular hazard; they should not be in an area where infants are on the floor. The chairs can slide across the floor, and infants' hands or feet can easily slip under the rocker.

BABY SWINGS

Even young babies can enjoy the effects of the back-and-forward motion of a baby swing. But there are some dangers attached to these swings, and their use in group care is usually inappropriate. Most baby swings are designed for home use for one baby where the adult is in close supervision. Multiple users probably put too much strain on the motor (if there is one) and the swing's structure.

The design of some swings requires the baby to be in an upright position, which can be inappropriate for two reasons. First, because the infant is top-heavy, he is very likely to fall forward and tip out of the swing. Second, an upright position may be inappropriate for those without back control; such babies may slump sideways or even slip out of the swing.

If baby swings are used, the baby should be strapped in at all times. In addition, baby swings should never be set up in high-off-the-ground positions, and they shouldn't be used on hard floors.

► Starting Points for Response

RESPONSIVE CAREGIVING

While responding to a baby's needs and supporting her through appropriate guidance tend to merge into similar nurturance, responsive caregiving tends to focus on providing for the most basic physical needs and guidance strategies to support emotional and psychological needs.

At 6 weeks to 3 months, infants are initiating social contact as well as responding to people. Through these relationships their needs are met. Adults need to read a baby's extensive cues; she uses crying, a range of sounds, body language, and facial expressions to let us know what she wants. She may want attention or need time alone. She may experience sensory overload and need to tune out. Her need for stimulation is balanced by her need for quiet times. The adults to whom she is attached will encourage the baby's repeated actions through playful sequences. They will respond to her cues and enable the baby to discover her body and its competence. Allowing time for the baby to kick and swipe at the air helps to develop physical control and supports the baby's focus on what her body can do. Neurological connections are being made through this activity that are vital for later development. The baby needs to build schemes of understanding and is dependent upon the adults to provide opportunities, space, and time for her development.

SUPPORTIVE GUIDANCE

The baby, who is in desperate need of physical contact and response, will begin to "fall in love" with the adults who meet her needs. Attachment to primary caregivers is essential. The baby has the ability to make multiple attachments, but particular attachment will come about only from continuity of responses. Infants who transition to group care need to have their emotional needs met just as much as they would in a home situation. Supporting physical needs is only the beginning of meeting infants' needs so they can blossom as human beings.

FACILITATING DEVELOPMENT

Babies' emotional well-being comes from the satisfaction of their physical needs and the establishment of nurturing relationships. For some adults, meeting infants' needs is relatively easy; for others, reading infants' cues can be challenging. The challenge can lie in mismatched temperament styles and patterns of behaviour, or the ill health or disability of either the adult or baby. Parents can be assisted in reading their baby's cues, but this needs to be done sensitively; it is ineffective to teach a skill if the educator undermines the parents' confidence.

A balance between stimulation and quiet time continues to be important at this stage. Babies need to make sense of their environments, and the adults in them, in a multi-sensory way, but too much information can be challenging to process. Enormous gains in brain development occur at this time, but the core stimulation needs to be relationship-based rather than object-based. As the baby's sensory acuity increases, his world of learning broadens. The baby will become more interested in physical experiences. The adult will learn when this happens from the dance of communication and from the baby's responses to the immediate environment.

Adult responses allow the infant to begin a process of **individuation**, where he starts to see himself as a separate person. The emergence of a sense of self needs support through responsive attention and meeting the infant's needs.

HOLISTIC RESPONSE

Activities 5.1 and 5.2 encourage a holistic response to infants. Activity 5.1 suggests ways of engaging in young babies' experience and extending your interactions with them. Activity 5.2 helps you to observe each infant and to develop activities that are targeted to individual interests and skill levels.

Activity 5.1

Responding to the Changing Needs of Infants at 6 Weeks to 3 Months

As your skills increase, you will be able to develop more activities that match the baby's stage of development. As you identify their emerging skills through careful observation, you will be able to enter the moment and enjoy the experience of playful exchanges with each baby. In this activity you will support the give-and-take, or turn-taking ability of the baby. This will, with extended play sequences, assist the baby's development in ways that lead to expressive language.

Activity 5.1

Responding to Changing Needs of Infants at 6 Weeks to 3 Months

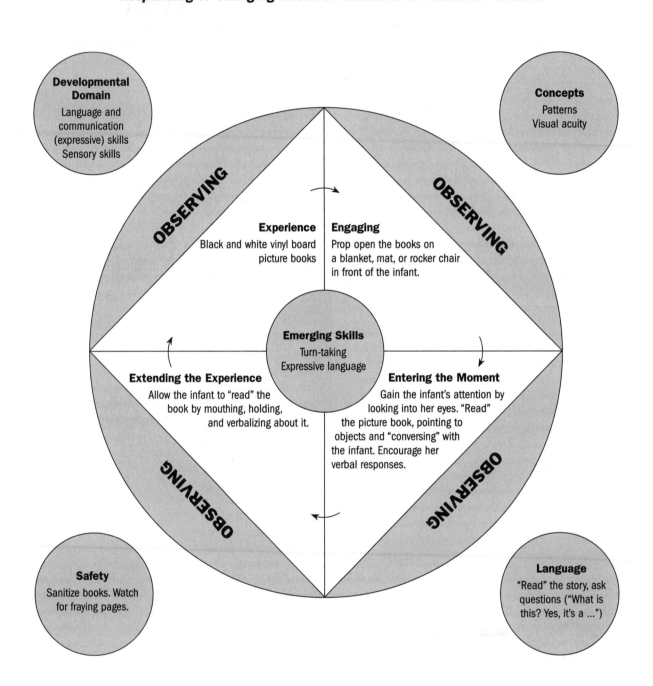

Developmental Domain
Language and communication (expressive) skills
Sensory skills

Concepts
Patterns
Visual acuity

OBSERVING

Experience
Black and white vinyl board picture books

Engaging
Prop open the books on a blanket, mat, or rocker chair in front of the infant.

Emerging Skills
Turn-taking
Expressive language

Extending the Experience
Allow the infant to "read" the book by mouthing, holding, and verbalizing about it.

Entering the Moment
Gain the infant's attention by looking into her eyes. "Read" the picture book, pointing to objects and "conversing" with the infant. Encourage her verbal responses.

OBSERVING

Safety
Sanitize books. Watch for fraying pages.

Language
"Read" the story, ask questions ("What is this? Yes, it's a ...")

Activity 5.2

Creating Responsive Curriculum for Newborns at 6 Weeks to 3 Months

By observing the full range of a baby's emerging skills, you can develop a wide range of experiences or activities that are supportive. Consider the skills that you see in the baby you are working with. Following some of the ideas given below, develop some simple activities that involve safe materials and your direct involvement with the baby.

Developmental Domain	Observation of Emerging Skills (Things You See)	Responsive Experience/Activity
Physical skills	– evidence of eye–hand coordination – reaching and stretching – rolling from side to side – visually tracking objects – increased strength of back muscles – ulnar (whole hand)/mitten grasp	Dangle items at a reachable distance. A crib gym may be useful. Roll balls and toys in front of the baby so that he can track the movement of these objects. Prop up the baby's head with pillows and rolled quilts while interacting with him. Provide stack blocks or cubes, cuddly small stuffed animals, rattles, bottle toys.
Language and communication	– associating words with actions – cooing, beginning babbles – receptive language skills	Visually connect with the infant and take turns in "conversations." Mimic sounds. Smile. Sing nursery rhymes and songs. Talk through your actions (e.g., "Your bottle is heating up now," "Here is your bib," "Let's put you in your chair").
Cognitive skills	– displaying purposeful behaviours – understanding cause-and-effect – recognizing faces	Shake rattles for noise. Swipe at hanging objects. Show photos of people to promote the discovery of others' facial features.

Developmental Domain	Observation of Emerging Skills (Things You See)	Responsive Experience/Activity
Social/emotional skills	– forming self-concept/ identity – forming sense of trust	Use the infant's name often when speaking. Respond to individual needs by tuning into the baby's cues. Discuss emotions while tending to his needs (e.g., "You're fussy because you need a diaper change," "Are you hungry? I'll heat your bottle"). Encourage self-soothing techniques (pacifiers, sucking/mouthing objects).

Three experiences follow that are suggestions for what might be appropriate for babies of 6 weeks to 3 months of age. Each of them addresses the physical and social skills that are emerging at this stage. Make sure to introduce them at a time when the baby appears hungry for stimulation and back off if she fails to attend to your idea. If she engages, you can enter the moment with her. If the time is right, repeat what she finds pleasurable. Then, possibly, extend the activity following the suggestions or develop your own ideas in accordance with the baby's responses.

Responding to Changing Needs

Infants at 6 Weeks to 3 Months

EXPERIENCE 1

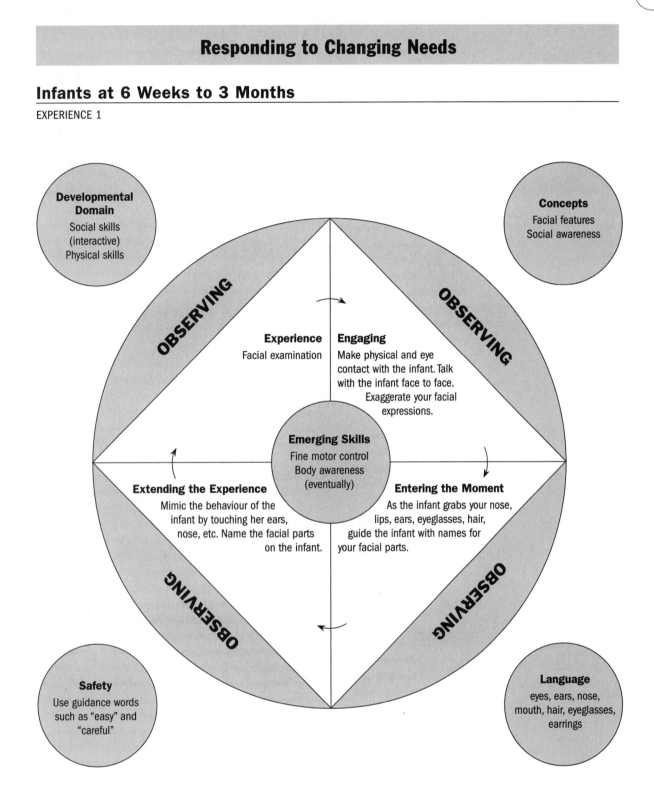

Developmental Domain
Social skills (interactive)
Physical skills

Concepts
Facial features
Social awareness

OBSERVING

OBSERVING

Experience
Facial examination

Engaging
Make physical and eye contact with the infant. Talk with the infant face to face. Exaggerate your facial expressions.

Emerging Skills
Fine motor control
Body awareness (eventually)

Extending the Experience
Mimic the behaviour of the infant by touching her ears, nose, etc. Name the facial parts on the infant.

Entering the Moment
As the infant grabs your nose, lips, ears, eyeglasses, hair, guide the infant with names for your facial parts.

OBSERVING

OBSERVING

Safety
Use guidance words such as "easy" and "careful"

Language
eyes, ears, nose, mouth, hair, eyeglasses, earrings

Responding to Changing Needs

Infants at 6 Weeks to 3 Months

EXPERIENCE 2

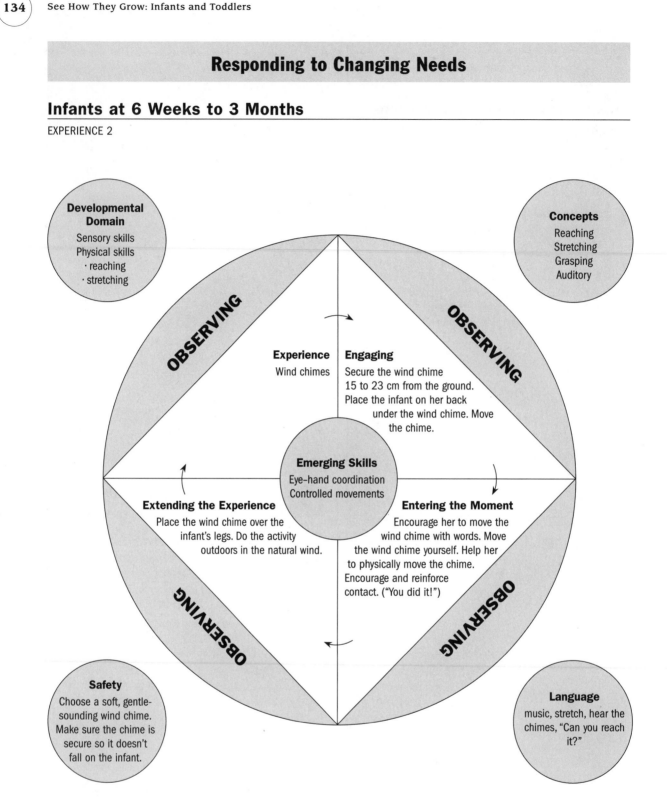

Developmental Domain
Sensory skills
Physical skills
· reaching
· stretching

Concepts
Reaching
Stretching
Grasping
Auditory

OBSERVING

OBSERVING

Experience
Wind chimes

Engaging
Secure the wind chime
15 to 23 cm from the ground.
Place the infant on her back
under the wind chime. Move
the chime.

Emerging Skills
Eye-hand coordination
Controlled movements

Extending the Experience
Place the wind chime over the
infant's legs. Do the activity
outdoors in the natural wind.

Entering the Moment
Encourage her to move the
wind chime with words. Move
the wind chime yourself. Help her
to physically move the chime.
Encourage and reinforce
contact. ("You did it!")

OBSERVING

OBSERVING

Safety
Choose a soft, gentle-
sounding wind chime.
Make sure the chime is
secure so it doesn't
fall on the infant.

Language
music, stretch, hear the
chimes, "Can you reach
it?"

Responding to Changing Needs

Infants at 6 Weeks to 3 Months

EXPERIENCE 3

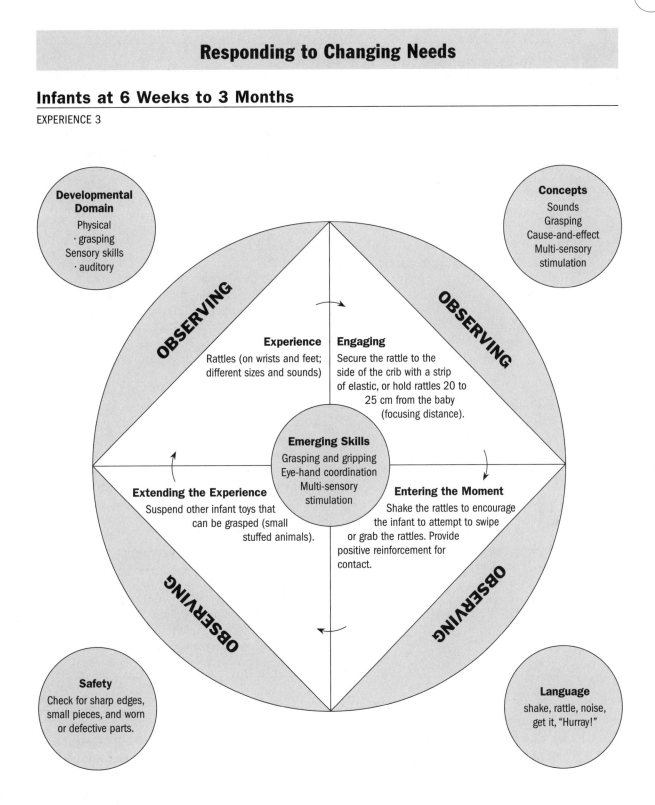

Developmental Domain
Physical
· grasping
Sensory skills
· auditory

Concepts
Sounds
Grasping
Cause-and-effect
Multi-sensory
stimulation

OBSERVING

OBSERVING

Experience
Rattles (on wrists and feet; different sizes and sounds)

Engaging
Secure the rattle to the side of the crib with a strip of elastic, or hold rattles 20 to 25 cm from the baby (focusing distance).

Emerging Skills
Grasping and gripping
Eye-hand coordination
Multi-sensory
stimulation

Extending the Experience
Suspend other infant toys that can be grasped (small stuffed animals).

Entering the Moment
Shake the rattles to encourage the infant to attempt to swipe or grab the rattles. Provide positive reinforcement for contact.

OBSERVING

OBSERVING

Safety
Check for sharp edges, small pieces, and worn or defective parts.

Language
shake, rattle, noise, get it, "Hurray!"

Further Experiences and Interactions

Further Experiences	Interactions
Suction cup toys (dangling toys)	Hold or attach favourite toys in front of the infant and encourage her to reach for them. Hold them closer if she is unable to reach them; gradually pull farther away.
Brightly patterned sheets	Occasionally drape sheets over the side of the crib, or lay the infant on her stomach over these sheets for visual stimulation.
Teething rings	Place rings in a freezer, fridge, or in warm water to achieve varying degrees of temperature for sensory stimulation when mouthing.
Squeaky toys	Hold the baby in your lap. Place the toy in front of her so she may reach for it. Squeak the toy and reinforce her attempts with smiles, words, and hugs.
Sensory quilts	Place the infant on her stomach on the quilt. Lay down with her, face to face. Encourage her attempts at propping and reaching.
Small pillows and toys	Lay the infant face down on top of the pillow so that the upper body is supported, and arms and hands are free to explore. Encourage reaching for toys.
Baby pictures and posters	Hang the pictures and posters at eye level in infant areas.
Nursery rhymes and songs	Face to face interaction. Sing, chant, and visually connect while reciting rhymes. Use exaggerated facial gestures. Insert infant's name in songs.
Neighbourhood walks	Describe the sights, sounds, temperature, and weather as you hold the baby while exploring the great outdoors.
"Where is your . . .?"	Sing songs that include body parts, and point to the parts on the infant.

Responsive Guidance for Infants at 6 Weeks to 3 Months

Age/Stage: Infants 6 Weeks to 3 Months

Situation	Response
• Portia isn't making the same kind of cooing noises that her sister made at the same age. • Meghan is the same age as Sarah, but Sarah isn't raising her head on her own yet and Meghan has been doing so for a couple of weeks. • Amee seems to cry for no reason, while Andy seems to take everything in stride. Developmental Issue: Language	**Developmental Issue: Comparing Babies' Development** Just as no two adults are alike, neither are two infants. Developmental norms are useful broad ranges of progress for assessing developmental lags in normal infants. The range covers the expected time frame most infants will achieve a certain skill in. All babies develop at different rates. Differences among infants are common within the first year. Infants progress at different rates and will often even out after the second year. If you feel your infant is lagging behind for the range identified by a stage of progression, consult a pediatrician. Similarly, infants inherit different temperaments from their parents, and the nurturing environment must be adapted to facilitate a responsive match to suit their needs.
• Michael hears English from his caregiver and French from his father. Will this delay or confuse his language acquisition? • I am bothered because many of our relatives talk to Tyron in "baby talk." What is the right way to talk to him?	**Developmental Issue: Language** Infants pick up the language that is spoken to them. What is important is to talk to your infant a lot, right from the beginning. Name objects around infants, sing songs, read stories, and expose them to a variety of language. As children grow, they will acquire the language around them; the gift of communication comes from a stimulating, responsive environment. Adults serve as stimulators and models for language whenever they interact with infants.

Manufactured Toys and Play Materials for Infants at 6 Weeks to 3 Months

Toy/Material	Uses	Group Care	Home
Rattles, Stroller rattles	Infants will delight in hearing the sounds created from the objects. Place the rattles within, or close to, their reach. Allow infants to grasp and create the sounds themselves.	√	√
Mobiles	Place mobiles 30 cm from the baby and slightly off to the right or left. (Use musical, rotating mobiles for variation.)	√	√
Plastic baby mirrors	Discuss what the baby can see in the mirror.	√	√
Dangling cloth ball	Dangle ball within 25 cm of her position. Gradually prop the baby up for reaching and stretching.		√
Activity centre	Watching and interact as the infant giggles and coos at the colourful, spinning motion and different noises.	√	√
Mouthing toys	Sucking and mouthing objects will aid in self-comforting and soothing regulation.	√	√
Puff balls, Squeeze toys	Grasping, grabbing, and squeezing stimulates gross and fine motor skills.	√	√
Multi-sensory toys	Bright colours, textures, and sounds stimulate sensory skills.	√	√
Tactile plush toys	Babies hug, touch, hear, mouth, and see a variety of experiences.	√	√
Tactile pillows	Provide soft, furry, nubbly, smooth surfaces for propping up infants.	√	√
Safety wall mirrors	Mirrors placed at eye level delight infants as they discover their reflections.	√	

▶ Summary

Many child-care centres accept infants from around 6 weeks of age, an age that corresponds to the end of some mothers' maternity leave. This may be changing in some areas, because parental leave has been extended. Separation may be a more significant issue for mothers than infants, because babies are more interested in having their needs met than in who is meeting them. Nevertheless, infants need to be supported through this transition. The greater the continuity of care, the better they settle into their new environment. Infants are able to make some attachments to several people. With a predictable pattern of care from the new caregiver, these attachments can be made successfully.

The individual style of an infant is clearly observable; his temperament may well be a fairly constant part of his individuality through the following months and years. Caregivers must identify individual patterns of behaviour if they wish to provide appropriate and responsive care.

An infant's sensory abilities are the core elements of her learning about her world. Very gradually, she receives information about her immediate environment and creates schemes of understanding in relation to those experiences. Although the infant's physical skills are not yet well coordinated, she will make some deliberate attempts to repeat sequences of behaviour that she finds pleasurable. This is the sensory-motor stage of cognitive development, when there is a significant step forward in creating a mental representation of the world. Practising actions leads to increased motor control. It also expands the infant's appreciation of how things happen; the infant makes connections between actions and results and can feel some control over the environment.

At this age, an infant begins to gain the sense that he is a separate person. He doesn't have a clear concept of self, only an understanding that he can bring about some responses in adults and with objects. Consequently, it is important for the infant to be able to build strong emotional ties with adult caregivers. He is building trust, an important element of emotional growth that will influence every other domain of development.

▶ KEY TERMS

assessment
binocular vision
cephalocaudal
developmental milestones
egocentric
habituation
individuation
maturational readiness
mental schemes
multiple attachments
myelination
positron-emission tomography (PET)
postnatal depression/baby blues
primary circular reaction
reciprocal relationships
resilient/resilience
screening
self-regulation
sensory-motor development
separateness
separation
sudden infant death syndrome (SIDS)
temperament
visual acuity
visual schemes

▶ DISCUSSION QUESTIONS

1. If you had to choose between centre-based care and private home care for your baby of 2 months, what would you choose, and why?
2. Discuss the maturation process and the difference adult involvement makes to developmental patterns.
3. If the temperament of a new infant seemed "difficult," what might you do?
4. If a baby were born prematurely, what difference might it make to her development at 8 weeks?
5. How might you help a mother to provide breast milk for her baby while she is at work?

▶ ADDITIONAL RESOURCES

▶ Further Reading

Allen, K.E., & L. Marotz. (2000). *By the Ages: Behavior and Development of Children Pre-Birth through Eight.* Albany, NY: Delmar.

Bassett, M. (1994). *Infant and Child Care Skills.* Albany, NY: Delmar/ITP.

Cassidy, J., and P. Shaver. (1999). *Handbook of Attachment: Theory, Research and Clinical Applications.* New York, NY: Guilford Publications.

Cryer, D., and T. Harms (eds.). (2000). *Infants and Toddlers in Out-of-Home Care.* Chapel Hill, NC: National Center for Early Development and Learning.

Gandini, L., and C. Pope Edwards. (2003). *Bambini: The Italian Approach to Infant/Toddler Care.* St. Paul, MN: Redleaf Press.

Goldberg, S. (1997). *Parent Involvement Begins at Birth: Collaboration between Parents and Teachers of Children in the Early Years.* Needham Heights, MA: Allyn & Bacon.

Kaplan, L.J. (1978). *Oneness and Separateness: From Infant to Individual.* New York: Touchstone/Simon and Schuster.

Klaus, M.H., J.H. Kennel, and P.H. Klaus. (1995). *Bonding: Building the Foundations of Secure Attachment and Independence.* Reading, MA: Merloyd Lawrence/Addison-Wesley.

Kotulak, R. (1996). *Inside the Brain: Revolutionary Discoveries of How the Mind Works.* Kansas City, MO: Andrews and McMeel.

Murray, L., A. Fiori-Cowley, R. Hooper, and P. Cooper. (1996). The Impact of Postnatal Depression and Associated Adversity on Early Mother–Infant Interactions and Later Infant Outcome. *Child Development* 67(5): 2512–2526.

Warner, P. (1999). *Baby Play and Learn: 160 Games and Learning Activities for the First Three Years.* St. Paul, MN: Redleaf Press.

Weissbourd, B., and J. Musick, J. (eds.) (1981). *Infants: Their Social Environments.* Washington, DC: National Association for the Education of Young Children.

▶ Useful Web sites

The role of touch in early communication
www.arts.uwaterloo.ca/~ma3rober/311lecture03_19.pdf
PBS resources
www.pbs.org/wholechild/providers/index.html
Psychology resource
www.psy.pdx.edu/PsiCafe/Areas/Developmental/CogDev-Child/
Indicators of child abuse
www.gnb.ca/0017/Protection/Child/general.html
The great child care debate: attachment (CCCF)
www.childcarecanada.org/resources/CRRUpubs/op7/7op3.html
Athabasca University Psychology Resources (including development, reflexes, attachment)
psych.athabascau.ca/html/aupr/developmental.shtml

CHAPTER 6

Grasping the World: Infants at 3 to 6 Months

A smile is a clear indication of the baby's increasing social skills. Here, an adult interacts warmly with a very young baby.

Learning Outcomes

After reading and studying this chapter, you should be able to:

- identify the observable characteristics of development of infants at the 3-to-6-month stage
- explain the significance of behaviours of infants from 3 to 6 months in a developmental context
- recognize and respond to the developmental diversity of 3-to-6-month-old infants and discuss issues pertinent to this stage
- assess the development of infants in the 3-to-6-month stage
- respond to the health, safety, and development of 3-to-6-month-old infants with appropriate nurturance, activities, protection, and caregiving
- develop strategies to work with parents as partners in the care and education of their infants

Scene: A conversation between a father and an educator at the start of a day

"Babies seem so much more human when they smile," commented a young father as he brought his baby of 3 months into the child-care centre. "It's easy to love a baby, but you see the real person in there when they make this connection with you."
"This is a milestone of development," explained the educator. "It is wonderful when you get a smile. It shows there is really a two-way social relationship."
"I can see that you are enjoying Sam," continued the educator. "We really love him, too." "Yes . . . but during the night when Sam wants company I get quite annoyed, and I feel bad about that," disclosed Dad. "I know what it's like to do without sleep. That seems quite usual to me: try not to feel bad about it . . . babies do well if the basic relationship is good . . . none of us has to be perfect," replied the educator, as she took Sam from Dad's arms. "Any chance of you catching up on some sleep?" she asked. "No, I'm already late for work," said Dad. "After a busy night it looks as though Sam wants to sleep now," said the educator, as the baby closed his eyes. "Just my luck," said Dad, as he kissed Sam softly on the cheek. (See Box 6.1 for a discussion of parental and centre patterns of care.)

At this stage, we find that babies will smile at anybody, but soon that won't always be the case. We particularly enjoy young babies at this stage: they get to know us well and we make strong attachments to them, as well as the other way around. But sleep patterns are not always as regular as parents might wish.

Smiling signifies a change in behaviour that has significance to each domain of development but, most importantly, an advance in social interaction. Babies respond to smiles and will show you how much they are interested in you and everything in the world around them. Even though the sleep patterns are not entirely predictable, you will notice that 3-month-old babies are awake and taking notice for longer periods. They look interested in many of the things around them. You will probably notice that the baby has become a "real person" and is happiest with people he knows. Strangers don't pose a threat, and the little person will be content to look at a new face and swipe at it with his fist.

BOX 6.1

PARENTS CARE FOR THEIR BABIES IN DIFFERENT WAYS: SHOULD YOU FOLLOW THE PARENT'S PATTERN OR DO WHAT YOU THINK IS BEST?

There are many reasons why parents rear their children the way they do. These reasons are social, economic, and cultural. Generally, a caregiver should follow the pattern of care established by the baby's parents. One of the challenges in infant care is to make the baby's experiences consistent between home and the child-care agency. Parents' child-rearing practices are quite likely to be similar to the agency's. However, some small differences may be meaningful or symbolic for the parents, and you need to respect them.

You need to listen and sometimes ask sensitive questions to find out what happens at the infant's home, so that you can adopt the same pattern of care. In most situations, you can accommodate the parents' style or wishes or reach an acceptable compromise. For example, if the parents want particular creams used at diaper changing, there's no reason not to use what they provide. Also, if the parent plays with the baby in a particular way, and responds to certain cues, it is a good idea to know this and do similar things. It's good to know if the baby is quickly calmed by being walked up and down. Imitating the parents' style can be appreciated by the baby and family.

Some practical issues don't influence the child's experience directly, so there's little need for the centre's practice to be the same as that of the parents. For example, a parent may ask why the agency seals soiled cloth diapers, when at home the parent soaks them in a pail. Explaining the risks of cross-contamination will usually assure the parent that there is a good reason for a different practice in group care.

Some aspects of the parents' style may reflect their culture or their beliefs about babies. Most culturally determined child-rearing practices can be easily accommodated within the agency. These might relate to adult expectations of babies, the degree of independence expected and encouraged, the type of play activity and adult involvement, the types of behaviours that are encouraged or discouraged, and how this is done. Other patterns that can be accommodated include individual feeding schedules, the transition to "adult" foods, different patterns of activity, the frequency with which infants are held or carried, the way they are clothed, their sleeping arrangements, and familiar smells, images, and sounds.

Different parents may present you with a range of requests for their babies' care. Some may want their babies to be fed particular foods. Others may want you to reinforce self-help skills. Some parents may want their babies to have physical play and be tickled; others disagree with tickling. You may find a parent who wants you to keep the baby awake in the hope the infant will sleep at night. This is a request that is unlikely to be met. A parent may want a baby protected from the cold in many layers of blankets or diapered only in cloth diapers. These things, with some modifications, might be accommodated. Some accommodations are reasonable and the program can make minor changes to fit the baby's need or that of the parent. Other requests do not fit a program's philosophy. If ever this occurs the issue should be discussed with the parents. Students should address challenging issues indirectly via their supervising teacher.

Some babies are used to being swaddled, or wrapped firmly, because the parent thinks that helps the baby to feel secure. You can do this, too, with a very young baby, but by the time a baby is 3 months old she will need some time to kick. You might reach some compromise by suggesting to the parent that you have noticed the enjoyment that the baby gets from a period of free kicking. A trusting relationship with the parents can enable you to learn from each other.

Although there is a wide range of acceptable practices in child-rearing, there should be some limitations, particularly concerning physical or emotional safety. You may encounter a situation where, even allowing for cultural or individual differences, the parents' style is really inappropriate. In such cases you might find it productive to handle the baby in a more appropriate way, and be a positive role model. Parents may notice that you manage situations differently, or respond more sensitively to the baby's needs, and may learn from your example.

A simple explanation of what you are doing can be helpful, but avoid any judgment of the parents' skills. It may be necessary to address the gap between the parents' child-rearing style and what happens within the agency, but this should be a sensitive discussion. It is more likely that the difference is created by a lack of knowledge on either side, poor communication, or a temporary situation brought about by stress. The support of the agency staff can be enormously helpful to the infant's family.

More often than not, parents want the same things for their children, even if they have different ways of achieving them. Parents want their infants and toddlers to be safe, contented, comfortable, and happy. They all hope that their children will be supported so that they can reach their potential, however they define success.

▶ What to Look For

PHYSICAL DEVELOPMENT

Growth

Babies may double, or nearly double, their birth weight by about 6 months of age (Illingworth, 1990). This pattern may be different for low-birth-weight infants. The outfits that were so big at birth will be outgrown within a short time. Babies' heads also grow quite rapidly. This is most noticeable between 3 and 6 months of age, when the head circumference will increase as much as 1 cm or 3/8 inch per month (Allen and Marotz, 2003). This increase is important because it is an observable indicator of brain development. A baby's length will also increase as much as 1.3 cm or 1/2 inch a month (Allen and Marotz, 2003) and this will be particularly noticeable when she is kicking and stretching. Her legs may be quite bowed, but she does not need them yet for walking, so this is usual. Her bones are still malleable, because the ossification and calcification processes have not yet hardened them. It is important to notice how well a baby's clothes fit, because any restrictions can influence growth and the formation of bones. Observing weight, height, and head circumference increases is essential when monitoring changes—these measurements are major indicators of health.

A notable effect of having infants sleep on their backs—as a safety measure to lessen the chance of succumbing to sudden infant death syndrome (SIDS)—is that babies are more frequently seen as having a head that is somewhat flatter at the back. This does not appear to have any lasting effect, and because of the skull's malleability it will return to a more rounded shape in time. For the same reason, the baby may have a bald spot at the back of the head, as the head rubs against the sheet. The hair does grow back and it is not an ongoing issue.

Infants at this stage may appear more chubby or filled out than they did in their first months. Although weight gain varies, increases should be charted. Feeding patterns, activity levels, and individual differences all contribute to the baby's growth.

Physical Skills

The new physical skills of a baby of this age enable increased learning. The coordination required to see objects and learn how to hold them is a complex skill gained during this stage. The baby goes from swinging an arm or leg at a dangling object to being able to grasp items with her whole hand. Once she can grasp objects and practise this skill, she will soon discover how to pass them from hand to hand (Allen and Marotz, 2003). These actions allow her to have a small amount of control over the physical world. Play objects must be safe for the baby to explore and should be the right size to be grasped by tiny hands, but not too small. Because objects grasped by the baby will inevitably make their way to the baby's mouth, items should be kept as clean as possible. As babies progress through these months their bodily control increases significantly.

Gross Motor Skills

The physical actions of reaching and grasping help babies find out about the world through their senses. When they are able to sit, at first propped up with support, they see the environment differently from when they are in a lying position. During these months, babies are likely to increase their back control and may be able to sit, supported at first and then unsupported, for short periods. Even when they can sit without some support, they can topple over because they are not yet able to rotate their upper body. Also, their high centre of gravity—top-heaviness—makes this difficult. If a baby's back "collapses" and he rolls to one side, he may not be ready for real sitting. This skill will be mastered a little later. High chairs and other hard forms of seating may be uncomfortable for the baby who has not yet gained control of his back. He may grow to dislike the seated position and even slide out of a chair if he is not well supported with firm cushioning.

Gradually, the baby will be able to sit straighter and for longer periods of time. As we mentioned in previous chapters, the baby's increasing neck and then back control is an example of the cephalocaudal sequence—that is, the usual sequence of bodily control, which starts from the head and works downward. Another significant sequence of control goes from the centre of the body outward. In keeping with this proximodistal sequence, you may see increasing back control followed by arm and then hand control.

When a baby of this age is placed on her front or back (with supervision), she may discover how to roll over. This often happens unexpectedly. There are some safety risks attached to the baby's increased movement, especially since, at first, rolling over is not a controlled action. After the baby learns to roll over, her range of movements begins to expand. When lying on her front, she may find a way of moving forward by "swimming" with her legs. At first this is accidental; in later months it may allow her to crawl. Spending longer periods on their backs may alter the patterns of pre-crawling actions. The "back to sleep" advice from pediatricians should be followed when babies are put in their cribs to sleep, but there may be a temporary change in developing gross motor skills that delays crawling or leads the baby to skip the crawling stage!

Fine Motor Skills

A baby's ability to grasp objects increases her access to sensory information. Often you will see her putting objects in her mouth. This is more likely for the sensation of touch than of taste. Mouthing objects is also satisfying because, by the end of this stage, the first teeth may be nearing readiness to erupt (Snow, 1998). It is interesting that one emerging skill—such as mouthing objects—coincides with a need to gnaw objects. In many ways development is not a linear progress of skill acquisition but a process that is interdependent—each domain influencing other domains.

Through the 3-month-to-6-month stage there is a big increase in the baby's hand control. His ability to perform deliberate actions is increased and frequently he does them over and over just for enjoyment. The repetition reinforces neural pathways, so it has an important function. Early playfulness and experimentation is aided by the baby's gaining a little control of the objects he grasps. At the beginning of the stage, the baby may not yet manage to manipulate any objects: grasping, and then letting go of the object he grasped, is challenging enough. In time, he will be able to pass items from hand to hand, but coordinating his eyes and watching his own actions proves difficult, as he doesn't know where items are in space. He may even knock himself with the object he grasps. Items are often wet from the drool from his exploration; this makes handling the item particularly tricky. You may see a whole-hand grasp—called a **palmar grasp**—so the things he can pick up have to be just the right size to fit in the palm of his hand. Letting go remains a difficulty for some—particularly if he has grabbed your hair, earlobes, or glasses! A simple game that involves grabbing and letting go may bring almost endless amusement.

In time, the baby will examine her hands and watch attentively as she grasps things. She may try to grab something and pass it to her other hand—perhaps not realizing that the second hand already has something in it. Accidentally at first, the baby may knock two items together—one in each hand. Finding amusement in this may keep her occupied for a while. As it occurs to her that banging things together makes a desirable noise, this may encourage the repetition. Passing things from one hand to the other, reaching to grab things without toppling over or as she lies on her back, and modifying her actions to fit different things that she handles may be features of her fine motor control at 6 months. Lying on her tummy poses particular challenges, because her arms are not as free to reach and grasp things. Some babies enjoy this position more than others. The sitting position may be preferred because she can see around her and make more successful attempts at grabbing, but time on her back also offers a different perspective.

COGNITIVE DEVELOPMENT

Senses and Perception

At this stage, babies' senses are acute. A baby prefers to hear human voices but is influenced by a wide variety of sounds (Allen and Marotz, 2003). She may find that kitchen appliances make interesting sounds, but some high-pitched sounds could be uncomfortable for her. As time goes on, the baby's ability to differentiate—or distinguish between—sounds increases.

Responses to smells may produce facial expressions similar to those of adults. Facial expressions have been found to be fairly similar across different cultures and among people of differing ages and experiences. They are not learned behaviours. Facial expressions are part of an inborn mechanism to allow for communication without benefit of language. Certainly facial expressions are part of the overall body language that allows communication of a baby's fear, joy, anger, and other primary emotions. This provides the adult with a way of reading a child's reactions to stimuli, needs, and preferences and seeing how to further communicate. Charles Darwin initiated interest in universal emotions, but this work was extended by Caroll Izard at the University of Delaware. Joseph Campos extended the list. Further studies may include other emotional expressions. Please see the Appendix for a chart of fundamental emotions demonstrated by infants and toddlers.

Facial Expressions

Facial expressions are fundamental and appear to be consistent across cultures. Combining the research of Izard, Campos, and others yields the following list of basic emotions:

interest—observable when the child has visual acuity to attend to faces or objects

shame*—dependent upon understanding of social expectations

shyness*—personality type or style, resulting in negative social experience

guilt*—dependent upon understanding of responsibility, although a young child may feel this mistakenly

joy—evident soon after birth

disgust—evident soon after birth, shown in reaction to discomfort or unpleasant taste

surprise—evident in startle reflex—refined in later months

sadness*—depends on self-awareness; later dependent on self-reflection and/or negative experience

anger—evident soon after birth, possibly a refinement of disgust

pride*—dependent upon sense of self and accomplishment

embarrassment*—depends on recognition of self and, possibly, the reactions of others

distress—evident from birth

empathy*—dependent upon cognitive understanding of the feelings of others

pain—evident from birth

The expressions that have an asterisk (*) beside them can be thought of as social emotions; they are acquired through social relationships as the infant develops into a toddler and preschooler.

With a continued liking for sweet tastes, most babies will reject some foods or the taste of some objects. At the age of about 4 to 6 months, infants are introduced to purées, their first "solid" foods. Although babies have general and personal preferences, there is a clear need to feed them nutritious foods without added sugar.

So far we have discussed the 3-to-6-month-old baby's sensory acuity as it relates to hearing and smelling. Acuity is the degree to which the sense organ is effective. We will now look at other types of sensory acuity.

At this stage, a baby can more easily follow moving objects with her eyes and by turning her head, because she is able to see a little farther away and has improved head control (Sheridan, 1997). This expands her access to visual stimulation. She has binocular vision and, consequently, some sense of spatial dimensions (Yonas et al., 1987). Binocular vision is the ability to coordinate the two separate images from the two eyes to create one image with indicators of three dimensions. The images that she receives can be interpreted so that she can have an improved idea of where things are in relation to her.

At 5 to 6 months, babies will reach for objects that they can see and that are within their grasp. Early attempts at judging distances may be incorrect, but trial-and-error helps her learn to gauge how far away objects are. The baby is particularly interested in visual information as her acuity increases. She will appear to enjoy looking at contrasting patterns, bright colours, and particularly faces (Fantz, 1965).

The infant's sense of touch is often underestimated. The skin is the baby's largest sense organ, and it sends many messages to the brain. Babies' skin is soft and particularly sensitive to temperature, texture, pleasure, and pain. Most babies enjoy gentle touches, but some are irritated by too much touching. The infant's ability to regulate her body temperature will probably have improved, but, because she is unable to tell us if she is hot or cold, we must pay attention to such considerations. It is worth repeating that the temperature for a baby lying on the floor can be lower than for an adult moving around the room. Caregivers must be aware of this possible difference.

The process of sensory stimulation and how it promotes the brain's development is not fully appreciated, but it is understood that early stimulation is highly desirable. The brain needs stimulation so that it can make neurological connections. In this stage of development, sensory discovery is extremely significant, but there must be a balance between times of high and low stimulation.

Sensory-Motor Behaviour

At the age of 3 months, babies are likely to take an increasing interest in their world and can be seen playing with people and objects that are within their sight and grasp. Their behaviours will be changing from random movements to more controlled, deliberate actions. Piaget (1952) describes this as the **sensory-motor stage**. Consider the following discussion of circular reactions in connection with the description of the chain of the sensory-motor substages found in the Appendix. The chain of substages will clarify the sequence of circular reactions observable in the infant. His actions help him to make sense of all the sensory stimulation he receives. Some of the things that he did by chance will now become part of his range of skilled movements. Many actions will be repeated—creating cycles of action. His thinking will allow him to anticipate some events, particularly if they have to do with his own needs. For example, you may notice that he becomes excited when you go to get his bottle, or displays displeasure when he sees that you are about to take him to the change table.

Mental Schemes and Circular Reactions

The infant will gain some understanding of her world as she experiences it. Gradually she will create a mental map of preliminary concepts connected with her firsthand experience. These are called cognitive **schemes**. They involve neurological activity at a level beyond previous achievements. Examples of early schemes might include how her blanket feels, the smell of mom, or, in the case of combined information, how she feels, sees, and smells her soapy bath water. These schemes reflect her understanding of her external world and consequently affect her actions. Everyday happenings and material are babies' most important stimuli. They enjoy simple things, like holding a small object and squeezing it to make a sound, or swiping at a face. Their explorations will move into patterns when they perform actions that cause a response. This is called a **primary circular reaction**. Babies will repeat actions many times, which shows us that they have some sense of deliberation and an ability to decide to do something, even if they cannot carry it out successfully.

Later in the stage, the repetitions of action will become more complex, what we call **secondary circular reactions**. The baby's actions will be concerned with the external environment rather than with her own body. When the baby notices that something has happened by chance, she will repeat the action that brought about the result. This shows that the baby has some basic understanding of cause-and-effect and knows that objects are separate from her.

Concentration Span

A baby may show enjoyment by playing for longer periods during these months. He might also show happiness by his facial expressions and by making cooing sounds. The range of expressed emotions becomes wider, as do his social relationships. You will probably find that his moods alter quite quickly (Allen and Marotz, 2003). Boredom with a simple activity may indicate that he needs a new source of interest. Familiarity with objects can be a source of comfort, but he may habituate from boredom and look away. Physical agitation, such as wriggling, leg-stretching, and sound changes, indicates the need for a change of scenery or a new object to handle and mouth.

The baby of 3 to 6 months is particularly interested in new things to look at. Her attention is drawn to novelty; anything that is of interest. Her visual **preferences**—the things she likes to look at most—continue to be faces, which she scans in outline and in some detail. But she is also interested in patterns of high contrast. Knowing this, adults have often responded by providing black-and-white images—particularly in mobiles that are within the baby's field of vision. However, the baby's attention to patterns can also relate to colour images—so we shouldn't limit the visual discovery of the infant.

Babies have different styles that lead to different patterns of attention. Some like frequently changing things to see or pay attention to and tire quickly of what is presented; they want to be exposed to action and change. Other babies will concentrate longer on a face or picture or stay with a playful activity longer. Their calmer style does not necessarily suggest a better focusing ability that will lead to the ability to keep at a task longer. These are merely style differences and may indicate that their learning will take different paths—neither path more effective than the other.

COMMUNICATION AND LANGUAGE

We have already looked at the baby's sensory acuity and determined that all five senses are usually working effectively at this stage. Because the senses are the primary means of learning and communi-

cating, they are very significant. Early screening and close observation are necessary to ensure that a baby's senses are enabling her to play and communicate. The senses of sight, touch, and hearing are probably the most important. Difficulties relating to the sense of touch are rare; there is a higher incidence of visual and hearing impairments. For communication purposes we generally depend on both sight and hearing, so early intervention may be necessary for babies who show a deficit in either sense.

At this stage, babies have the ability to recognize the range of sounds that are found in speech. It will take a while before they can use language, but they soon learn that your pitch and the way you speak have meaning. A baby may begin to recognize her own name during this stage (Allen and Marotz, 2003). She will begin to understand what is happening to her by associating sounds with seeing adults do things. She may enjoy hearing your voice talking or singing. There is comfort in the human voice and the patterns of adult conversation even when they are not understood.

Research into **language acquisition**—how babies learn to communicate verbally—indicates that exposure to the sounds that are integral parts of two or more different languages (such as English and Spanish) exposes the baby to a wider variety of sounds than would be experienced in a monolingual (one language) context. This may be beneficial, because it allows the baby to experiment and shape her sound production in ways that ultimately correspond to the languages of her immediate environment. However, at 3 to 6 months, the baby will make the same sounds regardless of the language she hears: contented sounds, cries, and a few more differentiated noises. The sounds may have meaning attached to them. For example, a particular cry can indicate to adults that she has a particular need. This does not necessarily mean that she makes particular sounds in order to get the responses she desires. But gradually her sound production will become more controlled and deliberate. At first there may be a somewhat disjointed to-and-fro of communication, with the baby sending messages by chance or deliberately. Adults also send messages that are only partly understood. When there is effective communication through body language, the way the baby is handled and played with, there is reinforcement of shared meaning.

Sound, by way of real language, conveys meaning, but so far the baby does not have a very broad understanding of language and depends on context for any shared understanding. For example, at around 5 months, the baby may raise her arms and make an "ah–ah" sound, which is translated by the adult as "lift me up now." Similarly, the adult may talk to the baby and emphasize key words. The sound coupled with an action—within a context—may offer meaning. "I'm going to change you now," said repeatedly while taking the child to the change table, may have the effect of linking sounds and action that, together, have meaning for the baby.

There is a big difference between a baby's receptive and expressive language. The meaning or understanding that a baby associates with a particular vocal sound is **receptive language**—hearing and knowing what a sound means. Toward the end of this stage, babies may have some limited receptive language, but it will remain context-dependent for some while. The beginnings of **expressive language** are found in crying or cooing. They can tell us what the baby is feeling; but as yet she is not making the sounds deliberately. Over the next few months the baby will make vocalizations that are deliberate—she is expressing herself, even if we don't know her meaning. In time, she will use a wider range of sounds that are part of one or more languages. Simultaneously, she will make stronger associations between sounds and meanings. Babies are also interested using objects to make sounds (Furuno et al., 1993). They like to hold a spoon and bang it against another object, thus having some control over the sound production.

Infant Communication

As yet, the baby's communication skills are rudimentary, but they can be adequate if we take time to interpret the message she sends. You can see babies communicating at this stage through **body language**, facial expressions, sound production, and responses. Babies are not able to tell you what they want or even to point to it, but they have a remarkable ability to let you know when they are pleased or unhappy. Crying can indicate unhappiness, but it can also be used to get a response when attention is required. Calm or agitated movement can be another cue for adults. Facial expressions and states of awareness (Quilliam, 1994) are still other indicators of mood and responsiveness. Many of these are not deliberate communications, but they can be interpreted and responded to as though they were.

Some of the baby's communication is not deliberate, but during this stage the baby may make deliberate attempts to communicate with adults. These attempts are called **intentional communications** (Greenspan and Greenspan, 1985) and involve the infant initiating connections with an adult, using sound and body language. As well, the baby is likely

to respond to the adult's attempts to communicate. Early communication sets the pattern of reciprocity: the fact that communication requires give-and-take, or sending and receiving. It is a two-way, turn-taking process.

Babies are especially likely to respond to adult language if it is relatively high-pitched, simple, repetitive, and accompanied by eye contact and exaggerated facial expressions. This type of communication is called **motherese** (Fernald, 1989), or **parentese**, and appears to reflect an innate ability of adults to communicate successfully with infants.

Young babies are becoming familiar with the language spoken around them. Their early babbling contains some sounds of that language. The language environment is important to language learning: conditions that encourage language development include positive relationships, exposure to simple language, and reinforcement of the infant's sound production.

Sending and receiving messages is a necessary part of communication. We can become more familiar with the dance of communication between adult and child by observing such interactions closely. This dance requires that both infant and adult listen and "speak." Developing reciprocal communications depends on the adult and infant having enough relaxed time to share experiences.

Communicating with parents is essential for reinforcing educator–infant interactions. It helps to synchronize communication strategies to avoid confusing the baby. Parents for whom English is a second language may benefit from sharing the infant's experiences through video (see Box 6.2).

EMOTIONAL AND SOCIAL DEVELOPMENT

It is most interesting to observe babies at 3 to 6 months because it is then that real social relationships begin to emerge. Infants' curiosity about the world and their eagerness to have it respond to them is amazing. In addition, their increasing physical control allows for more sensory discovery. The infant is starting take hold of the world!

Smiling and Attachment

The emotional growth that babies experience at this stage is reflected in their use of smiles. A baby may initiate an interaction by making a facial expression that is similar to a smile. When the adult responds positively, the baby repeats the expression. As the interaction proceeds, the baby's enjoyment is indicated by her real smiles. The baby finds the give-and-take of the social interaction pleasurable: a clear sign

BOX 6.2

BUILDING CROSS-CULTURAL COMMUNICATION SKILLS: USING VIDEOS

Parental permission must be obtained before any videotaping can be done. But it's a great way of showing parents what happened during their child's day while they were at work.

Using a video camera is relatively easy; with a little practice, the educator will gain sufficient skill to make a good image and capture significant parts of the child's day. Showing these video segments at parent meetings, making them available for lending to the parents, and using them as an integral part of your assessment process will be a useful addition for all parents, but for those who speak a language outside your own scope they can be invaluable.

You might have a particular intention in your recordings. You may want to highlight each baby's individual temperament, or capture behaviours that show the baby's skills.

of emotional growth. The social smile is a clear indication of the emotional well-being and sociability of the baby. Many adults relate better to babies when they have reached this stage because of their openness to social relationships. Laughter comes later—but the smile is captivating.

There is something about a smile that makes people respond to a baby—even adults wrapped up in their own business open up in response to the smiling baby. This may be another part of the baby's protective system; he seems appealing and yet vulnerable. A phenomenologist writing over 50 years ago (Buytendijk, 1947) tells of his fascination with the first smile and wonders, ". . . what is the essence and meaningful significance of a certain expression, such as a smile?" (p. 2.) Answering his own question, Buytendijk speculates that perhaps the smile exists without an inner life—an animalistic response without human experience. Perhaps the smile brings a human reaction that creates a first human experience, he suggests. He compares it to a parrot's greeting—it is clever mimicry but has no humanity. This may be disappointing for the phenomenologist expecting to meet early signs of human experience. Buytendijk thinks that a truly human encounter—which we might find when two people connect with each other—is ". . . not just the appearance or sensory perception of the presence of someone else . . . but the discovery of a 'thou' who engages with me in relation" (p. 9).

From a scientific perspective, it may be difficult to know what is behind the smile. Louise Kaplan (1978) agrees with Buytendijk, but she comes to the issue from the psychoanalytic school of thought. It is not the first smile that is particularly interesting, she thinks, because it has ". . . no psychological meaning"(p. 44); it is merely a physical twitch. Later, the smile becomes a part of the infant's social repertoire of communication skills, and with these new,

truly joyous and responsive smiles there appears to be a real expression of human experience. "Eye to eye contact and smiling are inborn responses that speak of our human preparedness to become attached to other human beings," suggests Kaplan (p. 75). The seemingly simple act of smiling becomes increasingly complex over time and takes on a wide variety of meanings as the infant develops and increases her social relationships. Kaplan suggests that the baby's smiles tend to be context-specific and can be "read" accurately only by the person who is engaging with the baby—this is the **specific smile**. The specific smile is characteristic of an attachment to an adult that can usually be observed in this 3-to-6-month period. Kaplan notes that at this stage the baby smiles more often as a result of hearing human voices, especially the ones she recognizes. By 3 months, she is often looking into her mother's eyes as she smiles, rather than looking through her or past her.

At, or shortly before, 3 months, the baby reaches a stage that Kaplan characterizes as "leaving limbo and entering oneness" (p. 89). With the attachments that the baby makes that are evidenced by smiles, the baby can feel secure to explore her world. As she does this, she begins to see herself as a separate, autonomous (self-directed) "person." This depends on attachment—babies who are unable to make such human connections will not see themselves as separate human beings, an enormously significant psychological step in emotional development.

At around 5 months, the baby will start moving outside what is called the **shared orbit**, her physical and emotional circle. This is a sign of strong attachment and risk-taking. The baby knows through experience that when the adult goes away she comes back, or there is certainly some continuity—her needs are being met both emotionally and socially. At the same time, that separation becomes harder. Because the bond to the **primary caregiver** (most significant attachment figure) can be counted on as being reliable, the baby appears to be fearful if separation from the primary caregiver occurs. This may seem strange, because the relationship is stronger than it has been—but so too is the emotional turmoil when the caregiver disappears.

As a baby becomes increasingly able to differentiate between people she knows and does not know, she can be seen to respond differently to different people.

Both Mary Ainsworth and John Bowlby have contributed significantly to the study of attachment. Their separate findings, with a common agreement on there being a **secure base relationship** at the root of attachment, have been reinforced over 25 years of subsequent research. Attachment theory is based on the idea that a strong and consistent relationship is needed for bonding (the process of making the attachment) to occur. Elaborating on the work undertaken on attachment over the years, Waters and Cummings (2000) are attempting to test the theory and see how it holds up to cross-cultural examination. Indications are that the broad base of attachment theory is applicable across different populations. This means that looking at *how* attachments happen might be less important than the fact that they *do* happen. This is not to imply that attachments are anything other than relationship-based, but that adults and infants may solidify their connections in a variety of ways. In one culture this may mean having the baby in close proximity for long periods and in another it might include meeting the baby's needs in a reliable way. This should alert us to the fact that caregivers and parents may have different styles that contribute to making sound attachments with babies—there is more than one way of forming attachments with a baby. There can be a variety of ways of making **secure attachments**—the most fundamental human relationships.

The challenge presented by infants who have made specific attachments—attachments to particular people—is that handling separation can be difficult. For an infant, **separation** can be a traumatic event. For very young babies this is not usually the case, although they may be calmed more easily by those who are familiar with the infant. It may be that once the caregiver is out of sight she might also be out of the baby's thoughts, so the less mature baby has less to worry about. The cries of the baby who is undergoing a separation can seem heart-wrenching; prolonging the act of separating may make matters worse.

Often a sense of **people permanence** is experienced before **object permanence**, which is at about

8 months, so people permanence may occur during the latter part of this age period—possibly at 6 months. The concept of object permanence is that when an object goes out of the baby's sight and she then seeks it, she is looking for the missed object because she can hold it in her mind. People permanence is similar—when a familiar person goes out of sight, the baby still remembers the person. So it's possible that some babies show some signs of **separation anxiety** because they have the concept of people permanence. Separation anxiety can show itself in several ways, depending on the stage of the baby, her ability to communicate, and her personality. Typically she might show fear or distress and cry for some period. Babies who do not cry at the time of separation have either not made a secure attachment or, more likely, they are still too young to hold in their minds the person who is gone. Several studies have found that the type and security of attachment that is made in the early months is critical to emotional development, in particular, as well as to other domains of development. The baby's style of interaction is also important in attachment and separation behaviours; even babies at 3 to 6 months have observable styles that influence the way they become attached to adults. Similarly, the adult's style shapes attachment and separation. If the two styles differ, there can be concern. Parents may have to develop strategies to handle the friction that results.

The baby may be distressed when he is with unfamiliar people, although he is likely to be comforted if his needs are met. Prolonged upset at separation from those most familiar is unlikely until the baby is a little older. Although there are differences of opinion on how many people can, or should, make bonding relationships with a baby (Berk, 2000), it is certain that infants at this stage are able to make initial attachments with several adults (Maccoby and Feldman, 1972). Despite some predictions that these multiple attachments might be detrimental, it has been found that the baby can make a small circle of attachments with adults or older children.

Self-Concept

We have already mentioned some aspects of self-concept—the idea that the baby knows that she is a separate human being. Margaret Mahler, who had a strong influence on Louise Kaplan's work, developed a complex theory of **separation-individuation** (1975) that explains how infants perceive themselves. At first, there is no dividing line between who the baby is and who the mother is. Through developing a strong and secure attachment with the mother (here

Mahler's work focused on mother and child), the infant finds that she can influence her immediate world and the people in it; then the infant could see herself as a separate individual. Mahler describes an interesting relationship of interdependence that she calls **symbiosis**. The mother and the infant find that they have need of each other, and the baby has some feeling of power that leads to **ego** development (creating a sense of self). The discovery changes shape over time, but the symbiosis is never completely severed. Typically even adults have a loving interdependence with their parents, and they with them!

Social relationships help a baby to discover and assert his separateness. Only in a relationship can a baby discover that he has influence. This helps the baby understand a human cause-and-effect connection. At 3 months, the baby finds that his behaviour brings a response from the adult. He smiles, and the adult smiles back. He cries, and the adult supplies what the baby wants. The baby becomes an agent of change and is empowered to take some control in his social world. The development of the baby's self-concept and self-esteem depends on the baby having a sense of control over his world. He needs to have some idea that he makes a difference and that his needs matter. Basic trust in the adult to support his needs and desires, and the beginnings of trust in himself, form the emotional roots from which confidence and self-esteem can later grow.

Current research appears to support the idea that forming a secure attachment is a critical part of an infant's development. It may also be essential to later emotional adjustment. This is being revealed through many studies of children who have not been successful or who present behaviour problems later in childhood. An infant's attachment to her caregivers is important, but the way it occurs in different infant–adult dyads may vary. Possibly, infants discern early in their experience that different people do different things for them, or do the same things differently; this may be the start of internalizing role models, as well as establishing different qualities of relationships with different people. The issue of whether or not these attachments are different is not an excuse for poor-quality relationships—the infant needs secure attachments with both caregivers and parents in order to build trust and a clear sense of self.

Temperament

Babies are far from being all alike; we have already mentioned this in relation to making attachments. Temperament styles are clearly evident in the pat-terns of reaction that babies demonstrate (Chess and Thomas, 1996). Some babies are quick to respond; others take time. Some babies are more fearful than others. There are infants who accept comforting rapidly; others hold on to their moods. Some babies have a tendency to observe what is happening, while others are more inclined to initiate communications. These different temperaments are observable in even very young infants.

Temperament styles have some biological basis, as we have discussed in previous chapters, and consequently the baby's traits tend to remain fairly consistent over time. An adult who is sensitive to the infant's patterns of behaviour will find that two-way communication becomes more effective. By modifying his own patterns of response, the adult will find that they become increasingly synchronized. Repetition helps this process, which is easy because the baby tends to repeat behaviour sequences.

The rhythm of the baby and her responses to stimuli may influence social relationships as well as the types of activity that the baby enjoys. Careful observation and sensitive responses will help you to determine her needs.

One way of supporting the regular exchange of information between adults is to develop Daily Information Charts as discussed in Box 6.3 (page 152).

▶ Particular Needs

Because young infants are discovering their world but have no idea of danger, they must be carefully protected. Safety issues are identified later in this chapter. Essential as these issues are, emotional considerations are just as important. Box 6.4 (page 153) lists some of the ways caregivers can respond to the needs of infants at this stage.

TRUST AND RESPONSIVENESS

Infants' relationships with adults are mostly based on trust. Babies are likely to trust adults if their needs are met in a regular and reliable way. We must be sensitive to the fact that babies need consistency. They need to see the same faces and be responded to in ways that allow them to predict patterns of adult behaviour. This is part of their discovery of how the world works. If babies do not have a small number of adults who provide reliable, sensitive attention and with whom they can form lasting attachments, they may have difficulty later forming relationships or suffer other social or emotional challenges.

BOX 6.3

A USEFUL STRATEGY FOR SHARING CARE: DAILY INFORMATION CHARTS

Parents are often extremely distressed when the time comes to leave their young infant at a child-care centre. They may have wide-ranging fears about what will happen to their child while they are away. Addressing these fears may involve preparatory meetings or parental observation of the centre "in action." The caregiver should take time to hear the parents' concerns, explain how the child's needs will be met, give parents information about the centre and its philosophy, and organize processes to help share information about the child. In addition, the parent can be encouraged to stay with the infant until both parties are ready to separate. The caregiver might also arrange meetings that allow the new parents to meet and chat with the parents of other children at the centre.

Infants need to be responded to in ways that are positive. The cues that they give us tell us what they need; we must learn their system of communication. When hungry, they must be fed; when uncomfortable, they must have attention and comforting. They may also convey the need for love and physical contact. Responses to all these needs build trust.

STIMULATION

At this stage, infants need sensory stimulation and the opportunity to play safely, both alone and with the assistance of an adult. Without this play, much early learning will be limited and the infant's thinking skills will be affected.

Along with times of stimulation, babies also need downtime, or opportunities to be quiet and relaxed. Reading the infant's cues will tell the caregiver when to provide stimulation and when to provide a calmer environment.

LANGUAGE AND COMMUNICATION

Careful reading of a baby's cues is the most important part of the adult's role. This leads to a reciprocal relationship, where messages are sent and received by both parties.

Before she can learn a language, a baby needs to hear the language spoken and have adults imitate and reshape her **vocalization**. It is essential that a baby be nurtured in a language-rich environment. At this stage, adults should speak in a very clear and direct way to the baby. Her early vocalizations will be framed within the language in which she is nurtured.

NUTRITION

Infants need good nutrition, preferably breast milk, during these months. A breast-feeding mother whose baby is in group care may be able to express her milk so a caregiver can give it to the baby in a bottle. Alternatively, if the mother is nearby, she may be able to come by to feed at regular times. Some mothers maintain morning and evening breast-feeding, and the infant is bottle-fed during the main part of the day. During this stage, the infant may begin to take some solid food, but the main nutritional source remains milk. He should be held closely when fed. If that is not possible, he can sit up, propped in a chair, once he is able to do so.

PHYSICAL CONTACT

Most babies thrive on lots of physical contact and affection. There can be exceptions to this; a few babies are not so receptive to touch and prefer emphasis on other types of communication. Infants are supplied with warmth and a feeling of trust when they experience the adult in close proximity. Infants need physical contact, not just to have their obvious physical needs met. Caregivers need to plan for the close times and be able to create them spontaneously when the opportunity arises and the baby is responsive.

When several infants are being fed together, low chairs in a semicircle may promote improved contact. This is an important social time. If this opportunity for closeness is missed, it cannot be repeated as successfully at another time, because there is a strong association between physical closeness, warmth, comfort, and feeding.

BOX 6.4

GETTING IN TUNE WITH INFANTS OF 3 TO 6 MONTHS

Below are some starting points for building your responsive skills with a 3-to-6-month-old infant. Tune in with respect and:

- support any routine that the infant has established
- identify the infant's temperament and work with his style in all activities and communications
- supply all the infant's basic needs: stimulation, food, diaper-change, physical contact, etc.
- check that the infant is dressed appropriately for the weather
- prop up the infant when he is trying to see
- respond quickly to the infant's cries and other cues for attention
- build trust by being consistent and loving
- provide simple toys and safe objects for mouthing
- assist separation from other adults by providing continuity
- place the mother's belongings near the infant so he is comforted by their sight and/or smell
- place mobiles within the focus of the infant
- provide visual stimulation in the form of pictures, faces, and patterns
- observe the infant's responses to a wide variety of music and sounds to see which he prefers
- raise the pitch of your voice and repeat simple words for the objects and actions that the baby sees
- provide simple sensory experiences within the baby's reach (e.g., food, textures, or objects to touch and see)
- allow the infant to sleep when he wishes
- rub the infant's back or soothe him by stroking his tummy
- pat the baby's back to help him expel gas
- keep the baby comfortable with appropriate skin care
- take time to sing songs and play finger/toe rhymes
- use warm bath times for play, talk, and massage
- place dangling toys within reach or for swiping at
- check all objects/materials for their safety
- try some mild rough-and-tumble play, lifting the baby high up or swinging him round, holding his body, not arms (stop if he's not happy)
- make a variety of sounds with shakers, etc., for the baby to follow visually
- use foam blocks to prop the infant in differing positions
- do tummy nuzzling and playful repetitive movements
- try infant "aerobics," playfully extending the baby's limbs in symmetrical movements
- help the baby to tune out by decreasing stimulation
- identify the trance state that leads to sleep
- acknowledge the baby's feelings by labelling them and acting appropriately
- make sounds (popping, tongue-clicking) to engage the baby
- imitate the infant's own vocalizations
- smile frequently and respond to the baby's smiles
- tuck a pillow under the baby's chest so he can play in a lying position (supervise the baby carefully)
- take the infant for walks outside in a stroller when she can be propped up to look around
- ensure the infant is protected from all kinds of harm
- place the baby on his back to sleep

OPPORTUNITY TO MOVE

The chance to stretch, move, and explore physical capabilities must be a regular part of the infant's day. Sometimes it is possible for the infant to go without restrictive clothing, but colder climates may make this difficult to arrange. In this case, the infant needs to wear clothing that is warm but does not limit movement. Movement is an important feature of physical skill acquisition and finding out about the body.

ACCOMMODATION OF INDIVIDUAL STYLES

In centre-based care, it can be difficult to ensure that all infants' needs are met. Those who have styles that get attention rapidly are more likely to have their needs met. Educators must make sure that even the most contented babies receive the attention that is essential for their well-being.

▶ Developmental Variation

Many of the reasons for variations in developmental patterns have been discussed in earlier chapters. Some developmental differences may not have been identified in the first three months of life. These may be congenital, chromosomal, metabolic, or other conditions. The most severe will probably have been diagnosed. Less severe conditions may be discovered at this stage because of the diligent observation of the adult caregivers.

BIRTH WEIGHT

Infants who had low birth weight may have weight increases that vary from the usual pattern (Snow, 1989). Premature babies may have continuing difficulties beyond those of weight. Sometimes they have long-term breathing problems. You may notice sensory deficits, and they may also show some skills a little later than other babies. Most will catch up, but it is important to observe such babies carefully. Developmental information from the adult caring for the infant can be essential, because the baby may need special support.

MALE–FEMALE VARIATION

There are minor differences at this stage between the development of boys and the development of girls. Girls tend to grow slightly faster and acquire vocalization skills slightly earlier than boys. The differences at this stage are extremely small and will probably be unnoticeable among a small group of infants in a child-care centre.

Studies have shown that adults respond in distinctly different ways to male and female infants. You may see babies as young as 3 to 6 months experiencing treatment according to their gender. Girls are sometimes treated more sensitively than boys. Boys' cries tend to be responded to less quickly. Ideally, you will not see this type of treatment. Caregivers may use language and display distinct expectations in accordance with the infant's gender. To treat children equitably, you must be sensitive to this issue. Avoid responding to boys and girls purely on the basis of whether they are girls or boys.

▶ Developmental Alerts

You will see developmental variations in every baby. As an educator, you are responsible for supporting development and identifying possible concerns if they arise. Although your task does not involve making a diagnosis, your observations can be very helpful and lead to the appropriate supports. Avoid making assumptions about the reasons for differences, but always respond if you think there might be a developmental concern.

During or at the end of this period of development, you may observe some things that could indicate a cause for concern and the need for further assessment and referral. These include:

- uneven weight increase
- prolonged food refusal
- too rapid or slow an increase in head circumference
- lack of response to facial expressions
- no smile
- lack of interest in visual stimuli
- staring without response to stimuli
- little excitement for people
- prolonged periods of sleep without alert phases
- eyes not converging on objects
- lack of vocalizations
- prolonged periods of crying without response to comforting
- lack of crying
- not being startled by loud sounds
- not turning head toward sound
- not following moving object within expected field of vision
- not grasping small objects put into hand
- not reaching for objects
- head lolling (leaning or rolling without control)
- asymmetrical appearance
- continuing rounded back (does not sit supported)

- failure to use hand and mouth for sensory discovery
- no anticipatory behaviours (e.g., for feeding)

▶ Health Concerns

A few health issues apply particularly to infants of this age. Teething, ear infections, viruses, coughs, colds, and other common health concerns are usually the cause of the problem, but any significant change in behaviour or health status should be documented. These changes may have a variety of causes, which can be identified by a health professional. A baby's presentation of any of the following signs and symptoms should be reported to the parents:

- refusal to feed
- regression from previously acquired skills
- unformed or offensive stools or diarrhea
- rashes or flaky skin
- bumps, bruises, or new marks on the skin
- soreness of the skin in the diaper area
- soreness of the mouth or white coating on the tongue
- crying without taking comfort
- disturbed sleep pattern
- colour change of any part of the body
- runny nose
- difficulty breathing; coughing and/or wheezing
- fever (take temperature with a thermometer)
- sunken or bulging fontanels
- seizures (convulsions)
- unconsciousness or partial consciousness
- vomiting
- bleeding from any part of the body
- swollen glands in neck or groin
- reaction to immunization, food, or new material

All accidents must be documented and reported to parents. Any breathing difficulty, significant bleeding, loss of consciousness, choking, convulsion, or other significant symptom should receive an immediate first-aid response and referral to a qualified medical practitioner.

At around 3 months, some babies experience tummy pain that is distressing and causes them to stretch out their legs until rigid and cry angrily. There are differing medical explanations for this and many home remedies. Any treatment must be checked with the parents—frequently you will find that they have developed strategies to cope. A parent might take the baby and safely put him in a secure restraint in the car; the ride tends to be calming. You cannot do this as a centre-based caregiver, but as an alternative you might try carrying the baby in a sling, walking with him on the hip, or laying him in a baby carriage and going for a walk. The rocking motion can calm the baby.

The sharp pains—from colic or other digestive problems—should be attended to by a doctor if they persist. Mention your concerns to the parents promptly; they may already have experienced the problem during the night. Gently rubbing the baby's tummy and keeping him warm often seems to help. Some parents like to offer warm, rather than cold, fluids and burp the baby to ease the gas. You might follow the parents' strategies.

THE FLOOR

To most adults, the floor is simply for walking on, often in shoes that have been worn outside. Yet young infants are often put on the floor to play. There are three issues to be considered here: hygiene, temperature, and safety.

- *Hygiene:* Adults must not wear street shoes in rooms where infants are on the floor at any time, even on a blanket or rug. The risk of infection is too high. Slippers, socks, or "house shoes" can be worn if they are clean. Outdoor shoes should be left outside the infant rooms.
- *Temperature:* The floor can be cold, and the infant's ability to regulate his temperature is poor, so check that he is warm enough. A child-care planner might consider installing under-floor heating.
- *Vulnerability:* When infants are on the floor, they should not be in a position where adults have to climb over them or pass things above them. Particularly risky are hot foods or liquids such as tea or coffee. These should not be consumed in the infant room.

▶ Signs of Potential Neglect or Abuse

Very occasionally, the caregiver might come across signs that raise real and immediate concerns for an infant. Suspected abuse or neglect is a difficult issue, and the caregiver must be aware of many considerations. You should monitor all signs of potential abuse and document them carefully, but you must not judge or diagnose the problem. Obvious symptoms can be responded to quickly, but other signs may be much harder to decipher. Be aware that a sign that seems to point to abuse or neglect could just as easily have another explanation. Inadequate levels of supervision, medical treatment, nutrition, or protection may constitute neglect, but these may be difficult to distinguish from accidents, faulty decision-making, poverty, or different values.

This is not to minimize the possibility of encountering real neglect or abuse. Remember that neglect or abuse can happen in any type of family or any social or economic status. At this age, the baby is especially vulnerable to shaking, which can cause brain damage. Any behavioural changes, bruises, marks, or other concerns must be documented and responded to if unexplained.

Neglect may be more difficult to observe than some of the more obvious outward signs of physical abuse. When a baby's needs are not met, there may be no physical sign other than a lack of developmental progress. Yet, as we have seen earlier, there can be many reasons for such a lack of progress, many of which are not due to neglect. However, in some cases, it may reflect a "failure to thrive," which is caused by emotional harm (Spitz, 1946; Sameroff and Chandler, 1975). Failure to thrive is a condition where inadequate human contact and absence of attachments leads to physical decline (the baby stops or slows down feeding, the child becomes apathetic and disinclined to move or play).

As noted in earlier chapters, in all cases of suspected abuse or neglect the protocol of the individual child-care centre should be followed and any cause for concern must be reported to the local child protection agency.

▶ Everyday Safety Issues

Infants at this stage must be supervised at all times when they are awake and closely monitored at sleep and rest times. Their vulnerability stems from their inability to anticipate, recognize, or move away from danger. An infant at this stage is completely dependent upon adults. He can attempt to grasp things within his reach, but this constitutes an additional potential hazard. Since after grasping an object the baby will likely take it up to his mouth, caregivers have to exercise particular caution.

For infants at 3 to 6 months, caregivers should always:

- Lay the infant on his back to sleep.
- Ensure cleanliness in all elements of infant care, hygiene, and food safety.
- Use car seats that are appropriate for the age and weight of the infant and make sure the infant is secured in the car seat in accordance with the manufacturer's instructions.

- Make sure that an infant cannot roll off the surface onto which he is placed.
- Choose items big enough to prevent choking.
- Make sure that the area around the baby's position on the floor is free from obstacles or harmful objects.
- See that there is an appropriate amount of space between crib bars, so that the baby does not get his head stuck between them.
- Avoid pillows and large stuffed toys that could cause suffocation.
- Carefully watch the infant when he is in a lay-back seat, so that he does not fall forward and that the chair does not slide off a surface.
- Closely supervise all play with food, water, or messy materials.
- Keep one hand on the baby at all times during diaper changing.
- Be sure that the infant is collected by the person identified by the parent.
- Check that environments are relatively soft, to reduce likelihood of injury.
- Avoid ties on soothers or any clothing with ribbons or strings that could choke an infant.
- Use a harness or fitted restraint in any seat or stroller to prevent falling forward.
- Check all equipment for its stability and appropriate use.

Maintaining a balance between a hygienic environment and allowing exploration, and between protection from risks and careful risk-taking, poses a challenge for adults. Here, the sensory advantages of young babies becoming aware of each other and their surroundings as they play in the fall leaves outweigh concerns about children playing on the ground.

- Offer puréed food and avoid food that could cause choking.
- Hold an infant while feeding him or, if necessary, place him in a chair (i.e., avoid propping bottles).
- Avoid microwave heating of formula, which may scald the baby.

▶ Starting Points for Response

RESPONSIVE CAREGIVING

The infant looks to the adult to provide what she wants and needs, as a trusting relationship, one based on love, emerges. Social smiles may indicate secure attachments. Responding to the infant's cues remains the highest priority for caregiving. Body language and facial expressions may provide useful hints to help us understand the baby. These will have evolved into more complex patterns that adults need to be able to read. Compared with those given at earlier stages, infants' cries have a wider range of meaning. Their sound production is more differentiated and therefore more likely to send messages. Their body control has increased, and their bodily responses can be linked with likes or dislikes and positive or negative responses. Entering the two-way dance of communication is essential for social interaction. The adult has to tune in to the infant as the baby tunes in to the adult. Reciprocal communication builds the foundation for later language learning and more complex social communications.

SUPPORTIVE GUIDANCE

Enter the moment with the baby and find experiences where there can be shared meanings. The baby needs to receive loving care and continuity for emotional growth attachments and the development of self. This type of care requires carefully supported transitions between the adults responsible for the baby. Multiple attachments can form if the child is exposed to several adults, but support is best offered in such a way that the same people are with the child each day. A primary caregiver model can be particularly supportive at this stage. Under such a model, the infant is in a small group of babies who receive care from the same person or people each day.

Meeting the baby's psychological needs requires supporting her through the processes of separation and individuation. She needs firm attachments to ensure that her sense of oneness develops. Continuity is essential for emotional well-being.

FACILITATING DEVELOPMENT

At this stage, babies are still entirely egocentric, and their focus is on ensuring that their own needs are met. A baby finds her place in her family and learns that she is loved when her basic needs are met and she receives the attention she craves. Adults can support her development by being there and providing what the infant needs at that time. She needs to have the opportunity to play with adults, to move, to hear voices that are directed to her, to be in an environment in which she is accepted and responded to rapidly, and to be propped up so she can see more of the world. Some sensory stimulation can be found in everyday experiences. A baby needs the time, space, reciprocal communication, and opportunity to discover people and objects. Such discovery will improve the handle she is beginning to have on her world.

HOLISTIC RESPONSE

Activities 6.1 and 6.2 encourage a holistic response to infants. Activity 6.1 suggests ways of engaging in the experience of babies at this stage and extending your interactions with them. Activity 6.2 (page 159) helps you observe each infant and to develop activities that are targeted to individual interests and skill levels.

Activity 6.1

Responding to the Changing Needs of Infants at 3 to 6 Months
The exciting skills that are emerging show you that there is also new thinking going on. Using the following model, implement an activity for a baby of this stage. Depending on her interest and response, modify what you do. If the baby isn't ready for peek-a-boo, try an eye-contact game.

Activity 6.1

Responding to Changing Needs of Infants at 3 to 6 Months

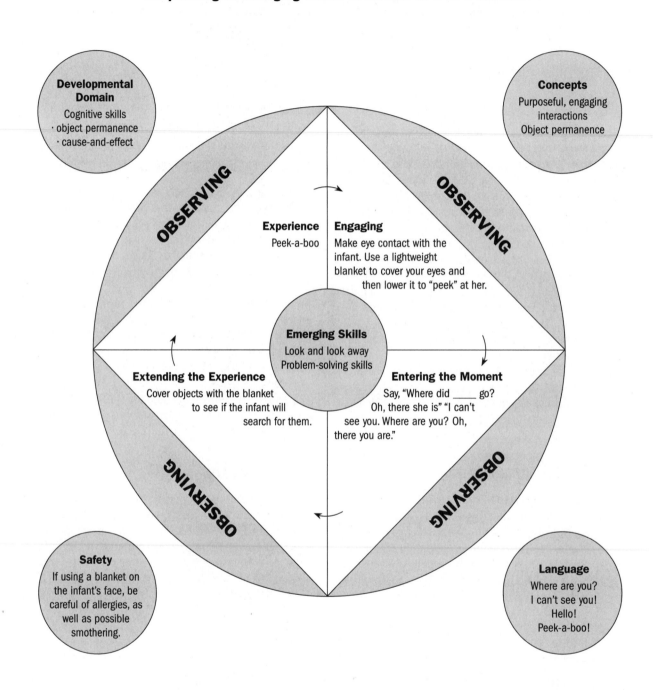

Activity 6.2

Creating Responsive Curriculum for Infants at 3 to 6 Months

When you combine the social skills and the baby's physical capabilities you might see how the domains interact. Design and implement an activity based on the baby's emerging physical and social skills. Review the chart for some behaviours you might see.

Developmental Domain	Observation of Emerging Skills (Things You See)	Responsive Experience/Activity
Physical Skills	– lifting head while on stomach – following objects with eyes and turning head – rolling over – reaching for objects – grasping objects – bearing some weight on legs in standing position when arms are held – sitting without support – turning in direction of voices	Allow baby to spend more time in a propped-up position, giving her a better view of the world. Monitor the safety of the environment constantly. Continually re-evaluate his developing skills. Provide a variety of grasping/reaching items. Pass multiple toys to the baby to encourage him to switch hands.
Cognitive skills/language and communication	– paying attention to small objects – laughing out loud – following objects; turning head in direction of the path – smiling spontaneously – vocalizing some vowel–consonant sounds – grasping for objects presented to him	Talk to the baby as you move around the room. Play peek-a-boo and other hiding games. Provide wrist and foot rattles to help him locate his body parts. Respond to his verbal responses/initiations. Imitate vocalizations and facial gestures.
Social/emotional skills	– laughing out loud – smiling purposefully at reflection in mirror – looking to your face after seeing your reflection in a mirror (may appear confused by the "two yous")	Interact frequently. Name body parts. Talk to him as you move around the room. Be sensitive to his individual cues and needs. Play peek-a-boo games. Use his name and yours while speaking to him.

The following section offers a series of experiences that might be planned for infants at 3 to 6 months. Some babies are more responsive than others to new experiences, so introduce them sensitively when it appears that the baby is alert. Rather than try to get her attention when she is involved with something else, try to find the right moment when she seems to want activity but has not found something by herself. Distracting a baby's attention when she is engaged with something meaningful to her is not a good idea.

Try out one or more of the experiences, and extend them if she seems to be ready. Frequently repeating the same pleasurable experience is better than jumping to things that are completely new. This, of course, depends upon the baby's temperament. Unlike using some manufactured toys, the materials used in these experiences are not safe for play when the baby is alone. Not only supervision, but complete involvement with the baby, is necessary throughout the experiences.

Responding to Changing Needs

Infants at 3 to 6 Months

EXPERIENCE 1

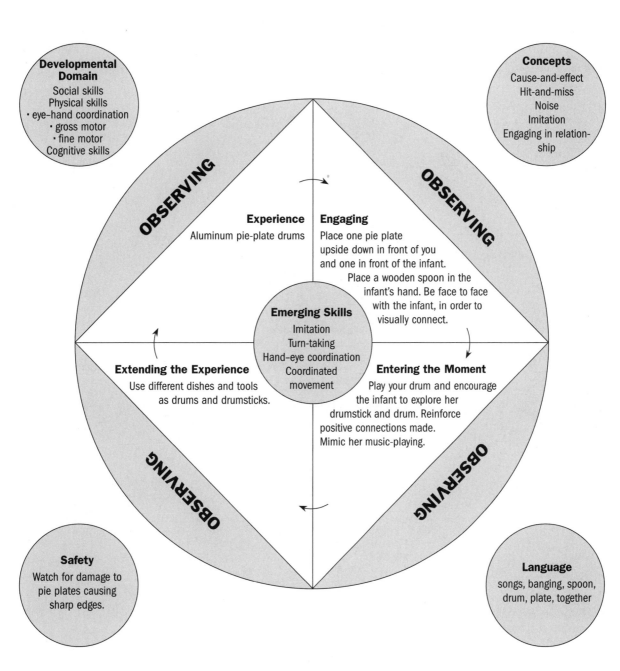

Developmental Domain
Social skills
Physical skills
· eye–hand coordination
· gross motor
· fine motor
Cognitive skills

Concepts
Cause-and-effect
Hit-and-miss
Noise
Imitation
Engaging in relationship

OBSERVING

OBSERVING

Experience
Aluminum pie-plate drums

Engaging
Place one pie plate upside down in front of you and one in front of the infant. Place a wooden spoon in the infant's hand. Be face to face with the infant, in order to visually connect.

Emerging Skills
Imitation
Turn-taking
Hand–eye coordination
Coordinated movement

Extending the Experience
Use different dishes and tools as drums and drumsticks.

Entering the Moment
Play your drum and encourage the infant to explore her drumstick and drum. Reinforce positive connections made. Mimic her music-playing.

OBSERVING

OBSERVING

Safety
Watch for damage to pie plates causing sharp edges.

Language
songs, banging, spoon, drum, plate, together

Responding to Changing Needs

Infants at 3 to 6 Months

EXPERIENCE 2

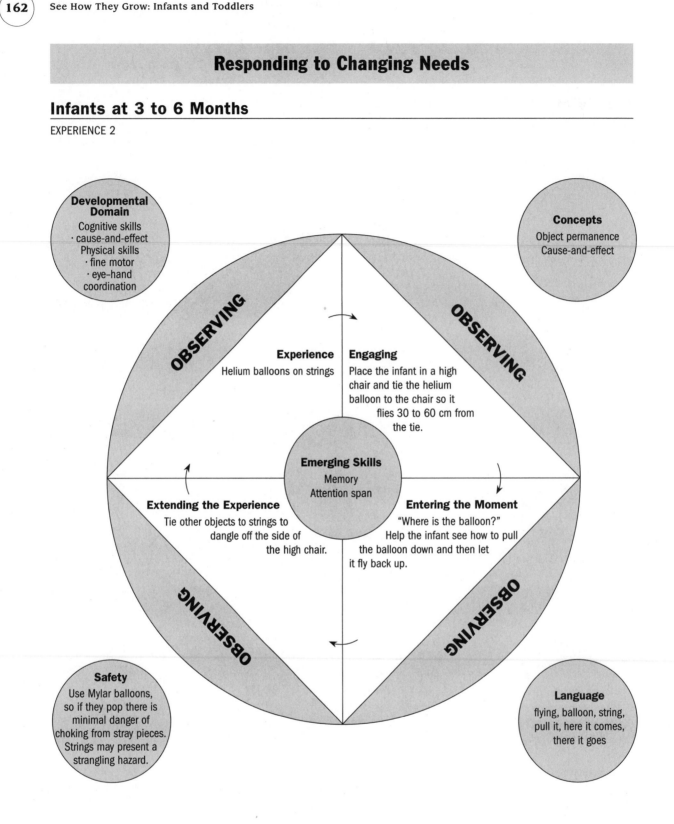

Developmental Domain
Cognitive skills
· cause-and-effect
Physical skills
· fine motor
· eye–hand coordination

Concepts
Object permanence
Cause-and-effect

OBSERVING

OBSERVING

Experience
Helium balloons on strings

Engaging
Place the infant in a high chair and tie the helium balloon to the chair so it flies 30 to 60 cm from the tie.

Emerging Skills
Memory
Attention span

Extending the Experience
Tie other objects to strings to dangle off the side of the high chair.

Entering the Moment
"Where is the balloon?" Help the infant see how to pull the balloon down and then let it fly back up.

OBSERVING

OBSERVING

Safety
Use Mylar balloons, so if they pop there is minimal danger of choking from stray pieces. Strings may present a strangling hazard.

Language
flying, balloon, string, pull it, here it comes, there it goes

Responding to Changing Needs

Infants at 3 to 6 Months

EXPERIENCE 3

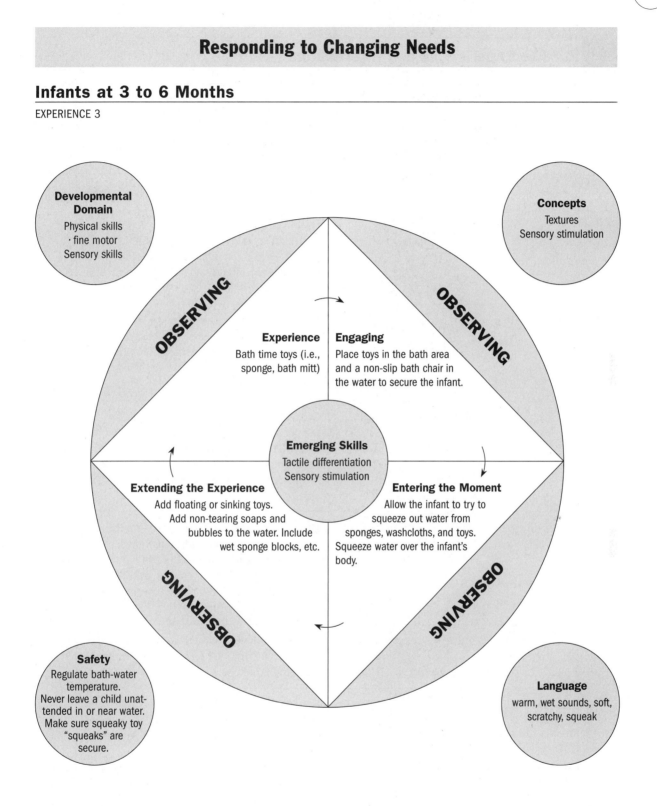

Developmental Domain
Physical skills
· fine motor
Sensory skills

Concepts
Textures
Sensory stimulation

OBSERVING

OBSERVING

Experience
Bath time toys (i.e., sponge, bath mitt)

Engaging
Place toys in the bath area and a non-slip bath chair in the water to secure the infant.

Emerging Skills
Tactile differentiation
Sensory stimulation

Extending the Experience
Add floating or sinking toys. Add non-tearing soaps and bubbles to the water. Include wet sponge blocks, etc.

Entering the Moment
Allow the infant to try to squeeze out water from sponges, washcloths, and toys. Squeeze water over the infant's body.

OBSERVING

OBSERVING

Safety
Regulate bath-water temperature.
Never leave a child unattended in or near water. Make sure squeaky toy "squeaks" are secure.

Language
warm, wet sounds, soft, scratchy, squeak

Further Experiences and Interactions

Further Experiences	Interactions
Rolling side to side	Move toys around to the infant's sides to encourage rolling over (front to back first, then back to front).
Propping-up games (Pat-a-cake)	Use pillows, quilts, rolled-up towels, etc., to prop the infant into a sitting position. Legs should be spread apart and the props arranged securely so that the infant is supported. Hold the infant's hands while making eye contact, and sing "Pat-a-cake" or other finger plays.
Transferring objects in hands	Use stacking blocks or cubes and sit the infant upright (use props if necessary). Talk with the infant about the block or cube and encourage her to grasp, hold, mouth, and manipulate the toy.
Activity gyms (strollers and floor models)	Describe the objects as the infant grabs, swipes, holds, pulls, and squeezes the toys. The infant could lie under, be propped to a sitting position in front of, or sit unassisted at the gyms. Try to make eye level consistent.
Dangling items from adult clothing (human mobiles)	Use elastic strips (and safety pins on the adult end) to attach rattles, plush toys, bells, etc., to your shirt. The objects will dangle off your clothes while you interact with the infant during routine times (diapering, etc.) as well as playing times.
Balancing games (muscle-strengthening)	Support the infant's hands and arms while she attempts to pull herself into sitting or standing positions.
Horsey rides	Support the infant under the arms while she sits astride one of your knees. Bounce your knee and sing galloping songs while making eye contact with the infant.
Imitation of babblings	If the infant appears to want to interact with you, imitate her vocalizations, pausing to allow her to take turns. Introduce new syllables when it is your turn to lead.

Further Experiences	Interactions
Book-reading	Hold the infant in your lap so that both of you can read the book together. Describe the pictures, point to the contents, and allow the infant to "read" herself. Reinforce her vocalizations.
Rhythms	While singing songs and reciting poems and finger plays, lightly tap the infant's legs or arms in rhythm to the rhyme.
Have conversations	While vocalizing your activities to the infant ("I'm heating your lunch now," etc.), pause and allow the infant to respond with babbles. Then proceed.
Hide-and-seek	Use toys, rattles, and plush and lightweight blankets. Cover the toys with the blanket in the child's view. Encourage her to find the "lost" items. (You may want to begin by covering the item only partially and then progress from there.)
Fishing	Use plastic infant chains to attach rattles, toys, etc., to the high chair. As the infant inevitably drops the toys, encourage her to grasp the chain and pull it back up.
Balls (varying sizes)	Roll balls back and forth between the infant and yourself. Encourage the infant in any attempt to roll the ball.
Pacifiers and other mouthing objects (teething rings)	Provide these items at times of distress to help the infant with self-comforting techniques. Continue talking calmly and soothingly to the infant during these emotional times, describing the experience.

Continue responding to her cues of distress. Continue vocalizing all of your interaction activities with the infant. Continue making eye and physical contact while engaging and interacting with the infant. Continue smiling and having fun while enjoying this period of her life!

Responsive Guidance for Infants Aged 3 to 6 Months

Age/Stage: Infants 3 to 6 Months

Situation	Response
• "Mac is always rolling over when I try to change his diaper. How can I get him to stop?" • "Is it ever too soon to prop my baby into a sitting position?" • "Lani is always pushing with her legs and attempting to stand. Isn't she too young for this yet?" • "Charlie can use a sipper cup to drink water."	**Developmental Issue:** **New Physical Skills** Providing plenty of opportunities for infants to expand their repertoire of physical skills is beneficial to the child if she appears ready for the experience. Watch for infants' cues to indicate their readiness to develop new skills. Only they know for sure if it is too early. Be prepared for achievement of quick developmental milestones. Help the child attain these skills while providing a safe and nurturing environment.
• Jill makes eye contact with adults when they are speaking to her, and then vocalizes something when they pause. • Nicky seems to "tune out" when adults talk around him. • Maryann seems to respond with squeals or whimpers when placed in certain situations.	**Developmental Issue:** **Talking with the Infant** Infants in this range are perched on the verge of language development and are experiencing communication in a new light. Words are beginning to have meaning and infant responses to them are beginning to be purposeful. Both receptive and expressive language are undergoing transformations. A number of caregiving strategies will benefit the infant's language acquisition. Speaking slowly, clearly, positively, and succinctly to infants using simple words will prove to be advantageous for both the adult and the infants. Allow infants the opportunity to reflect on your words and give them time to respond. Imitation and mimicking still assist in turn-taking rules that govern conversations.

▶ Summary

The emerging personhood of the baby is becoming obvious to all the adults in the infant's life. Individual personality, style, and response patterns are becoming clearly evident. Adults are likely to respond positively to the social smile that emerges during this stage. When a baby realizes that her smile engages adults, she will repeat it and use it to get attention. A happy baby is one whose cries are responded to quickly. This helps to build her trust in the key adults in her life. One or more attachments to an adult will aid in emotional development through the establishment of trust and in the emergence of a basic self-concept.

The dance of communication between a caregiver and a baby in this period is interesting to watch. There is a clear process of dialogue as both partners listen, watch, and wait. The infant's vocalizations will usually be more extensive in this period; the repertoire of sound production increases to cooing, happy sounds. Exposure to real language will gradually allow the infant to pass from undifferentiated sound production

Manufactured Toys and Play Materials for Infants 3 to 6 Months

Toy/Material	Uses	Group Care	Home
Rolling rattles, stroller rattles	Multi-functional noisemakers provide extra stimulation as the infant is required to manoeuvre the rattles in a number of ways.	√	√
Table top toys with suction cups	These toys allow the infant to grasp and manipulate their properties without loosening them.	√	√
Activity centres	Fine motor skills are developed by the pushing, pulling, popping, and playing involved with these centres.	√	√
Baby gyms	Sensory skills are stimulated by the sights and sounds that go with these adjustable playthings.	√	√
Mobiles	Use as stimulation while changing diapers, administering medications, etc.	√	√
Crib toys	Individual quieter times allow infants the opportunities to reflect and explore at their individual paces.		√
Soft/washable, sensory/sorter blocks	Infants poke, pull, and twist the patterns and delight in the sounds produced as they squeeze them.	√	√
squeeze toys	Small animals/cars/tools are mouthed and squeezed. They are easy to clean and comfortable to grasp.	√	√

to the sounds necessary to learn a particular language. Much of the infant's communication is through gestures, crying, gazing, and non-language sounds. There is a marked difference between receptive and expressive communication. She will usually find that adults respond to her needs by translating her cues. It is therefore essential for adults to be able to interpret all the signs that a baby is sending, not only her deliberate communications.

For the baby to thrive, she needs lots of physical contact, along with talking, singing, and other noises. Because she is not yet mobile, or even able to sit without much support, she is likely to enjoy seats that allow her a good view or to be held in such a way that she can see around her. Physical skills development is usually evident at this stage, in increased neck and back control, which leads to sitting. The baby's fine motor skills repertoire will be increasing; she may be able to release a grasp as well as hold on tightly to something in her hand. She can bring objects to her mouth and discover parts of her own body.

Interest in the environment is particularly evident at this time, although the baby can handle only those things that are within her reach. Everything is taken to the mouth for sensory exploration, so all toys and play materials must be clean. All kinds of sensory stimulation are necessary, but infants at this stage also need times of relaxation. Reading the signs of overstimulation is just as important as interpreting signs of boredom. Increased motor control, combined with sensory discovery, allows the infant to repeat and perfect some basic actions and add to her mental schemes.

▶ KEY TERMS

body language
ego
expressive language
intentional communication
language acquisition
motherese/parentese
object permanence
palmar grasp
people permanence
preferences
primary caregiver
primary circular reaction
receptive language
schemes
secondary circular reaction
secure attachments
secure base relationship
sensory-motor stage
separation
separation anxiety
separation–individuation
shared orbit
specific smile
symbiosis
vocalization

▶ DISCUSSION QUESTIONS

1. How might you handle a situation where a mother is reluctant to leave her infant with you?
2. What kind of stimulation might be appropriate for infants at 3 to 6 months if their development is fairly typical of the stage?
3. If you were to observe bruises on an infant's legs when you changed her diaper, what might you do?
4. When a mother wants you to give sugared drinks to her 5-month-old baby, what response would be appropriate?
5. How do you deliver a positive response to someone who says that your work with infants is "baby-sitting"?

▶ ADDITIONAL RESOURCES

▶ Further Reading

Caplan, F. (1995). *The First Twelve Months of Life: Your Baby's Growth Month by Month.* New York, NY: Bantam.
Fenichel, E., and L. Eggbeer. (1990). *Preparing Practitioners to Work with Infants, Toddlers and Their Families: Issues and Recommendations.* Washington, DC: Zero to Three.
Greenspan, S., and N.T. Greenspan. (1989). *The Essential Partnership: How Parents and Children Can Meet the Emotional Challenges of Infancy and Childhood.* New York, NY: Penguin.
Hyson, M. (1994). *The Emotional Development of Young Children: Building an Emotion-Centered Curriculum.* New York, NY: Teachers College Press.
Kaplan, L. (1978). *Oneness and Separateness.* New York, NY: Touchstone/Simon & Schuster.
Pimento, B., and D. Kernested. (2000). *Healthy Foundations in Child Care.* 2nd ed. Scarborough, ON: Nelson.
Snow, C.W. (1998). *Infant Development.* 2nd ed. Englewood Cliffs, NJ: Prentice Hall.
Wilson, L.C., L. Douville Watson, and M. Watson. (1995). *Infants and Toddlers: Curriculum and Teaching.* 3rd ed. Albany, NY: Delmar.

▶ Useful Videos

Getting in Tune: Creating Nurturing Relationships with Infants & Toddlers. (1992). Sacramento, CA: California Department of Education.
  Description: 24 minutes; study guide.
  Series: Program for Infant/Toddler Caregivers.
Exploring First Feelings. (1985). Washington, DC: Institute for Mental Health Initiatives.
  Description: 21 minutes.
The Separation-Individuation Process. Van Nuys, CA: Child Development Media.
  Description: an 84-minute, 3-part video depicting the separation-individuation process:
  Part I: "Symbiosis and the Differentiation Subphase: 0 to 8 Months."
  Part II: "The Early Practicing Subphase Proper: 8 to15 Months."
  Part III: "The Rapprochement Subphase and On the Way to Object Constancy: 13 to 36 Months."

CHAPTER 7

Me and You: Infants at 6 to 9 Months

Many babies are introduced to child care between the ages of 6 and 9 months. Group care can be warm, responsive, and individualized.

Learning Outcomes

After reading and studying this chapter, you should be able to:

- identify the observable characteristics of development of infants at the 6-to-9-month stage
- explain the significance of behaviours of infants from 6 to 9 months in a developmental context
- recognize the developmental diversity of 6-to-9-month-old infants and discuss issues pertinent to this stage of development
- assess the development of infants in the 6-to-9-month stage
- respond to the health, safety, and development of 6-to-9-month-old infants with appropriate nurturance, activities, protection, and caregiving
- develop strategies to work with parents as partners in the care and education of their infants

"They really sit up and take notice of everything going on," said a student after her first week of work with infants. "They seem to watch you all the time and are incredibly smart in how they try to get your attention," she continued. "I didn't always know what they were thinking, but they made lots of connections. When I went to the refrigerator and got out a bottle of formula, one 7-month girl would get so excited. If the bottle wasn't for her I had to hide it."

Much of babies' learning is observational, as the student suggested. As well, their increasing awareness of the world and their part in it makes being with babies at this stage really exciting. When they are awake, they can pay attention to all sorts of things. It's important to make all those learning experiences very positive.

Students notice that being with infants at this stage is different from working with younger babies. Their personalities are more clearly observable. They seem to respond in accordance with their temperament style, and they demand that you pay attention to them.

Their capacity to learn is obvious, as they examine everything that they can reach. Their own bodies are also a source of interest, and they may spend time finding out what their bodies can do. This is an essentially physical time. Infants enjoy the effect they can have on things and people, and will repeat many actions with objects. They enjoy the surprise of a playful exchange with adults and will do the same thing with them many times over for pure enjoyment.

Infants at this stage have adapted to their caregivers in a more sociable way. They like to spend a lot of time with adults. They enjoy interactions and will imitate people in subtle ways. Particular adults become important to the infant, and they may become distressed when a familiar adult leaves. Relationships are made with particular adults, so it becomes increasingly important to have the same people caring for the baby.

▶ What to Look For

PHYSICAL DEVELOPMENT

Growth

At the beginning of this stage, many babies will have doubled their birth weight, although weight gain patterns can vary considerably. Then the rate of growth slows down slightly, but the first year of life is the time of most rapid increase in size (Illingworth, 1992). The usual weight gain is about half a kilogram (one pound) per month (Allen and Marotz, 2003), so at this stage the baby may weigh between 6 and 10 kg (15–21 pounds) (Stoppard, 1983), depending upon age, birth weight, sex, body type, and general health. A fairly steady gradual increase in weight is more important than reaching an "ideal" weight. Sometimes growth slows if the baby has been unwell, but the baby usually catches up quite quickly. Chubby babies used to be considered healthy, because they had weight to fall back on if they became sick, but we now know that overweight babies tend to retain that pattern. Slight chubbiness is not a reason to reduce the fat content of the baby's diet. The baby needs some fats to increase neurological functioning. The baby is likely to be making the transition to some solid but puréed foods by this stage.

Gains in length and height drop off slowly, but growth remains more significant than in later years. This may mean growth of 1.2 cm (½ inch) per month (Allen and Marotz, 2003). At this stage, babies may vary in height from 62 to 71 cm (24 to 28 inches) (Stoppard, 1983).

The circumference of the baby's head and the chest are roughly equal (Allen and Marotz, 2003). The baby's body proportions are noticeably changing. The head becomes smaller in proportion to the body as the body grows considerably more rapidly than the head. Brain development is not dependent on significant size increase of the baby's head.

For some babies, teething is observable by a flushed appearance on the cheeks and increased drooling. The first tooth may come through at about 6 months (Berk, 2000), but this varies considerably. A few babies are born with teeth; others will not have any teeth until after their first birthday.

Gross Motor Skills

The slow change in body proportions, along with increase in muscular control, allows the baby to gain more bodily control. At about 6 months, most babies are able to sit unsupported for short periods. The length of time the baby can sit up gradually increases over the next few months. By 9 months the baby will probably be able to remain sitting while leaning forward to pick up an object and be able to roll from a lying position to a sitting position or vice versa (Furuno et al., 1993).

Usually, rolling from front to back comes before back-to-front rolling (Sheridan, 1997). However, at 6 months, a baby lying on her back may roll over quite easily; when this happens she may repeat it over and over for pleasure (Biasella, 1996). You may also see early attempts at **crawling**. If she finds herself on her front, she may pull herself up on her extended arms and will later attempt a "commando crawl" using her arms to move forward. Gradually her legs will gain control. She will then be able to propel herself backward or forward in a more proficient crawl (Allen and Marotz, 2003).

In recent years it has been noticed that babies are altering their crawling behaviours. This is likely due to having them sleep on their backs, which is essential for their safety and protection from the possibility of sudden infant death syndrome (SIDS). The Back to Sleep campaign has been successful in that caregivers are following its advice. However, having babies lie on their backs can mean that they do not gain the muscle control of either their arms or legs that is necessary for crawling. Observational evidence suggests that some babies are crawling later and even more babies are bypassing the crawling stage entirely. A few babies will be ready to demonstrate some sort of crawl by 9 months, but do not imagine there is anything wrong if the baby doesn't crawl for several months—or never crawls at all. Incidentally, the peak period for SIDS is over by the 6-to-9 month stage, but the possibility remains for some months to come. Following the Back to Sleep policy is necessary even when babies can roll over.

Some babies do not crawl in the usual way: they may do a crab crawl, moving sideways, or they may not crawl at all, finding that they can shuffle in a sitting position to get from place to place. Toward the end of this stage, the baby may become mobile and it is noticeable that her legs are gaining control, including strength and directioning; this comes from lots of practice at kicking.

If the baby is held in a standing position, she is likely to push her feet down and bounce, taking most of the weight on her feet (Furuno et al., 1993). In time, her foot movements will become more controlled, and she will step on each foot alternately (Sheridan, 1997). Opinion is divided over the advisability of encouraging a child to stand before she does so independently. At 9 months, few infants can lower themselves from standing without dropping to the ground in an uncontrolled way. No long-term advantage exists in encouraging babies to acquire skills ahead of a natural progression. Some competitive adults want their babies to be developmentally advanced and associate early physical skills with improved all-round development. Evidence suggests that "pushing" is more likely to be detrimental.

Fine Motor Skills

Much of the development of the fine motor skills of an infant at this stage is displayed in her ability to grasp objects. At 6 months, a useful but unrefined grasp is possible. This **palmar grasp** involves the whole hand. Practice and deliberate attempts to reach for smaller objects lead to an **intermediate grasp**, which uses the fingers in a more defined way (Illingworth, 1992). Intermediate grasp, a grasp that involves the whole hand with some degree of thumb–finger opposition, may be observed in some infants. But it is unusual for infants at this stage to be able to use a **pincer grasp**, with the fingers and thumb in true opposition. In any group of infants, we see that developmental patterns vary from one infant to another. By 9 months, the infant may use her fingers more precisely. In addition to developments in grasping, she may use her index finger to point.

Initially, the infant spends time looking closely at items she picks up. She will frequently play games that involve picking up objects or banging together items held in both hands. Releasing items from the hand presents greater challenges than grasping them. If a toy drops from her hand, she is likely to watch it rather than try to pick it up. This might be because she is interested in the act of dropping things, but it is more likely that when it goes out of sight it is also out of mind. Yet by 9 months, the infant will drop and pick up things if interested (Sheridan, 1997). At about 8 months, the infant may reach for an item that is partially hidden, displaying the beginning of a sense of **object permanence**. At 9 months, she may attempt to find something that has disappeared from view. It is interesting that with many infants **people permanence**, remembering that people continue to exist when they are out of sight, occurs before object permanence.

Outdoor discovery can be even more exciting than indoor play and can help the child to develop both gross and fine motor skills, such as the grasping shown here.

COGNITIVE DEVELOPMENT

Senses and Perception

Vision

Infants at this stage are **visually insatiable** (Sheridan, 1997)—they cannot have too much visual information; they spend much of their waking time looking around them and taking in a lot of what they see. The infant's visual acuity is improving, and she begins to have the ability to see across a room. In time, she will focus on distant objects (Furuno et al., 1987). At 6 months, the baby's vision is not yet clear and focused at a distance as far as across a room. During this stage, her long-distance focus becomes sharper. Vision continues to improve as the infant matures. The eyes move in unison (Sheridan, 1997), and the baby can follow moving objects without turning her head. She is still interested in looking at faces and patterns.

In this stage of development, the infant usually relates size to distance (Deiner, 1997). She consequently understands that near objects look larger than the same object farther away. Depth perception has been studied using a visual cliff (Campos et al., 1970), an artificial construction involving a glass, or plexiglass, table with a surface that is split in two. On one side, the surface appears to be directly below the glass, while on the other the surface appears to drop several feet. Infants of 6 to 9 months will crawl across the "shallow" surface, but not the "deep" one. This indicates that they have a sense of depth.

The attachments that the baby has with particular adults are seen not only in physically close relationships; now she will look around for the adult's face to check in that everything is all right. This **social referencing** is particularly noticeable when the baby is confronted with something new—she seeks emotional support through eye contact. The combination of improvements in her visual acuity allow the baby to widen her perception of her world: she gets to look at objects and people both close up and a little farther away. Having depth perception and generally improved vision allows the baby to see her environment and manipulate objects within it.

Infants of 6 to 9 months may understand that images found in books and pictures represent real objects, but they may prefer to look at the "real" three-dimensional aspects of an object rather than a picture of it (Fogel, 1997). The same applies to television images.

That a baby can be interested in the visual patterns that a television screen presents does not mean the screen provides her with significant learning. First-hand experience is far more important. She needs the knowledge about the properties of materials that comes from interacting with concrete (real) objects. To a limited extent, babies know that images represent real objects. Adults might therefore think that babies learn through watching television or videos. However, her interest is little deeper than being engaged by staring at a revolving mobile—interesting at first, but boring after a while. She cannot follow an abstract story line, either. Also, the baby has no control over the image and cannot remove herself from it, except by looking away from the screen. We need to ensure that the baby doesn't experience sensory overload. Watching television may even be damaging because of that lack of control; the baby must learn how to interact with her environment and experience the effect of her actions—TV doesn't allow this.

Hearing

The 6-to-9-month infant has increasingly good auditory discrimination, that is, the ability to hear sounds and tell them apart. Human voices are preferred over any other sound, and familiar voices are listened to most carefully.

One interesting experiment found that infants in this age period could recognize the differences between different short tunes (Trehub, Bull, and Thorp, 1984). The amount of experience of different sounds seems to make a difference. The greater the exposure to particular sounds or music, the more likely the baby is to remember the sound. Clearly, sound differentiation depends on memory as well as auditory acuity.

When auditory and visual stimuli are presented simultaneously, the baby will more likely pay attention to the sound than to the image. This indicates that auditory perception is the dominant sense of the two at this stage. That said, it is also clear that **multi-modal stimulation**—that is, stimulation of several senses—holds greater interest than stimulation of only one sense.

Interesting research outcomes have some application to our work with infants. Ongoing research into infants' multi-modal sensory stimulation (Lickliter & Bahrick, 2000) suggests that the typical **uni-modal stimulation** approach to sensory stimulation that is favoured by many infant caregivers may be insufficient. (This refers to stimulating the baby's vision, hearing, or other senses separately.) Although uni-modal sensory stimulation may enable the baby to focus more deliberately on one type of sensory information, it lacks the simultaneous processing possibilities of multi-modal stimulation. There is some suggestion that multi-modal stimulation supports learning more successfully because the dual or multiple channels reinforce one another. The brain's neurological pathways strengthen as they receive multiple sources of sensory input. In the world of the adult, experience is multi-modal. Adults hear, see, and so forth all at once. Early learning experiences may prepare infants for that world. As they grow up, children find themselves confronted with technologies that require multi-modal processing and may be in classrooms that are busy places, with many sources of stimulation bombarding them. Younger children might be on track to deal with this if they learn skills in excluding superfluous sensory information—learn to tune out what they don't need and focus on what is most relevant. But excluding uni-modal learning is probably a mistake, because attention to detail, conscious focus on specific sensory data, and refinement may all be necessary for particular skill acquisition. Learning to play a musical instrument or becoming a visual artist might depend on focus on the use of one sense and tuning out other sensory channels. This might seem distant from infant experience, but early artistic expression is found in the early months and years, and the skills are rooted in early experience. Entering into the musical world of the infant, as well as providing materials for discovery, might be the earliest human experiences in art and music.

Touch

The skin remains a very sensitive organ through which the infant absorbs new tactile information. Handling objects with increasing skill enables the infant to learn about new textures and the feel of toys and other items. He will enjoy the sensory discovery of domestic objects, gaining increasing knowledge of their attributes. The mouth remains an important part of the body for taking in tactile information. Most objects find their way to the baby's mouth, but for purposes of feeling rather than tasting.

Taste

Infants may be fed their first solid foods at this time, although some babies may have been **weaned** somewhat earlier. Babies who experience a wide range of tastes early in life are more likely to accept a variety of foods. Nonetheless, adults should be cautious about offering the baby too wide a choice too quickly. Babies may perceive new tastes differently than adults do (Beauchamp, Cowart, and Morgan, 1986). Infants prefer some tastes to others and, of course, have individual preferences.

Giving babies solid food too early can be counterproductive, because their digestive systems are not ready to process anything but milk. At about 6 months, babies need more nutrients than can be supplied by mother's milk or infant formula.

Babies may dislike the taste of some foods, or react negatively to the smell of certain foods. If the baby does not like what is presented, remove the item and try it again later. The following points have been made by the Canadian Paediatric Society to help adults decide when solid foods can be offered.[1]

How can parents tell if their baby is ready for solid foods? If parents answer yes to most of the questions below, it is probably time to start solid foods:

> Does your baby drink breast milk or formula eagerly?
>
> Does your baby want more when the bottle is empty?
>
> Does your baby seem hungry earlier than usual?
>
> Does your baby sit up without support and have good control of her neck muscles?

Smell

Smell may play a part in establishing attachments (Lamb and Campos, 1982). Clearly, babies respond positively to smells associated with the adults they know well. Infants may withdraw and turn away from unpleasant odours, but their preferences are not the same as those of adults.

Sensory-Motor Intelligence

The baby's brain is capable to an amazing degree of acquiring, processing, and storing information. It is not surprising that babies tune out from time to time when they are in sensory overload! Much of the infant's time awake is spent taking in bits and pieces of information and trying to make sense of them with reference to what he already knows from previous experience. Increased ability to grasp, hold, and mouth objects, along with improved visual acuity, allows the baby to take some control of the sensory input.

Throughout infancy, the baby progresses through the substages of the **sensory-motor** period (see Appendix). Piaget (1952) offers insight into the typical

---

1. Canadian Paediatric Society (2002).

patterns of action and reaction that we can observe. At 6 to 9 months, the baby's abilities to see and move enlarge his world somewhat. He can see and touch more objects and has a broader experience of people. Some things in his world become predictable and he discerns some sequences. Certain actions from the adult bring responses from the baby ahead of what is actually happening. When experiences are enjoyable, he wants them to go on and on. Sequences of playful exchange between the infant and adult provide great satisfaction when they are repeated many times. The repetition reinforces neural pathways essential for learning. It is as though practice play lays down the foundations of learning. Just as adults do things like practise their golf swing or keyboard use repeatedly to improve skills, so does the infant, without any instruction!

New information is assimilated as the baby's senses send data to the brain. As this information is processed, and the baby compares, filters, and adds new parts to his existing **schemes**, the sensory input continues. Almost simultaneously, the infant goes through the **secondary circular reaction stage** (Piaget, 1952). The baby repeats many deliberate actions, particularly when they involve things around him. He varies his actions to bring about different responses. This recognition that particular actions bring about certain effects is called **cause-and-effect** learning.

This period is one of tremendous sensory input, as increased physical skills allow extended periods of discovery. New information is **assimilated** with previously absorbed information. The infant then goes through a process of **accommodation**, in which his existing patterns of thought change in accordance with the new information. The cycle of assimilation and accommodation is integral to his learning. Bits and pieces of information are gathered mentally to create schemes of understanding.

Although infants at this stage are remarkably open to sensory input, we must be careful not to over-stimulate them. Such overstimulation will likely only frustrate the baby and make her feel bombarded. She may even tune out too much, because her inner world is more peaceful and less frantic.

Box 7.1 deals with the issue of trying to hurry development. This is an issue that feeds into some adults' insecurities. They may want what they think is best, but their efforts backfire when they make an infant or child overly stressed. David Elkind (2001) strongly advocates for children's right to develop naturally without being harmed.

BOX 7.1

ISSUE: CAN WE HURRY DEVELOPMENT TO MAKE INFANTS SMARTER AND MORE COMPETENT?

We are more likely to slow down an infant's development than speed it up. Lack of knowledge about the infant's development and about the particular needs of infants can lead to reducing the possibility of the child reaching her potential. So it's more important that we support emerging skills and subtle changes, making sure that we don't miss something that is essential to the developmental process.

The best way of looking at this issue is to appreciate the complexities of early development and do everything possible to facilitate it. This means that we have to consider our role in supporting the process, but first we have to understand something about the child's potential.

Years ago, it was thought that a child's potential was completely determined at birth. We now know, as a result of neuroscientific research, that the child's potential is determined, to some extent, by his genetic inheritance, but this isn't an absolute. Potential can be considered to be somewhat plastic. Given the optimal circumstance for development, that potential can be stretched to some extent. For example, a child who has an average aptitude at something may do slightly better in an enriched environment. But most aspects of potential have a limit. An infant will not learn to walk at an earlier age because we encourage her to stand on her feet. These skills appear according to an inner maturational schedule.

Limited, short-term advantages have been observed in infants and toddlers who have been subjected to intensive programs, but these offer dubious benefits. In the case of toddlers who are taught to read, it has been found that advantages may be at the cost of other developmental

There is a fine line between providing optimal experiences and pushing the child. Sometimes putting undue pressure on a very young child or having expectations that are very high can have the opposite outcome.

So we have the power to limit children's development by failing to provide for all the child's needs. We have the responsibility to facilitate development and provide an optimal environment, appreciating how competent the infant and toddler really is. But we won't be successful if we try to push the child, have overly high expectations, or provide developmentally inappropriate experiences; these are more likely to be counterproductive.

A number of well-known educators have expressed their concern about pressuring young children. The most notable, David Elkind, writing in *The Hurried Child* (2001), focuses on the experience of childhood that involves a drive to ever-higher achievement, a loss of spontaneous play, and early entry into adulthood. Elkind thinks that the focus of adults in children's lives can be inappropriate: he favours an approach that is sympathetic and allows a child the freedom to enjoy childhood and develop naturally. We might see Diane Ehrensaft's (1997) perspective as a child psychologist as being similar, but she concerns herself with families who are dysfunctional because the child is given too much control. In her view, children should be protected by having clear parameters of behaviour, and being exposed to childhood matters—not the realities of the adults. Ehrensaft shares Elkind's view that there are current problems in parenting and educating children, but her approach is quite different.

Children are hurried from a very early age, claims Patricia Thomas (2000), a clinical counsellor. In her experience, many children from infancy onward are exposed to pressure and unnecessary stress. Echoing Elkind's claims, she suggests that pressure intended to produce children who are smarter, more skilled, and better able to enter the adult world is in fact causing children to experience fear of failure, have insufficient time to play and amuse themselves, have chronic psychosomatic complaints, and be unhappy, even depressed, lethargic, or unmotivated.

Infancy should be a time of discovery, happiness, little achievements, maturation, playfulness, and close relationships—along with some risk-taking in everyday activities, getting over minor failures, learning to deal with other young children, learning by doing, building trust, trial and error, building preliminary concepts, recovering after short periods of unhappiness, and taking in everything they can about how the world works. Hurrying infants and toddlers does not make them smarter. Infancy should be an amazing sheltered but free experience, not a race.

Information Processing

Several studies show us that infants at this stage cluster together bits of information to make sense of what they take in through their senses (Caron et al., 1982; Cohen and Strauss, 1979). By 7 months, infants tend to categorize everything they see (Younger and Gotleib, 1988), although they do not have the language to label their thoughts. They will be gaining basic schematic understanding of the properties of objects and what is linked with what. By simple association, babies may predict what will happen and find pleasure in cause-and-effect actions.

The infant's memory of events tends to lengthen as she gets older. Sometimes you can observe that an infant remembers a person, object, or event, and performs an action that indicates this memory.

There are several components of **information processing**. One concerns memory. Probably because her memory is relatively short, and the infant responds positively to new stimuli, she tends to be distracted relatively easily. However, her attention span may be longer than before, due in part to her increased interest in playful activity. Toward the end of this stage, the infant looks for items gone from sight, showing her concept of object permanence and, possibly, her increased memory and understanding of objects.

Other components of information-processing involve external characteristics that can be observed in the baby's **trial-and-error** learning, **imitation**,

cause–and–effect discoveries and **action–reaction** sequences. When the baby is experiencing something new, or rediscovering something familiar, she will try out some actions to see what the response will be. She gains significantly through trial-and-error learning as she mouths objects, grabs, and generally discovers what she can do with the things within her reach. Similarly, many bits and pieces of learning will occur because she finds out such things as that banging her hand hurts or bashing something hard makes a loud noise; she links an action or "cause" with an "effect" or result.

Imitation appears to be present in a primitive form in very young infants—it seems to be an unconscious activity. As the baby reaches the 6-to-9 month stage some imitation will be more complex. She may copy the action of another baby or try out moves that mimic an adult's action. So far she does this as she sees the action, but soon her imitation may become deferred as well as immediate. **Deferred imitation** occurs when the baby copies someone else's action some time after the event. She might wave goodbye in a situation after she has seen others wave or she could make a stirring action after she has watched an adult bake cookies. Although deferred imitation is only just emerging at this time, it can lead to a very early indication of a type of symbolic understanding. With experience, the baby discovers that for most of her actions there comes about a reaction. When she cries she gets attention or when she knocks a toy off her high chair it disappears. At the same time she is getting to know that things still exist when they go out of sight, so her action–reaction sequence may become a repeated activity that causes a humorous response.

IMITATION

Imitation of adults encourages the development of language and social skills in the infant. Lots of adult contact will usually, quite spontaneously, involve **reciprocal imitation**—the infant and child imitate each other. Adults can encourage this by making sounds, facial expressions, and simple actions that the baby can imitate. The baby can be encouraged with smiles and verbal cues.

Facial expressions may be copied, with or without the accompanying emotion. So babies may be demonstrating an emotion that they are not really feeling—but this is fleeting. Sound patterns that are similar to words may be repeated frequently after they are offered by the adult. This imitation may be part of a play sequence or an element of social interaction during a diaper change. Words and phrases may be copied without meaning or full articulation of consonants. Sounds first heard on recordings or uttered by other babies may be of interest to the baby. If they are within her vocal range she may copy them immediately or, more surprising, make the sound a little later.

Actions may also be copied, but these tend to be single movements rather than complex multi-part actions. When imitating an action, it is common for the baby to perform it with both hands simultaneously.

Play

Much of the infant's play activity is solitary—by herself. Babies familiar with a group setting do observe each other, but they treat other infants more as objects than as people. This is because babies' thinking is essentially **egocentric**—from their own perspective. Yet, although they cannot appreciate the perspectives of others, they are intrigued by the presence and actions of others.

Adults who enter into play with an infant at this stage can do much to assist the give-and-take of communication. The infant is usually delighted to have the attention. Infants will respond to simple nursery rhymes (and make attempts to imitate the adult's accompanying actions). Some infants at this stage initiate play with adults, but others are more likely merely to respond to the adult's advances. This may have as much to do with temperament as with developmental stage.

Sensory play allows the infant to discover new materials, but caution must be exercised. The infant has little fear and even less ability to predict what might happen in potentially dangerous situations. Newly acquired reaching and grasping skills further complicate matters. Yet, under safe conditions, the infant learns much from repeating actions of grasping and observing material. Increased mobility leads to more physical activity. The 6-to-9-month infant enjoys practising the movements that lead to getting from place to place, but many early movements are performed for pure joy rather than as attempts to go somewhere specific. Indeed, playful rolling or crawling can lead to the baby moving farther away from a target, rather than advancing toward it!

Communication and Language

Before they are 9 months old, babies commonly lift both arms to communicate their desire to be picked up. This is a peak time for **preverbal cues**—indicators without words—so the process of communicating depends upon adults interpreting infants' messages and responding to them. The infant needs to learn the give-and-take nature of communication. You can see this being practised in the many "dances" the infant has with adults.

The adult needs to be able to "interpret the infant's intentions" (Fogel, 1997), because the baby will be sending out signals that are **intentional communications**—deliberate efforts to communicate—as well as signs that are unconscious. Babies tend to develop their own action-based communication style, although some signs are relatively universal. For example, a symmetrical pushing down of the legs might mean "my tummy hurts." Other signals need to be read in relation to an individual baby's previous communications.

In addition to the smiling seen at earlier stages, the baby now laughs, and laughter can be prompted by all sorts of give-and-take situations, such as playing tug with an object pulled on one end by an adult (Fogel, 1997). Her smile is truly social. **Social smiling** indicates a rich human experience—it is more complex than the reflexive or physical smile.

The 6-month-old baby's vocal apparatus is becoming more like that of an adult (Fogel, 1997). She can make several different sounds, because she is now breathing through her nose more than her mouth. She is likely to vocalize tunefully to herself (Sheridan, 1997). At this stage, a baby can probably make a full range of vowel sounds and may begin to make some consonant sounds, such as *r, s, z, th*, and *w* (Allen and Marotz, 2000). Increasing ability to vary the airflow allows the infant to make a range of sounds by varying loudness and pitch (Zlatin, 1973). The sounds that she makes at this stage are called **babbling** and bear some resemblance to speech. This babbling is partly based on imitated sounds and intonation patterns, the up-and-down flow of spoken language (DeBoysson-Bardies et al., 1984). Babbling also stems from the baby's discovery of her voice potential. The language the baby hears will influence her sound production. (This was discussed in Chapter 6.)

At 9 months, the infant's repertoire of sounds has increased so that she "babbles loudly and tunefully in long repetitive strings of syllables" (Sheridan, 1997, p. 16). Many of the babbling sounds contain two or three syllables, such as "ma-ma" or "aga-aga-aga." The babbling may begin to have some meaning, but most babies at 9 months are not yet using words to convey a meaning. They do, however, understand some associations, such as the link between waving goodbye and the word "goodbye."

The 9-month-old baby might be observed in lengthy **dyadic** (two-way) communications. Attracting the attention of the adult, she raises both arms, interpreted by the educator as "up," and initiates a pointing and reaching sequence while looking toward toys, and sustaining the look until given the toy.

SOCIAL DEVELOPMENT

The infant's increased communication skills support the social relationships that he is building. As we have already discussed, the infant has a wider range of physical skills involving handling things and interacting with people, an increased knowledge of his world through exploration and discovery, a broader range of communication skills, a longer memory, and an increased ability to pay attention to details. All these skills make possible more complex social relationships.

At 6 to 9 months the baby has a clearer idea that she is a separate human being. Margaret Mahler (1967) calls this a **second birth**—a psychological birth. In essence, the psychological birth is the time when the baby comes to know that she is a person in her own right. She begins to understand the effect that she has on others and see herself as "me" as opposed to "you." We cannot imagine that this is a scheme that can be expressed verbally, but her behaviour leads us to understand the separateness. Frequently the baby will expand her view of her world; this reinforces her separateness. Only with a relationship of close attachment can the baby have the confidence to branch out on her own and play independently.

During this stage, the child's attachments to adults begin to change. Her links with particular adults become more intense, and her anxiety increases when those to whom she is attached are absent. This is the stage of **clear-cut attachment** to particular adults. It is essential that the infant have the possibility of forming these clear-cut attachments to one or more people. These attachments contribute to the infant's ability to build trusting relationships, the most important issue that underlies all social development. Erik Erikson (1987), known as the father of psychosocial development, describes the first task of infancy as the creation of trust. Without it, the infant cannot build a separation of himself from others, a positive sense of self, or lasting relationships with anyone.

If their needs are met consistently and responsively, babies will develop secure attachments and will learn to be generally more trusting. If this does not happen, **mistrust** toward people, the environment, and even themselves, can result. If early attachments fail to occur, the subsequent mistrust may be very difficult to remedy later on. There are examples of babies who have been placed in institutions and who were deprived of loving care having difficulties later on with social relationships. Fortunately, some early interventions can be effective and trust can be built over time with consistency. Generally, though, the older the child, the more difficult it is to make up for lost nurturing.

If the opportunity to form strong attachments is missing in an infant's life, key experiences can be re-created to try to repair the missing psychological framework of trust. But this intervention has met with only limited success. Several studies have looked at the quality of infants' care in relation to the quality of their attachments. There appears to be a strong link between the two: sensitive care allows infants to develop more secure attachments (Sroufe, Cooper, and DeHart, 1996). It is encouraging to know that, even when there are poor attachments between parents and infants, there can be some remediation if high-quality care is provided, in which trusting relationships are built (Howes et al., 1988).

At 6 months, the infant may not yet be concerned about moving from the care of one adult to that of another, but this will soon change, causing the infant, and the adults, considerable stress. By 9 months, the infant may experience **stranger anxiety** if passed to an unfamiliar adult or placed in unfamiliar surroundings with adults to whom he is not attached (Bowlby, 1973). The most disturbing scenario for the infant is when an unfamiliar adult comes into familiar and predictable surroundings (Brookhart and Hock, 1976). The baby's response is likely to be negative because the unfamiliar person seems to spoil the pattern of predictability.

Separation anxiety tends to appear at 8 to 9 months of age (Bowlby, 1973). The infant becomes distressed and may protest loudly at being removed from the care of a person to whom he is attached (Snow, 1989). Adults who observe the infant's distress may assume that there is something wrong with the infant or that the adult who is rejected has done something inappropriate to the child. This is not the case. Such distress is a sign that the infant has made a healthy attachment (Snow, 1989). Although the manifestations of separation anxiety should not be a cause for great concern, the baby needs comfort and support through any transition of care.

Babies have different responses to people who are familiar and those who are not. A baby's ability to distinguish intimates and strangers at this early stage may be an evolutionary skill that protects the infant from the unknown.

EMOTIONAL DEVELOPMENT

The emotions that are expressed in infants of 6 to 9 months tend to be ones that are easily understood by adults; they are more focused and are more likely to be related to particular experiences than previously. Also, the baby reacts to people and events in a more clear-cut way, so adults can determine why the baby feels the way she does. The range of feelings that are observable through facial expressions are the basic emotions, or **proto-emotions**, that tend to be similar across all cultures. Socialization and experience have the effect of expanding the baby's range of emotional expressions.

One of the most obvious new emotions is fear (Izard, 1977), which an infant may demonstrate in a variety of situations. Anger may also be seen in infants at this stage. Anger may result from frustration at not being able to reach something or from waiting for a bottle that isn't produced fast enough.

As the range of emotional expression increases, so does the infant's ability to read emotions on the faces of familiar adults. By about 6 months, the infant may respond to the expressed emotions of a person in an appropriate way, matching the emotion (Michalson and Lewis, 1985). For example, an infant may smile back when she is smiled at, cry when someone speaks to her in a loud, angry voice, or make a face in response to one made to her (Snow, 1989).

By 9 months the infant may actively look for the expression of an adult as a sign of encouragement or discouragement. This is called **social referencing**, and may be an early indication of wanting to please and needing the security that comes from adult approval.

Frequently the baby will look back at her caregiver and seek some eye contact that reassures her that everything is all right. It is most frequently observed when we see the baby confronted with something or somebody new. It is as though she were saying to the adult, "Is this okay?" or "Should I feel threatened?" Her action can tell us as much as if she had used the actual words.

As we discussed before, social relationships with increased emotional contentment help the infant to distinguish himself from others. However, the development of a real concept of self is a slow process. The 6-month-old infant sees himself as a separate entity from his mother, the result of a process called **self-differentiation**. However, the baby still does not have a full appreciation of self. A baby of this age will look at himself in a mirror with some interest, but he does not yet appreciate that he is looking at himself.

The next step is **self-permanence**, which is related to the concept of object permanence. This involves the conceptual understanding that the "self" continues to exist. Infants typically develop this concept between 8 and 9 months (Deiner, 1997). It involves developing the **self–other scheme**, which is essential for the development of other aspects of self-concept. The self–other scheme requires the separation of self, identification of the two entities, "self" and "other," and the connection between the two.

SELF-IMAGE

The infant needs to discover herself and build positive elements into her concept of self. The adult can support this need by responding positively to the infant, by seeing her as a competent little person, and by encouraging small advances in development. As we saw in earlier chapters, caregivers too can help the development of a healthy self-image by ensuring that the child-care environment reflects all children in their care (see Box 7.2).

TEMPERAMENT

As the adults in the infant's life become more familiar with the infant's personal style, they are more likely to categorize the pattern of behaviour into a particular type. Chess and Thomas (1996) were responsible for the New York Longitudinal Study, which researched temperament in individuals from infancy to adulthood. They identified nine temperament types and three temperament constellations—easy, slow-to-warm-up, and difficult—into which most of these types fall. (See the Appendix for a list of all nine categories of temperament.) In their study, which may have used a fairly representative sample, about 40 percent of infants appeared to be easy in their style. They were mostly regular, positive, and adaptable infants who were found to be less challenging to work with than infants of the other styles. Much more challenging were the approximately 10 percent of infants who were difficult. They were irregular in functioning, had negative responses to stimuli, and found adapting to new situations more challenging. The slow-to-warm-up category constituted 15 percent of the sample. The balance of the sample comprised of mixed temperament types, and didn't fit into these constellations.

▶ Particular Needs

EXPLORATION

Infants at this stage are beginning to take control of their immediate world and enjoy being able to affect their surroundings. Consequently, they need to be in a safe environment in which they can mouth objects and find out about everything within reach.

BOX 7.2

AN AGENCY WITHOUT BIAS

Everything that we do in child care has a value; we discussed this in the first chapter. The value that you want to transmit is one of respect, so, for parents who speak languages other than English, you will need to do this through the program you offer and the communications you have with parents and their children. Respect can be considered an active as well as a passive value; but what speaks the loudest is what we do.

The child-care environment should reflect the cultures of the children and families for whom it provides care. It should also mirror positive attitudes about differing family styles, cultural practices, and individual differences of ability and appearance (Derman-Sparks et al., 1989; Hall and Rhomberg, 1995).

The choice of all materials must be filtered through an anti-bias review, and additions must be made that address differences. Every part of the environment, including the common parts of the building, such as hallways and waiting areas, should be considered. Pictures must represent a variety of cultures, toys must reflect appropriate positive images, photographs can create a representative picture of the diversity of the group, culturally significant artifacts can contribute to an atmosphere of inclusion, and books and scripts can be in different languages.

Be sure that inclusive representation is an ongoing focus, not just something done for effect. Making a novelty of cultural differences can be offensive. All cultural representations should be integrated, with none held up as foreign or "other."

PHYSICAL NEEDS

Feeding

At this stage, the infant will usually have been introduced to baby food or puréed "adult" food to provide some nutrients not found in milk. However, breast milk or formula is still important for protein, calcium, and fat. Since fats support neurological growth, babies should not be fed low-fat milk.

Diapering

Bowel or bladder control is not yet possible, so the infant needs regular diaper checks and to be changed when the diaper is wet or contains feces. At this stage, babies often wriggle on the change table, which may present challenges for the caregiver. This wriggling can be a safety hazard; the increased bodily control can lead to the baby showing dislike by moving and twisting. Some educators like to have babies focus on the diaper-change process to become more aware of their bodies. Other adults prefer to distract the child from the experience with mobiles, games, and rhymes. Whichever approach is taken, the diapering should be a positive experience for the infant.

Rest and Sleep

Infants vary in their sleep requirements, and their individual needs should be met. Usually, educators and parents are able to read the signs that the infant is tired. Adults need to be in tune with the infant's sleep pattern and provide an environment that is as conducive to rest and sleep as it is to stimulation. Babies in group care learn to tune out sounds that might keep other babies awake. Silence is not necessary, but most babies sleep best in relatively quiet environments with no bright lights. Some parents believe in co-sleeping—infants and adults sleeping together in a family bed. Co-sleeping remains a debatable issue. The U.S. Consumer Product Safety Commission (CPSC) is warning parents and caregivers about the "dangers of placing babies to sleep in adult beds." A CPSC study published recently in *Archives of Pediatrics and Adolescent Medicine* found that placing babies to sleep in adult beds puts them at risk of suffocation or strangulation (Nakamura, 1999). The risk warning was echoed in a 1999 joint statement, *Reducing the Risk of Sudden Infant Death Syndrome in Canada*, from Health Canada, the Canadian Institute of Child Health, the Canadian Foundation for the Study of Infant Deaths, and the Canadian Pediatric Society: "Bedsharing is a common practice for many families . . . The risk of SIDS is increased if the person who shares the bed is a smoker, or has been con-suming alcohol or taking other drugs that may decrease their responsiveness." Nevertheless, there are parents and some professionals who remain attached to the practice of co-sleeping and hold to the view that the supposed benefits outweigh any possible negative outcomes. Jan Hunt of the Natural Child Project and Dr. William Sears, a well-known media person, both advocate co-sleeping. Hunt claims that parent–child relationships are enhanced by it, there is easier access to breast-feeding, and responding to an infant in crisis is more immediate. Sears's stance is that, following his own research on the subject, there are numerous physical and psychological advantages for the baby as well as for the parents. Other commentators insist that the quality of sleep and its overall benefits to the attachment process, and the engagement it encourages between parents and infants, is vastly underrated. Fortunately, this is not an issue pertinent to child-care situations, although caregivers may be asked their opinion. The safe approach is to reiterate the position of the Canadian and American child health experts.

▶ Developmental Variation

Variation in developmental stages broadens as infants get older. At 6 to 9 months, some infants may not yet be able to sit, even with support, while others may already be attempting to crawl. When parents are concerned about their child's development, they should check it out with their family doctor, pediatrician, or other appropriate specialist, even if the educator doesn't think there is a problem.

Both parents and educators may be alarmed if an infant's development remains stuck in the same place for a period of time. Although the majority of infants progress smoothly and predictably, some do not. Significant concerns should be presented to specialists, although many of these developmental worries will turn out to be within the bounds of the norm.

▶ Developmental Alerts

SENSORY DEFICITS

An infant who fails to respond in an expected way to visual or auditory (sound) stimulation should be checked by a specialist. At 6 to 9 months, hearing and visual problems may be more apparent than they were earlier. As Box 7.3 indicates, parents and educators should compare observations and discuss how to proceed. This is important for at least two reasons. First, the educator may have information that will supplement the parents' observations. Second, educators are better able to support the child's needs if they fully understand what these needs are. In many cases, hearing and sight issues can be corrected, improved, or supported in ways that prevent a **multiple disability**. If either vision or hearing challenges go undetected, the baby can miss crucial sensory information, which can have a negative impact on the child's learning.

SEIZURE DISORDERS AND FEBRILE CONVULSIONS

Seizure disorders or febrile convulsions may result from brain injury or other neurological difficulties. Infants may have such slight **seizures** that they appear as no more than a twitch or a temporary detachment from attention. Other more serious seizures can also occur, sometimes resulting in a complete loss of bodily control, prolonged whole-body spasms, and a trance-like state that persists even after the seizure is over. Many things can trigger a seizure, including lights, smells, fever, fatigue, and other environmental conditions. Sometimes they occur for no apparent reason. Careful observation may help you determine what sets off a seizure; those conditions can then be avoided.

Infants who had birth injuries in the form of **cerebral irritation**—pressure on the brain—may experience seizures, so these injuries should be identified on their health history. Also, even young infants can have **epilepsy**. Educators may never witness infant seizures, but they must be able to recognize them and manage the situation in accordance with parental direction. Babies with epilepsy may or may not experience regular seizures (especially if under control). Special treatment is usually not required when a seizure happens, but a baby prone to seizures may need daily medication to control the condition.

Febrile convulsions, which are seizures not associated with epilepsy, occur fairly frequently. Indeed, between the age of 6 months and 6 years, about 3 percent of normal children have at least one such seizure (Canadian Paediatric Society, 1992, p. 132). Most of these result from a sudden high fever. Although such episodes might be alarming, they rarely lead to significant medical problems. However, because they might indicate the onset of a serious fever such as **meningitis**—inflammation of the meninges around the brain—a baby who has such a seizure should be evaluated by a physician as soon as possible.

DOWN SYNDROME

As mentioned in Chapter 4, **Down syndrome** is a congenital condition that results from a chromosomal abnormality. It affects about 1 in 600 children (Canadian Paediatric Society, 1992). There are varying levels of severity of the syndrome. Children with Down syndrome have a rounded face and their hands have short, relatively fat, fingers. They may have heart problems and their brains may function at below-normal capacity. However, the levels of functioning vary from baby to baby. Only rarely are medical interventions necessary. An infant with Down syndrome can usually be integrated into a child-care setting without difficulty. The group environment may provide the stimulation that the baby needs.

BOX 7.3

A USEFUL STRATEGY FOR SHARING CARE: ASSISTING WITH REFERRALS

A central part of conversations between parents and educators should consist of the educators sharing their observations. These can be written or more informal, but there needs to be some documentation of the child's progress.

Any question, concern, or observation voiced by the parents must be responded to with the educators' own thoughts and observations. If either the parents or educators think there is a difficulty, they should consider seeking the opinion of another professional. Referrals can be sought for a variety of reasons. Questions about hearing and sight are probably the most common, but there may be other health or developmental issues. The educators can provide print resources and phone numbers that help the parent obtain a professional assessment. Many health concerns are best handled by the educator suggesting that an opinion be sought from the family doctor or pediatrician. Since some services are without cost while others have a fee attached, educators should be careful about the range of possibilities that they suggest.

HEART CONDITIONS

Eight out of 1,000 children are born with a **congenital cardiac condition** (Canadian Paediatric Society, 1992). In addition, young children can acquire a heart condition as a result of rheumatic fever or Kawasaki disease, another illness characterized by fever. Some heart problems that haven't previously been detected by medical staff or parents might be observed by educators. Observable characteristics can include blue lips, difficulty breathing, limited growth, or weight gain from fluid retention. Infants and young children with heart conditions may be particularly susceptible to respiratory infections. This issue is significant for a child placed in a group setting. The increased exposure to infection from contact with other children could present risks to the child.

▶ Health Concerns

IMMUNIZATIONS

It is essential to ensure that infants at this stage are immunized against the most serious childhood infections. The Canadian Paediatric Society suggests that infants should receive their third and fourth immunizations at the beginning and end of this developmental stage. These are against diphtheria, pertussis (whooping cough), tetanus, poliomyelitis, and hemophilus influenza type b infections, including meningitis. Child-care centres must have a policy to ensure that young children have received their immunizations. There can be cases where parents object to immunization on religious, ethical, or other grounds. Agencies must decide how they will manage this eventuality. Although immunization programs vary, the chart in the Appendix presents a typical immunization schedule.

TEETHING

A few babies are born with teeth, but most infants will experience the soreness and eruption of their first teeth during this period. There is great variation in how this occurs. In some cases, there is very little trouble as the teeth break through the gum. Other babies might have sore gums, pink cheeks, and possibly a slightly raised body temperature and digestive upset. Sleep can be disrupted for short periods, but the most common sign of teething is that the baby gnaws on objects and drools prolifically—possibly causing some soreness on the chin.

Behavioural or symptomatic changes should be indicated to parents. Only if parents request it should any special treatment be given. In most child-care centres children will be excluded while medicated, or given only medication labelled by a pharmacist or prescribed by a doctor. Cold rings, gel toys, and other objects to mouth can be comforting. Extra cuddles might also be needed and plentiful liquids are usually acceptable. Gnawing on hard biscuits or vegetables may be a way for the baby to acquire new tastes and textures while easing through the new teeth.

THE TRANSITION TO SOLID FOOD

As we mentioned above, infants at this stage may start eating solid foods. Solid foods should be offered when the child is hungry. Although solid food may be offered, breast milk or formula remain central to the baby's diet. New foods should be introduced one at a time to see how well the infant likes and tolerates each food. Small amounts of puréed food may be offered. Often parents choose to start their infants on cereals, but there is some nutritional evidence that vegetables should be tried first. The baby's sweet tooth might reveal itself in a preference for sweeter foods, but the baby should be offered several different foods over time, of various colours, textures, and tastes. The best idea is to increase the baby's range of foods gradually. The baby's food does not have to be seasoned, even if it seems bland to the adult.

Introduce new foods one at a time, allowing three to four days between each new food.

Choose the least allergenic foods first. These include:

- rice cereals
- other single-grain infant cereals
- carrots
- bananas
- squash
- sweet potatoes
- peaches
- pears
- veal
- beef
- lamb
- poultry

In the early months, feed solid foods after milk as a supplement, so as not to replace milk. It is unwise to offer egg products to a baby not yet 1 year of age: allergic responses may occur, typically in response to egg white. For food safety, honey, in any form, should not be fed to young infants. For babies in a vegetarian or vegan family, consultation with a nutritional expert is advisable—some dietitians provide useful information, or you might consult a pediatrician. Babies who are breast-fed and weaned before 9 months should be given an iron-fortified formula. If given formula, it should be iron-fortified for the first 9 to 12 months of life (Canadian Paediatric Society, 1991). Formulas contain added vitamins and minerals to approximate the levels present in breast milk. No additional vitamin supplementation is needed when infants are formula-fed. The use of iron-fortified formula eliminates the need for additional mineral supplementation of full-term infants.

▶ Signs of Potential Neglect or Abuse

INDICATIONS OF NEGLECT

The Canadian Paediatric Society (1992) has produced a checklist of items that might indicate that a child is being neglected. These include:

- poor physical growth
- poor hygiene
- inappropriate clothing
- lack of supervision
- persistent hunger
- repeated injuries
- poisonings
- unattended medical needs

Some of those conditions might be in place for a short period; others may exist because of poverty or homelessness. It is not for the educator to investigate what is happening. The educator is required by law to report any signs, symptoms, or causes for concern to the child protection agency. The child protection agency is trained and has the legal responsibility to look into any reported neglect or abuse, without acknowledging the source of the concern. Please review the Appendix to review the types of neglect as defined by the U.S. National Clearinghouse on Child Abuse and Neglect Information.

FAILURE TO FORM AN ATTACHMENT

As we have seen, the need for an infant to make sustained attachments with one or more adults is of profound importance. There may be many reasons why a parent is unable or unwilling to offer the support that a child needs to ensure secure attachments. Reasons for ignoring the baby's attachment needs might include:

- poor birth experience
- parental depression
- psychiatric illness of the parent
- poverty
- homelessness
- job worries
- partnership difficulties
- the infant resulting from an unwanted pregnancy
- stress
- lack of understanding about the infant's emotional needs
- lack of parental coping skills
- discontinuity of life (changes of residence, etc.)
- a poor personality fit

At this stage some social engagement is usually evident in the baby. The style of interaction and its sophistication might vary, but there is cause for concern if there is poor attachment to the key people in the child's life.

Careful observation of the infant with the educators and with the parents is a normal part of practice; the intention is usually to maintain continuity, but the result may sometimes be that you notice apathy or detachment on the part of the adult. As with all situations of this sort, follow-up is necessary. Your perceptions can be checked out with other professionals.

Early intervention may help prevent or ameliorate attachment difficulties. Family support systems may help the parents, but in complex circumstances success becomes less likely. Where the infant is inadequately attached, parents may need to receive assistance and instruction on how to be competent caregivers. Although, through her personal resilience, the baby may not be displaying many negative signs of failure to attach, this is nevertheless a serious situation. In some cases the infant and family may need to be referred to child protection workers.

▶ Everyday Safety Issues

Before we review the specific safety issues related to infants at this stage, we should stop to consider the place of safety in the overall scope of adult responsibilities. There should be no real separation between safety, health care, guidance, nurturance, and responsivity in practice. Adults' actions must reflect a merging of all these components of the adult role. It is necessary to be mindful of all the needs of each infant simultaneously and do whatever is required. In being with infants, the adult protects them and ensures that they are loved and cared for—all at once. For example, there may be some safety concerns during feeding times, but this should not deflect the adult from nurturing and strengthening attachments or responding to the baby's cues during feeding. The safety and caring components are not a lesser part of the role; upon them depends the possibility for supporting higher-level infant needs. Refer to the interpretation of Maslow's hierarchy of needs in the Appendix; this model explains the necessity for basic needs being met as a precondition for ensuring that more complex personal and psychological needs can be met.

The baby's increasing mobility presents new challenges for both parents and educators. At this stage, the infant becomes better able to control his world, so that world needs to be safe. Because he can move around more and can reach, roll, and perhaps even crawl, he is able to fall off high surfaces, roll off a bed, or wriggle out of a high chair. Constant supervision is very important.

In addition, ensuring the high quality and safe use of items within the child-care centre is vitally important. The following is a checklist of considerations for various pieces of furniture and equipment.

High chairs/low chairs

- must be stable
- must have straps to secure the infant
- should not allow the infant to slide out
- should have no sharp edges that could cut exploring hands

Cribs

- must be stable and strong
- should have firm, well-fitted mattresses
- should have bars that are narrowly spaced so that the head can't be caught
- should not be painted with toxic or lead paints
- should have crib bumpers that prevent entanglement and suffocation
- should not have pillows
- should have toys of appropriate size without any small detachable parts

Change tables

- need to be used with caution (keep one hand on the baby)
- may be safer if there is a barrier around the edge

Playpens

- are better used for toy storage than infant imprisonment
- should be of stable construction
- should be constructed so it is impossible for the child's hand or head to become entrapped
- should not be used instead of adult supervision

Car seats

- must be checked for size, weight, and anchoring within the vehicle.

Adult beds, kitchen tables, and other furniture

- can present hazards: they are inappropriate places for infants who can roll

Strollers and baby carriages

- must be of an appropriate size
- need to be checked for durability, stability, and breaks
- infants must be strapped in and monitored at all times

Swings, seats, and walkers

- must be checked to see if they are appropriate for the size and weight of the baby
- must have padded mats underneath
- may require straps to secure the infant

Caregivers should justify the choice, use, maintenance, and appropriateness of each piece of baby equipment. Some pieces are clearly unnecessary and can even be dangerous. For example, baby walkers are of dubious developmental use. Their potential danger is too great to justify their use. In addition, over-the-door bouncer seats present hazards because they are positioned in high-traffic areas. Moreover, their benefits to the child are very limited. Too often, caregivers leave babies in them for prolonged periods.

Particular care should be taken when using secondhand or used equipment. Check to see if the equipment is old or worn. Repairs can be made as necessary, but faulty equipment should not be used. It is important to remember that equipment designed for home use may not stand up to the rigours of a group care setting. Consequently, centre staff must be cautious when purchasing equipment or accepting gifts of secondhand material.

BOX 7.4

GETTING IN TUNE WITH INFANTS AT 6 TO 9 MONTHS

Below are some starting points for building your responsivity skills with a 6-to-9-month-old baby. Tune in with respect and:

- allow the baby time to observe you
- emphasize physical forms of encouragement through touch
- show the baby how much you enjoy being with him
- maintain eye contact
- enable the baby to see what is happening around him
- identify characteristics of the baby's personality
- enjoy simple rhymes with actions together
- provide the baby with space to move on his tummy
- repeat actions and reactions over and over
- put safe objects within the baby's grasp
- hide items from view and then have them reappear
- offer visual stimulation with black-and-white and brightly coloured patterns within the baby's visual pathway
- put bells on the baby's socks to help him to be aware of his body
- have a firm surface that the baby can kick against
- talk and sing using clear sounds and lots of repetition
- pass objects in a circle around the baby and respond if he reaches out to grab things
- have lots of differently textured fabrics for touching, grabbing, and mouthing
- offer taste experiences, introducing one new food at a time
- introduce toys that have a cause-and-effect function
- show pictures of domestic objects (laminate the pictures and stick them to the floor)
- assist the baby to make links between events by providing a routine
- provide objects of interest and use these to lure him to an activity or experience
- tell the baby what you are about to do
- produce lots of objects that can be grabbed and mouthed (kitchen objects can be good)
- play games of give and take
- build up cardboard boxes to be swiped at and knocked down
- respond to the baby's cues for basic needs
- anticipate the baby's feelings
- respond when he cries by acknowledging the reason for the crying
- play tug of war with a suitable object
- offer safe mirrors so the baby can see himself
- mimic the baby's sounds
- support transitions and acknowledge distress
- label feelings and actions
- engage in communications with gestures
- assist with concept development with materials to explore
- accommodate varying social response patterns
- blend your caregiving strategies with those of the parents
- allow the baby to play when undressed, encouraging body awareness
- make diapering an intimate time for one-on-one dialogue
- encourage curiosity
- praise effort
- acknowledge new skill acquisition
- check the baby's hearing and visual abilities through playful experiences
- respond quickly to signs and symptoms of illness or discomfort
- use music to shape the mood

▶Starting Points for Response

RESPONSIVE CAREGIVING

As at earlier stages, caregivers must be able to interpret the baby's cues and respond quickly and appropriately. Box 7.4 provides some strategies for responding to infants of this age. Adults should also help to guide the baby's exploration. This is important for safety reasons and so adults can help support the baby's growing understanding of his world. Increasing communication between adults and the baby is also key at this stage. It helps the infant make secure attachments to particular adults. These attachments should be supported by continuous patterns of interactions from adults. Separations may be increasingly difficult times for the baby, and both parents and caregivers should think of ways to make these as smooth and easy as possible.

SUPPORTIVE GUIDANCE

The continuing development of a sense of self is important at this stage. Adults must think about how they are supporting this emerging sense of self. Providing rapid responses to requests and reading the complex cues that the baby sends out are important. The dance of communication is reciprocal: the baby enjoys the adult's interactions and tries to engage the adult in play. He may identify other children in close proximity, but his primary interest is to charm adults into communication and getting what he wants. The baby's intentional communications lead him to a pattern of trial-and-error play scenarios in which the adult can have a part. The baby has acquired the knowledge that things continue to exist even when he cannot see them. This information contributes to a new way of seeing the world, and shows that the baby has a symbolic representation of his world. Games of peek-a-boo allow the baby to incorporate this new knowledge of object permanence into his play.

FACILITATING DEVELOPMENT

Cognitive advances are pronounced at this stage, and the infant's physical ability to sit up and pay attention makes him a much more competent person. Stimulation is particularly important at this stage. Adults will find that the infant's information-processing skills are advancing and that his memory is increasing and new situations are better understood. The adult needs to take responsibility for the careful selection of toys and play materials. These need to be safe and chosen on the basis of how well they support the baby's emerging development.

Language skills are not yet evident in terms of real speech, but babbling has become more complex and may take on the sounds of the language around the child. The infant needs to hear that language and may enjoy rhymes as well as conversation. The use of **motherese** is particularly important. As mentioned in earlier chapters, in motherese the higher-pitched emphasis on sounds, coupled with exaggerated facial expressions that correspond to the sounds, is important in helping the baby figure out which sounds to pay attention to.

HOLISTIC RESPONSE

Activities 7.1 and 7.2 encourage a holistic response to infants. Activity 7.1 suggests ways of engaging in the experience of babies at this stage and extending your interactions with them. Activity 7.2 (page 188) helps you to observe each infant at 6 to 9 months and to develop activities that are targeted to individual interests and skill levels.

Activity 7.1

Responding to the Changing Needs of Infants at 6 to 9 Months

Object permanence is a concept that comes suddenly rather than gradually; this is what many educators notice. Observe a baby of 6 to 9 months and determine, through this game, whether or not she has grasped this concept. What reasons do you have for thinking she has (or has not)?

Activity 7.1

Responding to Changing Needs of Infants at 6 to 9 Months

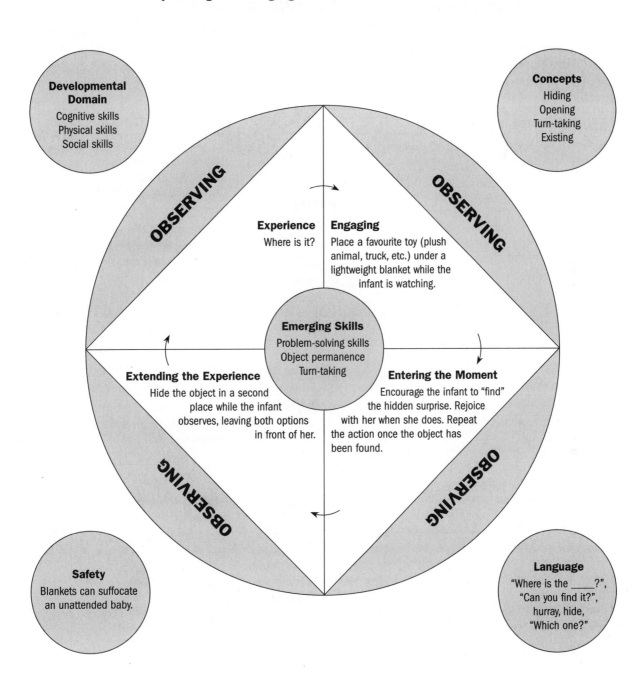

Developmental Domain
Cognitive skills
Physical skills
Social skills

Concepts
Hiding
Opening
Turn-taking
Existing

OBSERVING

OBSERVING

Experience
Where is it?

Engaging
Place a favourite toy (plush animal, truck, etc.) under a lightweight blanket while the infant is watching.

Emerging Skills
Problem-solving skills
Object permanence
Turn-taking

Extending the Experience
Hide the object in a second place while the infant observes, leaving both options in front of her.

Entering the Moment
Encourage the infant to "find" the hidden surprise. Rejoice with her when she does. Repeat the action once the object has been found.

OBSERVING

OBSERVING

Safety
Blankets can suffocate an unattended baby.

Language
"Where is the _____?",
"Can you find it?",
hurray, hide,
"Which one?"

Activity 7.2

Creating Responsive Curriculum for Infants at 6 to 9 Months

Just as the baby's perspective of the world alters when he can sit up and then stand, how he handles new experiences alters, too. Observe a baby of 6 to 9 months in play. What new play behaviours do you see? Design an activity or experience to support his interests in play.

Developmental Domain	Observation of Emerging Skills (Things You See)	Responsive Experience/Activity
Physical skills	– sitting without support – self-feeding (holding his own bottle) – standing with support – manipulating/grasping small objects (pincer grasp) – pass things from one hand to the other – pulling herself up to standing position – clapping hands – coordinating body movements to surroundings	Provide sturdy objects/furniture for the infant to use as support for pulling himself up. Provide squeezable objects that can easily be manipulated and transferred from hand to hand. Sing songs, play music, and tap/clap rhythms. Encourage kinesthetic activity by dancing with the baby. Talk to the baby as you move around the room.
Cognitive skills/ communication and language	– looking for dropped objects – looking in the direction of vocalizations – babbling – imitating adult body movements (to some degree) – evidence of depth perception – manipulating objects and exploring properties (turning an object over and around) – banging objects – understanding of object permanence – waving goodbye when goodbye is said – responding to own name	Provide hiding places for objects that the infant can manipulate. Play the dropping and picking-up game. Provide various objects to explore. Play peek-a-boo. Provide items that can do things (i.e., with lids that open or pop up). Talk about the items that the infant is looking/pointing at.

Developmental Domain	Observation of Emerging Skills (Things You See)	Responsive Experience/Activity
Social/emotional skills	– showing stranger anxiety – identifying strangers among familiar people – indicating desire to be picked up – laughing out loud – showing preference in caregivers	Cuddle and provide physical comfort to infant. Laugh with the infant. Respond to the infant's needs. Place pictures of familiar people in the environment. Play hide-and-seek. Name body parts.

The following suggestions for experiences that might be appropriate for infants at 6 to 9 months allow the infant to demonstrate and practise some of her emerging skills. Activities that encourage sensory discovery are useful at this age and will be exciting for her. She will delight in repeating some of the sequences that she finds particularly fun. Improving physical skills will be entirely enjoyable if the infant is engaged in the activity. Modify the experiences if some part of them seems unsuitable. For example, you might want to change the size of the balls used in Experience 3, depending on the size of her hands and the strength of her grasp. It is not wasting time for a baby to do things time and time again. The repetition might reinforce some of the neural pathways essential for learning. Always pay attention to safety issues and be sure to stay with the baby throughout the experiences using non-manufactured toys, as they pose a greater risk than items tested in toy factories.

Responding to Changing Needs

Infants at 6 to 9 Months

EXPERIENCE 1

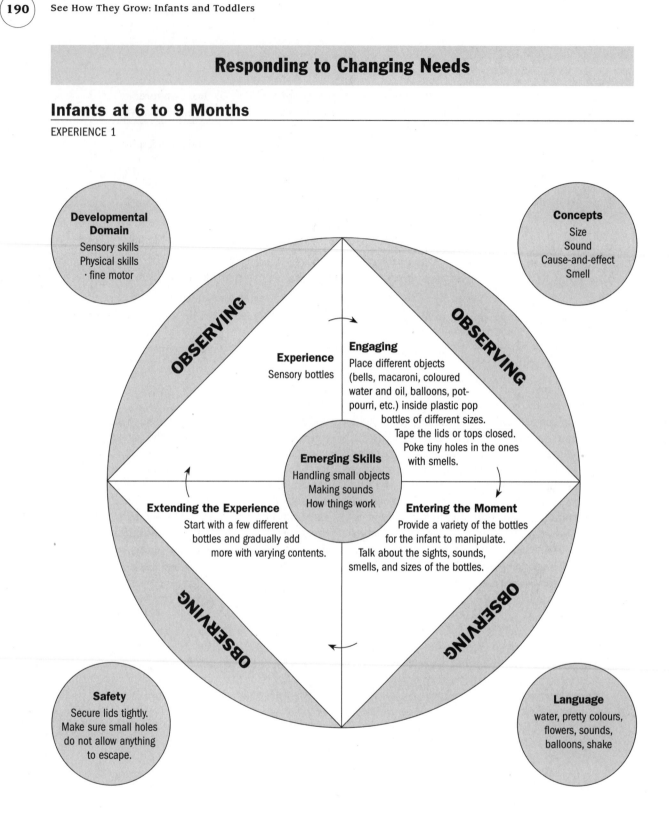

Developmental Domain
Sensory skills
Physical skills
· fine motor

Concepts
Size
Sound
Cause-and-effect
Smell

OBSERVING

OBSERVING

Experience
Sensory bottles

Engaging
Place different objects (bells, macaroni, coloured water and oil, balloons, pot-pourri, etc.) inside plastic pop bottles of different sizes. Tape the lids or tops closed. Poke tiny holes in the ones with smells.

Emerging Skills
Handling small objects
Making sounds
How things work

Extending the Experience
Start with a few different bottles and gradually add more with varying contents.

Entering the Moment
Provide a variety of the bottles for the infant to manipulate. Talk about the sights, sounds, smells, and sizes of the bottles.

OBSERVING

OBSERVING

Safety
Secure lids tightly. Make sure small holes do not allow anything to escape.

Language
water, pretty colours, flowers, sounds, balloons, shake

Responding to Changing Needs

Infants at 6 to 9 Months

EXPERIENCE 2

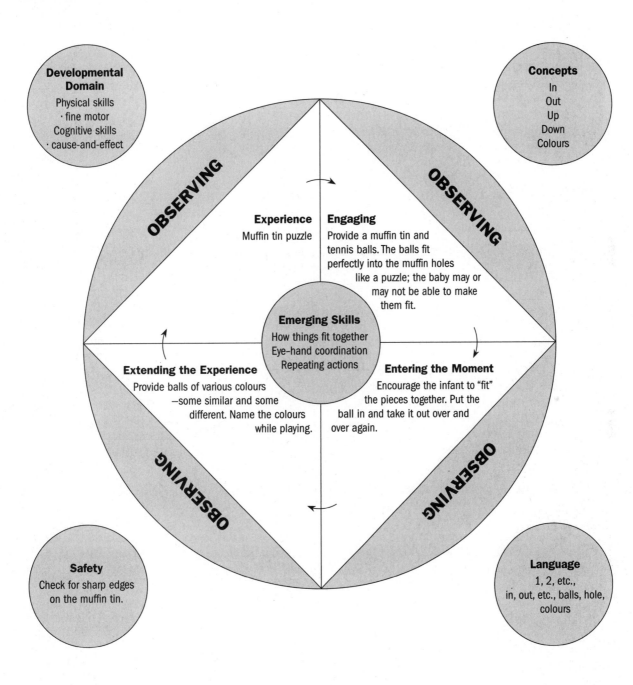

Developmental Domain
Physical skills
· fine motor
Cognitive skills
· cause-and-effect

Concepts
In
Out
Up
Down
Colours

OBSERVING

OBSERVING

Experience
Muffin tin puzzle

Engaging
Provide a muffin tin and tennis balls. The balls fit perfectly into the muffin holes like a puzzle; the baby may or may not be able to make them fit.

Emerging Skills
How things fit together
Eye-hand coordination
Repeating actions

Extending the Experience
Provide balls of various colours —some similar and some different. Name the colours while playing.

Entering the Moment
Encourage the infant to "fit" the pieces together. Put the ball in and take it out over and over again.

OBSERVING

OBSERVING

Safety
Check for sharp edges on the muffin tin.

Language
1, 2, etc.,
in, out, etc., balls, hole, colours

Responding to Changing Needs

Infants at 6 to 9 Months

EXPERIENCE 3

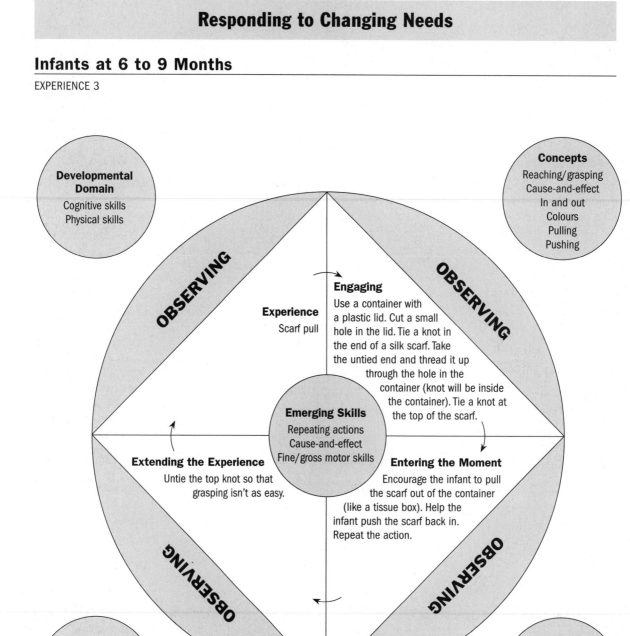

Developmental Domain
Cognitive skills
Physical skills

Concepts
Reaching/grasping
Cause-and-effect
In and out
Colours
Pulling
Pushing

OBSERVING

OBSERVING

Experience
Scarf pull

Engaging
Use a container with a plastic lid. Cut a small hole in the lid. Tie a knot in the end of a silk scarf. Take the untied end and thread it up through the hole in the container (knot will be inside the container). Tie a knot at the top of the scarf.

Emerging Skills
Repeating actions
Cause-and-effect
Fine/gross motor skills

Extending the Experience
Untie the top knot so that grasping isn't as easy.

Entering the Moment
Encourage the infant to pull the scarf out of the container (like a tissue box). Help the infant push the scarf back in. Repeat the action.

OBSERVING

OBSERVING

Safety
Strangulation may result from long scarves.

Language
pull, push, in, out, colours

Further Experiences and Interactions

Further Experiences	Interactions
Songs that encourage clapping: "Pat-a-cake"	When changing the infant's diaper or during other one-on-one times, sing and clap with the infant.
Cymbals (two pot lids)	Play the cymbals as an extension to clapping games.
Water play	In the bathtub or in small plastic pools, add plastic dishes, bath toys, and squeeze toys. Encourage splashing. *Constantly supervise this activity; children can drown in 1.25 cm of water.
Follow-the-leader	When the infant is crawling, cruising, or walking, follow her around, mimicking her mobility (i.e., if she crawls, you crawl). Encourage the infant to follow you, too.
Come and get it	Provide interesting or favourite objects slightly out of the infant's reach. Encourage her mobility.
Drop the bucket	Provide many objects that can be dropped and picked up at will. (Be prepared to be the one who does the picking up while the infant does the dropping.)
Talk to the animals	Encourage the babbling of the infant. Talk to the plush animals, pictures on the wall, play phones, etc. Pause and allow the infant time to speak as well.
Read books	Sit so that the book is accessible to both you and the infant. Encourage the infant to read the book. Respond to her pointing, naming the objects. Allow the infant to turn pages.
Sing nursery rhymes and other songs	During routine times and other times, including transitions, encourage finger plays and actions, clapping, etc.
Hide objects inside shoeboxes	Put favourite toys into boxes with lids. Encourage the infant to open the box and take out the surprise.

Further Experiences	Interactions
Juice lid drop	Gather the ends off of concentrated juice cans. Using a large margarine container with a slot in the lid, encourage the infant to put the juice ends through the slot.
Balls	Roll various balls back and forth.
Hide-and-seek	Play this game with mobile infants: while the infant is observing you, crawl out of her sight. When she follows, delight in her ability to find you. Repeat game.
Pots and pan drums	Encourage the music of this ever popular drum kit using wooden spoons as drumsticks.
Stacking blocks	Infants delight in knocking down the adult-made towers.

Responsive Guidance for Infants Aged 6 to 9 Months

Age/Stage: 6 to 9 Months

Situation	Response
• Christopher cries when his mother leaves the room, but he settles quickly. • Sandy cries when the neighbours and her relatives come over to visit. She used to smile when they came over. • Sarah is always fussing and demanding attention from the adults in her life. When she receives the attention, she appears content, but quickly demands it again if their attention wavers.	**Developmental Issue: Attachment/Separation Anxiety** Infants in this age range like to spend time with familiar adults. It is a sign of healthy attachment that the infant fusses or cries in the absence of her primary caregivers. Infants are beginning to distinguish individuals who are familiar from those who are unfamiliar. They will show a preference for family caregivers. It is considered a healthy sign of attachment if the infant settles relatively easily once the primary caregiver leaves. Wariness of strangers (depending on temperament style) may disappear sometime in the next year.
• Grace is pulling herself up by grasping any object within her reach. • Jack has begun crawling all over the house. • Karlie has started to toddle, taking a few steps before she falls down.	**Developmental Issue: Mobility** Childproof your home. Infants are increasingly becoming mobile. They are determined to get from one place to another and are literally seeing the world from new heights. The best way to determine the potential dangers that face the mobile infant is to look at the world from her perspective. Get down on the ground and view the possible hazards. Some things to look for are strings or tablecloths that hang down or stick out, electrical outlets and cords, unstable furniture, possible climbing instruments, ashtrays, houseplants, sharp corners, possible areas of entrapment, heaters/radiators, stairs, fireplaces, scatter rugs, floor clutter.

Manufactured Toys and Play Materials for Infants at 6 to 9 Months

Toy/Material	Uses	Group Care	Home
Activity centres	Toys can be manipulated, pushed, pulled, twisted, popped, dialled, etc.	√	√
Sensory nesting blocks	The ability to put things inside other things is beneficial (though the order in which this is done may be off). Colours and textures appeal to their senses.	√	√
Busy baby rattle sets	Rattles are eye-catching and feature parts that can be manipulated.	√	√
Sensory stacking rings	Rings can be hooked over a stand. Each ring has a different texture and sound when squeezed.	√	√
Soft infant climbers	A series of soft ramps, steps, and levels that allow babies to climb, crawl, roll, and slide around in a safe environment.	√	
Adjustable tables and chairs	Infant-size chairs and tables that allow stability and security of size.	√	
Shakers	Various sounds, sizes, shapes, and weights.	√	√
Small blocks (2.5 cm square)	Manipulate, move from hand to hand, or attempt to stack beside each other or on top of each other.	√	√
Ball pools	Plastic or blow-up pools that can be filled with balls, water, sand, shredded paper, etc.	√	√
Push toys	Trucks, cars, and/or animals that the infant can push or pull along.	√	√

▶ Summary

A major task of the 6-to-9-month infant is to get to know that she is a separate person, that other people respond to her, and that, together, there can be shared understanding. This can come about only if the trusting relationship remains constant between the baby and the adults she is familiar with. That predictability supports object permanence and people permanence, cause-and-effect, and action–reaction understanding. These adult–baby relationships need to be sustained, with mutual enjoyment helping the learning experience. The enjoyment is maximized if the adult can read the infant's cues and respond accordingly.

Patterns of behaviour are becoming increasingly observable and the baby's temperament style becomes more clearly evident. The adult can use this understanding of behaviour and style to promote their relationship. Looking to the adult for support and encouragement, the infant finds ways of seeking and sustaining attention. She desires playful as well as domestic experiences.

Development varies between children at this and every stage, but there are common processes for discovery learning. The sensory-motor intelligence of the infant provides a mechanism for building mental images from his sensory experience. Through the joint processes of assimilation and accommodation he builds mental schemes. He enjoys a wide variety of materials from which he discovers textures, smells, and shapes. However, the baby needs adult attention to thrive.

The baby's intentional communication and increased physical skills allow her to be more active in learning about her environment and in building relationships. Grasping, mouthing, and reaching are physical characteristics of this stage. She may imitate the adults around her, babble incessantly at times, and try to get adult attention through various means, including crying, gaining eye contact, and using facial expressions. Although many of the signs that she sends adults are not deliberate, she offers many cues to adults so that they can meet her needs. When her psychological and physical needs are met, she learns the trust needed for further relationship building.

▶ KEY TERMS

accommodation
action and reaction
assimilation
babbling
cause-and-effect
cerebral irritation
clear-cut attachment
congenital cardiac condition
crawling
deferred imitation
Down syndrome
dyadic
egocentric
epilepsy
febrile convulsions
imitation
information processing
intentional communication
intermediate grasp
meningitis
mistrust
motherese
multi-modal stimulation
multiple disability
object permanence
palmar grasp
people permanence
pincer grasp
preverbal cues
proto-emotions
reciprocal imitation
schemes
second birth
secondary circular reaction stage
seizures
self-differentiation
self–other scheme
self-permanence
sensory-motor
separation anxiety
social referencing
social smiling
stranger anxiety

trial-and-error
uni-modal stimulation
visual insatiability
weaned

▶ DISCUSSION QUESTIONS

1. What advantages, if any, are there for infants in trying to speed up their development?
2. What are the most significant concerns you might have seeing infants at this stage grasping everything around them?
3. Describe the observable elements of an anti-bias philosophy.
4. Donny, the youngest of three children, doesn't like being cuddled and seems irritable much of the time. When his mother tells you that she's having problems relating to his behaviour, what might you do?
5. You are getting tired physically and mentally from caring for infants. What might be some useful strategies for coping?

▶ ADDITIONAL RESOURCES

▶ Further Readings

Acredolo, L., and S. Goodwyn. (1992). *Baby Signs: How to Talk with Your Baby before Your Baby Can Talk*. Chicago, IL: Contemporary Books.

Carey, W.B. (1997). *Understanding Your Child's Temperament*. New York, NY: Macmillan.

Chess, S., and A. Thomas. (1996). *Temperament: Theory and Practice*. New York, NY: Brunner/Mazel.

Dombro, A. et al., (1997). *The Creative Curriculum for Infants & Toddlers*. Washington, DC: Teaching Strategies.

Dunst, C. *et al.,* (1996). *Supporting & Strengthening Families: Vol. 1: Methods, Strategies and Practices*. Cambridge, MA: Brookline Books.

Furuno, S., et al., (1993). *Helping Babies Learn: Developmental Profiles and Activities for Infants and Toddlers*. San Antonio, TX: Communication Skill Builders.

Karen, R. (1994). *Becoming Attached: Unfolding the Mystery of the Infant–Mother Bond and Its Impact on Later Life*. New York, NY: Warner.

Karmiloff, K., and A. Karmiloff-Smith. (1999). *Everything Your Baby Would Ask if Only He or She Could Talk*. New York, NY: Golden Books/Random House.

Powell, D.R. (1989). *Families and Early Childhood Programs*. Washington, DC: NAEYC.

Segal, M. (1998). *Your Child at Play: Birth to One Year– Discovering the Senses and Learning about the World*. New York, NY: Newmarket Press.

Sroufe, L.A. (1997). *Emotional Development: The Organization of Emotional Life in the Early Years*. Cambridge, U.K.: Cambridge University Press.

Stoppard, M. (1983). *Baby Care Book: A Practical Guide to the First 3 Years*. London, U.K.: Dorling Kindersley.

——. *Responding to Infants: The Activity Manual*. (1983). Minneapolis, MN: T.S. Denison.

▶ Useful Videos

Safe Seating in the Kid Zone: Car Time 1-2-3-4 (1999). Transport Canada.
Description: A short video illustrating the practicalities of infant car safety.

First Feelings. Nova.
Description: This video outlines the stages of emotional development of infants and toddlers. It explains research and theoretical ideas in meaningful ways.

Seeing Infants with New Eyes. NAEYC.
Description: Magda Gerber's exemplary program dramatically illustrates how adult interactions with infants can make a significant difference. (26 min.)

▶ Useful Web sites

Links to Canadian child, youth, and society:
www.youth.society.uvic.ca/webliography.htm
infant feeding:
meds.queensu.ca/medicine/fammed/infantfd/if-CommercialFormula.html
parent resources:
www.parentscanada.com/babycareonline/30learning.html
separation anxiety/home child care:
www.gov.on.ca/CSS/page/brochure/caregivers/cchc-03.htm#Separation anxiety
family violence:
www.hc-sc.gc.ca/hppb/familyviolence/pdfs/childabs.pdf
Caring for kids/Canadian Paediatric Society:
www.caringforkids.cps.ca/
Canadian Paediatric Society—solid foods:
www.canoe.ca/HealthCPS/solidfoods.html

CHAPTER 8

Raring to Go:
Infants at 9 to 12 Months

Babies progress in slightly different ways. Here, the infant finds her
own way of pulling herself up and collapsing back into a sitting or
crawling position.

Learning Outcomes

After reading and studying this chapter, you should be able to:

- identify the observable characteristics of infants at 9 to 12 months
- explain the significance of behaviours in infants from 9 to 12 months in a developmental context
- recognize and respond to the developmental diversity of 9-to-12-month-old infants and discuss issues
  pertinent to this stage of development
- assess the development of infants in the 9-to-12-month stage
- respond to the health, safety, and development of 9-to-12-month-old infants with appropriate protection, caregiving, and guidance
- develop strategies to work with parents as partners in the care and education of their infants

Scene: Parents meet the supervisor of a child-care centre to discuss how their whole family will be involved in their baby's transition from home care to centre-based care. Although their baby, Marcia, is only 11 months old, she is to be placed with a group of toddlers, because she is mobile and has adapted to a regular routine. The parents want to be sure that Marcia's language skills are encouraged.

"Marcia jabbers away all the time," said Janet, the mother of an 11-month baby. "I'm not sure what she's talking about, but she loves the sound of her own voice." Marcia interrupted the conversation by tugging on her mother's hair and adding her own contribution, "Bada bada bada." "I think she wants to join in our chat," observed the educator. "She already knows how to make sure she's not left out!"

The educator and mother continued their talk while enabling Marcia to be part of the conversation. They talked about how infants at this stage have picked up a range of social skills by copying adults and seeking solutions to problems such as how to get noticed. Then Marcia's mother confessed, "I'm worried that Marcia's communication will be held back when she's in the centre; the educators have several children to care for at one time." The educator's reply encouraged her. "We do lots of things here to help the infants let us know what their needs are. We help them to find ways of communicating and we play lots of games and sing rhymes to encourage language. Also, there is some benefit in Marcia being with toddlers who are beginning to say real words. At this stage babies copy each other as well as adults! We play many games with sounds and words, so it will be a positive place for talking." By the time she departed, Marcia's mother was feeling better about leaving her infant at the centre. In subsequent days, she noticed that the educator's reassurances had been accurate. Staff did spend a lot of time talking and playing with the children.

▶ What to Look For

PHYSICAL DEVELOPMENT

At this stage of 9 to 12 months, infants are larger and heavier, have increased physical skills, are more interested in the world around them, play with anything within reach, and communicate with increasing effectiveness.

Growth

The infant's weight continues to increase by about half a kilogram (one pound) per month, with actual weights ranging between 7 and 11 kg (15 and 24 pounds) at 9 months and between 8 and 12 kg (17 and 26 pounds), with an average of 10.5 kg (23 pounds), at 12 months (National Center for Health Statistics ([U.S.], 1982). If you were to examine patterns of weight gain in infants, you would likely find that at 12 months the baby is about three times her birth weight. At 9 months, the infant may be 66–76 cm (24–30 inches) tall; at 12 months, height is likely to be 70–80 cm (27–32 inches). Boys continue to be both slightly heavier and taller than girls, but the variation is individual and depends upon birth size, ethnicity, family patterns, health status, body frame, and nutrition. Although growth patterns are useful indicators of healthy development, the infant's own pattern is more significant than his growth compared with the norm.

Pediatric examinations will usually include measurement of head circumference; this measurement is likely close to that of the infant's chest. Both the infant's body and head are growing, but the latter at a slower pace, so the infant is gradually becoming less top-heavy.

Gross Motor Skills

The downward, **cephalocaudal**—from head to toe—progression of physical control now allows the infant to have increased control over her legs and the lower part of her body. At 9 months, she may creep on her hands and knees (Furuno et al., 1993b), lower herself to a sitting position from standing, and maintain good balance while sitting (Allen and Marotz, 2003). At 10 months, she will usually stand briefly (Furuno et al., 1993b) and may walk, or **cruise**—with a sideways shuffle—as she holds onto furniture in a standing position. Some infants find that crawling remains a faster method of getting around; most babies at this stage attempt to walk but revert frequently to their own method of crawling.

There is wide variation in the time frame for walking, and this appears to be a problem for parents whose baby takes longer than the average. Yet, there is no real cause for concern if the infant is not attempting to walk and shows little interest in being held in a walking position. Particularly if she is mobile in other ways, the baby has little reason to struggle to her feet.

It can be interesting to review familial patterns of skill acquisition. Most parents remember the age when their child first walked. This may have some bearing on other members of the family. Early walkers do not necessarily become the most proficient athletes!

When children become walkers, they are often referred to as **toddlers**. The term comes from the characteristic wobbly gait of the early waddling walk.

The term may also be used to refer to children of a particular age, usually over 12 or 15 months. At this stage, the infant may be placed in the toddler room at a child-care centre. This move may be decided on the basis of the child's age, stage, or the number of children at a centre.

Fine Motor Skills

With increased bodily control, the young child has a greater ability to move toward the objects that interest her. If her efforts are successful, she will grasp items with her thumb and fingers working in opposition. As we saw in Chapter 7, this early **pincer grasp** is called an intermediate grasp (Illingworth, 1990). By 12 months, the infant will probably display a more mature grasp, one that involves the thumb and index finger working in careful opposition. This is a pincer grasp; now even small objects can be grasped.

With this increased control of her hands, the baby will want to manipulate any objects that she can reach. When she has blocks or other items in both hands, she may bang them together, enjoying the sound that the action produces. She may hold her hand out as though offering an item to someone (Illingworth, 1990), but she finds releasing objects more challenging than grasping them. The infant is likely to be interested in putting things into and then taking them out of containers. At the end of this stage, she may make appropriate links between objects, putting a spoon in a cup or a hat on a doll's head, for example. This is called **functional-relational play** (Fenson et al., 1976), and marks a new type of play activity. In the same way, you may see an infant grab a spoon and attempt to feed herself. Although her actions are not very accurate, the infant wants to do this herself and needs practice to perfect the skill.

Another new skill that emerges at this stage, usually around 9 to 10 months, is the infant's ability to point with her index finger. She will also often use her hands to signal interest or to convey a message. Given the opportunity to imitate an adult, she may wave goodbye.

COGNITIVE DEVELOPMENT

Vision

The ability to see objects at some distance prompts the infant to want to find out what is happening. The baby has been able to identify adults from across the room for some time, but now visual acuity is improved and she is likely able to identify who adults are from their faces and their bodies.

The infant is able to see tiny objects, such as food crumbs or raisins (Sheridan, 1997), which she in turn

wants to pick up. This promotes the practice of manual skills such as pointing and grasping. Having better visual acuity also means that infants at this stage may stare at moving objects some distance away. They may watch television for short periods, although this may not be considered desirable, but they prefer to see the three-dimensional activity of people and are very interested in street action or any movement of people in the room. At this stage, the infant takes more notice of people and things around her when she is taken outdoors.

Hearing

Differentiated hearing allows the infant to listen to his own voice and select sounds to listen to from a multitude of surrounding noises. He is particularly interested in human voices, tuning in to hear them. He experiments with his own vocalizations, which is a sign of hearing ability. When he shapes some of his sounds to resemble the language that surrounds him, he is indicating that he hears those sounds. He replicates them and makes up his own. By 12 months, the infant can usually respond to his name and understand a few single words. He may also imitate mechanical sounds (Allen and Marotz, 2003).

Touch, Taste, and Smell

It can be useful for parents and caregivers to know that infants have taste buds that differentiate among sweet, bitter, salty, and sour tastes. Babies may even have a fifth set of taste buds that are receptive to umami—monosodium glutamate (Lowry, 2001). Different parts of the tongue have taste buds receptive to different types of tastes. Coupled with the sense of taste is the textural experience associated with foods. Now that the baby is being offered a bigger range of "adult" puréed food, she will experience mouth feel, aroma, tastes and aftertastes. Chemical receptors stimulate the taste receptors on the tongue to register a reaction at the same time that the baby experiences the texture and smell of the food. Feeding is a multimodal experience. Facial expressions are very good indicators of how well the baby is accepting a new food. At this stage, the introduction of foods that have a mildly bitter taste may be problematic—the baby has a more acute sense of bitterness—for instance, with some green vegetables—than she had in earlier months.

Babies who are breast-fed are exposed to a variety of tastes as they receive milk that has been filtered through the mother's digestive system into the mother's milk supply. Mothers may report babies reacting in particular ways after eating spicy foods. Mothers who continue to breast-feed for some if not all feedings are providing ideal nutrition and health protection for their babies. Ideally they should be supported in child-care settings so that the mother can feed her baby when necessary, or that the baby is fed mother's milk that has been previously pumped and stored. The experience of feeding is as important as the nutrients that are delivered. Closeness, cuddling, bodily warmth, and the smell of the adult all contribute to the development of attachments to adults; the senses of touch and smell are important to the bonding process. When parents are not available to feed their babies, it is desirable that conditions as close as possible to the breast-feeding scenario be created: holding the baby, providing a close nurturing relationship, talking to her, and being responsive to her feeding patterns are all important aspects of feeding. The fact that babies are able to hold a bottle and lie propped up is no reason to deprive the baby of the nurturance that a good feeding situation should provide.

Much of the infant's learning happens as a result of the receptivity of all his senses. At this stage, he is responsive to **multi-modal stimulation**—that is, he can absorb several types of sensory input at once. This requires more complex processing than single modality. The infant's nervous system has to process this multiple input using a cross-modal perceptual process. As mentioned in Chapter 7, multi-modal stimulation (such as breast-feeding) reinforces neural pathways.

Infants at this stage assimilate a tremendous amount of information from grasping, feeling, and experimenting with objects and materials. During the 9-to-12-month stage, the infant is less and less likely to take items to her mouth for discovery (Sheridan, 1997), although this remains a common behaviour. Perhaps her increased manipulative skills allow her hands to make the discoveries instead. Although some infants are quite adventurous with new textures, tastes, and smells, most need time to accommodate totally new experiences. For this reason, new foods should be introduced gradually and all types of sensory stimulation should be balanced with quiet times.

Sensory-Motor Behaviour

Greater deliberation in play is observable at this time. Piaget (1952) identified characteristics of this substage of the sensory-motor stage as "co-ordination of **secondary circular reactions**." The infant is beginning to be able to solve little problems, such as how to get the feeding bottle the right way round into his mouth, or what to do when a toy rolls away, out of easy reach. Review Piaget's substages of sensory motor development in the Appendix. This is an exciting time: adults can see a new type of behaviour

that is really "intelligent" (Snow, 1989) and that shows flexibility of thought.

The infant retains an **egocentric** way of seeing things and does not yet appreciate the perspectives of others. He does, though, observe adults closely and is interested in the activity of other infants and older children.

After the infant understands that objects and people continue to exist even when they are out of sight, some new behaviours become evident. Mastery of the concept of **object permanence** is an indication of a new type of mental scheme that involves holding information in mind even when immediate sensory input offers no reminders of it. The infant may look for something that is hidden and enjoy games of peek-a-boo. In both cases, the infant is excited about finding a lost item. However, the infant's memory is not very long, and he may soon become distracted. This doesn't mean that the concept of object permanence is not, at least partially, appreciated.

Awareness of object permanence demonstrates the capacity for early **symbolic thought**: to appreciate object permanence, the infant has to have a symbolic representation of the object in mind. You might observe other examples of symbolic thought at this stage. The linkage of a meaning to a word shows that the infant understands that one thing stands for another. When he lifts his arms as you say "up," he is showing you the connection. If he responds to a single word, without another prompt, he has clearly used a basic form of symbolism. The use of language relies on symbolic thought, so this is an essential cognitive skill.

Information Processing

The infant at this stage does not have a very long attention span. However, it is possible for the adult to prolong the infant's interest in objects (Belsky, 1980), particularly if the child usually has a short span of attention. In social interactions, babies' play can be lengthened by adults' careful intervention. Engaging in the child's own interests is particularly helpful. Also, extending fun experiences by increasing stimulation or making efforts to highlight what is happening can lengthen the infant's focus. Often repeating simple play sequences can help the baby keep her focus on something. In time, the baby will use these strategies herself, but her attention span is determined as much by her personality as her maturation.

Learning through **imitation** is particularly important at this stage before the child can speak. If an action has similarities to previous behaviours, the infant is more likely to imitate it (Fogel, 1997). Thus, simple actions that are like ones imitated earlier are easier to learn. Actions that accompany nursery rhymes are soon learned because they have the added advantage of prompting memory with association of sounds.

▶ Play

STARTING POINTS FOR UNDERSTANDING THE INFANT: MAKING RELATIONSHIPS AND GETTING TO UNDERSTAND HIS IMMEDIATE WORLD

Infants **play** without having to be taught how (Sroufe, 1977), and this remains the core activity for learning. Play allows infants to acquire a wide range of new skills and practise old ones.

Play becomes a little more complex for the infant as he comes to understand object permanence, uses symbolism, has greater physical skill, and uses some imitative actions. You may observe the baby playing by herself. This is **solitary play**. She may explore objects and repeat actions that cause a particular response. Soft cuddly toys are sought by some infants for comfort, but there is not yet real doll play involving pretend things. Typically, infants are intrigued by new toys and ideas and, although they want enjoyable activities repeated, they also like things that have novelty value (Snow, 1989). An infant will sometimes take notice of crib toys that he had previously ignored because they were too difficult to operate. These may challenge him to press a button or roll an item to create a noise.

This stage allows for wonderful advances in the infant's play behaviours. Until now the infant's physical ability to manipulate objects and basic schemes associated with her experience has limited the scope of her play. Leading up to this stage has been discovery play—which will continue in increasingly complex forms. This involves the baby performing actions to find out about materials and objects in her world. Essentially the play has been physical. Playful activity involving the infant's actions remain at the centre of her discoveries, but now her mental schemes are becoming more detailed—she knows how certain things feel and finds out what happens if she tries out particular actions.

Swinging her fist around for the sheer enjoyment of physical movement, she sees that a tower of small blocks is knocked over—and she sends them flying all over the place! She enjoys the fact that she has influence—she can make something happen. Repeating the activity many times provides amusement as well as essential learning.

This kind of play involving her senses, action, and repetition is called **sensory-motor play** or **practice play**. The accidental discovery that certain things happen leads to activity that is more organized. Soon intentional actions are incorporated into the play. Next time she sees a tower of blocks, she takes a deliberate swipe at them and the result is the same. Repeating this is fun and she does it over and over until her dad gets tired of building the towers! The infant has found that she has some power. She has controlled the blocks to make them fall down and she has controlled Dad because, for a short time at least, he has cooperated in rebuilding the tower. Their shared experience is even more meaningful because Dad provided some key words and exclamations as the game preceded.

Playing with objects is important at this stage, so the baby needs items she can handle—and she is insatiable in her craving for different kinds of materials, textures, and sizes of things. This is a peak time for sensory discovery and the baby wants to get right into liquids and semisolids like dough, Jello, and safe sensory materials. She also likes less messy objects that she can handle, bash together, throw, and bang. Often materials found in the kitchen are every bit as exciting as bought toys and play material. Babies often like to play with items such as wooden spoons, plastic containers, plastic sieves, boxes, used containers (clean and checked for safety) and other items readily at hand.

Early types of **symbolic** or **make-believe play** can be seen as the baby imitates the adults and children around her. You are likely to observe the copying of simple actions, but so far the baby doesn't have a full concept of the role behind the actions. Symbolic play is any play that involves using one object to represent another, or using an action or sound to represent something else. Symbolism is seen in the baby performing an action copied from an adult. It might also be observed when she is using a block to represent a car as it goes along. Early in this stage, symbolism is more likely to be observed in a baby making the action of baking a cake or "feeding" a baby doll (stirring with a spoon but with no cake mixture present). At 11 to 13 months, babies will usually need items that are realistic substitutes for the real thing. The infant will often use the small-sized version of the adult item in predictable and realistic ways. Adults cannot always tell the degree to which the infant is using symbolism, because she may have an idea in her mind that we cannot interpret from her actions. As the baby's first words appear—they, too, are symbols, since words stand for meanings—the infant's symbolic play may become enriched. It is now more likely that we will observe early make-believe.

Some **goal-directed activity** is seen embedded in the infant's physical play. Her greater intentionality leads her to make simple plans to achieve something. Observing closely, we may see her mentally holding on to an idea—such as reaching for something outside her range of movement—and using small strategies to get what she wants. Sometimes her goals are thwarted because her strategies are unsuccessful, but this trial-and-error activity continues until she is frustrated or turns her attention to something else. It is part of the **tertiary circular reaction pattern** (Piaget, 1952) of the sensory-motor stage (see Appendix) that leads the infant to repeat an activity and then elaborate the sequence by varying her tactics. This may help her achieve her goal. This level of complexity in play may not be seen regularly until 12 to 13 months, when the infant's play usually takes on a more experimental approach.

Children at about 1 year of age will play for increasingly long periods of time if they are engaged in the experience. In particular, they will extend the play if they have greater control over what happens—they like activities where they can control some element of the outcome, and with toys that offer a response to the baby. Although infants seem to have an innate ability to sort and organize things, the baby does not yet categorize objects according to their attributes. She may match two or more items that seem to belong together, but her sense of belonging may not be the same as ours. Where we might sort by shape or colour, the baby might sort by what she likes or what she doesn't like, or some other criteria we cannot determine. We might observe infants playing with stacking cups, but they are unlikely to seriate them (order them by size) or manage to put them all inside each other; that involves complex understandings of size, shape, and sequence. Objects will be played with to discover their feeling, weight, and other attributes. But descriptive language is still some time in the future, so schemes might be developed before the language that reinforces those concepts. Playing with a variety of objects, whether or not they are designed for particular purposes, is a good idea. For example, the baby might explore the edges and shapes of big puzzle pieces long before she can fit them into the cut-out spaces they are designed for.

During this stage, the infant may be involved with object play in increasingly specific ways. In **functional-relational play** (Belsky and Most, 1981), the infant connects two or more objects. Very young infants may play with multiple items without making any obviously meaningful connection between them, but by 12 months most have made connections based on the functions of the objects. The infant might put a phone handset back on the receiver, for example, or place a small figure inside a toy car.

The infant's centredness on herself is apparent, but she enjoys lots of adult involvement in her play. She likes the adult to repeat activities, such as partially hiding a toy and recovering it, building up towers of blocks so she can knock them down, and repeating the same short rhyme. The adult may also encourage the infant to pull himself up, stand, cruise, or, later, walk. By the end of this stage, many infants will be playing interactive games such as pat-a-cake (Sheridan, 1997).

Infants at this stage are not too young to enjoy books, although they tend to see the images in illustrations as representing objects rather than as part of a story (Hughes, Elicker, and Veen, 1995). Some books for very young children include furry, smooth, and rough textures in the illustrations; infants may enjoy exploring these with their fingers. Cuddling with an infant while reading a very simple story or pointing out a few objects in a book is a positive break from other play situations. It helps to build a child's vocabulary and establish a familiarity with books as sources of learning and enjoyment. Books are also an excellent way to present culturally familiar images to children of diverse backgrounds.

TEMPERAMENT

Sensitive adults will be able to identify the infant's temperament type among the nine sets of characteristics or three constellations suggested by Chess and Thomas (1990) (see Appendix). It is possible that an infant's temperament may not mesh well with an adult's style. This can present a challenge to even the most responsive adult. Being aware of the goodness of fit is important. It highlights discrepancies between the expectations and interactions of adults and the infants that they care for. If a match has some troublesome aspects that challenge the caregiver, the child could be labelled difficult. This could place the child at a long-term disadvantage (Goldstein, 1992) that creates developmental difficulties.

How infants approach new situations, how they play, and their routine patterns are all shaped by temperament. Adults can learn to respond effectively to infants of various temperament styles, and help children recognize their own style and learn to manage that style as they mature. However, as mentioned above, not all adults' and children's styles make good combinations. Parents must find ways to work with the combinations that exist in their families; in extreme cases they might need some professional support to develop strategies that make the relationships work. In child-care centres we can alter staffing arrangements to some extent to create more effective combinations. Patterns that are either too similar or very different can present the greatest challenges. Although no adult should come to a hasty conclusion about a child in any respect, this is particularly true for temperament styles. These cannot be gauged in a short time. To look at what characteristics are consistent over time takes time. At this stage of the infant's development, it is more likely that the infant's temperament style can be discerned. Also, remember that there are characteristics that are developmental—such as the willingness to go to strangers, gesturing, openness to new ideas, and responsiveness to stimuli. These are more likely to be indicators of her stage of development than her temperament.

LANGUAGE AND COMMUNICATION

Body Language

With a wide repertoire of gestures and vocalizations, the infant may make herself understood without the use of real words. If her cues receive an appropriate response, the infant is likely to have her gestures reinforced, and so will repeat them (Quilliam, 1994). Skillful educators and parents may extend the infant's **gesture vocabulary** by using a broader range of actions than the child would use spontaneously (Garcia, 1994).

Infants can use body language so successfully that some parents become concerned that their toddlers may choose not to talk. It is true that infants whose body language is well understood may be later in gaining a spoken vocabulary. Information may be more easily conveyed and understood through gestures and facial expressions than through one-word exchanges with an infant at this stage. Use of body language enhances the infant's communication skills and encourages greater sensitivity between adult and child. The adult who uses both gesture and words simultaneously offers the child an advantage in communication skill acquisition.

Receptive and Expressive Language

The use of gestures along with the spoken word can reinforce of the meaning of the words. It is likely that an infant at this stage understands several words if they are heard in context. This is her **receptive lan-**

guage. Even at 9 months, an infant can usually understand a simple instruction associated with a gesture. For example, the instruction "give it to Daddy" may be understood if Daddy has his hand outstretched at the same time he utters the words (Sheridan, 1997). By 12 months, the infant may obey simple instructions given in short phrases, like "Knock down the blocks" or "Give me the soother."

The infant at this stage is beginning to reshape early vocalizations into sounds that approximate those of the language spoken around her. They are early attempts at expressive language. The child experiments with her ability to make sounds. She hears sounds, imitates them, and, with lots of reinforcement from adults who imitate her sounds, remodels them into word-like sounds. This sounds like a complex process, but it happens without most adults realizing what is taking place—they are just enjoying the interactions.

Imitation doesn't explain the whole language-acquisition process, though. It is apparent that infants have an ability to acquire language in a way that cannot be fully explained by imitation theories. They are, it appears, **pre-wired** to gain language in infancy as long as they are exposed to language (Chomsky, 1968). Infants at this age are at a critical period for acquiring language. If they are not exposed to it now, they are unlikely to catch up later.

To express oneself using spoken language is an exciting step toward realizing one's potential. The **syllabic repetitions**—that is, the **babbling** repetition of single sounds—by the 9-month infant show the likelihood that language will be acquired. "Da-da-da" is reshaped by an adult and sounds like "dad dad." When Daddy hears this, he thinks the infant is saying his name. "Wow! Dad. Yes, come to *Dad*," he says. This is a simple example of the work adults do in supporting language. It can be described as a process of **scaffolding**, or providing structures to assist new learning (Bruner, 1983). By 12 months, the infant may speak two to six real words in context (Sheridan, 1997).

For receptive or **expressive language** to occur, several conditions must already exist. The infant needs to have the physical attributes of adequate hearing, vocal chords to produce sound, and a neurological system that is ready to process language data. In addition, the infant needs the ability to imitate, motivation to communicate, symbolic understanding that words have meaning, memory for words, surroundings in which language is used, adults who will simplify language to make it accessible, a close relationship in which communication is personal, and an environment about which there is information to share. When any of these conditions are compromised, the infant's language-acquisition process can become difficult.

SOCIO-EMOTIONAL DEVELOPMENT

There is some evidence to suggest that emotional development is subject to many of the same conditions as language (Poisson and DeGangi, 1992). Both are essentially social aspects of development, although we may see them as separate domains.

Stage of Emotional Growth

At 9 or even 12 months, infants do not understand emotions that are expressed and cannot label them. However, they are responsive to adults' facial expressions. They are also responsive to moods, and tend to be fussy when the adult is anxious and contented when the atmosphere seems calm. The range of emotions expressed by infants of this stage is still limited. They do not yet appear to appreciate expression of emotions such as shame, shyness, or guilt (Izard and Malatesta, 1987), which require a knowledge of self and others that is beyond them.

Greenspan and Greenspan (1985) describe the 9-month-old infant as entering a period focused on the "emergence of the **organized sense of self**." The infant is beginning to conceptualize emotions. For example, she relates love to nice experiences, hugs and kisses, and attention.

Greenspan and Greenspan assert that while this time is one of considerable physical advancement, the infant's emotions too are taking leaps forward. Significant for many adults is that the baby will show much clearer behaviours associated with her feelings. For example, ways that she might show that she is pleased may involve sound production, smiling, and reaching out. In many other situations there will be synchronized actions and expressions. Frequently these lead to her being able to express her feelings quite effectively—particularly to the adult who takes time to read her cues. You may observe the baby making more links between things. Occasionally she may imitate an adult's action and elaborate the sequence using her own imaginative ideas. At other times, she might use one object in place of another and think that the result is funny. Whether or not she really appreciates the incongruity (things in the wrong place) is not always certain, but she'll laugh because others are laughing even if she doesn't quite get what is funny. (Review Greenspan and Greenspan's chart of emotional milestones in Appendix.)

A further advancement of this stage can be seen in the baby's efforts to gain greater control over things and people. She takes initiative in communication and will respond well to others' efforts to communicate with her—as long as she has established a strong bond with them. The trusting relationship is the basis of her ability to try things independently, and she needs encouragement to do this. Depending on her temperament style, you are likely to see a baby who is not only taking physical control over her environment, but having a real effect on the adults around her. Being focused on the child, we might overlook the influence the young child is having on the adults and other children—she finds ways of making her mark!

Taking the initiative to explore is very important—and is an early sign of independence based upon **trust**—the core of a stable relationship. As her mobility increases, you may see her extend her own physical boundaries but check back for approval by way of a smile or positive facial expression. If she gets the encouragement she seeks, she may extend the circle of discovery around the adult but with regular **social referencing** as she seeks an adult's approval. Interestingly, if she gets a negative response—perhaps the adult shows mock horror at her impending action—she may be sufficiently influenced that she stops what she is doing or returns to be closer to the adult. The adult's emotions influence the infant significantly at this stage and an indication of a strong bond is that she tunes into the adult's feelings. As she reads the adult's expressions, she notices the mood that is reflected. She may take on a similar emotion to that of the adult or respond with a questioning face.

As a caregiver it is essential to note the effect of one's own feelings. Even feelings that we think are hidden may be absorbed by infants. Earlier on in the baby's life the effect may have related only to being unhappy if the adult was agitated, or to being easily soothed if the adult was calm and peaceful. Now the infant is more in tune with adults than we might imagine.

The emotional partnership that the infant has with adults is particularly important for emotional growth at this time. The emphasis in this partnership needs to be on building trust (Erikson, 1959). The adult must be physically and emotionally close and extremely consistent and responsive to the infant's needs. An increased opportunity for emotional closeness exists now that the infant can communicate a little more.

Erik Erikson's psychosocial explanation of trust as cornerstone of the healthy development of every infant is echoed by other theorists, but his emphasis on trust places it at the centre of all later emotional crises and challenges. It is understandable that in the first few months the baby's experience of **basic trust** lies in having her needs met and her world externally regulated. By the time the infant reaches 6 months or so her basic trust—that is a physical rather than conscious feeling—matures into trust in specific people and in familiar surroundings. This new type of **trust** takes on consciousness that is evident in her behaviour. Now that she has built specific attachments, her trust is in those people with whom she has bonded.

If the adult fails to live up to the expectations that the infant may have of particular adults, she may experience a feeling of **mistrust**. This is an emotion where, within the infant's concept of the predictability of this adult's actions, she becomes disappointed. Seemingly small changes in the adult's response to her—such as if a parent is temporarily emotionally disengaged because she is unhappy about an event, or the fact that her primary caregiver is not present for her (although another person well qualified for the job is available to her), she may come to be mistrustful. Although Erikson was of the opinion that such problems could be corrected and that infants—as well as older individuals—could recover from a temporary spoiling of the trusting relationship, he was sure that the issue had to be addressed. If trust was not required there could be ongoing difficulties for the child. The environment, too, must be routine and predictable for the child at this stage; disorganized patterns are particularly troublesome for some very young children.

"Infants of 4 to 12 months are developing more differentiated and organized systems of emotions and behaviour during this period and their internal control is expanding," comments Martha Bronson (2000) in her work on self-regulation in early childhood. "They are developing more complex strategies for soothing themselves, including moving toward or away from caregivers." What this tells us is that the baby's seemingly innate capacity to sort and organize people and objects is becoming meaningful in an emotional as well as a concrete sense.

At the same time, the infant begins to regulate her own emotions, gaining some degree of control over how she feels and how she behaves. The baby's awareness of her own feelings is enabling her to make these attempts to control her behaviour (**self-regulation**). She may be able to soothe herself when unhappy, prepare herself for sleep, disengage herself from over-stimulation, and amuse herself for short periods. As yet these behaviours may be only rudimentary, but they become increasingly evident if the baby's relationships, predictable environments, and

regular routines have enabled her to build trust. The ability to regulate her own emotions is very important for all later pro-social development. But in the short term the baby will be more content if she is supported in her self-regulation.

Bronson suggests that a number of practical conditions, in addition to trust, allow the baby to regulate herself. For example, the caregiver must ensure that when the baby first becomes assertive her refusal to carry out simple requests should be understood as part of her effort to control her environment. The caregiver can observe the baby's efforts to initiate interactions and play behaviours involving other adults or children and make appropriate responses. This may mean that the adult follows the baby's lead in a game or that she does as the child requests—as determined through her body language, gestures, and expressions. Frequently these games involve repeated sequences in which the adult follows the baby's play sequence, just as the baby has her part—like dropping items over the edge of the table for the adult to pick up and return. Also, as the baby internalizes routines, the caregiver needs to offer a simple sequence of happenings during the day, and for them to be repeated every day. Although the routine may seem rigid, it provides the predictability and comfort that lets the baby know what comes next.

Toward the end of this stage, the baby may have observed adults going about their usual domestic activity and tasks. This **observational learning** is essential and provides a model the baby can use to internalize roles. Immediate **imitation** involving simple copying of the whole action or part of it at the time or soon after may frequently be seen. She may demonstrate a stirring or dusting action or hold a real or imaginary item that she "pours." Attempting to put a hat on her head is another type of behaviour that suggests that she has linked an object and its purpose. At times the baby may surprise us by imitating an adult's action some time after the event was first seen. This is an example of **deferred imitation**—mimicking after the action has disappeared. These may appear to be disconnected and separate actions, but they have some internalized meaning, if only the recognition that "this is what grown-up people do." We might see a baby reaching out her arm and dropping things—this might be an imitation of the educator handing out items to each toddler, but we cannot always be correct about the links that the infant makes between actions and their meanings. So far any of these imitations tend to be short sequences. In time they will lengthen and involve stringing together a series of actions; this will be a demonstration of **role-modelling**. Real objects tend to prompt role modelling for the very young child, so items like a play phone, a cup, or other small object might promote acting out a role. Interestingly, infants at this stage may also copy each other in their actions—this is observational learning—but the infant is still behaving in a way that is mostly characteristic of **solitary play**.

Child-care centres' programs can be so busy that the children have little time to amuse themselves. Providing opportunity for the baby to feel that she is by herself (of course infants and toddlers are not really to be left unsupervised), to follow through with her own discoveries, or to try to calm herself when upset is advisable. Many older children find it difficult to play spontaneously or amuse themselves because they did not have the opportunity to become familiar with quiet times, talk to themselves, make "something out of nothing," become aware of their own feelings or inner voice, or use their imagination. This is not to suggest that infants at this stage should be left alone, but that a balance seems desirable between external stimulation and the opportunity for internal regulation.

Early **self-regulation** leads to later **pro-social skills** (positive emotions and behaviours). Unless children have some understanding of their own feelings, and have some control over them, they will be unprepared for a much greater advance in social and emotional development later on. Emotional well-being and self-regulation are essential for happiness and relationship-building through childhood and into adulthood. It seems unlikely, if they are without emotional self-regulation, that young children would ever be ready to take the perspective of others and imagine others' feelings. It would involve moving away from the egocentric thought of infancy and gaining empathy for the other person's feelings. Even so, supporting the infant's ability to regulate her feelings and actions requires only basic support and opportunity.

She needs to be given some opportunity to be alone and to comfort herself. Adults should support the child's efforts to calm herself, and not take over in such a situation. Infants at this stage are becoming more able to direct their anger purposefully (Sroufe, 1979). This is part of the infant's development of goal-directed activity (Fogel, 1997).

Not always does a young child's behaviour indicate the complexity of meaning that might be read into it in an older child. Although we might see an action performed by an infant, it does not necessarily mean that she has the deeper structures of meaning that we might infer from an older child. The early concept development of the infant remains at a **schematic stage**. She has a cognitive cluster of fairly primitive bits of information that have come about from her actions with objects and people. The baby's schemes at this stage are expanding but are entirely dependent upon experience. The ideas that she has about what adults do will come not from her imitation of them but, primarily, from the direct engagement she has had with adults. Some of her actions might lead us to think that she has a deeper appreciation of the thoughts and motives of adults than is possible, particularly when some of the actions we see her perform come from her imitation of adults. But these are surface-level imitations and cannot reflect complexities or any real understanding of what it's like to be an adult. Nevertheless, the relationships that the child and adult enjoy are completely genuine. But it is as though "what you see is all there is." Existentialists might disagree, but there is nothing in the child's behaviour that can lead us to think that her conceptual understanding or consciousness of an adult role is much more than a scheme related to her limited experience.

Infants at this stage have made specific secure attachments to the key adults in their lives, particularly their parents and caregivers, who are significant and consistent figures. It is evident that the infant, particularly at this stage, is able to make **multiple attachments** with a small group of people (Maccoby and Feldman, 1972).

Earlier research had emphasized the mother–infant attachment (Bowlby, 1969) rather than any bonding with other adults in the child's life. One might question the motives of some researchers at times—and this is one such time—when the outcome of their work underscored the need for mothers to stay at home to care for their children. If attachments to other people were impossible, it would seem that the mother had no other choice. Social and political motives will always influence research, and the very fact that it is conducted is similarly influenced. However, what we now know is that because the baby can make several secure attachments, it is possible for fathers, extended-family members, and unrelated caregivers to offer adequate care to babies. Of course, for the attachment to occur, certain conditions must be present. The baby's basic needs must be met and, more importantly, her psychological needs must be provided for. This requires emotional engagement with the baby, responsive nurturance, trust-building, and continuity of care.

The phrase **quality of attachment** refers to the degree of security felt by the infant in an attachment.

Quality of attachment seems to be rooted early in the infant's first year (Ainsworth et al., 1978), later attachments being affected by the bonds made in the first few months. This does not necessarily mean that infants will be damaged if they make no very close attachments in their first days. Although Bowlby (1969) suggested that this was the case, later studies argue that he overstated the necessity for mother–infant bonding in the first week of life (Rutter, 1979). Nonetheless, attachment behaviours are essential for healthy emotional development, and later weeks and months are just as important. The quality of attachment depends on the baby's circumstances. When researchers and educators observe infants, they look to see if the quality of attachment is strong—if it is what is called a **secure attachment**. Infants demonstrating secure attachments are more likely to be the babies who are offered consistent loving care. Secure attachment is one of the main conditions for later resilience. If life experiences become less desirable later on, the child is more likely to cope with the stressors.

By about 9 months, the infant is likely to enter a reciprocal stage of socio-emotional development, where she can return some of the love that has been given to her since birth (Sroufe, 1979). She may hug, kiss, smile, and share a real chuckle with her caregiver.

Self-Concept

As we discussed previously, the trust relationship and the ability to link cause and effect enable the infant to realize that she is not only a separate person but one who can influence her surroundings. These things help the infant develop a concept of an **existential self**—that is, that she exists and has some power. If the individual is to flourish, this concept of self is crucially important.

For an infant, having control over objects and herself is part of the process of discovering what she can do. Adults have traditionally underestimated the importance of this area of development. A child's self-concept can either enable her to succeed or limit the realization of her potential.

In Jungian psychotherapy, **motivation** propels elements of the developmental stages of the individual—parts that include the concept of self (Kast, 1992). In contrast, Freud would consider the drive to be **instinctual**, innate or biological. The reason this matters is that adults need to be able to support the child's **self-concept**, so how it develops must be of importance. If the creation of the self emanates from a force that is predetermined, then we can have little control over its coming to be. We can only help the

child to realize what she might have control over—her behaviour—but not her feeling of self. On the other hand, if the self is dependent upon motivation (although that, too, could be biological), then we can intervene and support her motivation to discover herself. In Kast's interpretation of Jung, she says, "When we turn to the self it becomes clear that a utopian goal (because its completion is impossible) motivates the process of **individuation** (the initial separation from mother to become a separate person), for the self motivates self-realization" [my parentheses]. "Individuation is understood not only as becoming one with ourselves, but also as realization of the self" (p. 5). According to Jung, the self acts **a priori,** as the creative principle that guides the structure of the **ego**. At the heart of the self is the origin of the psyche's self-regulation.

What this means to adults is similar to our understanding of attachment; it is essential for the child to be trusted by the adult, and to trust the adult. The adult–child trust is reciprocal, so the self emerges as a result of attachment and the baby needs to feel that attachment to know of her symbiosis (togetherness and interdependence) with the adult before she can experience separation. The separation has to be experienced before the sense of oneness or individuation can occur. At Kast suggests, this is utopian inasmuch as it can never be complete—we can never completely cut the cord that ties one to the other. The self is a result of separation, but the separation cannot be final.

In the drive toward self-realization, as the infant is motivated to find out about the world, she takes literal and emotional steps away from her attachment figures. To find herself she needs this separation—but it can only occur because she is attached!

Being an Infant

Several times in this chapter we have mentioned **consciousness**. Before this stage it is difficult to know to what extent the baby has consciousness. She obviously does in the sense of responding to stimuli, building schemes of understanding, being alert, and making relationships, but to what extent is she reacting on a biological level? True consciousness involves being aware of being aware. So, using that definition, when does the baby become conscious? Some answers come from phenomenologists, but they reframe the question. They are more likely to wonder what it's like to be a baby. They think they are most likely to get some idea about a baby's consciousness through that exploration. Several interesting studies have been conducted using a phenomenological research method. Rather than try to answer the question in relation to all children in all situations, most phenomenologists choose to focus on one area of a baby's experience.

In seeking the baby's experience, it is assumed that experience includes some level of consciousness of that experience. The following situations are some that have been explored in order to try to reach the essence of the baby's experience: finger play, diapering, crying, and breast-feeding. The conclusions cannot be **generalized**—taken as applicable to other situations—but reading them gives a sense of how the baby experiences her world. Even casual observation conducted at the child's eye level can bring some interesting perspectives. We cannot "unknow" what we know, so this presents particularly difficult challenges for the infant phenomenologist. Our perceptions of childhood, made up of our memories of experience, being with other children, perhaps rearing our own children, and, of course, studying children from the traditional approaches of behaviourism, cognitive psychology, or other schools of thought, further compromise our ability to understand what it feels like to be an infant. One way to try, when documenting the experience of being a baby from your own perspective, is to leave aside your perceptions and analysis of the infant (called bracketing) and try to get into the moment by engaging with the infant. Being part of the dyad is more likely to enable you to reach the child's perspective.

Another way to try to understand the baby's perspective is to read sympathetic writings describing infants. Selma Fraiberg's (1959) understanding of early childhood shines through her account, *The Magic Years*. In particular, her description of "becoming a person" is delightfully sensitive and, although recorded from the adult's perspective, offers detail that leads us to understand who the child is, her behaviour, and, most importantly, what is going on underneath her behaviour. Only by entering her world through careful observation, reflection, and engagement can we begin to know what it is like to be a baby.

▶ Particular Needs

Trusting relationships need ongoing connection and the supplying of basic needs. The infant needs human contact and physical connection, not only food, clothes, and diaper changes. Her psychological needs are of paramount importance because of the critical period of her socio-emotional development.

MOVEMENT AND STIMULATION

Mobility, whether in the form of crawling or walking, changes the child's perspective and alters the way he can take hold of the world and make it his own. Many infants continue crawling for some time. Even when they can walk, their crawling skill allows them to get where they want to go much faster. An infant needs lots of time and opportunity to move. Warm, uncluttered floor space is essential, but he also needs large pieces of furniture that he can use to cruise along when he is ready. He especially needs objects that he can safely use to pull himself to his feet.

With his improved physical control, the infant wants to explore his environment. He needs to be enabled to do this. Because the infant is able to crawl, or otherwise move toward, desired objects, he needs playthings that require the use of fine motor skills. Sensory exploration is the central theme of development at this stage, so the adult must provide a variety of safe and interesting materials. The infant may continue to mouth objects, so everything must be safe and clean.

LANGUAGE

Infants at this stage are extremely receptive to what they hear and see. They copy many of the sounds that adults produce. Adult involvement in assisting language acquisition is essential. This scaffolding is needed to make links among objects, people, and actions so the baby can make meaning for herself, using simple clear words, reinforcing them with gestures, and repeating the actions and words. This can be made fun in games, action rhymes, looking at board books, and in everyday domestic situations. In this way, babbling and real language can be bridged.

SOCIAL CONNECTIONS AND EMOTIONAL SUPPORT

Infants at 9 to 12 months are very interested in people and will try to get adults to join their games. Adult involvement in an infant's activities is essential to offer encouragement and stimulation and to increase the infant's comfort with such social situations. Adults need to be able to read the child's expressions and body language to interpret meanings. Shared meanings are a key part of the child's social development. Only time and attention to the infant can develop these shared meanings.

Infants at this stage search the faces of adults for familiarity and encouragement. The adults must be available to the infant for prolonged and uninterrupted periods. If the infant makes attachments with multiple adults, these need to be reinforced with ongoing consistent caregiving.

NUTRITION AND MEALTIMES

Although food should never be associated with reward, feeding can begin to be a very pleasant social occasion. It is never too early to provide a positive role model, so you spend time with the infants, modelling "proper" behaviour at the table, and setting the tone for the social interactions. Babies continue to need milk as their primary source of nutrients. Of course, breast is best.

By this stage, infants will usually have tried a variety of different foods and might have some clear preferences. Offer small portions of foods the child dislikes along with ones he likes. If the infant is hungry, he will eat some of each. Although balanced nutrition is most important, you want to avoid battles over eating. Mealtimes should not be associated with stress.

▶ Developmental Variation

Growth charts indicate that infants at this stage present a widening range of weight and height. Although many babies will triple their birth weight in

Mealtimes can be very messy, but the baby enjoys the social interaction and will gradually gain the skills to feed himself.

12 months, not all babies will reach this milestone as soon, and many others will surpass it. Remember that gradual progression is more important than actual measures. Professional use of growth charts can be helpful in detecting signs of nutritional or developmental issues.

A wide range of developmental stages is also evident at this age. While some babies are trying to sit unsupported, others will have control of their legs and will have been crawling for some time or will have progressed straight to cruising and walking. Parents and educators may have concerns about these differences, but development is not a race. Those who are "ahead" have few advantages over those who develop at a slower pace.

Concerns about developmental differences might lead parents to have their infant assessed by a specialist. Such an assessment may reveal a problem but is far more likely to indicate an individual pattern that remains within the norm. Educators and parents can help each other by sharing information and discussing developmental issues. If a thorough assessment is needed, both parties can contribute to this; both the parents and the educators have pertinent information to offer during the assessment process. Once the results of an assessment are known, frequently the parents and educators can devise a plan to support the infant's development.

AUTISM

Autism is a little-understood syndrome that results in severe introversion or self-absorption. Autistic children are unable to form relationships, may have difficulties with speech and language, repeat behaviours for prolonged periods, and respond negatively to new circumstances. Since young children may display these kinds of behaviour for a variety of reasons, the disorder can be difficult to diagnose. With the variety of symptoms, it may take time to arrive at a diagnosis of autism. By the same token, children may be assumed to be autistic when in fact they are simply slow to warm up to people or to communicate or are onlookers rather than doers.

Educators have to guard against a tendency to be hasty in suggesting that a child may be autistic. Some young children may have attachment difficulties or communication styles that are wrongly attributed to autism. Children may also make attachments to objects, which is a characteristic of autistic children, but this may simply be a phase. These children need support, but not to the degree that follows a diagnosis of autism.

The suspicion that a child is autistic may come from the observations of parents or educators, but a diagnosis can be made only after clinical assessment. Infants and young children with autism can usually be accommodated within a child-care centre. The typical management technique is to retain the same behavioural expectations for these children as for others of the same age. Parents are likely to be concerned that caregivers and educators provide adequate care and proper strategies for the autistic child. Educators should work closely with the parents to carry out the directions of the specialist.

▶ Parents as Partners in Care

Effective communication between parents and educators is always important, but never more so than when there are development concerns about an infant, especially ones as serious and difficult to diagnose as autism. Yet educators can be so concerned about communicating important information to parents that they forget that listening is also essential for two-way communication. Box 8.1 outlines strategies for developing listening skills, which are indispen-

sable if educators are to work effectively with parents in the care of children.

As we saw in the introduction to this chapter, a few moments spent in conversation with the parent who is dropping off a child at the centre can help to reassure a nervous parent that the child is receiving responsive, high-quality care. This is also a good time for the parent to inform the caregiver of particular concerns or requests. However, since at this time the caregiver may be responsible for several children, a more involved conversation might have to be rescheduled for off-hours, as Box 8.1 suggests.

▶ Health Concerns

HYGIENE

As infants become mobile, they are increasingly able to get into everything in sight. Thus, caregivers must be extremely careful about the hygiene of the environment and the spread of infection. Steps need to be taken to ensure that all toys are washed and they are not passed from mouth to mouth. Child-care centres

---

BOX 8.1

DEVELOP YOUR LISTENING SKILLS

It is particularly important for educators to develop their listening skills when they are communicating with parents. Such skill development can include ensuring that the atmosphere is conducive to talking, providing the time for communication, encouraging the parent to share her or his thoughts, making listening "noises," paraphrasing what the parent said to show that you are listening and understand what's being said, adding "I hear you" comments to acknowledge the parent's feelings, mirroring body language to show sympathy, maintaining appropriate eye contact, and responding positively so that the parent feels heard.

All this can be challenging, especially while you are on duty with infants or toddlers. You might find it helpful to set aside some time for such conversations in the early evening. Alternatively, you might arrange for a telephone conversation at a mutually convenient time or have another staff person cover for you so you can talk without interruption.

As early childhood educators are aware, communication is not always verbal. Heightened awareness of body language and reading young children's cues can lead us to apply the same skills to adults. This can be useful, but it can also lead to some assumptions that can be particularly misleading when the parent cannot tell us, in English, that we have misunderstood. English-speaking people themselves come from various traditions and have many socially learned behaviours that are particular to their background. These behaviours include their body language. Culturally shaped behaviour, for example, leads some people to indicate yes with a sign that, for others, means no. These are just two examples in which gestures could be read incorrectly. You will want to become familiar with the cultural styles of your parent group before jumping to any conclusion about what their body language says.

must have enough toys that they can be washed and that more than one infant can play with the same sort of toy.

Just as the environment must be hygienic, the same concerns apply to people within the environment. The best way to limit the spread of infection is to wash hands. This includes the infant's hands as well as your own.

DENTAL HEALTH

Teeth come through at different times and by this stage many infants will have some teeth. As soon as a child has one tooth, dental hygiene becomes important. Each child should have his own toothbrush, and brushing should occur regularly. A smear of toothpaste on a cloth or soft brush will enable you to clean the baby's teeth. The possibility of dental decay can be reduced if fruit juices or sweetened drinks are avoided, especially at sleep time.

▶ Signs of Potential Neglect or Abuse

GUIDANCE AND DISCIPLINE: WHAT IS TOO MUCH?

Guiding a child's behaviour involves supporting the child's development in a positive and encouraging way. Discipline may use many of the same techniques as guidance, but it attempts to control and shape behaviours in accordance with the adult's perspec-

tive. With guidance strategies, the child learns self-control and is empowered to operate independently; with discipline, the child learns who is boss and who holds the power in the relationship—and it's not her.

There are historical differences in the emphasis given to guidance and discipline. These differences reflect changing views of the nature of children and the role of adults. Current thinking focuses on the need to support and guide the young child rather than mould and discipline her. The role of the adult has changed to fit this child-centred approach. But not all people agree with this approach. Some educational circles have returned to more adult control, presumably in reaction to a perceived lack of self-discipline in older children.

In addition to historical differences, diverse cultures may emphasize guidance over discipline, or vice versa. Some cultures believe that infants and toddlers should be entirely unrestricted. Others believe that firm discipline is essential. In some families, parents from different backgrounds may not agree on the level of discipline. This may result in one parent thinking it necessary to meet every need and desire of the young child, while the other thinks the baby should be left to cry rather than be spoiled with too much attention. (Box 8.2 addresses the question of whether babies can be spoiled when adults give them everything they want.)

As educators, we will find that our work with families continually leads us to question the values that underpin our practice. What is desirable, what is acceptable, and what is not? A useful indicator may be what we know about children from experience and

---

BOX 8.2

ARE WE SPOILING INFANTS WHEN WE GIVE THEM EVERYTHING THEY WANT?

Infants cannot have a want that is not also a need. They think in the here and now, and can only have wants that relate to physical needs. Thus, giving infants what they want or need cannot spoil them. Another way of looking at the question focuses on what spoiling really is. When we use the term, we usually mean that the child will, in some way, be damaged. Could an infant be damaged by having his needs met? Of course not.

Desmond Morris (1995) said, "A spoilt baby is one who has been disciplined, not one who has been pampered." He went on to say that "a schoolchild may well be one who has been disciplined too little, but a spoilt baby is one who has been disciplined too much." He clearly believes that imposing some kind of external control on the infant might solve an adult's problems, but it can, at the same time, break down a relationship of trust. You can see this in a situation where the adult decides not to respond to a baby's cries for attention. In time, the infant may stop crying. The adult is happy in the short term, but the baby has stopped crying because he has lost the hope that the adult will respond to him. His trust is diminished.

from our child development study. If we use this knowledge wisely, we might realize that children develop their potential if they feel positive about themselves and their achievements, if they know who they are and can make decisions about what is right or wrong, if they internalize role models and can think critically, given the chance. If these observations are accurate, they suggest that guidance is more appropriate than discipline. Thus, we can contend that positive guidance is desirable, and that discipline, with its connotations of power and control, is not.

So are parents who use discipline being abusive or neglectful? Many of the classic definitions of child abuse include mention of a community standard that is commonly accepted. This standard is clear in extreme cases, but it is muddier in other situations where values conflict. To further complicate matters, child protection workers are charged with major legal and moral responsibilities, and yet agencies are often understaffed and overburdened. As a result, workers may be forced to make hasty decisions and apply personal values as well as subtle interpretations of the law. Is the parent who does not respond to the baby's crying after bedtime being abusive? In light of the values in this book, yes. But this alone will probably not attract the attention of child protection agencies. If the parent were poor or on welfare or had a history of petty crime, or lived in a place with thin walls, the child protection agency might be alerted to the crying baby. These other factors might influence people's perception of the situation, further muddying the supposed community standard.

Child abuse or neglect exists where a child is treated improperly, physically hurt, denied basic needs, emotionally manipulated, or otherwise damaged. That means that, while discipline can be considered acceptable, inappropriate use of power over the child is definitely wrong. The shades of grey in between will remain a topic of discussion in later chapters. See the section on neglect in the Appendix.

▶ Everyday Safety Issues

Because of the increasing mobility of 9-to-12-month-old infants, new safety concerns have to be considered. Here are some of the practical steps you should take:

- Remove all small objects that might come within range of the mobile infant.
- Check that the corners of all furniture are not potentially dangerous.

- Remove glass-topped tables and sharp objects (these should never be in a group setting, but might be present in a private home).
- Check that stairs have gates top and bottom.
- Childproof all low cupboards by installing child locks.
- Remove all hazardous materials, such as bleach, detergent, and cleaning materials, from low cupboards and lock them away on high shelves or discard them.
- Cover electrical outlets with safety covers.
- Remove objects from the floor that can present falling hazards.
- Discard all plastic bags and other dangerous items that the mobile infant might manage to reach.
- Install gates to ensure the child cannot get out of a room.
- Ensure that all outdoor play areas are fenced.
- Ensure that water troughs, paddling pools, swimming pools, and all containers of water that have the potential to cause drowning are removed, drained, and/or fenced.
- Check on the child's ability to climb out of a crib and avoid soft toys or bumper cushions that might provide steps out of the crib.
- Create increased visibility around doors so one can see if infants have crawled behind them.
- Ensure that baby equipment cannot be climbed when the child is on the floor.
- Check all toys and furniture to ensure that children cannot climb to danger.
- Increase diligence of supervision to track the movements of a mobile infant.
- Ensure that infants have bare feet, shoes, or rubber-coated socks on slippery floors.

▶ Starting Points for Response

RESPONSIVE CAREGIVING

Emerging skills are the focus of this period. The caregiver needs to observe each infant to determine individual patterns of development. Responses must always combine emotional and practical support. The infant still needs lots of cuddles, smiles, and playfulness. The caregiver's job is to make experiences enjoyable and to extend learning opportunities as they appear. Tuning in to the infant's needs remains important. Box 8.3 offers suggestions for getting in tune with an infant at this stage. The infant will be able to let you know whether what you are doing is right or wrong.

Box 8.3

GETTING IN TUNE WITH INFANTS AT 9 TO 12 MONTHS

Below are some starting points for building your responsive skills with a 9- to 12-month-old infant. Tune in with respect and:

- Enter the infant's space carefully; wait for her to include you.
- Invite the infant to you; accept any response.
- Encourage shared meanings through activity.
- Ensure close proximity when the infant wants or needs it.
- Experiment with different types of encouragement, usually through touch.
- Enjoy play experiences on the baby's level.
- Imitate the baby's sound production and assist by reshaping sounds into words.
- Respond quickly to needs and requests.
- Provide simple choices.
- Identify and accommodate the baby's level of mobility, providing space and large objects/furniture for pulling herself up into a standing position.
- Offer a variety of objects that can be grabbed and passed from hand to hand.
- Carefully select toys and play material for mouthing and handling.
- Have pictures visible of the infant and family members.
- Introduce a few safe, smaller objects to test the baby's pincer grasp.
- Offer taste or smell experiences in play.
- Introduce board books and a wider range of pictures.
- Play peek-a-boo around large objects.
- Share situational jokes.
- Have items available that make sounds.
- Build towers of blocks so the infant can knock them over many times.
- Demonstrate caring behaviours with dolls.
- Expand the infant's gesture vocabulary to aid communication.
- Use words and gestures simultaneously; repeat words and simple phrases with actions to make links.
- Provide a language-rich environment with conversation, rhymes, poems, and stories.
- Sing action rhymes.
- Sing along with the baby's babble.
- Slightly exaggerate your facial expressions.
- Maintain eye contact, particularly as the infant begins to move away from you.
- Make the day predictable in its main sequence of events.
- Acknowledge the range of the infant's feelings as they are demonstrated.
- Extend the baby's social world by overlapping relationships as transitions occur.
- Enable the baby to experience other babies.
- Acknowledge/accommodate babies who need supported transitions.
- Allow safe risk-taking so the baby experiences minor consequences.
- Whenever possible, try to organize staff so that the babies choose their caregivers.
- Ensure that floor space is warm when infants are on the floor for extended periods.
- Tape textured materials on the floor so the infant can crawl over them.
- Position furniture for safe cruising.
- Provide expressive encouragement.
- Encourage the baby to be actively involved with dressing/undressing.
- Talk through the infant's actions (e.g., "Now you're sitting up").
- Talk through your actions (e.g., "I'm going to change your diaper now").

SUPPORTIVE GUIDANCE

The infant's developing self-concept needs support. The infant knows that he is a separate person and that he can have some effect on the people and things in his world, but he doesn't yet recognize himself in the mirror. He likes to play games where he can repeat enjoyable actions, and he is starting to solve little problems as he plays. Play opportunity is the core activity of this age. The infant needs opportunities to discover everything, with the adult's help. Transition times can be challenging, because the infant tends to be firmly attached to one adult. Caregiving strategies need to take into account his fear of strangers and possible separation anxiety.

FACILITATING DEVELOPMENT

Sensory exploration as well as body exploration is playful learning at this stage. You might remove the infant's shoes and socks so he can reach and explore his toes. Light clothing—or none at all—allows the infant to more fully experience the sensations of rolling, sitting, and looking at himself.

External stimulation should match the infant's interests. At this stage, babies tend to be attracted to bright colours and patterns. A baby wants to engage adults in his play because he likes the attention and they provide him with increased understanding of what is happening. His language may start to emerge soon. At this stage, the baby needs lots of talking and listening to prepare for the language explosion that is about to occur.

HOLISTIC RESPONSE

Activities 8.1 and 8.2 encourage a holistic response to infants at 9 to 12 months. Activity 8.1 suggests ways of engaging in the experience of babies at this stage and extending your interactions with them. Activity 8.2 (page 218) helps you to observe each infant and to develop activities that are targeted to individual interests and skill levels.

Activity 8.1

Responding to the Changing Needs of Infants at 9 to 12 Months

Your interactions with the infant at 9 to 12 months must be responsive to her needs and emerging skills. To assist you in engaging in the infant's experience, the activity that follows offers suggestions that may extend your interactions. Careful observation is necessary so that you introduce the idea at the right time and in the appropriate way. Each suggestion includes ways to extend the idea, if the infant is ready. This activity also illustrates the safety, communication, conceptual, and developmental issues that you, as a child-care professional, need to keep in mind as you respond to the infant at 9 to 12 months.

Activity 8.1

Responding to Changing Needs of Infants at 9 to 12 Months

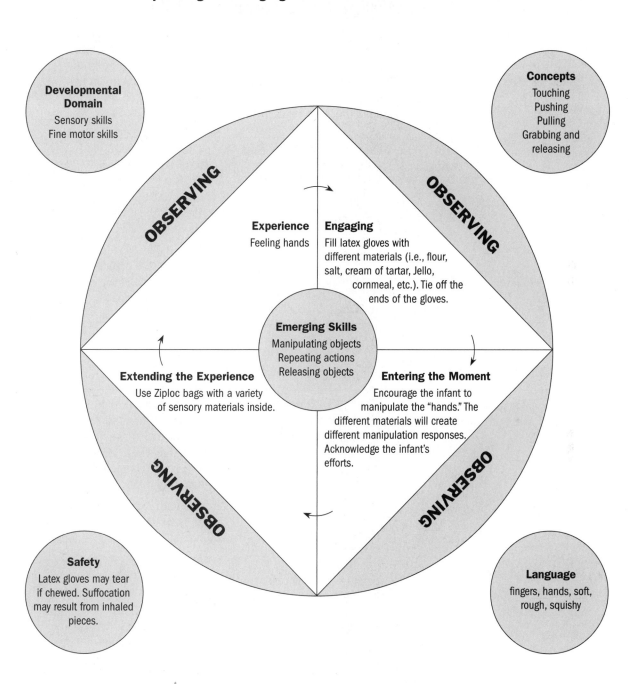

Developmental Domain

Sensory skills
Fine motor skills

Concepts

Touching
Pushing
Pulling
Grabbing and releasing

OBSERVING

OBSERVING

Experience

Feeling hands

Engaging

Fill latex gloves with different materials (i.e., flour, salt, cream of tartar, Jello, cornmeal, etc.). Tie off the ends of the gloves.

Emerging Skills

Manipulating objects
Repeating actions
Releasing objects

Extending the Experience

Use Ziploc bags with a variety of sensory materials inside.

Entering the Moment

Encourage the infant to manipulate the "hands." The different materials will create different manipulation responses. Acknowledge the infant's efforts.

OBSERVING

OBSERVING

Safety

Latex gloves may tear if chewed. Suffocation may result from inhaled pieces.

Language

fingers, hands, soft, rough, squishy

Activity 8.2

Creating Responsive Curriculum for Infants at 9 to 12 Months

Activities for the infant at 9 to 12 months should evolve from their own interests and skill levels. There cannot be a set "curriculum"! The adult's role is to tune in to the infant's world and create experiences that are mutually enjoyable, that celebrate her current abilities, and offer opportunities for continued development. The following ideas will help adults to observe each infant at 9 to 12 months and assist them in providing some meaningful experiences.

With confidence, the adult can extend these ideas yet further.

Developmental Domain	Observation of Emerging Skills (Things You See)	Responsive Experience/Activity
Physical skills	– standing with support – pushing self into sitting position from a lying position – cruising/possible walking – standing alone – drinking from cup independently – picking up objects between forefingers and thumbs	Provide sturdy objects/ furniture for the infant to use for cruising the environment. Provide toys that demonstrate cause-and-effect (pop-ups, dials, etc.). Allow the infant to attempt skills and provide support as needed.
Cognitive skills/language and communication	– saying first word(s) – understanding "no" – vocalizing a lot of gibberish – waving goodbye – gesturing or pointing as a communication method – manipulating and exploring the properties of objects – ripping paper – beginning to use objects appropriately (i.e., pushes buttons, hugs plush animals) – following simple instructions – imitating adult actions – responding to name	Provide a language-rich environment. Infants respond better to communication directed to them than they do to language used around them. Provide both words and gestures when communicating. Provide names for objects pointed to. Provide toys or objects that can be manipulated (and demonstrate cause-and-effect). Provide a varied environment that includes access to the outside world/ community. Provide creative materials (crayons, chalk, variety of types of paper).

Developmental Domain	Observation of Emerging Skills (Things You See)	Responsive Experience/Activity
Social/emotional skills	– clinging to familiar adult due to separation anxiety – checking in with parent when roaming – displaying assertive behaviours – attaching to toys or objects – repeating behaviours that get attention	Provide physical comfort and support to infant as needed. Use the infant's name (as well as the names of others) when talking with the infant. Talk with the infant, responding to her communication attempts. Encourage and provide positive reinforcement for all initiatives.

The following three experiences are suggestions for what might be suitable for the infant's emerging skills at 9 to 12 months of age. It is best to follow the infant's lead—she will usually show us what she is interested in. Try offering her some new activities, because she is likely to be open to novel experiences. If they are successful, you might find that repeating them, or doing them again in slightly different ways, will be interesting to her. Engage in the activity with her, but withdraw the activity if it isn't received well. You might want to try again later, but do things a little differently so she doesn't repeat any negativity. Extend the activities as suggested or, better still, follow her responses. These experiences may provide a good starting point. A list of further experiences may be a helpful guide. Offer any of them to the baby in a similar way to the first three. Think through how you will engage with the infant, enter the moment, and extend the experience. You could try planning those experiences using blank experience charts in the format offered in the book. Now that you have an understanding of the baby's development at this stage, you will appreciate the appropriateness of the activities, but adjust them to individual infants. The guidance strategies offered on the following pages may also be helpful, but develop your own to fit your philosophy and the particular child. A list of manufactured toys that might be suitable for this age range (9 to 12 months) is suggested, but many household items can become excellent toys or play materials.

Responding to Changing Needs

Infants at 9 to 12 Months

EXPERIENCE 1

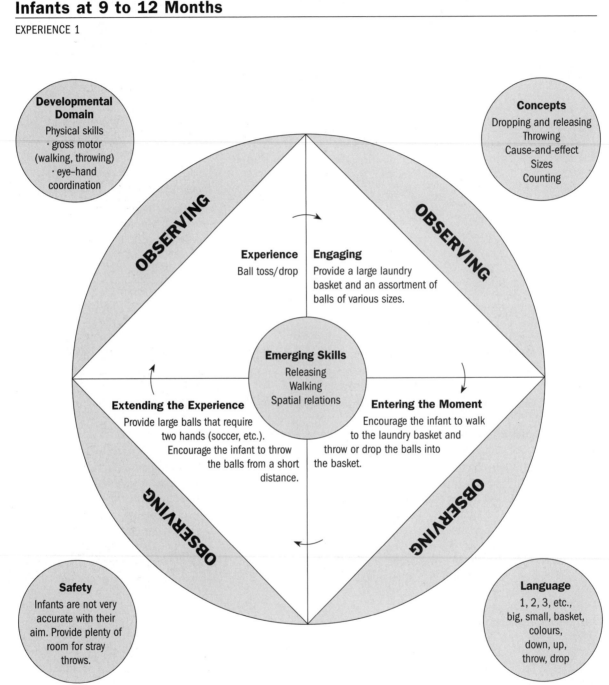

Developmental Domain

Physical skills
· gross motor (walking, throwing)
· eye–hand coordination

Concepts

Dropping and releasing
Throwing
Cause-and-effect
Sizes
Counting

OBSERVING

OBSERVING

Experience

Ball toss/drop

Engaging

Provide a large laundry basket and an assortment of balls of various sizes.

Emerging Skills

Releasing
Walking
Spatial relations

Extending the Experience

Provide large balls that require two hands (soccer, etc.). Encourage the infant to throw the balls from a short distance.

Entering the Moment

Encourage the infant to walk to the laundry basket and throw or drop the balls into the basket.

OBSERVING

OBSERVING

Safety

Infants are not very accurate with their aim. Provide plenty of room for stray throws.

Language

1, 2, 3, etc., big, small, basket, colours, down, up, throw, drop

Responding to Changing Needs

Infants at 9 to 12 Months

EXPERIENCE 2

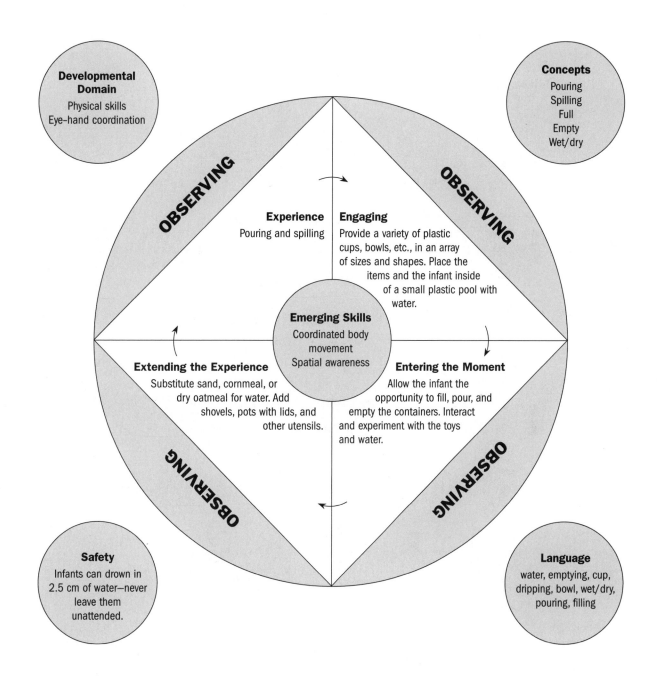

Developmental Domain
Physical skills
Eye-hand coordination

Concepts
Pouring
Spilling
Full
Empty
Wet/dry

OBSERVING

OBSERVING

Experience
Pouring and spilling

Engaging
Provide a variety of plastic cups, bowls, etc., in an array of sizes and shapes. Place the items and the infant inside of a small plastic pool with water.

Emerging Skills
Coordinated body movement
Spatial awareness

Extending the Experience
Substitute sand, cornmeal, or dry oatmeal for water. Add shovels, pots with lids, and other utensils.

Entering the Moment
Allow the infant the opportunity to fill, pour, and empty the containers. Interact and experiment with the toys and water.

OBSERVING

OBSERVING

Safety
Infants can drown in 2.5 cm of water—never leave them unattended.

Language
water, emptying, cup, dripping, bowl, wet/dry, pouring, filling

Responding to Changing Needs

Infants at 9 to 12 Months

EXPERIENCE 3

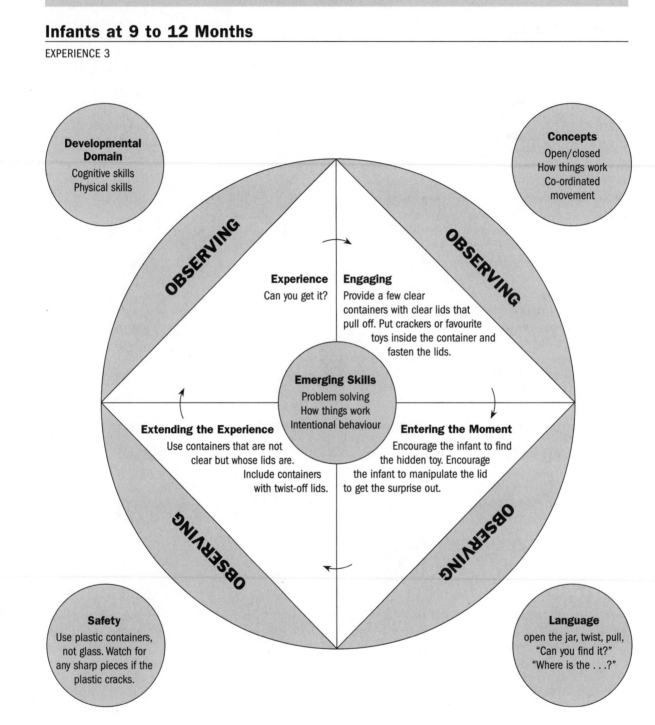

Developmental Domain
Cognitive skills
Physical skills

Concepts
Open/closed
How things work
Co-ordinated movement

OBSERVING

OBSERVING

Experience
Can you get it?

Engaging
Provide a few clear containers with clear lids that pull off. Put crackers or favourite toys inside the container and fasten the lids.

Emerging Skills
Problem solving
How things work
Intentional behaviour

Extending the Experience
Use containers that are not clear but whose lids are. Include containers with twist-off lids.

Entering the Moment
Encourage the infant to find the hidden toy. Encourage the infant to manipulate the lid to get the surprise out.

OBSERVING

OBSERVING

Safety
Use plastic containers, not glass. Watch for any sharp pieces if the plastic cracks.

Language
open the jar, twist, pull, "Can you find it?" "Where is the . . .?"

Further Experiences and Interactions

Further Experiences	Interactions
Stacking cups/nesting cups	Encourage the infant to stack the cups on top of or inside each other. Encourage her to knock the towers down.
Foam blocks	Allow the blocks to get a little wet (play with them in the bathtub). The blocks will then stick together when piled on top of each other.
Banging sticks (wooden spoons, drumsticks, etc.)	Provide a variety of items to bang, hit, and create "music."
Give-and-take	Encourage the turn-taking involved in passing toys back and forth between you and the infant.
Thick/bold crayons	Provide a variety of thick crayons and paper (tape paper down to the table). Allow the infant to stand at a low table (or sit in a high chair) and draw.
Routine-time language	Continue to discuss what happens at routine times—i.e., what will happen next, what is coming up, what to expect, etc.
Pointing power	Infants begin to point at about 11 months. Encourage this means of communication by responding to the gesture. Name the objects they are pointing to and help them to fullfil their need. Elaborate on or explain what is happening.
"This Is the Way . . ."	Sing this popular song along with whatever task you are doing with the infant.
Rolling balls	Provide a variety of balls and roll or pass balls around the room. Encourage the infant to follow the balls.
Shoebox hiding	Place a familiar item inside one of two shoeboxes—close both lids. Encourage the infant to find the item. Provide positive reinforcement.
Parallel-play games	Encourage the infant to play in proximity to other infants. Discuss the fact that these infants are playing with similar toys. Help the infants be aware of the others.
Extra eating utensils	Provide a variety of spoons, dishes, etc. Encourage the infant to attempt self-feeding, but continue to assist the infant to ensure she receives enough to eat.
Sensory doughs	Encourage the infant to push, pull, pound, bend, and tear the dough.

Responsive Guidance for Infants Aged 9 to 12 Months

Age/Stage: 9 to 12 Months

Situation	Response
• Jamal is speaking, but only his mother and father seem to understand what he is saying. • Janine is not saying any clear words, but is using a lot of gestures to communicate her needs.	**Developmental Issue: Language Acquisition** At around 9 months of age, infants are conveying their needs and desires through beginning sounds and gestures. By the 12th month, many infants are uttering their first words. The more familiar the caregiver is with the cues and styles of the infant, the easier it is to understand her communication attempts. Strategies to help the infant's language development include: • naming/labelling everything in the environment, giving the infant the words she would use if she could • listening and responding in turn to the infant's "words" • explaining what is happening during events or tasks • using descriptive sentences to describe things when appropriate • talking like a grown-up, but using simplified sentences (i.e., "bottle," not "baba") • encouraging the infant's attempts at language and communication • keeping directions simple • speaking correctly • not forcing the infant to repeat words • reading and singing to the child • providing both words and gestures when communicating
• Arnold doesn't play with the other children in his play group. • Barbie, Tyrell, and Arthur always seem to fight over the toys in the room. • Angela is very shy when we go out into the community.	**Developmental Issue: Social Skills** An infant is not yet a sociable being in the sense that most adults would expect. Infants are not yet able to recognize the needs and desires of others. Infants are just beginning to recognize that they are separate persons and that they have an influence on their surroundings. Peers are treated as other objects. Immediate desires are satisfied without consideration for others. They are just not ready to play with other children. Including familiar adults in their play is as sociable as infants can be during this period of their lives.

Manufactured Toys and Play Materials for Infants at 9 to 12 Months

Toy/Material	Uses	Group Care	Home
Activity garden kitchens	Many areas and objects to manipulate.	√	√
Activity tables	Spinners, dials, sounds, spinning balls, mirrors, flip-flops, etc., provide many opportunities to see how things work.	√	√
Stacking/ nesting	Can be used on their own, in the sandbox, or in the bathtub. Used for stacking and knocking down, lining up, and nesting inside one another.	√	√
Musical plush toys	Soft, cuddly animals provide music when hugged or squeezed.	√	√
Tunnels	Cause-and-effect and physical skills are enhanced as infants explore these passageways.	√	√
Musical instruments	The infant can bang, tap, chime, ring, or shake the instrument. Cause-and-effect instruments provide feelings of power and accomplishment.	√	√
Sensory books	Zippers, squeaks, and different textures add a new dimension to reading.	√	√
Books with real pictures	Stories describe daily events in the infant's life.	√	√
Soft play-ground climbers	A series of soft ramps, steps, and levels allow infants to climb, crawl, cruise, and walk in a safe environment.	√	√
Soft plastic animals	Durable plastic animals can be grasped, carried, and manipulated easily.	√	√
Easy puzzles with knobs/ handles	Two- to four-piece wooden puzzles of pictures familiar to the infant. Large knobs help the infant to manipulate the pieces.	√	√

▶ Summary

The increased physical skills, size, and the infant's improved ability to handle items in her environment have led to more sophisticated activity. She tends to want to discover the properties of materials, enjoys object play, and is actively involved with everything around her. With her increasing attention to detail and longer attention span, she plays in a solitary way as well as with adults. Her play may show features of symbolism as she learns through observation and imitation of adults and older children.

When confronted with new situations or materials, she enjoys sensory discovery. When she does something by accident the first time she may repeat the actions for fun: this also has an important neurological function. Her endless practice play can be demanding for the adult, but she enjoys being able to attract attention and have the adult play her game. She sends out messages to adults that can be read; her gestures, facial expressions, crying, and other sound productions are the adult's cues. Her babbling involves experimentation with sound and a lot of repetition, but it is influenced by the particular language sounds that she hears. She gradually increases her understanding of what adults are saying and makes deliberate attempts to use approximations of words.

Symbolism in language coincides with symbolism in the infant's play. The baby, whose thinking remains egocentric, develops new strategies for learning that are part of the sensory-motor stage. Repetitions in language, play, and other actions all have a part in her learning.

As her cognitive development advances, so does her social and emotional development. Hopefully, the baby has secure attachments to adults, but because she has a clearer understanding that things, and people, continue to exist even when they are out of her sight, she is anxious when separated from those significant people. Doing things more deliberately than before is a characteristic of this stage. We see this in play, emotional situations, and social relationships. Frequently she initiates communication with adults, and those adults who are responsive find that she enjoys prolonged engagement.

She sees herself as a separate person—something that has occurred because of the trusting bond she has with adults—and she does have some power over the people and objects in her environment. With increased consciousness, the baby appears to have an awareness of herself, the people around her, and the immediate environment. If she is enabled to feel secure through having reliable people around her and having all her needs met, she will be successful in passing through the first emotional challenge of her life. Our memories of our own infancy are not accessible, but we may gain insight into what it is like to be a baby if we get down on the child's level and try to see things from her perspective.

▶ KEY TERMS

a priori
autism
babbling
basic trust
cephalocaudal
consciousness
cruise
deferred imitation
differentiated hearing
ego
egocentric
existential self
expressive language
functional-relational play
generalized
gesture vocabulary
goal-directed activity
imitation
individuation
instinctual
make-believe play
mistrust
motivation
multi-modal (stimulation)
multiple attachments
object permanence
observational learning
organized sense of self
pincer grasp
play
practice play
pre-wired
pro-social skills
quality of attachment
receptive language
relational play
role-modelling
scaffolding
schematic stage
secondary circular reactions
secure attachment
self-concept

self-regulation
sensory-motor play
social referencing
solitary play
syllabic repetitions
symbolic play
symbolic thought
tertiary circular reaction pattern
toddler
trust

► DISCUSSION QUESTIONS

1. At a staff meeting, educators discuss how well they are meeting the attachment needs of the infants. "I think I'm too focused on physical needs," says one educator. How might you reply? What strategies might you suggest to improve attachments?
2. You made a mistake when you interpreted a parent's looking away as lack of interest in what you were telling her about her child. How could you repair the situation?
3. You and your colleagues can choose five new items for the infant room for the infants who are pulling themselves to standing positions. What do you buy?
4. How much of your behaviour do infants imitate, and how does this influence what you do?
5. When an infant of 9 months chokes on some mashed peas, what should you do?

► ADDITIONAL RESOURCES

► Further Reading

Bronson, M. (2000). *Self-Regulation in Early Childhood: Nature and Nurture.* New York, NY: Guilford Press.

Cryer, D., T. Harms, and B. Bourland. (1987). *Active Learning for Infants.* New York, NY: Addison-Wesley.

Fraiberg, S. (1959/1996). *The Magic Years.* New York, NY: Fireside/Simon & Schuster.

Karen, R. (1994). *Becoming Attached: Unfolding the Mystery of the Infant–Mother Bond and Its Impact on Later Life.* New York, NY: Warner Books.

Lally, J. et al., (1995). *Caring for Infants and Toddlers in Groups: Developmentally Appropriate Practice.* Washington, DC: Zero to Three.

Pimento, B., & D. Kernested. (2000). Healthy Foundations in Child Care. 2nd ed. Scarborough, ON: Nelson Thomson.

Rimer, P., and B. Prager. (1997). *Reaching Out: Working Together to Identify and Respond to Child Victims of Abuse.* Scarborough, ON: ITP Nelson.

Silberg, J. (2001). *Games to Play with Babies.* 3rd ed. Beltsville, MD: Gryphon House.

Allen, K.E., et al., (2002). *Inclusion in Early Childhood Programs: Children with Exceptionalities.* 3rd Canadian ed. Scarborough, ON: ITP Nelson.

Berk, L.E., and A. Winsler. (1995). *Scaffolding Children's Learning: Vygotsky and Early Childhood Education.* Washington, DC: NAEYC.

Shore, R. (1997). *Rethinking the Brain: New Insights into Early Development.* New York, NY: Families and Work Institute.

Weitzman, E. (1992). *Learning Language and Loving It.* Toronto, ON: Hanen Centre.

► Useful Videos

Let Babies Be Babies: Caring For Infants and Toddlers with Love and Respect. Winnipeg, MN: The Manitoba Child Care Association (MCCA).

Understanding Special Needs Videos (Videos #31–35).
#31. *Caring for Infants Exposed to Crack/Cocaine and Other Drugs.* (1993).Georgetown University Child Development Center and the National Maternal and Child Health Resource Center, Washington, D.C.

Description: This video was developed to show birth parents, foster parents, adoptive parents, grandparents, and other family members how to care for infants exposed to crack and other drugs. It is also recommended as a training tool for providers of services to these infants and their families. The video illustrates the difficult behaviours that these babies may demonstrate and identifies specific techniques to deal with these behaviours. It also identifies specific techniques that can be used to help a baby go to sleep, respond during alert times, reach and kick, and eat well. It emphasizes throughout the important role of the baby's primary caretaker.

Early Messages: Facilitating Language Development and Communication. WestEd, Center for Child and Family Studies, California Department of Ed., Child Development Division.

Together in Care: Meeting the Intimacy Needs of Infants and Toddlers in Groups.

This video presents three child-care program policies that will lead to special care. Those policies include Primary Caregiver Assignment, The Use of Small Groups, and Continuity of Care.

WestEd, Center for Child and Family Studies, California Department of Ed., Child Development Division.

▶ Useful Web sites

Infant phenomenology:
    phenomenologyonline.com/articles/
        template.cfm? ID=286
    www.atl.ualberta.ca/po/textorium.cfm
Infant nutrition:
    www.heinzbaby.com/
    www.theparentreport.com/resources/ages/infant/
        nutrition.html
Self regulation:
    www.science.mcmaster.ca/Psychology/2aa3esum/
        Emotion.PDF
affect
    www.psychoanalysis.net/wwwcrl/Affect
Infant autism:
    www.ont-autism.uoguelph.ca/utm.shtml
physical development
    www.growinghealthykids.com/english/
Language development:
    www.kidsource.com/kidsource/content4/speech.
        develop.baby.pn.html
National Network for Child Care (US):
    www.nncc.org/Child.Dev/child.dev.page.html

CHAPTER 9

New Horizons: Infants as They Become Toddlers

As infants become toddlers, they display many new skills. Here, a mobile toddler displays skillful imitation and prolonged concentration while at play.

Learning Outcomes

After reading and studying this chapter, you should be able to:

• identify the observable characteristics of toddlers 12 to 15 months old

• explain the significance of behaviours of toddlers from 12 to 15 months in a developmental context

• recognize and respond to the developmental diversity of 12-to-15-month-old toddlers and discuss issues pertinent to this stage of development

• assess the development of 12-to-15-month-old toddlers

• respond to the health, safety, and development of 12-to-15-month-old toddlers with appropriate protection, guidance, and caregiving

• develop strategies to work with parents as partners in the care and education of their toddlers

Scene:

> "In the infant room we have a number of children who are up on their feet. We think of them as being mobile infants rather than toddlers," said the educator as she answered a student's question. "Sometimes we have parents visiting who ask us why they are not in the toddler room, because they are walking. I tell them that children at this age may be walking but they still have many characteristics that mean they require infant care rather than toddler care."
>
> Parents are not the only ones who can be confused by the distinction between infants and toddlers. Back in class, a student asked, "So when does an infant become a toddler?" "That's a hard question; it depends on whether you are deciding on age or stage," responded the instructor.
>
> "I see that some infants seek attention. Is this a sign of maturity?" asked the student. "It can be," replied the instructor. "There are many aspects to maturity: physical skills, language, cognitive advances, emotional control, and so on. But young children don't progress smoothly, they take big leaps in one domain and tiny steps in others. That's what makes the developmental process so individual, so complicated."
>
> The student added her observations to the instructor's comments. "I've noticed that infants at this stage are trying to make sense of everything. They get into everything, and that's a safety problem. It's as though they are trying to see how everything works. But they take stuff apart, and can't put it back together." The instructor paused for a moment, and said "You've noticed an important characteristic of this stage, one that Piaget called 'the little scientist.' But every child is different and they go about things in individual patterns. Have you noticed how very young children approach things and people differently?"

Children at this age, probably more than any other, display broad variations in skill acquisition. Some children are not yet mobile; others move about rapidly. A few may be self-directed; others are more dependent. Some infants may be able to walk but still need a great deal of emotional support. Such children are probably not yet ready for a group situation in a toddler room. Other more autonomous toddlers may be striving for their independence and may fit more easily into the toddler environment. As is always the case with young children, caregivers and educators have to observe each child carefully and respond to individual differences in a supportive way.

► What to Look For

PHYSICAL DEVELOPMENT

What characterizes this period is the increased skill in the use of the body. For many young children at this stage, the most significant change is in their perspective of the world. Toddlers are beginning to see everything from a standing-up position, and they are better able to get hold of things within their reach. The toddler's new horizons present some new hazards and provide the opportunity to develop new skills.

Growth

Height typically increases from about 70–80 cm (27–32 inches) at 12 months to 73–83 cm (29–33 inches) at 15 months (National Center for Health Statistics (U.S.), 1982). Weight increases from 9–12 kg (20–27 pounds) at 12 months by about .11–.23 kg (¼–½ pound) per month (Allen and Marotz, 2003). Through the processes of **ossification** and **calcification**, the infant's bones become harder, and this prepares her to stand and walk.

The head does not continue to grow very significantly, and at this stage the infant's chest becomes bigger than his head (Allen and Marotz, 1994). The infant has a protruding abdomen and rounded appearance, but the body proportions are becoming more adult-like. Please review the growth charts in Chapter 3 for an overview of the patterns of growth. Remember, every child is different, and their personal growth patterns are most revealing—much more than any comparison with the norm.

Gross Motor Skills

The infant at this stage may have a variety of techniques for getting from place to place. It is likely that he is a proficient crawler (Bayley, 1969), although infants have different crawling styles. Some do a crab crawl, moving in a sideways action; others are more successful in moving backward than forward or sideways. A few infants do not crawl but become mobile using a bottom-shuffling technique. Others like to use a bear walk on all fours (Sheridan, 1997).

Usually the infant will be able to pull himself to a standing position and **cruise** around furniture, using a sideways shuffle. Independent walking may be evident at this stage. However, it is not uncommon, or a cause for concern, if the infant is not yet walking. Larger infants may take longer to start walking, but this has no long-term disadvantage. Infants who start to walk early in this stage are likely to have a short-term lead on mobility as the stage continues.

Because muscles have not yet fine-tuned the process, an infant's early gait—the way she walks—is quite wobbly. After a few steps, the infant may collapse into a sitting position or catch her balance by holding on to a person or object. At first the infant walks using a tremendous amount of concentration, but very soon the movement becomes an automatic behaviour.

When sitting, the infant has the skill to reach forward or sideways. She can also roll from back to front or front to back. Body movement gives the infant considerable pleasure, and she may repeat movements at which she is successful. Some movements may prove too difficult; the infant may become frustrated when she lacks the problem-solving skill to get herself out of a position. All the effort in moving can be tiring, and the infant's sleep requirement may temporarily increase.

Fine Motor Skills

During this period, the infant practises a variety of grasps. She can pick up small objects, hold them to examine them, and put them in the appropriate places, such as a peg in a hole (Furuno, 1993). The infant is likely to enjoy the effects she can have on the items in reach. The 15-month-old infant may stack two small blocks, pick up small toys, mark a paper with a crayon, turn a container upside down, or put items inside each other. The infant is also likely to be interested in handling a spoon, but her first attempts at putting the spoon in her mouth are rarely successful as a part of feeding. Consequently, feeding time can be very messy, and educators who encourage **self-help skills** should be prepared for long mealtimes and a lot of cleaning up afterward. Another early self-help skill may be observed when the infant tries to help as she is being dressed. You may see some degree of cooperation. At the same time, it is possible that she will register her dislike of something and deliberately refuse to assist.

Although the infant may indicate a **hand preference**—favouring the right or left hand—this may not be stable (Furuno et al., 1993b). The infant will use her index finger to point at things without having to be taught to do so. She may point at items or people across the room or at pictures in books (Sheridan, 1997). The act of pointing leads to having her needs met.

COGNITIVE DEVELOPMENT
Vision

The infant's ability to attend to details of pictures is observable. He is likely to recognize objects if they are simple images. It is difficult, though, to know how much of an image he recognizes, because he doesn't yet have the language to tell us. If the image is in any way obscured—half-hidden behind a door, for example—the infant may not recognize that what is represented is part of a whole. Recognition of some objects is clearer because the child's response shows us she knows what the picture represents.

Visual **acuity** is improving but is not yet 20/20. The infant may be interested by moving objects and people and can look with "prolonged and intense regard" (Sheridan, 1997) at action occurring some distance away.

It is noticeable that the infant may sit for quite a long period staring at an image. Looking closely, we see that she is scanning the image in a particular way. Infants like looking at faces. These can be adult, child, baby, or animal faces. The infant is fascinated by the image. At times, she might point to a picture and make a sound, perhaps something approximating a real word, as though she is trying to identify the picture. She particularly likes to look at photographs of her immediate family members and appears to know who they represent. Images in board, paper, or cloth books can also provide interesting things for a baby to look at; it's a good idea to display pictures around the room at the infant's eye level.

She may look intently at people nearby or those at some distance across a room. Some effort to imitate the actions she sees tells us that she is taking notice of the people's actions as well as their faces or bodies. In fact, she remains more interested in faces than bodies—her eyes move from faces to hand actions. The **imitation** and **observational learning** that come about because of her fairly good visual acuity is necessary. However, babies whose visual acuity is not so good tend to rely on their other senses to make sense of what is around them. Toys and play materials tend to be visually appealing to infants—if the sense of sight is below average the baby may be more likely to mouth and feel objects, as well as hold them up close, to experience their attributes. Mouthing is also associated with teething and may also be a behavioural pattern linked with some personality types—so don't immediately conclude that the baby has vision difficulties if she continues to mouth objects!

Hearing

Imitating different sounds and responding to music and other domestic sounds are the clearest indications that the infant has a functional sense of hearing.

Her sound production may become more like the language sounds that she hears. Early speech tells us that her hearing is likely to be adequate.

Infants at this stage are able to follow moving sounds, respond to the rhythm of music by waving their hands about, and enjoy making sounds using one or more objects and banging them together or against a hard surface. Not all sounds evoke a positive reaction, however. A startled response to a loud sound indicates some fear, but the infant is usually calmed when she realizes there is no threat. Sounds that seem threatening at first may bring a different reaction when the infant finds out they are not associated with anything negative.

Information Processing

A busy room or outdoor environment may produce many noises, but the infant is able to tune out some sounds and pay increased attention to human voices or a particular sound that interests her. This is an example of the process of **habituation**. Learning is dependent on this process; without it, there would be **sensory overload**. When the baby hears, feels, sees, or otherwise experiences simultaneous perceptions, she may not be able to sort out what to attend to.

Learning is built on the infant's exploration, using her senses in a single or **multi-modal** way (Allen and Marotz, 2003). She can take in information through more than one sense simultaneously and process it in complex ways (Siegler, 1991). Consequently, we need to balance stimulation with downtime. The infant requires quiet time to filter, sort, and memorize relevant features of information and forget the rest. It may be difficult for an infant to assimilate information when it is too complex and delivered by several media at once, but different babies respond differently.

When interacting with infants, adults instinctively tend to isolate pieces of information, make images clearer and simpler, and emphasize key sounds or other sensory information. One example of this is the use of parentese or motherese, in which the adult simplifies and clarifies the message, emphasizing key words and using a high-pitched tone of voice with an open facial expression. This is a form of **child-directed speech** that supports the child's focus on the "right" details. While this is useful, we should not underestimate the infant's ability to process information that is delivered in complex ways. The fact that a sound and image are delivered simultaneously may assist the child's understanding rather than interfering with it.

Sensory integration occurs when the infant translates sensory information into action. For example, the infant might see a picture of a cup and then reach for his cup, thrusting it out for the adult to fill with juice. Alternatively, he might hear a piece of music that he associates with bathtime and react by getting a towel and dragging it across the room to the adult.

Sensory-Motor Behaviour

This period is the beginning of the **tertiary circular reaction** substage of the sensory-motor stage. During this time, the infant performs deliberate actions that bring desirable consequences. More than simply repeating enjoyable actions, the infant begins to try little experiments. We can observe this when the infant explores objects in ways that are new. Although her increased bodily control can assist this process, the significant aspect of the stage is the learning that comes from discoveries of new materials and domestic objects. It is as though the infant is starting a quest to find out what properties are found in all materials.

In this stage of development, it is very clear that the infant's actions help her to construct a reality of the world (Piaget and Inhelder, 1967). As she meets new situations, she matches or compares them with what she already knows and adjusts her **construct of reality** accordingly. The infant assimilates newly experienced information into existing schemes of understanding. In accommodating the new information within her existing understanding, she widens her knowledge of the world. Although this process will continue as her learning becomes increasingly complex, this stage is notable for its dependence upon concrete experience and sensory stimulation. The adult will have many opportunities to see the infant engaged in sensory activity and experimentation.

At this stage of 12 to 15 months, the infant has a particular interest in things that are new. Rather than meeting situations and objects in ways she has used before, she now tries completely new solutions. She now uses **trial-and-error** in a deliberate way—rather than in the random actions she would have much earlier to try to find solutions. Her tertiary circular reactions are applicable to many situations, including problem-solving. In playing with an adult or older child she has fun with objects. She may like to repeat actions that involve disappearing and reappearing, such as peek-a-boo. However, rather than do this again and again in exactly the same way, she might start looking for the person out of sight or try to cover her own face in an attempt to disappear. She can't see the adult, so she assumes that he can't see her! Without having gained **object permanence** and **people permanence**, the baby won't find this especially funny, although she might smile at the surprise.

During this stage, the mobile infant may try using some objects in different ways. Sometimes she might find ways of recreating interesting events. In this situation, you might see the infant imitating an adult's actions. She makes many more connections between events, and in recreating an event she may incorporate small details that might not have seemed significant to the adult. Because her perspective is **egocentric**—she can see things only from her own point of view—she pays attention to the features of an event that have meaning for her. Amusing behaviours might result from this: she might copy a funny expression that an adult showed her; imitate an adult's mannerism, like putting glasses on and taking them off; or she might act out the sequence of bathing a baby doll, focusing on shampooing her doll's hair. Her memory for some aspects of an event may lead her to focus on particular aspects of the event rather than the sequence as a whole. On the other hand, it may happen that her egocentric thinking will lead her to recall actions as they pertained directly to her.

LANGUAGE AND COMMUNICATION

Body Language
There is usually an emergence of a new type of **body language** at the beginning of this stage, and it is quite easy to read. The infant uses her finger to point. Pointing may coincide with saying a word or just a sound. We'll discuss this exciting stage in language development in a moment. But the finger-pointing is an effective tool because we can often understand what the infant wants more easily than before. The newfound ability may have the baby using pointing to her advantage, and have her caregivers running to get what she wants. Although this might seem a demanding stage—and she will often want an item that she can see but that is not intended for her—it is not spoiling her to respond to her requests. The meaning she intends isn't always as obvious as we might imagine. For example, pointing at a bottle does not necessarily mean that is what she wants, or pointing to her crib may not mean that she wants to sleep.

Reading the cues the infant sends us is important. By trial-and-error we can determine if our assumptions were correct. One of the basic cues relates to the infant's **state of consciousness**. Susan Quilliam

(1994) suggests that we try to determine which of four basic states the child is experiencing. As we saw in previous chapters, Quilliam calls these **uptime**, **downtime**, **trance**, and **sleep**. These states are observable in people of all ages, but they are particularly important for the educator or parent to notice because they have significant impact on the kinds of stimulation, support, and personal space the individual infant needs.

Consciousness and Sleep: Reading the Cues
Uptime is the time of energetic exploration, response to stimulation, and quick reactions. The eyes tend to be bright and alert, the head is upward-looking, concentration is directed, and physical functions such as breathing are synchronized with the child's action. In *downtime* the child is quieter, more reflective, less responsive, and tends to sigh, look downward, pause for periods of time, and tilt the head. The *trance* state is one that is very relaxed: the pulse is slow, breathing is deep, responses to stimuli may be negligible, vocalization is minimal, and the eyes stare in an unfocused way. *Sleep* is perhaps the most obvious state, but there are differing levels within this state. Periods of REM (rapid eye movement) and restlessness in sleep are easy to observe. In deep sleep the body is usually at its slowest pace and is least responsive to the environment.

While on the subject of sleep, it might be useful to compare infant and adult sleep patterns. As many parents know, the patterns are not always similar, however much the adult tries to adjust routines to make them similar. However, a baby's sleep is like an adult's. The REM—rapid eye movement sleep—is a light sleep during which dreams occur and the eyes move rapidly back and forth. At this stage babies may sleep for about 14 hours, but the variation is considerable. About half of the infant's sleep is **REM sleep. Non-REM sleep** has four stages that are observable: the first stage involves drowsiness, when the eyes droop or maybe open and close and the baby dozes. In the second stage, there is light sleep—you may notice that the baby moves and may be startled or jump if there are sudden sounds. In stage three, the sleep is deep and the baby is quiet and does not move. During stage-four sleep, which is the deepest level, the baby may seem so still and quiet that the adult observing her may be worried. Parents sometimes wake their infants at this stage because they fear that they are not all right. This is an important level of sleep, because it often determines how awake, alert, and responsive the baby is during the day. If you observe the infant's readiness to sleep, you are likely to assist the baby to go through the **cycles of sleep** most successfully. The infant is probably ready for sleep when she rub her eyes, yawns, looks away frequently from any stimulation, and starts to fuss or get physically agitated. During the longest sleep time of the day—hopefully at night—the baby will go through several sleep cycles, from stage one through stage four, and back again.

Of course the baby is more agile at the 12-to-15-month period, but it is still suggested that she be put to sleep on her back or side for safety reasons. Homes and child-care centres sometimes use music to encourage infants to go to sleep, or use back-rubbing. This may seem helpful, but some caregivers suggest that the baby may become dependent on the music to put her to sleep. Conversely, others claim that quiet music enables the infant to get herself back to sleep if she awakens. Having the baby go to sleep in the adult's arms, at this stage, is probably not very helpful in the long run, because the baby may fail to develop the ability to get herself to sleep without an adult's presence. Sleep, like many aspects of life, has cultural patterns associated with it and is linked with strongly held beliefs. Caregivers should be slow to criticize parents' ways of managing their families unless they need to point out, appropriately and sensitively, that a significant safety issue needs to be addressed. Night-time breast-feeding during co-sleeping, getting the child to sleep by dropping off yourself with the infant, walking around until the baby sleeps in your arms, wrapping babies tightly for supposed security, having infants asleep on the sofa with a parent until their bedtime, all might seem unusual to you but could be useful strategies for some families. In child-care centres there may be practices that parents question or even, in time, imitate. And although continuity between home and centre is desirable, the infant is likely to learn what happens in which context.

Quilliam's explanation of states of consciousness gives us some idea about times when the baby is at peak alertness. However, this doesn't offer an explanation of how the infant is aware of herself or her environment. We have to look more closely at her behaviours to know how she sees herself. For example, looking at herself in the mirror might not produce a response that indicates that she knows who she is. At a deeper level, her awareness is greater than it was earlier in infancy, but her consciousness must be shaped by her limited language and conceptual understandings. It is possible that consciousness is not merely a cognitive or neurological experience, but perhaps something that transcends scientific dis-

covery. Research does, though, offer us some insight into the association between different levels of **consciousness** and different parts of the brain, the link between perception and consciousness, consciousness and its dependence on language, and the connection between consciousness and the concept of self (or **"I" concept**).

There are some important implications of the relatively well-known studies of consciousness. Although such studies have been out of fashion during the years that behaviourism, social learning theory, and developmental psychology come to the fore, there is a new interest in the **phenomenon of consciousness** on the part of neuroscientists, linguists, and philosophers. How the baby is conscious of herself and her world is of importance to her, but also to the adults who are involved in her life. How aware she is of herself and things and other people has great significance to how we engage with her.

The perceptual view of consciousness is important because of its relationship with infant sensory-motor learning. Consciousness seems evident in sensory perception (such as vision, audition) and bodily sensations (such as pain) as well as non-sensory aspects (such as emotion, memory, and thought). All of these conscious states can be seen as elements of consciousness. Also, most conscious states can be seen as being about something: objects, the world, or her own body. Infants are sensory learners and require physical skills combined with sensory information for their learning and, according to this view, their consciousness. The perceptual approach to consciousness recognizes that an infant's consciousness can be at various levels, but that it exists in the act of perceiving. Although this consciousness may not be like adult consciousness, it involves successions of response to external stimuli involving all of the five senses. Here a new concept is helpful to us, one that can be applied also to adult levels of higher consciousness. William James's powerful metaphor "stream of consciousness" suggests that consciousness is not a stop-and-start process but rather one that is associated with the perceptual responses that an individual experiences. This stream depends not on language but merely on awareness of sensory information.

Consciousness and language are related in many ways. We use language to describe our conscious experiences. These verbal utterances are a means for investigating human consciousness. What is said, it is thought, opens the door to our conscious mind. We consciously experience linguistic stimuli such as words and sentences, and we process them unconsciously. A person's language arguably helps to structure his or her conscious experience. Many researchers have asserted that language is essential to consciousness, and that infants who are **pre-lingual** (without language) have little or no real consciousness. The challenge that this view presents is that it seems that the research is conducted on the basis that "only what can be measured exists." Because we cannot get into the mind of the pre-lingual child, she is supposed to have no consciousness. However, most parents would disagree once they enter the world of their infant and see her responses to them and to her world, even though they may be only through physical forms of communication.

Myrtle McGraw, an infant observer who worked in the 1930s, studied consciousness and infant judgment. Her research challenged both behaviourism and maturationism, which advanced environmental and genetic theories of human development. She tried to show that infants possess consciousness and the judgment needed to guide their own development. Perhaps she challenged what might have appeared to her as simplistic views of development that focused on measurable characteristics but avoided other issues related to consciousness. Unfortunately, most views of consciousness, McGraw thought, avoided looking at the essence of the infant's conscious experience from the baby's own perspective and world-view. She argued that the infant's ability to think, develop strategies for action, and solve problems clearly indicated that there was infant consciousness.

Merleau-Ponty attempted to address the issue of consciousness from a different angle. He was greatly influenced by the study of developmental psychology and thought that phenomenology of perception was closely tied to the concept of the body schema. His work also shaped his philosophical conclusions concerning the experience of "self" and "others." Merleau-Ponty considered the observation of conscious phenomena in terms of how consciousness is lived out *bodily*. Expanding his theory, a new branch of biological philosophy called **neurophenomenology** emerged in the early 1990s. It blended the science of the brain with a new appreciation of consciousness based on brain functioning. Whether or not infant consciousness can be discovered through brain imaging techniques coupled with an appreciation of how the infant experiences the world, it might be helpful to our quest to understand the nature of infant consciousness. However, questions about the mysterious relationship between the brain's functions and awareness go back at least as far as classical Greek philosophy. So what does all this tell us about the consciousness of the infant?

It might be that it is centred on awareness of the body—and we know that the infant at this stage does have a preliminary concept of her body. It is possible that consciousness exists only if there is language—but some researchers think that is a limiting view of consciousness and we do see evidence of consciousness in the pre-linguistic stage. There is a chance that consciousness depends on a concept of the self—which is evident in the case for our infant at 12-to-15-months, or earlier. Finally, there is clear indication, from the infant's responses to stimuli, that some level of consciousness does exist before the 12-to-15-month stage. Because the baby is considered to be conscious in a scientific sense, we have some basis for understanding what that consciousness is about. This is only the measurable component of consciousness; we have yet to explain consciousness in a spiritual sense, but maybe that's a question of belief. Interestingly, babies do seem to have a conscious awareness at levels that might seem beyond the here and now but that cannot, from a cognitive perspective, be thought logical or dependent upon a belief system. There remains the possibility that the baby is unencumbered with the adult conception of the world and its complex belief systems, and lives in a state of consciousness that is at one with a reality that accepts what is rather than questioning what that reality means. By taking this view we do not see the baby as a blank slate but as an individual who is living with a consciousness of the present involving an awareness of the stimuli that her world presents; her "self" and the actions she makes on her environment; and her interactions with others—the people who exist within her world. Many adults claim there is a special quality of peacefulness that exists when the baby's pure acceptance of living in the moment opens up her conscious world to us.

The science of sleep is not particularly advanced as yet. However, recent brain research has brought sleep closer to the forefront of research attention. Clearly there is a strong link between good sleep and positive learning. But what is required to get good sleep is difficult to do and even harder to understand. One new research project at the University of Connecticut (Carol Lammi-Keefe, 2000) suggests that sleep patterns can be enhanced if nursing mothers increase their levels of DHA. To do this they must regularly consume some types of fish. Although the study needs replication (repeating for verification) the implication is that increased consumption of DHA encourages the development of the brain and central nervous system that then brings about deeper and quieter (stage-four) sleep. They are not suggesting that infants at this stage be fed fish directly but that the indirect consumption of DHA is thought to lead to improved motor and mental scores.

Most higher animals appear to sleep and it is assumed that this is for restorative or adaptive purposes. Restorative because it makes the sleeper feel more energized while awake and improves his memory functions, and adaptive because it allows the animal to protect itself from harm and to search for food at appropriate times of the day. If this is the case, and if these two theories have merit, should we imagine that the more infants sleep, the better their thinking skills and memories will be? And if their sleep follows a different pattern from their parents', is it because the baby's needs are not being met?

Receptive and Expressive Language

The infant at 12 to 15 months is on the brink of language use. From the time of the first real words, there is usually a rapid increase in receptive language. This means that the infant knows the meaning of some words even though she may not yet be able to articulate them.

However, **babbling** continues during this stage and the infant does a lot of experimenting with her own voice. Often you will hear the repetition of sounds that seem appealing to her or ones that she hears in the language around her. Consonants, particularly *m, p, b, t, d* and *n*, which are made at the front of the mouth, are repeated. This shows an advance in sound production. She does something else that indicates that she is listening to the language she hears. It is called **echolalia** and it's an attempt to imitate the sounds of whole phrases; it involves a parrot-like imitation of sounds, syllables, or words. Previously the sounds that the baby made were picked up and repeated by the adult. Now she is imitating the adult and is on the verge of acquiring real language. When listening to the baby babbling at this stage you might hear a combination of sounds. If overhearing her when she is in her crib you might hear babbling, echolalia, words, and rhythmic sounds that are like singing.

Some, but not all, of the baby's sounds and words will have meaning. Those sounds that are "words" may not have a meaning to the baby that is consistent over time. They may have different meanings for her in different contexts. "Ra-ra" might mean her toy doll when she's in her bedroom, but it might mean a different toy in her child-care centre.

The infant's babbling at this stage becomes more complex. **Variegated babbling** is the term for babbling sounds that are more closely associated with real language. Variegated babbling combines consonants and vowels—and often results in some wonderful words of the baby's own creation: "gabada" and "namana" are two examples. They may change with the context, so they mean one thing during a monologue (such as when she is in her crib talking to herself) or in a dialogue (as she "converses" with her caregiver in the playroom). The inflections she uses—the emphasis on particular syllables—is also of interest to the observer. The way that she makes the sounds, emphasizing particular parts of the sounds, is frequently similar to the voice patterns of the adults around her. At this stage, infants may utter **protowords**: words that do have a particular and specific meaning, although they are not real words with a commonly understood meaning. Protowords may include such inventions as "gege," meaning "go home," or "uh-uh," meaning "pick me up."

When using a word or sound that has a meaning—like "bo-bo" for bottle, or "mama" for mommy, she may be trying to convey a variety of meanings. In the case of "bo-bo" she might mean "Can I have a bottle now?" or "That's my bottle!" The use of one word to convey an entire thought, whether or not its meaning changes, is called a **holophrase**.

Within the 12-to-15-month stage, or a little later, we may hear the infant using a word such as "dada"—she means daddy, but she uses it to refer to all men. (This could be embarrassing for mom when she points to a stranger and shouts "dada"!) She may call all animals "dog" or uses the word "ba" to mean anything associated with water—not just bath time. We call these language errors **overextensions**—one sound or word has a variety of meanings. In time she will reorganize her thinking and will revise her concepts and vocabulary to fit conventional patterns. In a similar mis-understanding of words and categories, the infant may also use **underextensions**—these are heard in situations where the infant uses a general word for a single object—often something that belongs to her; for instance she may have a blanket and call it "blankie" and not be able to use the same term for other people's blankets.

Infants during this period commonly understand words in context, but the words usually have to be isolated from the flow of everyday language. From the infant's responses you can see that she knows the meaning of some key words such as bottle, cup, bed, bath, and other domestic things. Owens (1996) suggests that this early receptive language is dependent upon perceptual abilities involving hearing and discriminating between sounds.

Songs and rhymes are more fun with actions. The adult emphasizes the meaning of key words with her own actions. The toddler imitates the actions but not the sounds.

Early words fulfill the intentions that were earlier expressed with gestures, expressions, and sounds. To begin with, there may be a range of sounds that express different functions. Intonation varies within each sound production (utterance)—probably imitated from the adult's emphasis as he uses parentese.

At 12 months, the infant may say one to three words (Allen and Marotz, 2003). Within three months of starting to talk, she may be able to use as many as 50 words. Vocabulary gains vary considerably, and learning language somewhat later than the norm is not, in itself, indicative of a problem. As we saw in Chapter 8, infants who are easily understood when they point or use other gestures may not be as quick to say words, but this is not a lasting difficulty. The communication of meaning is probably more important than the utterance of particular sounds.

The acquisition of language is an extremely complex process. Although infants seem to "learn language" without consciousness and have little awareness that they are moving into an adult world of shared meanings that involves absorbing rules (**grammar**), gaining a vast vocabulary, and appreciating meanings (**semantics**) and purposes or intents (**pragmatics**) of the language. As discussed in Chapter 3, there are some interesting explanations for how this happens. The theory that seems to make the most sense is that the infant is **pre-wired** for it. Having the brain circuitry in place, the infant needs to experiment with sound production, have her sounds imitated, and also hear the language. At this stage of

language development, we see most of these things happening. We hear the infant making her own sounds, and we say back to her what she says. We talk to her, emphasizing important bits of language, and she in turn copies us. Expanding her repertoire of sounds and linking them with experiences or objects, she creates and understands some meaning and her vocabulary increases. So far, so good. Soon she will make her language more complicated and that cannot be explained using the idea of imitation alone—otherwise she would never say anything that she had not already heard. To explain this, there must be some way that she knows how to learn language—she must be wired for the experience!

Essentially language acquisition is a social process: it is not just hearing words spoken. Even if the infant listens to voices on television or radio, she cannot acquire language; at this stage, and later, she needs a mediator to help her. This is someone to respond to her sound-making, create a reciprocal communication process, help her associate words and meanings, and extend her vocabulary. These things will be done by the people she has made attachments to. The supportive process, as mentioned in previous chapters, is called **scaffolding** (Bruner, 1983). Scaffolding involves the adult providing a variety of supportive strategies, such as the ones already mentioned, to enable the baby to progress. The scaffold offers a structure—just like the scaffolding used in house construction—that enables the child to do things that she couldn't do without the help. Ultimately she will be able to use language without that support.

EMOTIONAL DEVELOPMENT

Stage of Emotional Growth

This time represents a stage of transition from babyhood to toddlerhood that is observable not only in terms of mobility but also with reference to psychological change and a move toward self-help and independence.

The new emotions of shyness and contempt appear in this stage (Izard and Malatesta, 1987). These may indicate an increased understanding of the self and the infant's relationship with others. These emotions may be observed when the infant meets new people or attributes something she doesn't like to a particular person. For example, when taken in for a medical exam, an infant may seem shy when she meets the doctor. If the doctor performs a procedure that the infant dislikes, the infant may demonstrate contempt toward her.

By 12 months, infants are usually gaining a **complex sense of self** (Greenspan and Greenspan, 1985; and see the Appendix for a full description of Greenspan's stages of emotional development). The infant is becoming organized in her thinking and with her emotions, but this presents some inner challenges. Her ability to communicate takes on more sociable patterns: for example, smiling when an adult grins at her. There tends to be greater integration of her actions and communications. She will show her raw emotions and direct them at the person she is connected with.

The infant's moods can change quickly and may be influenced more by her current activity than her ability to regulate her moods. There are some situations where she **self-regulates**. She might calm herself and attempt to deal with a frustration, but her focus will not last and she can easily be distracted. A better course, though, is for the caregiver to help the infant to recognize the emotion and then solve the underlying problem. Caregivers who label the child's feeling—"You seem angry" or "You are having fun"—can be helpful, because supplying the language is the first step in controlling that feeling. While finding ways of solving problems can be difficult—especially in a group context—adults can show the infant how to deal with the situation, or how to divert the emotion. Greenspan points out (p. 86) that as the infant gets to feel more competent and masterful, and is praised for her efforts, she will come to enjoy the partnership of adults. The infant will take the initiative in play with adults, but she often needs the adult to help her through situations that become chaotic.

Leaving the adult's side creates inner conflict. She wants the security associated with the adult, but also some freedom. As her mobility increases, so will her circle of discovery—her world will become larger. At 12 to 15 months this is erratic, because her feelings fluctuate, but when she is feeling alert and confident she will make some attempts at being autonomous. The increase in independence is strongly associated with mobility, but will not occur without emotional well-being based on strong and secure attachments.

Emotional Resilience

Resilience refers to the infant's ability to protect himself from unpleasant or negative experiences. The child's resilience is strongest when such experiences are relatively rare and the child has significant emotional support from his attachments to one or more adults. Such strong attachments tend to act as a buffer against bad experiences. If negative experiences are more common, or if the child does not have the reassurance of strong attachments, he cannot sustain his resilience (Carnegie Task Force on Meeting the Needs of Young Children, 1994). The short-term effect may be disconnection and apathy. In the longer term, the infant may grow up to be a child with social maladaptations and emotional problems.

Psychosocial Stage

Erikson (1980) described the second and third year of life as the stage of "autonomy versus shame and doubt." The infant has the urge to become independent. He needs to be able to strive for **autonomy** and make mistakes and not be shamed for them, or he will doubt himself. Infants early in this stage show signs of wanting to do things themselves. They may grab a spoon or wave around an undershirt in an attempt to feed or clothe themselves. While these efforts might be unsuccessful, it is important to remember that the behaviours are indicative of a significant developmental change. As mentioned earlier, the conflict that results from the infant wanting to be independent and needing adult support takes some months to be resolved.

SOCIAL DEVELOPMENT

Through the use of more refined communications, the infant's social relationships are becoming more complex. In this period, the infant likes a lot of adult attention (Allen and Marotz, 2003) and likes to know that an adult is nearby. She may even have new fears regarding familiar situations (Furuno et al., 1993b). As her circle of attachments broadens we can see that the baby's social skills are developing. She initiates and responds to other people and likes to imitate them and play simple games that are repetitious.

Attachment and Separation

Clear-cut attachment to a small group of adults remains evident. These relationships are extremely important: the infant continues to rely on those adults to be responsive to her needs (Berk, 1996). The infant may take steps to ensure that an adult stays in close proximity. She may hug or hold on tight, grasp the adult's legs, try to keep the adult involved in her game. The adult is a secure base from which the infant can make discoveries. She frequently uses the social referencing technique of looking back at the adult to check in and seek approval.

Significant **separation anxiety** may result if the adult to whom he is attached leaves the infant, however temporarily. Even though the infant knows that the adult continues to exist when out of sight, this provides little comfort. The infant may be angry at the adult for leaving him. Transitions at this stage need to be handled sensitively. Merely trying to distract a 12-to-15-month infant is insufficient. He needs to have concrete reassurance that the adult will return.

Separation is a serious issue and can be damaging if handled badly. The classic research undertaken by Robertson and Robertson (1989) documented the heart-wrenching stories of children at this stage separated from their mothers for periods of a few days. Even when they were reunited, there appeared to be significant emotional damage to the young child.

Convincing an infant of 12 to 15 months that "their" adult is going to return is easier if there is a small group of people to whom he is attached. The transfer from one person to another is challenging at times, but if there is consistency in how the transitions are made and in the circle of people he relates to, this won't be as difficult. It is a staffing challenge to maintain this continuity, but it is essential to high-quality child care.

The practice of constantly changing staff from one room to another, or from one centre to another for their professional development can have its merits, but the cost may include disruption in the emotional lives of the infants. At this stage, although their memory is not very long, infants need to be securely attached. This is not something that can be considered an administrative inconvenience. The best way to ensure that staff have appropriate vacations, time off, and professional development opportunities, is to rotate staff so that there is always someone with whom the infants are familiar and to whom they are attached.

Addressing the infants' need to build trusting relationships is not a high ideal—it is the foundation of good practice. In meeting the needs of infants, the recognition that separation anxiety and **stranger anxiety** are developmental characteristics that must be understood and accommodated should be the cornerstones of planning—not a nice afterthought!

When handled well, infants learn to appreciate that their needs will always be met. They also learn that different people will meet those needs—and that each of those people will add a new dimension to their social world. Of course infants need to know that when adults go away, they also come back—but they can do this only if supported—not if they feel abandoned. Fear of abandonment is a basic fear that can damage the individual's emotional well-being throughout life.

No one is suggesting that emotional damage need occur when parents leave their children at a child-care centre every day. The point is that parents and caregivers have to be aware of the depth of the child's distress when the adult to whom she is attached is no longer nearby. They need to work together to develop strategies to reassure the child.

Self-Concept

We return to the concept of self because of its over-riding importance. Mahler (1968) describes a **separation-individuation** process in which the 10-to-15-month-old infant is "practising" being separate. Moving away from the mother and finding out that he has control over some outcomes of action and play and that he has a body distinct from the mother's allows the infant to understand that he is a distinct individual. This view is interesting, because it explains how the child gains a self-concept, but it has not been accepted by some theorists outside the psychoanalytic school. Stern (1985) has another explanation for the gaining of self. He suggests that infants at this stage discover that there are other people besides themselves "out there." Stern's stages are cumulative rather than progressive. This means that infants' existing concepts remain pertinent while they gradually layer on new concepts. Particularly important are the primary relationships, rather than special defining moments of **self-concept** development. Yet another explanation, offered by Lewis and Brooks-Gunn (1979), suggests that the emergence of self-concept is related to the child's cognitive ability to recognize the permanence of himself and others.

The child's use of his own name can be an indicator of self-concept, but this rarely happens before 15 months (Brooks-Gunn and Lewis, 1982). Then the infant refers to himself by name rather than using a pronoun.

As discussed previously, the self-concept—sometimes called the "I" concept—can be thought as a turning point in the infant's recognition of self and evidence of a conscious awareness of herself. At this stage, the infant may begin to refer to herself by her name but will not call herself "I" for some time. It is unlikely that this indicates that she is without consciousness of either herself or her immediate world; scientific investigation often neglects to appreciate early forms of consciousness that are pre-lingual.

Personality

There are several different and conflicting theories of personality. Freudian theory would suggest that the infant in this period is in the latter part of the first stage of personality development, what Freud called the **oral stage** (Freud, 1940). Pleasure and frustration are experienced through the mouth, and feeding is the dominant part of the infant's life. Freudian theory contends that there must be neither too much nor too little **oral gratification** (that is, pleasure from the mouth) at this time; the consequence would be an oral fixation. While infants are extremely focused on their physical needs associated with feeding and sucking and use their mouths for sensory discovery, this theory has been challenged by those who think that Freud overestimated the effects of oral gratification. They disagree with his belief that deep and lasting psychological damage could be done on the basis of denying oral gratification or indulging it.

As mentioned in earlier chapters, **temperament** is a core part of personality development. One approach focuses on temperamental **traits** or characteristics, rather than on where those traits came from.

A contrasting view is presented in Maslow's theory of **self-actualization** (Maslow, 1970), in which the infant is seen as progressing through levels related to his will to be what he wants to be. (See the outline of Maslow's theory in the Appendix.) Self-actualization is the motivational factor that shapes personality development. The self-concept is the key part of personality that starts developing in early infancy and continues through life. The infant needs basic physical things and a sense of love. He strives to have these needs met so he can, ultimately, realize his potential. **Humanistic theory**, of which Maslow's theory is a part, emphasizes the concept of self as the core of personality development, but it focuses on this as an end in itself rather than as a means to an end. Educators may interpret this to mean that self-concept and self-esteem are such vital parts of development that they are the focus, rather than a byproduct, of development. It would be a healthy approach to address self-concept development and the creation of positive self-esteem as issues that need to be considered rather than left to chance.

▶ Particular Needs

SELF-HELP SKILLS

One of the signs of the increasing independence of infants as they become toddlers is that they want to do things for themselves. At this stage, they still need a great deal of adult assistance and encouragement to develop their self-help skills. Adults can offer immediate assistance during the task itself, but they can also improve the toddler's chances for success by simplifying the task—making sure the child's clothing has easy fasteners rather than tiny, unmanageable buttons, for example. Children need lots of time and opportunity to practise dressing, undressing, grooming, and feeding themselves. These tasks can be time-consuming and, in the case of feeding, messy. Infants and toddlers need to have their efforts encouraged, even if they are taking a lot of time and making more work for the caregiver. At this stage, an infant is more likely to try to assist the adult than perform a task by herself. Whatever efforts she makes, these should be praised and encouraged if we value independence.

TOILET-LEARNING

Many adults think that toddlers at this stage are ready for potty-training. However, our current understanding of young children's psychological processes and physical control over bowel and bladder suggests that 12 to 15 months is too early. The infant is not yet naturally striving for control over personal needs. Thus, toilet-training is often more of an adult "need" than a child's need. The term toilet-training or potty-training, emphasizes the adult's role in training the child. In contrast, **toilet-learning** focuses on the child's learning, with or without adult direction. The toddler needs to be able to learn to use the potty or toilet without pressure, in her own time. Box 9.1 deals with the rather contentious issue of toilet-training.

LANGUAGE

As the toddler's language skills rapidly increase in this period, adults need to offer **parentese**, the clear and repetitive use of simple language. Toddlers also need to hear rhymes, songs, and lots of ordinary spoken language.

At this stage, toddlers are better able to understand language than to express it, so adults must continue to be able to interpret toddlers' body language to understand their needs. In particular, the adult must be able to read the child's state of awareness and receptivity to stimulation. From this time onward, the baby's expressive language emerges. She needs encouragement, rather than correction of the many mistakes that she will make. Use appropriate but simple language, and avoid any hint that the infant is wrong. Her language will emerge, given confidence!

BOX 9.1

TOILET-TRAINING: WHY ARE PEOPLE SO OPINIONATED ABOUT IT?

Why do people want to "train" young children? There may be several reasons. Toilet-learning is tied to some profound issues related to being human, being clean, valuing privacy, and being in control. Although we know that children will, in time, want to conform to social expectations and use the toilet like everyone else, there is social pressure to do this as soon as possible. Historically, there has been a competition over who can train the earliest. Merit has been attributed to the adult's training achievement, as well as the infant's trainability. If we relax in the knowledge that it is unlikely that the child will go to school in diapers, and that there is no developmental advantage in performing on request, this pressure may be lifted.

The control issue runs deep in adults, although they may deny it. Yet, in practical terms, this is the adult's issue, not the child's. Indeed, the controlling adult might be more in need of training than the child. When a battle of wills occurs in the toilet-learning process, there is no winner.

More acceptable reasons for wanting to train the child to use the potty or toilet might be economic. Diapers, whether they are cloth or disposable, cost money. Parents on a limited budget might cite this as their motivation. Although money might influence the adult's perspective, it doesn't lead to the child's readiness.

As a stage of development, using the pot or toilet is a badge of advancement to some parents and educators. Where there are limited diaper-changing facilities, toilet-learning may be a prerequisite for entering a program. This is understandable, but again doesn't make allowances for the child's readiness to learn. Many educators have found that parents' claims about their child's toilet use are exaggerated. Of course, a new environment might cause a child to regress and lose gains in self-help skills. Under normal circumstances, the child might really be toilet-trained.

It's easy to see why there is such a focus on getting young children to use toilets rather than diapers. It's easier, cheaper, and demonstrates an important development. But what are the costs to the child pressured to use a potty or toilet? Opinions of child-care experts vary as to the degree of harm that pressure puts upon the child. Stoppard (1983) and others think that all toilet-training is unnecessary and inappropriate. Erikson (1950) was concerned with the damage done to the child's psychological well-being by coercive toilet-training. Some people believe that learning to deal with pressure is an important life skill. They think that it does no harm and has little connection to later emotional or personality development (Garber, Garber, and Spizman, 1987). A moderate approach is taken by Campbell and Webster (in Kilbride, 1997), who lean toward the reduction of pressure while being sensitive to culturally diverse perspectives on child-rearing practices. Generally, undue stress on performing any behaviour is inappropriate, and the general atmosphere of the child's environment is more significant than the particular focus on toilet training (Leach, 1997; Brazelton, 1992).

Infants and toddlers don't need to be toilet-trained. They will learn in time, given role models, opportunity, and a little encouragement. Recent studies (Berk, 1996) suggest that toilet-training after 2 years of age is quicker and presents fewer challenges for both the child and the adult. Avoidance of stress is clearly advisable, because it has the potential to do some harm. As educators, we can try to appreciate parental perspectives on toilet-learning and support parental initiatives while diffusing undue stress for the child.

PLAY EXPERIENCE

Infants and toddlers like to play with objects, so they should have the opportunity to experiment with a variety of playthings. At this stage, sensory experience is particularly important, because it allows the child to learn about the properties of materials. Adult involvement can help the young child focus, pay attention to details, and label things with words; it can also prolong the play sequence and make it more enjoyable.

Although play may occur without adults, some adult involvement is essential for learning. Adults need to take the role of scaffolder as they provide a bridge to new understandings through language, play, and discovery. A variety of strategies, including demonstration and reinforcement, will be helpful.

In recent years there have been a number of videos and toys that claim to offer brain-based activities. The manufacturers claim that their products will enhance the infant's brain functions, as though they somehow provide superior ways of supporting brain development. Some of these are benign: they don't actually do any harm. But the claim that certain experiences are brain-based is usually a marketing tool, without significant evidence as to their effectiveness. Any experience that the infant has is brain-based; it is not necessary to purchase something especially for that purpose. The most effective brain development occurs when we provide developmentally appropriate experiences, offer consistent nurturing that promotes secure attachment, and engage in the infant's spontaneous play and efforts to communicate. The "Mozart effect" was behind several products claiming advanced learning—in some cases advanced mathematical understanding—in young children. The idea was that by exposing infants to music—in particular, new recordings of Mozart's work (which doesn't seem like a bad idea in itself)—that infants' brains would somehow be advanced. This practice is unlikely to cause damage, but it's supposed benefits are not supported by solid research. Play Mozart's music if you think that's a good idea, but it is not necessary to purchase materials especially marketed to parents and caregivers.

EMOTION READING

As the infant enters the toddler stage, the range of emotions becomes broader. Her feelings of frustration may begin to mount as she finds that she wants to do things that are beyond her physical capabilities. Consequently, adults must be able to recognize, label, and understand the toddler's emotions. Though they are starting to do things by themselves, toddlers still have great dependence upon adults and need emotional security to launch out into the world independently. Rather than become frustrated with a child who shows anger or negative emotions, recognize her feelings in a calm manner.

As the 12-to-15-month-old moves toward greater independence, she encounters frustrations that are challenging for the adult. When she seems to be fighting adults the most, she is really trying to overcome her own conflicted feelings. To help her regulate her feelings and actions, there needs to be a place that she can crawl to so she can calm down—perhaps where stimulation is reduced. Learning to remove herself from frustrations can be a technique that builds on her natural disengagement when stimuli become overwhelming. In addition, she needs help to recognize what she is feeling, though it is too early for much understanding of words that describe abstract concepts. Provide comfort rather than add to her emotions by projecting your own onto the situation. Also, read her signs of tiredness and different levels of alertness, because your response to those indicators may keep events from becoming overwhelming for the young child.

▶ Developmental Variation

This is a time of contrasts within each child, as well as enormous contrasts in developmental stages within the group of children the same age. There is great variation in physical skills and concentration span. Fine motor control and self-help skills vary too. Some children attempt a wide range of independent activities, with some success, while others are more content to play placidly. Some toddlers begin to use words, while others will not talk for some time yet. Because the educator of a group of young toddlers will likely find a very wide range of competence, any programming must be individual rather than collective. Open-ended activities are the most successful for a group, because all the children can participate at their own level.

The well-prepared and experienced practitioner will sense if there are behaviours or other indicators leading to the need to examine the infant's development more closely. Usually such concerns should be shared with the parents, who will then seek the advice of appropriate experts. The practitioner may be asked about average behaviours for the infant's age. Care should be taken to mention to parents that there is a very wide variation of development at this stage and at others. If it is consistent with your philosophy and practice, you might want to use a developmental screening tool to get a better picture of the infant's overall development. The Brigance Infant and Toddler Screen (Brigance and Glascoe, 2002) or other observation method or assessment tool might provide a meaningful profile, but this should not replace further examination by a physician, pediatrician, or expert in special needs.

Accommodating children who have special needs can be an additional challenge to your usual responsibilities, but by working on the premise that you are treating all children individually and that all activities are open-ended, you can probably accommodate infants at this stage more easily than when they are older.

CHRONIC ILLNESS: HOSPITALIZATION AND ITS EFFECT ON DEVELOPMENT

This chapter emphasizes emotional development, so we are looking at various situations that might compromise the child's sense of trust and well-being. Young children who have had to be hospitalized for specific treatment may appear to be behind other children of the same age in some areas of development. This is simply because they have not had the same opportunity to play, explore, or be with other children. In most cases, if hospitalization is not prolonged, the child will catch up fairly quickly. Where there has been longer-term **institutionalization**, the prognosis may not be as good.

Infants do not have to suffer emotional deprivation because of hospitalization, but active steps have to be taken to ensure their emotional well-being. Failure to do so can, in extreme situations, result in damage that cannot be repaired, even with later intervention, play therapy, or other types of support. Avoiding emotional damage is the only way to ensure the child develops healthily. Fortunately, hospital care for infants and young children in North America and most European countries is mindful of the child's emotional needs and encourages attachments and provides whatever play experience is possible, given the child's condition.

Emotional development seems to be the key developmental domain at this stage; if something is compromised in this area, other domains are also affected. The infant or toddler whose maternal attachments were damaged in infancy due to long-term hospitalization may have social and cognitive functioning damaged as well. Early experiences do make a difference to later ones. It is as though the brain cannot forget the hardships, cannot repair the damaged attachments, and cannot reconnect the neurological connections.

Perhaps the most worrying part of emotional damage is that it may not be entirely evident. It is possible that the infant or young child who is emotionally hurt appears to be quiet and accepting of the situation. They may, in fact, make many superficial connections with adults—but they lack the trust in any one adult to have any deep, secure attachment. Such children may appear responsive to people, but, to the child, those people are little more than a momentary visual or auditory distraction. In earlier times, there was a belief that the infant's memory is short at 12 to 15 months and that she has no **autobiographical memory** (remembering of one's own personal story); because of this, emotional damage was thought to be transitory and repairable. Unfortunately, some professionals subscribe to that belief to this day. In fact, even if there is no memory of the event—such as hospitalization or placement in an orphanage—there is profound damage to the child's ability to build trusting relationships. Furthermore, the child will have trouble in the individuation process. If the infant does not show anxiety at the time of separation, this is not because she is accepting of separation; it is because she hasn't made a meaningful relationship in the first place. All situations in which the child is placed in a situation other than the primary circle of attachments should be planned carefully. There must be the strong presence of at least one person with whom the infant is attached, along with a supply of objects that are associated with home. It is important to accept that there will be some negative reactions associated both with being away from home and with any treatments given (particularly if they are invasive). The same parameters for behaviour at home and in hospital help the child to feel that there are consistent elements in her world.

CEREBRAL PALSY

The condition can range from quite mild to severe, with different levels of performance as a result. Cerebral palsy can result from birth complications, motor accidents, or even child abuse. The movements of children with cerebral palsy may appear ungainly, and their posture may seem awkward. The child's motor skills may lag behind those of his peers.

Prior to a diagnosis of cerebral palsy, educators may notice that an infant's motor development is a concern and share these observations with the parents. After the disorder has been diagnosed by a specialist, parents can work together to improve the child's motor skills. Some assistive devices might become necessary, and adults may need to learn how to position her sitting or standing to help her to become more independent. Despite the challenges of cerebral palsy, many children with the condition function well in other areas of their development.

CYSTIC FIBROSIS

Cystic fibrosis (CF), a genetically inherited condition, is most common among Caucasian people. Although infants and children with this condition experience different levels of severity, common symptoms are respiratory difficulties that include coughing, spitting, repeated lung infections, and congestion. Children with CF may also show some signs of poor growth and failure to thrive. Young children with CF will usually have salty sweat and unusually bulky and offensive-smelling stools. Depending on the individual child's symptoms, toddlers and older children can do well in small group settings. However, given their increased susceptibility to infection, exposure to large numbers of people can be undesirable. Medication is usually required for children with CF, and they need special care in hot weather to ensure that they drink sufficient fluids. These children are more likely to do well if they have a good balanced diet and if educators become familiar with the condition so that they can administer medication and perform necessary supportive functions. The impact of CF on the child's overall development is variable. Seeking good supports and professional expertise is essential to achieve optimal outcomes for each child.

SICKLE CELL DISEASE (ANEMIA)

This rare inherited disease occurs most frequently among people of Afro-Caribbean descent. It is a form of anemia that can cause tiredness, lethargy, pain in the abdomen and bones, and episodes of crisis. Ongoing medication might be necessary, as the child is susceptible to serious infection. Participation in a child-care program can be successful, but there may be blocks of time when the child is absent because of the disease. Educators need to work with parents to understand the particular needs of a child with sickle cell disease and try to develop strategies that meet the needs of each child and family.

THALASSEMIA

Thalassemia is another type of inherited anemia. This disease is most common among people of Mediterranean background. When both parents carry the gene, the child is more likely to be severely affected. Successful integration in a child-care program depends on the severity of the disease. Some children would experience no difficulties being included in a program. For others, transfusions, medications, and the symptoms of lethargy and pain might prevent their being able to participate in parts of a child-care program.

▶ Health Concerns

TOILETING AND DIAPERING

As the child takes a more active part in her diapering and toilet-learning, there is increased need for hand-washing. The infant might touch the potty, toilet, used diaper, and diapering materials, and can easily transmit germs to her mouth and spread them to other children. Teaching hand-washing as part of the procedure is a good idea. If the hand-washing is fun, children are more likely to do a thorough job. Using **universal precautions** is the most effective way of controlling infection. Child-care centres will follow exacting procedures to protect both the adult and child.

PINWORMS

Pinworms, or threadworms, are small, white, wiggly worms that live in the intestines of those infected. They lay their eggs around the anus, where they can cause an itch. If the child scratches the itch, the eggs can become attached to her fingers or fingernails and can infect another child. The eggs can survive for some time outside the body and can be transmitted easily when a child touches something that has eggs on it and then puts her fingers in her mouth. This is a very common infection, particularly prevalent among toddlers and preschool children, although adults can be infected just as easily. Treatment requires prescription medication.

EAR INFECTIONS (*Otitis Media*)

Ear infections (**otitis media**) occur frequently and are one of the most common reasons for parents to take their child to the doctor. Irritability is the most obvious sign of a problem, but the child may have other symptoms, such as those similar to the common cold. Naturopathic or medical doctors can make a diagnosis of otitis media, but only medical doctors can prescribe **antibiotics**. Some young children who have severe and repeated ear infections may have tubes surgically inserted into the ear to drain fluid. These children require little extra special attention from child-care staff.

How or why these infections occur so regularly is debatable, but ear infections are extremely common.

BOX 9.2

SUPPORTING FAMILIES WHO ARE NEW IMMIGRANTS

Transition to a new culture is a significant experience for anyone. Even if outwardly they seem to fit in, the majority of people who arrive from another country experience culture shock—that is, a profound feeling of disorientation. Culture shock affects the whole family, regardless of age and economic status. Culture shock may be worse for those who lack material comforts, speak a different language, or differ noticeably from mainstream society.

Families need help to make the transition to a completely new environment, but they may not see the educator as an appropriate person to assist them. Rather, they may see the educator as a figure of authority who is unapproachable or even threatening. So educators need to tread carefully and build a relationship of trust with the parents. This can take a frustratingly long time, but educators need to be persistent in providing opportunities to communicate, and at the same time remain sensitive to the parents' perceptions of them.

The most fruitful way to build a relationship with families who have recently immigrated is to provide conscientious, respectful care for their child. The example of what you offer a child calms parental fears for the child's health and safety.

Naturopathic doctors and chiropractors both have strategies to treat young children who experience frequent bouts of these infections, but many parents feel that medical intervention is essential. Among the medical community there is divided opinion about prescribing young children antibiotics every time they have an infection. To what extent ear infections can be transmitted to other children is uncertain, but caregivers must be cautious in order to protect all the children. This is why staff will exclude a child on antibiotics. Also, children may have reactions to the antibiotic that are more effectively dealt with at home. Young children may experience side effects from the drug as well as the misery caused by symptoms of the infection. It should be noted that many parents become frustrated over the frequency of their child's ear infections. Not only do parents have to manage an irritable child but must also be absent from their workplace. Some centres do offer facilities for children who are mildly ill; they develop their own criteria for whether a child can be accommodated.

Recent concerns about the overuse of antibiotics are worrisome. Experts fear that these drugs are losing their ability to fight some infections, and that the arsenal of new antibiotics is not keeping pace with bacterial mutations. Only parents and their physicians can decide what is appropriate treatment, but child-care centres often have policies excluding children from the agency for a set period while on antibiotic treatment. Some children who have repeated ear infections and long-term antibiotic treatments may have interruptions in their child-care

life that can be emotionally difficult for them. Considering the big picture, we need to be concerned that as a result of the overprescribing and misuse of antibiotics new antibiotic-resistant diseases are being identified. Particularly in overcrowded inner-city areas, the prevalence of antibiotic-resistant tuberculosis is increasing. Even if we are not affected by this directly, all adults can address the situation by avoiding any request for an antibiotic prescription where the condition is viral rather than bacterial. And even for some bacterial infections, antibiotic treatment may be unnecessary. Keep antibiotics for when we really need them.

▶ Parents as Partners in Care

Communication between parents and caregivers is essential, especially in cases where children have health or developmental problems, such as some of the conditions outlined above. Parents and educators must be able to discuss their initial concerns, the diagnoses and recommendations of medical professionals, and strategies for helping the children cope with the challenges they face.

Communication between parents and caregivers should not, of course, be limited to such serious situations. Educators should take care to talk to parents regularly about their child's progress. At this stage, one of the rites of passage that marks a child's progress is the move from an infant room to a toddler room at the child-care centre. This is a hurdle for the child, parents, and infant staff alike, and can best be handled as a gradual transition. At some point, it is helpful to hold a transition meeting with the toddler's parents. Although this meeting should be personalized, there can be mutual benefits if two or more sets of parents who have children at the same stage meet together. They can share their concerns and apprehensions with the educator and one another. The educator can explain what happens in a toddler room, including changes in environment, routine, and staff–child ratios. Offering parents access to resources that explain toddler development can have great benefits for shared care at this stage.

As we saw earlier in this chapter, another significant issue for children at this stage is separation anxiety. The parents and caregivers should work together to develop strategies that support a smoother and more reassuring transition for the toddler between parental care and group care.

Diverse challenges can exist for educators trying to enlist parents as partners in care. For instance, unique challenges arise when the parents are new immigrants. Box 9.2 (page 245) deals with some of the ways that educators can offer support to and gain the trust of newly arrived families.

▶ Signs of Potential Neglect or Abuse

Infants who are making the transition to toddlerhood pose some challenges to parents and caregivers that were not present earlier. Their increased mobility combined with their continuing lack of any sense of danger makes managing their behaviour very demanding. As the infant strives for independence, she also needs the adult to provide a safe base for her. This seems to send a contradictory message to the adult at times—and can cause great frustration. Combine that with the child's own frustration, because she wants to achieve things that her body will not allow, and the result can be volatile. Parents who are not well prepared for their job can misunderstand the messages the infant is sending them, and feel unable to stop the child's anger and challenging behaviour. Compounding the problem, the parents' feelings of apparent failure can cause them to lose patience. All these issues contribute to a parent reacting inappropriately toward the child. The demands for comfort that the infant can make may seem excessive and the parent can turn away from the child's needs. A multitude of family or financial pressures can leave the parent tired, stressed, and without

the resources to cope. If they are unable to manage their own emotions, they may lash out at the child, causing irreparable emotional damage to the child as well as physical damage.

As practitioners, we need to do what we can to address the issue of stress in the life of individual parents and provide both support and resources to help them cope. Parent education is extremely helpful; this includes the positive role model that the educator should present.

It should not always be assumed that parents are the only potential perpetrators of neglect or abuse. Family friends and relations may have similar problems that manifest themselves in projecting anger and damage to the child. Possibly worse than that, educators can also be the perpetrators of abuse. They, too, experience stress and can lack the skills to manage challenging and demanding situations.

Earlier chapters have outlined the procedures to be followed when educators suspect that child abuse has occurred. This is a very stressful position for caregivers. In cases where the parent is the suspected perpetrator, the educator should not approach the parent directly. However, this will not necessarily protect the identity of the person raising the issue of potential abuse. Although child protection agencies promise anonymity, it may be obvious who has raised the issue. In addition, child-care staff may be asked to offer evidence, and it may be clear that the information supplied could have come from no one other than the educator.

If the situation is difficult when the suspected abuser is a parent, it can be even more challenging when the perpetrator is a colleague. The agency should have a policy to cover this contingency. If so, it should be adhered to diligently. Only those directly involved should have any knowledge of the issue. This is not time to seek friendly advice or a professional opinion. If you have sufficient cause for concern, then the information must be directed to a child protection officer. Despite the stress and unpleasantness, reporting suspected abuse is a professional responsibility. The child's safety and protection come before all other considerations. Please refer to the Appendix for a review of issues related to neglect and abuse. In later chapters we will look again at issues related to caregivers and the potential for abuse or neglect.

▶ Everyday Safety Issues

Mobility leads to exploration, climbing, and getting into a wide variety of new difficulties. Safety is of great importance, but we do not want to spoil the toddler's chance for discovering the limits of his body or enjoying his newfound abilities.

INDOOR SAFETY

The walking—and soon to be climbing—toddler needs to be protected from his inability to spot danger. He may have some fear of falling, but he may get on top of things without realizing there is drop. Stairs are a major hazard. Even a crawler can climb the stairs and look down to see the floor below. He does not know the risk of falling and how much he could hurt himself. Consequently, stairs must be gated.

All kinds of furniture can be used for climbing. The 12-to-15-month-old child is capable of some interesting problem-solving when it comes to reaching what she wants. Chairs can become launching pads for efforts to climb onto countertops or other unsuitable and dangerous places. Falling when climbing up or down is not the only danger. When she reaches the summit, she may find tools and materials that are potentially dangerous for her to handle. Close supervision can help prevent these dangers, but the child's skill at moving fast should not be underestimated.

Now that the infant is mobile, this is the time to take an inventory of the environment to determine potential hazards before an incident occurs. Families need to take special notice of dangers within their homes. There are many safety resources available. Some provide checklists of things to check, others offer explanations of how to handle the most common home injuries. Typically, the mobile infant needs to be protected from electricity, choking hazards, strangulation hazards, water, sharp objects, objects that can be swallowed, falling, and poisonous substances, including cleaning materials and medications. The child-care centre environment must address the same issues as pertain to the home, but additional care must be taken to ensure that the whole environment is suitable for groups of children.

OUTDOOR PLAY AND CLIMBERS

Small climbers can present the mobile infant with physical challenges that are developmentally appropriate, but the child may not use the equipment according to the manufacturer's instructions. She may try getting onto it with the help of a chair, climb up the slide, try to put wheeled toys inside as a garage, or any other imaginative use. All of these present dangers. The choice of suitable equipment is only the beginning of safe practice. Educators need to

ensure that children are using equipment in ways that present no undue risk.

To soften falls, soft mats should be placed under all areas where the child could jump or fall. Climbing apparatus must reach the standards set by the major safety organizations. A mobile infant must not be able to jam her head, catch her fingers, or become trapped inside the structure. The surfaces of equipment should be smooth, without splinters. Swings should be set up so that the child cannot get into or out of the swing without assistance. Always remember that, as the child's physical capabilities increase, so do the situations in which there is potential danger.

▶ Starting Points for Response

RESPONSIVE CAREGIVING

Often the toddler at this stage wants to try everything independently, even though she might be unsuccessful. The adult needs to make the mobile infant feel that her attempts at self-help skills are worthwhile. To have the opportunity to be successful, the toddler needs adults to respond to her initiatives with a positive attitude and lots of encouragement. Frequently, frustration stems from the mismatch between what the toddler wants to do and is able to do. Responsive caregiving involves offering interesting alternatives in which frustration can be replaced by success. Box 9.3 (page 248) lists some strategies for working with a toddler at this stage. Reading the child's cues can assist the caregiver who doesn't yet understand the child's broadening vocabulary of sounds and real words.

Recognizing the cues is the key to responsivity. At this stage, the infant demonstrates a wide array of emotions. These need to be acknowledged and understood. Recognizing the child's alertness or state of consciousness allows the caregiver to enter the moment with her.

SUPPORTIVE GUIDANCE

Supporting the child's self-esteem is an important issue at this stage of development. Frequently the adult has to provide support, both emotional and practical, to allow the child some self-direction. The mobile infant's understanding of self is gaining complexity, but remains dependent upon the trusting relationships that she has built. The greatest challenge is to accept the child's varying moods and develop

BOX 9.3

GETTING IN TUNE WITH TODDLERS AT 12 TO 15 MONTHS

Below are some starting points for building your responsivity skills with a 12-to-15-month-old infant. Tune in with respect and:

- observe the infant before engaging with him
- respond positively to the infant's dance of communication
- observe the infant's modes of seeking attention
- have fun with the baby
- encourage the baby's efforts (to walk, to do a puzzle, etc.)
- tap into the infant's interests and curiosity and enable him to explore
- provide lots of sensory discovery experiences
- enable the infant to choose toys and play material
- respond quickly to the infant's needs
- acknowledge and label feelings
- assist at times of extreme frustration
- demonstrate practical problem-solving (e.g., putting hand in mitts)
- anticipate quick movements
- respond to changing interests
- sustain the infant's focus on current activity
- provide opportunities for walking outside, in shoes or with bare feet
- offer toys that lead to practical skills (e.g., putting objects in postbox)
- offer names of objects, particularly when the baby points at them
- post pictures on the walls; have laminated pictures and artwork within the baby's sight
- offer unconventional sound-making objects
- play as a partner in sensory experiences
- use exaggerated vocal tone and facial expressions
- provide domestic objects for play
- build up blocks for the infant to knock down
- extend play activity when she's responsive
- tap into peak uptime with physical games and rhymes
- allow for quiet times with solitary activity
- respond warmly to a request for your involvement
- provide a variety of board books and picture books
- be playful in imitating the baby's variegated babbling and attempts at words
- enable the infant to assist in getting dressed
- provide consistent responsiveness
- encourage independence and cooperation
- be accessible emotionally, even when the baby has moved away
- be sensitive during the transition process
- expect mild regression when the infant is tired, and comfort him when he is frustrated
- offer foods that the baby can feed to himself
- ensure that physical and emotional needs are met
- offer a sufficient variety of playthings to avoid the need to share
- provide an empathetic role model, exaggerating caring behaviours
- tune in to temperamental styles and individual rhythms
- respond to signs of distress
- assist the infant to solve his own difficulties
- allow for personal space
- enable the infant experience the consequences of his actions (safely)
- talk to the infant about what you are doing
- extend conversation with gestures and expressive animation

strategies to enable the infant to regulate her own feelings and actions. Appreciating both stranger anxiety and separation anxiety should lead the educator to make appropriate staffing arrangements.

FACILITATING DEVELOPMENT

Lots of opportunity to play, experiment, and enjoy sensory experiences is essential. The mobile infant responds well to the adult's enthusiasm, but really enjoys it when she can orchestrate the play herself. Reciprocal communications provide a structured way of sending and receiving ideas. The adult provides new language, which the toddler imitates. Gradually the child creates meaning through basic symbolism in play and language. Her learning is supported through sensory discovery, scaffolded responses, and extending communication and early language.

HOLISTIC RESPONSE

Activities 9.1 and 9.2 encourage a holistic response to mobile infants at 12 to 15 months. Activity 9.1 suggests ways of engaging in the experience of mobile infants at this stage and extending your interactions with them. Activity 9.2 (page 251) helps you to observe each toddler and to develop activities that targeted to individual interests and skill levels.

Activity 9.1

Responding to the Changing Needs of Infants as They Become Toddlers (12 to 15 Months)

Your interactions with the mobile infant at 12 to 15 months need to be responsive to her needs and emerging skills. To assist you in engaging in the infant's experience, the activity below offers suggestions that may extend your interactions. Careful observation is necessary so that you introduce the idea at the right time and in the appropriate way. Each suggestion includes ways in which the idea can be extended if the infant is ready. This activity also illustrates the safety, communication, conceptual, and developmental issues you, as a child-care professional, need to hold in mind as you respond to the infant at 12 to 15 months.

There are many other activities that are appropriate besides the ones listed below; your skill in developing them will come as your experience and enjoyment increase!

Activity 9.1

Responding to Changing Needs of Toddlers at 12 to 15 Months

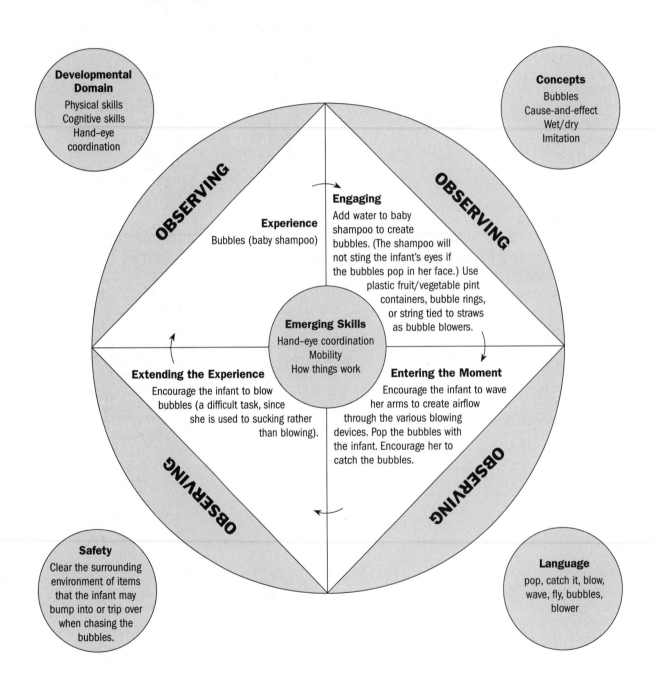

Developmental Domain

Physical skills
Cognitive skills
Hand–eye coordination

Concepts

Bubbles
Cause-and-effect
Wet/dry
Imitation

OBSERVING

OBSERVING

Experience

Bubbles (baby shampoo)

Engaging

Add water to baby shampoo to create bubbles. (The shampoo will not sting the infant's eyes if the bubbles pop in her face.) Use plastic fruit/vegetable pint containers, bubble rings, or string tied to straws as bubble blowers.

Emerging Skills

Hand-eye coordination
Mobility
How things work

Extending the Experience

Encourage the infant to blow bubbles (a difficult task, since she is used to sucking rather than blowing).

Entering the Moment

Encourage the infant to wave her arms to create airflow through the various blowing devices. Pop the bubbles with the infant. Encourage her to catch the bubbles.

OBSERVING

OBSERVING

Safety

Clear the surrounding environment of items that the infant may bump into or trip over when chasing the bubbles.

Language

pop, catch it, blow, wave, fly, bubbles, blower

Activity 9.2

Creating Responsive Curriculum for Infants at 12 to 15 Months

Activities for the mobile infant at 12 to 15 months should evolve from their interests and skill level. There cannot be a set "curriculum"! The adult's role is to tune into the infant's world and create experiences that are mutually enjoyable, that celebrate her current abilities, and provide opportunity for continued development. The following ideas will help the adult to observe each infant at 12 to 15 months and assist in providing some meaningful experiences.

With confidence, the adult can extend these ideas yet further.

Developmental Domain	Observation of Emerging Skills (Things You See)	Responsive Experience/Activity
Physical skills	– beginning to view the world from a new vantage point (standing) – quicker and more refined grasping, reaching, grabbing, pulling, and clutching skills – reaching behind himself while in a sitting position without falling over – place objects inside another (pegboards) and stacking one or two items on top of each other – pointing at things and people	Do not underestimate the abilities of infants/toddlers. They develop daily. Provide an environment with sturdy furniture. Provide different levels and surfaces for practising balance. Items found in the environment should have multiple uses. Allow the infant to manipulate and explore the objects. Provide pictures of real objects at the toddler's eye level. Encourage pointing by naming what he sees.
Cognitive skills/language and communication	– using senses in a multi-modal way (i.e., information is taken in through the senses and processed in complex ways) – acting upon his perceptions and actively exploring his environments – increasing receptive language – using holophrases and saying many words	Activities that encourage the use of more than one sense will help increase their accuracy and eye–hand coordination. A rich, stimulating environment with items that can be explored is important. Provide music, tape recorders with microphones, and a language-rich environment. Children are using their eyes to receive feedback on what their body is doing.

Developmental Domain	Observation of Emerging Skills (Things You See)	Responsive Experience/Activity
Social/Emotional skills	– testing independence, trying to do things on his own and attempting to help himself – frustration arising from physical immaturity (i.e., not being able to move and accomplish what he wants) – recognizing himself as a separate being	Provide support and encouragement for what the toddler can do. Read the cues exhibited and respond appropriately. Continue to provide assistance in a nurturing and trusting relationship. The toddler thrives on close, enthusiastic adult relationships. Allow the toddler to lead the interaction.

The following experiences may suit the emerging skills of the mobile infant at 12 to 15 months. Before you plan any of them, observe the infant's skill levels and interests. Either scaling down the activities to make them simpler, or adding to their complexity, may make them appropriate for the mobile infants you know. At this stage, most infants enjoy messy activities, but some children do not. These experiences are not ones that you might think appropriate for children left alone. Although challenging sensory experiences, they can present safety issues if you are not actively engaged with them as they play.

Responding to Changing Needs

Toddlers at 12 to 15 Months

EXPERIENCE 1

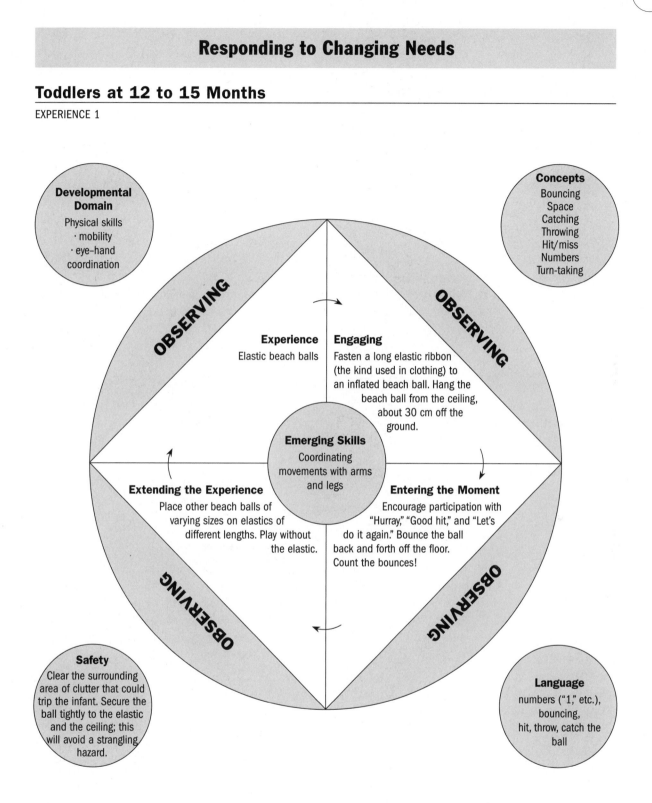

Developmental Domain

Physical skills
· mobility
· eye–hand coordination

Concepts
Bouncing
Space
Catching
Throwing
Hit/miss
Numbers
Turn-taking

OBSERVING

OBSERVING

Experience
Elastic beach balls

Engaging
Fasten a long elastic ribbon (the kind used in clothing) to an inflated beach ball. Hang the beach ball from the ceiling, about 30 cm off the ground.

Emerging Skills
Coordinating movements with arms and legs

Extending the Experience
Place other beach balls of varying sizes on elastics of different lengths. Play without the elastic.

Entering the Moment
Encourage participation with "Hurray," "Good hit," and "Let's do it again." Bounce the ball back and forth off the floor. Count the bounces!

OBSERVING

OBSERVING

Safety
Clear the surrounding area of clutter that could trip the infant. Secure the ball tightly to the elastic and the ceiling; this will avoid a strangling hazard.

Language
numbers ("1," etc.), bouncing, hit, throw, catch the ball

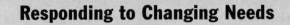

Responding to Changing Needs

Toddlers at 12 to 15 Months

EXPERIENCE 2

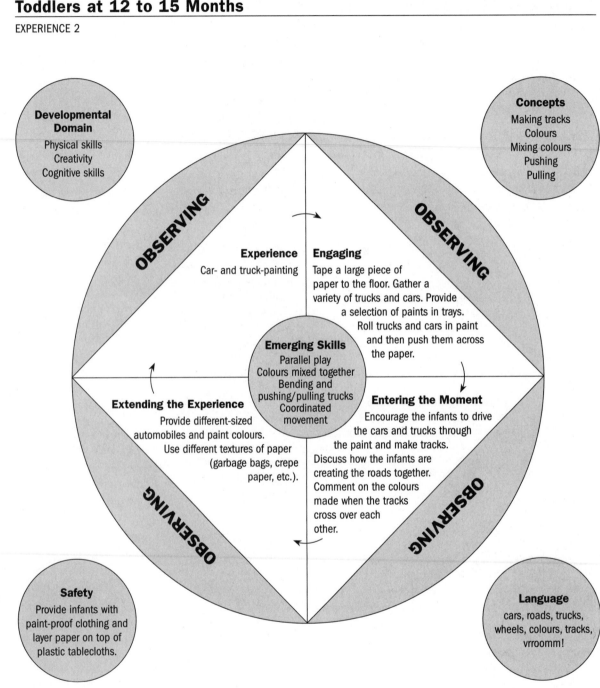

Developmental Domain
Physical skills
Creativity
Cognitive skills

Concepts
Making tracks
Colours
Mixing colours
Pushing
Pulling

OBSERVING

OBSERVING

OBSERVING

OBSERVING

Experience
Car- and truck-painting

Engaging
Tape a large piece of paper to the floor. Gather a variety of trucks and cars. Provide a selection of paints in trays. Roll trucks and cars in paint and then push them across the paper.

Emerging Skills
Parallel play
Colours mixed together
Bending and pushing/pulling trucks
Coordinated movement

Extending the Experience
Provide different-sized automobiles and paint colours. Use different textures of paper (garbage bags, crepe paper, etc.).

Entering the Moment
Encourage the infants to drive the cars and trucks through the paint and make tracks. Discuss how the infants are creating the roads together. Comment on the colours made when the tracks cross over each other.

Safety
Provide infants with paint-proof clothing and layer paper on top of plastic tablecloths.

Language
cars, roads, trucks, wheels, colours, tracks, vrroomm!

Responding to Changing Needs

Toddlers at 12 to 15 Months

EXPERIENCE 3

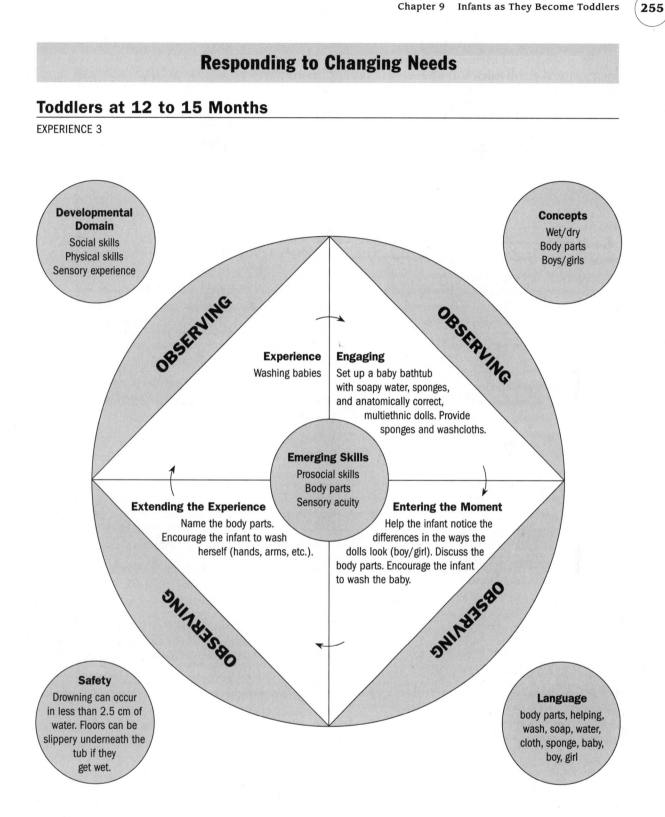

Developmental Domain

Social skills
Physical skills
Sensory experience

Concepts

Wet/dry
Body parts
Boys/girls

OBSERVING

OBSERVING

Experience

Washing babies

Engaging

Set up a baby bathtub
with soapy water, sponges,
and anatomically correct,
multiethnic dolls. Provide
sponges and washcloths.

Emerging Skills

Prosocial skills
Body parts
Sensory acuity

Extending the Experience

Name the body parts.
Encourage the infant to wash
herself (hands, arms, etc.).

Entering the Moment

Help the infant notice the
differences in the ways the
dolls look (boy/girl). Discuss the
body parts. Encourage the infant
to wash the baby.

OBSERVING

OBSERVING

Safety

Drowning can occur
in less than 2.5 cm of
water. Floors can be
slippery underneath the
tub if they
get wet.

Language

body parts, helping,
wash, soap, water,
cloth, sponge, baby,
boy, girl

Further Experiences and Interactions

Further Experiences	Interactions
Painting wall pictures	Use a large sheet of paper taped to the wall. Allow the infants to use hands, brushes (large household paintbrushes as well as small craft brushes), combs, sponges, etc., to paint with. Use a variety of colours.
Baskets with handles	Encourage the infant or toddler to fill her basket with toys and carry them around the environment.
Homemade mobiles	Use pictures from old books, shovels and pails, and other items that are important to the toddler. Hang the items up as mobiles.
Table-painting	Use the same tools as with wall pictures, above, but tape paper to a child-sized table.
Finger plays	Chant and sing a variety of finger plays that encourage body movements in conjunction with the words and songs.
Sensory table play	Fill tubs with sand, cornmeal, goop, oatmeal, etc. Include shovels, pails, small animals, and other utensils.
Sounds in the room	Use a tape recorder (perhaps with a tape of animal sounds) or other noise-making objects. Help the toddler identify where the sound is coming from and what the source is.
Head and shoulders games (and other body parts)—"Where is my . . .?"	Sing and identify the body parts of the toddler. Encourage the toddler to do the actions, and/or sing along.
Beanbags	Use these to throw and catch. Try to throw them at a target (i.e, a large laundry basket, box, etc.).

Further Experiences	Interactions
Texture and pop-up books	Sew your own texture books. Laminate pictures and sew them in behind fabric swatches. Encourage the toddler to explore the properties of the books.
Plastic eggs in egg carton	Encourage the infant to manipulate this activity as a puzzle.
Follow me	Encourage the toddler to imitate you. Touch parts of your body, clap, bang things, stomp your feet, etc.
Marble-painting	Find a large Tupperware container. Tape a piece of paper to the bottom of the container. Drop one or two marbles into different colours of paint. Place the marbles into the container and cover with a lid. Encourage the toddler to shake the container. Open the lid and view the creation.
Music-dancing	Play music (tapes or instruments) and encourage the toddlers to dance to the rhythm.

Responsive Guidance for Infants Aged 12 to 15 Months

Age/Stage: 12 to 15 Months

Situation	Response
• Jarod bangs everything he gets his hands on, with his hands or any object he happens to pick up. • Kylie squishes her food between her fingers and mashes it around the highchair table. • Francesca dumps all the toys out of their boxes and baskets. • Denzel pushes everything off the table or highchair every time it is put back on.	**Developmental Issue: Cognitive Development (Cause-and-Effect)** Children in this stage are starting to figure out that they can make things happen. These children are beginning to explore their power over the environment. As they figure out how things work, they take them apart or manipulate them. Provide a stimulating environment that allows for exploring and investigating. By using all of their senses, these children are developing a real understanding of the objects. Children feel successful when they are allowed to actively explore their environment. Caregivers need to prepare a safe, nurturing environment that produces successes for the infant or toddler.
• Roxann always attempts to take the spoon out of her caregiver's hand when she is eating. • Nicholas has discovered how to unsnap his trousers and seems to enjoy undressing himself. • Eddy seems to enjoy his newfound mobility. He spurns any attempts to be carried or to hold his hand. • Laticia is capable of washing her own hands and face.	**Developmental Issue: Self-Help Skills** Allow infants and toddlers to participate independently as much as possible in routine activities so that they can gain a sense of accomplishment. As the infant or toddler gains independence, provide him with simple choices (but do not overstimulate him) to help him feel a sense of autonomy. Provide an environment that encourages his independence and accomplishments. Provide child-sized equipment, choices, and a variety that reflects his new skills, interests, and abilities.

Manufactured Toys and Play Materials for Newborns at 12 to 15 Months

Toy/Material	Uses	Group Care	Home
Walker toys	Manipulative activity centres on wheels that move with the infant or toddler, providing some mobility support for them.	√	√
Pull-along clacker	Sounds are generated as the infant or toddler moves around the room.	√	√
Duplo blocks	Provides fine motor manipulation while connecting and pulling blocks apart.	√	√
Jack-in-the-box	Surprises the infant or toddler as she causes Jack to pop (demonstrates cause-and-effect).	√	√
Hammer and peg toy	Eye–hand coordination is improved as the infant or toddler pounds the pegs into the bench.	√	√
Giant nuts and bolts	Demonstrates how things fit together as the infant or toddler twists, turns, and fits the pieces together.	√	√
Shakers	Shows cause-and-effect as the infant or toddler understands her power to make things happen.	√	√
Two- or three-piece puzzles	Shape discrimination, spatial awareness.	√	√
Picture books	Language development, imagination, and creative thought.	√	√
Fine motor challenge games: zippers, locks, fasteners	Fine motor dexterity and self-help and dressing skills are encouraged.	√	√
Giant dump trucks	Pushing and pulling motor skills that help coordinate movement. Fine motor skills as truck is filled and emptied.	√	√

Toy/Material	Uses	Group Care	Home
Bowling	Coordination of movement as well as bending, rolling, and eye–hand coordination.	√	√
Music boxes	Encourage the infant or toddler to sing and dance to the music.	√	√
Play rings	Eye–hand coordination and spatial relationships as the rings circle the stand.	√	√
Baby swing	Body movement and coordination as the infant or toddler pumps and swings.	√	√
Blow-up knock-down inflatable bouncer	Emotional reactions, spatial relations, and motor skills as the infant or toddler manoeuvres the bouncer.	√	√
Play house	Symbolic play as the infant or toddler practises experiences.	√	√
Rag dolls or teddies	Prosocial and self-help skills develop as she cares for the dolls and teddies.	√	√
Play brush or comb sets	Self-help skills, body awareness, and self-concept are enhanced.	√	√
Thick paints or finger paints	Self-calming and soothing emotional skills, creativity, and fine motor skills are developed.	√	√

▶ Summary

This chapter describes the dynamic changes that the infant goes through as she becomes mobile and extends her world. As she begins to crawl, walk, and even climb, she shows a dramatic increase in mobility. Fine motor skills become a little more advanced, and she is able to grasp items and point more carefully and deliberately. We can see that the infant is a competent individual.

Simultaneously, advances in her language development are marked by more complex babbling and then first words. The complexities of her language are apparent in the way that she associates language and meaning. The mobile infant makes many attempts to communicate and also responds to the communications initiated by others. The feelings that she has may be overwhelming at times and she finds it challenging to regulate either her emotions or the behaviour associated with them. Frustrations are frequent because of the array of the emotions she experiences and her unsophisticated ways of dealing with difficulties. Reading the infant's body language can be difficult because her feelings change quickly, but we can recognize her cues and respond accordingly. Her states of consciousness vary during the day. It is best for the adult to tune in to the infant's world and try to maximize shared experiences in a stream of consciousness.

Although she is interested in the things around her and wants to discover how her world works, the infant depends upon adults to help interpret and make a bridge between what she already understands and any new information. She has a variety of strategies to cope with situations, including trial-and-error and simple problem-solving. Her sensory-motor intelligence has made advances into a more complex set of circular reactions; these enable her to try new ideas and organize her thinking more successfully.

Throughout this stage of 12 to 15 months, the infant experiences conflict between wanting to become autonomous and needing the security of the adults with whom she has become attached. Without a secure attachment, the infant's emotional development is compromised. Many negative experiences can have long-term effects on the child's emotional well-being. The mobile infant has an inner ability to organize her world—and has mental schemes that incorporate these understandings. Attachment and security are essential for the infant's development of a healthy self-concept. This necessitates careful handling of separations and people who are strangers.

▶ KEY TERMS

acuity (visual)
antibiotics
autobiographical memory
autonomy
babbling
body language
calcification
child-directed speech
clear-cut attachment
complex sense of self
consciousness (state of)
construct of reality
cruise
cycles of sleep

downtime
echolalia
egocentric
grammar
habituation
hand preference
holophrase
humanistic theory
"I" concept
imitation
institutionalization
multi-modal (senses)
neurophenomenology
non-REM sleep
object permanence
observational learning
oral gratification
oral stage
ossification
otitis media
overextensions
parentese
people permanence
phenomenon of consciousness
pragmatics
pre-lingual
pre-wired
protowords
REM sleep
resilience
scaffolding
self-actualization
self-concept
self-help skills
self-regulation
semantics
sensory integration
sensory overload
separation anxiety
separation–individuation
sleep (state of consciousness)
stranger anxiety
temperament
tertiary circular reaction
toilet–learning
trait
trance
trial-and-error
underextensions
universal precautions
uptime
variegated babbling

▶ DISCUSSION QUESTIONS

1. If a parent asks you to put a child on the pot every hour, on the hour, what might you say and do?
2. You are caring for a young child of recent immigrants. How might she be affected by her parents' culture shock?
3. How does an infant get to know that she is a separate person?
4. How resilient are infants to inappropriate child-rearing practices and traumatic events?
5. If an infant constantly mouths everything she can grab, what might you suggest to her father, who asks, "Why does she do this when it makes her mouth so sore?"

▶ ADDITIONAL RESOURCES

▶ Further Reading

Canadian Paediatric Society. (1999). *Well Beings: A Guide to Promote the Physical Health, Safety, and Emotional Well-Being of Children in Child Care Centres and Family Day Care Homes.* Vols. 1 and 2. Toronto, ON: Creative Premises.

Crowther, I., et al. (2000). *Infants & Toddlers: Curriculum & Teaching.* Scarborough, ON: Nelson.

Dombro, A.L., L.J. Colker, and D.T. Dodge. (1997). *The Creative Curriculum for Infants and Toddlers.* Washington, DC: Teaching Strategies.

Elkind, D. (1994). *A Sympathetic Understanding of the Child: Birth to Sixteen.* 3rd ed. Needham Heights, MA: Allyn & Bacon.

Erikson, E.H. (1980). *Identity and the Life Cycle.* New York, NY: W.W. Norton.

Morrison, G. (2003). *Fundamentals of Early Childhood Education.* 3rd ed. Upper Saddle River, NJ: Prentice Hall.

▶ Useful Videos

Program for Infant and Toddler Caregivers

Modules include:

Social-Emotional Growth and Socialization (3 videos, 3 video magazines, 1 curriculum guide, 1 trainer's manual, English or Spanish)

Group Care (4 videos, 4 video magazines, 2 curriculum guides, 1 trainer's manual)

Learning and Development (2 videos, 2 video magazines, 2 curriculum guides, 1 trainer's manual)

Culture, Family, and Providers (2 videos, 2 video magazines, 2 curriculum guides, 1 trainer's manual)

Description: Comprehensive training system for both centre-based and family child-care providers for caring for infants and toddlers. Order info: California Department of Education, 1-800-995-4099.

Touchpoints Video Series

Vol. 3. *First Year through Toddlerhood*

Description: Great resource for parents. Based on the work of T. Berry Brazzleton, who developed the videos as a guide for parents to help them understand and enhance their children's emotional and behavioural development. Covers topics by age, and touches on challenging behaviours such as sleep, sibling rivalry, and discipline. Order info: Consumer Vision Incorporated, 1-800-756-8792.

Useful Web sites

Infant/toddler safety
   www.theparentreport.com/resources/ages/toddler/safety/73.html
Parenting education
   www.cfc-efc.ca/docs/cwlc/00000861.htm
Current health issues (*Globe and Mail*)
   archives.theglobeandmail.com/hubs/health.html
Toys for children with visual challenges/CNIB
   www.cnib.ca/eng/national/cyf/toys.htm
Parental disengagement
   www.cjnr.nursing.mcgill.ca/archive/30/30_4_barnard.html
Growing healthy
   www.growinghealthykids.com/sheets/Factsheet1.htm
Infant/toddler sleep
   www.cincinnatichildrens.org/Health_Topics/Your_Childs_Health/Growth_and_Development/Wellness/Infant/infhab.htm
Encyclopedia of philosophy—Merleau-Ponty
   www.utm.edu/research/iep/m/merleau.htm

CHAPTER 10

Signs and Symbols: Toddlers at 15 to 18 Months

Lauren builds with large blocks. She also likes to knock them down! Here, she adds a block to a tower built with adult help.

Learning Outcomes

After reading and studying this chapter, you should be able to:

- identify the observable characteristics of toddlers at the 15-to-18-months stage
- explain the significance of behaviours of toddlers between 15 and 18 months in a developmental context
- recognize and respond to the developmental diversity of 15-to-18-month-old toddlers and discuss issues pertinent to this stage of development
- assess the development of 15-to-18-month-old toddlers
- respond to the health, safety, and development of 15-to-18-month-old toddlers with appropriate protection, guidance, and caregiving
- develop strategies to work with parents as partners in the care and education of their toddlers

Scene: Mom arrives at the child-care centre to take Garreth (16 months) home. She seems agitated and explains she has heard that early childhood should be a time for intensive learning because more development happens before 3 years than later on.

"I've been hearing on the news that if you don't educate young children before they're 3, it's too late," said Garreth's mom. "Do you think I've wasted too much time? Should I have been teaching Garreth?" "No, of course you haven't," replied the staff member. "Garreth doesn't need you to teach him for him to learn. You've done heaps of the right things: talking, playing, showing him pictures and books, and being with him while you do ordinary everyday activities. This is the heart of learning: making connections, getting to know each other, and helping Garreth find out about his world!"

The mother seemed somewhat reassured, but she wasn't entirely confident of her abilities as mother and educator. "I haven't always done the right thing. Sometimes I get home from work and I'm so tired I just let him play by himself for a bit. That can't be right, can it?" Garreth's caregiver smiled and went on, "No parent is perfect. And it's not such a bad idea for children to learn to play by themselves for short periods—children can benefit from learning to occupy themselves. Even if you did this quite often, Garreth's development wouldn't necessarily be harmed. Children have some resiliency—it's what human beings have in order to survive in an imperfect world." Garreth's mom continued expressing her concerns as the educator listened attentively.

An early childhood education student who had overheard this exchange later asked the caregiver for clarification. "How come you told Garreth's mom that it was okay to leave him to play by himself?" "That's not exactly what I said, but it's important to build parent confidence and for her to understand that she's not a bad parent because she can't be perfect," said the caregiver. "With our current understanding of brain development, we can't dismiss the notion that the earliest years are the most important for learning, but we know a bit more these days about children's resiliency. We need to balance these views."

"Well, that's okay, then," said the student. "I was wondering how I turned out okay when my mom didn't know much about child development." "That's another question," replied the caregiver. "Who knows how any of us would have turned out given a different set of circumstances in our early years?

I'm glad you picked up on this issue, though. It's highly debatable whether or not it's all over by 3. I think that the earliest years are likely to be the most important, but the subsequent years are pretty significant, too. We need to read the research and listen to the arguments of the experts so we can form our own opinions based on fact."

▶ What to Look For

PHYSICAL DEVELOPMENT

This is the time for the big "E," suggests Fogel (1997): "expression, exploration, and experimentation." He then adds "energy" to the list!

Growth

After an increase of about 25 cm (10 inches) in height in the first year, the rate of growth decreases. There may be about 13 cm (5 inches) more growth in the second year (Rolfes and DeBruyne, 1990). Typically, the toddler will be about 73–83 cm tall (29–33 inches) at 15 months and grow to about 76–86 cm (30–34 inches) at 18 months. The rate of weight gain slows, with 15-month-old toddlers weighing 9–13 kg (20–29 pounds), increasing by .11–.23 kg (¼–½ pound) per month. Obesity can become a concern at this stage. Box 10.1 discusses some of the issues surrounding obesity in toddlers and what caregivers can do about it.

The toddler's bones are a little less malleable, because they have **ossified** and **calcified**. The toddler's fontanels are closing after the considerable head growth during the first year of life. Muscle mass has increased a little, and body fat has decreased (Berk, 1996). The body continues to assume more adult-like proportions, with a smaller head in proportion to trunk and legs. The walking toddler takes on a more childlike appearance than that of an infant.

Gross Motor Skills

Most toddlers are walking by 15 months, and those who have not yet managed their first steps are likely to be successful fairly soon. Typically, the toddler will manage to walk alone in a cumbersome way with uneven steps. She frequently bumps into things and falls down into a sitting position or onto her hands and from there twists into a sitting position. By 18 months, after a good deal of spontaneous practice, the infant will walk with improved flow of movement. She will be able to walk automatically, without having to concentrate on each separate action. Also, she will

BOX 10.1

OVERWEIGHT TODDLERS

Raymond appeared confident as he strutted into the toddler room. He was later to start walking than many of his peers, but he had caught up and was obviously enjoying his newfound mobility. At 15 months, Raymond weighed almost 13 kg and he was continuing to gain weight. His chubbiness was appealing, though, and staff at the centre enjoyed his bubbly personality. His caregiver had some concerns, which she discussed with her supervisor. "Raymond is a delight, unless you have to carry him. He refuses to get in the stroller when we are out walking, and frequently we have to carry him back. I'm a bit concerned about his weight, really. His mother is a large woman herself and she says all of her children, of whom Raymond is the youngest, are 'tanks.' Should we be getting Raymond to eat less? He eats a lot—as much as some of the staff at lunch, and then he's first at the snack table mid-afternoon."

Weight is a complex and sensitive issue for many reasons. First, it is linked with major issues of acceptance and desirability. In our culture, thinness is desirable, so fatness is equated with being less than perfect. In a few societies, fatness is equated with health and, for women, fertility, but that is not the case in North America.

Second, food is linked to love. For parents and their children in particular, this link is difficult to separate. Feeding is one of the main ways adults build attachments with their infants. Mothers offer the breast for nourishment, but this care and closeness also meets the baby's emotional needs. This connection is continued when the parent provides food at the table. Freudian psychologists also link feeding with oral satisfaction—this is certainly part of food's association with pleasure. One can derive comfort from food and enjoy the tastes, textures, and eating experience.

Within all families, there are two factors that determine children's weight. The first is the genetic inheritance of body type, physiology, and physical potential. The second is the style of the family. If Raymond's mother and siblings are all large, it may be that the family has a genetic predisposition to obesity. On the other hand, the family may not share society's obsession with thinness and may feed family members accordingly.

Being overweight is a health issue, but experts' thinking about weight and health has changed over the last generation. Fifty years ago, a fat, rounded baby was considered a healthy baby. Health professionals thought that it was good for a baby to have some weight to fall back on in times of illness. Current thinking is different. A child is considered to be obese if she or he reaches the 95th percentile on the growth chart (Edelstein, 1995). Raymond's weight puts him in this category. The question is, What should be done about it?

Action should not involve putting Raymond on a reduction diet (Pimento and Kernested, 2000). Raymond is still growing very rapidly. He needs foods from all the food groups (Canadian Paediatric Society, 1992), but portion size should be carefully monitored, and healthy snack choices should be available. It's a serious mistake to offer low-fat foods and skim milk. Raymond still needs the fats, in reasonable amounts, for healthy growth and, in particular, for neurological development (Rofles and DeBruyne, 1990). In addition to monitoring Raymond's diet, caregivers could encourage him to be more active.

Although educators need to appreciate what they can do to assist obese toddlers and their parents, they have little control over the issue. Changes in nutrition require parental support; the child-care centre cannot be effective on its own. Meal and snack ideas and nutritional information in the form of bulletin boards, handouts, and parent-night information sessions might be useful. However, you need to know the parents well so you can decide how to reach them.

Because Raymond's mother was herself overweight, it was important to approach her with sensitivity. In such cases, it might be best to approach the issue indirectly. For example, the educator might chat about Raymond's general progress and make a comment about his appetite or ask a question about Raymond's walking and whether he demands to be carried. Non-threatening comments and open-ended questions can be helpful. Raymond's mother was extremely receptive to quick, healthy meal ideas that the caregiver offered on half-page recipe cards. Ultimately she recognized that she was feeding all the children the same size portions even though Raymond was younger and smaller.

be able to start and stop more easily, although she will retain the characteristic legs-apart posture for a little longer.

At this stage, toddlers may attempt gross motor movements that they cannot yet perform successfully. For example, a toddler may walk toward a ball to kick it, even though she is not yet able to stand on one foot to kick (Furuno et al., 1993b). The ball may move as the toddler bumps it or falls against it. Although she may feel a sense of achievement because she did make the ball move, she may also be frustrated that she cannot control her body as well as she wants to.

The toddler may continue to crawl because it is faster than her slow, purposeful walk. Going down an incline or down a couple of steps may require a backward crawl, which many toddlers can do easily. Backward movements may also be displayed when the toddler learns to reverse into a chair to sit down (Sheridan, 1997).

Given the opportunity, a toddler who has been walking for a few weeks may attempt to climb stairs while holding a rail (Furuno et al., 1993b). She may look downstairs with pleasure but react to the depth with some fear (Walk and Gibson, 1961). Parents and caregivers need to prepare for these new skills. Climbing is a newly discovered competence, usually appearing later in this stage. We need to watch out in case toddlers try to get up onto higher levels where there is something that interests them. The toddler may also run for a few steps but may have difficulty in stopping or negotiating obstacles (Sheridan, 1997).

On flat ground, the toddler might, at this stage, drag along a pull toy, but the coordination involved in pulling, turning to see the toy, and walking may be too challenging. Proficient walkers may manage to carry an object, such as a ball or a doll, as they walk (Furuno, 1993), but they usually stop when they pay attention to the toy. Pushing is a little easier than dragging or carrying. At this stage, toddlers like to push large lightweight boxes or toys by putting their weight behind the object. By 18 months, the toddler may be able to squat while playing or to pick up a fallen toy (Sheridan, 1997). This indicates that he has increasing control of his leg muscles. All these physical skills enable the toddler to be increasingly mobile and using the skills can make the toddler more tired than in previous months.

Fine Motor Skills

Although the toddler may show a **hand preference**—that is, a pattern of preferring to use either her right or left hand—it is not always consistent or permanent. Her increasing skill at using her hands is significant.

Feeding herself, assisting with tasks, playing, and imitating adult actions all help the toddler refine her **manipulative skills**.

During this period, a toddler will be able to hold a spoon and bring it to her mouth, hold a drink in a cup with a little adult help, carry objects using a whole-hand grasp (palmar) or holding them against her body, and pick up items using a delicate **pincer grasp** (Sheridan, 1997). She may be able to hold a crayon and scribble with a back-and-forth movement that mirrors the sway of her body.

The toddler is likely to use her finger to point at things and people. The pointing can be done in relation to books or other objects, television, or real-life action. As her interest in small things increases, she notices the details of pictures, and points and attributes names to the illustrations. She may turn the pages in a book (Furuno et al., 1993b) but not always in a left-to-right sequence. While the toddler may want to help with tasks in the kitchen, her **manual dexterity** is not yet up to the job. There is considerable increase in the toddler's ability to handle objects and she does this with great care and concentration. This shows a new level of **hand–eye coordination** that allows the toddler to play in different ways and be more successful with basic toys and puzzles.

Self-Help Skills

At this stage, the toddler may want to help as she is dressed or undressed. Her actions may not be well directed, but these efforts should be encouraged. Success is shown when she can take off items such as socks or a hat. She may also have mastered action to help with the dressing process, raising her leg to put on pants or holding out her hands for mitts. Interestingly, her actions will not always be in the correct sequence, and she may try to put on a coat before her undervest.

Mealtimes can take a long time, as she is likely to want to feed herself. Although her fine motor skills are not yet sufficiently refined for careful use of a spoon, she usually wants to try it herself. She is eating more adult foods, and she may manage many of these with her fingers.

At this stage, the toddler can usually make some connections between bowel and bladder fullness, the urge to urinate or defecate, and the feeling of evacuation and diaper-soiling. This does not mean that all the signs of readiness for **toilet-learning** are yet in place. However, some parents may already be encouraging their toddler to use the potty or toilet, and the parents' choices should be respected. Although it is commonly agreed that learning should not be stressful, there is considerable variation in how parents interpret that.

Please review Figure 10.1 for the criteria on early toilet-learning.

COGNITIVE DEVELOPMENT

Senses and Perception

Each of the five sense provides information to the toddler's brain, and she is able to process this efficiently. Her perceptions are limited more by lack of experience than lack of sensory acuity. The toddler's **visual acuity** is approaching that of an adult. Her hearing is quite acute, and she is able to differentiate between sounds quite accurately. She also has particular taste preferences and may have food jags, during which she refuses particular tastes. However, she is likely to try new flavours if the foods are presented one at a time with other familiar food. The toddler now uses her hands, more than her mouth, for feeling objects, but she may still use her mouth for discovery of new textures and objects. The toddler will respond to "good" and "bad" smells. She may notice the smells of food cooking, bathroom toiletries, or play materials that she likes, and respond negatively to the smells of the contents of her diaper, the garbage bin, rotting

---

FIGURE 10.1

Criteria for Early Toilet-Learning

Physical readiness

- has gained mobility
- enjoys bodily discovery
- has awareness of being wet and uncomfortable
- able to dress herself
- can sit still for a few minutes
- has bowel movements at fairly regular times
- remains dry for a period of an hour or so
- seems to recognize when she is going to have a bowel movement or pass urine
- can get the potty by herself

Social/emotional stage

- has a desire for independence
- has built a trusting relationship with an adult
- takes pride in doing things well
- wants to please adults
- wants to do what older children/ adults do
- likes to be clean

Cognitive /language skills

- uses words or signals
- aware of the process of elimination (through example)
- understands what the potty and toilet are for
- expresses interest in the process
- demonstrates imitative behaviour
- wants to put things "where they belong"
- can follow instructions
- seems to recognize when she is going to have a bowel movement or pass urine
- understands the association between clean underwear or diaper and use of potty or toilet

Notes on beginning toilet-learning

- think of the process as learning rather than training
- ensure consistent process between home and child care or home and other places where she spends her waking day
- avoid potentially stressful periods such as birth of sibling or moving house
- bowel control usually happens before bladder control
- ensure that there is no pressure, but use appropriate praise at effort
- change diapers in the bathroom if possible—to make appropriate association
- choose a period when adult and child can spend time together for at least three months
- girls tend to achieve toilet-learning earlier than boys
- place potty so it is accessible
- it can be helpful to place a potty so that the child discovers it, rather than having the adult introduce it to her
- draw attention to her bowel movement or urine in her diaper
- dress the child in clothes that are easy to remove
- place bowel movement in potty from diaper and transfer to toilet so that the child sees what happens
- suggest flushing away bowel movement in the toilet
- read to the child or allow her to play while seated on the potty so she is relaxed
- show no concern over accidents
- give up without concern if the child does not produce anything in the pot
- expect toilet-learning to take place over a period of months—it varies considerably among children

vegetables, or fish at the market. Interestingly, the associations she makes between smells and enjoyment may last a lifetime, even though she may not remember particular incidents.

As she matures, the toddler becomes better able to pay attention to information received through one sense and is able to process **multi-modal** information. Experience with all kinds of sensory materials enables the toddler to perform actions that are increasingly complex and from which she gains significant conceptual understanding.

Sensory-Motor Behaviour

The 15-to-18-month-old toddler is in the latter half of the **tertiary circular reaction** substage of the **sensory-motor** stage (Piaget, 1950). (Please see the Appendix for an overview of these stages.) You may see her handling materials in a slightly different way. She may perform actions to gain greater understanding of the properties of materials. The toddler might, for example, press different tools into dough to make a range of shapes. She might repeat these actions because they are pleasing to her, but she is also likely to extend her discovery by finding other objects to press, whether they are appropriate or not. Lots of **discovery play** is evident as she builds increasingly complex schemes of understanding about materials. New experiences might be treated cautiously, but soon the toddler will be squeezing, pressing, prodding, lifting, and dropping things just to see what happens. After she sees the results, she may repeat her actions or modify them in some way. When sensory experiences are extended using a variation of what is familiar, the toddler is interested in the novelty but remains confident of her previous learning.

The sensory discovery of materials remains the primary way that the toddler learns. She has great fun finding out what objects and materials will do. At 15 to 18 months she responds well to many new sensory activities. Through these, she extends her mental **schemes**, clustering together many bits and pieces of information to lead to fuller **concepts**. The toddler now knows how materials work after she performs a variety of actions on them. Extending initial discoveries happens every day, so the same materials can offer the toddler new discoveries repeatedly. Minor changes, such as making the dough a different colour, or providing different-shaped pieces of paper, will extend the learning even more. Gradually she will build conceptual understandings of colour, shape, and so forth. This will happen before true language has surfaced, but once language can be applied to

experience, the understanding is consolidated. Every time the toddler has a new experience, or a variation of an old one, her original concept is challenged. She will take in, or **assimilate**, this new information and change, or **accommodate**, her existing concepts accordingly. Most of the toddler's learning process involves discovery, assimilation, accommodation, and **equilibration** (balancing between taking in and altering schemes). The toddler's world has expanded because of her mobility and manipulative skills, so concept development occurs rapidly.

Brain Development

The most important thing that we need to understand about the brain development in this toddler stage is the significance of **synaptic connections**. Within the different areas of the brain, each having different purposes, are billions of nerve cells (**neurons**) that send messages to each other across **synapses**. These neurons, synapses, and the pathways between them (synaptic connections) are like the wiring of the brain. They enable all the different areas of the brain to communicate and coordinate their functions. At the time of birth, nearly all the neurons that will be needed have already been formed. So what we think of as brain development is actually the increase in connections between the neurons. New synapses are being made, but, at the same time, other neurons are being pruned or lost. The pruning is essential, because it increases the efficiency of the brain. Infancy and early childhood are the prime times for synaptic growth, but they are dependent upon the child's experience. However, too much pruning can occur; this happens if the child is deprived of important early experiences.

There are some areas of the brain that are less adaptable than others. These parts of the brain become less **plastic**, or less able to change after certain time periods. This gives us the idea that there are important periods in the child's life when key experiences are essential for brain development. We can reasonably assume that when those peak times or **windows of opportunity** are over or closed, certain learning cannot easily occur. Appreciating the significance of this is especially important in the first three years, because these windows of opportunity can be missed.

Many of the areas of the brain are responsible for different functions, such as hearing, sight, language, and so on. Neuroscientists have some idea of which areas are responsible for which functions, but some skills and abilities have not been related to particular areas. As yet, the scientific experts are uncertain about the purposes of a few areas of the brain. Caregivers and other adults in the lives of children may find this interesting. You may want to research this further, but for our purposes we need to know how all this translates into practice.

Our primary responsibility is to protect young children. This means not only protection in the physical sense—ensuring that they come to no harm—but protection in the neurological sense, to ensure that children are not put into any situation that could be injurious to their brain development. As mentioned above, brain development is dependent upon appropriate early experience. Neglect, trauma, abuse, institutionalization, prolonged hospitalization, inadequate parenting, lack of play opportunity, parental depression, lack of attachment and emotional well-being, along with many other negative situations, can be damaging to brain development—especially in the first three years (Hawley, Zero to Three: An Ounce of Prevention, 2000).

The next responsibility is to ensure that the young child receives age-appropriate, nurturing experiences. As many of us realize when trying to learn a second language as an adult, there is a **sensitive period** of learning that we missed! It is a hard task for monolingual adults to acquire new languages; they might have been more successful had they been given the window of opportunity at a much earlier stage. We need to know when these sensitive periods are—in this case what is a sensitive period, and for what kind of learning, and what sort of experience should be provided, during what stage of toddlerhood.

It is a good thing that current neuroscience has reinforced previous understandings about:

- the conditions for very young children to make secure attachments to adults (parents and out-of-home caregivers)
- socio-emotional development
- sensory experiences, perception, and sensory-motor intelligence
- what constitutes quality child care
- the characteristics of stage-appropriate activities
- when important sensitive periods occur

What we know now that we didn't know before the publication of recent brain research, is the reason why all of these things are so important. Sara Gable (2000) has interpreted a large amount of the core research. Gable's suggestions to infant and toddler caregivers who aim to establish relationships that promote brain development are as follows:

- Learn to read the physical and emotional cues of the toddlers in your care.

- Recognize the individuality of each child and sensitively respond to these differences.
- Assign a primary caregiver to each toddler in your program to work with this child and his/her family.
- Observe and record toddler behaviours that are indicative of early brain development.
- Share these observations with other caregivers who play an important part in the children's lives.
- Accept toddlers' strong emotions as signs of their desire to communicate with you and the world.
- Respond quickly and appropriately to these communications, giving meaning to these emotional communications.
- Find a balance between being over-involved and being under-involved.
- Recognize the child's current developmental status and create opportunities for each child to reach beyond her capabilities.[1]

The sensitive periods of the toddler stage lead us to pay particular attention to certain parts of the child's experience. All experiences are not equally important. For example, having experiences that lead to secure attachments are more important than playing with sand (not to imply that sensory discovery is unimportant!). The emotional experience is a profound one that enables other types of learning to occur. If the toddler does not have a secure attachment, she might be uninterested in venturing out to play with the sand, and even if placed in front of it she might lack the motivation essential to discover its properties. The following list of key experiences differentiate between **profound experiences** and **essential experiences**. Each is based on current understandings of the toddler's brain development.

Profound Experiences:

1. being loved
2. having all physical needs met
3. being respected as a separate person and having opportunity for self-discovery and self-regulation
4. enjoying physical proximity, comforting, and cuddling
5. having consistent caregiving, based on mutual trust
6. having adults respond to toddler-initiated cries, gestures, expressions, and language
7. being in a reliable and consistent environment with regular routines

---

1. Sara Gable, *Nature, Nurture and Early Brain Development.* (University of Missouri—Columbia).

8. having adults mediate between the child and the child's world
9. being competent, successful, and enabled to be independent
10. recovering from temporary negative situations

Essential Experiences:

1. having safe space to explore her own body and the environment
2. being offered a wide range of sensory discovery and experiencing the natural world, with adult encouragement
3. enjoying the time, opportunity, and space to play—with adult facilitating
4. being immersed in spoken language, and having adults support the toddler's language acquisition through scaffolding
5. having opportunity for social interaction with other children and being part of a group
6. being given opportunity for the discovery of music, song, story, and experimentation with sound
7. being offered a wide variety of visual stimulation
8. being offered regular opportunity and experience to identify, sort, order, build concepts, recall, organize, and solve problems
9. having the opportunity for minor risk-taking and finding out the consequence of actions
10. being offered the opportunity and materials for imitative, creative, symbolic, pretend, block, object, role-play, and imaginative play

Play

Accessing a full range of sensory discoveries is the central theme of play activity at this stage. Most of this will be **solitary play** and may last for prolonged periods of time. Improved motor control assists the toddler to perform more complex actions and move about to play more easily. Standing or sitting at a table may be possible for a few activities, but the floor is often preferred.

Toddlers at this stage will draw for short periods using chubby wax crayons. The marks they make on the paper are pleasing to them. Frequently these will be arc-like scribbles or back-and-forth or even up-and-down lines. Toddlers may also enjoy making dots by repeatedly stabbing at the paper. The toddler's scribbles mostly follow her body movements, because the arm is moved as an extension of the body rather than as a flexible tool.

The toddler may display actions that relate to hiding and finding toys or other objects. These games give great satisfaction and reinforce the concept of

object permanence. Simple hide-and-seek, played with an adult, also provides the reinforcement of people permanence.

Destruction is evident in knocking down towers of blocks or taking apart toys and domestic items. This is a natural stage toward construction, which is soon evident as the toddler builds stacks of blocks two or three high (Hughes, Elicker, and Veen, 1995). **Block play** is an important opportunity to learn some basic mathematical concepts.

The toddler may spend some time as an onlooker, particularly if there are other toddlers at play. She may play alongside them in early **parallel play**, using similar materials, but she is more likely to play in a solitary manner. Parallel play may be seen in a group situation where two or more toddlers do the same thing, such as splashing water, running, playing with dough while sitting in adjacent seats, or playing with pretend objects. **Egocentricity** prevents the toddlers from playing together, but mutual activity is common with toddlers as long as there are enough playthings. Toddlers are not capable of sharing or understanding that another toddler has her own perspective, but they do know that other children have feelings, because they hear their cries and acknowledge their laughter. They may also show a toy to a child of the same age or even invite another child to play (Hughes, Elicker, and Veen, 1995) and engage in some **shared meanings**, where there is a common understanding, whether spoken or not.

You may see some toddlers involved in **imitative play**. This can be immediate copying or a **deferred imitation**, where the toddler copies an adult some time after the initial observation. Deferred imitation is more complex than basic imitation because it involves memory and some degree of **symbolism**. It may also involve some association that the toddler makes between objects and their function. Some play sequences may involve pretend actions, but this is more typical of slightly older toddlers.

Information Processing

Observational learning is particularly important at this stage. This means that the toddler learns about the world from watching it. From observation comes some imitation of what is seen. Such imitation shows that the observations are more than visual stimulation—they are processed in some way. When you see a toddler copying a parent's actions with the vacuum cleaner, you can see direct learning from imitation. As we saw in the discussion of imitative play, sometimes toddlers will show deferred imitation. In one memorable example, the day after a visit from her uncle, a

17-month-old toddler was seen holding a crayon to her mouth to imitate him smoking: not all observational learning turns out to be positive.

Some memory functions can be seen as early as 15 to 18 months in the play sequences. The toddler recalls actions in relation to **scripts**, or mental representations of a sequence of actions. These scripts not only provide a method of recall but their creation allows the child to sort information, filter it to decide what is important, and put it into memory. Toddlers' scripts are very simple at this stage (Bauer and Hertsgaard, 1993), but they are useful devices for improving memory.

Deciding what to pay attention to is a challenge for toddlers who are bombarded with sensory information. Adults assist the process by isolating key features—pointing to a picture in a book or emphasizing a particular naming word, for example. Yet much of the toddler's attention has to be directed by herself, without adult intervention. Although the process is supported by adults, toddlers achieve the ability to attend to information independently. Selecting and **attending** to information is, to some extent, driven by the toddler's interests and motivation. Attending is a way we have of describing how the child pays attention to some aspect of what she is experiencing. She may attend to texture, for example, rather than any other perceptual information. Attending to some features of an object or experience is essential for learning. Without this ability, the child cannot single out characteristics or see how details relate to each other. Her ability to attend is variable and is shaped by her interests, maturational stage, state of alertness, sensory acuity, and skill level. But there is another element to attending to information: it is a question of experience and practice. Neurological (synaptic) connections are made and reinforced with this practice; probably the most significant skill for later success in school (Berk, 1996).

Practice play, when the toddler repeats sequences of actions, is not only important in reinforcing synaptic connections, but is also pleasurable for the toddler. Appreciating the significance of repetition, we can enter into the toddler's fun, knowing that there is a significant reason why it's important. Practice play often involves playing with objects. So **object play** is not necessarily a different type of activity; it's just defined separately by adults because they see that it has a different function. Object play is play that involves discovering the properties of the object.

In toddlerhood, object play takes on greater complexity than it did in earlier months. Now it might involve more than one object and can involve discovering the relationship of one object to another. The toddler loves to put things inside other things. For example, she will put a toy car in a box or put a dolly in its crib. In doing this, she is demonstrating some relationship between one object and another. It might be that one item is smaller and therefore will fit inside the other, or, as in the case of the doll, she may understand that dolls go in cribs. Knowing the function of objects is more sophisticated than just identifying what they are. Sometimes toddlers will be amused if objects are used wrongly. If they have built a concept in which, for example, "shoes go on your feet," they might laugh if they see you putting a shoe on your head. This shows that they understand the appropriate and inappropriate use of objects—but this involves only things that have domestic familiarity.

Sometimes you might see a **mental substitution** in toddler play (Hughes, 1999). The toddler might use one object to represent another. For example, you might see a toddler use a stickle brick on his face as a shaver to "shave like daddy" or pull along a telephone and say "bzzzzzzz bzzzz" to symbolize a car. So far, the toddler uses objects to represent other objects rather than indulge flights of pure imagination. Consequently, the toddler needs plenty of objects that might strike her imagination as representative of other things. This **symbolic play** has various levels during toddlerhood. At first, the symbolism involves things in relation to herself—as her egocentricity might suggest. She might use an object as mommy's purse and carry it around. Later it might involve playing alone as she acts out the caregiver handing around snacks to the children. She might use the stuffed animals close by and another object for a plate. In a few months the symbolism could involve thinking that is **decentred**—moving away from pure egocentric thought. In this case, you might observe the toddler in a pretend sequence involving several separate elements of pretence. In an example that also shows early role-playing, the toddler dresses in a pretend coat and waves as she pretends to leave—just like mommy.

Role-playing has yet to become very sophisticated, possibly because toddler language does not allow for complexity. However, you may see some imitative actions embedded in play behaviour. When observing play, you might want to categorize what you see to help make sense of what is happening. Our adult interpretations of play show that several components of play happen simultaneously. For example, a toddler might be playing in a solitary way as she pretends, with objects, to imitate an adult. This involves at least some elements of solitary play, object play, imitative play, sensory-motor play and symbolic play—all at once! Of course the child's perception of what is happening is more closely associated with pleasure, and he wouldn't be doing it if he were not internally motivated. So there are many ways of trying to understand what is happening in a play sequence.

LANGUAGE AND COMMUNICATION

Body Language

Toddlers who are active, as most are for all their waking time, may display some preference in their sensory interests. This is not to suggest that musicality or some other special talent is identifiable at this stage. There is a wide variety of opinion on that matter. Rather, the point is that observable differences exist in the way toddlers prefer to take in information. Some prefer seeing, while others prefer hearing or touching (Quilliam, 1994). If you look for the responses of toddlers to different stimuli, you can determine their preference. Quilliam suggests that we can detect these differences by observing the child's posture, movements, eye patterns, facial expressions, speech, skin, heart rate, and breathing. Toddlers who receive information through the **channel of preference** will tend to sit upright, move toward the source of stimulation, open their eyes wide, and smile. Their skin colour may deepen and their heart rate and breathing will quicken—except in the case of hearing music, when it may synchronize with the music. A negative response may indicate that the stimulation is not through their favoured channel. Negative responses include being startled, withdrawing, frowning, going blank, getting paler, whimpering or crying, closing the body by becoming stiff or shrinking inward, covering the head or ears, turning away, or shutting the eyes. The same positive or negative responses can be used to determine if a toddler is comfortable with multimodal stimulation, receiving sensory information via two or more channels at once.

It can be very helpful for the adult observe and interpret these largely involuntary responses. At the same time, though, adults need to assist toddlers' deliberate communication. Joseph Garcia (1994/1999) suggests that toddlers' communication can be assisted if adults add a language gesture to their actions. These gestures, he thinks, can be offered before, during, or after the specific actions. His experience with toddlers indicates that they are receptive to this communication method and can gain a repertoire of motions that can assist them to communicate their needs and ideas, and to respond to adults, while their oral language skills are still limited.

Garcia's communication enhancement is through baby **signing**. It is a somewhat controversial approach to assisting infant and toddler communication, because some practitioners think that there is no long-term advantage to offering these skills to young children, even if, in the short term, it enables them to express themselves and opens a channel of communication with adults as they try to have the child understand them. For infants and toddlers who are experiencing hearing impairments, this modification of **American Sign Language (ASL)** for infants and toddlers it is likely to offer a very useful communication tool. There are some child-care centres that accommodate both hearing and hearing-impaired children who are using this method of supporting communication, and they consider it advantageous. Garcia has the support of the well-known pediatrician Burton White and the signing method's research base, but further observation of signing in practice would be helpful for the field of early childhood education.

Another positive aspect of gestured communication is that it involves turn-taking, which helps to smooth the transition from preverbal to verbal communication (Hulit and Howard, 1997). Toddlers who are familiar with adults, play with them frequently, and interact with them through gestured communication become socialized into the turn-taking behaviour necessary in spoken language (Bloom, Rocissano, and Hood, 1976).

Receptive and Expressive Language

The toddler's receptive language grows quickly at this stage. She may respond positively to requests to do simple things (Sheridan, 1997) and appear to understand words used in context. Comprehension is enhanced when the adult emphasizes key words, but the toddler may understand phrases as well as single words. She is likely to know the action that accompanies phrases such as "It's tidy-up time" or "We're going up the stairs." Also, she may understand the word no and appreciate what it means (Sheridan, 1997). Of course, hearing the word no might be received negatively. Some educators avoid the word no, but there is little concrete evidence to show that using it is detrimental. The toddler does need to hear constructive language, but she also needs to understand boundaries.

The toddler may already be using words to refer to his mother and father, such as "mumma" or "duda," but this ability varies considerably. As the child focuses attention on walking, language advancement may temporarily plateau (Furuno, 1993). The toddler may use a vocabulary of 10 to 20 or more words accurately and clearly, but some toddlers will talk more, others less. The earliest words relate to objects in the immediate environment and are one- or two-syllable words (Hulit and Howard, 1997). The toddler is likely to make her needs known, whether using verbal language or gestures. Frequently, words and actions are communicated simultaneously. A few toddlers may manage to articulate some two-word phrases by the end of this stage (Furuno, 1993).

There is likely to be a lot of **variegated babbling** or tuneful jabbering (Sheridan, 1997), a form of babbling that takes on the sounds and intonations of real language. The toddler likes to hear her own voice and may make singsong sounds with many complex repetitions and modulations of sounds. **Tuneful babbling** usually has a greater range of sounds that are based on melodic experimentation.

The enriched language environment that is offered by the adult is enormously important to the toddler's language acquisition. Toddlerhood, as we previously discussed, is a sensitive period for acquiring language. Unlike the early infant stage, when it did not matter exactly what you said to the baby, because she was in need of hearing comforting adult voices and absorbed sound patterns rather than actual words, toddlerhood is the time to be careful about the content of your own language. Parents are sometimes unpleasantly surprised when the toddler imitates some of their words. The toddler is receptive to words said in a particular context, particularly when they are emphasized. This is not the time to use any ripe vocabulary! Toddlers need conversation rather than the passive language of television, radio, or audiotapes. These are not necessarily damaging at this stage, but the time spent viewing or hearing might better be spent on real two-way conversations. Television is a controversial issue for many. Rather than a learning tool, its greatest benefit at this stage might be to give the adult a break from tiring work. Television is more likely to be helpful if it is a shared experience. Language learning needs to be interactive—the child should not be left in front of the television by herself.

Books, stories, and action rhymes provide wonderful opportunities for interaction and offer closeness and mutual enjoyment. The toddler's attention span may not be long, but when the adult is truly engaged with her you may be surprised at how long she stays on task. Reading to toddlers is a pleasant experience, but the toddler will want to see the book's pictures. At bedtime or nap time, stories provide comfort as she hears the adult's voice; we cannot imagine that she is always following the story or understanding what the pictures mean, even if she seems to be staring at the book. There are divided opinions about reading to children just as they drop off to sleep. A few people think that the toddler then associates books with sleep—not a very positive approach for later studying. It's the experience of most educators and parents that toddlers get used to a routine story before bedtime. This provides a nice downtime and we can make the last few minutes of the ritual talking. If we read the signs of tuning out, we don't have to continue reading until they are asleep!

Identifying, labelling, and making sense of her world is supported through language. Conceptual understandings are underscored with the addition of language. Some academics link language and thought so closely that they seem symbiotic (mutually helpful). Clearly it is possible to have some thought without language—and language without meaning, but the association of the two allows the toddler to elaborate her learning through the progress of her conceptual development.

EMOTIONAL DEVELOPMENT AND SELF-REGULATION

Shame and **guilt** are relatively new emotions for toddlers at this stage (Izard and Malatesta, 1987). They signify the gradual emergence of an emotional conflict between **autonomy** and shame or doubt (Erikson, 1980). The toddler is attempting to do things independently, but is also becoming increasingly aware of her dependence and need for approval from an adult. She feels shame (a new condition) when she doubts her ability to act independently. These feelings mark the emergence of the toddler's sense of power and her fear about having it, or losing control. She may try to exercise this power in a variety of ways. Soon she will start to say "NO!" and find behavioural ways of showing us that she is an independent person with a different opinion.

The toddler usually has a good laugh at this stage—and she probably needs it to balance some of the other negative emotions she experiences! Her smile can be in response to an adult or she may initiate a smile in trying to engage an adult. This is usual within her circle of adults with whom she is attached—she is more likely to be cautious of strangers. It is a terrific experience to be part of a toddler joke—we can laugh along with her even if we don't get what is funny. The emotion behind the expression of laughter is based on finding small incongruities (things being used incorrectly), physical exertions, or as a result of physical handling. There is divided opinion about adults deliberately tickling children; some believe it is intrusive or makes the child lose control of herself. Whatever your opinion, the adult's unintentional acts can produce laughter. In addition to giving social smiles, the toddler may be seen to smile when alone; this appears to be in relation to how her activity strikes her as pleasing.

Moving toward 18 months, the toddler has an increasing sense of self, in what Stanley Greenspan call "the **emergence of an organized sense of self**" (1985). The toddler is better able to take initiative in a variety of situations. It is noticeable that even toddlers who were previously considered relatively passive will start conversations with adults, extending their physical proximity from the adult, playing spontaneously, and exerting their independence. The toddler's emotions may seem extreme, but she is gaining some control over their extremes. Although she may not seem as though she wants to have her independence reined in, the toddler needs to have a clear sense of boundaries, She may not accept "no" very well, or may need to be distracted from something that is inappropriate, but she needs the feeling that there are some external controls on her overwhelming feelings. Greenspan and Greenspan suggest that a number of behaviours that usually occur at this stage can be explained using his idea of emotional milestones.[1]

1. *Emotional partnership and complex imitation*– where the child is capable of reciprocating and copying adult behaviour and emotions
2. *Expressing needs and interests through taking initiative*–where the child begins to instigate activities based on her own needs and desires rather than by imitation alone
3. *Independence and distal communication*–where the child leaves the adult for a short time in order to explore; she feels connected with the adult from a distance by using her hearing and vision
4. *Originality*–where the child adds her own interpretation to things she has been taught, and uses objects or toys in ways she has not been shown
5. *Understanding function and meaning*–where the child begins to understand the uses and meanings of people and things
6. *Toddler-to-toddler relationships*–where the child can begin to develop a shared relationship with a toddler who is a regular playmate that goes beyond parallel play
7. *Recognizing emotional polarities*–where the child begins to realize that people are composed of

different emotions–that even though daddy may be mad at mommy, he still loves her at the same time
8. *Ability to communicate with words*–where the child begins to communicate with gestures, sounds, and a few words
9. *Accepting limits and using the distal mode*–where the child begins to respond to your setting limits verbally or with a gesture

The toddler period marks significant advances in self-regulatory abilities (Bronson, 2000). The increase in voluntary control during this stage is likely to come about because the toddler has a strong motivation for self-direction. It is noticeable that as the toddler tries to gain control over as much as possible, there is a change in the way she tries to be assertive. Because the toddler has increased language abilities and can represent ideas symbolically, she can become more aware of herself and what she wants. This may mean resisting external controls, which can be very frustrating for both the adult and the toddler. Gradually she will be able to accept some of the external controls placed upon her, in an effort to please the adult. Now she has an understanding that adults have different feelings from hers, and she has the ability to influence the adults that she has a growing need to please. She wants to get positive responses from adults, even though her will is very strong and she may not want to comply. Pleasing the adult can be a reward for good behaviour, and that reinforces behaving well. Also, the toddler has some rudimentary appreciation of what is socially acceptable behaviour, and watches closely to see what reaction she is getting from the adult. Knowing what is right is internalized in such a way that it constrains what she really wants to do. Fortunately, this inner conflict leads to further effort to curb some of her basic desires.

The struggle between autonomy and doubt is such that the toddler is prone to temper tantrums. Some toddlers feel frustration more than others; for some it may be that their personality style leads them to a more assertive style and stronger emotions; for others, adult interactions might lead them to manage their feelings more effectively. A sensitive balance is needed between appropriate external controls and ones that are coercive and forceful. Although a forceful parent may elicit an immediate compliant response, in the long term there is a negative effect on internal controls (Lepper, 1983).

Self-regulation takes a significant step as the toddler becomes more autonomous and is able to act more independently. However, much of the toddler's

---

1. Adapted from S. Greenspan and N. Thorndike Greenspan, *First Feelings (1985)*, p. 93.

learning is shaped by the culture in which she is nurtured (Berk, 1996). Behaviours that are desirable in one culture may be inappropriate in another. In fact, the move toward independence itself is highly regarded in some cultures while others are more comfortable with longer-term dependence.

The quest to use adults for social referencing, to check in with adults to seek their emotional response, aids the toddler in her ability to control her feelings. As the toddler becomes better able to control her feelings, she begins to define herself in relation to them. By 18 months, the toddler, whose language has been limited to object-related speech, will start to use words to label feelings.

Between 15 and 18 months, toddlers become increasingly interested in pictures of themselves (Berk, 1996), although they do not usually recognize themselves in a self-conscious manner (Lewis and Brooks-Gunn, 1978). However, they do have a clear sense that they exist. This sense of existential self emerges from the close two-way relationship the toddler has had with her primary caregiver throughout infancy.

As the toddler gains a clearer sense of the fact that she exists, and achieves an emotional separation from her adult attachment figures, she is gradually accumulating some ideas about her personal attributes. Although she is not yet ready to identify or describe what those characteristics are, she nevertheless develops a sense of how she feels about herself.

The thoughts and feelings that she has about her competence and security are created by the experiences she has and the way she is treated. At this stage, 15 to 18 months, it is important for her to hear and feel encouraged about the initiatives that she takes. As she goes about trying to become more independent, the adult needs to let her go. When the toddler finds out that when she returns to the adult after a little exploring in the big world and the adult is there to greet her and praise her for her courage, the experience is enriched. The adult is largely responsible for the child's self esteem—how she feels about herself. Whenever the toddler makes an effort, whether successful or not, she needs to know that it is okay to try things out. Also, having adult support allows her to find out that it's okay to make some small mistakes; that, too, is part of autonomous living. The toddler's **self-esteem** can be firmly established if she receives positive, but not shallow, encouragement from the adults who are special to her.

The toddler needs a world that is stimulating, but one where she can meet challenges with some measure of success. So parents and educators need to ensure that play material is developmentally appropriate, not just from the intellectual perspective but in the sense that it presents problems that she is able to solve. Self-esteem must be rooted in genuine success, not hollow praise. If we offer toys that are too challenging, the toddler becomes bored or frustrated with them. With a new challenge, the toddler may need adult help. Perhaps some strategies for solving the problem can be suggested. For example, showing a toddler how to identify the different shapes to be slotted into the right spaces can be a bridge to her doing it independently. More **open-ended activities** are suitable at this time, because they allow the toddler to set her own pattern of play with them and also to challenge herself to solving the problems that she creates for herself. Open-ended activities often involve materials that can be used in a variety of different ways, so there is no intrinsic right or wrong way to use them. The toddler might be happy to play with a series of empty boxes, to respond to an armful of different large pieces of cloth, or to experiment with Play-Doh and a selection of cookie cutters. Each of these experiences is open-ended, so there is little scope for failing at the activity.

As the toddler's repertoire of skills broadens, she is likely to set her own goals. She will show noticeably greater deliberation in her play. This can lead to successes and failures. Whenever the toddler comes to a situation that seems particularly challenging, she needs to develop skills that enable her to solve her own problem. Dealing with her frustration is necessary; so is managing disappointment and going back to try again—and she is likely to need adult help to support her through these difficult times. Dealing with a situation that does not work out as she wanted it to can be a significant learning experience and one where she discovers that she can overcome emotional obstacles. These playful and domestic situations provide the best opportunity for the toddler to learn about herself and become aware of how she feels in relation to what she is doing. They are essential for self-learning and the emergence of a positive self-esteem.

Using positive language supports the toddler's self-esteem. It can be based on all the toddler's strengths and effort that she makes. Pointing out new achievements, pinpointing successes, remarking on the child's effort to do a good job as well as commending the toddler on the nice things she does, builds healthy self-esteem. A toddler needs to know that she is loved and she must know that her activity is acknowledged as being important. Adults must ensure that the toddler's routine includes cuddle time, story time, and time for intimacy. It is essential that whenever her body is hurt, her feelings are recognized. As the toddler gains some idea of what is **socially acceptable behaviour**—acting in accordance with prevailing social norms—her efforts to behave according to the social rules should be recognized. Such things as the toddler's natural curiosity, her interest in how things work, or her efforts to pay attention to a story are all worthy of praise. There are plenty of things the toddler does right! Adults may overlook this when they feel assaulted by the toddler's extreme feelings, challenging behaviour, and frustrations. This approach to supporting the emergence of the toddler's strong self-esteem can also be helpful to the parent or educator. It can remind us of all the advances that the young child is making.

▶ Attachment

Close observation of the behaviour patterns of a toddler can tell parents and caregivers how well the toddler is attached to the adult. Susan Goldberg (2000) provides an excellent definition of **attachment** that can be used as a lens through which to observe the toddler: "Attachment is usually defined as an emotional bond between two individuals based on the expectations of one (or both) members of the pair that the other will care for and provide protection [to] in times of need" (p. 134). Goldberg's definition is particularly helpful to us at this stage because it highlights a consciousness on the part of the toddler—as well as the adult—as though there were some kind of unwritten contract between the two parties!

Toddlers are capable of doing things in a conscious way and it appears that they are aware of the attachment relationship even though they cannot yet articulate their thoughts in language. However, their behaviour is a good indicator to adults of whether or not they are attached to one or more adults.

All attachments are not equal. Many forces come into play to enable attachments to be made. Some of these forces are biological, or what we might call nature. The toddler's personality, brain-wiring, and potential for communication are largely determined by her genetic inheritance. The experiences that she has are what we call nurture; these include what adults are there, the circumstances of the family into which she is born, and everything that happens to her. How she makes attachments depends upon both **nature** and **nurture**, as well as the interaction of nature and nurture. So we can see there are infinite varieties of human attachments. An additional issue

that must be remembered as we observe toddlers is that attachment behaviour—which is one part of the toddler's emotional development—is linked to all the other developmental domains. The toddler's attachments are very likely to shape the child's:

- *emotional development*—because through attachments she builds a sense of security and trust, and the ability to recognize and regulate her behaviour
- *cognitive development*—because she needs to be secure to play, explore, and learn
- *social development*—because secure attachment shape her ability to make positive relationships
- *personality development*—because she needs to have a secure attachment so that she can develop her own personality
- *moral and character development*—because her security and trusting relationships provide the backdrop necessary to internalize positive role models and learn what is socially acceptable
- *language development*—because language acquisition is dependent upon adults with whom she is attached
- *physical development*—because she needs to feel secure and confident to have the motivation to move, explore, and acquire skills
- *resilience*—because having a secure base allows her to cope with difficulties that she encounters

The essential source for our understanding of attachment stems from the pioneering work of John Bowlby (1953) and Mary Ainsworth (1969) and Klaus and Kennel (1976), who each, separately, focused on the attachment of mother and child or parent and child. Bowlby called this **monotropy**, a bias to have a hierarchy of attachment preferences, with one primary attachment figure—usually the mother. Today our understanding of attachment is somewhat broader and there is some disagreement about applying the same theory of attachment to all attachment relationships. That said, the ways in which infants and toddlers make these attachments tend to fall into three main categories (Ainsworth 1973), shown below with some of their behavioural characteristics at the toddler stage:

- **secure attachment**
  - not overly stressed
  - demonstrates a range of emotions
  - attempts to self-regulate
  - trusts that her needs will be met (relatively calm about hunger, thirst, etc.)
  - confident in becoming independent (will move away from adult for periods of time)
  - casual relaxed physical contact

- uses regular social referencing (checking to see if the adult is there)
- shows curiosity
- lengthy attention span
- acquires pro-social skills earlier
- demonstrated spontaneous play
- expects support of adult
- relaxed in reunion behaviours

- **avoidant attachment**
  - neutral affect (emotion)
  - does not seem happy or unhappy with separations or being reunited
  - unconcerned about mother/adult presence/absence
  - makes little attempt at self-help skills
  - unresponsive to stimuli
  - avoids social contact with other children/adults
  - may appear distant or blank
  - behaviour erratic and unpredictable at times
  - imitates others emotionally
  - apathetic in play situations
  - makes limited eye contact

- **resistant/ambivalent attachment**
  - overly dependent
  - seeks attention
  - frequent temper tantrums
  - behaviour is not socially acceptable (with reference to the norm)
  - ignores play/exploration
  - difficulty in settling
  - shows no pro-social skills
  - fails to regulate extreme behaviours
  - poor attention span
  - tests adults
  - exhibits helpless or baby behaviour

A fourth category was introduced by Mary Main (1990):

- **disorganized/disoriented attachment**
  - not easily comforted
  - emotions/reactions unpredictable
  - moves from one adult to the next without engagement
  - not focused on tasks
  - easily distracted
  - emotions change very rapidly
  - plays with objects without following through a play sequence
  - short attention span
  - picks up toys and drops them, moving on to something else

- wanders aimlessly
- erratic contact with adults
- loses interest quickly
- has little curiosity
- acquires many skills later than average
- fails to categorize, organize, or put objects where they belong

By the time the toddler has developed to this stage, it is hoped that she has made some secure attachments to the important adults in her life. As discussed in previous chapters, attachment depends upon an ongoing, reliable, consistent relationship with an adult who meets the needs of the young child. If the toddler has had some difficult life experiences involving relationships that have been damaged because of neglect, abuse, or emotional unavailability of adults, there can be significant long-term difficulties for the child. If the toddler is experiencing attachment difficulties, immediate support should be provided. **Early interventions** may provide the dyad of toddler and adult with some strategies to help support the formation of an attachment. At the 15-to-18-month stage, parents and caregivers should be concerned if the toddler is *not:*

- seeking the support of an adult when distressed
- showing interest in her immediate environment
- responsive to adults trying to engage her
- demonstrating a wide range of emotions
- demonstrating typical play behaviours for her age
- showing distress at the time of separation from her primary caregiver/parent
- showing anxiety in the presence of strangers
- demonstrating secure attachment behaviours (as above)

The behaviours listed here are typical of toddlers of about 15 to 18 months. If the toddler does not demonstrate a cluster of these behaviours, a sharing of observations and consultations between the toddler's parents and caregivers and a recommendation to seek expert advice should be made. Of course, all toddlers are different in their stages of development, experiences, and personality, so any one or more of these behaviours is not necessarily cause for alarm—they are indicators of potential **attachment difficulties**. True **attachment disorders** require closer observation by experts; they are characterized by pathological behaviours that can be diagnosed only by a clinician. Referral to experts, such as pediatricians involved in early intervention programs, can be made through the family's general practitioner or directly, depending on local protocols. Many early interventions are successful in that they result in much healthier attachments. The behaviours outlined above can give some indication as to where there might be a problem; most early interventionists work collaboratively with parents and child-care educators to support the emotional needs of the child.

By the time the infant becomes a toddler it is likely that the circle of people to whom she is attached will have widened. There will be **primary caregivers** and possibly secondary caregivers, depending on how big the child's social world becomes. Observations of the toddler recorded by both the parents and child-care staff can lead to a better understanding of the difficulty. In addition to looking for the behaviours listed above, or the lack of them, adults might take notice of a toddler who:

- is indiscriminately friendly (makes a superficial relationship with every passing adult but is not distressed at their departure)
- shows no preference for one adult over another
- has a preferred caregiver but clings to that adult in a distorted manner
- appears disorganized/disoriented (relative to expected behaviour)
- engages in reckless activity (more dangerous than is typical even at the toddler stage)
- spends long periods alone rocking herself or banging her head

THE STRANGE SITUATION

Although the phrase might sound like a title from a horror movie, the **Strange Situation** is actually an interesting technique devised to assess infant attachment. It is based on the work of John Bowlby and was developed initially by Mary Ainsworth (1979). It involves naturalistic observations of infants—usually between 12 and 18 months of age—in a contrived situation. The Strange Situation provides an opportunity to see how the infant balances her need to explore—with appropriate toys made available—and her attachment to her mother (although other significant attachment figures have been used in some experiments). Through a series of separations and reunions the infant's behaviours are videotaped and then coded. The interpretation of the infant's responses involves categorizing the documented behaviours into one of three groups: avoidant, secure, or resistant. In later research, a fourth category was added: disorganized attachment. It should be mentioned that infants were not allowed to be distressed by the research experiment, and those infants who seemed unhappy were reunited with their mothers. Coding the behavioural responses presented some difficulties. A newer approach to attachment research

involves using the Strange Situation method but incorporates a "Q sort" methodology—using previously determined categories of behaviour into which the child's actual behaviour is then fitted. As discussed earlier, each infant's different responses are thought to identify the quality of attachment that the infant experiences. Conducting the research in different communities revealed similar proportions of infants in each category of attachment. Various explanations can be found for this, but it appears to indicate that there is a typical pattern of infant attachment across different populations.

Personality and Temperament

In earlier chapters, we discussed Chess and Thomas's temperament types. Another, simpler, way of analyzing temperament is the three-dimension model of Buss and Plomin (1984). This model posits that temperament can be identified according to degree in each of three dimensions: emotionality, activity, and sociability. This is a useful way of considering the temperament characteristics of toddlers, whose patterns of behaviour are more easily discernible than they were at earlier stages. *Emotionality* is the tendency to become upset or distressed, easily and intensely. *Activity* is the level of any behaviour—the amount of movement, speed of talking, quantity of energy put into activities. Finally, *sociability* involves seeking and being gratified by rewards from social interaction and preferring such interaction to solitude.

Most theories of **personality** development that focus on **temperament** consider personality as something attributable to the child's nature—his genetic inheritance. This might lead us to believe that adults cannot do much to change the basic temperamental style. There may be some truth in this—we are unlikely to change an individual's personal style. And we probably don't want to tamper with what makes the person who they are. We can, however, work with the child's style to help her to function effectively, and we can also help the child grow in awareness of what that style is. This helps the child to identify her personal characteristics and to maximize her potential by developing strategies appropriate to her style.

At the 15-to-18-month stage there are very clear indications of the characteristics of each toddler. If you are working in a group child-care setting, the combination of temperamental styles might present particular challenges. If the group of toddlers is made up of children who are high on the activity dimension, you will have a very busy, noisy, toddler room with lots of action. Toddlers tend to be emotional at this stage anyway, but if your group includes mostly those who are high on the emotional dimension, you will find the group very demanding and in need of a lot of attention.

The best group dynamic is probably one that includes a balance of temperament dimensions among the toddlers. In practice, we rarely get the choice—but if we do, we might want to aim for some balance within the group.

The Toddler's Consciousness

In this chapter so far, we have looked at the behavioural characteristics of toddlers in each domain of their development. These are the things we see when we observe children and are seeking some understanding of where they are at and how we might respond. But we might be in danger of forgetting to look at how the toddler perceives his world from the inside out. What is it like to be a toddler?

Looking at how the toddler responds to stimuli is the traditional way of trying to understand his experience, but there is another route that seems at once simpler and much harder—it seeks to appreciate the world of the toddler through his eyes or, rather, through his **consciousness**.

What is the toddler's consciousness? Of course we cannot generalize very successfully because we know that consciousness is individual. However, we can try to see the world from the toddler's general perspective. We have mentioned the toddler's understanding of trust, attachments, imitation of others, cognitive skills, and so forth. Each of these things demands a level of consciousness—not just being awake or alert. To feel trust from a toddler's viewpoint is difficult to understand. What is he feeling or knowing associated with trust? This question is of enormous importance to philosophers. They call it the "hard question." (They're right!) The easy question of consciousness is what they think science can answer—from MRI machines, PET scans, experiments, and theoretical concepts. They don't have the answers to the easy questions yet—but they are answerable, given time. However, we can attempt to look at the hard question. To the scientists this question—"What is consciousness?"—is hard because it cannot be answered using scientific methods.

A famous philosopher tried looking at consciousness this way. He posed the question "What is it like to be a bat?" This is much the same sort of question as "What is it like to be a toddler?" But we have an advantage, because we ourselves were toddlers once, even if our autobiographical memories don't let us back into that world very easily. The answer to the questions might be "We don't know."

The way the **phenomenologists** have of trying to understand what it's like to be a toddler (or anybody else) is by making a systematic attempt "to uncover and describe the structures, the internal meaning, of lived experience" Van Manen (1994, p. 10). So what is the meaning of being a toddler as they live their experience? We are hampered because we know the toddler doesn't have the language to tell us—that would be an easier route. For older people, we might ask them or read what they say it's like. For toddlers, what can we do to reach their lived experience? We might try to use what knowledge we have about toddlers' development and lives to help us appreciate their structures. But these are adult ways of looking at toddlers, rather than their way of looking at us. However, some cognitive phenomenologists do use their theoretical ideas about what is happening inside children's minds to try to understand their world. Appreciating the child's egocentricity might be helpful—she see things from her own point of view most of the time (but does she know she is doing this?—probably not). The toddler thinks in sensory-motor ways. She doesn't know the chart of substages, but she does have some consciousness of how her actions give her ideas about her world! These theoretical ideas can help us to appreciate something of the child's consciousness.

A helpful concept in understanding what it's like to be someone else—in this case a toddler—is to understand the notion of **qualia**. It's an odd term meaning "the qualitative content of mental states" (Dennett, 1991). The idea is to understand the essence of what makes the thing, or person, what it is. For example, the qualia of the colour red is its redness. So the qualia of being a toddler is . . . in being a toddler. It doesn't sound like we are much further ahead. But we are approaching an answer. The essence of being a toddler is *being*—it's fairly simple, if you are not a scientist! However, qualia are not the same across individuals—being Larry is not the same as being Lenny. Possibly, we can position ourselves to "be" alongside the toddlers "being"—this way we can enter the toddler's lived experience.

We can ask an associated question: "What is it like to be real?" The rabbit in the book *The Velveteen Rabbit* asks this question and continues, "Does it mean having things buzz around inside you with a stick-out handle?" In the story, the rabbit get this response from the skin horse: "Real isn't how you are made. It's a thing that happens to you. When a child loves you for a long, long time, not just to play with, but really loves you, then you become real." Later the skin horse elaborates: "It doesn't happen all at once.

You become . . . it takes a long time. That is why it doesn't happen often to people who break easily, or have sharp edges, or have to be carefully kept. Generally, by the time you are Real, most of your hair has been loved off and your eyes drop out and you get loose in the joints and very shabby. But these things don't matter at all, because once you are Real you can't be ugly except to people who don't understand."

▶ Particular Needs

PROFOUND AND ESSENTIAL EXPERIENCES

Earlier in this chapter we were introduced to the idea of the toddler requiring certain profound experiences"—without which she cannot develop healthily—and essential experiences. Neither set of experiences is optional: both must be provided. The profound needs have to be met as a priority at this stage, because of the sensitive periods in the toddler's development. The essential experiences will be meaningful only if the profound experiences are being provided. Consider the lists of these important experiences and plan accordingly to ensure that each toddler is given experiences that fit his developmental needs.

ATTACHMENT AND EMOTIONAL NEEDS

In discussing attachment in previous chapters, and focusing in this chapter on the attachment needs of the toddler, we have a clear idea of what the toddler needs. It is essential that we observe the toddler's attachment behaviours to see if secure attachments have been made. The details in the earlier section on attachment indicate the kinds of behaviours to watch for. How to respond to the attachment needs becomes apparent when we realize what is necessary to make secure attachments. The most important issues are to provide all the child's basic needs, consistent and loving care, and to be there in a relationship that allows the toddler to become independent because of the trust that has developed.

Greenspan and Greenspan's overview of emotional stages in *First Feelings* offers a good structure for examining the child's stage of emotional development and for ensuring that the toddler's emotional needs are met.

Careful observation and documentation is essential for monitoring the child's progress. In the event that the toddler is having attachment difficulties or is displaying behaviours that are of concern, discussion

with parents is vital. There may be need for a referral to an expert. Following the advice of the external agency and family and working collaboratively with them is the best way of meeting the toddler's needs.

▶ Attachment and Emotional Needs

AUTONOMY AND EMOTIONAL SUPPORT

The toddler must be offered opportunities to try to do things for herself. Behaviours that indicate a need for autonomy are not an indication that the toddler doesn't want adults, although it may seem that way. She needs adults' approval to make choices, indicate negativity, express feelings of joy and frustration, and take the time to do things her way. Despite the toddler's focus on autonomy, she needs the calm and nurturing support of the adults she knows. This provides her with a sense of trust and security.

PARAMETERS FOR BEHAVIOUR

The toddler needs to have a clear understanding of what is acceptable behaviour. While focusing on positive behaviour is necessary, her limited grasp of language means she will have to hear the word no on occasion. Knowing the boundaries increases her security.

As she begins to learn what is socially accepted behaviour, she needs to have positive role models and lots of encouragement as she learns to do the right thing.

SELF-HELP SKILLS

Toddlers learn by imitation and want to be as grown-up as possible. They tend to want to please, unless they have developed a strong idea of how they want to do things their way. Provide lots of opportunity for her to help get dressed and perform domestic helping tasks (even if it's more trouble than doing them all yourself).

SENSORY MATERIALS

The toddler can rarely have too much sensory activity. Water, sand, Jello, cornstarch and water, foodstuffs of all sorts, dough, and so on are all wonderful opportunities for play and discovery. Try offering the same experience many times over—it is always new to the toddler. You can vary the activity by changing its colour and the items that you add to the activity. Play alongside the toddlers and extend their play.

LANGUAGE

Lots of talking, stories, books, pictures, and rhymes provide opportunities to extend the toddler's receptive and expressive language. Use parentese to emphasize key words, and spend time with each child as you support all of their communication skills. Scaffolding is the adult's responsibility. When you provide a bridge to language acquisition, the toddler extends meanings, gains new words, and develops new ways to express himself. You might consider using toddler-signing with toddlers if their parents think it is a good idea.

ENTERING THE TODDLER'S WORLD

Make sure that you spend lots of time at the same eye-level as the toddlers. Let them take the lead in their games. Follow their instructions—they'll be given to you through gestures, facial expressions, and signs. Be quiet at times and mirror the mood of the toddler—except when she is overly frustrated or angry. Anticipate her actions by observing where she is looking. Take note of her observational learning and the times that she imitates others. You might extend the imitation yourself and see how the toddler enjoys having you enter the game. Be open and think in the present for as long as your responsibilities will allow.

EXPERIMENTATION

The toddler needs lots of experiences and the time to explore them. She also needs to find out about materials by taking them apart, being messy, and being free to explore and experiment with them. Of course she also needs an adult present to ensure that these activities are safe. Discovery learning needs to have lots of open-ended activities so that there are many ways for the toddler to be successful.

FAVOURED CHANNEL

Toddler styles differ. The toddler needs the adult to understand, tune in to, and provide activities that are in his favoured channel, whether auditory, visual, or some other.

Refer to Quilliam's (1994) outline of sensory channels to determine each toddler's favoured channel. Then develop activities that are consistent with the child's channel for learning and playing.

▶ Developmental Variation

A quick look in a toddler room might lead the casual observer to think that the toddlers were at a similar stage, but this is far from the case. Most, but not all, toddlers are walking by this stage; many are running and climbing, too. Fine motor skills, cognitive and language skills, and emotional control are all likely to vary even more than gross motor behaviours. In addition to these differences, some children may have been diagnosed with special needs. The disabilities of some of these children will be readily observable, but others may have significant conditions that are harder to detect.

DIABETES

Juvenile diabetes is a medical condition in which the pancreas fails to produce sufficient insulin, an essential hormone that helps the body to use and store sugars. Diabetic children must have their blood-sugar levels monitored and may need insulin injections. A good diet and exercise help to manage the condition. Symptoms of the disease include excessive hunger, thirst, urination, and weight loss, but these will be alleviated with appropriate treatment. Children with diabetes can thrive in a group child-care setting and can usually participate fully. Parents can provide information on how to meet their child's needs, and the caregivers should provide the parent with feedback on their child's progress.

ALLERGIES

Allergic reactions vary in severity, but should always be taken seriously. Some allergens can produce anaphylactic shock, a severe reaction that can cause death. Child-care agencies can take steps to exclude all signs of a known allergen, which can mean that an agency becomes a peanut-free zone or a feather-free place, depending on the allergies of its children. Allergic responses to a wide variety of materials, airborne particles, bee stings, animals, or foods can vary from a mild skin rash, itchiness, or wheeziness to a whole-body reaction that blocks the airway and stops the heart. Most of the time children with allergies appear not to have any difficulties, but they must be kept away from their allergens. Allergies to foods must be discussed with parents and all staff. Reminders of food and other allergies should be posted in a place where they will be noticed. It's desirable for known allergens to be excluded from the agency for all children. Educators need to be informed about what to do in the event of an allergic response for each child who suffers allergies; measures may include seeking medical attention immediately and administering epinephrine.

ASTHMA

Asthma is a chronic breathing disorder in which the child wheezes, experiences shortness of breath, and has particular difficulty breathing out. The severity of the disorder varies, but about one in 10 children are affected to some extent. The majority of children who have asthma can participate in a group child-care program and will benefit from it significantly. Child-care staff can work with parents to ensure that the child avoids circumstances such as weather conditions or allergens that might trigger asthmatic responses. The child is likely to have prescribed medications, some of which might need to be administered to the child at the appropriate time in the agency.

▶ Health Concerns

Increased social contact can heighten the risk of cross-infection. Several common conditions can be prevented, or at least reduced in frequency. Simple precautions, such as hand-washing, are the most effective measures to prevent cross-infection.

DIARRHEA

Diarrhea manifests itself with watery stools and frequent bowel movements but may also produce abdominal cramps, fever, or general lethargy. It is not a disease, but a symptom that can be caused by a wide variety of things, including lactose intolerance (a reaction to milk products); water contamination or food allergies; a parasitic, bacterial, or viral infection; or the consumption of too much sugar. Only a physician can diagnose the cause. Dehydration is a risk for the child with diarrhea, and parents and caregivers must ensure that the child takes in enough fluids.

Staff at the child-care centre must always take steps to reduce the possibility of infection. Hand-washing—by both adults and children—is the most effective defence against the spread of diarrhea. In addition, the environment of the centre must be kept clean, with toys and surfaces sanitized and materials changed regularly. Scrupulous hygiene in the bathroom and kitchen is essential. In some cases, the child with diarrhea might have to be sent home to

prevent cross-infection. If diarrhea affects the group, caregivers need to be open with parents in discussing the reason for the outbreak and the steps being taken to address it.

IMPETIGO

Impetigo is a skin infection at the site of a scrape or insect bite. Although it is not a sign of poor hygiene in itself, its spread can be prevented with hand-washing. Symptoms include clusters of red bumps that ooze and create a crust. Diagnosis and treatment by a doctor is necessary. To prevent cross-infection, children with impetigo are usually excluded from a child-care agency until treatment is under way.

SCABIES

Scabies is a common, highly communicable skin disease caused by mites that live on, and burrow under, the skin, causing a rash. It requires medical attention, and treatment is usually given to everyone in the family. In addition, clothing and bedding must be washed. Infected children are usually excluded from child care until they have received treatment.

RINGWORM

Ringworm is a fungal infection that causes a rash with a ring-shaped itchy edge. It requires medical treatment and, because it can spread, children with ringworm should be excluded from child care until treatment has started. Caregivers can help reduce the spread of the fungus by ensuring that staff and children wash their hands frequently and do not share brushes and combs.

HEAD LICE

Head lice are tiny insects that like the warm environment of the scalp. Their eggs, called nits, are laid on the hair shafts close to the scalp; they are hard to remove because they stick to the hair shaft and defy hair-washing. They are not caused by poor hygiene: a child may have clean hair and still have head lice. They may cause itching, but not all infected children will scratch their heads. Treatment is essential, and children should be sent home with their bedding, clothes, and soft toys. Parents are responsible for treatment and for returning the personal items after they have been washed. Meanwhile the educator should check that no other children have been infected—it is very likely that they are. All bedding, dress-up clothes, and washable items should be laundered in hot, soapy water and dried in a hot dryer. Carpets should be vacuumed thoroughly. Head lice are responsible for many lost days of work, child care, and school, even though they are relatively harmless—at least in the sense that they do not transmit any serious disease.

▶ Parents as Partners in Care

Clearly, when caregivers encounter highly communicable conditions such as head lice and ringworm, they must work with parents to make sure the condition is properly diagnosed and treated. They may also need to pass information along to the parents of other children at the centre. Parents must inform caregivers about their children's allergies so that together they can establish steps for prevention and response. Special diets may be needed for children with food allergies as well as for children with juvenile diabetes. Conditions such as severe allergies, asthma, or diabetes may require that the caregiver administer medication supplied by the parents. As in so many other cases, communication and cooperation between parents and caregivers is the most effective strategy for quality care.

A strategy that can involve both parents and educators and can integrate some of these health concerns with more routine or pleasurable items is the use of portfolios. As we saw in Chapter 2, a portfolio is a personalized collection of information about a child that celebrates that child's life and accomplishments. Parents and educators can contribute items to a child's portfolio. These might include health records, observations, daily charts, assessment results, individual program plans, contextual questionnaires, photographs, tape and video recordings, favourite items, artwork, and any other items that tell the story of the child's development. Documenting a child's progress has both a developmental and a sentimental purpose, each equally important to parents and educators. The portfolio can accompany the child as he moves from the infant room to the toddler room and can be developed as the child develops. When he leaves the centre, the portfolio can be given to the parents.

Some of the items in the child's portfolio may be designed to honour the culture of her family. Including such items is one way to communicate to parents that you are interested in their culture. Another way is through celebrations that have cultural connections. It is important to be sensitive to parental concerns when deciding what occasions to celebrate. Having some familiarity with the cultures of the families who have children at the centre will be helpful. For example, parents from some cultures are very happy to celebrate birthdays, but others may feel such celebrations are inappropriate on religious grounds. Although religious holidays can be another occasion for a celebration, some parents may think that non-religious observance of a religious occasion is disrespectful. In other cases, parents may be uncomfortable with their children participating in a celebration of a religious holiday that is not connected to their culture. For example, Christmas is part of a Christian celebration that is not shared by everyone outside that faith or culture. Halloween, too, can have negative connotations for some people, so costumes and trick-or-treating at the child-care centre may not be appropriate.

These considerations shouldn't lead you to bypass all celebrations. Most centres are able to develop a strategy for deciding which occasions to highlight and for creating their own celebrations. Discussions at parent meetings should give some indication of which celebrations are appropriate, but be careful to solicit everyone's opinion. Involve the parents in planning the celebration and invite them to attend the actual event.

▶ Signs of Potential Neglect or Abuse

The toddler's increased mobility, coupled with insatiable curiosity, leads her to explore everything around her. Parents or caregivers who are not aware, or who are insufficiently careful about the toddler's safety, may neglect to protect her adequately. Many accidents are not really accidental—they could have been prevented. At this developmental stage the toddler cannot anticipate what is going to happen when she explores the home or other environment. Some of the most common injuries that occur to toddlers as a result of inadequate supervision (which is a form of neglect) are burns and scalds (mostly from heaters and stoves), falls from such places as kitchen countertops and shopping carts, poisonings from household cleaning chemicals, choking on a variety of small objects, strangulations from such things as blind cords, inappropriate clothing or ropes, and the consumption of medications. Toddlers should not be left alone at any time, should be unable to access rooms in the house while parents sleep, need to have their play experiences selected wisely and monitored, and need to be protected from their own curiosity.

THE ROLE OF THE CHILD PROTECTION AGENCY

When a child protection agency receives information from the general public, or from educators and teachers, it has a legal and moral responsibility to investigate. If the matter is urgent, it will be referred to the police. The child protection worker's investigation may take several avenues. Information may be gained from the adults who work directly with the child, neighbours and family acquaintances, the parents, the supposed perpetrator, observation of the child who is the supposed victim, social welfare agencies working with the family, the family doctor, and any other source of relevant information. The child protection worker is trying to establish whether there is reasonable cause for concern and whether the child is at risk. Although child protection workers will work alongside the police investigation, their task is not to find someone guilty but to protect the child.

Confidentiality is an issue in these investigations; sources of information are not revealed by the worker. However, sources may become obvious if the case comes to prosecution and evidence is needed. Child protection workers are more concerned with the child's health, emotional well-being, development, family interactions, and safety than anything else. They take a holistic view rather than basing their action on single incidents. Although people who report suspicions of abuse to protection agencies may have reasonable grounds for concern, the child protection worker does not assume that everything inferred by onlookers necessarily reflects what is actually happening. The worker is trained to work with families, determine what is happening, and make decisions about the child's best interests.

Uncovering what happens in a family, neighbourhood, or child-care agency is a complex and demanding job. Many child protection workers have a large caseload and need all the assistance they can get. Educators can be of enormous help by providing documented observations. Educators and caregivers may occasionally feel that the decisions of protection agencies seem inappropriate. However, the educator is not usually in possession of all the facts and should accept that the decisions that are made are in the best interests of the child.

▶ Everyday Safety Issues

Stranger anxiety peaks in toddlers at around 15 months. After this time, the toddler starts to trust people in a broad sense, particularly if he has been securely attached to his parents and educators and has no reason to feel distrust. The toddler's trust marks important emotional growth, but it can bring with it new dangers.

STRANGER DANGER

The toddler is physically incapable of protecting herself. In addition, the trusting nature of toddlers can make them particularly vulnerable to strangers. Toddlers at this stage may begin to trust all adults. They are too young to understand why they shouldn't take candy from someone they don't know or be led by the hand by a stranger. It is too early to teach the toddler about such dangers, so parents and educators must remain vigilant. Now that they are mobile, toddlers can easily stray. Concern about strangers is legitimate, but more children have bad experiences with people they know than with strangers.

EMOTIONAL SAFETY

Toddlers need a tremendous amount of emotional support and encouragement. Without it they can become unhappy and even emotionally damaged. Feeling successful and knowing that adults are always there when he needs them gives the toddler a base of emotional safety. Protection from psychological harm is every bit as important as other safety issues.

TRAVEL SAFETY

The growing toddler may resist sitting in his car seat. This is not the time to give in to requests for autonomy—here, the adult knows best. But you can make the car seat more fun by providing the strapped-in toddler with new playthings. His continued growth means that the adults should often check the appropriateness of the car seat size. Be sure the opening mechanism is impossible for the toddler to operate, despite his improved fine motor skills.

ANTICIPATING DANGER

Toddlers live in the here and now, and this reality presents another danger to the age group. They cannot predict what is going to happen. They might walk behind a swing, not realizing that it will hit them, pour milk from the carton and spill most of it on the floor, or fail to get out of the way of a bigger child pedalling toward them. Time and experience will help, but for now toddlers need to be in an environment where they can't get into things that are potentially harmful. In addition, they must be supervised closely so that they won't be hurt by things they can't predict.

▶ Starting Points for Response

RESPONSIVE CAREGIVING

Autonomy is something that the toddler wants, and should have. Toddlers want encouragement to do things for themselves. Caregiving strategies should include making available a few choices, having activities in which the toddler can be successful, praising all efforts, making self-help skills fun, and showing the toddler you are proud of her desire for independence. Box 10.1 lists some of these strategies.

Supportive Guidance

Emotional support is the backbone of toddler autonomy, so providing consistent nurturance is important. It must be offered when the toddler wants it, not only when you have time to give it. Because the toddler learns from observation, many of your guid-

---

BOX 10.1

GETTING IN TUNE WITH TODDLERS AT 15 TO 18 MONTHS

Below are some starting points for building your responsivity skills with 15-to-18-month-old toddlers. Tune in with respect and:

- demonstrate openness in your body language
- observe the toddler's use of personal space and distancing
- determine the toddler's favoured style of engagement and approach
- get down and follow the toddler's lead
- let the toddler direct the activity and make safe choices
- enjoy the child's energy as he explores
- provide a variety of sensory experiences and play alongside the toddler
- encourage the toddler's natural curiosity
- allow the child to experience some consequences
- provide space for movement
- dance to a variety of types of music, imitating each other's actions
- sing songs or action rhymes and repeat them frequently
- respond to what the toddler finds funny
- offer simple tools for doing a task (shovelling, scribbling, etc.)
- sit on the floor and extend puzzle play
- build towers with blocks and let the toddler knock them down
- crawl through a tunnel and play peek-a-boo
- hide objects in boxes
- have bags to put things in
- roll out textured dough and press things into it
- accept downtime or unwillingness to respond to stimuli
- have messy play materials ready for finger-painting and testing out what the toddlers will do
- play simple hide-and-seek around big boxes or pieces of furniture
- encourage shared meanings through playful interactions
- offer stories and talk about pictures
- reinforce simple sequences of actions
- encourage toddlers to acknowledge one another and play parallel to one another
- offer simple roles or tasks that can be copied
- label feelings as you acknowledge them
- identify the child's sensory preferences and provide experiences in the selected channel

- add gestures to communications
- emphasize key words
- imitate and extend the child's tuneful jabbering
- enable the child to be independent or dependent as he wishes
- encourage cooperation in non-frustrating ways
- reinforce a sense of success/achievement when appropriate; acknowledge effort
- notice and praise efforts at emotional control
- remain in close proximity for social referencing, enabling eye contact
- encourage continuity of caregivers
- try various strategies to deal with the child's frustration: distraction, acknowledgment, and/or problem-solving
- acknowledge the process of the child's activity as well as the product
- remain calm, even when he is extremely emotional
- show your joy at being with him
- respond to signs of change, illness, or upset

ance strategies will involve positive role-modelling. You will need to show the toddler how to eat and perform all kinds of domestic tasks; she will want to copy you and gain your approval when she tries to get it right. The internal conflict between independence and dependence may cause frustrations at times; these may need to be deflected in some way. For example, providing a new play situation may help the toddler move past an emotionally challenging situation. It's too early to talk things out, as the child doesn't yet have adequate language. The toddler does need to know how to handle emotionally difficult situations, but she may be overwhelmed by the intensity of her feelings and need adult support and distraction. There are some concerns about using distraction too often. The toddler needs to work through some of her challenges. If, for example, sharing is a problem, the adult can introduce turn-taking. Having enough toys to reduce such difficulties is also effective. The toddler might copy sharing behaviours, but as soon as the child has to give up something she has, conflict is likely. The educator needs to handle this with the understanding that the toddler cannot delay her gratification. She wants what she wants now, and talking about it will help only a little. It is important for the centre to have enough toys that these conflicts are reduced.

FACILITATING DEVELOPMENT

The toddler's play behaviours show her interests and competences. She plays with materials differently now; she wants to perform little experiments to see what will happen. The trouble is that she is not aware of danger; the choice of play materials on offer must reflect this reality.

Playing alongside other children can allow the toddler to mirror the actions of her peers. Opportunity for this kind of parallel play should be provided. A large enough number of playthings should be available to minimize conflict. The toddler really wants to please, so positive and helpful behaviours as well as early demonstrations of empathy should all be praised.

This toddler rides her tricycle by trundling rather than pedalling it. In time, she will develop the coordination needed for the more complex task of pedalling.

Language skills can be supported in all situations: adults can use lots of labelling words and repeat short sentences so that the toddler can focus on the important part of what is being said. She is likely to love books, stories, pictures, rhymes, and songs, but tends to want them in a quiet moment rather than in a group circle. Toddlers love to make music with percussion instruments, so set out the instruments on days when you don't have a headache!

HOLISTIC RESPONSE

Activities 10.1 and 10.2 encourage a holistic response to toddlers at 15 to 18 months. Activity 10.1 suggests way of engaging in the experience of toddlers at this stage and extending your interactions with them. Activity 10.2 (page 289) helps you to observe each toddler and to develop activities that are targeted to her individual interests and skill levels.

Activity 10.1

Responding to the Changing Needs of Toddlers at 15 to 18 Months

Your interactions with the toddler at 15 to 18 months must be responsive to her needs and emerging skills. To assist you in engaging in the toddler's experience, the activity below offers suggestions that may extend your interactions. Careful observation is necessary, so that you introduce the idea at the right time and in the appropriate way. Each suggestion includes ways the idea can be extended if the toddler is ready. This activity also illustrates the safety, communication, conceptual, and developmental issues that you, as a child-care professional, need to keep in mind as you respond to the toddler at 15 to 18 months.

There are many other appropriate activities besides the ones listed below; your skill in developing them will grow as your experience and enjoyment increase!

Activity 10.1

Responding to Changing Needs of Toddlers at 15 to 18 Months

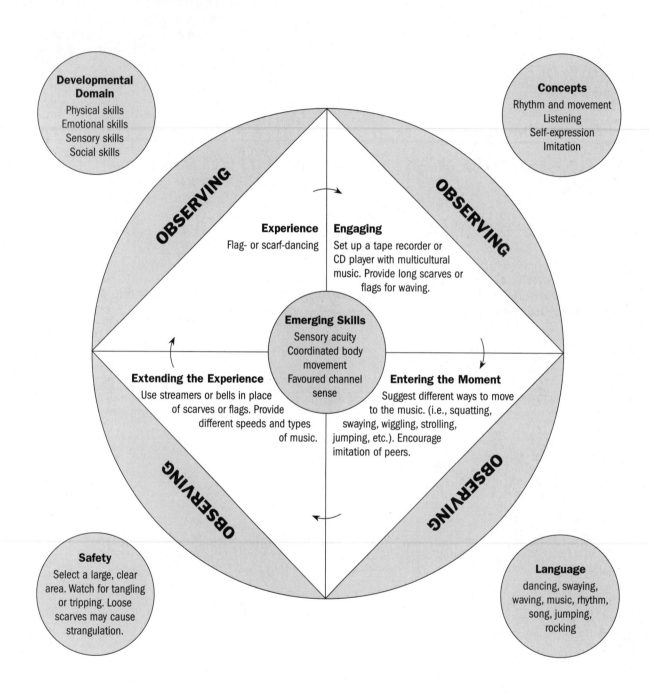

Developmental Domain
Physical skills
Emotional skills
Sensory skills
Social skills

Concepts
Rhythm and movement
Listening
Self-expression
Imitation

OBSERVING

OBSERVING

Experience
Flag- or scarf-dancing

Engaging
Set up a tape recorder or CD player with multicultural music. Provide long scarves or flags for waving.

Emerging Skills
Sensory acuity
Coordinated body movement
Favoured channel sense

Extending the Experience
Use streamers or bells in place of scarves or flags. Provide different speeds and types of music.

Entering the Moment
Suggest different ways to move to the music. (i.e., squatting, swaying, wiggling, strolling, jumping, etc.). Encourage imitation of peers.

OBSERVING

OBSERVING

Safety
Select a large, clear area. Watch for tangling or tripping. Loose scarves may cause strangulation.

Language
dancing, swaying, waving, music, rhythm, song, jumping, rocking

Activity 10.2

Creating Responsive Curriculum for Infants at 15 to 18 Months

Activities for the toddler at 15 to 18 months should evolve from their interests and skill levels. There cannot be a set curriculum! The adult's role is to tune in to the toddler's world and create experiences that are mutually enjoyable, that celebrate her current abilities and provide opportunity for continued development. The following ideas will help the adult to observe each toddler at 15 to 18 months and assist in providing some meaningful experiences.

With confidence, the adult can extend these ideas yet further.

Developmental Domain	Observation of Emerging Skills (Things You See)	Responsive Experience/Activity
Physical skills	– pushing and pulling toys along in his explorations – stopping and starting walking – difficulty in negotiating around objects and stopping while running – walking with wide-leg gait – crawling backward down stairs and taking a few backward steps – showing a hand preference – deferring imitation of activities – scribbling – throwing overhand	Provide activities that encourage the toddler's increased mobility and fine motor skills to help him feel confident in his abilities. Provide activities that encourage whole body coordination and, in particular, large motor development. These are of more interest to toddlers in this period than fine motor development.
Cognitive skills/language and communication	– continuously picking up, throwing, and dropping objects – pointing at objects, pictures, and people of interest – exploring and experimenting with the properties and possibilities of objects – using a 10-plus word vocabulary – increasing visual acuity, approaching that of an adult – trying out new manipulative actions on items and objects – deferring imitation – refined sensory acuity	Create a learning environment that can be actively explored. Balance stimulation with safety when setting up the active learning space. Label the toddler's gestures before, during, and after specific actions. Exchange gestures while conversing with the toddler to help him understand the rules of spoken language. Keep requests simple and repeat key words when speaking to a toddler.

Developmental Domain	Observation of Emerging Skills (Things You See)	Responsive Experience/Activity
Social/emotional skills	– solitary playing with little interest in other children – referring to himself by name – helping to undress himself; lifting his legs for pants and extending arms for shirts (taking off is much easier than putting on) – enjoying the sound of his own voice; singing and babbling out loud – emerging autonomy and shame and doubt – decreasing separation anxiety – emerging self-regulation of behaviours – using words to label his feelings – appearing interested in pictures of himself	Help toddlers to engage in brief interactions with their peers. Keep groups small in order to provide a positive experience. Provide positive role-modelling to help a toddler's social development. Provide support and guidance, helping the toddler establish a sense of identity. Help the toddler express his feelings by labelling his cues. Provide an environment that offers choices and opportunities for success.

Responding to Changing Needs

Toddlers at 15 to 18 months

EXPERIENCE 1

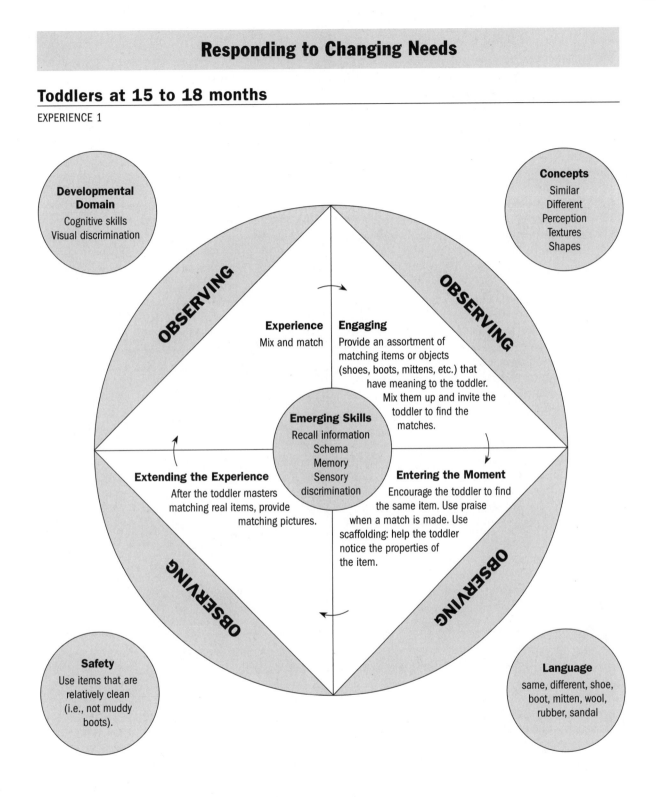

Developmental Domain
Cognitive skills
Visual discrimination

Concepts
Similar
Different
Perception
Textures
Shapes

OBSERVING

OBSERVING

Experience
Mix and match

Engaging
Provide an assortment of matching items or objects (shoes, boots, mittens, etc.) that have meaning to the toddler. Mix them up and invite the toddler to find the matches.

Emerging Skills
Recall information
Schema
Memory
Sensory discrimination

Extending the Experience
After the toddler masters matching real items, provide matching pictures.

Entering the Moment
Encourage the toddler to find the same item. Use praise when a match is made. Use scaffolding: help the toddler notice the properties of the item.

OBSERVING

OBSERVING

Safety
Use items that are relatively clean (i.e., not muddy boots).

Language
same, different, shoe, boot, mitten, wool, rubber, sandal

Responding to Changing Needs

Toddlers at 15 to 18 months

EXPERIENCE 2

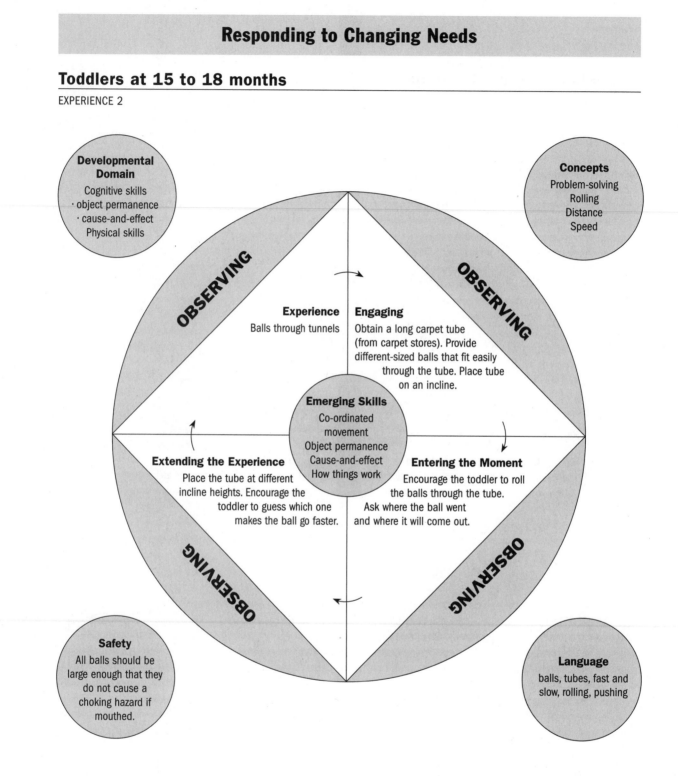

Developmental Domain
Cognitive skills
· object permanence
· cause-and-effect
Physical skills

Concepts
Problem-solving
Rolling
Distance
Speed

OBSERVING

OBSERVING

Experience
Balls through tunnels

Engaging
Obtain a long carpet tube (from carpet stores). Provide different-sized balls that fit easily through the tube. Place tube on an incline.

Emerging Skills
Co-ordinated movement
Object permanence
Cause-and-effect
How things work

Extending the Experience
Place the tube at different incline heights. Encourage the toddler to guess which one makes the ball go faster.

Entering the Moment
Encourage the toddler to roll the balls through the tube. Ask where the ball went and where it will come out.

OBSERVING

OBSERVING

Safety
All balls should be large enough that they do not cause a choking hazard if mouthed.

Language
balls, tubes, fast and slow, rolling, pushing

Responding to Changing Needs

Toddlers at 15 to 18 months

EXPERIENCE 3

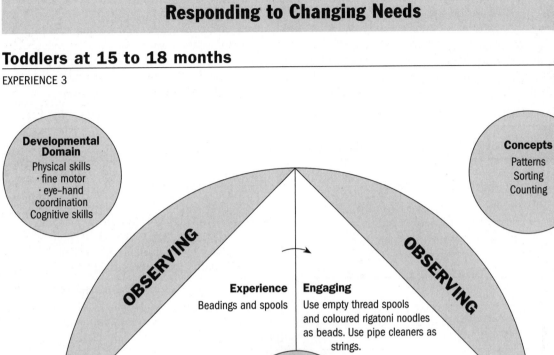

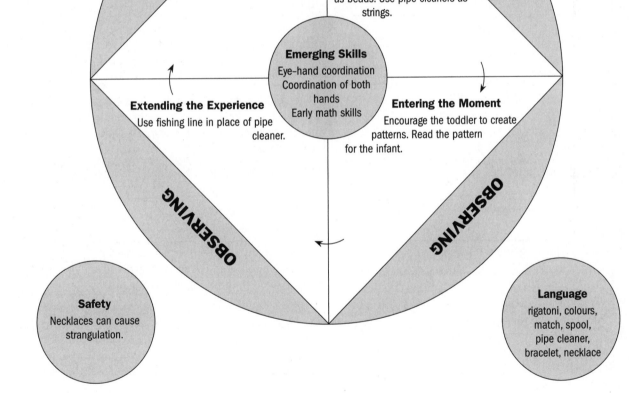

Developmental Domain
Physical skills
· fine motor
· eye–hand coordination
Cognitive skills

Concepts
Patterns
Sorting
Counting

Experience
Beadings and spools

Engaging
Use empty thread spools and coloured rigatoni noodles as beads. Use pipe cleaners as strings.

Emerging Skills
Eye-hand coordination
Coordination of both hands
Early math skills

Extending the Experience
Use fishing line in place of pipe cleaner.

Entering the Moment
Encourage the toddler to create patterns. Read the pattern for the infant.

OBSERVING

OBSERVING

OBSERVING

OBSERVING

Safety
Necklaces can cause strangulation.

Language
rigatoni, colours, match, spool, pipe cleaner, bracelet, necklace

Toddlers are likely to love the experiences that follow because they appeal to toddlers' curiosity and interests. You can make modifications to the experiences to suit the materials you have at hand. Also, depending on the individual toddler's response, you can add to the experiences or make them a little simpler. If a tod-dler takes the activities in directions that you had not planned, follow his lead and let him make of the opportunity what he wants. Monitor the safety implications of the activities, because there are hazards in using non-manufactured play materials and we cannot predict how toddlers might respond.

Further Experiences and Interactions

Further Experiences	Interactions
Obstacle course	Encourage toddlers to crawl under tables, chairs, and benches, over ramps, stairs, and ladders laid down, around balls, shelves, and furniture, and through tunnels and hoops.
Hats	Provide a variety of hats (police, fire, base-ball, sun, straw, winter, and top hats). Encourage the toddler to experiment with the hats.
Purses and bags	Provide a variety of different purses and bags for the toddler to fill and carry. Provide surprises in the bags and purses for the tod-dler to discover.
"Feely" bags	Place toddler-familiar items in fabric bags. Tie the bags closed. Encourage the toddler to feel and determine what is inside the closed bags.
Hide-and-seek	Hide from the toddler's view and encourage the toddler to find you. Switch roles.
Tearing paper	Collage the ripped magazines, pictures, colours, tissue, etc.
Drawing and scribbling	Use chalk, thick crayons, or washable felt markers on a variety of surfaces (corrugated paper, wax paper, tinfoil, newsprint, and so on).
Nature paintbrushes	Use feathers, pine branches, or vegetables (corn on the cob, carrots, and celery leaves) as paintbrushes.

Further Experiences	Interactions
Sensory doughs	Add cookie cutters, dishes, small animals, and little people.
Doubles and sufficient materials	Provide more than one supply of activities for toddlers. Encourage toddlers to be involved in similar, mutual activities. Although they won't play together, they may play at the same time at the same thing.
Prop boxes	Fill dramatic play boxes with items that will enable the toddler to imitate behaviours witnessed in the adults around them (i.e., phones, dishes, etc.).
Imitation games (follow the leader)	Encourage the toddler to follow you in dance, walks, and other physical movements. Follow the toddler in turn.
"This is the way . . ."	Sing this popular song while completing routine activities (i.e., pick up toys, wash our hands, clean our teeth).
Clothespin play	Encourage the toddler to manipulate clothespins onto the rim of a shoebox or can. Encourage the toddler to take them off again.
"If you're happy and you know it . . ."	Encourage the toddler to act out the behaviours described in the song.
Sensory blocks	Create your own sensory blocks. Use a variety of boxes that are decorated on the outside with sandpaper, cotton, felt, velvet.

Responsive Guidance for Toddlers Aged 15 to 18 Months

Age/Stage: 15 to 18 Months

Situation	Response
• Paulie, Debbie, and Jamal are in the same play group, but they don't play together. • David came home from his play group copying the behaviours of Jay (another boy in his play group). • The children in the toddler room hit, bite, and push each other when a new toy is introduced.	**Developmental Issue: Peer Relations** Toddlers still view their peers as objects; they are not capable of realizing that these "objects" have feelings, needs, and desires of their own. Toddlers are not likely to play with other toddlers because of their egocentric thinking. However, they are not oblivious to their peers' existence. Observation of other's behaviours is a learning experience for the developing toddler. Pushing, shoving, and other aggressive behaviours are also a result of the egocentricity of toddlers. They just don't realize that others want the toy as well. Having duplicate or numerous choices helps alleviate this problem. Through practice, exposure, and positive role-modelling, toddlers will begin to show pro-social behaviours toward others.
• Charlise is growing and changing in her abilities and interests quickly. Each week she seems more capable than she was the week before. • Tyler is very independent at times, but at others she appears to need to be comforted and alone with her primary caregiver. • Whitney is solving problems, insisting on her own choices, and exploring objects.	**Developmental Issue: Overall Development** This stage of toddler development needs to be facilitated with patience and an empathetic balance between leading and following the toddler's behaviours. While the toddlers' independence and sense of self are developing, they require nurturance, stability, and security. Toddlers need encouragement, opportunities to be successful, a fun environment that fosters self-help skills, and an opportunity to be proud of their accomplishments. While all of these things are essential to the toddlers' optimal development, so is the need for nurturance, safety, and assistance when their limited abilities prevent them from satisfying their desires.

Manufactured Toys and Play Materials for Toddlers Aged 15 to 18 Months

Toy/Material	Uses	Group Care	Home
Bags and baskets	Facilitate the clustering, carrying, and dumping tendencies of toddlers.	√	√
Containers	Carry, stack, and place things inside. Toddlers can manipulate them in many ways.	√	√
Large cardboard boxes	Endless possibilities as these boxes become houses, airplanes, boats, stores, etc.	√	√
Beanbags	Easy to grasp, catch, and throw as tiny hands mould them.	√	√
Balls	Pushing, rolling, and throwing as fine and gross motor skills are refined.	√	√
Fine-motor puzzles	Show how things fit together and enhance shape recognition and problem-solving skills.	√	√
Large wax crayons and papers	Easy to manipulate in a palmar grasp. Whole arm movements produce scribbles, an essential stage in art skill development.	√	√
Ride-on toys	Gross motor skills, body coordination, and balance are encouraged.	√	√
Finger paints	Emotional, expressive, and fine motor skills are refined.	√	√
Picture books with words and phrases	Language acquisition, visual acuity, and early literacy skills are developed.	√	√
Bells and shakers	Auditory acuity, rhythm and movement, and creative skills are facilitated.	√	√
Nesting toys	Visual acuity, eye–hand coordination, and fine motor skills are refined.	√	√
Bath-sponge toys	Emotional expression, cause-and-effect, physical skills.	√	√

Toy/Material	Uses	Group Care	Home
Play-Doh	Sensory acuity is enhanced	√	√
Chalk sticks	Sense of cause-and-effect and creative skills developed.	√	√
Push- or pull-along toys	Mobility and cause-and-effect are developed with these push/pull toys.	√	√
Peel-and-stick photo album	Self-help skills, social skills, and a sense of self are targeted.	√	√
Dump trucks	Push, pull, and math (measuring) concepts are evident.	√	√
Wind chimes	Auditory acuity, distance, and discrimination result from these pleasant instruments.	√	√
Sun-catchers	Visual acuity and environmental awareness are stimulated.	√	√
Large snap beads	Fine motor skills are refined.	√	√
Pots, pans, dishes; doll crib and blankets; doll bath and towels	Social, symbolic, and dramatic play emerge.	√	√
Drums	Cause-and-effect, rhythm , and movement skills are enhanced.	√	√
Hammer and peg toys	Fine motor skills, problem-solving and imagination are developed.	√	√
Sand toys (scoops and shovels)	Problem-solving and sensory acuity are developed.	√	√

▶ Summary

When young children make the transition from infancy to mobility, their perspective changes enormously. Their physical skills allow them much greater movement. The enjoyment they derive from seemingly pointless running or repeating a simple action reinforces the learning that comes from those experiences. Toddlers who are enabled to play, discover, and explore have the opportunity to find out how the world works. There are some safety issues associated with this, but there are even greater benefits.

A toddler is less likely to be playful and motivated to explore if her emotional development is hindered. This can happen if she is not experiencing secure attachments with the important people in her life. Only if her emotional needs are met can she play spontaneously and take risks and solve minor problems. There are some profound experiences that are essential for her development: without these key experiences she cannot develop in the other domains in any satisfactory manner. Once she experiences emotional well-being, she can then get on with the business of being a toddler. This involves learning through many different types of play. Through play activity she builds new conceptual understandings of her world. By performing many actions she finds out the properties of materials and what she can do with them. Her sensory-motor intelligence is taking steps forward as she thinks in ways that have greater degrees of symbolism.

The toddler's ability to communicate becomes a little more refined as she manages to use a few real words. Her repertoire for communicating involves using gestures, facial expressions, crying, and using some made-up words as well as a few real ones. She has a need to connect with adults and enjoys prolonged engagement, particularly if the adult follows her lead. If the adult uses scaffolding techniques, the child's language acquisition can be supported. In addition to using traditional language, the child may respond well to techniques that allow her to use a form of sign language.

There is even greater evidence at this stage of differing styles of behaving. The temperament style of each child can be categorized in several ways, but each child is different. Each child's own favoured channel of communication is something that the adult must discover. Using the favoured channel will help the toddler to communicate more successfully. Reading the toddler's cues and behavioural signs will help the toddler and the adult to understand each other better.

Entering into the life of the toddler requires being on their level and trying to see things as they might. Get down on the toddler's level, be still, listen, and follow the toddler's lead.

▶ KEY TERMS

accommodation
American Sign Language (ASL)
assimilation
attachment
attachment difficulties
attachment disorders
attending
autonomy
avoidant attachment
block play
calcification
channel of preference (sensory)
concepts
consciousness
decentred
deferred imitation
discovery play
disorganized attachment
early intervention
egocentricity
emergence of an organized sense of self
equilibration
essential experiences
guilt
hand–eye coordination
hand preference
imitative play
manipulative skills
manual dexterity
mental substitution
monotropy
multi-modal (sensory)
nature
neuron
nurture
object permanence
object play
observational learning
open-ended activities
ossification
parallel play
personality
phenomenology
pincer grasp

plastic (brain)
practice play
primary caregiver
profound experiences
qualia
resistant/ambivalent attachment
role-playing
schemes
scripts
secure attachment
self-esteem
sensitive period
sensory-motor
shame
shared meanings
signing
socially acceptable behaviour
solitary play
Strange Situation
symbolic play
symbolism
synapse
synaptic connection
temperament
tertiary circular reaction
toilet-learning
visual acuity
tuneful babbling
variegated babbling
window of opportunity

▶ DISCUSSION QUESTIONS

1. Compare the play behaviours of an infant at 6 months with those of a toddler at 18 months. What developments have occurred that make the play different?
2. If the favoured channel for a toddler is auditory, how might you provide appropriate experiences for her?
3. When a mother worries that her toddler's gross motor skills are not as advanced as those of other toddlers in the room, what might you say to her?
4. How might you find ways of entering into the life of a particular toddler you know?
5. What is the connection between language and thought? Does one come before the other?

▶ ADDITIONAL RESOURCES

▶ Further Readings

Allen, K., and L. Marotz. (2003). *Developmental Profiles: Prebirth through Twelve.* 4th ed. Albany, NY: Thomson Learning.

Eisenberg, A., H.E. Murkoff, and S.E. Hathaway. (1996). *What to Expect: The Toddler Years.* New York, NY: Workman Publishing.

Frost, J., and S. Wortham. (2001). *Play and Child Development.* Upper Saddle River, NJ: Prentice Hall.

Greenspan, S., and N.T. Greenspan. (1985). *First Feelings.* New York: Viking.

Kilbride, K.M. (ed.). (1997). *Include Me Too! Human Diversity in Early Childhood.* Toronto, ON: Harcourt Brace.

Marion, M. (2003). *Guidance of Young Children.* 6th ed. Upper Saddle River, NJ: Prentice Hall.

McCam, M., and F. Mustard. (1999). *Early Years Study: Final Report.* Toronto, ON: Canadian Institute for Advanced Research.

Santrock, J., and J. Mitterer. (2001). *Psychology.* First Canadian Edition. Whitby, ON: McGraw-Hill Ryerson.

Weiser, M. (1991). *Infant, Toddler Care, & Education.* 2nd ed. Upper Saddle River, NJ: Prentice Hall.

Weitzman, E. (1992). *Learning Language and Loving It: A Guide to Promoting Children's Social and Language Development in Early Childhood Settings.* Toronto, ON: Hanen Centre Publications.

▶ Useful Video

Joseph Garcia: *SIGN with Your BABY.* Northlight Communications.

▶ Useful Web sites

Links to child development research sites in Canada
    www.home.istar.ca/~cccns/ECD.html
    www.eccdc.org/catalogue/a_research.htm
Today's Parent (articles)
    www.todaysparent.com/baby/article.jsp?cId=477
Windows of opportunity
    www.cfc-efc.ca/docs/vocfc/00001087.htm
    members.aol.com/WStaso/windowsop.htm

Information for parents of toddlers
    getsetforlife.ca/zapfamily/zapfamily.html
        babyparenting.about.com/
Brain research/neuroscience
    muextension.Missouri.edu/xplor/hesguide/humanrel/
        gh6115.htm
    www.med.sc.edu:88/brochure/neurosci.htm
Play
    www.kidsource.com/kidsource/content2/
        nature.of.childs.play.html
    ericae.net/edo/ED307967.HTM
Child development/sensory-motor intelligence
    www.clc.cc.il.us/home/soc455/psycweb/develop/
        index.htm
    www.macbrain.org/resource.htm
    www.nncc.org/Child.Dev/todd.dev.html
    www.hlth.gov.bc.ca/ccf/child/publicat/comm/
        com026.pdf
Emotional development
    www.rti.org/child/links.html
    www.firstsigns.org/pages/about/advisory.html
Toddler health and safety
    www.cps.ca/nrc.uchsc.edu/CFOC/PDFVersion/list.html

CHAPTER 11

Feeling Around: Toddlers at 18 to 24 Months

Toddlers are almost always tiring. They are unlikely to sit still for more than a few moments. Adults need to keep fit to maintain their responsivity.

Learning Outcomes

After reading and studying this chapter, you should be able to:

- identify the observable characteristics of toddlers at the 18-to-24-month stage
- explain the significance of the behaviours of an 18-to-24-month-old toddler in a developmental context
- recognize and respond to the developmental diversity of 18-to-24-month-old toddlers and discuss issues pertinent to this stage of development
- assess the development of 18-to-24-month-old toddlers
- respond to the 18-to-24-month-old toddler's health, safety, and development with appropriate protection, guidance, and caregiving
- develop strategies to work with parents as partners in the care and education of their toddler

Scene: Outside the door of the toddler room a staff member starts to orient new students to the program.

"They leave you so tired at the end of the day," said the educator in the toddler room as she introduced two new students to the centre. "But it's so rewarding. You see the toddlers developing right before your eyes. I shouldn't admit that I have a favourite age range, but this is it. I just love watching them walk, talk, and become such interesting little people!"

The educator asked the students if they had spent any time with toddlers before. "Just a bit of babysitting," said the first student. "That was fun, but it was hard work. I couldn't guess what this little boy was going to do next." The other student added, "My experience is much the same, but the toddler I babysit is my nephew, so I've become familiar with him. I don't know if he's like other toddlers, but he watches me all the time and has a lot of fun copying me."

"You both have some idea of what it will be like here," observed the educator. "Yes, you will find it a hectic place, because the toddlers are so busy and into everything, but try to take time for some quiet moments—that is, if you can find any! The time goes quickly when you're busy, but I find it hard to stay awake at nap time on some days when they all go off to sleep and I'm tired! But I have to stay alert. All kinds of things can happen quickly with toddlers. I think you will have to prepare yourselves by keeping well and making sure you get a good night's sleep."

In her comments the educator gave the students confidence that they knew something about working with toddlers and agreed with them about the toddlers' activity level. But she also hinted to the students that toddlers' moods change quickly, and that they are responsive to close contact and the building of relationships. She concluded with some observations on the toddlers' curriculum: "Activities need to be fairly easy, although you might be surprised what some of the senior toddlers can do. We like to build curriculum on the toddlers' interests rather than watering down preschool ideas. We don't have themes and that sort of thing in the toddler room because the toddlers' learning comes from their interests, not ours!"

▶ What to Look For

PHYSICAL DEVELOPMENT

The 18-month-old toddler is extremely active and enjoys her new freedom to move about. During this stage, the toddler refines the skills that have been emerging and moves toward increasing independence.

Growth

The toddler's height continues to increase, but the rate of growth slows a little. At 18 months, toddlers may be 76–86 cm (30–34 inches) and at 24 months 81–92 cm (32–36 inches). Weight at 18 months is likely to be in the range of 9–13.5 kg (20–30 pounds) and, at 24 months, 10–15 kg (22–33 pounds).

Some growth trends can be observed. Increased mobility tends to reduce the amount of fat storage, and the toddler's shape becomes a little slimmer. Infants and toddlers of larger parents are more likely to be large themselves. It is also likely that children who begin life somewhat larger or smaller than average will maintain that difference (Deiner, 1997), but this is not always predictable. Racial differences are also observable (Edelstein, 1995), with those of Afro-Caribbean descent tending to be slightly larger than growth chart norms and those of Indo-Asian background tending to be a little smaller. Further differences can be noted when considering the growth patterns of First Nations and Inuit toddlers. Refer to Chapter 3 for growth chart information.

Gross Motor Skills

The awkward walking and running motion of the 18-month-old toddler is gradually refined during this period. The toddler's movements become more polished, and she can usually manoeuvre around obstacles with increasing ease. By 2 years of age, the toddler can run, stop, and start with no difficulty (Sheridan, 1997). She still has a wide-stance walk (Allen and Marotz, 2003), as her legs are closer together now than when she started to walk. The toddler's walking process usually involves a heel-to-toe pattern at this stage.

Most toddlers enjoy climbing, but don't appreciate the inherent dangers. They may climb stairs one at a time, always having both feet on one step before moving to the next one (Furuno et al., 1993b). They may also climb onto chairs or other furniture (Sheridan, 1997). Frequently toddlers will try to get a good view of the action going on. Because adults are usually carrying out domestic tasks at a higher level, the toddler will try to reach a good viewing position. Adult awareness of this issue can lead to effective planning. Some-times a small step stool can be provided for toddlers to stand on so they can reach the desired height. Of course, toddlers tend to forget that they need to take a step down as they return to the floor, so be careful when the toddler wants to descend. A toddler may walk or run toward a ball to kick it, but her movement will be erratic. She will usually have to stop and ponder before coordinating her feet to kick the ball (Furuno et al., 1993b).

During this stage, the toddler is likely to enjoy ride-on toys (Furuno et al., 1993b), but she will use her feet to **trundle** along rather than to pedal. Trundling involves the toddler propelling herself forward using alternate foot pushes as she sits astride the ride-on toy. Pedalling may take longer to learn, because it involves more complex coordination of movement.

Balancing on one foot becomes possible toward 2 years of age (Allen and Marotz, 1994), and the toddler may jump up and down or stand on tiptoes (Furuno et al., 1993b), but her balance is likely to be precarious. A typical position for a 2-year-old at play is squatting (Allen and Marotz, 1994). This posture may start at 18 months; by 24 months the toddler may play in this position for an extended period of time.

Fine Motor Skills

With refinement of various hand movements and a more precise grasp, the toddler is able to do some things that she couldn't do before. The scribbling seen at 18 months is refined, using a more effective **pincer grasp** of the thumb and fingers (Furuno et al., 1993b). Hand control and **hand–eye coordination** increase. Hand–eye coordination involves fairly complex movement and judgment as the toddler connects what she is looking at and the action she is endeavouring to make. Various different hand–eye coordination skills are emerging at this stage. They can be observed in

The skill levels of the two children at either end of this stage are quite different. Note the differing grasps and uses of paper.

the manipulative skill involved in undoing buttons, pouring from and filling containers, folding paper, stringing a bead, stacking objects, throwing a large ball, catching a large ball with arms outstretched, picking up small items, and holding a book and turning its pages (Allen and Marotz, 1994; Furuno et al., 1993b; Sheridan, 1997; Woolfson, 1995).

Self-Help Skills

The drive to do things independently can be frustrating for the toddler because her skills don't always match her will to do things by herself. In addition to the toddler making attempts to do things for herself, she may say something like "Leila wanna," speaking of herself. Such phrases can be one of the toddler's earliest phrases. She may refer to wanting to help with dressing or undressing, putting feet into shoes, using the toilet, feeding herself, delaying sleeping, or helping with household tasks (Allen and Marotz, 1994; Furuno et al., 1993b; Wilson, Douville-Watson, and Watson, 1995).

It can be time-consuming to deal with the toddler's need to try to do things herself. We can make it a little easier for her if we provide her with clothing that has relatively easy fastenings and items that are easy to put on and take off. Striving for independence is necessary at this stage, and in the long run it leads the toddler to the management of many life skills. Acquiring self-help skills requires hand–eye coordination and determination; both are challenged when the toddler becomes frustrated.

One aspect of toddler self-help that often appears to be of greater concern to adults than toddlers is **toilet-learning**, or toilet-training, as many people call it. Learning to use the potty for urination or defecation carries with it emotional overtones for adults who want to know that their child has gained the socially acceptable behaviours associated with toileting. As we discuss later, when reviewing Freudian interpretations of this stage and in discussions about independence and autonomy, this stage carries with it a heavy emotional load for parents and toddlers. Fortunately, most adults have learned that it is not fruitful to emphasize the issue by applying any sort of pressure on the toddler. We can leave the matter until the child is ready herself to control her bowel and bladder, presuming she has the physical capacity to do so, or at least provide the opportunity for toilet success without making a fuss over it. You might like to review the points made in Chapter 9 about the toddler's readiness for toilet-learning.

COGNITIVE DEVELOPMENT

Senses and Perception

Interest in the world is the most clearly observable characteristic of the toddler at this stage. With insatiable curiosity the toddler explores and experiments with everything within reach and spends time studying the details of objects and actions that interest her. Although she uses her hands more than her mouth, she still uses her mouth for some tactile exploration, and particularly for comfort. Refinement of her manipulative skills allows her to touch things and find out their properties. She is particularly interested in visual stimulation involving colours, patterns, and shapes. Movement intrigues toddlers. They may watch moving images—whether real or on television, video, or film—for prolonged periods, although this isn't desirable. Usually a combination of sound and visual stimulation is the most successful at holding their interest. Games and stories that involve hearing and vision are received particularly well. Taste and smell are not the most significant channels of sensory information, but they remain important parts of multi-modal perception; they tend to reinforce experiences and make them more memorable. At this stage, the toddler's sensory **acuity** is close to that of an adult, although her processing of the sensory material will be different because she has much less experience.

Sensory-Motor Behaviour

The toddler at this stage is likely to make a transition in the way she thinks and operates. She is entering the mental representational substage of the sensory-motor stage (Piaget, 1950). This means that she is making a progression from linking two objects together to making mental representations and linking them in combinations. Mental representations are symbolic ways of thinking about objects that are not physically present. This stage, 18 to 24 months, is the stage in which these mental representations help the toddler to understand reality. Her mental representations are her inner constructions of her real world. They allow her to think in symbolic ways such as deferred imitation—performing an action some time after she has observed it demonstrated—and in pretend ways in make-believe play. (We will discuss both of these symbolic functions later, because they are important elements of playing and learning.) We might see the toddler solving little challenges through symbolic means, by using internal images of objects that are out of sight or events that occurred previously. She will continue to use a trial-and-error technique to attack problems, but her new skills will involve various forms of symbolism. At this stage, a toddler can begin to think her way out of a situation that requires more than random tries at a solution. For example, imagine that a toddler's blocks keep falling over after she has stacked two or three. She may keep building, but eventually she will stop and think about the problem. Turning over the blocks, she may see a small stone on the bottom of the first block, which has caused it to rock when the others were piled on top. She will be able to make the connection, remove the stone, and then build her tower.

Brain development

"Risk is not destiny," claims Rima Shore (1997, p. 61). What she means is that there is hope for children who are exposed to detrimental experiences. The brain's ability to adapt to experiences that are both good and bad leaves us with some hope for children who have suffered various forms of deprivation or negative experiences. Parents sometimes worry if their toddler is exposed to a minor trauma or upsetting experience; they might reasonably think that this will have detrimental effects on the child's development. While there is clear evidence that young children can overcome some poor experiences, and come out of them seemingly unharmed, similar experiences might have a greater impact on one child than on another child. Children are individual in these responses, just as in every other area of their development.

One of our greatest difficulties is to determine what experience will bring about what response from each child. We can recognize some signs that one toddler is more sensitive than another, but predicting their responses is impossible. The degree to which a child is damaged by negative experiences is partially explained by the **plasticity** of the toddler's brain and is influenced by previous experience. It is hoped that positive early experiences will build some resilience. We do know that early intervention can ameliorate some of the damage that might be done. This can be done through **early intervention programs**, but it can also be addressed through the regular programming and home experience of the toddler. Generally speaking, the earlier the intervention, the more likely it is to be effective. The better the continuity and predictability of the environment, the greater the chances of success.

Preventive measures are always better than trying to put things right after they've gone wrong. If the toddler has mostly positive stimulating experiences within a context of consistent care, she is likely to be developmentally healthy. It has been determined that the human brain doubles in weight during the first year of life—starting at approximately .5 kg (1 pound) and weighing 1 kg (2 pounds) at the second birthday. "The increase in size and weight of the brain is due to an increase in the size of the neurons, elaborations of **dendric** elements, **myelination** of the **axons**, and an increase in the number and size of the **glial** cells" (Bergen & Coscia, 2001, p. 27). (Please refer to the Glossary for definitions of these terms.) What we must appreciate is the significance of this scientific understanding. This enormous brain growth indicates the interaction of both **nature** (genetic inheritance) and **nurture** (life experience). Stanley Greenspan describes this as an "... elaborate dance between biology and the environment" (Greenspan, 1997). Knowing that there is an interplay between the toddler's biology—in terms of each child's intellectual potential, emotional style, and temperament—and the early experiences for which the adults are primarily responsible, puts a heavy weight of responsibility on parents and caregivers. In fact, many brain researchers put weight behind arguments for strong and ongoing collaboration between parents and caregivers.

A central aspect of supporting brain development is **responsive care**. A recent analysis of brain research, to extrapolate scientific findings and provide a bridge to practice, has been undertaken by the Canadian Child Care Federation (CCCF, 2001). Their accessible materials are supported by the statement:

> Responsive care (also) helps to reinforce or strengthen certain neural pathways (connections between brain cells) that will later affect how the child behaves and succeeds in life. Repeated positive experiences (such as when a child needs a hug and gets one) make positive healthy connections. Repeated negative experiences (such as when a child is ignored or rejected) make just as strong connections, but the child will view the world as a less secure place.[1]

The CCCF fact sheet also details the way that caregivers should provide responsive care. The key points are that he or she:

- watches for the child's own individual cues and signals and learns to anticipate when it is time for food, a cuddle, rest, or a new activity
- exposes the child to new experiences and activities as and when the child is ready
- shares the child's activities and follows the child's interests
- watches for moments to extend the child's skills
- expresses affection and cheers specific accomplishments

We can see a strong theme running through current brain research and its applications: the cognitive and emotional aspects of development are intertwined. Earlier attempts to understand the workings of the brain tended to focus on cognitive functions rather than those associated with emotions and feelings. Indeed, intellectual activity now appears to depend on emotional security. Consequently, we have a clearer understanding that mental stimulation is relatively ineffective without emotional security. Meeting emotional needs must, therefore, come ahead of addressing any other developmental issue or domain.

Information Processing

The emotionally secure toddler uses a variety of techniques for learning; each of these is shaped by her motor intelligence. **Imitation** is an important part of learning, but now the toddler might extend the imitation into a game of her own design. Here is an example: after copying an adult driving a car, she might divert from direct copying to a more complex driving game. Starting at this time, the toddler increasingly uses elaboration and deferred imitation. Because the toddler can have mental representations of objects and events that are out of sight, she can hold an action in mind and play it out later. For example, the day after a toddler accompanied his father to the laundromat, he was observed acting out the scene, dumping clothes into a box and then trying to fold them with a smoothing action similar to his father's.

Direct and deferred imitation are both important activities that demonstrate the toddler's ability to think symbolically. Ultimately this ability will enable him to internalize adult roles that will lead to **sociodramatic play**. In time, the attention to detail of the toddler's imitation is startling. Because they don't realize the significance of behaviours, the toddler can copy many undesirable as well as desirable roles. There are times when parents and educators are taken aback when watching the imitation of their own behaviours and language in areas they might expect to be ignored by the toddler. Imitative learning

---

1. *Canadian Child Care Federation (2001), Nourish, Nurture Neurodevelopment* fact sheet, Responsive Care.

is at its height in the toddler period, but it is a form of learning that is used throughout life.

Increased memory function helps the toddler's cognitive skills; recognition and recall functions work well and are reinforced with practice. Making **mental combinations**—that is, linking one thing with another—helps memory. Mental combinations lead to the toddler's ability to make a wide variety of linkages. Things that match or go together may be features of puzzles and games that the toddler is now beginning to appreciate. The toddler may also link people and actions, making associations between, for example, people and the jobs they do, or things belonging to different rooms in the house. Frequently games involving this sort of matching are particularly challenging, because they require that the toddler hold in mind several details—something that still poses a cognitive difficulty for the toddler. However, simple games of sorting and matching can be helpful and they do assist in building memory skills. Frequently, undertaking activities involving the functions of things assists in remembering them. Toddlers respond well to games that involve linking things together. For example, they may enjoy a game with felt images in which they have to connect different people with the type of clothing they might wear.

Play

The toddler's play activity reveals many of her cognitive skills coupled with her socio-emotional stage of development.

Imitation and **deferred imitation** lead to **pretend play**. The characteristics of this type of play include decentration, decontextualization, and integration (Bretherton, 1984), each of which is a significant developmental advance. We will discuss each of these three characteristics separately.

Decentration involves the toddler's emerging ability to gain a new perspective. She is beginning to be able to move away from total **egocentric thought** and see things from the viewpoint of another person. We might see this when another child with whom the toddler is playing becomes hurt. The toddler may show some understanding that the child is upset.

Decontextualization refers to the toddler's ability to think and to act outside the context, or surroundings, where the learning initially took place. Thus, a toddler may pretend to prepare or serve food—actions she observed at home—in a game of food court at a child-care centre.

Lastly, with **integration** the toddler is better able to connect symbolic ideas. Thus toddlers might understand that skills acquired in one area are applicable in another. For example, a toddler who has learned how to mix paints to create colours may then try to mix other substances to create colours. Or after playing a game that involves matching items, she may apply matching techniques to other interests. By 2 years of age, toddlers may play **make-believe** games requiring deferred imitation of roles, skill in handling domestic items, and the acceptance of another toddler playing alongside.

It is noticeable that girls are somewhat earlier at displaying caring roles in their pretend play, but the reason for this is open to speculation. They may hug a bear or doll or pat a hurt child more readily than a boy would. Because they can both decentre, boys and girls may display some **empathy**, or understanding for someone else's feelings. However, in both real and pretend situations, girls show the ability to empathize earlier than boys.

Much of the toddler's play activity is very physical and boisterous. She loves to run around, just for the feeling it creates. As we discussed earlier, climbing is also characteristic of this stage. Toddlers like to use small climbers and slides and may repeat the action many times.

Increased skill in handling materials grows with practice. Toddlers of this age get much-needed practice through their play. Their manipulative skills enable them to carefully handle small materials, but frustration can result if tasks are too difficult.

A wider variety of play activities can be seen at this stage. Although you may observe toddlers playing by themselves in **solitary play**, they will more often play alongside each other in **parallel play**. Here the toddler may perform actions similar to those of another toddler near her, but she is not influenced very much by what the other child is doing. Toddlers who have more experience playing alongside other children, and who are developing well in the complexity of their play behaviours, may show some signs of **associative play**, but if we look closely we can see that their play remains focused on their own direction and shows very little sign of mutual activity or even sharing.

Observing toddlers playing with blocks can lead us to think that they are more interested in destruction than construction! Toddlers do enjoy knocking over towers of blocks, but they can also small build towers of a few blocks by themselves. The destruction phase is not damaging at all, but it may be prolonged if the adult continues to build the towers that the toddlers then knock down. The concepts that are built during block play are important in a mathematical sense. Toddlers are learning about space, weight, distance, height, and so forth. Their buildings tend to be made in straight lines along the floor or vertical constructions. Remember that toddlers cannot yet hold several characteristics in mind at once, so building in three dimensions is not yet part of their play. At this stage, the block play remains elaborate object play rather than true **construction play**, but there is evidence of emerging understanding about building.

A noticeable feature of toddler object play is that the use of the objects tends to relate to the purposes of the objects used. If the toddler uses a play telephone, she will usually use it for talking, and if she uses items from the house area she uses them in imitation of the real actions. That said, she might use some neutral objects in a variety of ways as they arise in her imagination. For example, water might become "juice" or pieces of paper might be pretend pizzas. The symbolism used in pretend play or play with objects can be characterized by adults as being both pretend play and imaginative play—the way that play activity is described can be confusing.

The adult's role in toddler play is vitally important. It is important to remember that we shouldn't spoil the spontaneous nature of the play—the play must come from the child, even if we have provided some materials that we think are suitable for toddlers of a given stage of development. Entering the child's play should be done very much the way a child observes the play of other children—as an onlooker.

Toddlers will invite the adult to play when they are ready. Be prepared to be a play partner in the activity—this involves following the child's lead rather than directing the play yourself. Your role may not be clearly defined, but avoid trying to use it as a teaching opportunity: that will make it boring for the toddler. Instead, play along with the toddlers as they wish to play, but take the opportunity to talk about what they are doing—as though you are a quiet narrator of their activity. This can encourage their awareness of their own actions and it adds language that makes the toddler's thoughts more solid.

Vary your part in the toddler's play to see what the children want you to be. Wherever appropriate, try to help the toddlers solve some of their own practical difficulties as they arise. Remember, they are not abstract thinkers, so assistance may mean demonstrating—but avoid doing it yourself. Also, resist any tendency to want to clear up, clean up, or otherwise organize the play until near the end of its natural flow. If it becomes essential to conclude a play experience sooner than the toddlers might want to stop, give them a warning or try to steer them into a mode that

brings about a happy conclusion. Since play is the centre of the toddler's learning, you want to ensure that you maximize its potential and demonstrate your respect for play through your own actions, language, and facial expressions.

LANGUAGE AND COMMUNICATION

The toddler's communication skills are improving in both spoken language and body language. Because toddlers at 18 to 24 months are more mobile and have more experience in the world, they have more to communicate.

Body Language

We can read toddlers' needs quite quickly if we pay attention to the messages being sent. Often they communicate using several signals at the same time—a sound, a gesture, and a facial expression, for example. The total is a very effective communication process. The toddler may point and make a sound that approximates the name of the object he wants. "Dondon wan nana" may indicate that Don (talking about himself) wants a banana.

Toddlers' facial expressions can convey a lot of information. The responsive adult can identify the toddler's apprehension, boredom, tiredness, enthusiasm, or his need to be rescued or reassured. Often these expressions are accompanied by body movements. You might read excitement not only in a facial expression but in the toddler's jumping up and down. The need to use the bathroom may be conveyed by a pensive stare and a dance up and down. Each child has particular body signs, but the experienced educator will notice that children have many signs in common, too.

Imitation is a big part of being a toddler, and adults can capitalize on this by providing detailed two-way communication techniques. Toddlers pay close attention to the details of communication and will copy them if the opportunity arises. This imitative process leads to **social learning** (Bandura, 1977).

Body language can be made more systematic if a **sign language** is introduced. In earlier chapters we discussed the potential for introducing **signing** to assist infant communication. Joseph Garcia's work on signing with infants and toddlers is based on the premise that "pre-speech infants have the intelligence to communicate specific thought and needs" (1994, p. 11) and that very young children who have already started to use formal language can have their communication enhanced through signing.

[S]ign languages are highly structured linguistic systems with all the grammar and complexity of spoken language. Just as English and Italian have elaborate rules for forming words and sentences, sign languages have rules for individual signs and signed sentences. (Hickok, Bellugi, and Klima, 1998)

If we are to believe that signs are more than separate entities—although that might be what they are at the start of the child's learning—conversational signing involves all the rules and complexities of regular spoken language. Garcia's work on signing is based on the **American Sign Language (ASL)** system, the one most commonly used in North America. Although its usefulness for toddlers who have hearing impairments is obvious, its use with toddlers who have average auditory capacities also appears to be valid. Interestingly, communicating by means of ASL and other signing systems uses the same area of the brain that is accessed when using spoken language, even though it depends on a different sensory channel. As yet there is little evidence of the long-term effect of early signing on those who can hear. Its use with deaf and hearing-impaired children is, of course, well appreciated.

Pay attention to each toddler's receptivity to imitation. It is not unusual for a toddler to follow you while imitating everything you do, but most toddlers are a little more subtle than that. They may notice, and later imitate, aspects of adults' posture, movement, expression, gaze, tone of voice and intonation, touch, and physical functions such as breathing (Quilliam, 1994). You can observe this when toddlers respond to a minor mishap by raising their eyebrows and saying "Uh-Oh," copying the adult's intonation. Alternatively, you can see them imitating an adult's reaction to something. "Ukky. No spider," they may say, as they make a disgusted face and push away with their arms, after witnessing an adult's negative reaction to spiders!

Receptive Language

Always understanding much more than she can articulate, the toddler has an extensive understanding of language. She will appreciate the meaning of many words if they are said clearly, but she may not understand the flow of adults' conversation. Toddlers listen attentively, although they can be confused about what they hear. Yet adults cannot assume that anything said in front of a toddler is confidential!

Toddlers will not usually assimilate talk that involves complex symbolism or concerns things beyond their experience. They are more likely to understand language if it is about concrete things and basic feelings. Understanding is also enhanced when actions accompany words. The adult might say, "We're having a story in a minute," and imitate opening a book. The toddler may now have sufficient language skills to understand and be calmed by reassurances like "Mommy will come back after play time."

Expressive Language

The language explosion at this stage is exciting to observe. Imitation assists the acquisition of new vocabulary, which typically grows very quickly. The toddler may use 50 or more words by 2 years of age (Sheridan, 1997). Some linguistic researchers think this estimate is low and the majority of 2-year-olds are using more like 150–300 words (Owens, 1996), but vocabulary depends upon toddlers' exposure to language, their cognitive and social skills, and their temperament. The words they use tend to be related to people and objects that are present. However, because toddlers now have some mental representations, conversation can be about things that are not immediately visible. The toddler's expression of ideas contains many mistakes. Rather than explicitly correcting the toddler with a "No, that's wrong," it is better simply to say back the words correctly, perhaps using an inquiring tone. Constant correction can inhibit toddler language development. Also, avoid laughing at the mistakes, even though they can be funny. You can seem amused, but make sure the toddler doesn't think you are ridiculing her.

At the beginning of this stage, the toddler will usually be using two-word sentences (Furuno, 1993). These will increase to three- and four-word phrases very quickly. Commonly, she will go from saying "Daddy home" to "Daddy's home now," or from "Hally up" to "I want up." The toddler may continue to babble using mostly consonant sounds and use jargon with strings of modulating sounds. She will also begin to use that all-important word "Mine!" as she comes to recognize her personal possessions.

Songs and rhymes hold particular interest for the toddler. She may want the same ones repeated, but is usually receptive to new ones as well. She will also listen and sing along readily. Sometimes she hears the song as a flow of tuneful sounds rather than as separate words. Hence, her repetition of the lyrics may sound peculiar, even funny. "Five little dicky birds" might be sung as "My little squitty dirds."

Although imitation explains the learning of vocabulary, there is more to language acquisition than vocabulary. The toddler connects words using a set of rules. Did she learn that, too, by copying? How is it that she can use phrases that she has never heard before? Chomsky (1957) thinks that toddlers acquire language because they already have a **universal grammar**, which is biological rather than learned. Piaget (1954) explained the process somewhat differently, as one of assimilation and accommodation similar to other cognitive processes. We discussed these concepts in earlier chapters. Regardless of how it occurs, this stage of language acquisition is an enthralling time for toddlers' caregivers because it takes a significant leap forward.

Along with the new use of a simple **grammar**, or set of rules, in her language, which we see as she attempts to string words together, there is another aspect of language that is noticeable and demanding. The toddler is likely to be asking her first real questions. Earlier she might have implied them by pointing and looking quizzical. Her first questions might be just one word, suggesting that the adult give her a name of something. For example, she may point at a fruit in the shopping bag and want to know what it is called. Soon she may demand a yes or no response to a simple question. She may ask, "Daddy gone?" and so ask if, rather than state that, Daddy has gone. She is likely to use an inflection in her voice that indicates that it is a question, and may point to the door that Daddy uses.

At this stage she may soon be able to pull together a two- or three-word phrase. Along with a spooning gesture, she might ask, "Moma want 'ing'?" meaning, does Mommy want pudding? Frequently early questions are accompanied by gestures and pointing to reinforce her meaning, and some words may have meanings only she understands. A favourite in our family was "Where's noing-noing?" The noing-noing was a **comfort object**—a soft piece of cloth that had to accompany its owner wherever she went. In asking where it was, she would perform an action indicating tucking the cloth under the chin and close to her body. This example not only illustrates the toddler's ability to ask a question, but it shows two other interesting things. Clearly she cannot ask for an object if she does not remember it—and clearly she does remember it even though it is out of sight. Also, the example indicates the emotional comfort derived from a soft object. It might remind you of Harlow's monkey experiments, where the infant monkey that is deprived of mother love prefers a soft covered object to a hard inanimate object. But avoid assuming that attachments to objects necessarily indicate maternal deprivation. All kinds of objects become very important to toddlers. Some toddlers insist that they must have their blue cup, have their old soother, or wear a

particular garment. They are not being intentionally difficult, they just have a strong emotional tie to the object. Only if the object is forced away from them might any long-term difficulties result. These issues rarely remain for more than a few weeks or months.

EMOTIONAL DEVELOPMENT

Stage of Emotional Growth

The ability to control emotions begins in the second half of the second year (Berk, 1996). The toddler faces a number of challenges that make emotional control difficult. First, the toddler has to know what she is feeling. This in itself is difficult, because the toddler's feelings swing from one extreme to the other very rapidly. Second, the toddler needs to understand the request to control her feelings or behaviour, if the request for control is external. This requires understanding of the language, particularly the words for the feeling that she has. It also means compliance with the adult's request. Third, if the control is motivated from within, the toddler must listen to herself as she attempts **self-regulation**—the ability to control her own feelings and actions. She has to know what she is trying to achieve. This requires having the memory to hold in her mind an adult's earlier request.

The complex capabilities of symbolic representation, self-awareness, and language enable the toddler to take greater control of her feelings and actions. These things lead toddlers to be "increasingly able to understand and obey external rules and restrictions and to hold themselves back from engaging in prohibited acts" (Bronson, 2000, p. 67). From this description we might think that the toddler is able to be completely self-controlled. Of course, that is not what is meant! The toddler is beginning to struggle with controlling herself, but she is frequently frustrated and needs much encouragement. For example, the toddler might see a cookie she wants, and although she has been told not to take one, she might hover over the cookies because she is tempted. Her inner voice is saying something like: "I want a cookie," but she knows that the educator has said that she cannot have another one. Whether or not she takes a cookie does not depend merely upon her understanding of right and wrong or whether or not she wants to please this adult: she is trying to overcome the strength of feeling associated with wanting the cookie. When lying down to sleep, she might be fearful of the shadows and cry softly for an adult. Hopefully someone will come, but perhaps nobody hears her quiet cries, so she might try to calm herself. These attempts at self-regulation occur throughout the toddler's day. Often she is successful, but frequently she is not. Sometimes the distress of the toddler because of her inability to regulate her feelings builds to a state of frustration. If the adult then shows disapproval of the resulting behaviour, the toddler can be disheartened.

At this stage, the toddler's emotions are particularly challenging because they are becoming more complex. The toddler may show signs of pride, doubt, empathy for others, or shame about some supposed failure. These are often called **social emotions**, because they are feelings associated with the toddler's relationships. This is the time to be extremely nurturing and understanding, while building on all the toddler's positive accomplishments. Enabling the toddler to have some sense of control is helpful. Offering choices can be good, but make the choice between just two things or activities—having more choices is difficult for the toddler to hold in mind and might increase his frustration. Phrasing requests in positive ways, such as "Stir the paint like this" (while demonstrating what you mean), is more effective than saying "Don't flick the paint." Supplying a concrete model of what is right is preferable to introducing a negative idea. A variety of **positive guidance strategies** will help the toddler improve her self-regulation.

Toddlers have a reputation for being challenging. Among the toddler's negative behaviours are biting, hitting, kicking, and having temper tantrums. Toddlers do not always learn these from imitation, but when they see that another child gets attention as a result of any of these acts this may prompt imitation. The behaviour that seems most troubling to both parents and caregivers is that of biting. This may be because it appears to be a kind of animalistic and primitive antisocial behaviour. Ann Gordon and Katharine Williams Browne (1996) offer a detailed plan for dealing with biting incidents in toddler programs that is consistent with our responsive caregiving and positive guidance approaches. The following suggestions are adapted from *Guiding Young Children in a Diverse Society* (p. 180).

When a biting incident happens

- Stop the aggressive behaviour swiftly and calmly.
- Try not to shriek or shout, but say firmly "Stop. No biting people."
- Comfort the victim.
- Show the biter the hurt and have them help you "fix it."
- Avoid lecturing or punishing the biter.

Afterward

- Find out more about what has happened—calmly.
- Ask each child what he or she wanted or didn't like.
- Suggest to both toddlers to use words, gestures, or signs to indicate their needs or wants.
- Give the toddlers a substitute for biting people (e.g., a teether).
- Practise what to do constructively in these situations (use role-playing or stories).

Later that day

- Talk to both sets of parents. Stay calm, and explain in developmental terms—avoid blame.
- Stay close and involved. The biter has much to learn and the bitten needs to be reassured.

For a few days or weeks

- Observe and anticipate, prevent, or redirect potential biting.
- Keep in touch with parents and explain what is happening.

The reason behaviours occur is usually more important than what actually happens, so it is better to avoid overreaction in any situation where the adult observes challenging behaviours. When we can appreciate the inner conflicts experienced by the toddler we can see why, so frequently, their behaviour is difficult to manage. **Temper tantrums** are challenging for adults as well as toddlers. Remember that when a tantrum occurs the toddler is not able to manage her own feelings—that is why it started. Try to remain calm, ensure her physical safety, and avoid giving in to whatever the display of feeling is focused upon. Toddlers respond in different ways to adult intervention. Some seem to want to be controlled by the adult and cuddled as this happens. Other toddlers may become increasingly angry if an adult is in any way involved with them. This may alter how you deal with the toddler, but the principle of remaining calm is essential.

Toddlers are most likely to have an outburst of emotion at a transition time during the day. A display of anger, physical acting-out, or a tantrum is most likely to occur when the toddler is tired, unwell, or stressed. Some toddlers are prone to tantrums because of their temperament type and the way they are handled by their parents and caregivers; some combinations of adult and toddler personalities result in calmer behaviours. Rushing at the end of the day is problematic for some toddlers. They can become overwhelmed by the stress and not understand the concept of time that is associated with moving quickly. It is better to schedule extended periods of time for transitions or, preferably, reduce them to a minimum, planning around the toddler's own schedule.

A resource for parents called *Toddler's First Steps* offers some practical advice that is appropriate for both the home and child-care settings (Government of British Columbia, 2002, p. 12). We have made some slight changes to fit our purposes.

Help the toddler to behave well by:

- letting each toddler know that you accept her feelings
- letting each child know that other children have needs, too
- offering solutions to problems
- being clear about behavioural limits
- offering explanations for limits
- helping toddlers see consequences of their actions
- redirecting behaviour and giving them something else to do
- offering simple choices
- helping toddlers express their feelings and desires
- being consistent in your responses
- letting the toddler know what is going to happen
- making sure that our actions don't reinforce whining, tantrums, or other negative behaviour
- offering a positive role model
- physically restraining the child if she is in immediate serious danger

Finally, the toddler does not yet have the language ability to express her feelings. Instead, she may act them out in apparently aggressive behaviour such as hitting, biting, and pushing.

It is not surprising that the toddler needs frequent reminders about appropriate behaviours and will benefit from sensitive guidance to support her attempts at inner control.

Toddlers at this stage are usually willing to please, so they often comply with an adult's requests. They frequently look at the adult to see if what they are doing matches the adult's expectations. This **social referencing** continues for a while. At the same time, although she still wants to please, the toddler has conflicting feelings of wanting to do things her way, in her own time, and on her own terms. This results in a challenge for this stage of development, where feelings of autonomy conflict with shame and doubt (Erikson, 1950).

The toddler's behaviour may often seem to move between extremes. She may be quietly compliant at times and extremely negative and assertive at others.

Adults find this frustrating. They must realize that both the positive and negative behaviours are indications of healthy toddler development. Even so, guiding the toddler to support her emotional development can be a challenge, particularly if the toddler's temperament differs from that of the parent or educator.

The **psychoanalytic school** offers another explanation for toddler behaviour regarding issues of control. It suggests that, during what is called the **anal phase**, the toddler gains pleasure from controlling her bowels and evacuating feces at will (Freud, 1940). Both Erikson and Freud would agree that this phase requires careful handling, because the balance between control and compliance is clearly a core element of toddler development. They argue that a toddler could suffer a fixation—getting stuck at this stage—if the balance between external control and support is not offered. For example, older children and adults might display uptight anal behaviours characterized by a high degree of control. While this theory has merit and explains the instinctive urge for control, some child-care experts think that Freud overemphasized the importance of bowel control. They note that, although the toddler is clearly striving for and gaining control over her body at this stage, bowel control is only one part of this process.

SOCIAL DEVELOPMENT

Toddlers' increased communication skills are part of the reason why their social competence improves. Practice with social relationships supports the acquisition of communication skills.

Attachments to adults remain close and physical. The toddler will demand lots of attention, encouragement, and cuddles. Having multiple caregivers is not a problem as long as the relationships are continuing and consistent (Lamb et al., 1985). The challenge for educators is to ensure that the patterns of response to the toddler are similar. Although toddlers know that they may get different responses from each adult in their lives, needless conflict is avoided if the patterns are not widely different. The child experiences greater security if adults agree on the parameters for the toddler's behaviour as well as the style of interaction used by the adults.

We have already outlined the major characteristics of the toddler's play, but they are worth revisiting as we consider how they relate to the toddler's social skill development.

The toddler is a frequent onlooker of the play of other children. She uses this as a device to know when to enter the play and how to conduct herself once engaged in it. She is also often an onlooker in her relations with adults, because she learns by imitating adults and internalizing aspects of their roles, creating an internal scheme of what adults do.

Onlooker behaviours are often considered to be a type of observational learning. As the toddler gains knowledge of the roles of adults and other children, she internalizes them as models of behaviour. This primary social learning skill is needed in many ways as the toddler learns what is socially acceptable and what is inappropriate behaviour. The adult models that are available to the toddler are probably the strongest influences in her social learning.

Solitary play remains a strong feature of toddler activity at this stage, but there are increasing examples of parallel play (Parten, 1932). Even in sociodramatic play—that is, make-believe play that involves other children—toddlers may imitate one another, but they do not collaborate, share, or have common goals. Learning to focus on one's own activity is an important step, and it must be taken before the toddler can hold in mind what she is doing and at the same time be aware of the presence of others. Parallel activity, followed by the gradual shift to increasing degrees of cooperation with others, provides the basis for success in later social interactions. Parents' and educators' support for appropriate social skill acquisition is essential for social learning. among toddlers. Because toddlers find it difficult to balance their own needs with those of others, frequent adult supports have to be offered. Although avoiding undue conflict is one suitable strategy, toddlers do need to learn how to deal with conflict. Adults can be present and suggest ways of dealing with conflicting views. Taking turns, providing reasonable choices between play materials, finding alternative activities, or offering future times to access a toy might be helpful approaches. Also, labelling—using a descriptive commentary of the experience they are each having—can help them to come to terms with the conflict. Try to remember that toddlers find it hard to wait for their turn at something and are stuck in an egocentric pattern of thinking. Learning that it is possible to recover from upset is also important, but this should not be considered a primary strategy for managing conflict.

Endeavour to give toddlers some opportunity to have their say, even though they may have limited language. This is when the adult can describe what is happening; it may be understood by the toddler before she has the ability to talk this through herself. Older toddlers and preschool children will be able to use their words to describe their thoughts about con-

flict, but, for the toddler, using the language required for articulating feelings about conflict is almost impossible, especially given the toddler's heightened emotions.

Self-Concept

Now that she has found her voice, literally and metaphorically, the toddler has discovered that she is a separate person who can influence her environment and the people in it. At this stage, a toddler's self-recognition becomes more clear-cut and she shows increased interest in her own face. This is an advance in the toddler's concept of self that is evident in the **rouge-and-mirror test** (Lewis and Brooks-Gunn, 1979). When the toddler sees herself in the mirror with her nose reddened by makeup she shows embarrassment. Before this time, the young child looked into the mirror and failed to recognize herself. When she looks and recognizes herself—knowing that her nose is not usually red—she feels very uncomfortable. The toddler has gained a mental representation of her own face, along with a sense of how it ought to look.

During the 18-to-24-month stage, the toddler becomes able to name herself, apply the pronoun "I" to her image, and identify herself in a photograph (Harter, 1983). Soon she will be able to categorize herself by gender and as having particular attributes.

> The self—the ME—of the young child emerges in this 18 month era with such a force that it feels more like a geologic event than a stage in development. After months and months of figuring out what is me and not me in the world, children are so anxious to put this new understanding to a test that we . . . often feel all we can do is to direct traffic. (Pruett 1999, p. 52)

Pruett's words echo what many parents and educators feel about the period of toddlerhood. However, Pruett is adamant that we do much more than just direct traffic!

His view is that adults need to take an active role in the toddler's life because it is essential to provide guidance in both practical and emotional ways. He reminds us of the implications of the toddler's striving for autonomy and a sense of self: the toddler gets to have a much clearer notion of what's hers—and this is at the root of many conflicts between toddlers and between adults and toddlers. The toddler's increasing selfhood also allows her to be positive in her feelings and behaviour. In her clarity of what is "you" and what is "me" she can show some signs of empathy within her social relationships. Differentiating between herself and others offers a clearer notion of the roles that people play; this is facilitated by her move away from totally egocentric thought.

There appears to be a connection between the toddler's attachment to adults and the formation of her sense of self. Goldberg explains it this way: "Attachment experiences are thought to result in internal working models that incorporate an appraisal of the self and the self in relationships which shape a general outlook on social experiences" (2000, p. 172). Although more research is needed in this area, it seems that secure attachments somehow enhance the development of the self-concept.

Personality

In a room full of toddlers, there will be as many personality types as there are children. We have already looked at some ways of classifying temperament in earlier chapters. Now we will examine some other ways of characterizing patterns of behaviour that may be more pertinent to toddlers and older children than the temperament models we have already examined.

There are several models of personality that categorize the **traits** of individuals. Traits are the particular characteristics of the individual that make him unlike anyone else. According to Allport and Odbert (1936), the English language may have 18,000 words relating to characteristics; this is a complex area.

Some trait theorists use a checklist of adjectives that apply to individuals. Others have adopted a list of opposites. Still others employ a five-factor model (Digman, 1990) that uses **factor analysis** (see below) or even a two-factor model that considers only extroversion and introversion (Campbell and Hawley, 1982). Some models consider core or central traits; others cluster traits to make a profile; yet others produce a map that can be compared with the norms for a particular type of individual. The Five Trait Theory is a trait theory that, as the name suggests, proposes five universal traits of personality: extroversion, agreeableness, conscientiousness, neuroticism, and culture. This trait model has evolved over a period of some years and has been critiqued at each stage of its development. Common criticisms are that it is insufficiently based on sound theory, involves subjective decisions, limits an individual's personality profile, fails to explain the causes of human behaviour, and does not embrace the idea that there are unconscious motivational issues. Most importantly, the five traits can be interpreted differently, depending on the understanding of the assessor. It seems undesirable to make lasting decisions about a toddler's personality on the basis of

limited criteria, but, at the same time, having any model of traits can help us to know what to look for as we try to determine the core characteristics of each child. Avoid the assumption that any personality profile is complete or permanent. Although traits are considered characteristics that remain constant over time, the toddler's behaviour patterns are influenced by many factors, such as mood, attachments, current struggles, and emotional issues. Data gathered over time are more significant than an assessment conducted on any single day. All of these models require reflection on the individual's style, or observation of responses in naturalistic or contrived settings. Analyzing traits prompts us to consider components of personality that might otherwise be elusive. To do this, we must identify the particular characteristics of individual children. For this information to be useful, it must be accurate. But how useful are existing models in our work with toddlers? Consider Cattell's model of opposite traits. Cattell is responsible for the development of trait theory. His model proposes 16 universal traits in the realm of personality. Cattell collected many relevant terms in his search of these traits, and through what were considered thorough research methods at the time, he narrowed his model down to 16 traits. In this model, a trait is considered to be a characteristic by which one person differs from another in a relatively permanent way (R.B. Cattell, 1980). Cattell's Factor Theory is one of the best-known trait theories. It uses a complex statistical technique called factor analysis, as mentioned above, to derive the 16 basic traits. The traits are presented in semantic opposites, in the following pairs:

- reserved and outgoing
- concrete thinking and abstract thinking
- affected by feelings and emotionally stable
- submissive and dominant
- serious and happy-go-lucky
- expedient and conscientious
- shy and bold
- tough-minded and sensitive
- trusting and suspicious
- practical and imaginative
- forthright and shrewd
- self-assured and apprehensive
- conservative and experimenting
- group-dependent and self-sufficient
- undisciplined and self-controlled
- relaxed and tense (R.B. Cattell, 1951)

It is an interesting list, but you might reasonably have some difficulties with it. Do you see all the traits as true opposites? Are they all, in fact, traits? Are some of the behaviours developmental? A major problem is that personality is such a subjective issue that each of us might look for different characteristics and measure the toddler's behaviour patterns differently. This subjectivity makes personalities difficult to assess.

Personality and Motivation

One of the key criticisms of the personality trait models is that they are concerned with overt behaviour rather than with underlying causes and motivations. One way of thinking about motivation is to explain it with reference to the **instinctual drives** that are part of the Freudian explanations for personality. This approach, based on biological interpretations of behaviour, sees **intrinsic motivation**—motivation from within—as being based in the biological pull to meet our physical and psychological needs. Thus individual differences are explained as biological variations. For example, some people are driven to climb mountains, while others focus on personal relationships. Just as in other aspects of the natural world, not all motivation patterns are the same. Within a culture or particular setting, the motivators might be quite similar between people—this is why some personality theories propose that some personality traits are shaped by societal influences. **Extrinsic motivation** comes from the toddler's environment rather than from within herself. The extrinsic motivators are provided by the adults who encourage the toddler, through activities and experiences that have built-in reinforcers, and by larger societal influences that assist the toddler to set goals and achieve what she is conditioned to want. Both intrinsic and extrinsic motivation are essential for personality development and govern learning in every aspect of the toddler's life.

The toddler's **locus of control**—the place where her control is located—can be both intrinsic and extrinsic. However, both can be damaged by negative experiences and lack of success. The toddler who gains the ability to manage her own feelings and behaviour (self-regulate) will be the toddler who has her intrinsic motivation supported. The toddler's intrinsic drive for autonomy leads her to be motivated to take the locus of control. Interestingly, the toddler does not have to be taught to strive for independence, but she is likely to need to have this brought into her consciousness. Offering a narrative description of what she is doing at the time of the behaviour helps the toddler to know she wants to be grown up. Although external supports and rewards are helpful,

the child's inner motivation is the true driving force for achievement. If the toddler becomes dependent upon adults for praise or support, she is less likely to remain focused on her own interests and goals. Socially accepted behaviour demonstrated by the toddler—an indicator of her drive for autonomy—can be reinforced by external motivators, but ultimately the toddler must follow her own drive. Adults can find out what these motivators are about, and feed into her interests and the challenges she sets herself, rather than impose tasks emanating from the adult's goals, however well-intentioned. Getting to know the toddler's personality traits is an excellent way to uncover the patterns of the child's behaviour. Trying to locate the reasons for the toddler's motivation to behave the way she does is also of great importance. Having the toddler recognize for herself the way she responds to situations and the motivators for success can be started at this stage, although a full understanding of her categorical self—how she describes who she is—will not come about until she attains the language and self-awareness of the preschooler.

The toddler functions more effectively, and with less conflict, if she is encouraged to follow her own interests. At this stage, some well-intentioned adults might think that the toddler's receptive mind can be supported by providing what they consider to be appropriate activities. They sometimes think that the toddler will learn well in accordance with the adult's goals for the toddler's development. This is an impertinence on the part of the adult! It is also counterproductive and a waste of time. Those frequently used planning sheets developed by adults to meet the child's needs, and to reach the next stage, are too often shaped by the adult's supposed knowledge of the child's development rather than on where the child's own interests lie. Here again, we need to trust that the toddler will develop successfully—according to a maturational schedule for which she is wired. Providing a **curriculum** in the sense of determining the content and delivery system for development will frequently be at variance with where the toddler is at. Rather than finding that the adult's curriculum design is too challenging, often we find that the toddler's learning is far ahead of the curriculum document (which, fortunately, she cannot read!). She is also more likely to develop as a more fulfilled, self-actualized individual if we enable her to follow her own motivations and interests.

What It Is Like to Be a Toddler

Getting down on our knees might be a good start at trying to understand how the toddler perceives her world—but it's only a beginning. Earlier in this chapter we tried to understand the toddler's behaviour as we observed it. And we have applied various theoretical and practical ideas to help us explain or find meaning in what we see. Some of these understandings offer insight into what the toddler's world is like. For example, appreciating the toddler's physical abilities, getting to understand why the toddler finds ways of doing adult things, coming to grips with her drive for independence and the consequent struggles that this imposes, trying to understand the egocentricity of her thinking and how she tries to solve problems, and observing the intricacies of the toddler's play can give us some precious gems of understanding of the tod-dler's own experience. Even appreciating something of her awareness that is on a conscious level, and what is lurking in her subconscious, gives us glimpses into her inner world.

You might have some other techniques for entering the toddler's world—ones that are intuitive rather than theoretical. Being able to sit quietly and listen and move into the child's activity might help. This is the author's phenomenological approach and it may offer you a framework for being in the world of the toddler. It is not presented as a correct model: only toddlers could tell us if it approaches their experience, and they cannot tell us in traditional language forms. Read Box 11.1 and see what you think.

BOX 11.1

WHAT'S IT LIKE TO BE A TODDLER?

I can, I think, I feel, I understand, I need, I want, I hear, I see, I must, I like, I pretend, I talk, I copy, I play, I listen, I make sense, I try, I love, I'm driven, I'm conscious, I am.

These notes offer a fairly simplistic view of what it might be like to be a toddler. It is almost too much of a challenge for adults to try to un-know what they have learned in the time since they themselves were toddlers. We have to forget the complex world that we currently live in, and all the social learning we have acquired over the years, as well as what we have learned through experience and from formal teaching. We also have to un-know our language; these are hard tasks. But let's try, because we might get a glimpse of what it's like to be a toddler. We are trying to take an inside view from a toddler's perspective. But remember, all experience is individual—no two toddlers think, feel, or respond in exactly the same way. We are endeavouring to under-stand the *qualia* (the raw feel) of being a toddler. Now try to imagine . . .

Me/myself	some consciousness of: "I am" (a separate person) . . . "I'm me" (an individu-ated person), "I can . . ." (a competent person), "I'm Tina" (but refers to self by name, not "I"), "This . . . is mine" (I possess), "My body" (identifies parts and some functions), "I am trying to . . ." (self-regulation)
Senses	some awareness of: sound, hearing, sight, taste, smell, and multi-modal input, deliberate actions to get sensory data
	experiences but not aware of: reflexive and automatic responses to stimuli, habituating, paying attention to details, being bored, perceiving, processing information, multi-modal input, paying attention to one aspect of multi-sensory experience
States of being	aware of: "being" or feeling: happy, sad, angry, comforted, fearful, empathetic, frustrated, hurt, and so on
	experiences without complete awareness: tiredness, happiness, irritability, her responses to stimuli, initiating, being content, being loved, being given atten-tion, trust, independence
Wants	conscious of wanting: food, drink, pleasure, movement, body comfort, play
	not always aware of wanting: comfort, calming, security, continuity, being loved, play partners, people who will communicate

Needs	<u>not aware of:</u> needing adequate nutrition, space, time, relationships, air, love, emotional support, intellectual stimulation, quiet, sleep, physical exercise, protection from harm, respect, psychological nurturance, continuity of care, protection from harm, health care
Drives	<u>instinctual drives (outside the toddler's consciousness):</u> curiosity, playing, observing, making relationships, categorizing, making practical sense, interpreting (making meaning), communicating, making sounds, attending to information, being attracted to visual and other stimulation, having preferences, being wired for language and learning
Her mind	<u>conscious thoughts:</u> identifying objects and people, associating objects with their purposes, understanding what happens in certain situations, e.g., cause-and-effect (if I do . . . then . . .), trial-and-error (if I try . . . this might . . .)
	<u>handling materials:</u> what their basic properties are (hard, soft, floppy, sticky, goopy, etc.) but may not yet have the language to describe
	<u>questioning:</u> when? where? why? how? what?
	<u>following very simple instructions:</u> recalling previous experiences, linking actions and places, matching, sorting, discerning similarities and differences
	<u>some conscious awareness of:</u> processing information, remembering (short-term memory may be more acute than long-term memory), linking ideas, associating objects and people, problem-solving
	<u>may not be conscious of:</u> conceptualizing (and may not understand/use associated language), but uses these and other basic concepts: colour, shape, distance, time, self, others, up/down, high/low, fitting things together, matching items, things that go together
	<u>determining patterns:</u> predicting what happens next, basic sequencing, having a mind, being conscious, functioning egocentrically
Symbolism	<u>representational thinking with some consciousness:</u> one object can represent another, copying adult actions, deferring imitation of adult actions, using words, recognizing that pictures represent real objects and people, internalizing roles, absorbing basic notions of right and wrong, basic fairness
Play	<u>some awareness of:</u> pretending, creating, imagining, hiding, building, role-playing, making things, using materials, practising
	<u>little awareness of:</u> learning through play, play and development, importance of play, etc., except via adult's respect of spontaneous play activity
Competence	<u>conscious of abilities:</u> walking, running, climbing, jumping, crawling, sitting, pedalling, throwing, basic catching, balancing, pulling up, grasping, turning, building, helping to get dressed, doing simple puzzles, helping mommy . . . (etc.), making people respond, imitating, watching people, doing things as grown-ups do, scribbling, squishing, tearing, knocking down, prodding, going to the toilet, getting dressed
Communication	<u>conscious of:</u> crying, making sounds, varying sounds, imitating adult sounds, saying single words, saying short phrases, listening, copying intonation of phrases, using singsong, getting adult responses
	<u>not conscious of:</u> taking turns in communicating, the meaning of all sounds heard, the rules of language

Enjoyment/ Likes/ preferences	<u>conscious pleasure in:</u> relationships, food, feeding and mealtimes, playing, bowel movements, urinating, being respected and accepted, talking, being successful, being praised, physical activity, listening to music, singing, doing the actions with rhymes, "reading" books, being like Daddy (or other adult), playing alongside other children, being social, being alone for short periods, doing things by himself, helping, food, messy activities, being a "grown-up," adults doing incongruous (funny) things, having her own place and belongings, knowing where things belong, being given choices, being shown how to solve conflicts, adult actions that have basic fairness, hearing simple explanations, having adults who read her cues, being given extra emotional support when unwell or stressed, adults who keep their cool, being part of a family, being accepted as part of a group, talking, repeating actions, predicting what comes next, making sounds, rhyming words, banging and making rhythmic sounds, moving to rhythms, taking small risks, discovering her own body, having control over her own body, sensory materials, bath time, having adults close by <u>may not be conscious of preferences such as:</u> visual interests, being with one person rather than another, using one particular channel of communication rather than another (e.g., visual rather than auditory), behaviours associated with her personality, temperament style differences, problem-solving behaviour patterns
Dislikes	<u>conscious dislike for:</u> some foods, being ignored, places or objects associated with discomfort, feeling abandoned, failing, being frustrated, being told no, disrupted routines, not having "his" cup (or whatever item is possessed), being washed, being taken away from what he likes doing, getting into a tantrum (and not being able to get out of it), not getting his way, being physically restrained, not being allowed to touch things that belong to others, hearing adults argue or fight, being bombarded with sound or other sensory overload, not knowing what is expected of him, having to share parental attention with a new sibling, overwhelming dreams and nightmares, erratic or inconsistent consequences for his actions, not knowing what is going to happen in the short term, angry adults, unpredictable adults, being handled roughly, being hurt, being required to be part of the group before he is ready, strangers, sitting still when asked, feeling out of control, interruptions as he plays <u>may not be aware of:</u> selecting one activity rather than another, excluding some options based on previous experiences
Challenges	<u>conscious of:</u> some social rules, and wants to please adults but finds it difficult to comply with sharing, take turns, do as she is directed, focus on what the adult wants her to do, sit still at circle time, rest or be left alone when she doesn't want to go to bed, give up bottles, soothers or other baby things, realize that hitting or biting hurts someone else, listen to reasons why something is unacceptable, be good, be stimulated and then told to be quiet, do the right thing

Experiences that are generally outside the toddler's understanding:

mess, untidiness, aesthetics, cleanliness, safety, adult needs, left- or right-handedness, the larger environment, what things cost, why people have to go away, why chores have to be done, fluctuating moods (lives in the present), fluctuating energy levels, the need for adults to perform some functions (like working, sleeping, shopping, etc.), hazards and why they prevent him from doing things that he wants to do, traffic and speed, violence (as seen on television), dressing for the weather, the need to visit the bathroom before leaving home, not talking about private things in public, the unfairness of the world, reasons why she cannot have something she wants, the need to hurry, adult relationships, personal space and possessions (of others), looking after things, deferring gratification (waiting until later), seeing things the way other people do.

Having tried to enter the toddler's world, you may want some ideas about what to do with your experience. Some adults interpret the toddler's consciousness of her world as something that lets us engage at the toddler's level. That might be useful, but it makes our response little more than being another a toddler! Better still might be to use the essence of the experience to enter the toddler's world as she expects us—as an adult with adult responsibilities. That way, we can conduct the adult role but with much greater sensitivity and the new ability to be a **facilitator** in the child's work. The idea of a facilitator offers a different approach to our role (as either parent or employee); it gets away from the idea that we are simply offering care—although care in many ways must be provided. And it is removed from educator because the role is more than teaching or supporting learning activities. Being a facilitator involves:

1. being there:
   being alongside the toddler in a mode of respect and accepting the toddler as a competent human being

2. observing and monitoring:
   observing the toddler, using all the adult's senses before moving in to be her play partner, and monitoring the maturational unfolding of her development

3. recognizing individual interests and developmental patterns:
   recognizing and supporting the toddler's intrinsic motivation, pre-wiring, and instinctual drives

4. interpreting:
   acting as an interpreter of body language, gestures, facial expressions, and sound production, and providing a channel for successful communication

5. environmental designing:
   assessing, designing, refreshing, and altering the environment in accordance with her interests, needs, and capabilities

6. offering responsive support and positive guidance:
   determining when the toddler needs support, and providing it in whatever form is necessary—and advocating for the child's rights

7. working with (not against) and accommodating individual styles, traits, and needs:
   celebrating the toddler's individual characteristics and providing a consistent safe base for emotional and physical security

8. honouring autonomy:
   accepting the toddler's drive for autonomy and enabling her to be successful at becoming independent

9. providing exterior construction (for interior construction):
   providing a scaffold for any aspect of the toddler's learning as it evolves naturally, and offering a bridge from where the toddler is functioning to where she aspires

10. consistent role-modelling:
    being a positive role model for the toddler's social learning and offering constructive strategies for successful relationship-building

None of these roles might seem extraordinary, given the philosophy of *See How They Grow*, but as we appreciate the infant as she becomes a toddler, we must adapt our role accordingly. Let us recall for a moment earlier discussions about the needs of infants and toddlers and the philosophical premise upon which we seek new understanding of very young children. As we discussed earlier, there are developmental stages and individual needs of toddlers. As we enter the toddler's world, we see that there is a hierarchy of toddler needs. At first there are the physical needs, and last of all are the psychological needs. This can be explained using Maslow's Hierarchy of Needs (see Appendix). The toddler's needs have to be met in sequence—higher-level needs are dependent upon earlier needs met. Like building blocks, the child's physical needs have to be met before his psychological needs can be addressed.

Some approaches to early childhood education are considered to fall in the medical mode: they simply address the child's needs for cleanliness, absence of disease, competent caregiving, and so on. These approaches tend to be thought of as old-fashioned. Current approaches to ECE tend to favour the responsive and educational approaches. Neither of these, in themselves, is wrong. And in reality both the medical and educational models have merit. As we have determined in our efforts to understand the toddler, we also need to appreciate what it's like to be a toddler and have some sensitivity for what that means. This phenomenological approach offers a higher-level response to the needs of toddlers—one that leads, one hopes, to the toddler's self-actualization. This is a somewhat abstract concept of psychological well-being that depends upon success on the toddler's own terms.

▶ Toddler Consciousness in the Age of the Brain

Scientific discoveries can help adults understand what the brain does and how it functions. These things apply to the lives of toddlers. Extrapolating from the research, we can try to enhance toddlers' experiences. The view of the scientist generally is that all mental processes, even the most complex emotional and psychological ones, derive from the operation of the brain. Recent research supports this **paradigm** (way of thinking). What we think of as being the mind is a range of functions carried out by the brain (Kandel, 1998). Within this paradigm, everything in our conscious life is caused by brain processes (Searle, 1995). Indeed, as one of these scientists claims, "You're nothing but a pack of neurons" (Crick, 1994).

Although the outcome of scientific research seems to hold up under scrutiny—a substantial amount of recent brain research is thought to be credible, valid, and reliable—some educators and philosophers think that taking this brain view to explain behaviour is dehumanizing. Elio Frattaroli (2001) writes: ". . . [no scientist] even pretends to have any idea how brain processes could possibly produce the mysterious and ineffable experience of human consciousness" (p. 8). He contends that what purports to be science doesn't stand the test of scientific method, although many people would disagree with him. At any rate, he does have one valid point: the true nature of consciousness lies outside the boundaries of science because it is entirely subjective—it is always a personal experience. This does not reduce the significance of the recent brain research, but it should lead us to a different kind of inquiry. This book does not focus on trying to dismiss the outcome of science, but rather aims to use it together with other **ways of knowing**. "Ways of knowing" is a phrase used by several researchers interested in the perspectives that are based on gender or other specific criteria.

The framework from which we approach the understanding of a phenomenon is likely to affect what we find. Thus, if we examine consciousness using a traditional scientific perspective we are likely to come up with a scientific answer! As adults in the lives of toddlers, when we ask the same questions about consciousness, we will probably get a response from an educational or parental viewpoint. Why should this be wrong? We can borrow from other world-views to inform ourselves, but there is nothing wrong with trying to understand a toddler's consciousness using an observational technique. Even scientific method demands that the observational method used should be appropriate to the phenomenon being observed. In this case, we use the detailed narrative observations that people in this discipline are familiar with.

By conducting many narrative recordings and informal observations we can get some answers to the questions of toddler consciousness. However, the answers remain focused on the observation of behaviour—what the child does on the outer level—rather than the inner experience of consciousness.

Much of the thinking of the 19th and 20th centuries was based on **positivism**—the idea that there is only one objective truth and that scientific discovery requires separation between the observer and the subject—the person being observed. Phenomenologists usually take a different view, one that accepts that truth (if there is such a thing) is created by the individual involved in the experience. So their consciousness is highly individual and subjective. Frattaroli, in addressing this issue, states clearly that: "It should be self-evident that the only way we can possibly know anything—scientific or otherwise—about conscious experience is through observing someone's conscious experience of it!" (2001, p. 170). We can agree with Frattaroli because we know that to understand the toddler's consciousness we have to observe her in her consciousness. We might or might not be sympathetic to any view of consciousness that involves a soul; phenomenology accepts that any subjective consciousness is valid, and there is room for a soul at the root of consciousness should we be inclined to posit one. (This view would not be tolerated within a purely scientific approach, where the approach might be that if it's not measurable and observable it doesn't exist.)

This might seem like a long route to underscoring what you knew anyway—that observing toddlers is the most effective way of understanding and entering into their consciousness. However, it was a path that we needed to take. With this kind of examination of the issue, we have validated the fact that experience is subjective and that there are more significant ways of approaching a toddler's consciousness than strapping her into a CT or PET scan to get a map of what centres of her brain are active during consciousness!

▶ Particular Needs

BEING IN THE TODDLER'S WORLD

True understanding of what it's like to be a toddler can come only from trying to see the toddler's perspective—and that includes getting down to her eye level and letting her take the lead in play activities. While academic learning can help us to understand behaviour, for us to understand her consciousness of the world we need to spend time with her.

ATTACHMENT AND SUPPORT

Toddlers need strong relationships with adults. They need those relationships to be consistently loving and caring. Nothing is more important. Offer physical and emotional support, but respect the toddlers' own boundaries and tune in to their individual styles.

THE COMPETENT TODDLER

Rather than focus on what a toddler cannot yet accomplish, we respect toddlers more and learn to meet their needs better if we see them as competent human beings. Looking at all the things that toddlers can do is amazing. They have achieved a lot in so little time.

SAFETY

One area that might be an exception to the last statement is that of safety. We need to plan, protect, and anticipate the toddler's actions because he is focused on his own development. The environment must offer some basic risk-taking opportunities, but this should be balanced with careful measures that match the

toddler's ability to climb, examine, and get into almost everything.

BRAIN WORK

Toddlers need stimulation and relaxation; learn to respond and initiate activities accordingly. Every experience must be positive and nurturing. Try to offer a wide variety of learning experiences, delivered in a loving and supportive manner.

SENSORY DISCOVERY

Materials that he has played with previously become completely new toys, because the toddler's skill at handling things and problem-solving behaviours are more sophisticated. Offer a range of materials that stimulate all the senses—hearing, tasting, touching, seeing, and smelling—but make sure they are safe.

COMMUNICATION

It takes two to communicate, and you are the person to respond and initiate gestures, signs, and real language. Use lots of descriptive language, but emphasize significant words so that the toddler can pick up what they are in context. Using lots of books, pictures, stories, tapes, music, sound experimentation, puppets, and rhymes, as well as everyday domestic conversation, is essential.

BEING A FACILITATOR FOR TODDLERS

You can consider yourself the toddler's translator. Offering a bridge between what she currently knows and what she is trying to find out is your prime job. This provides a scaffold for her learning that is impossible without an adult.

PERSONALITY STYLE

There are several ways of looking at a toddler's temperament: you may consider her temperament style, favoured channel of communication, or traits. Whichever way you go about it, make sure that you appreciate the different patterns of response from every individual toddler.

PLAY PARTNERSHIP

Toddlers lead; you follow. Start by observing quietly and move into the circle of play very cautiously. Follow the child's lead—she'll tell you what she wants you to do. Avoid teaching, but be there to help her strategize when things get difficult. Do what you can to extend the play experience to maximize its usefulness and learning potential.

ROLE-MODELLING

The toddler's imitative learning puts the adult on a challenging stage where the toddler watches everything. Make sure that your language, behaviour, facial expressions, and all your interactions are positive.

SELF-HELP

Toddlers want and need to do things themselves. Adults need to allow enough time to make this possible. Adults can also help to ensure that the toddler is successful by simplifying the task. For example, clothes that are easy to take off and put on make the task more manageable.

TAKING CONTROL

Toilet-learning—as well as other kinds of learning—can easily turn into a battle of wills. It is better to deflect this by not making toilet-learning an issue. The toddler is likely to want to feel grown up in this area, too, and decide for herself when to use the potty or toilet.

Toddlers need to be independent and make choices: this gives them a sense of control. She wants to do everything herself and she wants to do it her way. The toddler needs opportunities to make decisions, direct her own play, and involve adults in activities directed by her.

PRETEND PLAY

Opportunity and props for basic domestic play and simple role play are important at this stage. The toddler may like to put her doll to bed, drive a pretend car, or think up scenarios in which she can take a part. Early pretend play is not truly co-operative, so there should be enough props that several children can play at the same time.

DEALING WITH EMOTIONS

The frustrations of being a toddler, the powerful emotions that well up without much warning, the joy that makes the child unable to be still, the enthusiasm she brings to so many things she does—all this can be overwhelming. Parents and educators need to work together to help the toddler to label her feelings, accept how she feels, and gain some mastery over her emotions. The toddler needs to develop calming strategies. She may have learned some self-comforting techniques as an infant, but she needs to broaden her repertoire now, with adult help. Efforts at self-regulation need to be reinforced, and toddlers need to start expressing feelings rather than demonstrating them negatively. Toddlers need to have their feelings accepted rather than being directed to feel "appropriately."

RITUALS

Many toddlers find comfort in predictable sequences of events and enjoy some structure to their routines. This helps them to understand what is happening and what is likely to happen and gives them some sense of time and sequence.

Some children create **rituals** for themselves, or have adults participate in rituals that have some comfort. You might see this at nap time, when the toddler will not sleep if her cuddly toys are not in the preferred places. She may demand to eat and drink from a particular bowl and cup. Although the need for this seems trying to the adult, it should be understood as a developmental stage that will pass.

▶ Developmental Variation

Toddlers with specific developmental needs may be registered in a child-care agency at this age. Those who were cared for at home in their early months may now transfer to a child-care centre or a home child-care setting, where their individual needs can be met. Some of the more common and observable differences in development require considerable accommodation, but, with some professional assistance, most children can be included in toddler programs.

ORTHOPEDIC DISABILITIES

Orthopedic disabilities result from impairments to the bones, joints, or muscles. They can stem from a variety of conditions, including arthritis, spina bifida, cerebral palsy, or congenital malformations. The most obvious challenge that these children face is in the area of motor skills, but they may also experience debilitating pain. Moreover, their impaired motor skills might affect other areas of their development, such as language acquisition, cognitive development, and social skills.

Children with these disabilities vary considerably in the degree to which they are affected, so each child should be accommodated individually. Commonly, children with orthopedic impairments can be assisted with various devices that provide increased motor control, and they may benefit from physical positioning so that they can access toys, learn some self-help skills, and take part in the program. Toddlers with orthopedic disabilities may be helped by individually constructed structures that allow the child to play and explore in an upright position. The toddler educator can assist the child in a holistic way, not only to support her mobility or manipulative skills. Careful observation, good documentation, and individually responsive caregiving are essential.

HEARING AND VISION IMPAIRMENTS

The educator may be the first to realize that a child has a hearing problem. If, when observing the child, the educator discovers any kind of perceptual impairment, it should be shared with the parents. Everyday play experiences may give rise to concern. If the toddler fails to give typical responses to either hearing or visual stimuli, further observation and documentation should lead to professional assessment. It is the responsibility of the parent to ensure that the child receives appropriate assessment. Children who have either hearing or vision problems can usually be assimilated into the regular child-care program. Educators should be aware of each child's ways of learning and should accommodate them accordingly. **Assistive devices** such as hearing aids and eyeglasses can be enormously helpful. These children need to see specialists regularly, because their conditions can change rapidly. The most useful strategy for supporting children with any sensory impairment is to build on the child's strengths in areas of their sensory capabilities.

MULTIPLE DISABILITIES

Some children entering a child-care program may have more than one disabling condition. One condition may have caused the other, or there may simply be coexisting conditions. Each child's needs must be assessed. Determining how the child can best be accommodated must be a priority. Children who are multiply disabled may present challenges that can be overcome with special assistive devices, external support from community resources, training for the educators, or the addition of an assistant or specially trained resource teacher. Parental communication

and shared care can help the family and the agency to collaborate effectively.

▶ Parents as Partners in Care

During the period leading up to the second year of life, many toddlers with a developmental disability are diagnosed. Some of the signs and symptoms of disability might have been detected earlier, but this is not always the case, for a variety of reasons. At this stage, many caregivers and educators, along with the toddler's parents, observe behaviours that indicate some cause for concern. Knowing that early intervention is almost always beneficial, the caregivers should share their concerns with parents and request an exchange of information. The parents, as well as the staff, may have started to have the same concerns. Sometimes the parents do not respond to the situation until prompted by the staff. Young children who spent their infancy at home, or who were previously cared for by local baby-sitters, may not have been observed by professional caregivers. Being enrolled in a program within a child-care centre might offer a new opportunity for observing the toddler. Also, there may be some signs and symptoms that are new or have become more obvious during this stage. Consequently, many toddlers at 18 to 24 months are referred to specialists. There must be ongoing consultation with parents, and it is usual for the parents to make the appointments with specialists. This generally follows an initial consultation with the family doctor. It is the place of the professional caregiver to supply parents with adequate observational information, assist them in accessing resources, advocate for the toddler to ensure that her needs are met, keep appropriate relevant documentation, and make appropriate accommodations to the program, in accordance with the outcome of any assessment that is made. Frequent consultation between key professionals and parents is essential to support the toddler. Typically, an individual program plan is developed for the toddler that can be implemented both at home and at the centre.

It is understandable that parents might resist seeking a specialist consultation that might lead to an unwelcome diagnosis. From the time of pregnancy and birth, most parents anticipate a healthy child. Accepting that the child may not match their internalized image is an emotional struggle. Like any other type of loss—in this case the loss of the imagined perfect child—there are some typical stages that can be observed in parents. Although parents may show, or attempt to hide, their feelings in a variety of ways, there are some stages most parents have to pass through. Kay Wright Springgate and Dolores A. Steglin identify them this way:

Stage 1: Shock: During this stage, feelings of numbness, with an abrupt disruption in their normal thought and feeling patterns, are experienced. Irrational thoughts and patterns are common at this time.

Stage 2: Denial: This stage is characterized by feelings and thoughts of "This can't be happening to me," "It isn't true," and "There must be a mistake." This stage provides an emotional buffer to the crisis and even provides a temporary escape.

Stage 3: Sadness and anger: Many negative emotions flood the parents at this point. The anger may be channelled toward themselves, toward the child, toward the doctor, and toward others. Families may feel such a profound sense of sadness that they isolate themselves from family and friends. Some families share these intense feelings.

Stage 4: Adaptation: This fourth stage finds a lessening of emotions and anxiety, with a growing acceptance of the child.

Stage 5: Reorganization: The final stage finds a new sense of equilibrium in the family. The family redefines and restructures itself to accept and include the exceptional child. During this stage, the family finally achieves successful coping, when problems are addressed and solved.[1]

Professional caregivers and educators must not intrude into the lives of parents at any time. However, understanding the stages that parents go through when they learn that their child has a disability is a great asset in supporting effective communication with parents. It can be challenging for professionals to avoid getting caught up in the emotion of the situation. While it is not wrong to share and empathize with parents, it is the primary task of the caregiver to provide for the child's needs. Working with the child's parents is an essential part of this, but you cannot shield the parents from their grief. It is also worth remembering that parents may not progress through these stages within a set time frame. It can be the parent who initially appears to adjust well to the situation who reverts to earlier stages of grieving for no apparent reason.

Again we see that communication and shared care are particularly important when a child has disabilities or other problems that may require specialized care. In such cases, parents and educators can be excellent resources for each other. Parents can communicate the results of assessment and information about the abilities of, and the challenges facing, their child. In turn, the educator can provide the parents with observations of the child's progress or challenges and may be able to help with access to community resources.

Depending on the severity of the disability, parents are often under an unusual amount of stress and may be nervous about placing their child in care. The parents can be reassured by conversations with the educator, who convey the staff's knowledge of the child's condition and sensitivity to his needs.

The issues surrounding the special needs of children, requests by parents, and demands on educators raise the general problem of boundaries. One of the goals of a child-care centre is to be flexible and accommodating for all parents and children, not just for those with special needs. But how far can educators go, and how do they communicate limits? Box 11.2 raises some issues and offers strategies for communicating boundaries to parents.

▶ Health Concerns

Contact with a widening circle of people can lead a toddler to greater exposure to childhood illnesses. Only a medical doctor can diagnose such illnesses, but educators must be knowledgeable, and watch for signs and symptoms, and be aware of how to respond to any outbreaks. Local health authorities can provide parents and educators with up-to-date information on when to exclude children and what constitutes a notifiable disease. It is essential that toddlers receive immunizations in accordance with the required protocols before and during their time in child-care settings. Prevention of disease is an important issue—particularly early in life.

THE COMMON COLD

A cold is a viral condition that is infectious for a short time before the symptoms are experienced and for the next seven days. It is spread via droplets from

---

1. Adapted from Stages of Grief: Adjusting to a Child with Special Needs, from *Building School and Community Partnerships through Parent Involvement* (1999, p. 132).

BOX 11.2

COMMUNICATING BOUNDARIES

Educators of infants and toddlers can be so willing to please parents that they fail to convey clear messages about the parameters of their professional relationship—these are called **professional boundaries**. This can easily happen because of the intimate nature of infant and toddler work.

When we say to parents that we are flexible about the program, we may give the impression that all parental requests can be accommodated. It might be better to say exactly what is negotiable. For example, be specific about times between opening and closing when parents can drop off, visit, or collect their child. In the case of toddler care, you might want to restrict visiting or pickup during sleep time—but you must say so!

A more difficult challenge to boundary-setting can occur when the professional relationship is unclear. Sometimes, especially in small communities, parents and colleagues know each other outside the walls of the agency. In such situations, it is necessary to clarify the workings of the parent–professional relationship. Whether evening baby-sitting is a possibility should also be discussed.

Being involved in the lives of toddlers is a wonderful opportunity to offer seamless caregiving, but difficulties can arise around expectations on both sides of the relationship. While it is not wrong to be emotionally involved with a toddler and her family, the educator must maintain a professional relationship in everything associated with the delivery of the child-care service.

Having empathy for parents and even sharing the joys and disappointments of parenting are essential elements of the professional partnership. However, we need to learn how "to be a participant in the family social system, while avoiding entangling alliances," suggest Irene and Herbert Goldenberg (1996, p. 367). It is for the benefit of everyone that these boundaries are set and reinforced when necessary. The following suggestions might be helpful when setting professional boundaries.

- Try to separate your home life and your professional role.
- Communicate to parents the appropriate times and methods for exchanging ideas, concerns, and other information.
- Mention the parameters for confidentiality—and stick to them yourself.
- Discuss the professional role in group meetings with parents.
- Identify elements of the parent's role as they become necessary; for example, explain that parents seek medical advice directly from their doctor or that parents are responsible for various supplies, such as diapers and sunscreen.
- Show empathy for parental feelings, but avoid introducing your own family issues.
- Avoid leading a parent to think that you can offer therapeutic help. Instead, refer the parent to helpful resources.
- Respect the parent's background, religious beliefs, and political persuasion, but do not discuss issues outside your professional role.
- Help parents to solve their own problems rather than provide answers for them.
- Keep conversation within the range of your professional competence (apart from general pleasant remarks).
- While you might think of parents as more than acquaintances, they are not your friends or potential clients—for cosmetic sales, for inclusion at your own family gatherings, to use for marketing purposes as potential customers, as supporters of political parties or for fundraising, or as potential converts to a religion.
- Identify situations that are outside your experience, training, or professional responsibility, and refer parents to experts and suitable resources.
- Offer child-care advice based on your own experience, but label it as just that—"In my experience . . ."

- Parents expect professional behaviour, so be sure that you behave in an ethical manner.
- Tell parents "I don't know" when you do not know an answer to a question, but then try to access resources that can help.
- Refer parents to the staff member concerned or, if necessary, the centre's supervisor if they try to engage you in conversation about other staff.
- Accept that you are emotionally engaged with each toddler and her family, but recognize that the engagement should not disengage you from acting with professionalism.
- Open communication helps with boundary-setting.

Try to be as precise as possible. Ambiguous statements might be misinterpreted. If you have real problems with a parent's request, say so tactfully and try to reach a compromise. Calm, kind, and clear conversations assist mutual understanding.

sneezing or coughing, whether airborne or on hands or surfaces. A runny nose or congestion may reduce the child's appetite, but there is usually no need to exclude a child with a cold, unless she feels too lethargic to take part. Because toddlers share materials and play in close proximity, it is extremely difficult to avoid the spread of the common cold.

INFLUENZA

Influenza is often confused with the common cold, but it is much more severe. There are many varieties, but health experts predict their arrival and vaccinations are offered to counteract it. The flu can be very serious for infants and those suffering from immune-system problems. Exclusion from the agency is necessary, but the virus is likely to have been passed to other children before symptoms are evident. Protection from influenza can be provided by vaccine. Each year researchers develop vaccine to target anticipated influenza strains. Parents should seek the advice of their physicians regarding protection.

STREP THROAT

A child who has a fever and very sore throat will often be found to have strep throat. However, this diagnosis cannot be confirmed until medical personnel take a throat culture. Antibiotic treatment is usually prescribed. If she feels well enough, the child can return to the centre a day after treatment starts. Mouthing toys and being in close proximity to others can increase the spread of this infection. Although mild in most instances, strep throat can present serious health risks.

▶ Everyday Safety Issues

Although toddlers of this age benefit from being taken out and about, excursions present some safety issues. Short walks and visits to local events are better than travelling long distances for larger events that won't be meaningful for children so young.

INDOOR SAFETY

The curiosity and increased mobility of the toddler at this stage have to be addressed from a safety perspective. Every aspect of the toddler's environment must be evaluated and toddler-proofed. This should not, however, lead to making a sterile environment without play opportunities. Consider the following broad categories of potential risk and ensure that you take appropriate steps to manage the risk. This may mean the removal of a potential hazard or improved supervision.

The following potential hazards should always be assessed:

- *water,* including water for play purposes, sinks, and any running water
- *electricity,* including its connection with water, power outlets, lighting, fans, and all appliances
- *fire,* including all sources of heat, the flammability of all materials, microwaves, irons, laminating machines, and ovens
- *strangling,* including all cords from blinds, toys with pull-along cords, telephone wires, clothing, strings, and cords
- *choking,* including foods, toys, coins, and small items of play material
- *suffocation,* including all stuffed toys, plastic bags, soft materials, and pillows

- *falling,* including all items that could be used for climbing stairs, inadequate footwear, flooring, water on the floor, slippery materials, items to trip over, climbers, cribs, swings, and toddler toys
- *sharp objects,* including knives, plastic scrapers, fences, swing seats, dough cutters, and tins
- *pollutants,* including all potentially damaging solid, liquid, and gaseous materials, such as cleaning materials, paints, permanent markers, prescription and over-the-counter medications, illegal drugs, blood, excrement, aerosols, inadequate air quality, unwashed foods, play materials, and waste materials
- *collisions,* as a result of insufficient space for the type of activity, crowding
- *extreme temperatures,* including ice, exposure to hot spaces, cold, and inadequate clothing or bedding
- *miscellaneous hazards,* including firearms, weapons, laundry facilities, insect bites, the sun, kitchens, old fridges, walk-in freezers, syringes, condoms and found objects, non-custodial parents, strangers, warfare, terrorism, tornadoes, lightning, earthquakes, places where toddlers can get locked in, untested drinking water, rodents, wild animals, pets, poisonous plants, drunken adults, drug-takers, and unpredictable situations

This is not a complete list of hazards and is not intended for use as a checklist of items to assess. The parent or professional must keep current about safety hazards and be aware of every aspect of the environment. It is not suggested that adults keep toddlers away from all these hazards. Clearly, many of the items include play materials that can be used where there is appropriate adult involvement. Most materials and situations require **risk management**. This involves:

1. identifying the potential hazard
2. recognizing the developmental level of the child (and what dangers she might be in because of her skills and judgment—or lack of them)
3. assessing the risk of harm:
   - consequences too great, therefore avoid the material/situation completely
   - consequences mild, therefore allow only careful use of material/situation
   - consequences negligible, therefore allow open use of material/situation
4. altering the environment in accordance with the level of risk
5. monitoring the use of material/situation

In general, if the adult responsible for decision-making finds it difficult to make a risk assessment of a material or situation, it is advisable to avoid its use until further information can be accessed.

FIELD TRIPS

Any outing requires extensive preparation. There must be contingency plans for a variety of mishaps. Ensure that:

- parental permission has been granted for the trip
- liability insurance coverage is in place
- the toddlers know what is going to happen
- the supervisor knows where you and the children are going
- your trip has manageable travel arrangements
- you carry all the necessary medical supplies and first-aid equipment, cash, emergency plans, and phone numbers
- you take a mobile phone, if possible
- you have enough adults available
- you take changes of clothing
- you plan for toilet/potty/diaper arrangements
- you have antibacterial gel in case hand-washing is impossible
- you count the number of children regularly
- if walking in convoy, you have adults at the front and back
- you use strollers that are in good repair and have safety straps over the shoulders
- strollers are taken along for any children who become tired from walking
- you plan food and snacks and supply drinks
- sunscreen is applied if any skin is exposed (young children should not have skin exposed to the sun)
- you wear a hat in the sun
- you plan for cold, rain, or wet snow, or other extreme weather
- if the large group splits, which is better for toddlers, each adult is assigned specific children

For easy identification, you might consider clothing all the children in brightly coloured T-shirts. Be prepared to cancel the trip if:

- there are not enough adults to help
- the weather is poor or threatening
- some children seem listless or show symptoms of illness
- the children don't seem interested in going

▶ Starting Points for Response

RESPONSIVE CAREGIVING

This is an active phase of childhood, and the adult can find it challenging to keep up with the toddler. His

---

BOX 11.3

GETTING IN TUNE WITH TODDLERS AT 18 TO 24 MONTHS

Below are some starting points for building your responsivity skills with an 18-to-24-month-old toddler. Tune in with respect and:

- respond positively to attention seeking—what does the toddler want or need?
- listen to the toddler before you talk to her
- laugh with the toddler when she laughs
- enjoy physical fun with the toddler
- individualize all responses
- plan activities based on emerging skills
- provide plenty of space for mobility
- encourage simple problem-solving play
- introduce trundle or ride-on toys
- use tunnels and planks to construct an obstacle course
- respond quickly to needs, talking about what you are going to do and what she needs
- monitor climbing activities
- praise successes, pointing out what you think is good
- reinforce language and introduce new words and phrases
- label body parts, domestic objects, and the toddler's feelings
- offer books, pictures, and artwork
- play various types of music, associating them with moods and activity levels
- dance with the toddler
- support the toddler's initiatives to do things independently, and praise her initiatives
- provide child-sized grown-up items for imitative play
- sing songs, rhymes, and action verses
- provide stimulation for each of the senses together and separately
- sit at the child's level for puzzles and easy build-up/knockdown construction
- follow the toddler's lead in her play
- use concrete experiences and here and now for language
- support self-help skills and toilet-learning
- extend play into nature and the outside world
- discover how real objects work
- have materials ready for pretend play
- offer dress-up hats and draping clothes
- extend play episodes, adding new ideas
- model empathic responses, exaggerating key features of your role
- have opportunity for parallel play activity to encourage side-by-side acceptance of other children
- introduce games and puzzles with easy-to-handle pieces
- show how to be kind to dolls/bears
- use body language and words at the same time
- respond to invitations to play, and play along with the toddler's ideas
- acknowledge frustrations and point out ways of solving problems
- suggest diversions/distractions if feelings become extreme
- identify and respond to needs for personal space, rest, and sleep
- offer meals at the table in small groups, encouraging conversation
- be in the moment as the child interacts
- notice and support play sequences involving culturally specific activities
- speak clearly and offer long pauses to encourage two-way communication
- accommodate different styles of response
- reduce stimuli if the toddler is overwhelmed

interests may change quickly, but when he finds something to explore, he may stay with it for a while. He will not appreciate stopping, so you may give a warning about when that is going to happen. The toddler continues to need support and will look to adults for assistance when he needs it. He may have a clearer idea of who he is but, because his thinking is still egocentric, he is strong-willed about what he wants. The caregiver has to handle this in ways that prevent conflict with other children. Although the toddler likes to have the approval of adults and will do things to please them, his own immediate wishes are stronger. The cues he sends are blended with some conventional language, but the caregiver will do well to read his signs. The caregiver may be able to help the toddler recognize how he feels with simple questions that he can respond to with a nod or shake of the head. Box 11.3 provides strategies for building your responsivity to toddlers at this stage.

SUPPORTIVE GUIDANCE

Helping the toddler learn to control the tide of emotions that sweeps over him is an important guidance issue. The educator's calm manner and consistent approach is helpful, but clear strategies are necessary to assist this. Labelling feelings is helpful, but it doesn't, in itself, provide control. Fortunately, the toddler wants to regulate himself, so praising his efforts should encourage further progress. There will be times when the toddler is overwhelmed with emotion and will need distraction because he cannot control

himself. In such cases, the educator's empathy is particularly important. The toddler may sometimes find it difficult to make decisions. The educator can help the toddler by narrowing down the decision to a choice between two things.

FACILITATING DEVELOPMENT

Learning to play alongside others is an important social skill. The educator should ensure that the toddler has opportunities to do this. Play experiences involving basic construction, pretend play, and lots of sensory and discovery materials are starting points for supporting both cognitive and social development. Toddlers respond well to painting and to making things, but they need to be focused on the process rather than the product. At the same time as the toddler is playing, language is being learned. The adult has responsibility for supporting and extending play with lots of encouragement and the use of clear and direct words and phrases. Even when the toddler is engrossed in a chosen activity, he will look across to the adult for a supportive response.

HOLISTIC RESPONSE

Activities 11.1 and 11.2 encourage a holistic response to toddlers at 18 to 24 months. Activity 11.1 suggests ways of engaging in the experience of toddlers at this stage and extending your interactions with them. Activity 11.2 (page 331) helps you to observe each toddler and to develop activities that are aimed at individual interests and skill levels.

Activity 11.1

Responding to the Changing Needs of Toddlers at 18 to 24 Months
Your interactions with the toddler at 18 to 24 months need to be responsive to her needs and emerging skills. To assist you in engaging in the toddler's experience, the following activity offers suggestions that may extend your interactions. Careful observation is necessary so that you introduce the idea at the right time and in the appropriate way. Each suggestion includes ways in which the idea can be extended if the toddler is ready. This activity also illustrates the safety, communication, conceptual, and developmental issues you, as a child-care professional, need to hold in mind as you respond to the toddler at 18 to 24 months.

There are many other activities that are appropriate besides the ones listed below; your skill in developing them will grow as your experience and enjoyment increase!

Activity 11.1

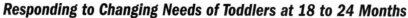

Responding to Changing Needs of Toddlers at 18 to 24 Months

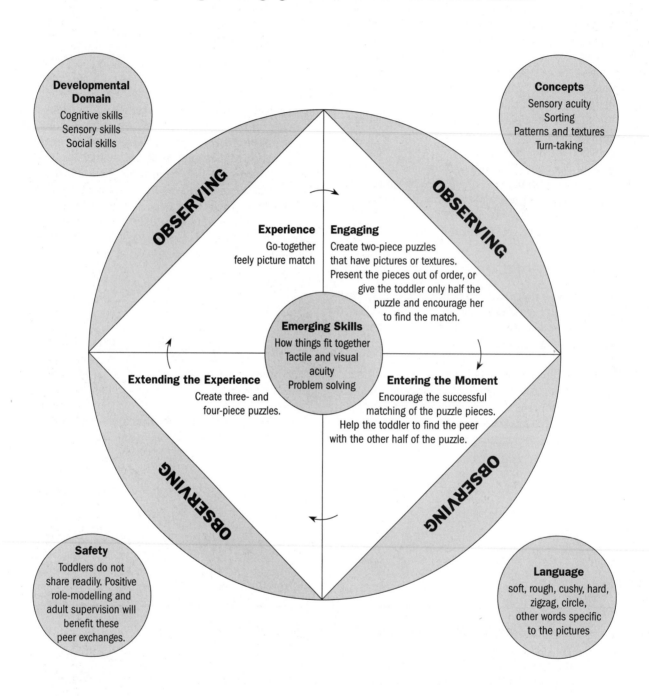

Developmental Domain
Cognitive skills
Sensory skills
Social skills

Concepts
Sensory acuity
Sorting
Patterns and textures
Turn-taking

OBSERVING

OBSERVING

Experience
Go-together
feely picture match

Engaging
Create two-piece puzzles
that have pictures or textures.
Present the pieces out of order, or
give the toddler only half the
puzzle and encourage her
to find the match.

Emerging Skills
How things fit together
Tactile and visual
acuity
Problem solving

Extending the Experience
Create three- and
four-piece puzzles.

Entering the Moment
Encourage the successful
matching of the puzzle pieces.
Help the toddler to find the peer
with the other half of the puzzle.

OBSERVING

OBSERVING

Safety
Toddlers do not
share readily. Positive
role-modelling and
adult supervision will
benefit these
peer exchanges.

Language
soft, rough, cushy, hard,
zigzag, circle,
other words specific
to the pictures

Activity 11.2

Creating Responsive Curriculum for Infants at 18 to 24 Months

Activities for toddlers at 18 to 24 months should evolve from their interests and skill levels. There cannot be a set curriculum! The adult's role is to tune in to the toddler's world and create experiences that are mutually enjoyable, that celebrate her current abilities, and that provide opportunity for continued development. The following ideas will help the adult to observe each toddler at 18 to 24 months and assist in providing some meaningful experiences.

With confidence, the adult can extend these ideas yet further.

Developmental Domain	Observation of Emerging Skills (Things You See)	Responsive Experience/Activity
Physical skills	– walking competently – early running – negotiating steps one step at a time – jumping with both feet – throwing and catching – turning the pages of a book one at a time – drawing large circles	Provide an environment that invites exploration on many levels. Sensory experiences (water play, sensory doughs, music, etc.) should be abundant in this environment. Provide indoor and outdoor environments that encourage gross motor skills. Provide materials and experiences that focus on the pincer grasp.
Cognitive skills/ communication and language	– imitating people around her – understanding new words daily – interest in sorting, shapes, size, and weight – increasing attention span and memory – beginning of pretend play	Encourage toddlers to be involved in the tasks of others (i.e., let them help you and encourage them to assist others). Provide the language that the toddler is seeking. Positively role-model the rules of language (i.e., grammar). Allow the toddler to manipulate objects (i.e., spontaneously sort and classify as they choose). Provide objects that encourage dramatic play. Provide a literature-rich environment.

Developmental Domain	Observation of Emerging Skills (Things You See)	Responsive Experience/Activity
Social/emotional skills	– aggressive behaviour (hitting, biting, pushing, etc.) – recognizing personal belongings and using the word "mine" – imitating others' behaviours and enjoying helping the adults in her life – showing interest in peers – demonstrating pro-social skills (although parallel play still predominates)	Help the toddler channel her emotions into appropriate avenues. Encourage language activities that describe feelings. Provide duplicate toys or activities with material that is easy to share (sand and water tables). Encourage social activities by providing patience and positive role-modelling. Provide personal space for the toddler within the room. Label the space so it is recognizable to the toddler. Encourage pro-social skills by providing activities that more than one toddler can play with at the same time.

Almost all toddlers will enjoy the experiences that follow. The first involves dramatic masks that may feed into the toddler's interest in dramatic play. If she is a little worried about the faces on the masks, make sure that she has plenty of time to examine a mask before playing with it. This may prompt conversation and a sharing of the emotions that it prompts. The toddlers' love of rhythmic movement and sound-making should make the maracas fun. Some toddlers will take off with them and play their own rhythms; others may take a little longer to warm up to the activity. Notice if the toddler wants to observe for a while before she joins in. If the toddlers are not yet ready to play the game as suggested, they may want to make up their own. Each of the experiences has a risk-management issue associated with it. Make sure that you offer adequate involvement so that you reduce the possibility of anyone getting hurt. Enjoy yourself as you follow the toddlers' lead.

Responding to Changing Needs

Toddlers at 18 to 24 months

EXPERIENCE 1

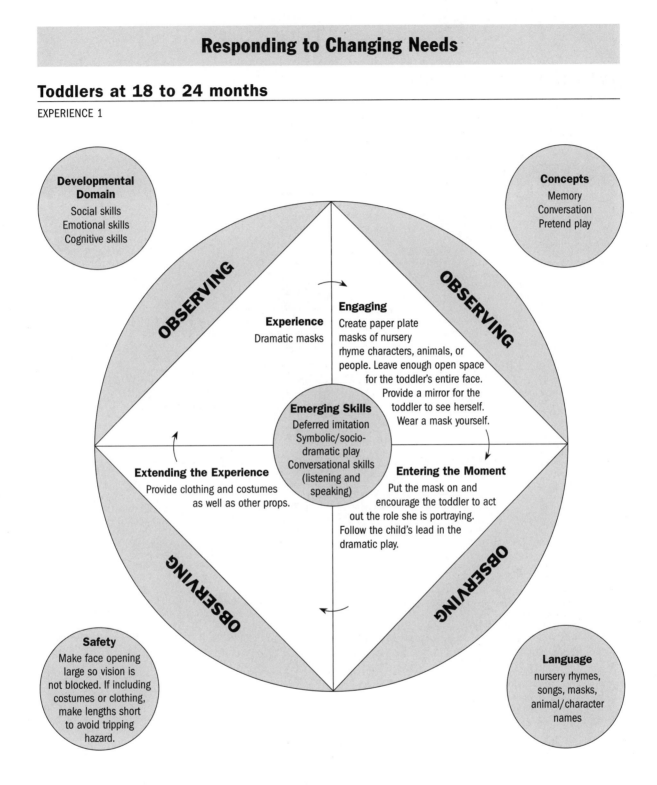

Developmental Domain
Social skills
Emotional skills
Cognitive skills

Concepts
Memory
Conversation
Pretend play

OBSERVING

OBSERVING

Experience
Dramatic masks

Engaging
Create paper plate masks of nursery rhyme characters, animals, or people. Leave enough open space for the toddler's entire face. Provide a mirror for the toddler to see herself. Wear a mask yourself.

Emerging Skills
Deferred imitation
Symbolic/socio-dramatic play
Conversational skills (listening and speaking)

Extending the Experience
Provide clothing and costumes as well as other props.

Entering the Moment
Put the mask on and encourage the toddler to act out the role she is portraying. Follow the child's lead in the dramatic play.

OBSERVING

OBSERVING

Safety
Make face opening large so vision is not blocked. If including costumes or clothing, make lengths short to avoid tripping hazard.

Language
nursery rhymes, songs, masks, animal/character names

Responding to Changing Needs

Toddlers at 18 to 24 months

EXPERIENCE 2

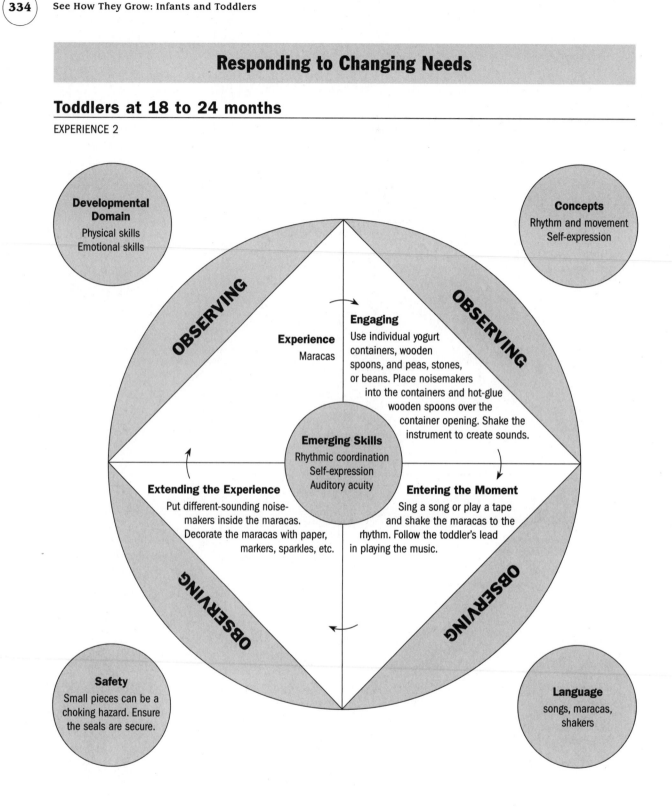

Developmental Domain
Physical skills
Emotional skills

Concepts
Rhythm and movement
Self-expression

OBSERVING

OBSERVING

Experience
Maracas

Engaging
Use individual yogurt containers, wooden spoons, and peas, stones, or beans. Place noisemakers into the containers and hot-glue wooden spoons over the container opening. Shake the instrument to create sounds.

Emerging Skills
Rhythmic coordination
Self-expression
Auditory acuity

Extending the Experience
Put different-sounding noise-makers inside the maracas. Decorate the maracas with paper, markers, sparkles, etc.

Entering the Moment
Sing a song or play a tape and shake the maracas to the rhythm. Follow the toddler's lead in playing the music.

OBSERVING

OBSERVING

Safety
Small pieces can be a choking hazard. Ensure the seals are secure.

Language
songs, maracas, shakers

Responding to Changing Needs

Toddlers at 18 to 24 months

EXPERIENCE 3

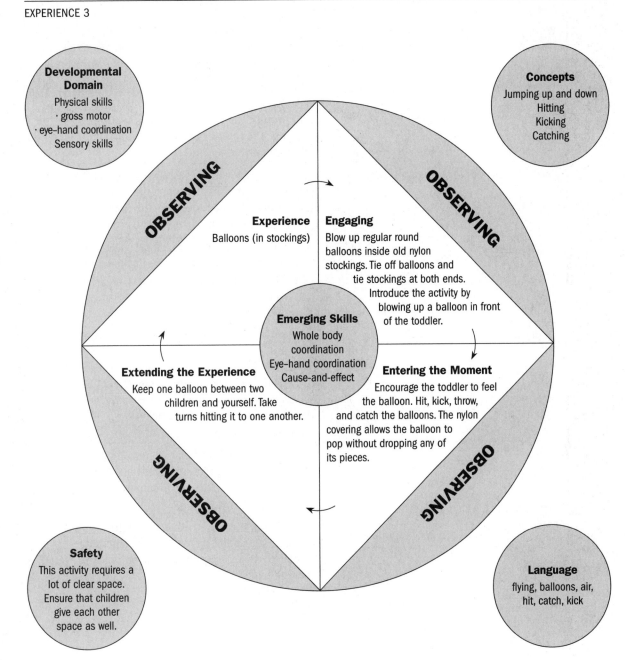

Developmental Domain

Physical skills
· gross motor
· eye–hand coordination
Sensory skills

Concepts

Jumping up and down
Hitting
Kicking
Catching

OBSERVING

OBSERVING

Experience

Balloons (in stockings)

Engaging

Blow up regular round balloons inside old nylon stockings. Tie off balloons and tie stockings at both ends. Introduce the activity by blowing up a balloon in front of the toddler.

Emerging Skills

Whole body coordination
Eye–hand coordination
Cause-and-effect

Extending the Experience

Keep one balloon between two children and yourself. Take turns hitting it to one another.

Entering the Moment

Encourage the toddler to feel the balloon. Hit, kick, throw, and catch the balloons. The nylon covering allows the balloon to pop without dropping any of its pieces.

OBSERVING

OBSERVING

Safety

This activity requires a lot of clear space. Ensure that children give each other space as well.

Language

flying, balloons, air, hit, catch, kick

Further Experiences and Interactions

Further Experiences	Interactions
Who's behind the blanket?	Ask one toddler to stand behind a blanket. Ask the other toddlers to identify who is missing from the group.
"Stop me from seeing . . ."	Encourage the toddler to explain what we see, hear, or taste with. Ask the toddler how she would stop you from seeing, hearing, or tasting. Encourage her to cover your mouth, eyes, or ears as a result.
Cooked spaghetti and glue sculptures	Encourage the toddlers to play, mould, and manoeuvre the spaghetti and glue on a sheet of waxed paper. Allow glue to dry overnight. Peel waxed paper off the creation.
Feely bags	Place Jello, shaving cream, whipped cream, mashed potatoes, oatmeal, etc., in separate Ziploc bags (using two bags is recommended for each sensory item). Encourage children to sculpt and squish.
Smelly cans	Use single-serving Pringles cans filled with different-smelling items (coffee, cinnamon, peanut butter, licorice, etc.). Tape or glue down lids and poke holes for smelling. A sheet of wax paper may be necessary between the can and lid to help stop spilling.
Picture books	Use family pictures or magazines or catalogues to create a picture book. Use photo albums or plastic sheets so the book can be changed.
Salad spinner art	Put a paper plate on the bottom of the spinner; place different-coloured paints on the plate. Cover the spinner, and spin. Spiral art is created.

Further Experiences	Interactions
Tightrope-walking	Tape a line of thick masking tape to the floor. Encourage the toddler to walk on the "tightrope" in different ways.
Pulling wagons or sleds	Encourage toddlers to pull plush animals or peers in wagons or sleds.
Eyedroppers and tongs	Use eyedroppers in water tables and tongs for other objects. Encourage the toddler to use the instruments.
Bubble Wrap and MACtac	Tape Bubble Wrap and/or clear MACtac (sticky side up) to the floor. Encourage the toddlers to walk, jump, stomp, and move over the different textures.
Read realistic storybooks	Read picture book stories to the toddler. Hold the toddler in your lap. The plot of the story should have relevance to the everyday life of the toddler.
Who is speaking?	Tape-record voices (of the toddlers, parents, teachers, or popular TV characters). Play the tape and encourage to toddler to guess who is speaking.
Matching shadow puzzles	Trace objects that are easily identified (toys with definite shapes). Show the "shadows" to the toddlers and encourage them to find the item that matches in the room.
The shell game	While the toddler is watching, place a small ball under one of three cups. Move the cups' positions a few times. Encourage the toddler to guess which cup the ball is under.
Colouring to music	Tape a large piece of butcher-block paper to the floor, wall, or fence. Play music of various kinds. Encourage the toddler to draw or paint to the music.

Responsive Guidance for Toddlers Aged 18 to 24 Months

Age/Stage: 18 to 24 Months

Situation	Response
• Don is fine when he is playing alone, but he often hits and pushes his peers if they get too close to his play activity. • Matthew has begun hitting his parents and caregivers when he doesn't get his own way. • Keith has started pulling the other children's hair. • Shirley grabs toys away from other children even if she wasn't playing with them before.	**Developmental Issue: Aggressive Behaviour** Toddlers still have very limited language skills and therefore don't always or often have the ability to describe their feelings. Any language they do have may not adequately describe the breadth of their emotions. Adult intervention is necessary to maintain a safe environment; however, a toddler can be guided appropriately if the caregiver has a clear understanding of the intent of the behaviour. The toddler does not wish to hurt others, but merely wants to express emotional desire. Positive role-modelling, providing words that fit the toddler's emotions, encouraging the language of feelings, and patience go a long way in helping the toddler navigate this developmental stage. Remember to provide a consistent environment that does not accept the child's aggression when it occurs.
• David will not lay down on his cot when we come in for nap time. • Marcia avoids putting her toys away during cleanup. She seems to have selective listening when it comes to tidy-up time. • Alex becomes restless after she is dressed for outside time. She begins pinching and hitting the other children who are getting ready. • Reyka fusses and fights her caregivers when they take her to have her diaper changed.	**Developmental Issue: Transition Times** Transition times pose some difficulty for many toddlers. With their increased memory and attention span, they are more tuned in to their activities, and sometimes it is difficult for them to change direction merely because the clock on the wall says it is time to do something else. A responsive environment will provide warning cues to the toddler before the routine changes (i.e., "We are going to go outside soon," "Let's read a story before nap time," etc.). Transition songs sometimes help the toddler regulate their own behaviour (i.e., "This is the way we pick up our toys, dress for outside," etc.). Toddlers should not be expected to wait for long periods of time with nothing to do during transition times. Provide transition activities (songs, etc.) to keep them engaged while they wait.

Manufactured Toys and Play Materials for Toddlers Aged 18 to 24 Months

Toy/Material	Uses	Group Care	Home
Large wooden blocks	Stacking, laying beside each other, knocking down, and carrying are all emerging construction skills.	√	√
Toy animals	Symbolic and pretend play is emerging at this time.	√	√
Climber	Emerging gross motor skills and body coordination are challenged here.	√	√
Large balls	Rolling, bouncing, catching, throwing, kicking, and other uses.	√	√
Dress-up hats	Pretend play is supported by these fun and easy accessories.	√	√
Child-sized soft furniture	Allows toddlers to feel comfortable at their own level.	√	√
Dolls of different cultures or ethnicities	Imitative play, sense of self, and empathy can be fostered by these dolls.	√	√
Bags	Excellent equipment for carrying special treasures.	√	√
Aquarium or pets (i.e., rabbit)	Empathy, problem-solving, and pro-social skills are engaged as toddlers care for the fish and other pets.	√	√
Doll carriage	Wheeled toys support gross motor skills. Imitative behaviours are developed as the toddler acts out adult behaviours.	√	√
Two- to six-piece puzzles	Encourage problem-solving, shape discrimination, and manipulation.	√	√
Large-sized cars and trucks	Gross motor skills, pushing and pulling, and pretend play are developed.	√	√

Toy/Material	Uses	Group Care	Home
Tray puzzles	Visual and shape discrimination, fine motor skills, and cause-and-effect are enhanced.	√	√
Stacking toys	Visual discrimination, fine motor skills, and problem-solving skills are encouraged.	√	√
Shape-sorters	Eye–hand coordination, understanding how things fit together, and shape discrimination emerge.	√	√
Ride-on toys	Gross motor skills and balance are encouraged and supported by this fun experience.	√	√
Small climber	Gross motor skills can be encouraged in the indoor environment as well as outside.		
Finger puppets	Stories, nursery rhymes, and songs or finger plays can be enhanced with these characters.	√	√
Bath toys and water wheels	Cause-and-effect, problem-solving, and emotional skills are supported in this soothing experience.	√	√
Sand-pit pails and scoops	Fine motor skills, measurement, and other math concepts emerge in this great experience.	√	√
Foam blocks	Easily manipulated and carried. If these blocks get wet, they stick to each other and bathtub sides.	√	√

▶ Summary

The stage of 18 to 24 months marks significant changes in all aspects of the toddler's development. There is clear evidence that every advance within each developmental domain is paralleled by advances in all the other domains.

The physical size and mobility of the toddler shows marked changes, as she is able to run, climb, and demonstrate a variety of gross motor and fine motor skill advancements.

Her sensory acuity is near that of an adult, but her limited experience and sensory-motor thinking limits the processing of her perceptions. At this stage, the toddler wants to discover materials and see what they can do. She performs actions upon everything she can handle to determine the properties of the materials and objects. The toddler cannot recognize the potential hazards of a situation and cannot predict outcomes of her actions. Because her grasp is more refined, she is able to manipulate objects and carefully handle small items, demonstrating her hand–eye coordination.

The toddler's play behaviours are increasingly complex and we see examples of imitative, pretend, role-playing, symbolic play, construction, and a variety of other solitary activities, along with some social interaction linked with parallel and even associative play. The play sequences tend to be longer and she enjoys adults playing with her; any social interactions are usually desirable. As she is in the latter stages of sensory-motor behaviour, we tend to observe characteristics of this stage of thinking in her play. These include imitation, deferred imitation, some shift away from egocentric thought, and more complex ways of solving problems. The toddler has intense curiosity that leads her to learn; identifying her interests is very important. Of course, every child is different in style and temperament, so we need to respond to each toddler differently. One way of looking at personality differences is to look at traits that are demonstrated fairly consistently.

Having established strong attachments to adults, and continuing make them with new people in her life, she usually demonstrates emotional security. That said, the toddler is striving for autonomy and we can see her trying to be independent in many different ways. She wants to do things for herself, so she helps with domestic tasks and with personal self-help activities, such as dressing and toileting. The toddler needs adults to be responsive to her changing needs. A variety of ways of doing this are supported in recent brain research.

Contrasting with the independence is the toddler's fear of being shamed. She has some idea of what is socially acceptable behaviour and tries to regulate her own feelings and actions, but she is not always successful. Temper tantrums are fairly common at this stage, but even when they are not demonstrated, many toddlers show ways of venting their frustrations. There are numerous positive guidance strategies that can help the toddler to manage her behaviour—overall, it is best to remain calm and to understand the developmental root of the behaviour.

The toddler's communication skills often include single-word, two-word, and even three-word phrases. She tends to use actions as well as sounds to indicate meaning. Learning a signing technique may advance the toddler's communication skills even at the pre-language stage. The ability to use language with some forms of grammar indicates that the toddler's brain has been wired for language. Her brain development continues; the actual size of her brain has doubled since birth. The activity of her brain is enhanced by positive experiences. Some negative experiences may not have long-term effects because there is some resiliency, but this should not be taken for granted. The adult's responsibility is to make the toddler's experiences as positive as possible. Brain research points to the necessity for supporting emotional development as a first concern. Other domains of development can be developed successfully only if the toddler is emotionally secure.

▶ KEY TERMS

acuity
American Sign Language (ASL)
anal phase
assistive devices
associative play
axons
comfort object
construction play
curriculum
decentration
decontextualization
deferred imitation
dendric
early intervention programs
egocentric thought
empathy
extrinsic motivation
facilitator

factor analysis
glial (cells)
grammar
hand–eye coordination
imitation
instinctual drives
integration
intrinsic motivation
locus of control
make-believe play
mental combinations
myelination
nature
nurture
orthopedic disabilities
parallel play
pincer grasp
plasticity
positive guidance strategies
positivism
pretend play
professional boundaries
psychoanalytic school
responsive care
risk management
rituals
rouge-and-mirror test
self-regulation
sign language
signing
social emotions
social learning
social referencing
socio-dramatic play
solitary play
temper tantrums
toilet-learning
traits
trundle
universal grammar
ways of knowing

▶ DISCUSSION QUESTIONS

1. Identify all the examples of symbolism that you can infer from a toddler's behaviour.
2. Compare the trait model of personality with any other model of personality or temperament.
3. What songs and rhymes might you sing with toddlers?

4. How does the rouge-and-mirror test indicate the concept of self?
5. What use are growth charts?

▶ ADDITIONAL RESOURCES

▶ Further Reading

Bailey, D.B., and M. Wolery. (1992). *Teaching Infants and Preschoolers with Disabilities.* 2nd ed. Englewood Cliffs, NJ: Merrill.

Goldberg, S. (1997). *Parent Involvement Begins at Birth: Collaboration between Parents and Teachers of Children in the Early Years.* Needham Heights, MA: Allyn & Bacon.

Greenberg, P. (1991). *Character Development: Encouraging Self-Esteem and Self-Discipline in Infants, Toddlers, and Two-Year-Olds.* Washington, DC: NAEYC.

Greenman, J., and A. Stonehouse. (1997). *Prime Times: A Handbook for Excellence in Infant and Toddler Care.* South Melbourne: Longman.

Heidemann, S., and D. Hewitt. (1992). *Pathways to Play: Developing Play Skills in Young Children.* St. Paul, MN: Redleaf Press.

Hodges, S. (1998). *Toddler Art: 18 Months–3 Years.* Torrance, CA: Totline.

Lally, J., et al. (1995). *Caring for Infants & Toddlers in Groups: Developmentally Appropriate Practice.* Washington, DC: Zero to Three.

Pruett, K. (1999). *Me, Myself and I: How Children Build Their Sense of Self.* New York, NY: Goddard Press.

Raver, S.A. (1991). *Strategies for Teaching At-risk and Handicapped Infants and Toddlers: A Transdisciplinary Approach.* Englewood Cliffs, NJ: Merrill.

Silberg, J. (1996). *More Games to Play with Toddlers.* Beltsville, MD: Gryphon House.

Stonehouse, A. (ed.). (1990). *Trusting Toddlers.* St. Paul, MN: Toys 'n' Things Press.

▶ Useful Videos

NAEYC videos

Ready for Life.

Description: This documentary follows the lives of six children and their families. It illustrates how children develop the strength and confidence to face life's challenges in emotionally healthy ways. Showing diverse family structures, the video is narrated by Ruby Dee and features the expert advice of Dr. Bruce Perry.

Dramatic Play: More Than Playing House: How Caring Relationships Support Self-Regulation, by Marie Goulet
Description: Children acquire self-regulatory skills through interaction with caregivers. The video and 50-page video guide explore child development, including what we know from brain research, in relation to self-regulation. Wonderful footage in care settings illustrates caregiver practices that support self-regulation at different ages.

Say It With Sign (Tape 1), by L. & S. Solow
Introduction to Sign Language: Signs You Already Know. Higher Learning Systems, Fairfield, CT 06430

▶ Useful Web Sites

Language and communication
www.hanen.org/Hanen2002/frames.htm
www.literacytrust.org.uk/Research/
 earlylanguage.html
www.highscope.org/NewsNotes/PositionPapers/
 infanttoddler.htm

American Sign Language
www.lessontutor.com/ees_asl_flashcards.html

Children with disabilities/early intervention
www.centreforability.bc.ca/bccaa/children/
 eipfaq.html
www.handsandvoices.org/resource_guide/
 18_videos.html

www.therapeuticresources.com/94-9toc.html
 psych.hanover.edu/vygotsky/iturondo.html

Play
www.cayc.ca/PlayPhilosophy.html
www.nncc.org/Child.Dev/intel.dev.todd.html
www.canadian-health-network.ca/html/
 newnotable/jul1a_2002e.html
www.cfc-efc.ca/docs/cccf/00000988.htm

Brain research
ericeece.org/pubs/reslist/braindev00.pdf
www.zerotothree.org/brainwonders/index.html
www.naeyc.org/resources/eyly/1999/13.htm

Emotional development
daycare.about.com/library/weekly/
 aa010800a.htm
eqi.org/emotions.htm
www.science.mcmaster.ca/Psychology/
 2aa3esum/Emotion.PDF

Parents of toddlers
www.babycentre.co.uk/general/539903
www.todaysparent.com/toddler/
 article.jsp?cId=6561
www.essentialbaby.com.au/Pinky/
 Pinky200205.cfm
www.search-institute.org/assets/toddlers.html

Guiding behaviour
www.hlth.gov.bc.ca/ccf/child/publicat/
 comm/com015.pdf
www.cfc-efc.ca/docs/cccf/00009_en.htm

CHAPTER 12

Here and Now: Toddlers from 2 to 3 Years of Age

Two-year-olds can be enormous fun. Their curiosity and energy is boundless.

Learning Outcomes

After reading and studying this chapter, you should be able to:

- identify the observable characteristics of toddlers from 2 to 3 years of age
- explain the significance of the behaviours of toddlers in their third year in a developmental context
- recognize and respond to the developmental diversity of 2-to-3-year-old toddlers and discuss issues pertinent to this stage of development
- assess the development of young children between 2 and 3 years of age
- respond to the 2-to 3-year-old child's health, safety, and development with appropriate protection, guidance, and caregiving
- develop strategies to work with parents as partners in the care and education of their 2-year-olds

Scene: The toddler room teachers at an infant and toddler child-care centre hold an evening meeting with a small group of tired parents.

"You can have a conversation with a 2-year-old," said one mother. "But such a lot of what Josh says I don't understand. And when I can make out what he's saying, I'm hearing him say 'no' and 'won't.' This feels so negative."

"I have some of the same difficulties," responded another mother, "particularly the 'no' part. I find that Adrienne wants to do everything herself and talks to herself as she does it. I feel as though Adrienne sees me as the biggest challenge in her life. I ask her to do something and she says 'no'; everything seems like a battle."

"Is it any help to hear that most 2-year-olds are like that?" asked the educator. The educator smiled sympathetically. "It can be a really demanding time when toddlers are at this stage. I try to deal with this by thinking of why the toddler is behaving this way, but it can be physically draining to keep up with the toddler and these behaviours can make you feel horrible." Several parents nodded in agreement. Adrienne's mom asked the educator what they did at the centre when a toddler was appearing to be so negative.

"We try to see the 'no' part, the refusal to do things and the wanting to do everything by themselves, as an important developmental stage. But it's hard to keep that in mind when you have to manage the situation. I think it comes down to the fact that now they are able to do some things for themselves, they like to feel independent. They have changed a lot in a short time; now they can show us just how independent they can be!"

Adrienne's mom seemed a little uncomfortable, but said that she was bothered by her daughter's attitude and negative behaviour when she picked her up from child care. While offering reassurance, the educator proposed a strategy to try to help matters. "You have such a challenging time because she is striving for independence and this means conflict with the people closest to her. I also think that you get a hard time when you collect her because she is tired. Adrienne, like the others her age, is so active that she gets cranky by early evening even when she's had a nap. Would it be a good idea if we made snack time a bit later in the afternoon, so she's not going home hungry, too?"

Mom didn't reply immediately, then said, "I feel silly, but Adrienne can ruin the evening. When I need to come home from work and have a few minutes of quiet, I feel that she assaults me with 'I want dinner' and 'No, not macaroni,' and so on. Yes, it might be an idea to give a later snack. Or perhaps I could bring her a snack in the car to keep her going."

Josh's mom had another idea: "I can imagine how you feel, I get tired, too! But, you know, it wouldn't be a bad idea if you collected Adrienne just a few minutes later, after you've had time for a drink and put your feet up. Having a few minutes to yourself might help." Adrienne's mother looked relieved, and responded, "Let's try those two ideas."

A parents' night at a day care can provide an excellent opportunity for parents to discuss their fears, problems, and frustration with early childhood educators. This meeting wasn't ideal—everyone was tired—but real issues were addressed. The educator should listen, empathize and respond with sensitivity. If possible, make practical suggestions that alleviate problems.

Box 12.1 (page 346) provides another example of an exchange between a parent and educator. The educator listens to the mother's concerns, reassures her that the situation is normal, suggests a strategy for dealing with the problem, and listens as the mother expresses her reservations. Listening skills, a knowledge of child development, and a sense of humour all contribute to the success of the exchange.

▶ What to Look For

The age range discussed in this chapter is broader than those in earlier parts of this book because the rate of change slows somewhat in the third year of life. Consolidation of development is apparent, skills are refined, conceptual understanding is gained through lots of hands-on learning, the notion of self becomes categorized, language becomes more complex, and the 2-year-old maintains a keen interest in everything around him.

PHYSICAL DEVELOPMENT

Growth

The growth rate is never again going to be as rapid as in the first two years, but the toddler continues to make gains in height and weight. At 24 months, the toddler's height might be 81–92 cm (32–36 inches) and at 36 months 90–100 cm (35–40 inches). Weight typically increases, so that at 24 months toddlers weigh 10–15 kg (22–33 pounds) and at 36 months

---

BOX 12.1

COMMUNICATING BOUNDARIES

Josh's mom told the early childhood educator that her challenge centred on how Josh constantly said no to her but was entirely agreeable with this father. "He can't wait to get home to see Dad. Dad does everything right! He wants to do everything like Dad. The good bit is that he wants to be with Dad on Saturdays when he does small contracting jobs. We got him some play tools, and he loves them. But is he learning that women stay home to do housework while men go out to work? He thinks that everything 'male' is superior and says no to domestic jobs."

"This is a tricky situation," agreed the educator. "It sounds as though you are worried about some sex role stereotyping, learning that boys do 'good,' interesting jobs and girls do boring home jobs. If that is what he's seeing, that is probably what he's taking in. But remember, Josh is at a stage when he's identifying with his father because he sees himself as male. This is healthy, but it's an emphasis that will probably not continue with such intensity for very long. You might have reinforced this by buying him his own tool set, but I would probably have done the same! Maybe there is a way of making traditionally female roles just as interesting to him. How about encouraging your partner to have a boy's night at home when Josh and his dad do the cooking and clearing up?"

Josh's mom replied, "That won't be easy, but it's an idea. Won't that make it look as though home jobs are done by males only on special nights?"

"You might be right," said the educator.

"Still, it might be too much to expect more," sighed Josh's mother. "I suppose I really want my husband to take on more home jobs."

"Well, that I can't help you with!" said the educator, as the two women laughed.

12–17.3 kg (27–38 pounds), although the average is 14 kg (31 pounds) (National Center for Health Statistics, 1982). As children mature, the range of height and weight becomes greater. As a rough guide, weight at 2 years of age is approximately four times that at birth (Allen and Marotz, 1994) and height is about twice that at birth. Boys continue to be larger than girls (Mott, James, and Sperhac, 1990).

The child's proportions continue to alter, with a more elongated body that is larger in proportion to the head. The toddler will continue to have a protruding tummy because the abdominal muscles have not yet developed fully. The toddler will likely have his first full set of teeth—twenty deciduous or milk teeth.

Internal changes to the bones and muscle continue. The child's bones are less malleable because they have hardened by **calcifying** and **ossifying**. Muscles are increasingly defined, but this is not really apparent through casual observation.

Breathing occurs through the mouth and nose and is a little slower than in the previous months. Body temperature can fluctuate in accordance with activity level and emotion, but the body is better at regulating itself than it was in infancy. Sexual development remains in a plateau that lasts for some years, until later hormonal changes (Tanner, 1990). The **lymphatic system**, which provides the child with the ability to fight infection, is in a stage of fairly rapid growth (Berk, 1996).

Brain Maturation

The process of **brain maturation** is important for all learning as well as all types of physical, perceptual, social, and emotional competence (Nash, 1997). The 2-year-old toddler's brain is approximately 70 to 80 percent of its adult size (Allen and Marotz, 1994; Tanner, 1990). Within the brain, the process of growth continues.

Each **neuron**—brain cell—contains an **axon**, a cell body, and numerous **dendrites**. It's the task of each neuron's axon to hook up with dendrites from other neurons, creating a **synapse**—that is, a connection. Learning involves making these synaptic connections; but they will occur only as a result of the biological existence of the neurons and the experience to which the child is exposed. We can describe this as nature and nurture working together.

It may seem overly technical to examine the complex actions within the young child's brain, but some extraordinary growth is occurring.

By the age of two, the number of synapses reaches adult levels: by age three, a child's brain has 1,000 trillion synapses—about twice as many as her pediatrician's. This number holds steady throughout the first decade of the child's life. In this way a young child's brain becomes super dense. (Shore, 1997, p. 19)

All this brain activity leads us to understand that the young child's brain is "biologically primed for learning" (Shore, 1997). Educators may not need to know how the complex brain develops, but they do need to appreciate that there are significant consequences of this growth in terms of the child's learning potential—and their role in maximizing this potential.

Another important part of brain activity concerns **myelin**—the layer that forms around nerves and is found at low levels in the brain. The myelin sheath around nerves speeds the transmission of impulses through the nerve cells. The process of myelination accounts for the young child's increasing motor skills and generally improved bodily control. This is a result of the increasing efficiency of message transfers to and from the brain (Berk, 1996).

The part of the brain called the **cerebellum**, which aids in balance and control, is in an important stage of development that peaks at 4 years of age (Tanner, 1990). You can see evidence of this growth as the toddler gains motor control and ability to balance and manoeuvre around things.

Developments in the brain affect the child's level of alertness. You may notice that the toddler's concentration now can be relatively long, depending upon his interest in an activity. The **corpus callosum** has the largest bundle of nerve fibres and connects the brain's two hemisphere (sides) and enables the child to perform more complex tasks. The 24-to-36-month-old toddler is usually at a stage of thinking that increasingly involves problem-solving behaviours. Right-handedness or left-handedness is determined by the child's dominant cerebral hemisphere. Children develop hand preference by 2 or 3 years of age (Berk, 1996; Ramsey, 1980). It is inappropriate to force a child to be right-handed. Although many 2-year-olds are **ambidextrous**—that is, able to use both hands equally well—they should be allowed to play and use implements with the hand of their choice (Fogel, 1997).

Neurons, the nerve cells in the brain, have undergone an explosion of new connections. The axons that send signals and the dendrites that receive signals have made these connections as a result of all the child's sensory experiences. If those experiences hadn't occurred, the brain's potential would have been limited. The profusion of advances in brain science should drive educators to consider the quality of the programs that they offer young children. We now know that the early years of a child's life are windows of opportunity that, if not utilized, will severely limit the child's potential. After brain functions have atrophied from lack of use, they cannot be regenerated with much success.

Gross Motor Skills

The 2-year-old will run, walk, jump, squat, and climb (Furuno, 1993). From the time of her second birthday, she will increase her skills so that she can run faster and with more manoeuvrability, walk forward with less knocking into things, walk backward, jump down from stairs or other heights with better control, jump higher in the air, walk upstairs and downstairs taking one step at a time, squat for periods of time, and climb up onto chairs, climbers, and any other available structure. With her improved sense of balance, she may be able to walk for a few steps on a beam. Through all these actions, the child gradually extends her competence and increases her confidence (Allen and Marotz, 1994; Fogel, 1997).

Interest in music and movement may lead the 2-year-old to dance. Some dance trainers like to work with toddlers and young children, but many child development experts think that the child is too young and needs to explore her own body and its capabilities without direction. Her response to music allows the 2-year-old to move with rhythm, moving parts of her body while staying in one spot, or moving around the floor. Arm and leg movements are not usually coordinated. Later in the year, the child will probably have better physical control and might learn to move her arms and legs simultaneously.

Kicking a ball can pose some difficulties for the 2-year-old, but soon she will be able to coordinate her actions so that she doesn't have to run, stop, and then kick, but can flow from the run into the kick. Catching a large ball requires concentration for the 2-year-old as she extends her arms. Coordinating the body and judging speed and direction are the challenges that face the child in her third year. By 3 years of age, the child may manage both kicking and catching with greater ease and alignment.

Pedalling a tricycle or mobility toy may be difficult. The 2-year-old may propel herself forward using **trundling**—using alternate feet to push forward—rather than pedalling. Some 2-year-olds find that the pedals of some tricycles are hard to use because they are positioned in front of the body rather than underneath, where the child can push down using her weight to pedal successfully. By 3 years old, children who have had experience with pedal vehicles can usually operate them.

Fine Motor Skills

Fine motor control is further refined in the third year of life. The 2-year-old can hold things using one hand in a careful **pincer grasp**, reach, grasp, manipulate a crayon or paintbrush, and operate a computer mouse. She will often attempt to dress and undress, putting her arms into sleeves, legs into pants, and feet into shoes. You may see the child using zippers and Velcro, and trying to use buttons (Furuno et al., 1993b). She may increasingly like copying basic shapes onto paper, but the drawings reflect motor skills rather than thoughts and emotions (Freeman, 1980). Opening doors using handles, turning book pages, constructing simple objects, gluing items onto paper, and knocking down and rebuilding towers of blocks are other fine motor accomplishments of the third year. Putting together puzzles of increasing complexity is an enjoyable pastime and a chance to increase manual dexterity (Fogel, 1997). Playing with

Many skills that started to emerge over the past few months are now being refined. With the help of her grandfather, this toddler follows the pictures in a new book and turns the pages carefully.

a variety of sensory materials such as dough, clay, and water gives the child the opportunity to develop the skills required for those materials, such as pouring, rolling, stamping, pressing, and squeezing. Matching-and-sorting activities, appropriate in the third year, also refine fine motor control. In particular, the child likes to scribble and draw on paper or with chalks. As yet, her actions generally follow her body movement, but some marks she makes are considered.

Eating is a little less messy than at earlier stages, but the 2-year-old may have difficulty using a spoon or fork. By 3, the child can usually manage a child-sized knife, fork, spoon, chopsticks, or whatever implement is familiar. Still, accuracy is likely to be imperfect, and the child may prefer to eat with her fingers.

COGNITIVE DEVELOPMENT

From Sensory-Motor to Pre-operational Thinking

There is a gradual, rather than abrupt, change in the 2-year-old's thinking. According to Piaget's model of development, she is moving from the sensory-motor stage to the **pre-operational stage**, in which the child uses greater symbolism and mental representation.

The **preconceptual thinking** of the 2-year-old—according to the Piagetian model—occurs because the child is not yet able to classify objects in a consistent way. (See the Appendix for a chart of Piaget's developmental stages.) This semi-logical thinking suggests that the child's understanding of concepts is only beginning to emerge. However, the 2-to-3-year-old child makes many attempts at ordering her world in ways that may be particular to her individual way of thinking, even though they may not conform to adult views of conceptualization. Therefore, the child does, during this stage, show some signs of concept-building, even if these concepts are more fluid than they will be in later months and years. Piaget tended to focus on what a child cannot yet accomplish, but there are other ways of viewing what she can do and how she does think. The emerging ability to make connections between ideas is particularly important, and her ability to understand some number concepts is also evident. Neo-Piagetians emphasize these abilities rather than focus on supposed deficits.

The cognitive advances can be seen in several ways. The child's language is not rooted only in the moment: she can speak about what she remembers and what she wants. **Deferred imitation** is increasingly evident in play, demonstrating that children can internalize what they see and act it out later. Sociodramatic play generally appears at about 2 years, showing how the child's **mental representations** have become increasingly complex. This kind of play reinforces several different kinds of mental functioning, including memory, language, reasoning, imagination, problem-solving, and creativity (Dias and Harris, 1990).

Although educators often look to Piaget for the most significant explanation of children's process of cognition, many child development experts (Berk 1996; Flavell, 1985; Sodian et al., 1991) think that his views underestimated some cognitive activity of young children, particularly in the areas of **egocentricity, symbolism**, and **logic**. Although Piaget tended to emphasize what the child could *not* do, rather than what she could do (Berk, 1996), we can learn from his model of cognition and apply it to what we see children doing.

You might want to look for some of the characteristics of the pre-operational stage by looking at the things children say, the things they do, and the mistakes they make. You will notice that the child's thinking remains mostly from her own perspective. This egocentricity may not allow her to know how another child thinks or feels. You may see her respond to a child in distress with some **empathy** or be able to take turns with an adult's help, but you are unlikely to see **cooperative activity**.

Because a child at this stage thinks **transductively**—that is, from event to event—she may have inaccurate understandings of cause and effect. For example, she may think that having fish sticks for lunch means the music man is coming, because he came last time they had fish sticks. This is a type of semi-logical reasoning that shows the child's ability to make associations, even though they may be incorrect.

Her inability to think through a series of actions means that a toddler cannot reverse her thought process. She may, for example, be confused about the route when returning from a walk to the park, even if the same route was taken on the way to the destination. This could also be a memory problem or a difficulty with perspective—things look different when you turn around and see them from another angle. Because she focuses on only one aspect of something, she can neglect important details when listening to a story or telling someone what happened. Her thinking is bound by perception. She makes judgments on the basis of what she sees in her immediate world.

At this stage a child may attribute personal qualities to objects. She might, for example, talk to objects and expect that they understand. This is most noticeable when she talks to her stuffed toys or dolls. Of course, we see older children doing this, too, but they know it is only pretend.

Lastly, the toddler is unlikely to be capable of **conserving** ideas. A lack of conservation means that she does not appreciate that something may have changed its form or appearance but stayed the same in number, quantity, length.

The young child tends to focus on what she sees. For example, she may be fooled into thinking that there are fewer vegetables on a plate because they are all heaped together, or she might think there is more juice in her cup because the level is higher than it is in another child's cup that is wider. Similarly, the young child may think that she hasn't been given the same amount of Play-Doh because hers takes on a different shape—even if she sees the shape being transformed. The child may not understand that quantity remains the same—is constant—even when transformed in how it looks. Similarly, the child may not hold in mind—or conserve—one category as she sorts out several different objects. When sorting a mixture of peas and beans she is likely to forget which type she has been separating a little time into her task.

These apparent problems seem to be of little importance to the child at this stage; as long as she gets whatever quantity she thinks is more or best! Because she does not hold in mind that weight, number, and so forth remain constant, she is more interested in how things appear. The ideas of **constancy** and **conservation** are important indicators of the child's stage of thinking. Although there are some reasons why this first phase of the pre-operational stage is called preconceptual rather than conceptual, we will consider these attempts to organize her thinking to be early concepts. Even though the child's thinking is likely to be incomplete and often inaccurate, her increasing ability to differentiate, categorize, organize, and try to understand the world provides us with ample evidence of early conceptual understandings.

Partial Conceptual Understanding

You will see evidence of several new cognitive skills as a young child progresses through her third year. She is developing **concepts**, in her early conceptual understanding.

You may see her developing **temporal concepts**, or concepts about time. She may understand the use of terms such as "before," "after," or "wait a minute," and expect that things will happen in a particular sequence. The toddler's spatial concept might be revealed in her use of space when playing or her use of words such as "near" and "far" or "up" and "down." The concept of speed is harder to observe, but you might see the child estimating how fast another child is going on a tricycle as she moves across its path, or she may talk about a car "going fast." Colour concepts are relatively easy to observe. The first stage involves colour differentiation and identification. At this stage children mix and match colours to see what the result will be.

The concept of number may be evident at this stage in the child's use of words such as "lots" or "hundreds," which may be used as a broad descriptor rather than as an actual number. Songs may help the child learn counting sequences—for example, "one two three four five / Once I caught a fish alive"—but they do not contribute to a real number concept. A toddler may count in sequence but not understand the correspondence between the spoken numbers and the number of objects in front of her. She may understand the difference between number shapes (what the number "1" looks like) and even recognize these by 3 years of age. True number concepts come from handling materials; experiencing quantities, and having an adult supply relevant language to assist understanding.

Many other conceptual advances can be observed in 2-to-3-year-olds. Listen to what they are talking about. They may use language that they don't understand, but this misuse and the way that children play with materials can give us insight into their conceptual thinking. Their understanding of the properties of materials parallels their experience of them, so observe carefully during these play times. You will notice some understanding of textures, temperatures, how things pour, and so on.

The way the adult can assist in the child's learning involves a number of different strategies, each dependent upon the type of play and learning as well as the child herself. Lev Vygotsky offers a useful model in what he called the **zone of proximal development (ZPD)**. Laura Berk and Adam Winsler, who have interpreted Vygotsky's work, describe the ZPD as:

> the hypothetical, dynamic region in which learning and development take place. It is defined by the distance between what a child can accomplish during independent problem solving and what he or she can accomplish with the help of the adult or more competent member of the culture. (1995, p. 5).

Some of the elements of the adult's role as they provide the backdrop for scaffolding—the support system for learning:

- engaging in collaborative activity
- creating a shared understanding about the task or activity

- providing the appropriate emotional tone for learning
- helping the child stay focused on the task
- promoting self-regulation
- relinquishing adult control of the activity
- gauging the level of effective problem-solving necessary for the task
- assessing the level of problem-solving skill on the part of the child
- devising strategies to assist the child
- supplying appropriate language to support the learning

Senses and Perception

Although sensory acuity is now close to that of the adult, the way the child processes the information is dictated by the cognitive processes of this stage. The toddler now has greater **sensory integration**, making better links between thought and action.

Information Processing

We can see evidence of a 2-year-old's memory when she recalls events, uses deferred imitation, or applies the same strategies that she used before to solve a problem. The child's memory is increasing, but still tends to be contextualized. Something is more likely to be memorable if it occurred in a particular situation, marked by sound, smell, or visual perceptions.

Persistence at a task usually lengthens during the third year (Fogel, 1997), and the child's attention span typically gets longer, depending on her motivation and interest. Toward the end of this stage, there is usually a surge in organizational skills. The child wants to sort, order, and classify objects. She can now do this according to several criteria, but she may not hold in mind the attributes as the activity continues. Tasks that involve matching items, sequencing a series of pictures, and classifying by one attribute often make pleasing games.

Multiple Intelligences

Howard Gardner (1983; 1993) has offered a model of intelligence, called the **multiple intelligences (MI)** theory, that is markedly different from others. This view focuses not on how a child comes to have a different mode or modes of intelligence but on what those modes mean to the way she learns. His theory presents eight or more intelligences that are observable in children. These include musical, bodily-kinesthetic, logical-mathematical, spatial, naturalist, linguistic, interpersonal, and intrapersonal. But Gardner's theory is not limited to these—it is likely that he will identify further ways of being smart!

Children at this stage are establishing their patterns of functioning, their favoured channels of communicating, and their particular interests. Because of these things, we can use Gardner's model to identify and promote dominant intelligences and find ways of supporting the less visible intelligences through the stronger ones. We might identify that a child has a particularly pronounced interpersonal intelligence and support her developing musical intelligence by providing activity bridges between the two. This support might mean encouraging the child to use her interpersonal skills to have older children help her with a musical skill. Alternatively, she might transfer her interpersonal intelligence to musical games that have the same give-and-take of the conversational style she has adopted—clapping rhythms between adult and child might do this. Gardner's model helps us to see the child's learning in a different light and to provide experience for the child that is not only developmentally appropriate but also individually and culturally fitting.

> Hand in glove with an accurate and accurately evolving description of each person's intelligence is the need for an educational regimen that helps every person achieve his or her maximal potential across the range of disciplines and crafts. (Gardner 1993, p. 229)

Rather than being a static theory, Gardner's model demands that educators, and others in the lives of young children, pay attention to the "individualization of intelligence" (p. 228). His ideal is to have an education system that can be tailored to the intelligence of each child; perhaps the toddler educator is better placed to do this, at a time when the adult–child ratio is more favourable for children than in later years. Gardner's view is in accord with brain research and is sufficiently flexible to incorporate new neuroscientific findings; he thinks these will uncover further understanding about the brain and behaviour.

By the age of about 2 years there is usually an observable pattern of the child's play and learning that indicates her style preferences and modes of thinking. Several publications claim to further the concept of multiple intelligences through supplying specific activities and prescribed curricula; these may not be consistent with Gardner's premise. His writings mention the Project Spectrum approach as one that does reflect his thinking. Many of the practical published resources suggest completing a personal inventory of intelligences that you yourself possess before attempting to understand the intelligences of

each of the children—and this does seem like an excellent idea. The open-ended nature of a portfolio system captures the multi dimensional aspects of each child's progress. Using this approach provides assessment coupled with individual learning profiles for each child. You may want to develop a portfolio system that focuses on each child's strengths or talents as a starting point for implementing a MI-based program.

Play

The symbolism, imitation, and memory aspects of the child's cognitive development show themselves in the play patterns of 2-to-3-year-olds. The toddler becomes more involved in imitative play (copying the actions of adults) and pretend play (using her growing imagination). Her social skills development comes from prolonged periods of social interaction. She is able to engage in **parallel play** and with increasing association, including some sharing and mutual interest. The give-and-take of social interaction provides opportunities for some sociodramatic play involving other children, but the ability of the child is not usually up to sustained conversation or developing joint goals.

Play still involves a lot of physical activity of various types. Climbers and other outdoor apparatus and lots of sensory activity support physical, exploratory, and sensory play. Fantasy play may also be seen in the latter part of this year. At that point, children's imaginations allow them to escape reality and indulge in fanciful and creative explorations in dress-up and other kinds of make-believe, some of which may be shaped by television, videos, or books. The 2-to-3-year-old is interested in many aspects of the real world, including other people, discovering how things are made, what everything does, and how her body works.

Puzzles, games, and sorting and matching activities (table play) allow the child to play in a more structured way than other totally spontaneous play activities do, but she will use these playthings in the way she wishes, and may not be tied to their conventional or expected uses. Games with rules are not easily played without adult guidance, but some sharing and turn-taking can be observed in spontaneous play if the children are familiar with one another and have had the opportunity to play together.

As we observe the 2-year-old's play, we can see many activities that we can categorize in a variety of ways. Some of these things that she does can be considered **creative play**—inasmuch as the ideas that go into her play are novel to her and she uses her imagination to develop her play sequences. Sometimes she might share these with other children. As she approaches her third birthday, you might notice more complex **sociodramatic play** that involves shared imagination and some fantasy. You might also notice the child's incorporation of ideas that have come from television, videos, or books. Although there are videos produced for this age group, they do not always promote improved play; the ideas and characters tend to be imitated rather than developed in more imaginative ways. Some of the children at this stage may be exposed to television characters unsuitable for their stage of development; because the child is so impressionable and internalizes negative and aggressive ideas, adults should be careful what children see and hear. Not all television is bad for children, but there are many playful activities that are more beneficial and enjoyable.

As we mentioned earlier, there are many ways of looking at what is happening in play; one activity might be labelled in several different ways, depending on the focus of the observer. Creativity can be found in imaginative play; fantasy and pretend are sometimes evident in object play, and so forth. Sometimes we see children solving their own challenges, or challenges that are embedded in the type of activity they are involved in. Observers may classify this as **problem-based play**; this is the kind of activity that prompts much learning from the play experience, but it might occur within another type of play that we label something else! Such is the complexity of the child's play at this stage that even experts have difficulty describing and naming it.

Creativity involves a thought process that is in some way new to its creator. In the case of the young child, she makes things, uses language, expresses herself in music or sound, imagines and plays within a wide range of creative activities. In the same way that play has its therapeutic purpose, so do all types of **creative thought**. Creativity allows children—and us—to combine logic and imagination, using both **convergent** and **divergent thinking**. It is most likely that divergent thinking produces the most creative ways of solving problems and making objects. This is why **open-ended activities** are most important at this stage of creative thinking. The child needs to be presented with materials for which there are no right or wrong ways of doing things. Open-ended activity allows the child to explore, discover, and then to create.

Often educators speak about offering a creative curriculum or providing creative activities (or sometimes, unfortunately, "a creative"—meaning some kind of supposedly creative play activity). What we supply for children should be the opportunity, space, time, and materials to develop their creative thinking processes. This is why it's essential to allow the child to make things her way rather than imitate the "correct" way of doing things. In society, we tend to honour representational art—images that look like the real thing—rather than expressions of thoughts and emotions relating to the child's imagination. Because of this, we may want to encourage representational picture-making and be enthusiastic when the child draws a picture that we can see depicts something "real." But it is far better to allow the young child to make images that express her thoughts and feelings—frequently they can be an opening to conversation with her. This has the effect of supporting her language development alongside her thinking skills.

Rarely do children make pictures that are truly representational at this stage, although they do convey ideas and perceptions. This is the stage when children's thinking can be spoiled by zealous educators who want the whole group of children to make identical objects, or the adult who draws to show the child what an object is meant to look like. Offering these prompts not only stunts the child's creativity but sends the message to the child that her own efforts have failed. We need to show that we value genuine attempts at creative thinking and making things. Below are some starting points for creative open-ended activities. Remember that to the child—whose development offers her new insights and skills on a daily basis—the same materials can be new each time they are offered. That said, you might want to vary the experience by making small changes that make the activity particularly novel. The materials themselves are not "creative": the child's thinking that flows from exploring and making is creative.

Some activities and experiences that promote creative thinking:

- clay—vary consistency, amount, and objects to press, cut, etc.
- earth—vary types and use for mud pies, growing things
- dough*—vary in colour and consistency— offer various cutters, rollers, extruders, and offer cooking tools, food ideas, construction materials, etc.; sometimes suggest making the dough with different types of flour or other materials

---

* Some adults have concerns about using food as a play material—in this case use alternatives to food unless using it to provide the children with edibles.

- pastry/cookie* dough—use rollers, cutters, and real pastry sheet (baking done only by adults)
- Jello/gelatin*—vary consistency and colour; offer containers
- cooking materials*—this may need a little more guidance if the items are to be eaten
- manufactured Play-Doh or other non-toxic malleable material; offer a variety of kitchen implements, stones, shapes, cutters, etc.
- painting with pudding*—provide thick paper or plastic trays; use fingers or dip with serrated shaped spatulas (corrugated cardboard can be used for this)
- water—vary colour; add bubbles; offer various containers, measuring cups, sieves, funnels, water wheels; sometimes allow for water–clay mixing opportunities; provide different temperatures of water (but not extremes); add items that float or sink; offer warm soapy water for washing doll clothes; offer baby bath for doll-washing, etc. (some authorities require individual water play bins because of the possibility of cross-infection)
- snow and ice—snow can be brought inside and melted, painted, and played with as a semi-frozen material with containers; outside, children can play in snow, build with it, press shapes into it, or paint it; ice can be used for a variety of play activities; add colour if making ice cubes (protect children's hands from extreme temperatures inside or outside)
- water and cornstarch*—add colour; offer a variety or implements to scoop and pour; vary colour
- flour/water "glue"—use for papier-mâché; vary colour; use for collage
- rice/peas/beans/lentils/dried pasta/cooked pasta*— provide scoops, funnels, and containers (be wary of potential choking hazard)
- paint—vary thickness; offer papers of different textures, shapes, and sizes; vary colour tones such as two or three pastel colours, some bright or fluorescent tones together
- paint with finger—paint with a variety of tools such as cardboard scrapers, brushes, or spatulas; offer kitchen implements; offer three-dimensional objects to paint or use their dough models; offer pine cones, feathers, and other natural materials for painting; suggest painting old large refrigerator boxes
- blocks—along with wooden floor blocks, Sticklebricks, Lego, and Duplo, offer shoebox building, pizza boxes; suggest building, painting blocks
- printing—offer paints in different colours and offer cotton reels, pine cones, feathers, leaves, cut-out shapes, puzzle shapes, and a variety of different papers; offer sponge shapes, vegetable shapes, textured surfaces, including three-dimensional objects
- collage—offer magazines, a variety of papers, pre-cut shapes to stick, stickers; use food materials,* smallish items for sticking onto paper or card, such as wood shavings; use safe glue that really works (avoid polystyrene chips because of potential hazard)
- shaking pictures—offer different papers, glue, and sawdust, confetti, dry soil, small paper shapes, or other safe little pieces to make picture and shake or sprinkle the pieces over them
- paper and crayons/markers/pencils—offer different colours, thicknesses of markers; suggest using wax crayons sideways to make rubbings
- sand—vary wet/dry; add a variety of water toys, containers, buckets, moulds, kitchen tools, a balance, scales, scoops, measuring cups, etc. (avoid glitter for safety reasons)
- chalk—sidewalk chalk outside on ground; chalkboard or dark papers inside
- sand and white glue—pictures can be made with glue; the glue can be coloured with paint or food colouring; sand can then be shaken (this too can be coloured) over the image so some sticks to the glue
- pictures on acrylic or plastic surfaces—offer thick paint or pudding* and use paint to scribble and make images; add spreaders; take a print of the picture onto paper
- cloth or felt—offer a variety of colours and textures; use paper, card, or more cloth and white glue; boxes can be covered; hats can be made; larger pieces of cloth can become capes, clothing, and promote fantasy and pretend play (avoid separating craft activities from dramatic play)
- containers and hammers—offer a variety of safe containers to bang and make sounds; offer brushes and wooden and plastic blunt sticks to make sounds; add corrugated card, textured card, plastic, and available clean waste materials that can also produce sounds; offer items that vibrate; homemade shakers; create a drum from an old tin and sticky-back plastic; play a variety of taped music to play along with
- music and movement; play music with a distinct beat and rhythm; offer a variety of music styles representing differing ethnicities and cultures; contrast lively and sleepy tunes; offer songs to sing along with, action rhymes, music that prompts movement and dance; use your own voice to sing

children's names; provide music in the background; and the foreground

- junk materials (small)—collect, store, and provide access to clean materials, such a paper rolls, egg cartons, food packages, paper bags, paper plates, straws, packing materials, etc.; offer glue; suggest painting whatever is made

- natural materials—can be collected by children and adults; use for painting, growing things (indoors and out), sorting, categorizing, experiments, collage, printing, etc; find stones, acorns, leaves, shells, pine cones, seeds, bulbs, vegetables, fruits, clover, flowers, nuts, plant cuttings, moss, soils, twigs, straw, grass cuttings, feathers, etc. (be aware of conservation issues, poisonous items, and children's allergies)

- junk materials (large)—collect, store, and make available, indoors or outdoors; tubes, large boxes, packing materials, wooden planks, cardboard pieces, etc.; provide balls for rolling through tubes—suggest making a house out of large boxes—allow safe construction (inside and out); combine with traditional manufactured construction materials (check for splinters, heavy weights, and sharp edges)

- wood—provide twigs, branches, and various sizes of prepared wood; add smaller pieces, such as waste materials, knobs; find soft balsa wood; suggest painting, printing, or gluing items; add to conventional art and construction materials

- old machines—supply old phones, keyboards, clocks, scales, etc.; to take apart and reassemble; allow for incorporation into pretend play (check for safety hazards such as small parts, electric hazards, batteries, etc.)

- old junk conversation box—provide a discovery box that offers items to identify, compare, contrast, sort, discuss, use as prompts for the imagination, etc. (offer under close supervision because of potential hazards); stimulate all of the senses; it might contain a wide variety of things, whatever you or the children find, such as spices, a camel's tooth, medals, buttons, natural objects, unusual foods, pieces of fabric with different patterns (from different cultures), pictures of people of different ages and backgrounds, an old record, coloured silks, prints of artworks by the old masters, a brass bell, clay sculptures, mini cooking pots, a miniature tea set, a bag of marbles, semiprecious gemstones, a mini-skeleton, pictures of hats from around the world, models, citrus fruits, exotic fruits, fabric swatches, paint colour samples, a box of three-dimensional shapes, Russian dolls that fit inside one another, a model of the teacher's teeth in plaster of Paris, free samples of face creams and perfumes (consider allergies), a dream catcher, a silver bracelet, a small spinning top (examples offered by a child-care centre in Ajax, Ontario)

Creative play can incorporate a very wide variety of activities. Some of these are social, but the child in her third year is more likely to **play associatively** except in some short episodes of sociodramatic play, when roles are clearly differentiated. The 2-year-old sees no problem with there being two mommies in the playhouse at the same time, and the children are not usually dependent upon each other for the play sequence to progress. When the child is involved in play that allows her to express her strong feelings, she is most likely to be in a solitary play activity. Although some anger is played out in pretend play, not all expressed anger is imitating adults. Sometimes we hear ourselves reflected in the child's pretend play; this can be a wake-up call for us to ensure that our behaviour is always appropriate.

It is possible that children's play has changed as a result of recent world conflicts. Children brought up during the troubles in Northern Ireland and those enduring the Bosnian conflict have been found to act out their concerns through play.

With the global conflicts that are current issues in world affairs, we all have concerns about how our children will manage both the social conflicts that are everyday parts of their lives and the larger conflicts in their world.

How well will the young child be prepared to deal with situations that we cannot yet anticipate? Frequently we are shocked because we see young children expressing anger as they play. Some of this may come from within them—resulting from the natural frustrations of their stage, but other aggressive play comes as a result of the images that they see and the adult conversation that they hear. While it is undesirable to offer children weapons with which to act out their fears and aggression, it is highly likely that some acting out is beneficial. We tend to think of all play as offering both a learning and therapeutic purpose, so we must provide opportunities for safe play that concerns children's fears and ways of coming to understand the warlike images they see. Much conversation and reassurance is needed, but we must first listen to what the children are telling us in both their language and in their play.

Some **aggressive play** is an unfortunate, if inevitable, offshoot of the times we live in—but we must provide the child with peaceful methods of communicating and ensure that nobody is physically or emotionally hurt. Acting out fears and concerns should be channelled into productive activity as much as possible. Above all, emotional support must be provided to ensure that the child does not feel she is under any immediate threat and knows that the adults around her will always be there to protect her.

Part of the reality of our times is that the world contains extreme political regimes and terrorist acts; these facts cannot escape young children, however much we try to protect them. Given this, we need to be particularly attentive to the fact that young children should not be exposed to the images that are presented in graphic form on television and in other media. However much we try to protect our children, they do overhear our concerns and experience our anxieties secondhand. Truthfulness is essential, we need to limit the child's world to one in which she is secure and trusting. Play can have a positive role in coming to terms with a range of difficult emotions. While we do not want to promote play that is warlike, terrifying, or fear-inducing, there may be times when the child needs the avenue of play to deal with ideas that might otherwise overwhelm her.

For children who have been directly exposed to violence or trauma of any kind, the benefits from play may be particularly therapeutic. While this kind of play may occur spontaneously, there are times when parents might be encouraged to consult a therapeutic professional who might incorporate play therapy into their treatment. Remember that the majority of children in their third year who exhibit extreme behaviours in their play are not being directly subjected to terrifying images, violence, or trauma in their lives. Even so, observe all children sensitively as they play and share any real concerns with other professionals on your team as well as with the child's parents. If further examination of the play behaviours or other aspects of the day are thought to be necessary, parents may seek a referral to an appropriate psychologist, psychiatrist, or other therapist.

Play behaviours, like every other aspect of the young child's development, are highly individual. There are many factors that shape how the child plays. To some extent, the child's nature, or biological makeup, will be a factor, but her experience too will shape the way she plays. At this stage, play serves various purposes that you can observe if you look carefully. These are some of the functions of play during the third year of life:

- learning about the properties of materials and how things work
- getting to know other people and how to communicate with them
- building concepts about weight, time, size, number, colour, etc.

- imitating and internalizing social roles and learning what is and is not socially acceptable behaviour
- improving memory and information processing functions
- organizing her world by sorting, classifying, sequencing, striating, and ordering
- refining her gross and fine motor skills
- exploring her emotions and gaining insight into why people behave the way they do
- acting out some of the anxieties, concerns, and issues that trouble the child
- escaping the real world and fantasizing, using her imagination
- discovering right and wrong and the consequences of actions
- regulating her feelings and actions
- increasing her pro-social skills
- increasing her communication and language skills

It is often during play sequences that we observe the child's particular interests and talents. Janice may be interested in how machines work and Eli may be interested in social relationships. Jasper observes closely before he moves into a sociodramatic activity involving shopping, and Robin spends long periods pouring and sifting lumpy sand. These may represent particular interests; if they become regular patterns of behaviour they are even more noteworthy.

The purpose of **fantasy play** is a challenge to figure out. It might be that the child is temporarily escaping the extreme feelings and demands of reality. It can also provide a pleasurable interlude from other types of play. Many parents become concerned about young children who remain in a fantasy stage for a prolonged period; some try to stop the child's imagination from running away with itself. It is likely to be more productive if the child is allowed to act out her fantasy, even if it is prolonged. Some philosophers consider fantasy a magical experience for children—one in which the usual laws of nature and society do not apply. Some educators sometimes feel that fantasy play—particularly fantasy that involves **superheroes** such as Superman—or whoever is publicized today as a character with extraordinary powers—provides an opportunity for the child to empower herself in a world where she is disempowered—or controlled by adults. A more pragmatic view, held by other educators, is that there is a link between fantasy play and each domain of development. This is confirmed in the statement "Self-directed fantasy play . . . is an essential feature in young children's cognitive and psycho social development" (Perry, 2001). Fantasy play remains more of a mystery to adults than other types of play, but it is obviously an important part of learning, even if we cannot easily analyze it. Freudian theory explains fantasy in terms of inborn longings, Jungian ideas centre on the acting out of archetypes, and phenomenologists, such as M.J. Langeveld, suggest a necessity for the child of creating a world of her own possibilities. This might mean an inner empowerment:

> In the modern world everything tends to become rationalized and is therefore more available to the adult. In contrast, fantasy may create an ordered world but only to work out possible arrangements within the confines of a world of open possibilities which is, after all, still a world in the style of the everyday and shared world.[1]

Some children at about 3 years of age get stuck in a role-playing fantasy that takes up much of their waking time. This is not a problem—except to the adult. Fantasy play hardly exists at the age of 2, but by 3 the adult can feel that fantasy has a strong pull on the child. But the child will have greater difficulty sorting out fantasy and reality if he is denied the possibilities of fantasy than if he is encouraged.

Many developmental psychologists tend to view the young child in terms of what she cannot yet accomplish, or how her thinking limits her abilities; we might find this a negative perception of the child. Watching her at play, we see her increasing competence in all domains of her development. Rather than focus on what the child cannot yet do, the most effective means of supporting her learning is to provide experiences and activities that build on her existing skills and motivations. Knowing when to be involved in the child's play is something of an art. As with younger children it is best to start with close observation and take your cue from there. The 2-to-3-year-old will want you to be part of her play, and she will realize how much you value her play activity through your respect for it, your sensitive involvement, and because you follow her lead.

Most children at this stage, or any other, do not have to be taught to play—only some of those children who have developmental difficulties might need some play intervention to teach them play skills. However, children may have their play experiences extended or promoted because a perceptive educator picks up on the children's interests. There can be children who are shy and who are slow to warm up or move into a play activity, but a child's prolonged observation of activity can be cause for concern. That said, some children do learn more through observational learning, so it might be just her style rather than a real issue. However, do be concerned if a child seems apathetic or uninterested in play. There may be reasons for this, so avoid jumping to any conclusions. There might be any of the following reasons for a child demonstrating atypical play behaviours: illness, tiredness, intense shyness, self-consciousness, abuse, neglect, poor infant experience, previous prolonged hospitalization or institutionalization, communicative disorder, sensory deficit, or some other disability. Children who are identified as experiencing these difficulties might benefit from early intervention.

It should be stressed that the majority of 2-year-olds are extremely active, curious, motivated, playful, ask plenty of questions, are messy, play for prolonged periods alone and alongside others, are strong-minded, want to please, explore everything within their reach, and show little thought for safety. Their physical exuberance can be both a challenge and a joy to the adults in the children's lives.

LANGUAGE AND COMMUNICATION

Body Language and Reading Emotions

Reading the child's body language and translating her cues remain important ways of understanding the child's thoughts, feelings, levels of awareness, and personal interests. This section looks at how we can observe the process of communication. First, remember that body language can be conscious or unconscious. The 2-year-old may be able to present some conscious body language, which sometimes even contradicts the truth, but on the whole the child will send clear and honest messages. Body language can also be innate or learned. In innate body language, the message comes from bodily functions, feelings, and reactions that are automatic. Learned body language involves shaping the language in accordance with a family, setting, culture, or context. Much of what we observe combines innate and learned behaviours, and we generally don't distinguish between the two.

It is important to appreciate that there are innate and learned factors that contribute to messages that are sent. On the whole, needs are communicated through innate means, and desires are communicated via learned methods. Body language and other signs can offer adults insight into what the young

---

1. M.J. Langeveld (1983), "The 'Secret Place' in the Life of the Child," *Phenomenology & Pedagogy:* 1 (2): 181–189.

Body Language: Reading the Signs from Toddlers and Twos

PHYSICAL ACTION	INTERPRETATION
Eye Contact/Use	
general eye contact	need for attention, social referencing, request for approval, anxiety, love
face-scanning	taking in visual information, attempt at recognition, searching for something
rapid movements (eyes open)	searching for something, scanning an object
rapid movement (eyes closed)	REM sleep, thinking but awake
eye avoidance	fear, respect
closed eyes	tired, excluding stimulation
gazing	signal of attachment
gazing into space	trance state, lack of interest
lowering eyes	submission, fear, disengaging, thinking about an emotion
pupil dilation	arousal, excitement, interest
eye-roving	lack of focusing, lack of interest, concentration difficulty
eye-rolling	boredom, thinks someone is stupid or silly
frowning with eye contact	disapproval, seeking assistance
blinking	too much light, startled, punctuating body language
looking up	visualizing, solving a problem, thinking of a sound
looks around the room at each child	anxiety, onlooker prior to making a move, lacking confidence, slow to warm up in social situations
Facial Expressions	
smile	happiness, anxiety, learned response to appear pleased, invitation to social connection, enjoyment through any sense
giggles	finds something funny, copying another person
laughs	finds something funny, enjoys activity, involved in pleasurable social activity
looking away with frown	feels embarrassed, shame
tongue out	concentrating, rude gesture, tasting something
looks at own reflection and makes silly face	embarrassed at own recognition
looks at own reflection and makes weak smile	unsure who the image represents

PHYSICAL ACTION	INTERPRETATION
Facial Expressions (cont'd)	
broad smile	open and happy
weak smile	tentative, fearful of social connection
grin (mouth closed)	cheerful (same as smile)
frown	sadness, emotionally upset, disappointment, didn't get their own way, questioning, uncertainty
nose twitching	smelling something
long face, open eyes, transfixed	fear, experiencing pain
tongue out/nose turned up	disgust, dislike
tonguing	hungry, thirsty
tense/distorted face	anger
flushed face	excitement, teething, too hot, wind/cold reaction, fever, allergy
pale face	cold, heat stroke (check signs and symptoms), tired, nauseous
yawning	tired, bored, imitation
"blank" face	aware of bodily functions, listening, tuning out
drooling	teething, sore mouth, loss of bodily control, palsy (check other signs and symptoms)
blank/lack of expression	attachment difficulty, tired, emotionally withdrawn
Head Movements	
head tilted sideways (may have open mouth)	interest
tilted down	shy, doesn't want to play, fearful
tilted up	confident, open to invitation
hiding face	anxiety, attempt to withdraw, unwillingness to respond
moving from side to side	listening to music, recreating a feeling
twisted away	dislike, rejects food, sound is too much, over-stimulated, tuning out
side to side	no/refusal (may be opposite in some cultures)
up-and-down head shake	yes/acceptance (as above)
head shake	strong dislike/frustration
head forward	interested, concentrating
head-banging	unable to communicate, emotionally upset, deprived of attention/stimulation, deprived of physical contact

PHYSICAL ACTION	INTERPRETATION
Gestures	
hands move up and down together	excitement
patting tummy	hunger, identifying where food goes
opening arms	invitation for a hug
clenched fist	anxiety, anger, response to stress
pointing at object/person	identification of something or someone, "I want that," assertiveness, "you"
pointing at own body part	"I hurt here," identification of part (e.g., "arm")
pointing to own chest	"me"
banging arms (on table, etc.)	anger, frustration, seeing what will happen
hand wave	goodbye, "I want you to go," something hurts
grabbing	"I want that," jealous
arms up	pick me up
arm waving	seeking attention, responding to music
sweeping arms across table/floor	destruction, anger, frustration
holding item to mouth	feeling temperature, texture, etc., for comfort, for taste
thumb/finger-sucking	comfort, nervousness, imitation
toe-sucking	"Look, I've found my toes"
dropping items over edge	playfulness, testing to see if objects are permanent, to see adult's reaction
chewing wrist	nervousness/insecurity
prodding an adult	"I want attention," "Come and do this for me," "Pay attention to this"
tickling someone	taking role of the one in control, testing another's reaction, imitating an adult
holding arm/fingers out (as if measuring)	indicating size, indicating intensity of feeling
pulling own hair	frustration, profound unhappiness
pulling someone else's hair	anger, checking to see response
eating refusal	not hungry, upset, unwell/nauseous, food dislike
Body Movements	
quick gross motor movement	excited, thrill at achievement, pleasure, energized, response to cold, response to music, response to open space
jumping up and down	all of the above, plus bowel or bladder fullness (holding it)
lack of responsiveness	unwell (check other signs and symptoms), poisoned (as above), tired, tuning out

PHYSICAL ACTION	INTERPRETATION
Body Movements (cont'd)	
slow movements	tired, overwhelmed, sad, hunger
wriggling	wants to get way, rejecting control, being playful
rhythmic movements	self-comforting, response to music
backward movement, then short forward movement	surprise, action preceding another response
rocking	self-comforting, playfulness, upset and feeling rejected
symmetrical movement	added vehemence, developmental—can only operate both sides together
holding/stroking genitals	comfort, anxiety
Posture and Stance	
relaxed but alert	ready for action
arched back	"I don't like being touched," "Go away"
turning away	dislike, rejecting what's being offered
hunched shoulders	"Keep off"
periodic turning away from others	disengagement, anger
leaning on things	tired
resting head on hands	tired, getting comfortable
leaning forward	interested, paying attention, seeking attention
slouching—rounded posture	tired, dejected, lacking in enthusiasm
throwing self on floor	frustration, loss of control, showing depth of feelings
clutching doll/blanket	providing security, for physical comfort
upright	confident, energetic/alert
Proximity	
closeness	comfort, attachment, interest/intrigue, wants more attention
moving in close	attempting to persuade
medium distance (across room)	needs closeness and independence, seeks adult help/assistance/involvement
distance	discomfort, prefers to be solitary, fearful, independent, onlooker, has given up on being close
moving close, then moving away	playing with automomy/independence, checking out abilities
holding on	needs reassurance, separation anxiety, stranger anxiety, enjoys closeness, feeling possessive

PHYSICAL ACTION	INTERPRETATION
Proximity (cont'd)	
sits by self (often in corner)	needs physical protection, wants emotional support, disconnection from others
refuses to join in	tired, feels incompetent, doesn't feel like sharing, not interested
matching activity (copying)	"I want to be alone," "Let me into your game"
looks more than joins in	lonely, observer or onlooker
plays with back to group	confident in being alone, ignores other children, showing upset
partial back to group	wants to join in, checking what others are doing, feels left out
Bodily Contact	
pats child	empathy/knows she's hurt
hits other child	anger, loss of control, frustration, doesn't know they hurt, too
hits adult	anger, frustration, loss of control, doesn't know they hurt, attention-seeking
smacks doll	venting frustration, acting out feelings, imitating adult behaviour
hugs adult	confident of being loved, needs reassurance, seeks physical contact
hugs other child	confident, expression of positive feeling
cuddles into adult	seeks reassurance, enjoys close proximity
kisses	sign of affection
strokes skin	need for contact
pulls away	wants to be left alone
Sound Production	
squeal	excitement, enthusiasm
shouts "ah"	surprise, mock surprise
whine	"I want something," "I'm unhappy," imitation or deferred imitation
sigh	boredom, dislike
cry—loud	"I'm hurt," "I'm uncomfortable," protest—"Don't go"
cry—stop and start	waiting for a response
cry—grizzling (continuous groaning-whine)	hunger, need for diaper change
cry—persistent/fairly loud	loneliness, boredom
cry—whimper	"I'm giving up," "No one is paying me attention"
cry—whine	"She did something to me," "Help me"

PHYSICAL ACTION	INTERPRETATION
Sound Production (cont'd)	
cry—groan	ache/hurt
cry—fierce	pain
singsong babble	content, exploring sound intonations
long babble	experimenting with own voice, imitating sounds or repeating them
no cry (prolonged period)	disengagement or unattached, content
Breathing	
rapid breathing	excited, feeling active, listening, exertion, anger, fear, disgust
rapid then calm	happiness
shallow breathing	attending to visual information, solving a problem
deep breathing	relaxed, happy, bored

child is thinking and feeling. The following indicators are adapted from Quilliam (1994):

- eyes and eyebrows—shape/gaze/openness/flickering/reddening/puffiness/eye contact/squinting/observing/looking away/focus
- mouth—open/closed/down-turned/ jaw dropped/ lips pushed forward/smile/laugh
- nose—wrinkled/flared
- body position—inward/pulled back/symmetry/ shoulders up or down/social space/frozen
- breathing—rapidity/deep or shallow
- skin colour—pale/change in colour/rash/blotchy
- gestures—use of learned signs/pointing/language and gesture together/symbolic actions
- physical proximity—space between child and another child/space between child and adult/ watches at what distance
- what the child says—thoughts/feelings/pace of speech/ability to articulate/sound production/ imitation/deferred imitation/role-playing
- play behaviours—actions/activity level/interest/ concentration span/type of play
- facial expressions—innate emotions/**social emotions**
- mistakes—errors in thinking/language mistakes/ memory function/incorrect associations
- congruity—action and language matching/action and expression matching/congruity between aspects of body language

- stimuli—alertness/consciousness/awareness/speed of response/lack of response/delayed response/ appropriateness of response

However, children's individual styles as well as their exposure to culture shape how body language should be read. Studies of children offer several alternative interpretations for most behaviours (see, for example, Izard, 1971; Izard and Malatesta, 1987; Morris, 1999 and 1995; Quilliam 1994).

Language

Two-year-olds are at the beginning of a period marked by lots of questions. They ask questions as an invitation to converse, to understand the world better, and to get a response. "Where" and "what" questions usually come first. Then come the "who," "how," and "why" questions. A few children, at the end of this stage, will extend their questioning to "which," "whose," and "when" (Bloom, Merkin, and Wootten 1982).

Although the child's questioning seems endless at times, she is using language in a variety of other ways. The child is likely to have quite a large vocabulary. However, there is tremendous variation; some children will be much earlier or later to talk. Studies estimate that, at 30 months, children know upward of 200 words (Sheridan, 1997).

The early use of new words may present some pronunciation difficulties. Commonly, children at this stage have trouble making the sounds for "r" or "l," and they tend to make them sound like "w." Other **consonants** present the same challenge. This is a temporary articulation difficulty that exists because of either hearing differentiation challenges or physiological immaturity.

As we saw in an earlier chapter, though, there is more to language acquisition than simple vocabulary. Language development is often looked at in terms of the increasing **mean length of utterance (MLU)**. This measures the average number of morphemes, or smallest units of meaning in language (these units include prefixes and suffixes as well as roots). Another consideration is the type of words used by the child. In his first, simple utterances, he generally uses nouns, or words that label things. Next he uses verbs, action words that indicate a relation between things. The MLU gradually becomes longer and begins to display rules of language. At the same time, sentence structure becomes more complex.

Children gain an understanding of language rules by hearing adults and other children speak, by hearing television and other media, and by trying to piece together communication in a meaningful way. Frequently toddlers create **overextensions**, or the incorrect application of a rule. Although their early attempts may be full of errors, toddlers are quite successful at making themselves understood.

This stage is the time for **private speech**—talking out loud to herself for self-regulation. Children may talk about what they are doing as they do it. Private speech might involve playing with sounds, practising saying something correctly, and even singing some lyrics. Sometimes children utter their private speech as if they were narrating their own activity. Private speech can also include the unheard voice of the child, as she uses language to structure her thinking.

During the explosion of language that can occur at this time, we need to remember that adults are the facilitators and mediators of the process. During the third year of life there is evidence of a combination of aspects of language development. Consider each of these as they occur simultaneously:

- practice with sound production associated with language (**phonemes**, **consonants,** and **vowels**)
- listening with greater acuity and attention to language-specific sounds
- increase in length of utterance—mean length of utterance (MLU)
- gains in labelling objects, people, ideas, and feelings—**vocabulary**—(**receptive** and **expressive**)
- increased appreciation of links between language and meaning—**semantics**

- use of language that has **symbolic** function—a word represents an object, idea, etc.
- increase in private inner speech
- internalization of organizational rules of language—**syntax**
- acquisition of the basic rules of language—**grammar**
- use of language to communicate needs, wants, and ideas
- questions increase
- follows commands—puts understanding into action

In earlier chapters we discussed theories that explain these amazing leaps forward in understanding and using language. The brain may be wired for language, but the amount of language learning that happens at this stage is staggering; never again will there be such great gains in the child's vocabulary and understanding of meaning and structure in language.

The adults' responsibility is to support the child's language learning—not only in increasing her vocabulary but in all the other aspects of her language that we just mentioned. A wide variety of strategies for language support are articulated by Elaine Weitzman (1992). She suggests addressing every aspect of the child's program, including the environment and how it is structured to support talking and learning, the adult's role in promoting conversation, supporting social interaction between children, and encouraging a variety of play activities, especially pretend play and play that encourages the use of the child's imagination. Some of Weitzman's strategies that involve adults include:[1]

- speaking in sentences so that children hear correct models, expansions, and extensions
- labelling objects, people, actions, and events
- telling children what is going to happen in the near future
- providing simple explanations
- offering intensive repetition
- timing responses to correspond to the child's focus of attention
- being slow and clear in everything you say
- positioning words that you want them to notice at the beginning or end of a sentence—and emphasizing them
- using real-life situations that the child has a real interest in

---

1. Adapted from E. Weitzman (1992), *Learning Language and Loving It: A Guide to Promoting Children's Social and Language Development in Early Childhood Settings* (Toronto, ON: Hanen Centre).

- supporting simultaneous first- and second-language learning—recognize that there are stages of second-language learning that might show themselves in a silent phase, code mixing, loss of first language, and lots of grammatical errors
- comfort the child in her first language if possible
- use correct forms but avoid correcting mistakes
- use music and rhymes to help with language acquisition
- introduce books, writing, and literacy materials into play situations
- help children use language to identify and solve problems
- use literal language rather than abstract ideas and metaphors
- extend the topic of interest to the child
- imagine and pretend along with the child

Clearly the child's acquisition of language occurs alongside her increasing understanding about her world. Language assists in the labelling, understanding, and categorization of objects and ideas. It also enables the child to convey her thoughts and feelings and respond to others as she hears what they say. The give-and-take of language helps build social relationships. Most importantly, the child's language supports her ability to think, and her increasing experience provides opportunities for language growth. We see the interdependence of all the aspects of her development within language development: physical—the ability to produce meaningful sounds; and social—in the interactions needed to build vocabulary and internalize the rules of language; and cognitive—in the thinking skills that result from being able to apply language and use it to form ideas and think abstractly. Vygotsky suggested that language and thought merge at around 2 years of age, producing verbal thought. Because mental operations are regarded as embodied within the structure of language, cognitive development results from an internalization of language. Whether Vygotsky is correct when he says language and thought become indivisible is, perhaps, less important than the fact that language and thought are without question mutually supportive.

Bilingual and Multilingual Learning

Children exposed to two or more languages have the opportunity to grow up speaking those languages. Although there can be some challenges for the child learning two or more sets of language sounds and rules, children's receptivity to language is wide open at this time. Of course, the child can become con-fused, use words incorrectly, and switch from one language to the other in mid-sentence. Yet these difficulties are relatively trivial compared with the cognitive and social advantages (Freire and Bernhard, 1997).

Supporting the child's first language is important. Among other benefits, such support demonstrates respect for the language and culture of the child and his family. Where possible, the educator might learn some words in the child's first language to try to provide a bridge to English. This can also have benefits for the educator's relations with parents, as Box 12.2 illustrates. It is important for the child to make connections between her heritage and the language she speaks (Chud et al., 1985), so we need to find practical ways of supporting that language learning.

Some parents may want their child to learn English while at the child-care centre and another language at home. Parental wishes must be respected, but the child's emotional well-being must be considered, too. Language acquisition is tied to profound emotions and has the potential for making a child feel either lost or well integrated.

▶ Emotional and Social Development

Both Freud and Erikson have given us models for understanding the complexities of emotional development. While controversial, these models offer useful explanations for the process. Freud's emphasis on the oral and then anal phases of development (Freud, 1940) seems to focus too much on possible pathology—that is, on what can go wrong. But the model does provide us with a loud warning of the damage that can occur if the stage is not handled well. Although Erikson's theory is more optimistic, it points to the importance of the early building of trust and the child's need for autonomy. Both theorists signal the importance of acknowledging developmental stages and ensuring that we respond to them.

EMOTIONAL INTELLIGENCE

Most educators and parents would agree that it is essential that young children have a positive sense of themselves and **self-esteem**. Recently the notion of self-esteem was revisited. It is now understood that esteem must result from the child's efforts and achievements rather than for just existing (this is not the same as being loved unconditionally). Self-esteem does not focus on what she is but on what she does. Experiencing **unconditional love** involves

---

BOX 12.2

LEARNING THE PARENTS' LANGUAGE OR FINDING AN INTERPRETER

Adult second-language learning is challenging but not impossible. The initial goal, which should be manageable, is to master only a few phrases in the language of the parents. To make you more comfortable, you might want to have some prompt cards with key phrases like "She's had a good day." These can be written phonetically so you can sound out the phrases. Parents are usually flattered that the educator is making an effort to talk to them in their own language. You may never be fluent, but your efforts will usually improve your relationship.

Sometimes there isn't enough time to learn the language of families new to the child-care community. The task might be daunting, and the information that needs to be communicated too complex. In these circumstances, you may find that written information in the parents' first language is insufficient and you'll need to find an interpreter. There are several ways to find one. Ask the parents themselves by using a written question in their language. Some families use their older children or other relatives to provide this service. If this fails, try to find staff or other professionals who might be able to translate. Interpretation services may be provided locally by federal, provincial, or municipal authorities. Other translation services may exist, but you should be aware that private services may be quite expensive.

---

a sense of trust and well-being that is important, but separate from self-esteem. Unconditional love requires the adult to accept, support, nurture, and love the child whatever her behaviour, whatever her mood—without any condition. To build self-esteem in the child, the adult offers plenty of opportunities for the child to feel good about herself because she tries to do things herself and meets with success. At times, her self-esteem will protect her from feeling a sense of failure if she doesn't measure up to her own expectations. It will also build a resilience that makes her want to try even harder. Adults may express their adulation, praise, and encouragement for the child's slightest efforts. She knows when she has made a real effort and may find the adult lacks authenticity if she receives praise that is not truly in line with the effort she has expended. Self-esteem results from genuine personal achievement and effort made for a purpose. Although children may be naturally competitive, it is not helpful to introduce competition into the child's day. It is more important that the child improve her own performance rather than aim to be first to put on her coat! Similarly, children may want to please the adult—this may be sufficient motivation along with their personal drive. Trying to be best or first is far less important than improving their personal performance.

Daniel Goleman's work on emotion has led him to believe that there is such a thing as **emotional intelligence** (Goleman, 1997). He presents this concept as a theory applicable to adult emotional growth, yet there seems little reason why it should not apply also to healthy emotional development throughout life. As we become aware of Goleman's five domains of emotional intelligence, it becomes apparent that some degree of that intelligence is likely to have developed in the early years of life. The following lists the domains with reference to the emotional life of toddlers and under-threes.

1. *Knowing one's emotions.* The root of emotional understanding is in knowing that she is a separate person, being in touch with how she feels, and having that echoed by the people she is attached to. Having her cues read and having her feelings acknowledged, not ignored, helps the young child to know her emotions.

2. *Managing emotions.* Having some positive feedback about herself, knowing that she is loved, and having a consistent attachment figure provides the child with a base for being able to manage her emotions. When her efforts to manage her feelings are rewarded externally, and with a sense of pride, the child feels success in managing her emotions. If she does not receive the support she needs and is shamed by her actions, her emotional regulation will be less effective and she will lack confidence in her ability to be in control.

3. *Motivating oneself.* Internal motivators lead the child to be curious about things, people, and herself. She is propelled forward with a natural motivation to strive and be successful. When adults interfere with that process and lead the child to

doubt herself and her competence, challenge her interests, or undermine her successes, then the motivation is spoiled. Adults need to allow the child to experience success and provide external encouragement until the child can motivate herself independently.

4. *Recognizing emotions in others.* Early attachment to adults provides the first two-way relationship in which the child finds that she has a sense of self and others. From this, she builds the relationship and mirrors the emotions of the other. In time, she becomes able to think less egocentrically and begins to know that others have feelings. With later appreciation of the perspectives of others, she is able to recognize and read their emotions. Gaining in social skills and emotional awareness, she gains a conscience. With internal and external supports and encouragement, she finds that recognizing the feelings of others is rewarding. Adults can spoil this process in many ways: by failing to meet the child's needs, by not providing a consistent, caring adult figure that the child can attach to, and by ignoring the need to reinforce emotional learning.

5. *Handling relationships.* Relationships that are built on trust in the early years provide the foundation for building mature relationships later on. The child's security in being loved and feeling positive about herself allows mistakes to happen. The child can continue to take small risks without her world caving in. The young child needs opportunities to launch into her social world from a secure base. If the conditions for healthy emotional growth are not provided, the child will not have the sense of security to manage social relationships.

Adding to the emotional intelligence concept, John Gottman (1998) has applied Goleman's model to children. Gottman's work focuses on the responsibilities of adults, particularly parents, to be "emotional coaches" for their children (1998, p. 75). The core of this responsibility involves:

- being aware of the child's emotions
- recognizing the emotion as an opportunity for intimacy and teaching
- listening empathetically and validating the child's feelings
- helping the child verbally label emotions
- setting limits while helping the child solve problems

▶ Particular Needs

Maturational changes underpin the developmental advances of the 2-year-old. She is now larger, stronger, and better able to help herself and think about her world. She has come a long way since birth. From now on, almost all skill development is a refinement of what has already emerged. To assist the 2-year-old's development, several important needs must be met.

EMOTIONAL SECURITY

Emotional security continues to be a core issue. It constitutes the foundation on which all the other domains are dependent. Security for the child at this stage means constancy, knowing what is expected, having clear parameters of behaviour, being understood and accepted, and knowing that he is loved and that what he does is important. Being sensitive to the child's fears is essential. Some planning might help avoid troubling images, but the child needs to act out and talk about his fears.

CONVERSATION

Toddlers need to listen and to talk. They need to be reminded that conversation is a two-way process. Vocabulary can be extended only by exposure to language, so all types of language activities are important. The child needs to listen to stories, hear rhymes, talk about activities and feelings, have conversation over mealtimes, and use fantasy and reality in play. She also needs to have the opportunity to talk with adults and other children.

SPACE

Children at this age are larger and more active and need an increased amount of indoor and outdoor play space. In this space, they need equipment that encourages safe gross motor activity. Climbers, bikes, hoops, and balls of all sizes are appropriate. The children also need space to respond to music. At this stage, they love to move to music in a free, unrestricted way.

HANDS-ON LEARNING

Children learn by doing. They need to touch, feel, explore, experiment, and find out how everything works, how it can be taken apart, what properties it possesses, and what they can create from it. Thus, children at this stage need a wide range of sensory, art, discovery, and construction materials.

SORTING OUT THE WORLD

The 2-year-old's ability to sort and match starts a quest to organize and sort everything in the world. He needs some help classifying dogs or sheep, for example, but soon gets the idea and wants to cluster together everything of the same kind. The child can now handle smaller objects, so he can sort things and put them away, matching them to picture labels on the containers. Play material with sets of animals, coloured items, and natural objects are needed for sorting.

FINE MOTOR ACTIVITIES

Children at this stage like to complete puzzles with a few pieces, play with table toys, paint and do other creative activities, and build things with construction blocks. They need the opportunity to repeat puzzles, even when they have done them successfully. New games also have interesting challenges. These activities assist fine motor skill development, but they also help develop concepts of size, shape, colour, and so on.

THE INVOLVEMENT OF ADULTS AND OTHER CHILDREN

Two-year-olds like to play alone and sometimes alongside other children, but they flourish when they get adult attention. The child feels empowered when he can drive the play activity. Adult involvement is needed to enhance or assist in elaborating the play, help the child attend to details, prolong his concentration, offer appropriate language, and provide strategies to assist in social skills. The adult should be a play partner, not a director.

Before the age of 2, the toddler usually does little more than acknowledge, tolerate, and play alongside other children. After 2 years, he is in a transition stage where his understanding of others increases. He is still egocentric, but he needs other children to help him become more socially competent.

IMAGINATION

Changes in the play behaviour of children this age happen because they are able to think symbolically. This enables them to play in both imitative and imaginary ways. Props and stories might encourage imaginative thinking. Fears are very real at this stage, and imaginative play can help the 2-year-old act out some of them.

PERSONAL AND INTELLECTUAL STYLE

The 2-year-old has a need to be understood. Adults can show that they respect a child when they take time to be with him and observe his patterns of responses. Part of the need is for adults to know how best to reach or engage a child. Box 12.3 provides some suggestions for sharing this information. The child will have a favoured channel of communication, a leaning toward one or more multiple intelligences, a **temperament style**, and particular **personality** traits that make him an individual. The child needs to have adults recognize all these characteristics and respond in an appropriate and supportive manner.

BOX 12.3

A USEFUL STRATEGY FOR SHARING CARE: COMMUNICATION SYSTEMS

A variety of communication devices can be used to assist the two-way communication that is desirable in a child-care setting. Many involve giving information, which is perfectly valid, but you will also need some hearing strategies. Bulletin boards, open nights, newsletters, daily charts, group meetings, and mini–resource libraries can assist with information offerings. Portfolios, assessment processes, parent meetings, and social activities can provide times for two-way information exchanges. Individual meeting times, evening telephone conversations, and informal chats at the beginning and end of the day can be times when parents are most likely to share their feelings.

▶ Emotional Intelligence Support

As the 2-year-old becomes better at articulating her feelings and regulating her actions, she becomes increasingly **competent** in what are now her life skills. Adults must understand that she needs to be independent but function in a social setting. As the adult appreciates her style, he can provide support as her social/emotional **coach**.

OPPORTUNITY AND RISK-TAKING

Learning to recover from emotional situations as well as learning from practical mistakes is essential to the child at this stage. She needs opportunity to play and discover and her environment needs to be safe but also offer plenty of risk-taking learning. This does not mean playing with dangerous materials, but ones that can be dealt with in open-ended way. Having some objects that can be dismantled and rebuilt is also enjoyable and offers the chance to find out how things work and to exercise different types of thinking skills.

SOCIAL SITUATIONS

The child in her third year needs plenty of opportunity to play with other children in a safe environment. During play situations conflicts will arise; the child needs to have these to learn that other people have different points of view. She needs the adult to act as mediator to help her bridge the gap between the two children and for each child to have a positive learning experience as a result.

SHARED MOMENTS

Above all the play and social situations that are essential for learning and development, the child needs adults to share moments with her. These may involve happiness or sadness, activity or passivity; but they all involve having a mutual understanding that transcends words. She needs you to be there.

▶ Developmental Variation

Particularly notable at this stage are the patterns of behaviour and communication in a few children that present challenges for the educator and parent and, of course, for the child herself. We think of these as behavioural issues, communication disorders, or maladaptive behaviours. They may be caused by many factors, including temperament style and other inherited characteristics, life experiences and nurturing, or medical conditions. Frequently the causes are multiple.

ATTENTION DEFICIT DISORDER (ADD) AND ATTENTION DEFICIT HYPERACTIVITY DISORDER (ADHD)

Attention deficit disorders are mentioned frequently by the media and by parents who are trying to explain the behaviour of their young children. Attention deficit disorders concern the child's inability to focus on tasks, organize herself in a way that is developmentally appropriate, or think in patterns that are generally accepted as normal. **Hyperactivity** is a term used to describe the child's inability to slow down or remain seated. Hyperactive children move around a lot and tend to be excitable. A diagnosis can be made only by a pediatrician, physician, psychiatrist, psychologist, or other specialist. Children with attention deficit or hyperactivity disorders present challenges for educators. They may appear to do poorly in some educational settings, which seems surprising because children with these disorders may have above-average intelligence. Although ADD can be treated with Ritalin and other drugs, such a response is controversial. Some people feel that children on Ritalin are being drugged out of difficult behaviours to make the educator's job easier; others feel that Ritalin is the only way for some children to be calm, focused, and successful.

ANXIETY DISORDER

Life events, abuse, traumas, styles of parenting, or temperament types, in any combination, can result in a young child suffering undue **anxiety**. Although the specific cause is sometimes very hard to determine, it may be particularly relevant to the solution of the problem. Two-year-olds normally experience a wide range of emotions, and fears normally take up a significant part of their emotional energy. Sometimes these show up as nighttime problems, including nightmares and fears, sometimes called **night terrors**. But if the fears take over, the result can be a pattern of anxiety that is difficult to break. An extreme form of this is an **anxiety disorder**. Anxiety can manifest itself in a variety of ways, including self-comforting behaviours. The child may stroke her body or masturbate, rock, or gnaw at her own hand or arm. She may have sleep problems, experience panic, or display prolonged or obsessive attachment to comfort objects. She may withdraw, be unable to interact with others, and be unwilling to interact with unfamiliar places or people. Treatment may be required from a pediatrician, early interventionist, or psychiatrist.

ATTACHMENT DISORDER

When infants fail to make secure attachments because their style differs from their caregiver's, or they make attachments that are later damaged or broken by significant changes in their lives, they may display **attachment disorders**. Children suffering from abuse are most likely to suffer attachment disorders, because the faulty dynamic of an important relationship has broken their trust. Even if the child does not seem particularly distressed, she can have an attachment problem if the normal boundaries of relationships concerning love and trust are distorted. In extreme circumstances, where infants have not had the opportunity to make attachments—in cases of extreme neglect, for example, or when infants have been placed in unresponsive care in orphanages—they may lose the ability to form attachments.

Many attachment difficulties respond to intervention. Parents and educators can be taught how to tune in to the child and improve the goodness of fit between themselves and the child. More severe forms of attachment disorder may be ameliorated, but it may not be possible to completely mend them. Those children can grow up unable to make or sustain adult relationships.

AGGRESSIVE BEHAVIOUR

Children become aggressive for a variety of reasons. They may have learned this behaviour from others, they may not have learned any self-calming skills or self-control, or they may lack adequate problem-solving skills; they may be unable to use language to articulate their feelings; they may be showing off their power. Children who display **aggressive behaviour** may simply be seeking attention and not know how to do so positively. Some aggressive behaviour may stem from pain, neurological damage, or intense frustration that overwhelms the child. The child who displays aggressive behaviour may feel very vulnerable, unable to take control. This child needs a lot of love and support. In many cases, particularly if the issue is addressed when the child is young, the behaviour can be modified by using behaviouristic techniques of reward or mild "punishment," by providing positive role models and strategies for overcoming frustration, and by deflecting the child's energies into activities where she feels successful.

CHILDREN UNDER STRESS

Children who live in an environment that stresses their parents are not necessarily stressed themselves. Yet they may experience the effect of the stressors, either directly or indirectly. In the latter case, they may catch the parent's stressful reaction and might receive less than ideal support from the parents. Stressors include major issues such as poverty, unemployment or underemployment, family illness, domestic violence, housing inadequacies, and separation or divorce. Parents who are able to cope with their circumstances and who have support systems may be able to protect their child from their direct stressors, but it is harder for them to protect the child from their own frustrations and worries. A child experiences this **stress** and can show it in many ways, including withdrawal, disengagement from play, slowed growth and development, temper tantrums and other behavioural problems, or communication difficulties. Removal from the source of stress may be helpful, but it doesn't guarantee that the child's stress is banished partly because it has become a pattern, and partly because removal from the source is likely to mean removal from the people to whom she is attached. Interventionists can help parents and children deal with stress constructively.

LANGUAGE DELAY

Delayed language does not always reflect a real problem. As we have seen, the range of language skills is very wide in children at this stage. However, educators may notice that a child is not cooing, babbling, or jabbering. The first step is to check perceptual acuity. Hearing is particularly important. If the delay is caused by a hearing deficit, the child might be helped by a hearing aid, tubes in the ears, or therapy to help the child feel vibrations. The physical components of sound production also need to be checked. If the **language delay** is linked to a cognitive deficit, the mode of treating the child might differ. Many educators work well with speech and language pathologists, reinforcing on a daily basis the efforts that the specialist makes.

COMMUNICATION DISORDERS

Communication disorders can take a variety of forms. They include autism, where the child has neurological difficulty in letting people into her life. Other communication difficulties include **aphasia** (a neurological condition that affects the ability to communicate), articulation difficulties, voice disorders, dysfluency (such as stuttering), and **orofacial defects** (such as cleft palate). In addition, culture shock can cause communication difficulties that have to do with an inability to speak English or emotional challenges in integrating into a new environment.

Support for children's language difficulties is best done when the child is young. A speech/language clinician or pathologist can diagnose and treat communication disorders. This person can also help parents and educators to use various techniques to assist language and communication.

▶ Health Concerns

Two-year-olds are very interested and capable of being involved in their own self-help in the area of health. The reader can view this section as the 2-year-old's health curriculum.

HAND-WASHING

Hand-washing should be a matter of routine before meals and snacks and after diapering or the use of the toilet or potty. Two-year-olds need encouragement and positive role models so that they will do this routinely. They need sinks they can reach, liquid soap they can pump, taps that they can turn on and off, and paper towels or single-use cloth towels that are washed and sanitized. Take care that young children are supervised when they use water. There is always some potential for drowning, even in a few centimetres of water. They can also scald themselves if the hot tap is too hot or soak themselves completely within seconds.

TOILETING

Two-year-olds may have the bowel and bladder control to use the potty or toilet. Some want to take a long time sitting on the potty, as though it were a regular social situation. There is little harm in this as long as they don't get cold. Other children will observe those using the toilet but will continue to prefer diapers. There should be no fuss about this. The atmosphere in the bathroom should be positive and non-controlling. Telling the children stories about bathrooms can be a good strategy to encourage the children to think of toileting in positive ways.

EATING

Most toddlers at this stage feed themselves with finger food but may want some help cutting up large pieces. They can usually use their fingers and some

can use a fork, spoon, or chopsticks. Children come to child care with various mealtime experiences. They need to make a gentle transition to self-help and feeling comfortable in the social situation of sitting at a table. Children usually look forward to lunch time or snack time and enjoy the adult conversation that occurs. Mealtimes should be associated with pleasantness. Children should not be forced to eat, nor should food be used to manipulate their behaviour. Appetites vary, and children should be encouraged to think about whether they are hungry, and eat accordingly. A variety of foods should be served on a regular basis. Encouragement, but not force, is desirable. Food not eaten should be removed without fuss. Children should hear positive messages about food making them strong or giving them energy.

Learning about food can be great fun. Matching picture cards and pretend food can be good ideas, but handling real food is best. Two-year-olds love to participate in food preparation. In doing so, they find out about colour and texture, about how food is prepared, and about basic rules of hygiene.

ENVIRONMENTAL AWARENESS

Children at this age can be shown how to sort items for garbage or recycling. This sense of order appeals to them. While they cannot appreciate global environmental issues, they do learn from example. If we waste paper, we send the message that this is acceptable. We need to send good messages. If we make messes, we need to take responsibility to help with cleanup. If we keep a recycling bin for scraps, we are sending a message that it's good to reuse things and not be wasteful.

DENTAL HYGIENE

Children's toothpaste and personal toothbrushes should be provided by parents for use after eating. Two-year-olds may not do a very good job and may chew the brush, but the effort is worthwhile. Adults need to monitor and help with tooth-brushing to make sure it is effective. Because the child will have her first set of teeth, they need to be protected from decay. The health of first teeth influences later dental health. Sugary foods and candy should be avoided for the sake of the child's teeth and dietary needs.

SLEEP HYGIENE

A schedule that includes quiet times and a mat or cot to sleep on are appropriate for children at this stage.

They welcome the predictable routines and rituals associated with sleep. Most children welcome snuggling into their favourite cuddly toy or holding a soft piece of blanket. The pattern for naps should be similar every day, so that the child becomes used to the sequence of activities that lead to sleep. Back-rubbing or playing soft music may be part of this, but whatever the educator offers on one day has to be available every day.

Disturbing dreams may waken the child. If this happens, provide reassurance. It may be helpful to avoid showing frightening images in books and on television.

EXERCISE

Two-year-olds do not need structured activities or sports. They need to run, climb, explore, and have fun outdoors spontaneously. The adult should provide space and opportunity for this. If the weather is really bad, children will need to run around in an indoor play space. Two-year-olds need to hear that running and stretching their bodies is healthy.

LABELLING FEELINGS

Young children will always point to the part of their body that hurts, but it is useful for them to acquire a vocabulary related to how their body feels and functions. "It hurts" can help a parent or educator to know what the matter is. "I feel ucky" can let the adult know that a child doesn't feel well.

A positive rather than shameful attitude toward bodies is essential, but children can be taught about being private. Although privacy is a socially learned behaviour, many children feel more comfortable if given their own private space. Children need to learn to request privacy.

▶ Signs of Potential Neglect or Abuse

SEXUAL ABUSE

Of all the types of abuse, child **sexual abuse** brings out the most emotionally charged response. Realistically, the educator and parents are the people closest to the child on a daily basis and thus best positioned to recognize behavioural changes and signs and symptoms of abuse. As in any other type of abuse or neglect, the educator must follow the agency's child abuse protocols, pass information to the local child protection agency, consider how medical advice can be sought, and ensure that the situation is kept confidential. Signs of sexual abuse may be evident in infants, toddlers, and 2-year-olds. These may include:

- any of the signs attributable to other forms of abuse
- behavioural changes
- withdrawal
- sleep problems
- fears
- body-flaunting
- masturbating or rubbing the genitals
- hiding the body
- refusing to remove clothes
- soreness of the vagina
- soreness of the penis
- anal soreness, bleeding, or itching
- bleeding or infected genitals (i.e., showing a discharge)
- soreness around the mouth
- bruises around the genitals or on the insides of the legs
- hand marks on the legs

Remember, it is not for the educator to determine whether abuse, sexual or otherwise, has occurred, but to document any observations that are pertinent and follow reporting procedures. The educator must contact the child protection agency if there is cause for concern. Extensive investigation is likely and it is essential that all concerned cooperate with staff from the child protection agency and with the police.

▶ Everyday Safety Issues

Two-year-olds can begin to take small steps toward increasing their own safety. They may be ready to learn the rules of the room, which can be demonstrated and mentioned when the situation arises. They can learn that:

- We are kind to each other (we don't hurt each other).
- We take turns (we don't push and shove).
- Paint stays at the easel (is not taken across the floor).
- We use words (we don't hit each other).
- Forks are for eating (not for jabbing the next child).
- We go down the slide one at a time (not all together).
- Messes need wiping up (or someone may slip).
- We walk around the swing (not across its path).

- We hold hands when we walk (we don't run all over).
- We have to wait our turn (we don't fight for food or a turn on the bike).
- Another child is first this time (not you, so don't push).
- Scissors go point down (to prevent accidents).
- You should look where you're going (rather than bump into things or people).
- We don't go outside without a grownup (it's not safe by yourself).

If these are offered in context, they are positive statements that are easily understood. But children at this age cannot hold two things in mind at once, so expect a lot of forgetting. Repeat the rule as necessary. Two-year-olds can feel most positive about taking control of a situation and following the rule, so the educator needs to say "Good waiting, Gianni," or "I like the way you are holding hands to be safe." Two-year-olds can learn some personal-safety techniques by learning to say things like:

- "No."
- "I don't like you hurting me."
- "I'll wait for Mommy at the window."
- "Don't touch me."
- "I don't want that."

- "I'll tell Mary that you did that to me."
- "Go away."

Although these statements sound assertive, they can be said in a variety of situations where there are everyday concerns or conflicts at play. The child is beginning to exercise her right to freedom and personal safety, which is part of her need for personal empowerment.

▶ Starting Points for Response

RESPONSIVE CAREGIVING

Two-year-olds are leaving behind their infancy and joining the wider world, where they are keen to become independent. But along the way, they feel vulnerable or need emotional support because things can seem too much. The educator needs to read the child's signs and respond to them accordingly. Sometimes the child needs approval, at other times protection. Her feelings change so rapidly she's not always aware of how she feels. The caregiver needs to help the child to understand her feelings and how to control them so that she can use them to her advantage. Box 12.4 provides some strategies for responding to the needs of a child at this age.

BOX 12.4

GETTING IN TUNE WITH THE 2-TO-3-YEAR-OLD CHILD

Below are some starting points for building your responsivity skills with a 2-to-3-year-old child. Tune in with respect and:

- Allow for uptime and downtime.
- Respond to cues, including facial expressions and gestures.
- Have fun in the child's play on his level and extend play experiences in partnership.
- Accept repetitive/ritual behaviours.
- Assist self-awareness and competence in labelling characteristics.
- Offer creative modes of expression, such as paint, clay, music, movement, etc.
- Show the child that you like to spend time with him.
- Enable the child's world to be safely enlarged.
- Support the emergence of self-help skills.
- Dance and place actively with the toddler.
- Offer many sensory discovery experiences, including ones that challenge the child's experience of the properties of materials.
- Suggest handing out snack items to others.
- Offer quiet spaces for the child to be alone.
- Enable the toddler to accept and help control his own feelings and recognize others' feelings.

- Provide choices of action and allow consequences to be experienced.
- Introduce small-group activities to increase social exposure and cooperation.
- Acknowledge the toddler's demonstration of empathy, taking turns, following practical directions, and working together.
- Accept frustrations, but help the toddler to get himself out of the challenge—be consistent and calm.
- Provide plenty of indoor and outdoor play space.
- Introduce items from nature (check safety).
- Reshape mistakes in language with playful demonstrations of the correct version.
- Provide tools to "help" adults.
- Respond to and assist the toddler's curiosity.
- Notice gender-specific play but encourage non-gendered approaches.
- Use stories and books for close one-to-one contact and to extend the child's experience.
- Respond to questions with simple answers or by suggesting ways the toddler can find the answer.
- Introduce playthings that challenge the development of fine motor skills (e.g., Velcro fasteners, zippers, etc.).
- Use domestic objects as playthings: e.g., chairs with large cloths can become tents.
- Introduce and reinforce simple sequencing activities.
- Talk about objects in terms of concepts (colour, counting, quantity, height, etc.).
- Offer a full dramatic play centre, including culturally familiar home objects.
- Suggest having a teddy bears' picnic.
- Go for walks and stop to talk about what you see.
- Introduce concepts such as yesterday and tomorrow, but appreciate limited use of the concepts.
- Identify the toddler's individual intelligences and build on those preferences.
- Use a conversational, give-and-take style in body language, talking, dance, and other activities.
- Offer achievable physical challenges in climbing, running, balancing, etc.
- Use large balls for rolling and catching with arms outstretched.
- Play hide-and-seek.
- Encourage the child to make connections between objects and actions, people and jobs, domestic items and where they belong.
- Access technological activities for short periods.
- Offer clear parameters of behaviour and simple consequences.
- Offer time, when it is requested or when there is a favourable response to your invitation for intimacy.
- Encourage use of transitional objects.
- Provide spaces for personal belongings and respect that the child has certain belongings that she does not wish to share.
- Mention the toddler's achievements to the parent, in front of the child.
- Demonstrate and encourage tidy-up times.
- Explain simply how you feel about situations and behaviour.
- Respond to signs and symptoms of distress, illness, or other issues.
- Provide mood-changing activities or experiences for when new directions are needed.
- Display the toddler's artwork with respect.
- Provide passive experiences that are relaxing (avoid overuse of TV or video).
- Talk about TV characters and stories.
- Aid the toddler's transitions, acknowledging her feelings.
- Support dual-language learning.

SUPPORTIVE GUIDANCE

There's so much to learn, and the 2-year-old wants to do it all, right now! She needs assistance in making choices, following through with an activity, and knowing the sequence of planning, action, and cleanup. These are the socially acceptable behaviours of the toddler room. She needs to know what is expected, and she may need many reminders because she can't always remember. Everything should have a set routine. Ritualistic behaviours help the child make sense of things.

FACILITATING DEVELOPMENT

The 2-year-old's need for order makes her interested in sorting and matching everything in sight. She starts to classify things, but forgets or changes the criteria for sorting partway through, so her activities may seem disjointed. Her imagination leads to more complex forms of play that might involve other children. With some signs of cooperation, she might be involved, too, in sociodramatic play, but the sequences will not be very long or complex. It is helpful if the adult provides lots of starting points and "why don't you . . ." suggestions. The child wants adult approval, but may not be as dependent on the adult in the activity of play. Conceptual understanding increases tremendously during this year, and language learning complements all the new understandings. The child likes lots of familiar stories and may sit for a while in a small group to listen. Creative music activities are usually well received. Children are stretching their capabilities to broaden the repertoire and refinement of motor skills. They enjoy practising them as they paint, draw, glue, construct, and play with sensory materials and a variety of games and puzzles.

HOLISTIC RESPONSE

Activities 12.1 and 12.2 encourage a holistic response to young children at 24–36 months. Activity 12.1 suggests ways of engaging in the experience of toddlers at this stage and extending your interactions with them. Activity 12.2 (page 376) helps you to observe each toddler and to develop activities that are targeted to individual interests and skill levels.

Activity 12.1

Responding to the Changing Needs of Young Children at 2–3 Years Old

Your interactions with the 2-year-old must be responsive to her needs and emerging skills. To assist you in engaging in the toddler's experience, the following activity offers suggestions that may extend your interactions. Careful observation is necessary so that you introduce the idea at the right time and in the appropriate way. Each suggestion includes ways the idea can be extended if the toddler is ready. This activity also illustrates the safety, communication, conceptual, and developmental issues that you, as a child-care professional, need to keep in mind as you respond to the 2-year-old.

There are many other appropriate activities, besides the ones listed below; your skill in developing them will grow as your experience and enjoyment increase!

Activity 12.1

Responding to Changing Needs of Toddlers at 24 to 36 Months

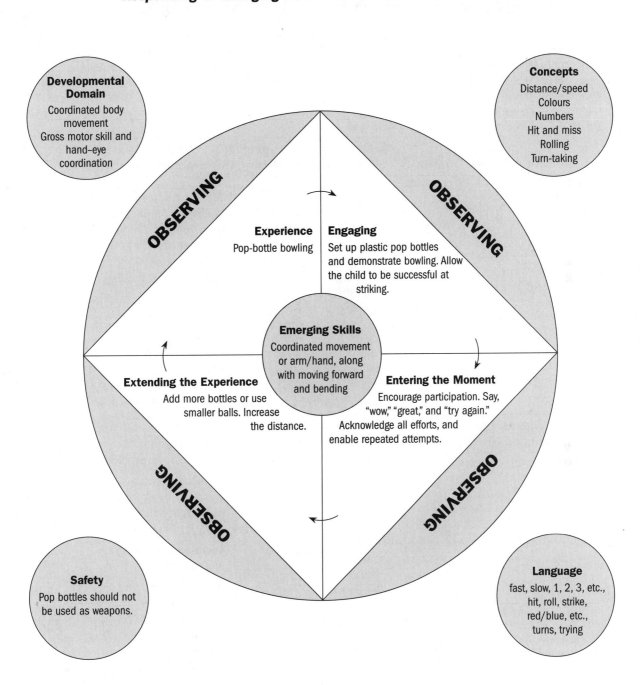

Developmental Domain
Coordinated body movement
Gross motor skill and hand–eye coordination

Concepts
Distance/speed
Colours
Numbers
Hit and miss
Rolling
Turn-taking

OBSERVING

OBSERVING

OBSERVING

OBSERVING

Experience
Pop-bottle bowling

Engaging
Set up plastic pop bottles and demonstrate bowling. Allow the child to be successful at striking.

Emerging Skills
Coordinated movement or arm/hand, along with moving forward and bending

Extending the Experience
Add more bottles or use smaller balls. Increase the distance.

Entering the Moment
Encourage participation. Say, "wow," "great," and "try again." Acknowledge all efforts, and enable repeated attempts.

Safety
Pop bottles should not be used as weapons.

Language
fast, slow, 1, 2, 3, etc., hit, roll, strike, red/blue, etc., turns, trying

Activity 12.2

Creating Responsive Curriculum for 2-to-3-Year-Old Toddlers

Activities for the 2-year-old must evolve from their interests and skill levels. There cannot be a set curriculum! The adult's role is to tune in to the toddler's world and create experiences that are mutually enjoyable, that celebrate her abilities, and provide opportunity for continued development. The following ideas will help the adult to observe each 2-year-old and provide some meaningful experiences.

With confidence, the adult can extend these ideas yet further.

Developmental Domain	Observation of Emerging Skills (Things You See)	Responsive Experience/Activity
Physical skills	– stepping with a pronounced heel–toe pattern – running with greater confidence, although changing direction and stopping suddenly are still difficult – jumping up and down on both feet and propelling wheeled toys – learning toileting skills – improved fine motor skills support self-dressing skills	Provide stimulating physical challenges in the environment while maintaining the safety necessary to support active exploration. Provide outdoor activities that present opportunities for mastering gross motor skills. Make sure there is large equipment (tricycles, wagons, etc.) to support the 2-year-old as he attempts to use toys in different ways.
Cognitive skills/ communication and language	– using objects in ways other than their intended purpose (symbolic play) – taking objects apart and putting them back together – sorting and classification skills – expanding vocabulary – talking in two-word phrases	Offer activities and experiences that stimulate the desire to solve problems. Provide materials that can be manipulated and used in more than one way. Arrange a rich dramatic play area that will foster pretend play. Provide choices that are simple and direct to help the child develop discrimination and self-regulating abilities. Provide a language- and literacy-rich environment.

Developmental Domain	Observation of Emerging Skills (Things You See)	Responsive Experience/Activity
Social/emotional skills	– beginning of sharing and empathy – expressing emotions through temper tantrums – helping with household chores – asserting his independence by saying no even if he complies with the request	Provide opportunities for social interaction between small groups of children. Allow children to discuss and experiment with their feelings in a trusting and accepting environment.

Responding to Changing Needs

Toddlers at 24 to 36 months

EXPERIENCE 1

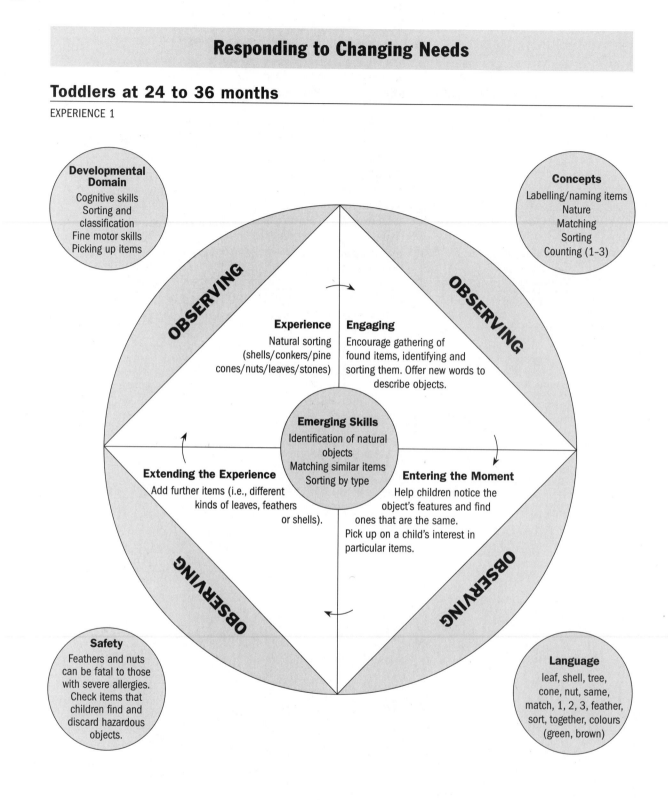

Developmental Domain
Cognitive skills
Sorting and classification
Fine motor skills
Picking up items

Concepts
Labelling/naming items
Nature
Matching
Sorting
Counting (1–3)

OBSERVING

OBSERVING

Experience
Natural sorting (shells/conkers/pine cones/nuts/leaves/stones)

Engaging
Encourage gathering of found items, identifying and sorting them. Offer new words to describe objects.

Emerging Skills
Identification of natural objects
Matching similar items
Sorting by type

Extending the Experience
Add further items (i.e., different kinds of leaves, feathers or shells).

Entering the Moment
Help children notice the object's features and find ones that are the same. Pick up on a child's interest in particular items.

OBSERVING

OBSERVING

Safety
Feathers and nuts can be fatal to those with severe allergies. Check items that children find and discard hazardous objects.

Language
leaf, shell, tree, cone, nut, same, match, 1, 2, 3, feather, sort, together, colours (green, brown)

Responding to Changing Needs

Toddlers at 24 to 36 months

EXPERIENCE 2

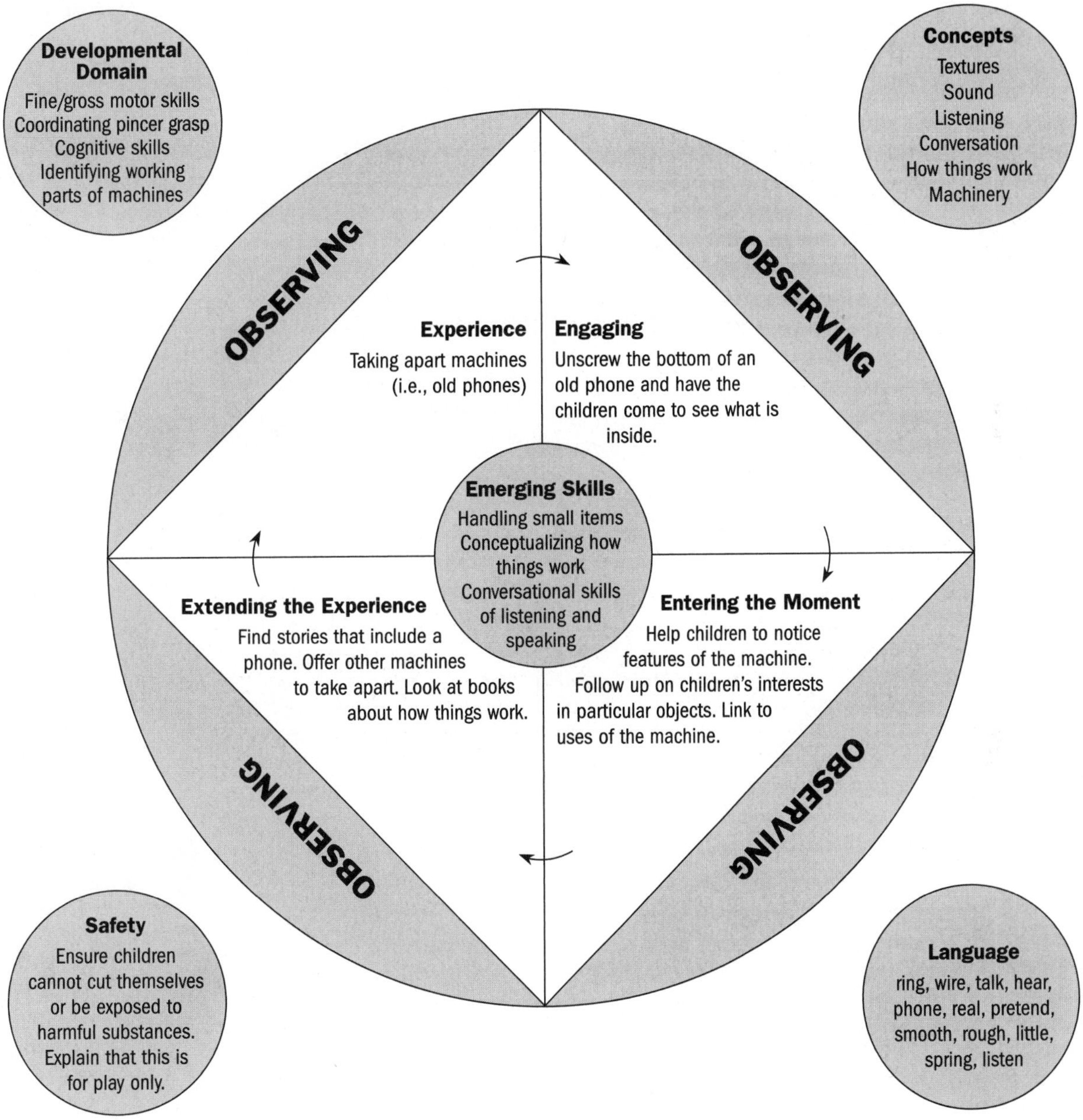

Developmental Domain

Fine/gross motor skills
Coordinating pincer grasp
Cognitive skills
Identifying working
parts of machines

Concepts

Textures
Sound
Listening
Conversation
How things work
Machinery

OBSERVING

OBSERVING

Experience

Taking apart machines
(i.e., old phones)

Engaging

Unscrew the bottom of an
old phone and have the
children come to see what is
inside.

Emerging Skills

Handling small items
Conceptualizing how
things work
Conversational skills
of listening and
speaking

Extending the Experience

Find stories that include a
phone. Offer other machines
to take apart. Look at books
about how things work.

Entering the Moment

Help children to notice
features of the machine.
Follow up on children's interests
in particular objects. Link to
uses of the machine.

OBSERVING

OBSERVING

Safety

Ensure children
cannot cut themselves
or be exposed to
harmful substances.
Explain that this is
for play only.

Language

ring, wire, talk, hear,
phone, real, pretend,
smooth, rough, little,
spring, listen

Responding to Changing Needs

24 to 36 months

EXPERIENCE 3

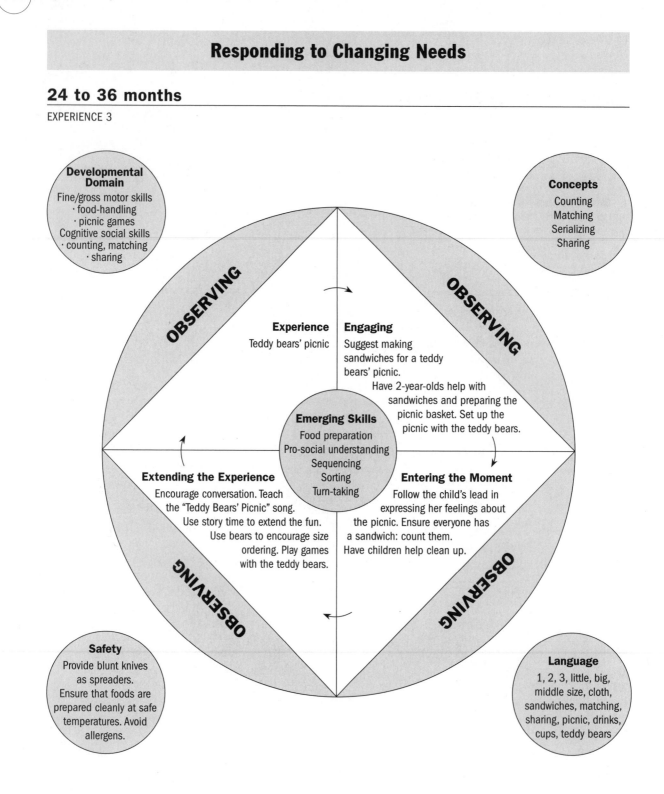

Developmental Domain
Fine/gross motor skills
· food-handling
· picnic games
Cognitive social skills
· counting, matching
· sharing

Concepts
Counting
Matching
Serializing
Sharing

OBSERVING

OBSERVING

Experience
Teddy bears' picnic

Engaging
Suggest making sandwiches for a teddy bears' picnic.
Have 2-year-olds help with sandwiches and preparing the picnic basket. Set up the picnic with the teddy bears.

Emerging Skills
Food preparation
Pro-social understanding
Sequencing
Sorting
Turn-taking

Extending the Experience
Encourage conversation. Teach the "Teddy Bears' Picnic" song. Use story time to extend the fun. Use bears to encourage size ordering. Play games with the teddy bears.

Entering the Moment
Follow the child's lead in expressing her feelings about the picnic. Ensure everyone has a sandwich: count them. Have children help clean up.

OBSERVING

OBSERVING

Safety
Provide blunt knives as spreaders. Ensure that foods are prepared cleanly at safe temperatures. Avoid allergens.

Language
1, 2, 3, little, big, middle size, cloth, sandwiches, matching, sharing, picnic, drinks, cups, teddy bears

Further Experiences and Interactions

Further Experiences	Interactions
Sensory doughs	Provide cookie cutters, rolling pins, and safety scissors to manipulate the dough.
Different surfaces and levels	Providing some carpeting, pillows, ramps, mats, grass, and sand areas allows the child the opportunity to master balancing and mobility in a variety of ways.
Floor puzzles	Start with large, simple puzzle pieces that have familiar, meaningful pictures for the child.
Manipulative blocks	Large connecting blocks stimulate the fine motor and cognitive skills. Large floor blocks will be explored, carried, and climbed.
Books with colourful, familiar, meaningful pictures	Create picture books with real photos. Allow the child to read and turn the pages on her own.
Stacking blocks	Stimulate spatial awareness (on, under, in, out, etc.).
Sequence puzzles	Cognitive skills are stimulated and a recognition of early literacy is enhanced (i.e., beginning, middle, and end to stories or events).
Dramatic play prop boxes	Pick themes for prop boxes and include a variety of materials that will encourage socio-dramatic play (i.e., restaurant box includes dishes, aprons, place mats, tablecloth, etc.).
Pull-along toys/push toys	Attach ropes to favourite toys so they can be pulled along on explorations (constant supervision is necessary to avoid strangulation).
Hide-and-seek items	Place surprises inside purses, luggage, or containers. Place sound-making devices (alarm clocks, metronomes, etc.) around the room and encourage children to find out where the noise is coming from.
Photograph albums and family pictures	Display albums and pictures around the room at the child's eye level.
Name songs and chants	Frequently use children's names in the songs and chants you use. Use these songs and chants during transition times to help identify their roles.

Responsive Guidance for Toddlers Aged 24 to 36 Months

Age/Stage: 24 to 36 Months

Situation	Response
• Shelly wants to dress herself when her mom needs to leave for work quickly. • Trina has a tantrum because her blue dress is in the wash. • Damian will accept his lunch only if it is in a blue bowl. • Mandy has to have her bears and dolls in certain positions before she will go to sleep. • Tom wants to use a cup like his big brother, but wants a bottle when he needs comfort.	**Developmental Issue:** **Autonomy and Ritualistic Behaviour** Two-year-olds are striving to do things independently but at the same time are dependent upon the adults in their lives and on experiencing a predictable routine. There is comfort in old familiar things and knowing what will happen next. Additionally, 2-year-olds may attribute cause-and-effect inaccurately and imagine that things must be done a particular way for almost magical reasons! Understanding these things is helpful, but you may want to plan your time accordingly to ensure that you avoid a battle of wills. Giving in to some requirements for things to be the way the 2-year-old wants is rarely problematic. But the 2-year-old needs to know her boundaries, and that whining don't mean winning!
• John refuses to sit still at circle time. • Kelley will eat, but only with her fingers. • Tatjana points to people who are strangers to her and says "Wot's dat?" • Helen takes off her underpants or trainer pants and lifts up her skirt so everyone can see her bottom. • Jeremy uses the word "share," but he eats all the snacks by himself.	**Developmental Issue:** **Acceptable Behaviour** There may be secondary reasons for some of these behaviours. These might include limitations of attention, inability to use implements, genuine inquiry, delight in the 2-year-old's own body, or an unwillingness to share—but each of these scenarios indicates the toddler's limited understanding of what is acceptable behaviour. Some of the behaviours might have been thought funny when they were first seen, but the adult may find them tiresome. Appreciating the cognitive difficulties in understanding the complexities of acceptable behaviour is a major hurdle and two years is insufficient to master them. Adults can reinforce good behaviours and ignore or redirect negative ones. Questions can be answered simply and correctly, but the strongest learning tool is the modelling of the appropriate behaviours by all the adults the 2-year-old meets.

Manufactured Toys and Play Materials for Toddlers Aged 24 to 36 Months

Toy/Material	Uses	Group Care	Home
Giant floor puzzles	Encourages cooperation and shape discrimination and manipulation.	√	√
Low tables and chairs	Allows children to sit and play at their own levels.	√	√
Wooden train set (a few pieces)	Encourages cooperation as well as understanding of space, shape, distances, and speed.	√	√
Large wooden blocks	Encourages children in construction and understanding of space, height, shape, and imagination.	√	√
Play foods	Children use their imagination in simple dramatic play. Encourages conversation and cooperation.	√	√
Farm animal set	Two-year-olds identify each animal, extend vocabulary, and may sort items.	√	√
Giant dinosaur collection	These may encourage dramatic play and use of the imagination. Many 2-year-olds identify each dinosaur.	√	√
Doll house (large wooden pieces)	Early dramatic play can be encouraged with home-like "house." Children may act out their fears.	√	√
Transparent boxes or baskets for toy organization	Children can help tidy up and find items they want. This helps with sorting skills as well as with organizational understanding.	√	√ (can be bought in stores)
Beanbag seat	A squishy beanbag seat can promote a focus on books, etc., and allow children comfort.	√	√
Large beads or laces for threading	There is a concern about small pieces presenting a safety issue. Choose large beads that can be manipulated.	√	√

Toy/Material	Uses	Group Care	Home
Light table	A table that has a translucent top with light underneath encourages close observation and discovery.	√	√
Dough cutters or rolling pins	These provide an extension to the dough experience and are fun with food.	√	√
Finger paints or brushes	Manufactured finger paint is easier to handle, but more expensive than making your own.	√	√ (make your own!)
Bowling/ skittles set	Older, better-coordinated twos may enjoy large plastic skittles, but avoid frustration!	√	√
Cars and roadway	Girls and boys enjoy cooperating to run their cars on a road. Ensure that each child has a car.	√	√ (make a roadway on cardboard)
Wagon	Children can pull themselves along or be pulled by an adult.	√ (depends on numbers and potential use)	√
Dump trucks	Filling and dumping sand or other items is fascinating for 2-year-olds.	√ (ensure trucks are sturdy)	√
Balls (various sizes)	Rolling, bouncing, feeling, and other uses are found by twos.	√	√
Percussion: musical instruments	Making sound and discovering rhythm can be exciting and encourages cooperation.	√	√ (try making shakers)
Xylophone	Encourages pitch discrimination and rhythm. Ensure item is tuned.	√ (but sharing can be problematic)	√
Toy phone	One of the best ways to encourage conversation. Have two or more!	√	√
Sidewalk chalk	Outdoor play can be enhanced by colouring the space. The rain will erase it.	√	√

Toy/Material	Uses	Group Care	Home
Paddling pool	All water play attracts children. It is cooling and involves discovery, but be safe.	√	√
Duplo/Lego	These blocks are the right size for small hands. Construction play is colourful and fun.	√	√
Sticklebricks	Building is easy with pieces that stick together easily.	√	√
Tray puzzles	Simple tray puzzles of two to eight pieces can be provided. They can be great for spatial learning.	√	√ (expensive)
Shape stampers and dabbers	These can extend painting and printing activities as well as coordination.	√	√
Tunnels	Climbing through the tunnel and playing peek-a-boo can enhance floor time.	√	?
Climber/loft	Gross motor skills are supported and a loft provides a quiet private space.	√	?
Child-sized coffee set, tea set, and crockery (use culturally diverse items)	Imitative play is delightful for 2-year-olds. This encourages conversation and cooperation.	√	√
Small-sized brooms and mini vacuum cleaners	Encourage play cleanup and copy adult actions. This may encourage taking responsibility.	√	√
Tape recorder	Use for playing music and sounds and for taping the children's own voices.	√	√ (can be expensive)
Low painting easel	Standing up to paint allows freer movement and creativity.	√	√ (but it takes up space)

Toy/Material	Uses	Group Care	Home
Non-spill paint pots	These tend to limit spilled paint and encourage brush wiping and control.	√	√
Stickers	Can be used on special occasions, but tend to encourage competition.	√	√
Baby swing with seat	This offers some limited fun but requires close supervision.	√	√
Glue and spatulas	Non-toxic white glue can be used for sticking, collages, and junk modelling.	√	√
Safety scissors	When the 2-year-old is ready, she may try cutting out shapes or items.	√	√
Teeter-totter rocker/ see-saw	This requires cooperation. Ensure that children are safe.	√	√
Plastic magnifying glasses	Discover the world close up.	√	√
Gardening implements, seeds, bulbs, and plants	The concept of growth is difficult, but encourage children to garden.	√	√
Toy camera	Imitate adults. This has fairly limited use, but can be popular.	√	√
Easy opening dress-up clothes	Complicated clothes should be avoided, but simple dress is fun and imaginative.	√	√
Bird feeder, birdhouse, birdbath	Encourage ecological sensitivity and learn about birds.	√	√
Magnets	See what attracts and explain the properties of metal.	√	√
Masks and mirror	These can be scary for some, but many children love to act out different roles.	√	√

Toy/Material	Uses	Group Care	Home
Beanbags	Throwing, catching, and aiming can be incorporated into many activities.	√	√
Dolls (various ethnicities)	Imitative play can be promoted with dolls. When you are small, it can be a good feeling to care for someone smaller! Dressing dolls can be difficult, but provide a blanket.	√	√
Low shelves	These enable all the toys to be accessible.	√	√
Stuffed toys	Soft animals can provide comfort and company.	√	√
Shape sorters (various)	Shape identification is likely to come before trial-and-error sorting or deliberate sorting.		
Picture books	There is lots to talk about in picture stories.	√	√
Step stool	Reaching adult or older children's things can assist with self-help.	√	√
Short-story books	Follow along with a short story and extend vocabulary.	√	√
Duplo blocks/ figures	Construction is easy with hand-sized blocks.	√	√
Dramatic-play playhouse	Basic imitative and dramatic play can be fostered in a playhouse or dramatic play centre.	√	√
Tents	Ready-made tents make great places to find a quiet moment.	√	√
Dramatic props (child-sized stove, sink, fridge, and/or table)	A variety of props assist in enriching dramatic play. This can lead to associative and cooperative play as children play together.	√	√

Toy/Material	Uses	Group Care	Home
Cause-and-effect toys	A variety of cause-and-effect toys can be enjoyable and can teach important skills.	√	√
Boats for the bath	Toys in the bath extend the experience.	√	√
Watering cans	Watering seeds helps twos to learn about growth.	√	√
Small tricycles	Gross motor skills can be developed with a variety of wheeled toys.	√	√
Picture-matching games/Lotto	Assist picture identification and matching skills with these simple games.	√	√
Water/sand toys (sand/water wheel, funnel, rakes, sieve, moulds, and shovels)	Indoors or out, sand toys give hours of fun and learning through experimentation.	√	√
Hand puppets	Stories are enriched with hand puppet characters.	√	√

▶ Summary

During the young child's third year there is an increased confidence, curiosity, and independence in the child, as we see that she wants to do things for herself. As her fine and gross motor skills are refined, she is able to increase her self-help skills involving dressing, toileting, mealtimes, and other everyday competencies. Now the child can improve the range of mobility skills and is able to climb, jump down from small heights, and become active inside and outside. Improving hand coordination allows the child to play with a variety of materials, including paint and crayons. Her grasp is more refined and she uses this skill to help her with eating and dressing.

The child usually enjoys a predictable routine and may demand that certain domestic actions be undertaken in a ritualistic manner. She may want to have things done in a certain way and may be adamant that she drink from a particular cup or wear particular clothes. Frequently we may see that the child has strong emotions that might change rapidly. Although she is able to regulate her feelings and behaviour to some extent, she often seeks the assistance of adults to help her manage situations. Having a small range of trusted adults is important as the child balances independence and dependence.

It is important at this stage that the child be given the tools to become emotionally intelligent. Many aspects of her increased self-regulation indicate an understanding of her self and others. Increasing this understanding can come about in a variety of ways, but it is predicated on solid relationships with adults and the opportunity for her to socialize with other children. She has some empathy for others but needs this reinforced. Having adults act as coaches assists her to become socially and emotionally competent.

The child's increasing cognitive skills can be attributed to her brain development, but also depend upon her having appropriate learning experiences. Usually the 2-year-old will be moving from the sensory-motor stage of thought to the preconceptual phase of the pre-operational stage, according to Piaget's model of cognition. At this stage, it is evident that the child has increasing abilities to categorize her world, even though her thinking is not yet constant. She has some difficulty holding ideas in mind, which can make her thinking appear semi-logical. She may also make some incorrect associations between ideas. Her attention span when engrossed in an activity increases over time. Children have different ways of being smart. The multiple intelligence theory explains how we can recognize each child's strengths and use these favoured channels to expand the child's learning.

At this stage, the child's play becomes broader and more complex. We may see a number of pretend games, but she remains interested in sensory play of various kinds as she becomes more sophisticated in how she handles the materials. Through play, the child increases her knowledge about the world, what it's made of, and how it works. In particular, she learns about the properties of materials, along with many preconceptual ideas. Her social relationships include others in her play behaviours, but her play tends to be parallel or associative rather than cooperative. Imitation continues to be important to her learning, particularly in understanding social roles. In her play we frequently see situations that are imitated or adapted from what she has seen in other situations. This deferred imitation is one signal of her symbolic thinking ability. We may see evidence of a more vigorous imagination in a variety of ways—particularly in her fantasy play.

Having an imagination and fluctuating emotions, along with an incomplete understanding of the realities of life, the child may experience a range of fears. Sometimes these are evident when she has nighttime problems, including nightmares and fears or night terrors.

It is very noticeable that during the third year the child's language expands tremendously. Not only does her vocabulary grow, but so does her use of the rules of language. This enables the child's communication skills to be increasingly refined. She manages to convey and understand many more ideas. The link between language, social development, and cognition is evident within language development. When a child is acquiring one or more languages at a time it is necessary to support both languages, even if some temporary confusions arise.

The child's parents are the most important adults in the life of their child. Working in partnership with parents can assist us to define what our role is in the lives of young children. Observing children, acting as their coach, providing scaffolding for their learning, acting as mediator, and enjoying their company are each essential elements of our role to support every part of the child's development. But we must see the child as a competent human being. Froebel provides us with some meaningful perspectives in understanding this role; the most important element is that we learn to be there for them.

▶KEY TERMS

aggressive behaviour
aggressive play
ambidextrous
anxiety
anxiety disorder
aphasia
associative play
attachment disorder
attention deficit disorders
axon
brain maturation
calcify
cerebellum
coach
communication disorder
competent
concepts
conservation
consonants
constancy
convergent thinking
cooperative activity
corpus callosum
creative play
creative thought
creativity
deferred imitation
dendrites
divergent thinking
egocentricity
emotional intelligence
empathy

expressive vocabulary
fantasy/fantasy play
grammar
hyperactivity
language delay
logic
lymphatic system
mental representations
mean length of utterance (MLU)
multiple intelligences (MI)
myelin
neuron
night terrors
open-ended activities
orofacial defects
ossify
overextension
parallel play
personality
phonemes
pincer grasp
preconceptual thinking
pre-operational stage
private speech
problem-based play
receptive vocabulary
self-esteem
semantics
sensory integration
sexual abuse
social emotions
sociodramatic play
stress
superheroes
symbolism
synapse
syntax
temperament style
temporal concepts
transductive thought
trundle
unconditional love
vocabulary
vowels
zone of proximal development (ZPD)

▶ DISCUSSION QUESTIONS

1. A mother and father tell you they are considering taking their child out of centre-based care, to put her in private home care, because of a recent incident in which their child was bitten by another child. What might you say and do?

2. Recent advances in brain science have improved our understanding of children's behaviour. How does this understanding translate into a change in the educator's role?

3. How could you organize your day with under-3-year-olds so that you can enjoy more shared moments with them?

4. What strategies might you use to assist a child of 30 months to integrate into your child-care setting, when he has had no previous exposure to other children and speaks only Farsi?

5. How can educators advocate for higher standards of child care?

▶ ADDITIONAL RESOURCES

▶ Further Readings

Brosterman, N. (1997). *Inventing Kindergarten: Nineteenth Century Children*. New York, NY: Abrams.

Burton, L., and T. Kudo. (2000). *SoundPlay: Understanding Music through Creative Movement*. Reston, VA: National Association for Music Education.

Fröbel, F. (1826). *On the Education of Man (Die Menschenerziehung)*. Keilhau/Leipzig: Wienbrach.

Gardner, H. (1993). *Multiple Intelligences: The Theory in Practice*. New York, NY: Basic Books/HarperCollins.

Goleman, D. (2000). *Working with Emotional Intelligence*. New York, NY: Bantam Doubleday Dell.

Gottman, J. (1998). *Raising an Emotionally Intelligent Child*. New York, NY: Fireside Books/Simon & Schuster.

Greenspan, S., and S. Wieder. (1997). *Infancy and Early Childhood: The Practice of Clinical Assessment and Intervention with Emotional and Developmental Challenges*. Washington, DC: Zero to Three.

Kaiser, B., and J.S. Rasminsky. (1999). *Meeting with Challenge: Effective Strategies for Challenging Behaviours in Early Childhood Environments*. Ottawa, ON: Canadian Child Care Federation.

Lerner, C., and A. Dombro. (2000). *Learning and Growing Together: Understanding and Supporting Your Child's Development*. Washington, DC: Zero to Three.

Lieberman, A.F. (1993). *The Emotional Life of the Toddler*. New York, NY: Free Press.

Liebschner, J. (1992). *A Child's Work: Freedom and Guidance in Froebel's Educational Theory and Practice*. Cambridge, U.K.: Lutterworth Press.

Lilley, I. (ed.) (1967) *Friedrich Froebel: A Selection from His Writings*. Cambridge, U.K.: Cambridge University Press.

Pawl, J., and M. St. John. (1998). *Learning & Growing Together: Understanding and Supporting Your Child's Development*. Washington, DC: Zero to Three.

Pawl, J., and M. St. John. (1998). *How You Are Is as Important as What You Do*. Washington, DC: Zero to Three.

Pruett, K. (1999). *Me, Myself and I: How Children Build Their Sense of Self–18 to 36 months*. New York, NY: Goddard Press.

Saracho, O., and B. Spodek. (1998). *Multiple Perspectives in Play in Early Childhood Education*. Albany, NY: SUNY Press.

Weitzman, E. (1992). *Learning Language and Loving It: A Guide for Promoting Children's Social and Language Development in Early Childhood Settings*. Toronto, ON: Hanen Centre.

Wilson, L. (1997). *Partnerships: Families and Communities in Canadian Early Childhood Education*. Scarborough, ON: Nelson.

▶ Useful Videos

Life's First Feelings: Growing Pains. NOVA. Closed captioned; 60 minutes (VHS).

Description: This video provides a close look at babies' emotional responses, clues about developing personality traits, and how parents help with socialization.

Ready for Life. KERA. 60 minutes.

Description: This intimate story of six children and their families—depicting the joys and sorrows they face as they begin to explore the world—displays how children begin to develop the strength and confidence to face life's challenges in emotionally healthy ways.

Nourishing Language Development in Early Childhood. Davidson Films. 31 minutes.

Description: Using vignettes filmed at an exemplary children's centre, students are introduced to the vocabulary of language studies. Dr. Honig describes the development of spoken language in infancy, toddlerhood, and early childhood.

Childhood Development: A Cognitive Approach to Developmental Psychology. Films for the Humanities. 5-part series; 25 minutes each.

Description: From the earliest stages of mental representation to advanced acquisition of language and social skills, this series presents various research methods, theories, and concepts of developmental psychology to promote understanding of a crucial period of development.

Babywatching. Films for the Humanities. Colour; 50 minutes.

Description: Featured zoologist and peoplewatcher Desmond Morris sets out, not merely to watch babies, but to watch, think, and see the world like a baby.

Let Babies Be Babies: Caring For Infants and Toddlers With Love and Respect. Manitoba Child Care Association. 6-part series; 16–30 minutes each.

Description: These videos and accompanying guides take viewers on a journey through current thinking on a variety of early care issues. Drawing on the personal experience of caregivers from both family and centre-based child-care settings, as well as the work of leading experts, this series provides the practical advice needed by today's caregiver.

▶ Useful Web Sites

Emotional development
www.science.mcmaster.ca/Psychology/
2aa3esum/Emotion.PDF
www.athealth.com/Consumer/issues/childsanger.html
Play
www.cfc-efc.ca/menu/play_en.htm
www.unbf.ca/education/ecc/gallery/mollie/
www.voices4children.org/factsheet5.htm
Brain development
www.childcarecanada.org/research/complete/
neurons.html
www.sparrowlake.org/
Movement and music
www.cfc-efc.ca/docs/cccf/00013_en.htm
www.menc.org/information/prek12/echild.html
Families
www.vifamily.ca/
www.unesco.org/education/educprog/ecf/
www.familiesandworkinst.org/
www.nafcc.org/
Language and cognition
www.igs.net/~cmorris/zpd.html
members.tripod.com/Caroline_Bowen/devel2.htm
www.cal.org/ericcll/digest/earlychild.html
www.ooaq.qc.ca/Fiches/en_pgFiches.html
www.learningtolisten.org/index.html
Froebel: philosophy and phenomenology
www.infed.org/thinkers/et-froeb.htm
www.froebel.com/
www.atl.ualberta.ca/po/articles/
template.cfm?ID=363
www.froebelfoundation.org/philosophy.html
Child abuse
www.hc-sc.gc.ca/hppb/familyviolence/
childsa.htm
www.childhelpusa.org/
Various EC topics
www.earlychildhood.com/Articles/index.cfm
ericeece.org/
www.educationworld.com/early_childhood/
www.unicef.org/

Appendices

▶ Nine Categories of Temperament

TYPES

1. Activity level: the percentage or degree of activity
2. Rhythmicity: regular or unpredictable
3. Approach/withdrawal: caution or clinging (in new situations)
4. Adaptability: resistance or flexibility (with change)
5. Intensity of reaction: the degree and length of reaction
6. Responsiveness threshold: the amount of stimulation necessary for a response
7. Mood: positive/negative (duration and degree)
8. Attention span and resistance: length and intensity of interest or scattered versus focused effort
9. Distractibility: the degree of reaction to unimportant stimuli, degree of attention

CONSTELLATIONS

1. Easy: 40% of children
   moderate intensity, adaptability, mostly positive mood
2. Difficult: 10% of children
   negative, fearful, easily distracted, not predictable, shifting moods, intense reactions, "movers"
3. Slow-to-warm-up: 15% of children
   difficult but not persistent, negative to start and then "warm up," less intensity

Average: the other 35%

Each child demonstrates different elements within the types. In the majority (65%) of children, there is clear evidence of one of the three constellations of temperament. The types help us to observe temperamental characteristics; the constellations offer a guide to the most frequently observed sets of characteristics. Remember to observe all characteristics carefully, without assuming a constellation.

Source: Chess and Thomas (1996), Temperament: Theory and Practice *(New York, N.Y.: Brunner/Mazel Publishers), p. 34.*

▶ Immunization Schedule

The following chart presents a typical immunization schedule for a healthy infant. Although there are Canadian guidelines for immunization, provincial variations exist. The U.S. and Europe have similar schedules, but differences exist because of the varying perceived risks of exposure in different countries.

Immunizations have not always eliminated the viruses that they target, but they are an important public health measure. Canadian children receive immunizations through the medicare system and do not have to pay for them. This is not the case in the U.S., where families without medical insurance and who are financially disadvantaged may not be immunized. This compromises their health and the health of those around them.

In general, each child is given an immunization card indicating what immunizations are to be given and when, and documenting when they have been given. Parents are responsible for ensuring these cards are kept up-to-date.

Age at immunization	DTaP	IPV	Hib	MMR	V	Hep B	PC	MC
2 months	X	X	X			X*	X	X
4 months	X	X	X			X*	X	X
6 months	X	X	X			X*	X	X
12 months				X	X		X	
18 months	X	X	X	X				
4–6 years	X	X		X				

* These immunizations are given in three doses at infancy or in preadolescence.

DtaP	diphtheria, tetanus, pertussis
IPV	inactivated polio virus
Hib	haemophilus influenza type b conjugate vaccine
MMR	measles, mumps, rubella
V	varicella
Hep B	hepatitis B vaccine
PC	pneumococcal conjugate vaccine
MC	meningoccocal C conjugate vaccine

Physicians, nurses, and nurse practitioners who administer the immunizations check on the overall health of the child before giving the immunization(s).

Children who have a severe allergy to eggs, a weak immune system, or who are sick with a fever are not normally given immunizations.

Child-care centre directors are responsible for making sure that every child enrolled is immunized in accordance with the appropriate schedule.

A few parents decide against immunization for religious or moral reasons. There are usually procedures that cover these situations. The family's physician may be asked to write to child-care centres verifying this. Not all the vaccines charted below are required for entry to child care—check with the centre or local health authority.

Mild reactions to immunization, such as minor swelling, redness, or a little pain, can be treated at home, and they are fairly common. Any significant reaction, such as a fever of 39.5°C (103.1°F) or greater, persistent crying, seizures, stiff neck, drowsiness, pale or blue skin, allergic reaction, or changes in behaviour, should be brought to the attention of a physician or emergency department at the nearest hospital.

Amended schedules can be developed for children who have not received their immunizations in accordance with the usual schedule. It is rarely too late to immunize.

▶ Neglect: An Overview

Note: The terms "child," "children," "infant," and "toddler" refer to infants, toddlers, and young children under 3 years of age.

DEFINING NEGLECT

The definitions of neglect include:

- physical neglect
- child abandonment and expulsion
- medical neglect
- inadequate supervision
- emotional neglect
- educational neglect

Neglectful actions may be undertaken by parents, parent substitutes, and other adult caretakers of children.

PHYSICAL NEGLECT

Refusal of health care
- failure to provide adequate health care for the newborn infant
- failure to provide or allow needed care in accordance with recommendations of a competent health-care professional for a physical injury, illness, medical condition, or impairment
- failure to provide appropriate health care for infants and toddlers who have disabilities

Delay in health care
- failure to seek timely and appropriate medical care for a health problem that any reasonable layman would

have recognized as requiring professional medical attention

Abandonment
- desertion of a child without arranging for reasonable care and supervision

Expulsion
- refusal of custody of the child, such as permanent or indefinite expulsion of a child from the home or child-care centre without adequate arrangements for care by others

Other custody issues
- custody-related forms of inattention to the child's basic needs
- leaving the child with others for prolonged periods
- providing inconsistent care without a secure home base

Other physical neglect
- conspicuous inattention to avoidable hazards in the home
- inadequate nutrition, clothing, or hygiene
- other forms of reckless disregard for the child's safety and welfare, such as driving with the child while intoxicated; leaving a young child unattended in a motor vehicle; failing to protect the child from sun, heat, cold, or inclement weather; or failing to protect the child from physical dangers that might reasonably be predicted

SUPERVISION

Inadequate supervision
- child left unsupervised or inadequately supervised

EMOTIONAL NEGLECT

Inadequate nurturance/affection
- marked inattention to the child's needs for affection, emotional support, attention, or competence

Chronic/extreme abuse or domestic violence
- chronic or extreme spousal abuse or other domestic violence in the child's presence

Permitting drug/alcohol abuse
- encouraging, administering, or permitting drug or alcohol use by the child
- exposing the child to drugs or alcohol, risking self-administration

Permitting other maladaptive behaviour
- refusing to take appropriate steps to protect child from transportation hazards, such as walking onto a road or street
- failing to control behaviour that has the potential for posing undue risk, such as climbing in unsafe places

- failing to control the child's behaviour in ways that are potentially dangerous, such as allowing a toddler to significantly hurt an infant

Refusal of psychological care

- refusal to allow needed and available treatment for a child's emotional or behavioural difficulties in accordance with competent professional recommendations

Delay in psychological care

- failure to seek or provide needed treatment for a child's emotional or behavioural impairment or problem which any reasonable layman would have recognized as requiring professional psychological attention

Other emotional neglect

- other inattention to the child's developmental or emotional needs not classifiable under any of the above forms of emotional neglect

EDUCATIONAL NEGLECT

Not applicable to infants and toddlers except:

Inattention to special education need

- refusal to allow or failure to obtain recommended services, or neglect in obtaining or following through with treatment, for a child's diagnosed special need without reasonable cause

ADDITIONAL SITUATIONS THAT MIGHT CONSTITUTE NEGLECT

- exposing the unborn child to drugs, alcohol, or other known teratogens
- failing to access emergency services after accidents or emergencies
- failure to provide appropriate first-aid treatment in the event of minor accidents
- exposing young children to, or failing to protect them from, known environmental pollutants
- failing to check the credentials of a person purporting to be a parent or legal guardian, and handing over a child to the care of such a person
- failing to protect the child from persons known to be violent or inappropriate
- placing a child in the care of a person too immature or incompetent to provide for the child's needs or to respond to hazardous situations

Adapted from The National Clearing House on Child Abuse and Neglect Information (U.S.), 2003.

Important note: Parents have the overriding responsibility for their infants and young children at all times. The early childhood practitioner, home child-care provider, guardian, baby-sitter, or other designated caregiver has a duty of care to all children in his/her charge. Any sign of potential neglect or abuse that is identified must immediately be reported to the local child protection or welfare agency, Children's Aid Society, Family and Children's Services, or the police. Any reasonable concern for the child's well-being requires this action. Finding proof of neglect or abuse is not the task of parents or caregivers; it is the task of the appropriate authority, applying its standard policies and procedures under the relevant legislation. It is not the role of any caregiver to confront, accuse, diagnose, analyze, or interfere with any child protection agency or police investigation. Caregivers should objectively describe, document, and date any relevant information, including, if applicable, child observations and health concerns.

▶ Essential Features of Constructivist Theory: Piaget's View

- focuses on the child's inner construction of the outer world—knowledge is not "out there" but an internal creation
- stage progression depends on the level of the child's cognitive processes, not age (age ranges are a guideline)
- stages are invariant (every child must go through them in sequence) and universal (applicable to everyone)
- there are four major stages in which there are structurally different types of cognition
- the theory is rooted in biological ideas involving adaptation
- based on the notion of intrinsic motivation (not external rewards)
- understanding the child's stage of cognition depends on close observation of behaviour and language—particularly the child's mistakes
- adaptation involves assimilation (taking in new ideas) and accommodation (changing existing thought patterns to incorporate new ideas)—i.e., acquiring more knowledge and different ways of thinking
- sensory-motor intelligence involves combining sensing and acting
- pre-operational thinking involves the child's use of symbolism, mental reasoning, and the use of concepts (before the stage of formal, logical, mental processes)
- responses to the environment depend on the situation and the individual's understanding of the situation
- children need to be active in their own development
- children may be supported in their learning by being confronted with moderately novel events that build on previous experience
- language and thought are intertwined

▶ An overview of Piaget's stages of cognitive development

Stage	Approximate Age	Characteristics	Activity/Play examples
Sensory-motor stage Substage 1 *Reflexive*	first month of life	reflexive activity automatic (unlearned) responses to external stimuli five senses available for input	sucks from the breast feels the texture of her quilt her random movements are symmetrical bangs her hand against the side of the crib gazes at adults
Sensory-motor stage Substage 2 *Primary circular reactions*	1–4 months	motor activity centred on the body senses available to absorb input coordination of actions establishes simple habits focused on own needs simple anticipation of events some reflexes disappear	repetition of enjoyable actions—sucks many objects stares and touches something at the same time combines grasping and sucking sucks on own hands cries when needs are not met but, initially, without deliberate attempts to get attention
Sensory-motor stage Substage 3 *Secondary circular reactions*	4–8 months	develops schematic ideas deliberate actions focus on repeating interesting effects direct imitation focused on self simple associations increased physical skills enable infant to handle materials more effectively	reaches for and grasps objects manipulates items repeats interesting or surprising actions copies another baby banging with a wooden spoon links objects by function sits and passes toy from one hand to the other
Sensory-motor stage Substage 4 *Coordination of secondary circular reactions*	8–12 months	begins to organize schemes intentional behaviour goal-directed activity object-permanence physical causality (beginning of problem-solving) imitation with alterations anticipates events makes efforts to change events recognizes that others exist but is focused on self	looks for hidden objects shakes rattle in different ways "hides" from Mom at bedtime copies adult putting on a hat but modifies what she has seen reaches for bib at feeding time makes deliberate cries to get attention plays peek-a-boo with older sibling

▶ An overview of Piaget's stages of cognitive development (cont'd)

Stage	Approximate Age	Characteristics	Activity/Play examples
Sensory-motor stage Substage 5 *Tertiary circular reactions*	12–18 months	discovers new means through active experimentation combines and extends ideas builds schemes through more complex actions elaborates schemes broader imitation stronger associations (links between objects and ideas) trial-and-error activity uses increased fine and gross motor skills to reach goals uses some basic symbolism uses simple language extends play experiences to make them more interesting recognizes that others exist but remains focused on self	uses new techniques to be successful in putting shapes through appropriate slots looks in several places for a lost item imitates parts of an adult role discovers the properties of Play-Doh action occurs within a wider physical space, such as organizing self to play in sand at a distance from the adult puts objects together that belong, such as a number of toy cars points to car and says "car" tries several ways of positioning puzzle pieces to put puzzle together correctly varies the way she performs actions as she experiments with snow activity with junk/found materials, where she combines materials and extends the enjoyment seeks adult help with play task plays alone with a doll watches older children playing
Sensory-motor stage Substage 6 *Internalization of schemes*	18–24 months	mental representation of reality internalizes images of things and past events beginning of true thought deferred imitation make-believe activity complex schematic under-standing acceptance of others but remains focused on self early categorization internalizes social behaviours	uses a variety of strategies to solve the problem of manoeuvring a chair into a small space pretends to be mother or father in house play play involves imaginary creatures anticipates the ball emerging from the other end of a tube uses words and simple language to convey needs and ideas plays alongside others (but without interaction) sorts a few items according to her own criteria—e.g., "things that I like" recognizes objects and people in pictures attempts to soothe another child when she is hurt, in imitation of adult response (not true empathy)

▶ An overview of Piaget's Stages of cognitive development (cont'd)

Stage	Approximate Age	Characteristics	Activity/Play examples
Pre-operational stage	2–3 years (continues through to 7 years)	symbolic thought egocentric perspective internalizes roles primitive reasoning deceived by appearances complex deferred imitation and elaboration builds concepts associated with direct experiences make-believe representation of ideas animism broader strategies for problem-solving transductive reasoning magical thinking constructs own reality categorization using one attribute wide range of conceptualiza-tions: colour, weight, size, things that float/sink, what to wear, things to eat, etc. rich imaginative thinking indications of creativity remembers and follows an instruction	plays alongside or with other children, having learned the concept of turn-taking has difficulty in understanding another child's perspective (why she wants the same toy) thinks that another child has more to eat because his portion is spread out over the plate involved in water play, discovers floating and sinking sociodramatic play sequences involving other children paints in ways that express her own ideas and feelings believes that her teddy can hear her talking (animism) thinks that the puppet lady is coming today because it is raining (because when she came last week it was raining) responds positively to request to put item into garbage bin refuses to go to bed without the ritual sequence of story—arrangement of toys on bed—good-night kiss sorts small toys according to colour (but forgets the criterion after a period of time)

► Charting Your Baby's Emotional Milestones

I. SELF-REGULATION AND INTEREST IN THE WORLD (BIRTH TO 3 MONTHS)

Increasingly (but still only sometimes):	YES	NO
– able to calm down	___	___
– sleeps regularly	___	___
– brightens to sights (by alerting and focusing on objects)	___	___
– brightens to sounds (by alerting and focusing on your voice)	___	___
– enjoys touch	___	___
– enjoys movement in space (up and down, side to side)	___	___

II. FALLING IN LOVE (2 TO 7 MONTHS)

When wooed, increasingly (but still only sometimes):	YES	NO
– looks at you with a special, joyful smile	___	___
– gazes at you with great interest	___	___
– joyfully smiles at you in response to your vocalizations	___	___
– joyfully smiles at you in response to your interesting facial expressions	___	___
– vocalizes back as you vocalize	___	___

III. DEVELOPING INTENTIONAL COMMUNICATION (3 TO 10 MONTHS)

Increasingly (but still only sometimes) responds to:	YES	NO
– your gestures with gestures in return (you hand her a rattle and she takes it)	___	___
– your vocalizations with vocalizations	___	___
– your emotional expressions with an emotional response (a smile begets a smile)	___	___
– pleasure or joy with pleasure	___	___
– encouragement to explore with curiosity (reaches for an interesting toy)	___	___

Increasingly (but still only sometimes) initiates:		
– interactions (expectantly looks for you to respond)	___	___
– joy and pleasure (woos you spontaneously)	___	___
– comforting (reaches up to be held)	___	___
– exploration and assertiveness (explores your face or examines a new toy)	___	___

IV. THE EMERGENCE OF AN ORGANIZED SENSE OF SELF (9 TO 18 MONTHS)

Increasingly (but still only sometimes):	YES	NO
– initiates a complex behaviour pattern such as going to the refrigerator and pointing to desired food, playing a chase game, rolling a ball back and forth with you	___	___
– uses complex behaviour in order to establish closeness (pulls on your leg and reaches up to be picked up)	___	___
– uses complex behaviour to explore and be assertive (reaches for toys, finds you in another room)	___	___
– plays in a focused, organized manner on her own	___	___
– examines toys or other objects to see how they work	___	___
– responds to limits that you set with your voice or gestures	___	___
– recovers from anger after a few minutes	___	___
– able to use objects like a comb or telephone in a semi-realistic manner	___	___
– seems to know how to get you to react (which actions make you laugh, which make you mad)	___	___

V. CREATING EMOTIONAL IDEAS (18 TO 36 MONTHS)

Increasingly (but still only sometimes):	YES	NO
– engages in pretend play with others (puts dolls to sleep, feeds doll, has cars or trucks race)	___	___
– engages in pretend play alone	___	___
– makes spatial designs with blocks or other materials (builds a tower, lines up blocks)	___	___
– uses words or complex social gestures (pointing, sounds, gestures) to express needs or feelings ("me, mad" or "no, bed")	___	___
– uses words or gestures to communicate a desire for closeness (saying "hug" or gesturing to sit on your lap)	___	___
– uses words or gestures to explore, be assertive or curious ("come here" and then explores toys with you)	___	___
– able to recover from anger or temper tantrum and be cooperative and organized (after five or ten minutes)	___	___

Later in stage and throughout next, increasingly (but still only sometimes):		
– uses your help and some toys to play out pretend drama dealing with closeness, nurturing, or care (taking care of favourite stuffed animal)	___	___

	YES	NO
– uses your help and some toys to play out pretend drama dealing with assertiveness, curiosity, and exploration (monsters chasing, cars racing, examining doll's body)	___	___
– pretend play becomes more complex, so that one pretend sequence leads to another (instead of repetition, where the doll goes to bed, gets up, goes to bed, etc., the doll goes to bed, gets up, and then gets dressed, or the cars race, crash, and then go to get fixed)	___	___
– spatial designs become more complex and have interrelated parts, so that a block house has rooms or maybe furniture, a drawing of a face has some of its features	___	___

VI. EMOTIONAL THINKING: THE BASIS FOR FANTASY, REALITY, AND SELF-ESTEEM (30 TO 48 MONTHS)

Increasingly (but still only sometimes):	YES	NO
– knows what is real and what isn't	___	___
– follows rules	___	___
– remains calm and focused	___	___
– feels optimistic and confident	___	___

	YES	NO
– realizes how behaviour, thoughts, and feelings can be related to consequences (if behaves nicely, makes you pleased; if naughty, gets punished; if tries hard, learns to do something)	___	___
– realizes relationship between feelings, behaviour, and consequences in terms of being close to another person (knows what to do or say to get a hug or a back rub)	___	___
– realizes relationship between feelings, behaviour, and consequences in terms of assertiveness, curiosity, and exploration (knows how to exert willpower through verbal and emotional communication to get what he wants)	___	___
– realizes relationship between feelings, behaviour, and consequences in terms of anger (much of time can respond to limits)	___	___
– interacts in socially appropriate way with adults	___	___
– interacts in socially appropriate way with peers	___	___

Source: Stanley Greenspan and Nancy T. Greenspan, *"Charting Your Baby's Emotional Milestones,"* from First Feelings. *Copyright © 1985 by Stanley Greenspan, M. D., and Nancy Thorndike Greenspan. Used by permission of Viking Penguin, a division of Penguin Putnam Inc.*

▶ Hierarchy of Needs: Abraham Maslow

Actualization is the life force that drives human development.

Progression through the levels* (or tiers) depends on resolution of the needs.

From the base level to level four, each stage involves a deficit. Without addressing the need, progression to the next level is impossible. Each of these levels of need creates a motivation—to correct the deficit.

To become self-actualized, all the lower tiers of need must be satisfied.

The possibility of reaching level five does not depend on social or economic standing (other than what is required to meet earlier needs).

Each person's experience is different; perceptions of self are idiosyncratic—even a diseased person in prison can reach self-actualization—however, Maslow thought that very young children were unlikely to be self-actualized. (Carl Rogers disagreed.)

Self-actualized persons remain in a situation of need; these needs include goodness, beauty, aliveness, playfulness, meaningfulness, as well as maintaining each of the lower four tiers.

It is a very subjective process trying to determine one's own levels of need; determining who might be self-actualized is even more difficult!

Maslow's perspective brings a humanizing element to psychology. It is both heuristic (offers a general idea) and qualitative.

* The tiered (wedding cake) illustration is an adaptation of Maslow's pyramidic diagram representing the different levels of need that, once satisfied, lead to self-actualization or transcendence.

Adapted from: Abraham H. Maslow (1968), Toward a Psychology of Being *(D. Van Nostrand), Library of Congress Catalogue number 68-30757.*

LEVEL FIVE: "BECOMING"

self-actualization (e.g., self-directed, maximizing potential, being whole, psychological health)

LEVEL FOUR: "DESERVED ACHIEVEMENT"

self-esteem needs (e.g., success, personal competence, status, recognition, dignity, affirmation, independence)

LEVEL THREE: "BELONGING"

belonging—love needs
(e.g., belonging to family, finding one's place, contact and safety needs)

LEVEL TWO: "DEPENDENCY"

(e.g., security, predictability, stability, protection, other physiological needs)

BASE LEVEL: "SURVIVAL"

(e.g., shelter, food, water, warmth, passing urine and feces)

Glossary

abuse   psychological, physical, or sexual injury inflicted on an individual

accommodation   the process that changes existing ways of thinking in response to new experience—reorganizing or creating new schemes in response to external stimuli (*refer to* Piaget)

action and reaction   the link or association between one action and a reaction that it causes

active play   involves whole-body movement; requires space and simple, safe equipment

activity level   the motor component in a child's functioning; the degree of activity

acuity   the degree to which one or more of the senses is functional

adaptation   the process of change within the individual—involves complementary processes of accommodation and assimilation (*refer to* Piaget)

aggressive behaviour   any action that is motivated to cause harm—socially unacceptable behaviour resulting from anger

aggressive play   play behaviour involving actions that cause harm to other people or to objects

ambidextrous   hand activity without hand dominance (left or right)

ambivalent attachment   an ineffective and unreliable relationship with an adult characterized by distress at separation and anger on return of the attachment figure (*refer to* Ainsworth)

American Sign Language (ASL)   a hand-signalling system used for and by those without hearing; like other sign languages, it incorporates grammatical rules (informally called Ameslan)

anal stage   the second stage of personality development, during which the superego takes form, toilet-learning usually occurs during this stage (*refer to* Freud)

analysis   the process of organizing or summarizing data and then making inferences that assist in creating meaning

anecdotal records   short narrative observations describing significant events; recorded after they have occurred

anti-bias curriculum   the curriculum and experience of the child that is designed and delivered in ways that address potential biases related to gender, race, culture, poverty, and other social issues (*refer to* Derman-Sparks, Rhomberg & Hall)

antibiotics   physician-prescribed courses of medication that target particular bacterial infections

antivirals   physician-prescribed medications that target specific viral infections

anxiety   a troubled feeling or state of emotional unrest—the state might be caused by something occurring within the individual or by particular circumstances

anxiety disorder   a feeling of emotional unrest that cannot be attributed to "real" concerns; may be associated with any one of several neurotic conditions involving irrational fears

Apgar   a standardized measurement instrument used to assess health indicators in the newborn infant

aphasia   a language impairment that may have resulted from damage to the central nervous system

a priori   a term used to identify a type of knowledge that is obtained independently of experience; a priorism is a philosophical position maintaining that our minds gain knowledge independently of experience through innate ideas or mental faculties

assessment   the process of gathering data (including observational information)—using informal or standardized instruments—and making deductions that explain behaviour

assimilation   the process of incorporating new learning into existing schemes (*refer to* Piaget)

assistive device   any device, such as a machine, leg brace, or computer, that enables an individual to be as able-bodied or intellectually functional as possible

associative play   spontaneous activity in which children play alongside each other and interact but involve themselves only with their own play (*refer to* Parten)

attachment   the positive emotional relationship that develops between two individuals—between adult and child (*refer to* Bowlby, Ainsworth)

attachment difficulties   situations that occur where the child is unable to form one or more appropriate positive relationships with adults because the child's experience is erratic or deficient (*refer to* Ainsworth, Greenspan)

attachment disorders   situations that occur where the child is unable to make one or more appropriate positive relationships, to such an extent that there may be long-lasting implications; intervention may be successful

attachment figure   the adult or older child with whom the child makes the affectional tie

attending   paying attention to a stimulus

attention deficit disorders   any disorder, in infancy or later in life, that impedes the ability to focus on tasks; ADD and ADHD are commonly known attention deficit disorders; most attention deficits impede learning; various interventions may be helpful

atypical development   patterns of human development that lie outside the range of the norm or average

atypical birth presentations any positioning of the baby immediately prior to or during birth that is not usual—e.g., breech

authentic assessment gathering of data—including naturalistic observational material—that is reviewed in a contextualized, sensitive, and individual manner (*refer to* Wortham, Martin)

autism a condition in which the individual demonstrates social isolation and communication difficulties

autobiographical memory memories of one's own life (limited by infant amnesia)

autonomy an inner drive to become independent and meet one's own needs; a sense of independence or self-government

autonomy versus shame and doubt the second stage of the life cycle, in which the psychological conflicts of toddlerhood can lead to healthy independence (*refer to* Erikson)

avoidant attachment an inadequate relationship with an adult, characterized by a lack of protest under stress (*refer to* Ainsworth)

axons the part of the neuron (brain cell) that transmits messages to other neurons, muscles, or glands of the body

babbling long strings of sounds produced by the infant; repeated consonant-vowel sounds (sometimes called canonical or reduplicated babbling)

baby signing the use of hand signals, gestures, expressions, and bodily movements that have shared meaning (*refer to* Garcia)

baseline observation a quick and efficient overview of the child's behaviour and health indicators (usually made at the start of each day) that provides a benchmark for change

basic emotions emotions that can be inferred from facial expressions; may be universally understood (*refer to* Izard)

basic trust versus mistrust the psychological conflict in infancy that can be resolved given appropriate support (*refer to* Erikson)

behaviour any demonstrated action, whether deliberate or not

behaviourism the perspective that development occurs primarily because of external influences in the environment (nurture) (*refer to* Pavlov, Watson, Skinner)

behaviour modification the processes of trying to change behaviour by using rewards or negative consequences

best practices ways of working (with children) that are accepted within the profession as exemplary

bias any distorted perception of other people or social groups, or a preference—such as visual preference

bilingual the acquisition of two languages

binocular vision the capacity to coordinate the sensory input from both eyes; results in the ability to perceive depth

biological clock one of the three clocks of life-span development—the influence of heredity and maturation

block play playful activity involving the use of manufactured or found materials to build or construct; observable stages of play behaviour are evident; such play may involve imagination and creativity, but will usually contribute to mathematical concept-building

body language messages, sent either deliberately or unconsciously, that are conveyed by the individual's posture, facial expressions, gestures, or other behaviour

bonding the close physical and emotional relationship (affectional tie) between an adult and child (typically mother and child in the early weeks after birth); Bowlby proposed that one key figure must provide a bonding relationship (*refer to* Bowlby, Klaus & Kennell, Rutter, Ainsworth)

bottom shuffling a method of infant mobility involving sitting on the buttocks and using leg movements to propel the body forward, backward, or sideways; sometimes preferred to crawling

brain the part of the central nervous system that is encased by the skull; has approximately 100 billion nerve cells (neurons), which are responsible for every type of bodily and mental function

brain maturation the biological process of growth and development of the structure and function of the brain

calcification the process of hardening, generally bone

caregiver a person responsible for meeting the physical (and other developmental and health) needs of an individual

catch-up the idea that, given certain remedial experiences, the child can resume a typical stage of development

cause-and-effect understanding that particular actions bring about (cause) particular results (effects)

categorical self the aspect of the self that is self-descriptive (of its own characteristics)—e.g., "I'm a boy" or "I can jump'"

centre of gravity concerning physical growth, the weight difference between the upper and lower parts of the body; the infant is top-heavy and thus has a high centre of gravity

cephalocaudal (principle) that development of the body following a sequence from head to foot

cephalocaudal/proximodistal (principles) the development of the body follows dual sequences simultaneously—from head to foot and from the centre of the body outward to the hands

cerebellum the part of the brain that uses sensory inputs to guide motor activity

cerebral irritation irritation of the brain caused by bacteria (or other foreign bodies) or pressure; it may result in difficulty in becoming calm; the condition may cause seizures

channel of preference (sensory) the individual's best or preferred way of communicating and functioning—e.g., visual or auditory

character the combination of traits that distinguishes an individual; the behaviour of the individual that demonstrates their moral understanding

charts prepared documents that are completed after specified behaviours or functions have been demonstrated and observed—e.g., infant feeding charts

checklist a method of recording observational information that documents the presence or absence of predetermined criteria

child care a full-time or part-time program offering care and education, usually licensed

child-care provider any person who meets the developmental needs of the child

child-centredness a philosophical approach to programming for children that focuses on the child's interests, motivations, needs, and developmental stage

children at risk infants or children who are vulnerable in some way that may result in academic or social challenges

chronic condition a health concern that continues and must be managed over time

chromosomes rod-shaped portions of DNA organized into 23 pairs within each cell; they are responsible for the transmission of hereditary characteristics

chromosomal disorders individuals who experience behavioural or developmental difficulties as a result of having abnormal chromosomes

chronological age the actual age of the child (as opposed to the individual's performance level)

clear-cut attachment the infant's attachment to a specific adult

CNS—central nervous system the brain and spinal column

coach the role of an adult or more mature child to encourage, support, and provide strategies for success

cognition the process of thinking, knowing, reasoning, and other mental functioning

cognitive development changes in the individual over time that result from increased intellectual functioning; may be considered within a framework of stages; depends on interplay of heredity and experience; includes aspects of the mind, brain growth, and behavioural changes

cognitive needs the specific experiences necessary for intellectual functioning

colic a condition characterized by acute abdominal pain

colostrum the first fluid secreted by the mother's breasts soon after birth, before true milk comes through

comfort object any object that the child finds particularly comforting; the object takes on particular significance—e.g., blanket, teddy bear, etc.

communication (skills) the ability to share meaning with others; typically involves a shared language or signing

system; includes ability to exchange ideas involving a sender and receiver of a message

communication disorder a broad term used to describe a structural or functional difficulty or deficit that impedes effective communication—may be a diagnosed disorder such as aphasia or hearing impediment

community a geographical area or neighbourhood; one or more cultural groups with a certain proximity; a group of people with a shared economic status; a system of people with overlapping or shared needs or desires; a group of people such as family members and friends

competencies the level of observable functioning of the individual, or specified knowledge and skills that are to be acquired

(the) competent child a view of the child that assumes that the individual has sufficient skill and aptitude (rather than a deficit model that views the child as helpless and waiting to become competent)

concept clusters of schemes that together create an idea

confidentiality the professional and ethical performance of a role that includes keeping information private and sharing information appropriately as the role demands

congenital cardiac condition a condition that was present from birth involving the structure or function of the heart

congenital condition a condition that was present from birth

consciousness a function of the mind that is awareness of a person's self, environment, and mental activity; may choose courses of actions; there are several observable levels of consciousness; the "problem of consciousness" lies in its complexity; philosophers, neuroscientists, and many others define consciousness differently; consciousness concerns functions of the brain, behaviour, mind, and soul or spirit (*refer to* Dennett)

conservation the understanding that physical attributes stay the same even when their appearance is altered—e.g., mass, number, weight (*refer to* Piaget)

consonants speech sounds, or letters of the alphabet, that are not vowels (*see* vowels)

constancy the idea that things remain the same in some respect, despite perceptual information to the contrary

construct of reality the inner representation of the outer world; creating an understanding of what is real

construction play spontaneous activity involving making, building, or creating; typically involving blocks or found materials; may involve imaginative aspects or make-believe; usually includes an end product—i.e., what is made

constructivism a philosophy of learning that considers reality to be self-constructed: the child, through stages, creates an inner construction of her outer world (*refer to* Piaget)

continuity (developmental)   the notion that the process of human growth and development follows a gradual progression

continuity of care   the design and delivery of child-care programs in ways that enable particular adults to maintain special and continuing relationships with particular children, ensuring that the routines and patterns of care remain the same

continuity/discontinuity (developmental)   the opposing notions that the process of human growth and development follows either a gradual progression or a step-by-step pattern

convergent thinking   thinking that requires a specific correct response

cooing   the squealing-gurgling, happy sounds made by babies from around 6 weeks to 4 months; non-speech sounds

corpus callosum   the area of the brain that contains the largest bundle of nerve fibres and connects the two hemispheres of the brain; allows the two areas of the brain to communicate

crawling   mobility involving propelling the body forward, backward, or sideways while on the knees; typically a stage of physical development prior to walking

creating emotional ideas   the fifth stage of emotional development, which typically occurs at 18 to 36 months (*refer to* Greenspan)

creative play   spontaneous activity with materials or ideas that involves understanding how to use objects or represent ideas, making something, and using innovative or new ideas

creative thought   activity of the mind that involves creativity (*see below*); may involve divergent thought, problem-solving, trial-and-error, or a combination of other thinking skills

creativity   an individual's capacity to produce new ideas, inventions or artistic objects of value; the process of creating and making things

critical period   the time when the child must be exposed to appropriate experiences for development to occur (*see also* "sensitive periods" and "windows of opportunity")

cruising   moving around by standing up and walking sideways while holding on to a stable object

cues   any indicator or message sent (deliberately or not) by an infant or young child that is read and interpreted by an adult or older child; may include facial expressions, sound productions, gestures, and bodily movements

culturally diverse   an environment that includes people of various cultures; an organization that welcomes people from different heritages; may also include individuals from various ethnic backgrounds, people of different religions, people from a range of geographic locations, people who speak different languages, and people living in different subcultures (groups within groups)

curriculum   traditionally refers to the prescribed content of what is to be learned within a designated time period; the philosophy of *See How They Grow* uses the term to mean every aspect of the child's experience, whether designed or not

CVS—chorionic villi sampling   a prenatal examination of the fetus to screen for developmental abnormalities

cycles of sleep   the patterns of sleep—repeated every 90 minutes or so—that involve up to five different types or levels of sleep

dance of communication   the two-way intentional communication that goes back and forth between two individuals

decentred   the ability to alter perspectives; seeing from the perspective of others

decentration   the degree to which a child is able to shift her focus of interest from herself to external objects

decontextualization   understanding something out of context, or outside its usual setting

deferred imitation   copying single behaviours or complex roles some time after the initial observation of the behaviour

dendrites   the neuron branch that is the major receptive surface of the neuron; it receives and processes signals from other neurons (brain cells)

depth perception   the integration of information from both eyes in order to gauge relative size or distance; seeing the world in three dimensions

deprivation   the state in which essential experiences, basic needs, or relationships are denied, absent, or inaccessible

development   the dynamic process of growth and change within an individual that occurs over time

developmental alerts   behaviours that are atypical (significantly different from the norm) of the child's stage, or otherwise indicate cause for concern; they usually require further observation and possible referral to appropriate agencies and professionals

developmental diversity   a group of individuals demonstrating a variety of developmental levels and stages

developmental domains   aspects of the individual's development; e.g., cognitive, social, emotional

developmental milestones   stages in the individual's development; commonly accepted advances that mark new achievements

developmental outcomes   the results of a program or intervention that demonstrate its success or failure; increases in individual performance measured over a period of time

developmental profile   an overview of an individual's development that may include written components and examples that illustrate their level of performance, or a chart indicating average performance levels at each age group

developmental psychology the study of human behaviour and the reasons for its manifestation; identification of discernable stages of change within the individual (*refer to* Piaget, Kholberg)

developmentally appropriate the notion that there are experiences, play materials, actions, etc., that are particularly suitable for children at particular stages of their development

developmentally appropriate practice (DAP) all aspects of children's programs and practices that are designed and implemented in ways that meet each child's developmental needs (*refer to* Bredekamp/NAEYC)

developmental delay an infant or child who has a specific deficit or group of difficulties resulting in developmental patterns that lie outside the norm (outside average)

diary records a series of anecdotal records recorded in sequential order; may provide a teacher with information about individual children or a group of children

(the) difficult child the categorization of a child's temperamental style as being challenging (*refer to* Chess & Thomas)

direct instruction a method of teaching where the adult takes responsibility for structuring learning experiences; adult may use demonstration and other strategies

discontinuity the notion that human growth and development follow a fluctuating pathway of progression and regression, rather than a gradual progression

discovery play spontaneous activity that involves finding out the properties of materials and how they work

discriminate attachment the second stage of attachment, in which the infant makes an attachment to a specific person who meets her needs

disengagement when the individual takes her attention away from a stimulus; may be deliberate or not

dishabituation the increase in responsiveness after stimulation changes

disorganized/disoriented attachment an inadequate relationship with an adult, characterized by the child showing inconsistent patterns of responding to stress (*refer to* Ainsworth)

divergent thinking thinking involving unusual responses; associated with creativity and "thinking outside the box"

DNA—deoxyribonucleic acid the substance in genes that contains information

domain (of development) an aspect of human development; includes physical, emotional, cognitive

Down syndrome a chromosomal abnormality characterized by distinctive facial features and intellectual deficits; also known as trisomy-21

downtime the state of consciousness where the individual is at a low level of response to stimulation

dream mental activity, usually involving imaginary events, that occurs during sleep (REM sleep); may be open to interpretation (*refer to* Jung)

dyadic any activity or relationship involving two, either an individual and an object or two individuals

early childhood assistant (ECA) a person prepared to work with young children; may hold a certificate

early childhood care and education (ECCE) programs and services for young children and their families

early childhood educator (ECE) a prepared individual who is qualified to meet the developmental, caregiving, health, and educational needs of infants, toddlers and preschool children (and sometimes school-age children; works with parents and families, in accordance with professional and ethical practices

ECE preparation (training) any program of study and practice leading to qualification for working with young children—e.g., ECE diploma, Bachelor of Applied Arts in Early Childhood Education, Specialist post-diploma in working with infants, Family Child Care Provider Certificate, B. Ed. in Early Years Education (note that such preparation varies enormously)

early intervention the practice of offering compensatory or other experiences to an infant or young child and her family with the intention of ameliorating (making better) any deficit, developing strategies for success, or addressing potential problems

early intervention programs comprehensive programs designed for infants or young children and their families to support the specific needs of that child/family

(the) easy child a characterization of the child's temperament (*refer to* Chess & Thomas)

echolalia the infant's repetitive babbling of one sound

eclectic (approach) a philosophical approach to working with children that takes elements of various different philosophies and combines them into a meaningful whole

ecological system the idea that human development occurs within and is influenced by complex social systems; involves concentric circles indicating differing social levels (*refer to* Bronfenbrenner)

educarer a prepared individual who is qualified to meet the developmental, educational, and caregiving needs of infants, toddlers, and 3-year-olds (*refer to* Gerber)

educating the process of facilitating learning—assisting in the learner's acquisition of knowledge, skills, and dispositions (attitudes)

ego the part of the individual that is rational and reasonable (*refer to* Freud)

egocentric from the perspective of the individual; in infancy, an inability to see from the perspective of others

egocentric thought thinking that does not take into account the perspective of others; in infancy, an inability to see from the perspective of others (*refer to* Piaget)

egocentricity   the state of seeing only from the individual's perspective; in infancy, an inability to think from the perspective of others (*refer to* Piaget)

emergence of an organized sense of self   the fourth stage of emotional development; typically occurs around 9 to 18 months (*refer to* Greenspan)

emotional development   changes in the individual over time that involve understanding the self and feelings, and regulating behaviour; occurs within stages (*refer to* Erikson, Greenspan)

emotional intelligence   acquiring skills that can be applied in social situations and becoming emotionally mature; ways of being emotionally "smart"; involves emotional development (*refer to* Goleman)

emotions   feelings; complex internal states (not directly observable, except through the interpretation of expressions and body language)

empathy   a social emotion; experiencing the emotions that someone else is feeling; the ability to understand the feelings of another individual

engagement   time spent paying attention to something or someone

entry-to-practice standards   a set of minimum requirements for work in a particular context or of a particular type—e.g., education; standards typically set out the knowledge and skills required for the role

epilepsy   disordered brain functioning characterized by seizures (or convulsions) of varying severity

equilibration   the process of human adaptation in which there is a drive to balance assimilation and accommodation (*refer to* Piaget)

essence   the core element of what makes individual people who they are; the phenomenon of discovering what makes another person different

essential experiences   experiences that are necessary for growth and development to occur at an optimal level

ethics   the values associated with good conduct; professional standards of behaviour; includes levels of practice, reliability, confidentiality

event sampling   a series of observational recordings focused on a specified category of behaviour; used to determine patterns and causes of behaviour; may be used for behaviour modification

experience   anything that produces a response, consciously or unconsciously; what happens around or to an individual; a planned or unplanned event (*refer to* Dewey)

exosystem   the parts of the ecological system that influence experience (but young children have little direct contact)—e.g., the parent's workplace (*refer to* Bronfenbrenner)

exploratory play   any spontaneous activity that involves finding out the properties of materials—e.g., water play

existential self   the individual knowing that she exists

expressive language   uttering meaningful sounds, words, phrases, and sentences

expressive volume   the level of loudness used in language

extrinsic motivation   encouragement, inducement, or support that comes from outside the individual

facilitating development   the role of the adult in organizing, observing, interacting, and supporting another individual's growth, adaptation, and change

factor analysis   a statistical method of managing large amounts of information that reduces the data to a limited number of core themes; commonly associated with research into temperament and personality

failure to thrive   a condition where a seemingly healthy baby fails to grow and develop normally; the individual may have her obvious needs met but lack physical contact (*refer to* Spitz)

falling in love   the second stage of emotional development—typically occurs during 2 to 7 months (*refer to* Greenspan)—or the process of establishing a special relationship

family   a group of individuals who share living space; a natural group in which members are related by birth, marriage, or other criteria and share a household unit

family child care   child care that is offered within a home environment, typically licensed with a trained adult and the supervision of a child-care agency; usually a multi-age program

family systems   the idea that groups of people who share living experiences create structures and function within them

fantasy   imagination unrestricted by reality; being whimsical; a creation of the imagination

fantasy play   spontaneous activity involving suspension of reality, imagination, pretending, and/or make-believe

febrile convulsions (convulsions)   non-epileptic fits in childhood

fine motor skills   learned behaviours involving the small muscles of the body—e.g., the hands manipulating an object

fontanels   the soft spot (anterior and posterior), front and back, on the infant's head, over which unconnected bones are lined with a protective material

genetics   the study of heredity; family patterns of disease; evolutionary patterns of behaviour (*refer to* Darwin, Vogel)

genetic counselling   offering advice to parents and others seeking information about heredity and patterns of genetically determined conditions

germs   microorganisms that might produce disease—e.g., bacteria, viruses, moulds

gesture   a deliberate action of the hands, head, or body, indicating an idea or feeling

gesture vocabulary   a range of hand and arm signs that have shared meanings

glial cells   supporting cells that form a protective coating and nourishment for neurons; they provide scaffolding for growing and developing neurons

goal-directed activity   an activity that results from an individual's efforts to do something deliberately

goodness-of-fit   the extent to which the caregiving style of the parent meshes with the temperament of the infant

grammar   the system of rules that governs syntax in language

gross motor skills   learned behaviours involving the large muscles of the body—e.g., walking

growth   increase in size of the individual; in infancy and early childhood it is typically assessed through measurement of height/length, weight, and head circumference

guilt   the feeling of remorse and responsibility for something that occurred, whether a real or imagined wrong; a product of conflicted feelings (*refer to* Erikson)

habituation   the decrease in the response to a stimulus that occurs after repeated presentations of the stimulus— e.g., looking away from a mobile after continued stimulation

hand preference   the individual's natural pattern of using the left or right hand

hand–eye coordination   the skilled connection between seeing something, reaching for it, and grasping it

health   a state of well-being in which individuals attain their own state of optimal activity and absence of disease, show positive mental functioning and a positive sense of self, have the opportunity to realize their physical potential, and are able to function effectively within social groups, while being emotionally stable and reasonably content

health professionals   physicians, nurses, paramedics, physiotherapists, specialists, and other personnel who contribute to managing health, emergencies, illnesses, conditions, and diseases

healthy development   a desirable level of human development in which the individual becomes a fully functioning person

HIV (human immunodeficiency virus)   a virus that attacks the immune system; transmitted when bodily fluids are transferred from one person to another

holistic response   any response to an individual that takes into account each interacting domain of the person's development

holophrase   one-word utterances that stand for a whole phrase; the meaning depends on the context

homemade checklist   a list of behaviours or other criteria developed by a teacher or parent, used for recording the presence or absence of each item

humanistic theory   a theory of development that concerns meeting the individual's needs; based on humanism (*refer to* Maslow)

hyperactivity   levels of physical activity that are higher than normal, sometimes associated with a disorder

I   reference to the self; the concept of being a separate person; a symbol identifying understanding of the self

id   the part of the psyche that is the seat of instinctual processes or passions (the ego and superego manage the impulses of the id) (*refer to* Freud)

imitation   the act of copying single actions of another person, or the copying of complex actions, as with role models

imitative play   spontaneous activity that involves the copying of single actions of another individual, or the acting out of an internalized role; may involve deferred imitation

imprinting   a response to a stimulus that continues long after the stimulus has disappeared

inclusion   integrating all children into a program, regardless of their ability levels or background

indiscriminate attachment   the infant can be comforted and have his needs met by any adult; he has no special responsiveness to the primary caregiver he has; typically observed during the first 3 months

individual   a separate human being

individual program plan (IPP)   a curriculum or intervention plan created especially for one child on the basis of her assessed needs

infantile amnesia   the phenomenon by which early experiences, typically from before 2 years of age, are not remembered later

individuation   the process of working on becoming a separate person

informal observation   casual or unrecorded observation

information processing   the approach to cognitive development that views the brain as a sophisticated computer with memory and symbolic functions

initiative versus guilt   the third stage of the life cycle, in which the young child needs to resolve the conflict of powerfulness against social pressures to behave well (*refer to* Erikson)

innate (behaviour)   characteristics that are inborn, preprogrammed, acquired but not learned

instinct   what is known or done without learning; feelings or thought based on knowledge without experience; behaviour emanating from pre-wiring

instinctual   concerned with innate capacities or drives

instinctual drives   innate motivations

institutionalization   placing an individual into an institution; typically refers to subjecting the individual to inflexible routines and lack of nurturing and physical contact; a rigid program detrimental to the individual's development

integration   accepting, accommodating, and welcoming individuals of all ability levels, cultures, and backgrounds into a program

intentional action   the emergence of goal-directed activity, typically seen at 8 to 12 months; one of the substages of sensory-motor development (*refer to* Piaget)

intentional communication   the third stage of emotional development—which typically occurs at 3 to 6 months (*refer to* Greenspan)—or any deliberate attempts to convey a message

intentional variation   the emergence of deliberate varying of actions; typically observed at 12 to 18 months (*refer to* Piaget)

intermediate grasp   a grasp that refines the palmar (whole hand) grasp; may involve scooping or some effort at thumb–forefinger opposition

internalization   the process of learning at a level where the tools used are mental, and their use is not visible to others; understanding and accepting an idea

internal world   the function of the mind; the conscious and unconscious workings of thought; awareness of one's own thinking; inner speech and emotion (*refer to* Greenspan)

intrinsic motivation   a drive that comes from within (rather than from external forces)

irreducible needs   the child's basic and essential needs that must be met for healthy development (*refer to* Greenspan & Brazelton)

kindergarten   literally, "the children's garden"; a program for young children; a philosophy of education involving respect for the natural unfolding development of young children and the adult's role as nurturer, educator, and facilitator (*refer to* Froebel)

lactating   the physiological process of producing milk (as in breast-feeding)

language acquisition   the process of becoming able to use a shared code or communication system involving rule-governed combinations of symbols

language acquisition device (LAD)   an innate mechanism that allows language to occur—involves pre-wiring (*refer to* Chomsky)

language delay   later-than-average acquisition of language

lanugo   soft hair that covers the fetus and newborn and helps the vernix stick to the skin

life cycle   the natural and ongoing sequence of birth, life, and death; life-cycle theory proposed by Erikson

locus of control   the perception of control over one's own destiny or future; the belief that one's actions are controlled by the self

logic   the aspect of the ability to think that involves reason and drawing conclusions

lymphatic system   the tissues of the body that screen out harmful substances and manage infection control

macrosystem   the part of the ecological system that broad ideologies emanate from; values and cultural patterns are transmitted through the institutions of the macrosystem (e.g., nations, governments, religious systems) (*refer to* Bronfenbrenner)

make-believe play   spontaneous activity involving pretend and imaginative ideas

manipulative play   similar to object play—spontaneous activity involving handling materials and discovering what they will do

manipulative skills   learned behaviours involving an increasing ability to handle materials and objects successfully

manual dexterity   the individual's ability to use the hands to achieve complex tasks

maturation   the biologically shaped, naturally unfolding course of growth and development (*refer to* Gesell, Illingworth)

maturational readiness   the notion that the child is ready for particular experiences at certain stages of growth

mean length of utterance (MLU)   the average length of the sentences that a child produces; average number of morphemes per utterance

meconium   fetal feces, usually expelled after birth

mediator   a person or structure that acts as an intermediary between the child and the environment; providing supports for learning

memory   a complex function of the brain to recall past events and experiences; storage and access to information previously obtained; elements of memory include recognition, recall, association, internalized scripts, control mechanisms, selection, and retrieval

meningitis   inflammation of the membranes encasing the spinal cord and brain; usually caused by bacterial or viral infection

mental combinations   putting together two or more ideas; holding in mind two or more attributes simultaneously

mental operations   the ability to think about actions that were previously done physically

mental schemes   (*see* schemes)

mesosystem a system of several microsystems that the individual functions within; for young children this might mean home and child care

metabolic disorders disorders that impede the breakdown of food and the production of energy

microsystem the smallest unit of the ecological system; the immediate environment (*refer to* Bronfenbrenner)

milia small white spots, mainly on the nose or the face, caused by blocked sebaceous glands; requires no treatment

mind the entity responsible for thought, feelings, and speech; the seat of consciousness; the function of the brain

modelling the process of demonstrating a social role performance; it is required for observational learning (*refer to* Bandura)

moral development the gradual increases and changes in understanding of right and wrong and the acquisition of values; acceptance of socially acceptable behaviours and moral reasoning, and appreciating societal attitudes and beliefs; stages of moral judgment (*refer to* Kholberg)

morpheme the smallest unit of meaning within language—a word, a prefix, a suffix

motherese changes in the mother's speech that emphasize particular sounds and the use of a higher pitch than normal when communicating with infants and young children; may be culture-bound

motivation the reasons or incentives for human behaviour, explained as basic drives in psychoanalytic theory

motor development the aspect of physical development that involves gross motor skill acquisition and mobility

multi-age programs a program for young children that is designed for and delivered to a mixed group of toddlers, preschool children, and/or infants and school-age children

multi-modal (senses) involving two or more of the modes of sensory input (hearing, sight, touch, taste, and smell)

multi-modal stimulation stimulating two or more senses simultaneously

multiple attachments having two or more secure attachment figures; having a series of important relationships involving significant bonding; typically these relationships are with parents, extended family members, and caregivers

multiple disabilities having two or more disabilities at the same time—e.g., having a hearing deficit and a congenital heart condition

multiple intelligences (MI) the idea that there are many ways of being smart—a theory that identifies seven or eight or more ways of being intelligent (*refer to* Gardner)

mutual interactions two-way communications, and actions that involve both individuals in meaningful exchanges

myelin a coating around the nerves (axons) that conducts electrical impulses from one brain area to another

myelination the process where myelin is laid down on the nerves of the brain; when parts of the brain myelinate, it allows or improves the function of that area, such as movement or vision

narratives written observations that conform to one of the standard methods of recording (running record, specimen record, anecdotal record, or diary record)

nature (development) the aspects of individuals that exist because of their genetic heredity (*see* nurture *and* nature/nurture)

nature/nurture (development) the interaction of genetic inheritance and life experience that contributes to making individuals who and what they are

neuron a nerve cell

night terrors the child's fears that emanate from misunderstandings, fears, nightmares, shadows, darkness; commonly experienced at night and in the dream world

neglect the denial of an individual's basic needs

neonatal the period of time around the birth of the infant—usually the first 6 weeks of life

neonate the infant at birth and for the first few weeks of life

neuron brain cells that store and send information; there are about 25 different types, each with a cell body, dendrites, and an axon

neuroscience interdisciplinary study of the brain and behaviour

non-participant observation an observation conducted from a distance without direct involvement in events or responsibility for what occurs

norms the average performance of a large sample of children at designated ages

normative profiles charts and tables indicting the typical patterns of growth and development at designated ages, of a particular population of children considered to represent the "norm"; often presented as percentiles (*refer to* Sheridan, Illingworth, Allen & Marotz)

numerical scale a form of rating scale that uses numbers to indicate the degree to which a behaviour is present or a characteristic is evident

nurture (development) the aspects of individuals that exist because of their experience of life (*see* nature *and* nature/nurture)

object permanence the realization that objects continue to exist when they are out of sight (*refer to* Piaget)

object play spontaneous activity that involves manipulating objects or materials for purposes of discovery

observation   watching behaviour and activities of children in care in a controlled, informed, educated, purposeful manner, often with specific goals, questions, or concerns in mind; usually involves making records

observation documentation   the professional written accounts of behaviour, development, and significant change; may form part of a portfolio; can be used as official documents in legal proceedings

observational learning   learning by watching people's behaviour

obstetrics   the branch of medicine concerned with childbirth and the care of the mother before, during, and after birth

occupational standards   levels of competence that are required within a profession

onlooker play   spontaneous activity in which the child watches another child or children at play; may ask questions or converse with those at play but does not get actively engaged with their play

open-ended activities   learning activities that do not have built-in correct or incorrect ways of handling materials or doing things

optimal conditions   the best possible situation; exemplary environment

optimal development   the best possible developmental outcome

oral stage   the first of a series of developmental stages characterized by the infant's drive to mouth objects and gain oral satisfaction (*refer to* Freud)

oral gratification   the emotional satisfaction gained from mouthing objects or feeding (*refer to* Freud)

orthopedic disabilities   the lack of muscular tone or mobility resulting from abnormalities in the musculoskeletal system

ossification   the process of converting cartilage to bone

otitis media   inflammation of the middle ear

overextension   the child's application of a language rule in a situation where it does not apply—i.e., extending it beyond situations where it does apply

over-stimulation   a situation in which the infant or older individual is unable to process sensory information because it has become overwhelming

palmar grasp   a hand grasp using the whole hand (and palm)

paradigm   a way of looking at a situation; a perspective

parallel play   spontaneous activity occurring alongside other children, without sharing or cooperation; playing separately at the same activity at the same time and in the same space

parentese   speech pattern used in talking to infants and young children; refers to either the male or female parent (*see* motherese)

participant observation   an observation made while the observer is engaged in activity or communication with the individual being observed

patterns of development   the predictable stages and changes that are observable within each individual; may involve frequent progressions and some regressions; may be continuous or discontinuous

pediatrician   medical doctor specializing in work with infants and children

people permanence   the notion that people continue to exist even when they are out of view (*see also* object permanence)

percentile   any value defined by dividing the group into 100 equal parts; a band that indicates the scores associated within that numerical range; commonly used in developmental profiles to indicate average performance levels and where a particular individual falls within the range

perception   the process of taking in, processing, and interpreting sensory information, through one or more sensory channels

perinatal   around the time of birth, before or after

permission   the professional requirement to ask parents if it is acceptable to observe, record, or conduct an activity

personal health   the factors that contribute to the individual's overall health and well-being—e.g., diet, exercise, nurturance, growth, development, and absence or presence of disease

PET scan   positron emission tomography is an imaging technique that uses a radioactive tracer to show the chemical activity of the brain

personality   the sum total of the enduring characteristics that differentiate one individual from another

phoneme   the smallest linguistically distinct unit of sound

phenomenon (plural: phenomena)   a thing as it appears; anything that can be perceived as a fact or occurrence (*refer to* Kant); experiences of the external world, experiences of the internal world, and experiences of emotion (*refer to* Dennett)

phenomenological approach   a philosophical approach to being and working with others that respects the consciousness of the other person and endeavours to enter into the person's life-world (*refer to* van Manen); a special technique of introspection involving becoming acquainted with the objects of conscious experience (*refer to* Husserl)

phenomenology   the systematic study of conscious experience; entering into the life-world of another person (*refer to* Dennett)

phenomenon of consciousness   awareness of the conscious world of oneself and others

philosophy   the investigation of knowledge and being; the perspectives and values that underpin practice

physical development growth and change of the individual over time; involves the individual's body, gross motor skills (large body movement and mobility), and fine motor skills (small muscles such as hand control)

physical needs the individual's basic requirements—including food, clothing, and protection—without which the individual would fail to grow and develop

pincer grasp the use of the hand where the thumb and forefinger work in opposition to each other

placental insufficiency the situation where the placenta is unable to deliver the essential nutrients to the fetus for its growth, health, and development

plasticity the brain's ability to change (its malleability, in other words) as a result of experience or injury; particularly changeable in early life

play spontaneous, intrinsically motivated, enjoyable activity resulting in learning; the child's work; a means of discovery, practice for adulthood; an activity to reduce stress; a means of fostering development; a route to self-discovery; a way of learning social skills; an activity for its own sake (*refer to* Hughes)

play partner one who acts as a facilitator of child's play in such a way that the child takes the lead and the partner follows directions or performs similar actions; partnership may involve making suggestions or providing new materials, but the partnership is led by the child

play therapy experiences that are structured to support emerging skills and competencies; especially designed activities that prompt the child to play in ways that address her psychological, physical, or other challenges

play therapist a prepared individual who is qualified to assess the developmental needs of a child and/or provide appropriate play experiences that address a child's particular or special needs

plaything any manufactured or found object used to promote and facilitate play

positive guidance strategies ways that an adult can support a child's learning and behaviour through encouragement, natural and logical consequences, coaching, using internal and external motivators and rewards that avoid the use of inappropriate punishments; relies on an understanding of the child's stage of development and understanding

positivism the idea that there is an ultimate truth and unquestionable reality, rather than personal perspective or construction of reality

postnatal depression/postpartum depression a period of time when some mothers experience depression, low energy levels, negative moods, or other symptoms; possibly a result of chemical or hormonal changes after giving birth; may need medical or psychiatric assistance

practice play spontaneous activity involving repeated actions that aid discovery

pragmatics the understanding of the use of language in communication; language use within a communication context

pragmatism/functionalism an approach to education that focuses on practicality, usefulness, social responsibility; focuses on child-centred learning (*refer to* Dewey)

preconceptual thinking basic thoughts or consciousness—usually based on sensory-motor activity—that exist prior to true concept development

preferences the individual's deliberate choice or the individual's most effective mode or channel

pre-lingual the stage before true language emerges

premature an infant who is born before full gestation; may be small and may experience health and developmental difficulties

prenatal the period before birth; the time from conception to birth; the three trimesters of pregnancy

pre-operational stage the stage of thought following the sensory-motor stage—typically 2 to 7 years—during which the child has some conceptual understanding but is limited because she hasn't acquired the means and "operations" to transform and manipulate ideas (*refer to* Piaget)

prepared checklists valid and reliable instruments that include lists of behaviours or other attributes; used as guides to observe and record information about a child's development

pretend play spontaneous activity involving imagination, imitation, and make-believe

preverbal cues the messages conveyed by means such as facial expressions, gestures, and sound production before true language is acquired

preverbal dialogue interactive communication between adult and infant involving intentional communication

pre-wired the idea that the brain is prepared or structured to acquire language or other learning prior to such learning occurring

primary caregiver the adult to whom the child has the strongest attachment

primary caregiver model a child-care system that is organized and delivered in such a way that each child has a caregiver who is designated to have the main responsibility for that child and has continuing contact with the child

primary circular reaction simple repetitive acts resulting from an enjoyable experience—typically observed at 1 to 4 months; a sub-stage of the sensory-motor stage (*refer to* Piaget)

principles of development the commonly agreed-upon ideas that explain human development—e.g., stage progression

private speech self-directed speech or utterances that children use to guide their own behaviour or use as a commentary on their own actions—speech that is turned inward and may support self-regulation (*refer to* Vygotsky)

problem-based play spontaneous activity that involves solving challenges presented by the play materials, by the child, or by a play partner; a method of informal action-based discovery learning

professional development ongoing education, training, study, or experience that contributes to the increase and updating of proficiency within a professional field—e.g., education

professional any person who is qualified to provide health services, social services, or child care and education, and who is also committed to upholding the ethical standards associated with those roles and responsibilities

profound experiences the idea that there are some key experiences that are essential for certain aspects of development to occur—e.g., resolution of conflicts

program (early childhood) any environment and curriculum designed and delivered for young children—e.g., an infant program in a child-care centre or a family home child-care program for young children of various ages

program standards (exit standards) the knowledge, skills, and dispositions (competencies) required for successful completion of a program—e.g., early childhood education

progression steps forward in development

pro-social skill learned behaviour that is intended to help others—e.g., helping or sharing

proto-emotions feelings that have not yet developed into specific emotions

proto-words/proto-conversation vocal interactions that resemble real conversation but lack real words or grammatical rules

proximodistal the principle that physical skill development goes in a series of stages from the centre of the body outward to the hands

pruning a process whereby unused synapses (connections among brain cells) are shed; experience governs which synapses will be shed and which will be preserved

psychoanalytic school children undergo a series of stages of development in which they experience difficulties in dealing with biological drives and social expectations; psychological well-being depends on successful management of these conflicts (*refer to* Freud, Mahler, Erikson, Winnicott)

psychological clock one of the three clocks of life-span development; the influence of inner needs and drives

psychological needs the conditions essential for the development of a healthy psyche, soul, mind, or self—e.g., love

psychosocial theory individuals develop a personality through undergoing a series of inner conflicts—these can be resolved with appropriate supports (*refer to* Erikson)

qualia the qualities of experiential states; the nature of the self or ego and its relation to thoughts and sensations; the mystery of consciousness; the introspectively accessible, phenomenal aspects of our mental lives; the "what it's like" character of mental states; the way it feels to have mental states such as pain, seeing red, smelling a rose

quality care the concept of exemplary services that meet the needs of children and families; indicators of quality include child–caregiver ratios and staff training

quality of attachment the degree to which a strong and secure bonding relationship has developed

rating scales measurement devices used to record the degree to which an attribute or behaviour is present or absent (may involve semantic differentials or numerical scales)

readiness the idea that there is a state of being when a child is ready to acquire a skill or experience something meaningfully

receptive language the infant's ability to understand the language that is being communicated to her

receptive volume the level of sound the individual can hear at

reciprocal imitation two individuals copying each other's actions

reciprocal relationships social relationships between two people where there is a two-way exchange and mutual benefit

reciprocity the process of giving and receiving in a meaningful manner

reflective practice professional practice that includes regular evaluation of the program and one's effectiveness within it

reflex an inborn, automatic response to stimulation

regression steps backward in development (opposite of progression)

REM sleep a stage of sleep characterized by rapid eye movement, especially during dreaming

resilience the idea that an individual can be prepared or strengthened to withstand and recover from negative circumstances

resource teachers adults who are prepared in a way that enables them to meet the needs of children with disabilities and special needs

responsive care a philosophy of care, education, and nurturance that meets the changing needs of the developing infant and young child and is sensitive to the individual differences of each child

responsivity the process of being responsive to the needs of each child; involves a philosophy and an attitude of mind

rhythmicity (regularity) the predictability or unpredictability in patterns of the child's behaviour (*refer to* Chess and Thomas)

risk management the careful and thoughtful assessment of risks associated with an activity or circumstance; decision-making on the basis of risk/benefit analysis

rituals the routines and sequences of behaviour linked with particular activities, relationships, or times of day; sequences of behaviour that can take on a spiritual significance

role-modelling demonstrating appropriate actions and reactions through behaviour; the set of actions associated with particular roles or jobs

rouge-and-mirror test an informal test to determine the child's understanding of the concept of self (*refer to* Gibson)

rough-and-tumble play spontaneous activity involving play-fighting, chasing, and close physical interactions such as tickling; may include adult–child interactions

routine the regular and predictable sequence of mealtimes, sleep times, and activity during each day

running records observational recordings that include everything the child does, everything the child utters, and the way all behaviours are demonstrated; the recordings are detailed, sequential, and as objective as possible

scaffolding the role of the adult (or other child) to provide, and gradually remove, a support to the child's learning; providing a bridge for the child to gain new understandings or skills (*refer to* Bruner, Vygotsky)

scheme an organized pattern of sensory-motor functioning; a preliminary cluster of ideas; early infant ideas (*refer to* Piaget)

screening the basic process of reviewing, checking, or assessing a group of individuals to determine if any meet specified criteria—e.g., hearing deficit, developmental delay; may lead to further investigation

script series of sequential steps to perform a task; a set of words and/or actions adopted within a particular situation

second birth the idea that individuals undergo a psychological rebirth during infancy (*refer to* Mahler)

secondary circular reaction actions the child repeats as a result of his becoming interested in the external results that they produce, typically observed at 4 to 8 months; a substage of sensory-motor development (*refer to* Piaget)

secure attachment a positive, trusting, and reliable relationship with an adult

seizures (convulsions) uncontrolled bodily movements resulting from problems with the brain or central nervous system; they vary in severity

self the distinct and separate individual; conscious awareness of being

self-actualization when the highest level of the individual's needs are met it is possible for the person to experience actualization; includes positive self-regard and productivity (*refer to* Maslow)

self-concept one's identity; beliefs about what one is like as a person

self-esteem an individual's perception of his or her own overall positive or negative self-worth; the degree to which one feels positive about oneself

self-differentiation seeing oneself as a separate and different person

self-permanence understanding that one continues to exist over time

self-recognition the ability to recognize oneself in a mirror (*see* rouge-and-mirror test)

self-regulation the ability to control feelings and emotions, or the behaviour that results from those emotions; the ability to modify or change behaviour as a result of managing inner emotions

semantics the meanings represented by language

sensation stimulation of one or more sense organs (sight, touch, taste, hearing, or smell)

senses the five faculties for taking in information (sight, touch, taste, hearing, and smell)

sensitive period the window of opportunity (*which see, below*) when the brain is most receptive to particular types of learning experiences

sensory concerning the senses

sensory acuity the degree to which one or more of the five senses can perceive stimulation

sensory integration making meaning out of information received through two or more of the five senses

sensory-motor (sensorimotor) the first stage of the individual's cognitive development; this stage has six substages (*refer to* Piaget)

sensory-motor play spontaneous activity demonstrating the characteristics of the substages of the first stage of cognitive development (*refer to* Piaget)

sensory overload receiving too much stimulation or information from one or more of the five senses; inability to make meaning from sensory input

sensory stimulation providing auditory, olfactory, visual, taste, or touch information through one or more sense

separateness the need to become, or the process of becoming, a separate person

separation awareness of being without a person or object

separation–individuation the process of becoming a separate and individual person

separation anxiety distress shown because of the departure, or impending departure, of a person to whom the individual is attached

separations a series of departures and returns of a person to whom the child is attached

sexual abuse   any abuse or maltreatment of an individual that involves the sexual organs of the perpetrator or victim, and/or unwanted or inappropriate touching, and/or damage to the sexual identity, privacy, or feelings of the victim

shaken baby syndrome   a form of physical abuse where the infant is shaken, causing brain or other damage; babies who are shaken typically display symptoms that are difficult to interpret

shame   a social emotion involving embarrassment or awkwardness about an imagined or real behaviour; includes a level of self-consciousness

shared meanings   communication involving eye contact, close proximity, language, play, or other ways of being at one with another person; exchanging understandings

shared orbit   the two-way communication and shared space of two individuals

small for dates   an infant who is smaller than average for that age; may have health and developmental difficulties

social development   the process of increasing awareness of self and others; understanding and adopting socially acceptable behaviour; absorbing values

social emotions   emotions learned through social interaction

sociodramatic play   spontaneous activity involving role-play, imagination, deferred imitation, and creativity

stress   a physical response to a stressor (a challenging situation)

superheroes   human-like figures in play and stories that have extraordinary powers; children involved in superhero play may feel especially empowered

sudden infant death syndrome (cot death/crib death)   unexpected death in infancy with no apparent cause

siblings   children who share the same parents; brothers and sisters

sign language   a system of communication, such as ASL (American Sign Language), that enables individuals who are deaf to communicate using gestures and hand signals

signing   the process of using a language of gestures and hand signals

skills   learned behaviours; require deliberate action and practice

sleep   a state of temporary loss of consciousness in which there are discernable cycles of approximately 90 minutes; characterized by five levels, measured by an electroencephalograph; a periodic state of physiological rest during which consciousness is suspended

(the) slow-to-warm-up child   a characterization of the temperament of a child (*refer to* Chess & Thomas)

social clock   one of the three clocks of life-span development; the influence of culture and society

social context   the human backdrop or environment in which something happens

social emotions   feelings that exist because of relationships—e.g., shame, empathy

social learning   a theory of learning that emphasizes observational learning, imitation and deferred imitation, and internalizing of roles (*refer to* Bandura)

socialization   the process of learning social rules and adapting to social expectations; becoming part of a social group

social referencing   using eye contact or touch to check with a person to whom there is an attachment; often used by child for emotional support and to seek encouragement

social smile   a smile that initiates contact or responds to another person; indicates some ability to be social

socially acceptable behaviour   any actions or language that are generally accepted as being appropriate in a particular situation or context

solitary play   spontaneous activity involving only the individual, not involving others

soul   the spirit or essence of the immaterial, nonobservable part of the individual; the fundamental nature of the person

special needs (a child with)   a child who has a diagnosed disability, deficit, or developmental challenge; a person who has particular difficulties; a child who requires particular supports to achieve optimal development

specific attachments   attachment to a particular person

spirit   the essence of an individual; elements of experience that transcend everyday reality; meaning found in experience; a person's own inner energy

spiritual development   the stages of human change that involve finding increasing understanding of personal meaning and values; finding the sacredness of life; having awareness of forces within and outside the self; sharing higher-order experiences

stage   a period of time at which the individual demonstrates behaviour associated with a labelled explanation—e.g., sensory-motor stage

strange situation   a sequence of staged episodes that indicate the strength of attachment between a parent (or other adult) and young child (*refer to* Ainsworth)

stranger anxiety   anxiety, distress, or uneasiness shown by a child when an unknown person is present

superego   the aspect of the individual's personality that represents a person's conscience; knows right and wrong (*refer to* Freud)

supportive guidance   providing the individual with appropriate encouragement, nurturance, and instruction, and reinforcing positive behaviour

syllabic repetitions   repeating sounds that have language-like characteristics

symbiosis   a close association between two individuals where each needs the other (the needs may differ in kind); interdependence

symbol   something that represents something else

symbolization   the emergence of symbolic activity—typically observed at ages over 18 months; the last of the sensory-motor sub-stages (*refer to* Piaget)

symbolic play   spontaneous activity that involves symbolism (*see below*); may incorporate pretence or make-believe

symbolism   the process of using objects, words, or actions to stand for something else

synapses   the connections between neurons through which nerve impulses travel

synaptic connection   (*see* synapses, *above*)

syndrome   a group of combined symptoms or signs that characterize a disorder

syntax   the rules for combining words to form phrases and sentences

teaching   the process of facilitating learning, involving direct instruction, demonstration, encouraging the learner's motivation, and offering information

telegraphic speech   sentences spoken by very young children that leave out the less significant words and include only the words that carry the most meaning

temper tantrum   a loss of control of emotions or the experience of conflicted feelings resulting in anger, crying, stamping feet, kicking, screaming, or other extreme behaviours; frequently occurs in toddlers when they cannot regulate their feelings and actions

temperament   the observable traits or patterns of behaviour of an individual; the way the individual behaves

temperament styles   the general or predictable way of responding to stimuli or going about a task that is particular to the individual

temporal concepts   the collection of ideas that makes up the individual's understanding of time

teratogen   any substance that has the potential for damage—e.g., smoking or taking certain drugs during pregnancy that could cause a birth defect

tertiary circular reactions   varying the repetitive actions to prolong and change the result—typically observed at 12 to 18 months; one of the sensory-motor substages (*refer to* Piaget)

toddler   the stage of the child after infancy when the child starts to walk or toddle; defined by age, a toddler may be 8 to 18 months, 12 to 24 months, etc. (variable according to practice and legislation)

toilet-learning   the individual's gradual maturational process of understanding and acquiring skills required to use the potty or toilet for bowel movements and urination (*toilet-training* is a more regimented approach)

traits   an individual's personality characteristics

trance   a level of consciousness similar to a hypnotic state; lack of awareness of the environment; loss of voluntary movement and lack of sensitivity to external stimuli

transductive reasoning   reasoning that relies on preconcepts; may attribute incorrect cause-and-effect

transitions   parts of the child's experience that involve a change of activity, people, or place

trial-and-error   learning through experimenting and making mistakes, as well as experiencing success

trundle   movement on a large wheeled toy that requires the use of alternating or simultaneous leg or foot movement to push the vehicle forward; pre-pedalling

trust   confident reliance on self or others

trust versus mistrust   the first of the stages of the life cycle, in which the infant needs to establish basic trust (*refer to* Erikson)

tuneful babbling   strings of sounds that have patterns of pitch and rhythm

twins   two individuals developing side by side during prenatal development; may be fraternal (developing from two separate zygotes—or dizygotic) or identical (developing from one divided zygote—or monozygotic)

typical development   human development that lies within the range of the norm or average

unconditional love   love that exists without conditions or dependence on particular behaviours or situations

unconscious   a level of mental experience not available to normal awareness

under-extensions   a child applies a word meaning to fewer examples than is generally accepted; restricted use of a word

uni-modal stimulation   offering stimulation through one sensory channel at a time—e.g., visual material

universal grammar   the internalized set of rules and principles integral to all existing languages (*refer to* Chomsky)

universal precautions   a principle of health and infection control that treats everyone as having the potential to transmit germs (bacteria, viruses); precautions such as hand-washing and the appropriate use of gloves are used consistently with all people as infection control measures (*refer to* Pimento & Kernested)

uptime   a level of consciousness characterized by an individual's high sensitivity and responsiveness to stimuli

urticaria   a hypersensitive reaction; showing large spots with a red centre; typically appears during the first week of life; not an infection

variegated babbling   long strings of different syllables used in the vocal experimentation of infants

vernix a protective creamy white waxy substance that covers some of the skin of the newborn baby

visual acuity the degree to which the individual can see

visual cliff an experimental apparatus intended to test depth perception in infants and toddlers (*refer to* Gibson & Walk)

visual insatiability the individual's unstoppable interest in looking

vocabulary the bank of available words

vocalization any sound production

voluntary grasping grasping that is deliberate and voluntary

vowel a speech sound or letter of the alphabet, characterized by the absence of obstruction in the vocal tract—e.g., A, E, I, O, U

vulnerability particular sensitivities to which the individual can succumb in adverse circumstances

ways of knowing the notion that there are different viewpoints or mental structures from which individuals construct their reality—e.g., women's ways of knowing (*refer to* Gilligan)

weaned/weaning the process of transition from one thing to another, such as from fluid to solid food

window of opportunity sensitive periods of time when the brain is particularly capable of learning certain things most efficiently and thoroughly; the time when a child can benefit most from appropriate learning experiences

zone of proximal development (ZPD) behaviours that are on the edge of emergence; the gap between the child's actual performance when operating alone and the child's potential performance when assisted by more knowledgeable adults or children (*refer to* Vygotsky)

References

Adamson, L. (1996). *Communication Development during Infancy*. Boulder, CO: Westview/HarperCollins.

Ainsworth, M. (1969). Object Relations, Dependency, and Attachment: A Theoretical Review of the Infant–Mother Relationship. *Child Development* 40: 969–1025.

———. (1973). The Development of Infant–Mother Attachment. In B.M. Caldwell and H.N. Ricciuti (eds.), *Review of Child Development Research* 3: 1–94. Chicago, IL: University of Chicago.

———. (1979). Attachment as Related to Mother–Infant Interaction. *Advances in the Study of Behavior* 9: 2–51.

Ainsworth, M., D. Salter, and B. Wittig. (1967). Attachment and Exploratory Behavior of One-Year-Olds in a Strange Situation. In B.M. Foss (ed.), *Determinants of Infant Behavior*, Vol. 4. New York, NY: Wiley.

Ainsworth, M., et al. (1978). *Patterns of Attachment: A Psychological Study of the Strange Situation*. Hillsdale, NJ: Erlbaum.

Allen, K., and L. Marotz. (1994). *Developmental Profiles: Pre-Birth through Eight*. 2nd ed. Albany, NY: Delmar.

———. (2003). *Developmental Profiles: Pre-Birth through Twelve*. 4th ed. Albany, NY: Delmar.

Allen, K., C. Paasche, A. Cornell, and M. Engel. (1994). *Exceptional Children: Inclusion in Early Childhood Programs*. Scarborough, ON: Nelson.

Allport, G., and H. Odbert. (1936). Trait-Names: A Psycho-Lexical Study. *Psychological Monographs* 47(211).

Amacher, N. (1973). Touch Is a Way of Caring. *American Journal of Nursing* 73(5): 852–854.

Apgar, V. (1953). A Proposal for a New Method of Evaluation of the Newborn Infant. *Current Research in Anesthesia and Analgesia* 32: 360–367.

Avard, D., and L. Hanvey (eds.). (1989). *The Health of Canada's Children: A CICH Profile*. Ottawa, ON: Canadian Institute of Child Health.

Bailey, D., and M. Wolery. (1989). *Assessing Infants and Preschoolers with Handicaps*. Columbus, OH: Merrill.

Bandura, A. (1977). *Social Learning Theory*. Englewood Cliffs, NJ: Prentice Hall.

Barnhorst, R., and L. Johnson (eds.). (1991). *The State of the Child in Ontario*. Toronto, ON: Oxford University Press.

Bauer, P., and L. Hertsgaard. (1993). Increasing Steps in Recall of Events: Factors Facilitating Immediate and Long-Term in 13.5- and 16.5-Month-Old Children. *Child Development* 64: 1204–1223.

Bayley, N. (1969). *Bayley Scales of Infant Development*. New York, NY: Psychological Corporation.

Beauchamp, G., B. Cowart, and M. Morgan. (1986). Developmental Changes in Salt Acceptability in Human Infants. *Developmental Psychology* 19: 17–25.

Beach, J., J. Bertrand, and G. Cleveland (1998). *Our Child Care Workforce: From Recognition to Remuneration: a Human Resource Study of Child Care in Canada*. Ottawa, ON: Child Care Human Resources Steering Committee.

Begley, S., et al. (1992). Mapping the Brain. *Newsweek*, April 20: 66–72.

Belsky, J. (1980). Child Maltreatment: An Ecological Integration. *American Psychologist* 35: 320–335.

———. (1986). Infant Day Care: A Cause for Concern? *Zero to Three* 6(5): 1–9.

Belsky, J., and J. Kelly. (1994). *The Transition to Parenthood*. New York, NY: Delacorte Press.

Belsky, J., and R. Most. (1981). From Exploration to Play: A Cross-Sectional Study of Infant Free Play Behavior. *Developmental Psychology* 17: 630–639.

Bentzen, W. (1993). *Seeing Young Children: A Guide to Observing and Recording Behavior*. 2nd ed. Albany, NY: Delmar.

Bergen, D., and J. Coscia. (2001). *Brain research and Childhood Education: Implications for Educators*. Olney, MD: ACEI.

Berger, M. (1982). Personality Development and Temperament. In R. Porter and G. Collins (eds.), *Temperamental Differences in Infants and Young Children*. Ciba Foundation Symposium 89. London, UK: Pitman.

Berk, L. (1994). Vygotsky's Theory: The Importance of Make-Believe Play. *Young Children* 50(1): 30–39.

———. (1996). *Infants, Children and Adolescents*. 2nd ed. Needham Heights, MA: Allyn & Bacon.

———. (2000). *Child Development*. 5th ed. Boston: Allyn & Bacon.

Berk, L., and A. Winsler. (1995). *Scaffolding Children's Learning: Vygotsky and Early Childhood Education*. Washington, DC: NAEYC.

Berman, P. (1980). Are Women More Responsive Than Men to the Young? A Review of Developmental and Situational Variables. *Psychological Bulletin* 88: 668–695.

Bertrand, J., et al. (2001). *Nourish, Nurture, Neurodevelopment Resource Kit*. Ottawa, ON: Canadian Child Care Federation.

Biasella, S. (1996). The First Year of Life: A Lot Happens in the First 365 Days. *Lamazebaby Magazine* 23: 30–40.

Birckmayer, J., et al. (1990). *Teens as Parents of Babies and Toddlers*. Ithaca, NY: Cornell University Press.

Blaxall, J., et al. (1996). *Children at the Centre*. Toronto, ON: Harcourt Brace.

Bloom, L., L. Rocissano, and L. Hood. (1976). Adult–Child Discourse: Developmental Interaction between Information Processing and Linguistic Knowledge. *Cognitive Psychology* 8: 521–552.

Bloom, L., S. Merkin, and J. Wootten. (1982). *Wh*-Questions: Linguistic Factors That Contribute to the Sequence of Acquisition. *Child Development* 53: 1084–1092.

Boothe, R., et al. (1985). Postnatal Development of Vision in Human and Nonhuman Primates. *Annual Review of Neuroscience* 8: 495–545.

Bower, T. (1997). *The Perceptual World of the Child*. London, UK: Fontana.

Bowlby, J. (1953). *Child Care and the Growth of Love.* London, UK: Penguin.

————. (1965). *Child Care and the Growth of Love.* 2nd ed. Harmondsworth, UK: Penguin.

————. (1969). *Attachment and Loss,* Vol. 1: *Attachment.* New York, NY: Basic Books.

————. (1973). *Separation: Anxiety and Anger.* New York, NY: Basic Books.

Brazelton, T. (1992). *Touchpoints: Your Child's Emotional and Behavioral Development.* New York, NY: Addison-Wesley.

————. (1995). *Neonatal Behavioral Assessment Scale No. 137.* Cambridge, UK: Cambridge University Press.

Brazelton, T., and B. Cramer. (1990). *The Earliest Relationship: Parents, Infants and the Drama of Early Relationship.* New York, NY: Addison-Wesley.

Brazelton, T., and S. Greenspan. (2000). *The Irreducible Needs of Children: What Every Child Must Have to Grow, Learn, and Flourish.* Cambridge, MA: Perseus Publishing.

Bredekamp, S., and C. Copple (eds.). (1997). *Developmentally Appropriate Practice in Early Childhood Programs.* Rev. ed. Washington, DC: NAEYC.

Bretherton, I. (ed.). (1984). *Symbolic Play: The Development of Social Understanding.* Orlando, FL: Academic.

Brigance, A., and Glascoe, F. (2002). *Brigance Infant & Toddler Screen.* North Billerica, MA: Curriculum Associates.

Bronfenbrenner, U. (1979). *The Ecology of Human Development.* Cambridge, MA: Harvard University Press.

Bronson, M. (2000). Recognizing and Supporting the Development of Self-Regulation in Young Children. *Young Children* 55(2): 32–37 (March).

Brookhart, J., and E. Hock. (1976). The Effects of Experimental Context and Experiential Background on Infants' Behavior towards their Mothers and a Stranger. *Child Development* 47: 333–340.

Brooks-Gunn, J., and M. Lewis. (1982). Affective Exchanges between Normal and Handicapped Infants and Their Mothers. In T. Field and A. Foel (eds.), *Emotion and Early Interaction.* Hillsdale, NJ: Erlbaum.

Bruner, J. (1978). *Learning the Mother Tongue.* Boston, MA: Allyn & Bacon.

————. (1983). *Child's Talk: Learning to Use Language.* New York, NY: Norton.

Buss, A., and R. Plomin. (1984). *Temperament: Early Developing Personality Traits.* Hillsdale, NJ: Erlbaum.

Buytendijk, F. (1947). The First Smile of the Child. (Trans. M. van Manen, 2000). *Phenomenology & Pedagogy* 6(1): 15–24.

Campbell, J.B., and C.W. Hawley. (1982). Study Habits and Eysenck's Theory of Extroversion–Introversion. *Journal of Research in Personality* 16: 139–146.

Campbell, L., B. Campbell, and D. Dickinson. (1996). *Teaching & Learning through Multiple Intelligences.* Needham Heights, MA: Allyn & Bacon.

Campos, J., et al. (1970). Cardiac Response on the Visual Cliff in Prelocomotor Human Infants. *Science* 170: 196–197.

————, et al. (1983). Socioemotional Development. In P. Mussen (ed.), *Handbook of Child Psychology,* Vol. 2: *Infancy and Developmental Psychology,* 4th ed. New York, NY: Wiley.

Canadian Child Care Federation. (2001). Supporting Breast Feeding in Child Care. Resource Sheet #57. At www.cfc-efc.ca/docs/cccf/rs057_en.htm

————. 25 March 2002. Draft Child Care Practitioner Occupational Standards. 4 March 2003. At www.cccf-fcsge.ca/subsites/ training/pdf/draftoccs_en.pdf

Canadian Child Care Federation and the Canadian Day Care Advocacy Association. (1993). *Caring for a Living: Final report.* Ottawa, ON: Canadian Child Care Federation/Canadian Day Care Advocacy Association.

Canadian Child Care Federation and the Canadian Institute for Child Health. (2001*). Nourish, Nurture, Neurodevelopment: Neurodevelopmental Research–Implications for Caregiver Practice.* Ottawa, ON: Canadian Child Care Federation/Canadian Institute for Child Health.

Canadian Council on Social Development. (1996). *The Progress of Canada's Children, 1996.* Ottawa, ON: Canadian Council on Social Development.

Canadian Paediatric Society. (1991). Meeting the Iron Needs of Infants and Young Children: An Update. CPS Statement N91-01. *Canadian Medical Association Journal* 144(11): 1451-1454.

————. (1992). *Well Beings: A Guide to Promote the Physical Health, Safety and Emotional Well-Being of Children in Child Care Centres and Family Day Care Homes.* Vols. 1 and 2. Toronto, ON: Creative Premises.

————. (1999). *A Guide to Promote the Physical Health, Safety and Emotional Well Being of Children in Child Care Centres and Family Day Care Homes.* 2nd ed. Ottawa, ON: Canadian Paediatric Society.

Canfield, J., et al. (1997). *A 4th Course of Chicken Soup for the Soul.* Deerfield Beach, FL: Health Communications.

Caplan, F. (1973). *The First Twelve Months of Life.* New York, NY: Bantam.

Cappe, M., and I. Felligi. (1996). *Growing Up in Canada–NLSCY Study.* Ottawa: HRDC/Statistics Canada.

Carnegie Task Force on Meeting the Needs of Young Children. (1994). *Starting Points: Meeting the Needs of Our Youngest Children.* New York, NY: Carnegie.

Caron, R., et al. (1982). Abstraction of Invariant Face Expressions in Infancy. *Child Development* 53: 1008-1015.

Carter, A. (1975). The Transformation of Sensorimotor Morphemes into Words: A Case Study of the Development of "Here" and "There." *Papers and Reports on Child Language Development* 10: 31–48.

Catlin, C. (1994). *Toddlers Together.* Beltsville, MD: Gryphon House.

Cattell, P. (1940). *The Measurement of Intelligence of Infants and Young Children*. New York, NY: Psychological Corp.

Cattell, R.B. (1951). A Factorization of Tests of Personality Source Traits. *British Journal of Psychology* (Stats. Sect.) 4: 165–178.

—————. (1980). *Handbook for the Sixteen Personality Factor Questionnaire*. Champaign, IL: Institute for Personality and Ability Testing.

Chalmers, D. (2002). The Puzzle of Conscious Experience. *Scientific American Special* 12(1): 90–100.

Chattin-McNichols, J. (1992). *The Montessori Controversy*. Albany, NY: Delmar.

Chasnoff, I.J., et al. (1992). Cocaine and Pregnancy: Clinical and Toxicological Implications for the Neonate. *Clinical Chemistry* 35(7): 1276–1278.

Chess, S., and A. Thomas. (1977). Temperamental Individuality from Childhood to Adolescence. *Journal of Child Psychiatry* 16: 218–226.

—————. (1990). The New York Longitudinal Study (NYLS): The Young Adult Periods. *Canadian Journal of Psychiatry* 35: 557–561.

—————. (1996). *Temperament: Theory and Practice*. New York, NY: Brunner/Mazel.

Childcare Resource and Research Unit. (1995). *Child Care in Canada: Provinces and Territories 1995*. Toronto, ON: University of Toronto. At www.childcarecanada.org/resources/prov_terr/prvtrrtoc.html

—————. (2000). *You Bet I Care! Reports 1, 2, 3, and 4: A Canada-wide study on wages, working conditions, and practices in child-care centres*. Guelph, ON: University of Guelph.

Chomsky, N. (1957). *Syntactic Structures*. The Hague: Mouton.

—————. (1968). *Language and Mind*. New York, NY: Harcourt Brace and World.

Chud, G., et al. (1985). *Early Childhood Education for a Multi-cultural Society*. Vancouver, BC: Pacific Educational Press.

Clarke-Stewart, A. (1982). *Day Care*. New York, NY: Fontana Paperbacks.

—————. (1989). Infant Day-Care: Maligned or Malignant? *American Psychologist* 44: 266–273.

Click, P., and D. Click. (1990). *Administration of Schools for Young Children*. 3rd ed. Albany, NY: Delmar.

Cohen, L., and M. Strauss. (1979). Concept Acquisition in the Human Infant. *Child Development* 50: 419–424.

Coon, D. (1992). *Introduction of Psychology: Exploration and Application*. 6th ed. St. Paul, MN: West.

Craft, M., and J. Denehy. (1990). *Nursing Interventions for Infants and Children*. Philadelphia, PA: W.B. Saunders.

Crick, F. (1994). *The Astonishing Hypothesis: The Scientific Search for the Soul*. New York, NY: Simon & Schuster.

Cryer, D., T. Harms, and B. Bourland. (1987). *Active Learning for Infants*. Menlo Park, CA: Addison-Wesley.

—————. (1987). *Active Learning for Ones*. Menlo Park, CA: Addison-Wesley.

—————. (1988). *Active Learning for Twos*. Menlo Park, CA: Addison-Wesley.

Davis, K. (1996). Learning to Move, Moving to Learn. *ACEI Focus on Infancy* 9(2).

DeBoysson-Bardies, B., et al. (1984). Discernible Differences in the Babbling of Infants According to Target Language. *Journal of Child Language* 11: 1–15.

Deiner, P. (1997). *Infants and Toddlers: Development and Program Planning*. Fort Worth, TX: Harcourt Brace.

Dennett, D. (1991). *Consciousness Explained*. New York, NY: Little, Brown.

Derman-Sparks, L., et al. (1989). *Anti-Bias Curriculum*. Washington, DC: NAEYC.

Dewey, J. (1963). *Experience and Education*. New York, NY: Collier Books.

Dias, M., and P. Harris. (1990). The Influence of Imagination on Reasoning by Young Children. *British Journal of Developmental Psychology* 8: 305–318.

Digman, J. (1990). Personality Structure: An Emergence of the Five-Factor Model. *The Annual Review of Psychology* 41: 417–440.

Dittmann, L. (ed.). (1984). *The Infants We Care For*. Washington, DC: NAEYC.

Doherty, G., and B. Stuart. (1996). *A Profile of Quality in Canadian Child Care Centres*. Ottawa, ON: Human Resources Development Canada.

Doherty-Derkowski, G. (1995). *Quality Matters: Excellence in Early Childhood Programs*. Don Mills, ON: Addison-Wesley.

Dombro, A.L., L.J. Colker, and D.T. Dodge. (1997). *The Creative Curriculum for Infants and Toddlers*. Washington, DC: Teaching Strategies.

Donatelle, R., and L. Davis. (1997). *Health: The Basics*. 2nd ed. Needham Heights, MA: Allyn & Bacon.

Doxey, I. (ed.). (1990). *Child Care and Education: Canadian Dimensions*. Scarborough, ON: Nelson.

Edelstein, S. (1995). *The Healthy Young Child*. St. Paul, MN: West.

Ehrensaft, Diane. (1997). *Spoiling Childhood: How Well-Meaning Parents are Giving Children Too Much—But Not What They Need*. New York, NY: Guildford. (ERIC Document No. ED413111)

Ehrlich, E. *Child Care: Quality Is the Issue*. Washington, DC: NAEYC.

Eisenberg, A., H.E. Murkoff, and S.E. Hathaway. (1996). *What to Expect: The Toddler Years*. New York, NY: Workman Publishing.

Elkind, D. (1994). *A Sympathetic Understanding of the Child: Birth to Sixteen*. 3rd ed. Needham Heights, MA: Allyn & Bacon.

—————. (2001). *The Hurried Child: Growing Up Too Fast, Too Soon*. 3rd ed. Cambridge, MA: Perseus Publishing.

————. (2001b). Much Too Early. *Education Next* (Summer).

Emmet. E. (1968). *Learning to Philosophize.* Harmondsworth, UK: Pelican.

Erikson, E. (1950). *Childhood and Society.* New York, NY: Norton.

————. (1963). *Childhood and Society.* 2nd ed. New York, NY: Wiley.

————. (1959). *Identity and the Life Cycle: Selected Papers.* New York, NY: International University Press.

————. (1987). The Human Life Cycle. In S.P.Schlein (ed.). *A Way of Looking at Things: Selected Papers From 1930–1985,* 595–610. New York, NY: Norton.

Erickson, M., and K. Kurz-Riemer. (1999). *Infants, Toddlers and Families: A Framework for Support and Intervention.* New York, NY: Guilford Press.

Eysenck, H., and M. Eysenck. (1989). *Mind Watching.* Scarborough, ON: McGraw-Hill Ryerson.

Fantz, R. (1963). Pattern Vision in Newborn Infants. *Science* 140: 296–297.

————. (1965). Visual Perception from Birth as Shown by Pattern Selectivity. In H.W. Whipple (ed.), *New Issues in Infant Development. Annals of the New York Academy of Science* 118: 793–814.

Farrell Erikson, M., and K. Kurz-Riemer. (1999). *Infants, Toddlers and Families: A Framework for Support and Intervention.* New York, NY: Guilford.

Feldman, R. (1997). *Development across the Life Span.* Upper Saddle River, NJ: Prentice Hall.

Fenson, C., et al. (1976). The Developmental Progression of Manipulative Play in the First Two Years. *Child Development* 47: 232–236.

Fernald, A. (1989). Intonation and Communicative Intent in Mothers' Speech to Infants: Is Melody the Message? *Child Development* 60: 1497–1510.

Flavell, J.H. (1985). *Cognitive Development.* 2nd ed. Englewood Cliffs, NJ: Prentice-Hall.

Fogel, A. (1997). *Infancy: Infant, Family, and Society.* St. Paul, MN: West.

Fowler, W. (1990). *Talking from Infancy.* Cambridge, MA: Brookline.

Fraiberg, S. (1959/1996). *The Magic Years.* New York, NY: Fireside/Simon & Schuster.

Frattaroli, E. (2001). *Healing the Soul in the Age of the Brain: Becoming Conscious in an Unconscious World.* New York, NY: Viking.

Freeman, N. (1980). *Strategies of Representation in Young Children: Analysis of Spatial Skill and Drawing Processes.* London, UK: Academic.

Freire, M., and J. Bernhard. (1997). Caring for and Teaching Children Who Speak Other Languages. In K.M. Kilbride (ed.), *Include Me Too! Human Diversity in Early Childhood.* Toronto, ON: Harcourt Brace.

Freud, S. (1940). *An Outline of Psychoanalysis.* New York, NY: Norton.

Friendly, M., et al. (1998). *Early Childhood Care and Education in Canada: Provinces and Territories: 1998.* Toronto, ON: Childcare Resource & Research Unit.

Froebel, F. (1967). *Friedrich Froebel: A Selection from His Writings.* Cambridge, UK: Cambridge University Press.

Furuno, S., et al. (1987). *The Hawaii Early Learning Profile.* Palo Alto, CA: VORT.

————, et al. (1993). *The Hawaii Developmental Charts.* Tucson, AZ: Communications Skill Builders, the Psychological Corporation.

————, et al. (1993b). *Helping Babies Learn: Developmental Profiles and Activities for Infants and Toddlers.* San Antonio, TX: Communication Skill Builders.

Gable, S. (2000). Nature, Nurture and Early Brain Development. University Extension, University of Missouri-Columbia, pub. GH6115.

Gable, S., and M. Hunting. (2001). Nature, Nurture and Early Brain Development. At muextension.Missouri.edu/xplor/hesguide/humanrel/gh6115.htm.

Gabriel, H.P., and R. Wool. (1990). *The Inner Child.* New York, NY: Ballantine Books.

Galton, F. (1875). History of Twins. In *Inquiries into Human Faculty and Its Development,* 155–173.

Garber, S., M. Garber, and R. Spizman. (1987). *Good Behavior.* New York, NY: St. Martin's Press.

————. (1993). *Monsters Under the Bed and Other Childhood Fears: Helping Your Child Overcome Anxieties, Fears, and Phobias.* New York, NY: Villard Books.

Garcia, J. (1994). *Toddler Talk.* Port Angeles, WA: Stratton-Kehl Publications.

————. (1999). *Sign with Baby: How to Communicate with Infants Before They Can Speak.* Seattle, WA: Northlight Communications and Stratton-Kehl Publications.

Gardner, H. (1993). *Multiple Intelligences: The Theory in Practice.* New York, NY: Basic Books/HarperCollins.

Gee, R. (1985). *Babies: Understanding Conception, Birth and the First Years.* London, UK: Usborne.

Gerber, M. (1998). *Dear Parent: Caring for Infants with Respect.* Los Angeles, CA: Resources for Infant Educarers.

————. (1998b). *Your Self-Confident Baby: Raising Your Child the Right Way.* Toronto, ON: John Wiley & Sons.

Gesell, A. (1928). *Infancy and Human Growth.* New York, NY: Macmillan.

Gilfoyle, E. (1980). Caring: A Philosophy for Practice. *American Journal of Occupational Therapy.* 34(8): 517–521.

Gilligan, C. (1982). *In a Different Voice: Psychological Theory and Women's Development.* Cambridge, MA: Harvard University Press.

Godwin, A., and L. Schrag. (1988). *Setting Up for Infant Care: Guidelines for Centers and Family Day Care Homes.* Washington, DC: NAEYC.

Goldberg, S. (2000). *Attachment and Development.* Texts in Developmental Psychology Series. London, UK: Arnold.

Goldstein, S. (1992). Young Children at Risk: The Early Signs of Attention-Deficit Hyperactivity Disorder. *CH.A.D.D.er Box* 5 (January): 7.

Goleman, D. (1997). *Emotional Intelligence.* New York, NY: Bantam.

Gonzalez-Mena, J., and D. Widmeyer Eyer. (1989). *Infants, Toddlers, and Caregivers.* Mountain View, CA: Mayfield.

Gordon, A., and K.W. Browne. *Guiding Young Children in a Diverse Society.* Boston, MA: Allyn & Bacon.

Gottman, J., J. Declaire, and D. Goleman (1998). *Raising an Emotionally Intelligent Child.* New York, NY: Fireside/Simon and Schuster.

Goulet, M. (2000). *How Caring Relationships Support Self-Regulation.* Video and video guide. Spring 2000. Washington, DC: NAEYC.

Government of British Columbia. (2002). *Toddler's First Steps: A Best Chance Guide to Parenting Your Six-Month to Three-Year-Old.* Best Chance Series. Toronto, ON: Macmillan Canada.

Greenberg, P. (1991). *Character Development: Encouraging Self-Esteem and Self-Discipline in Infants, Toddlers, and Two-Year-Olds.* Washington, DC: NAEYC.

Greenspan, S. (1997). *The Growth of the Mind and the Endangered Origins of Intelligence.* Reading, MA: Addison-Wesley.

Greenspan, S., and N.T. Greenspan. (1985). *First Feelings.* New York, NY: Viking.

——————. (1989). *The Essential Partnership: How Parents and Children Can Meet the Emotional Challenges of Infancy and Childhood.* New York, NY: Penguin.

Guy, K.A. (1997). *Our Promise to Children.* Ottawa: Canadian Institute of Child Health.

Hall, N. Saderman, and V. Rhomberg. (1995). *The Affective Curriculum.* Scarborough, ON: Nelson.

Hamner, T., and P. Turner. (1996). *Parenting in Contemporary Society.* 3rd ed. Boston: Allyn & Bacon.

Harden, B., and C. Harden. (1997). *Alternative Health Care: The Canadian Directory.* Toronto, ON: Noble Ages.

Harding, J., and L. Meldon-Smith. (1996). *How to Make Observations and Assessments.* London, UK: Hodder and Stoughton.

Harms, T., and R. Clifford. (1980). *Early Childhood Environmental Rating Scale.* New York, NY: Teachers College Press.

Harms, T., D. Cryer, and R. Clifford. (1990). *Infant/Toddler Environment Rating Scale.* New York, NY: Teachers College Press.

Harter, S. (1983). Developmental Perspectives on the Self-Esteem. In E.M. Hetherington (ed.), *Handbook of Child Psychology: Socialization, Personality, and Social Development,* Vol. 4. New York, NY: Wiley.

Hawaii Early Learning Profile. (1994). *Revised HELP Checklist.* Palo Alto, CA: VORT.

——————. (1997). *HELP Activity Guide.* Palo Alto, CA: VORT.

Hawley, T. (2000). *Starting Smart: How Early Experiences Affect Brain Development.* 2nd ed. Washington, DC: Zero to Three.

Health Canada. (1998). Infection Control Guidelines: Hand Washing, Cleaning, Disinfection and Sterilization in Health Care. *Canada Communicable Disease Report.* Vol. 24S8.

Helm, J., S. Beneke, and K. Steinheimer. (1997). Documenting Children's Learning. *Childhood Education* 73(4) (Summer): 200–205.

Hewat, R. (2000). Living with an Incessantly Crying Infant. *Phenomenology Online,* at phenomenologyonline.com/articles/template.cfm?ID=286.

Hickok, G., U. Bellugi, and E.S. Klima. (1998). What's Right About the Neural Organization of Sign Language? A Perspective on Recent Neuroimaging Results. *Trends in Cognitive Sciences* 2: 465–468.

Honig, A. (1983). Meeting the Needs of Infants. *Dimensions* (January): 81–84.

——————. (1995). Singing with Infants and Toddlers. *Young Children* (July): 72–78.

Honig, A., and H. Brophy. (1996). *Talking with Your Baby.* Syracuse, NY: Syracuse University Press.

Honig, A., and J. Lally. (1981). *Infant Caregiving: A Design for Training.* Syracuse, NY: Syracuse University Press.

Howes, C., et al. (1988). Attachment and Child Care: Relationships with Mother and Caregiver. *Early Childhood Research Quarterly* 3: 403–416.

Howes, P., and H. Markman. (1989). Marital Quality and Child Functioning: A Longitudinal Investigation. *Child Development* 60: 1044–1051.

Hughes, F. (1991). *Children, Play, and Development.* 2nd ed. Needham Heights, MA: Allyn & Bacon.

——————. (1999). Children, Play, and Development. 3rd ed. Boston, MA: Allyn & Bacon.

Hughes, F., J. Elicker, and L. Veen. (1995). A Program of Play for Infants and their Caregivers. *Young Children* (January): 52–58.

Hujala, E. (ed.). (1996). *Childhood Education: International Perspectives.* Oulu, Finland: University of Oulu Early Education Center.

Hulit, L., and M. Howard. (1997). *Born to Talk: An Introduction to Speech and Language Development.* Needham Heights, MA: Allyn & Bacon.

Hyde, A. (1977). The Phenomenon of Caring: Part VI. *American Nurses' Foundation* 12(1): 2.

Illingworth, R. (1990). *Basic Developmental Screening: 0–5 Years*. 5th ed. Oxford, UK: Blackwell Scientific Publications.

———. (1992). *The Development of the Infant and Young Child*. London, UK: Churchill Livingstone.

Isaacs, S. (1929). *The Nursery Years*. London, UK: Routledge and Kegan Paul.

Izard, C. (1971). *The Face of Emotion*. New York, NY: Appleton-Century-Crofts.

———. (1977). *Human Emotions*. New York, NY: Plenum.

Izard, C., and C. Malatesta. (1987). Perspectives on Emotional Development I: Differential Emotions Theory of Early Emotional Development. In J. Osofsky (ed.), *Handbook of Infant Development*, 2nd ed. New York, NY: Wiley.

Jacob, S. (1992). *Your Baby's Mind*. Holbrook, MA: Adams.

Jacobson, A. (1994). Starting with Infant Development: A Window to Planning Curriculum. *ACEI Focus on Infancy* 6(4).

Josephson, W. (1995). *Television Violence: A Review of the Effects on Children of Different Ages*. Ottawa, ON: Canadian Heritage.

Kaiser, B., and J. S. Rasminsky. (1995). *HIV/AIDS and Child Care*. Ottawa, ON: Canadian Child Care Federation/ Health Canada.

Kandel, E. (1998). A New Intellectual Framework for Psychiatry. *American Journal of Psychiatry* 155(4).

Kansas Stakeholders Advisory Committee, Early Childhood Education. (1996). *Quality Standards for Early Childhood Education for Children Birth through Eight*. Topeka, KA: Kansas State Board of Education.

Kaplan, L.J. (1978). *Oneness and Separateness: From Infant to Individual*. New York, NY: Touchstone/Simon and Schuster.

Kast, V. (1992). *The Dynamics of Symbols: Fundamentals of Jungian Psychotherapy*. (Trans. S.A. Schwartz). New York, NY: Fromm International.

Kelly, P. (ed.). (1989). *First-Year Baby Care*. Deephaven, MN: Meadowbrook Press.

Kendrick, A., R. Kaufmann, and K. Messenger (eds.). (1988). *Healthy Young Children: A Manual for Programs*. Washington, DC: NAEYC.

Kilbride, K.M. (ed.). (1997). *Include Me Too! Human Diversity in Early Childhood*. Toronto, ON: Harcourt Brace.

Kimura, D. (2002). Sex Differences in the Brain. *Scientific American Special* 12(1): 32–37.

Kitzinger, S. (1989). *The Crying Baby*. London, UK: Penguin.

Klaus, M., and J. Kennell. (1976). *Maternal–Infant Bonding*. St. Louis, MO: Mosby.

———. (1982). *Parent–Infant Bonding*. 2nd ed. St. Louis, MO: Mosby.

Klaus, M.H., J.H. Kennell, and P.H. Klaus. (1995). *Bonding: Building the Foundations of Secure Attachment and Independence*. Reading, MA: Merloyd Lawrence/ Addison-Wesley.

Kholberg, L., et al. (1987). *Child Psychology and Childhood Education: A Cognitive Developmental View*. New York, NY: Longman.

Kotulak, R. (1996). Children's Brains Greedy for Words from Infancy. *Toronto Star*.

Lally, J., et al. (1995). *Caring for Infants and Toddlers in Groups*. Washington, DC: Zero to Three.

Lamb, M., and J. Campos. (1982). *Development in Infancy*. New York, NY: Random House.

Lamb, M., et al. (1985). Infant–Mother Attachment: The Origins and Developmental Significance of Individual Differences in the Strange Situations: Its Study and Biological Interpretation. *Behavioral and Brain Sciences* 7: 127–147.

Lamb, M., K. Sternberg, and M. Prodromidis. (1992). Nonmaternal Care and the Security of Infant–Mother Attachment: A Reanalysis of the Data. *Infant Behavior and Development* 15: 71–83.

Lammi-Keefe, C.J., et al. (2000). Higher Maternal Docosahexaenoic Acid (DHA) is Associated with More Mature Neonatal Sleep State Patterning. Kansas City, MO: PUFA in Maternal and Child Health Meeting, September 10–13.

Langeveld, M. (1983). The "Secret Place" in the Life of the Child. *Phenomenology & Pedagogy* 1(2): 181–189.

Langeveld, M. (1984). How Does the Child Experience the World of Things? *Phenomenology & Pedagogy* 2(3): 215–223.

Leach, P. (1997). *Your Baby and Child: From Birth to Age Five*. New York, NY: Knopf.

Lear, R. (1990). *More Play Helps: Play Ideas for Children with Special Needs*. Oxford, UK: Butterworth-Heinemann.

Leavitt, R., and B. Eheart. (1985). *Toddler Day Care: A Guide to Responsive Caregiving*. Lexington, MA: Lexington Books/D.C. Heath.

LeDoux, J. (1996). *The Emotional Brain*. New York, NY: Touchstone/Simon and Schuster.

Leonard, M. (1977). *Nearly One Year Old*. Princes Risborough, UK: Shire Publications.

Lepper, M.R. (1983). Social Control Processes and the Internalization of Social Values: An Attributional Perspective. In E.T. Higgins, D.N. Ruble, and W.W. Hartup (eds.), *Social Cognition and Social Development*, 294–330. New York, NY: Cambridge University Press.

Lewis, M., and J. Brooks-Gunn. (1978). Self-Knowledge in Emotional Development. In M. Lewis and L. Rosenblum (eds.), *The Development of Affect*. New York, NY: Plenum.

———. (1979). *Self Cognition and the Acquisition of Self*. New York, NY: Plenum.

Lickliter, R., and L.E. Bahrick. (2000). The Development of Infant Intersensory Perception: Advantages of a Comparative Convergent-Operations Approach. *Psychological Bulletin* 126: 260–280.

Lieberman, A.F. (1993). *The Emotional Life of the Toddler.* New York, NY: Free Press.

Lowry, L. (2001). The Development of Taste during Infancy. At www.heinzbaby.com/HINI/taste.htm

Maccoby, E. (1980). *Social Development: Psychological Growth and the Parent–Child Relationship.* New York, NY: Harcourt Brace Jovanovich.

Maccoby, E., and S. Feldman. (1972). Mother-Attachment and Stranger-Reaction Patterns in the Third Year of Life. *Monographs of the Society for Research in Child Development* 37(1) (serial no. 146).

Main, M., and E. Hesse. (1990). Parent's Unresolved Traumatic Experiences are Related to Infant Disorganized Status: Is Frightened and/or Frightening Parental Behavior the Linking Mechanism? In M.T. Greenberg, D. Cicchetti, and E.M. Cummings (Eds.), *Attachment in the Preschool Years: Theory, Research, and Intervention,* 161–182. Chicago: University of Chicago.

Mahler, M. (1968). *On Human Symbiosis and the Vicissitudes of Individuation.* New York, NY: International Universities Press.

Mahler, M.S., F. Pine, and A. Bergman. (1975). *The Psychological Birth of the Human Infant.* New York, NY: Basic Books.

Marotz, L., M. Cross, and J. Rush. (1993). *Health, Safety, and Nutrition for the Young Child.* 3rd ed. Albany, NY: Delmar.

————. (1999). *Take a Look: Observation and Portfolio Assessment in Early Childhood.* 2nd ed. Don Mills, ON: Addison-Wesley.

McAfee, O., and D. Leong. (1994). *Assessing and Guiding Young Children's Development and Learning.* Needham Heights, MA: Allyn & Bacon.

McCain, M., and J.F. Mustard. (1999). Early Years Study: Reversing the Real Brain Drain. From *The Early Years Study: Three Years Later– Early Child Development to Human Development: Enabling Communities.* (2002). Toronto, ON: The Founders Network.

McKenna, J. (1997). Bedtime Story: Co-sleeping Research. *Human Nature,* October 1997, and at www.naturalchild.com/james_mckenna/bedtime_story.html

Maslow, A. (1970). *Motivation and Personality.* 2nd ed. New York, NY: Harper and Row.

Michalson, L., and M. Lewis. (1985). What Do Children Know about Emotions and When Do They Know It? In M. Lewis and C. Saarni (eds.), *The Socialization of Emotions.* New York, NY: Plenum.

Miller, K. (1992). *Things to Do with Toddlers and Twos.* Chelsea, MA: Telshare Publishing.

Montessori, Maria. (1914/1965). *Dr. Montessori's Own Handbook.* New York, NY: Schocken Books.

Morris, D. (1977). *Manwatching: A Field Guide to Human Behaviour.* St. Albans, UK: Triad Panther.

————. (1999). *Babywatching.* London, UK: Vintage/Ebury.

Morrison, G. (1997). *Fundamentals of Early Childhood Education.* Upper Saddle River, NJ: Merrill/Prentice Hall.

Mott, S., S. James, and A. Sperhac. (1990). *Nursing Care of Children and Families.* Redwood City, CA: Addison-Wesley.

Moyer, I. (1983). *Responding to Infants: The Infant Activity Manual.* Minneapolis, MN: T.S. Denison.

Nakamura, S., M. Wind, and M. Danello. (1999). Review of Hazards Associated with Children Placed in Adult Beds. *Archives of Pediatric and Adolescent Medicine* 153: 1019–1023.

Nash, J.M. (1997). Fertile Minds. *Time,* June 9:

National Center for Health Statistics. (1982). *Infant Development Growth Charts.* Washington, DC: U.S. Public Health Services.

Newberger, J. (1997). New Brain Development Research: A Wonderful Window of Opportunity to Build Public Support for Early Childhood Education! *Young Children* 52(4): 4–9.

Newman, N. (1987). *Small Beginnings.* Newton Abbot, UK: David and Charles.

O'Hagan, M., and M. Smith. (1993). *Special Issues in Child Care.* London, UK: Bailliere Tindall.

Owens, R. (1996). *Language Development: An Introduction.* 4th ed. Needham Heights, MA: Allyn & Bacon.

Parten, M. (1932). Social Participating among Pre-School Children. *Journal of Abnormal and Social Psychology* 27: 243–269.

Pawl, J., and M. St. John. (1998). How You Are Is as Important as What You do. in *Making a Positive Difference for Infants, Toddlers, and Their Families.* Washington, DC: Zero to Three.

Penn, H. (1999). *How Should We Care for Babies and Toddlers? An Analysis of Practice in Out-of-Home Care for Children under Three.* Toronto, ON: Childcare Resource and Research Unit.

Perry, J.P. (2001). *Outdoor Play: Teaching Strategies with Young Children.* New York, NY: Teachers College Press.

Phillips, D. (ed.). (1987). *Quality in Child Care: What Does Research Tell Us?* Washington, DC: NAEYC.

Piaget, J. (1950). *The Psychology of Intelligence.* New York, NY: International Universities Press.

————. (1952). *The Origins of Intelligence in Children.* New York, NY: International Universities Press.

————. (1954). *The Construction of Reality in the Child.* New York, NY: Basic Books.

Piaget, J., and B. Inhelder. (1967). *The Child's Conception of Space.* New York, NY: Norton.

Pimento, B., and D. Kernested. (2000). *Healthy Foundations in Child Care.* 2nd ed. Scarborough, ON: Nelson.

Poisson, S., and G. DeGangi. (1992). *Emotional and Sensory Processing Problems: Assessment and Treatment Approaches for Young Children and their Families.*

Rockville, MD: Reginald S. Lourie Center for Infants and Young Children.

Pruett, K. (1999). *Me, Myself and I: How Children Build Their Sense of Self (18–36 Months)*. New York, NY: Goddard Press.

Pugmire-Stoy, M. (1992). *Spontaneous Play in Early Childhood*. Albany, NY: Delmar.

Quilliam, S. (1994). *Child Watching: A Parent's Guide to Children's Body Language*. London, UK: Ward Lock.

Ramsey, D. (1980). Onset of Unimanual Handedness in Infants. *Infant Behavior and Development* 3: 377–386.

Raver, S. (1991). *Strategies for Teaching At-Risk and Handicapped Infants and Toddlers*. New York, NY: Merrill.

Reents, J. (2001). Safe Co-sleeping. *Geoparent*. At www.geo-parent.com/family/techniques/safecosleeping.htm

Restak, R. (1991). *The Evolution of Consciousness: The Origins of the Way We Think*. New York, NY: Simon & Schuster.

Rimer, P., and B. Prager. (1998). *Reaching Out*. Scarborough, ON: Nelson.

Roberts-Fiati, G. (1997). Observing and Assessing Young Children. In K.M. Kilbride (ed.), *Include Me Too! Human Diversity in Early Childhood*. Toronto, ON: Harcourt Brace.

Roberston, J., and J. Robertson. (1989). *Separation and the Very Young*. London, UK: Free Association.

Rolfes, S., and L. DeBruyne. (1990). *Life Span Nutrition: Conception through Life*. St. Paul, MN: West.

Rose, V. (1985). Detecting Problems with Growth Development Charts. *Nursery World*, Nov. 28: 6–7.

Rowland, S., and T. Lawhon. (1994). How Do I Love Thee: Enhancing Intimacy in Children. *Childhood Education* (Fall): 38–41.

Russell, B. (1960). *On Education*. London, UK: George Allen and Unwin.

Rutter, M. (1979). Maternal Deprivation, 1972–1978: New Findings, New Concepts, New Approaches. *Child Development* 50: 283–305.

Sagi, A., et al. (1994). Sleeping Out of Home in a Kibbutz Communal Arrangement: It Makes a Difference for Infant–Mother Attachment. *Child Development* 65: 992–1004.

Salkind, N. (1994). *Child Development*. 7th ed. Fort Worth, TX: Harcourt Brace.

Sameroff, A., and M. Chandler. (1975). Reproductive Risk and the Continuum of Caretaking Casualty. In F. Horowitz (ed.), *Review of Child Development Research*. Chicago, IL: University of Chicago Press.

Sanger, S. (1991). *Baby Talk/Parent Talk: Understanding Your Baby's Body Language*. New York, NY: Doubleday.

Schmitt, B., and R. Krugman. (1992). Abuse and Neglect of Children. In R.E. Behrman (ed.), *Nelson Textbook of Pediatrics*, 14th ed. Philadelphia, PA: W.B. Saunders.

Scientific American. (1998). Exploring Intelligence: A Search in the Human, Animal, Machine and Extraterrestrial Domains. *Scientific American Presents* 9(4).

Searle, J. (1995). The Mystery of Consciousness. *New York Review of Books,* Nov. 2: 60.

Secker, D. (2001). Interpreting Growth and Growth Standards. At www.heinzbaby.com/HINI/growth.htm

Seefeldt, C. (1990). *Continuing Issues in Early Childhood Education*. Columbus, OH: Merrill.

Seimens, H.W. (1924). *Die Zwillingspathologie*. Berlin: Springer.

Shaffer, D. (1993). *Developmental Psychology: Childhood and Adolescence*. 3rd ed. Belmont, CA: Brooks/Cole.

Shatz, M., and A. O'Reilly. (1990). Conversational or Communicative Skill? A Reassessment of Two-Year-Olds' Behavior in Miscommunication Episodes. *Journal of Child Language* 17: 131–146.

Shelov, S. (ed.) (1993). *Caring for Your Baby and Young Child: Birth to Age 5*. New York, NY: Bantam Books.

Sheridan, M. (1997). *From Birth to Five Years: Children's Developmental Progress*. London, UK: Routledge.

Shimoni, R., J. Baxter, and J. Kugelmass. (1992). *Every Child Is Special*. Don Mills, ON: Addison-Wesley.

Shonkoff, J., & D. Phillips (eds.). (2000). *From Neurons to Neighbourhoods: The Science of Early Childhood Development*. Washington, DC: National Academy Press.

Shore, R. (1997). *Rethinking the Brain: New Insights into Early Development*. New York, NY: Families and Work Institute.

Siegler, R. (1991). *Children's Thinking*. 2nd ed. Englewood Cliffs, NJ: Prentice Hall.

Silberg, J. (1993). *Games to Play with Babies*. Mt. Rainier, MD: Gryphon House.

———. (1996). *More Games to Play with Toddlers*. Belville, MD: Gryphon House.

Simkin, P., J. Whalley, and A. Keppler. (1991). *Pregnancy, Childbirth and the Newborn*. Deephaven, MN: Meadowbrook Press.

Singer, D., and T. Revenson. (1996). *A Piaget Primer: How a Child Thinks*. New York, NY: Plume/Penguin.

Snow, C.W. (1998). *Infant Development*. 2nd ed. Upper Saddle River, NJ: Prentice Hall.

Sodian, B., et al. (1991). Early Deception and the Child's Theory of Mind: False Trails and Genuine Markers. *Child Development* 62: 468–483.

Spitz, R. (1945). Hospitalism: An Inquiry into the Genesis of Psychiatric Conditions in Early Childhood. *Psychoanalytic Study of the Child* 1: 53–74.

———. (1946). Hospitalism: A Follow-up Report on Investigation Described in Volume 1. *Psychoanalytic Study of the Child* 2: 113–117.

Springgate, K.W., and D.A. Staglin. (1999). Adjusting to a Child with Special Needs. *Building School and Community Partnerships through Parent Involvement.*

Spock, B. (1996). Mommy, Don't Go! *Parenting* (June/July): 86–91.

Sroufe, L. (1977). Wariness of Strangers and the Study of Infant Development. *Child Development* 48: 731–746.

———. (1979). Socioemotional Development. In J. Osofsky (ed.), *Handbook of Infant Development.* New York, NY: Wiley.

———. (1988). A Developmental Perspective on Day Care. *Early Childhood Research Quarterly* 3: 283–292.

Sroufe, L., R. Cooper, and G. DeHart. (1996). *Child Development: Its Nature and Course.* 3rd ed. New York, NY: McGraw-Hill.

Statistics Canada. (1995). *National Longitudinal Survey of Children and Youth.* Ottawa, ON: Statistics Canada.

Statistics Canada. (1996). *1996 Census.* Ottawa, ON: Statistics Canada.

Steiner, R. (1982). *The Roots of Education.* London, UK: Rudolph Steiner Press.

Stern, D. (1985). *The Interpersonal World of the Infant.* New York, NY: Basic Books.

Stonehouse, A. (ed.). (1990). *Trusting Toddlers.* St. Paul, MN: Toys 'n' Things Press.

Stoppard, M. (1983). *Baby Care Book: A Practice Guide to the First Three Years.* London, UK: Dorling Kindersley.

Tanner, J. (1990). *Foetus into Man.* 2nd ed. Cambridge, MA: Harvard University Press.

Thomas, A., and S. Chess. (1977). *Temperament and Development.* New York, NY: Brunner/Mazel.

———. (1985). The Behavioral Study of Temperament. In J. Strelau et al., *The Biological Bases of Personality and Behavior,* Vol. 1: *Theories, Measurement, Techniques and Development.* Washington, DC: Hemisphere.

Thomas, P. (2000). Children and Stress: "The Hurried Child." Taconic Counselling Group. At www.taconicnet.com/childstress.htm

Trad, P. (1993). *Short-Term Parent–Infant Psychotherapy.* New York, NY: Basic Books/HarperCollins.

Trehub, S., D. Bull, and L. Thorp. (1984). Infants' Perception of Melodies: The Role of Melodic Contour. *Child Development* 55: 821–830.

Tremblay, R., et al. (1994). Predicting Early Onset of Male Antisocial Behavior from Preschool Behavior. *Archives of General Psychiatry* 51: 732–738.

Tronick, E. (1989). Emotions and Emotional Communication in Infants. *American Psychologist* 44(2): 112–119.

Turnbull, A., and H. Turnbull. (1997). *Families, Professionals, and Exceptionality.* 3rd ed. Upper Saddle River, NJ: Merrill/Prentice Hall.

United Nations. (1991). *Convention on the Rights of the Child.* New York, NY: United Nations Dept. of Public Information.

Van Hoorn, J., P. Nourot, B. Scales, and K. Alward. (1993). *Play at the Center of the Curriculum.* New York, NY: Merrill/Macmillan.

Van Manen, M., Ed. (1994). Writing in the Dark: Phenomenological Studies in Interpretive Inquiry. In *Researching Lived Experience: Human Science for an Action-Sensitive Pedagogy.* London, ON: Althouse Press.

Voices for Children. (2002). *Promoting Children's Healthy Development.* At www.voices4children.org.

Vygotsky, L. (1934/1962). *Thought and Language.* Cambridge, MA: MIT Press.

Wainright, G. (1985). *Body Language.* Sevenoaks, UK: Teach Yourself Books/Hodder and Stoughton.

Walk, R., and E. Gibson. (1961). A Comparative and Analytical Study of Visual Depth Perception. *Psychology Monographs* 75(15).

Waters, E., and E.M. Cummings. (2000). A Secure Base from which to Explore Close Relationships. *Child Development* Special Millenium Issue, Feb.

Watkinson, M. (1987). Examination of the Neonate. *Update,* November 1, 949–958.

Weiser, M. (1991). *Infant/Toddler Care and Education.* 2nd ed. New York, NY: Merrill/Macmillan Publishing.

Weissbourd, B., and J. Musick (eds.). (1981). *Infants: Their Social Environments.* Washington, DC: NAEYC.

Weitzman, E. (1992). *Learning Language and Loving It: A Guide to Promoting Children's Social and Language Development in Early Childhood Settings.* Toronto, ON: Hanen Centre.

Werner, E., and R. Smith. (1992). *Overcoming the Odds: High Risk Children from Birth to Adulthood.* Ithaca, NY: Cornell University Press.

Weston, P. (1998). *Friedrich Froebel: His Life, Times and Significance.* London, UK: Roehampton Institute.

White, B. (1988). *Educating the Infant and Toddler.* Lexington, MA: Lexington/D.C. Heath.

White, B. (1995). *The New First Three Years of Life.* New York, NY: Fireside/Simon and Schuster.

Whitebrook, M., C. Howes, and D. Phillips. (1990). *Who Cares? Child Care Teachers and the Quality of Care in America.* Final Report of the National Child Care Staffing Study. Oakland, CA: Child Care Employee Project.

Widerstrom, A., B. Mowder, and S. Sandall. (1991). *At-Risk and Handicapped Newborns and Infants: Development, Assessment, and Intervention.* Englewood Cliffs, NJ: Prentice-Hall.

Widerstrom, A., B. Mowder, and S. Sandall. (1997). *Infant Development and Risk.* 2nd ed. Baltimore, MD: Paul H. Brookes.

Wilson, L. (1997). *Partnerships: Families and Communities in Canadian Early Childhood Education.* Scarborough, ON: Nelson.

Wilson, L.C., L. Douville-Watson, and M. Watson. (1995). *Infants and Toddlers: Curriculum and Teaching.* 3rd ed. Albany, NY: Delmar.

Winter, S. (1995). *Outdoor Play and Learning for Infants and Toddlers.* Little Rock, AR: Southern Early Childhood Association.

Wolff, P. (1966). The Causes, Controls and Organization of Behavior in the Neonate. *Issues* 5(7).

Woolfson, R. (1995). *A to Z of Child Development from Birth to Five Years.* Toronto, ON: Stoddart.

Yeates, M., et al. (1990). *Administering Early Childhood Settings: The Canadian Perspective.* Columbus, OH: Merrill.

Yonas, A., et al. (1987). Four Months Old Infants' Sensitivity to Binocular and Kinetic Information for Three-Dimensional Object Shape. *Child Development* 58: 910–917.

Younger, B., and S. Gotleib. (1988). Development of Tract and Primitive Syllabification in Infancy: The First Six Months. *Purdue University Contributed Paper* (Fall).

—————. Categorization skills: Changes in the Nature or Structure of Infant Form Categories? *Development Psychology* 24: 611–619.

Zlatin, M. (1973). Explorative Mapping of the Vocal Tract and Primitive Syllabification in Infancy: The First Six Months. *Purdue University Contributed Papers* (Fall).

Index

Photo Acknowledgements

Chapter 1

Page 1: Sue Martin; courtesy of the YMCA of Greater Toronto Family Development Centre.
Page 12: Courtesy of Cathy Coulthard.

Chapter 2

Page 38: Sue Martin; courtesy of the YMCA of Greater Toronto Family Development Centre.
Page 55: Courtesy of Sue Martin.

Chapter 3

Page 62: Sue Martin; courtesy of the YMCA of Greater Toronto Family Development Centre.
Page 68: Courtesy of Cathy Coulthard.

Chapter 4

Page 87: Courtesy of Leanne Morton.
Page 93: Courtesy of John Riddell.

Chapter 5

Page 114: Courtesy of Leanne Morton.
Page 118: Sue Martin; courtesy of the YMCA of Greater Toronto Family Development Centre.

Chapter 6

Page 141: Courtesy of Cathy Coulthard.
Page 156: Courtesy of Leanne Morton.

Chapter 7

Page 169: Courtesy of George Brown College.
Page 171: Courtesy of Leanne Morton.

Chapter 8

Page 199: Courtesy of Sue Martin.
Page 211: Courtesy of Cathy Coulthard.

Chapter 9

Page 229: Sue Martin; courtesy of the YMCA of Greater Toronto Family Development Centre.
Page 237: Sue Martin; courtesy of the YMCA of Greater Toronto Family Development Centre.

Chapter 10

Page 263: Courtesy of Deborah Bailey.
Page 286: Courtesy of Sue Martin.

Chapter 11

Page 302: Sue Martin; courtesy of the YMCA of Greater Toronto Family Development Centre.
Page 304: Courtesy of Deborah Bailey.

Chapter 12

Page 344: Courtesy of Marc Trudel.
Page 348: Courtesy of Christina Tesolin.